REFERENCE

Key to 1:250 000 Maps, atlas pages 86-205

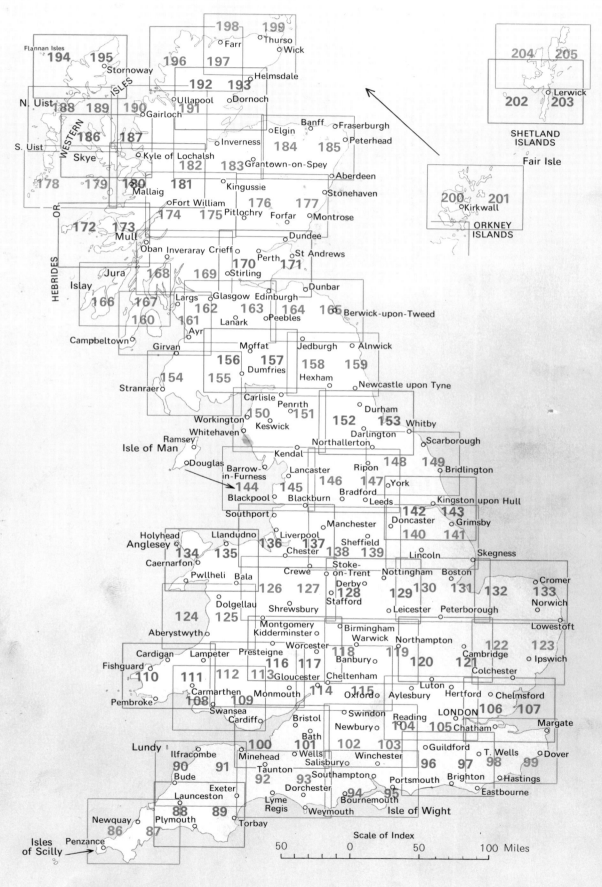

THE ORDNANCE SURVEY

NATIONAL
ATLAS
OF GREAT BRITAIN

THE ORDNANCE SURVEY
NATIONAL ATLAS
OF GREAT BRITAIN

ORDNANCE SURVEY
COUNTRY LIFE

First published 1986 by
Ordnance Survey   and   **Country Life Books**
Romsey Road   an imprint of
Maybush   *The Hamlyn Publishing Group Limited*
Southampton   *Bridge House, 69 London Road*
SO9 4DH   *Twickenham, Middlesex TW1 3SB*

1:250 000 maps (pages 86–205), index and endpapers by
Ordnance Survey, Southampton © Crown Copyright 1986

Arrangement and all other material, including national maps
(pages 8–83) © The Hamlyn Publishing Group Limited 1986

Reference section pages 8–83 created by Lionheart Books

Country Life Books ISBN 0 600 33316 7
Ordnance Survey ISBN 0 319 00071 0

Printed and bound by Jarrold and Sons Ltd, Norwich

CONTENTS

A SHORT HISTORY OF THE ORDNANCE SURVEY
The National Mapping Organisation

The formation of the Ordnance Survey owes much to the advocacy of General William Roy, a renowned surveyor engineer and archaeologist of the 18th century. As a young man he was responsible for the production of a military map of Scotland following the 1745 Rebellion. Later he directed the first scientific survey operation carried out in Britain; the precise measurement of a survey base line at Hounslow Heath (now London Airport) and the triangulation connection with France. The establishment of a national organisation to be responsible for survey and mapping of the country was not to take shape, however, until after his death in 1790.

In 1791, Britain found itself under threat of invasion from France. The British Army required accurate mapping of the south coast of England for military purposes at 1 inch to 1 mile scale. The survey was carried out by the Board of Ordnance, a Crown organisation, responsible for army engineering, artillery and other armaments at that time. The name Ordnance Survey stems from this time; their first offices in the Tower of London are commemorated today in the Ordnance Survey coat of arms.

As the threat of invasion receded, civilian applications for the mapping were identified. The industrial revolution was under way, with the associated rapid expansion of towns and road and rail networks, and politicians, administrators, civil engineers and others were quick to recognise the value of accurate maps. The survey was gradually extended to cover other areas of the country and Ordnance Survey was given the task of carrying out the work. Moreover, surveys were undertaken to produce maps at much larger scales to give even more detailed and accurate information. There were scientific applications, too, including the mapping of archaeological sites so that by the mid 19th century, Ordnance Survey had assumed its modern role of providing a national survey for scientific, military, government and public use. The authority for many of its activities is the Ordnance Survey Act of 1841.

As urban and industrial development continued, the demand for more detailed large scale maps increased. The original 1 inch to 1 mile series was retained as a general map but in 1840 the scale of 1:10 560 (6 inches to 1 mile) was authorised for the survey of northern England and Scotland which at that time had not been covered by 1 inch to 1 mile scale mapping. It was found, however, that even this scale was inadequate for all purposes, and there then followed a long controversy surrounding the choice of a suitable base scale for maps of Great Britain. This was resolved in 1863 when it was decided to adopt a scale of 1:2500 (25 inches to 1 mile) for cultivated areas, 1:10 560 (6 inches to 1 mile) for uncultivated areas of mountain and moorland and 1:500 (10 feet to 1 mile) for towns of more than 4000 population. Smaller scale maps including the one-inch map were to be derived from these large-scale surveys.

The first 1:2500 scale survey of cultivated areas was completed in 1893 and by 1914 the first revision had been completed. During the period of the 1:2500 survey there were considerable advances in map production, including the introduction of zincography (a process of etching the map image onto zinc plates for printing; previously the image had been transferred to or hand drawn on special smooth limestone blocks), photography and colour printing. The design and content of the mapping also developed in response to technical advances, user demand and economic pressures to stem the rising cost of the national survey. The latter led in 1893 to the abandonment of the 1:500 series of town plans unless locally funded.

Economies were intensified by World War I, and Ordnance Survey, in line with other government organisations suffered considerable cutbacks in manpower and resources, so much so that only revision of large scale maps covering areas of rapid change could be continued. It was unfortunate that these restrictions coincided with government legislation on land registration (1925), town planning (1925), land drainage (1926), slum clearance (1930) and land valuation (1931), all of which in one way or another required accurate mapping for implementation. By the early 1930s it became clear that Ordnance Survey had been left ill-equipped to supply sufficiently accurate maps. A Departmental Committee under the chairmanship of Sir

A contemporary sketch of William Roy's Survey of Scotland.

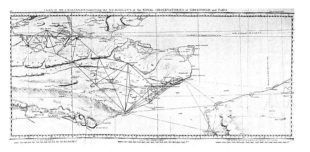

Triangulation connection between the Royal Observatories of Greenwich and Paris – a contemporary map showing the triangulation scheme connecting the Greenwich and Paris meridians; the connection took six years to complete.

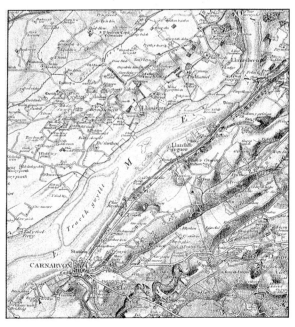

Extract from One-Inch map first published in 1841 – an interesting comparison can be made with the same area shown in the Landranger 2nd Series extract on the next page.

J C (later Lord) Davidson was set up in 1935 to consider how to restore the effectiveness of the national survey.

Its report, although published in 1938, could not be implemented until after World War II, but it formed the framework on which the present Ordnance Survey was developed. The major recommendations of the Davidson Report included: the introduction of a metric National Grid as a reference system for all large and small scale maps; the recasting of the 1:2500 series on national instead of county lines using a national projection (the method of depicting the earth's surface as a flat plane) rather than separate county projections which had caused problems of fit and accuracy along county borders; the introduction of a system of continuous revision for large scale maps; the testing of a larger 1:1250 (50 inches to 1 mile) scale of survey for densely population urban areas; the trial of a 1:25 000 (2½ inches to 1 mile) medium scale map which, if successful, was to be extended to cover the whole country.

After the war, these recommendations were implemented, with large scale surveys, metric conversion and revision proceeding at 1:1250, 1:2500 and 1:10 000 (6 inches to 1 mile) scales. Smaller scale maps of one inch to one mile, 1:25 000 (2½ inches to 1 mile), 1:250 000 (1 inch to 4 miles) and 1:625 000 (10 miles to 1 inch) were all published as derivations from the large scale surveys. The one-inch national series was converted to 1:50 000 scale in the early 1970s.

Today, Ordnance Survey is a civilian government department with headquarters in Southampton and a network of small local survey offices throughout the country. The resurvey task initiated after World War II in response to the Davidson Report has been completed and the emphasis now is on the revision of this huge archive of survey information, to keep it up-to-date and meet user demand. New technology has been used to aid the surveyors and draughtsmen in their task. An increasing number of Ordnance Survey 1:1250 and 1:2500 maps are being produced using automated cartographic techniques. Information collected and recorded by the surveyor in graphic form is converted by electronic means into digital form and stored in a computer databank. The graphic information is recorded as a series of numerical co-ordinates which identify the precise location of the feature on the ground. Once the information is stored on the computer it can be recalled to produce an exact scale map copy, or a larger scale or smaller scale copy as required. Furthermore, selected detail can be recalled rather than the whole map.

While the techniques of survey and mapping have developed and improved dramatically since the early years of the Ordnance Survey, and are still developing, the customers for accurate detailed maps remain basically the same. Computer generated maps are very much in demand from local government, coal, gas, electricity, water and construction industries and others concerned with the maintenance and development of the infrastructure of Great Britain. Ordnance Survey's objective is to continue to meet this demand as well as satisfying the general public's need for small scale derived mapping for educational, leisure and many other purposes.

Editor's Note

The reference section of this atlas has been compiled with the aim of providing comprehensive and up-to-date information on many aspects of Great Britain in the 1980s, from geology to government, climate to culture. Facts and figures have come from a wide variety of sources and have been interpreted in as objective a manner as possible. The most recent available statistics have been included but since there is often a lapse of some years before figures are published, the year of the latest information will frequently vary from subject to subject and exact comparisons have not always been feasible. The most recent census, for example, was in 1981 so demographic statistics are limited to that date. Metric units have been used throughout for consistency.

Extract from modern Landranger (1:50 000 scale) map – the dramatic hill shading of the early version shown on the previous page has been softened, towns and villages have grown in size and the spelling of some of the place names has changed.

Modern surveying – using an electromagnetic distance and angle measuring instrument (EDM Geodometer).

EVOLUTION

At any time in the geological past, the Britain of today would have been quite unrecognizable. High mountains, deserts, tropical swamps, shallow seas, deep ocean basins, freezing ice-caps – these have all occupied the area where the British Isles now lie. This bewildering array of landscapes supported populations of equally bizarre animals and plants. The proof of all this lies in the rocks all around. In the contorted rocks of Scotland and Wales, the roots of ancient mountain chains are to be found. The same regions also display vast thicknesses of shales, made from mud that once lay at the bottom of former oceans. Coal-measures mark the sites of ancient forests. In the Midlands, sandstones that carry the structures of ancient dunes

[For the complete geological timescale see the map key on page 11.]

show where deserts covered the land 370 million years ago. The shallow-water limestones of England's south coast show trails of footprints where, more than 130 million years ago, dinosaurs walked across limy mudflats looking for forage. The clay of the London basin contains fossils of crocodiles and palm kernels, showing that it was laid down at the mouths of muddy sub-tropical rivers. Throughout Britain, mountains are scarred with U-shaped valleys cut by Ice Age glaciers, and the adjoining lowlands are piled with glacial debris.

Geographical and biological studies of present-day Britain indicate that the land is still evolving and that the climate, landscape, flora and fauna will, in only a few million years, be quite different.

Geography of the past
The drifting of continents has had a profound effect on Britain's geological history. During the Ordovician (1), part of Britain lay on the North American landmass and part on the North European. An ocean lay between. In early Devonian times (2) these two continents collided, forcing up along the join the Caledonian Mountains. By the Permian (3), this combined landmass had fused with that of South Europe. The 'supercontinent' so formed then broke up, and by the Tertiary period (4) Britain was part of what we now call Europe.

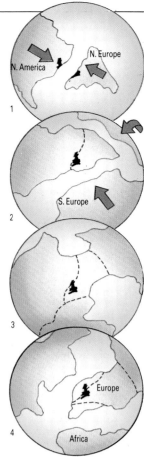

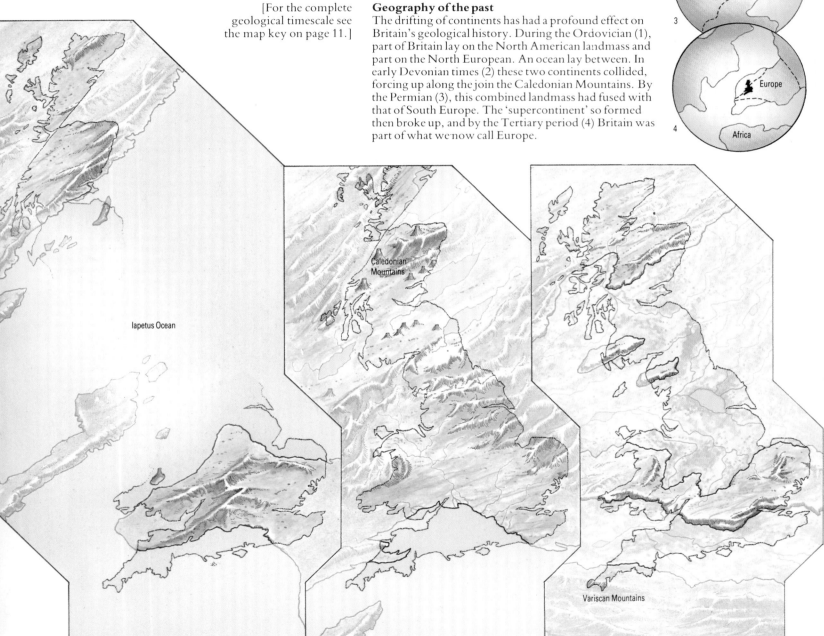

Iapetus Ocean

Caledonian Mountains

Variscan Mountains

Ordovician – 450 million years ago
During the lower Palaeozoic – the Cambrian, Ordovician and Silurian periods – the region that was to become Britain was split in two. The Iapetus Ocean, probably as great in size as the modern Atlantic, lay between them. Gradually the two continental masses moved together, with a great deal of volcanic activity between. Rocks formed in the lower Palaeozoic consist largely of shales.

Devonian – 370 million years ago
In Devonian times the two continents collided, obliterating the Iapetus Ocean and crushing up the vast range of the Caledonian Mountains in between. The northern part of Scotland was then forced into its present position. It was a time of deserts, and most Devonian rocks are desert sandstones. Fossils include, from northern Scotland, the first land-plants and freshwater lake fish, and, in the south, marine creatures.

Carboniferous – 300 million years ago
As the Caledonian Mountains eroded away, shallow seas spread over the area. The eroded debris from the mountains encroached on the seas and produced vast delta swamps, clothed in exotic forests. Mountain-building in northern Europe threw up the Variscan Mountains in the south of the region. The Carboniferous rocks include limestones from the shallow seas and coal deposits from the swamps.

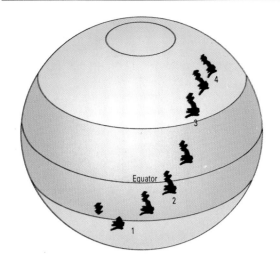

Shifting landmass, changing climate

Britain's climatic history is partly due to the movement of its landmass area across the globe over the past 400 million years. During the Devonian period (1), Britain lay in the southern desert belt of the Earth. By the Carboniferous (2), it lay across the equator, and rain forests flourished. The next period, the Permian (3), found Britain in the northern desert belt, and hot, dry conditions again prevailed. Since then the steady northward movement (4) has produced progressively cooler and moister conditions. (Steps 1 and 3 above correlate with steps 2 and 3 in diagram left.)

Ice Age – 400,000 years ago

The final stamp on the British landscape was placed during the Pleistocene period when, for reasons still unclear, world climate cooled, producing the Ice Age. Ice caps formed on the highlands, and these spread as glaciers into the lowlands, meeting up with ice sheets that reached across the North Sea from Scandinavia. The moving ice sheets modified the scenery significantly. But during the Ice Age there were several glacial phases, separated from one another by interglacial phases with a warmer climate than at present; each phase lasted tens of thousands of years. The map shows the extent of the ice sheet during the most extensive glaciation phase 430,000 to 375,000 years ago.

Permian – 250 million years ago

In Permian and Triassic times, another desert period followed. The Variscan Mountains continued to rise and the area of Britain consisted of mountains and desert basins. A shallow inland sea, the Zechstein, spread across from Germany. Gradually the Permian mountains were eroded to Triassic hills. Typical rocks of the time are desert sandstones. The land animals were mostly desert reptiles.

Jurassic – 150 million years ago

The Jurassic and Cretaceous periods had more equable climates. There were few hills now, and the area consisted largely of shallow seas and low wooded islands. The vegetation of conifers and ferns was browsed by dinosaurs. The marine shales and limestones of the time contain fossils of sea reptiles and molluscs. By the end of the Cretaceous the sea covered almost the whole area; deposits of chalk were created.

Lower Tertiary – 60 million years ago

By the Tertiary, the modern distribution of highlands and lowlands had been established. The shallow sea in south-east England was filling up with mud and clay washed in by rivers from the northern and western highlands. There was volcanic activity in Scotland as the newly created Atlantic Ocean continued to widen. Crocodiles and large mammals roamed the subtropical swamps and forests.

GEOLOGY

Probably no area in the world of similar size displays so great a richness and diversity of geological features as does Britain. Examples of most types of rocks, minerals, soils and land forms that exist in the world are to be found somewhere within the landmass of the British Isles.

Old fold mountains stretch south-west to north-east across northern and southern Scotland and Wales. Four hundred million years ago these formed a vast, almost continuous, mountain chain similar in size and form to the modern Himalayas. Now only isolated highland areas remain. Millions of years of weathering and erosion have cut deeply into the contorted sedimentary rocks and exposed the cores. Here the rocks have been subjected to great pressure and heat, creating new, metamorphic rocks, and the molten material forced up in the mountain-building process has solidified into the intrusive igneous rocks.

Evidence of later mountain-building some 280 million years ago lies in the Pennine chain and in the highland areas of Cornwall and Devon that form the heart of the south-west peninsula.

Relatively undisturbed sedimentary rocks form the rest of the country, and stretch out under the North Sea, where they contain great oil reserves. Being laid down in a gradual, sequential manner, the sedimentary rock layers give an unbroken record of events in Britain's geological history from the Carboniferous period onwards.

Although there is no modern volcanic activity in the area, large lava flows that formed less than 50 million years ago lie on the Scottish islands. Fingal's Cave on the Isle of Staffa is a fine example. And the remains of volcanic islands dating from 450 million years ago appear in Wales and in the Lake District. Notable examples are Cader Idris and Snowdon, which are both in Wales.

Igneous rocks are formed from hot molten material – magma – that has cooled and hardened. Sedimentary rocks are formed as fragments of rocks – pebbles, sand and mud particles – are deposited by rivers and seas then cemented together; the pressure of the upper layers forms rock material in the lower layers.

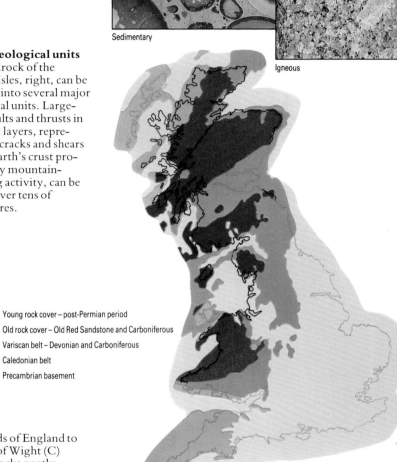

Sedimentary

Igneous

Main geological units
The bedrock of the British Isles, right, can be divided into several major structural units. Large-scale faults and thrusts in the rock layers, representing cracks and shears in the Earth's crust produced by mountain-building activity, can be traced over tens of kilometres.

Young rock cover – post-Permian period
Old rock cover – Old Red Sandstone and Carboniferous
Variscan belt – Devonian and Carboniferous
Caledonian belt
Precambrian basement

Sections through the landmass
Contorted and metamorphosed rocks of Scotland (section A) are cut by numerous faults. From North Wales across to northern England (B), the twisted rocks, more than 400 million years old, give way to gently folded sediments laid down 200 million years later. A section from the Midlands of England to the Isle of Wight (C) shows rocks gently folded by the same Earth movements that built the Alps far away to the south.

Section A   Length of Scotland

Section B   North Wales–Northern England

Section C   Midlands–Isle of Wight

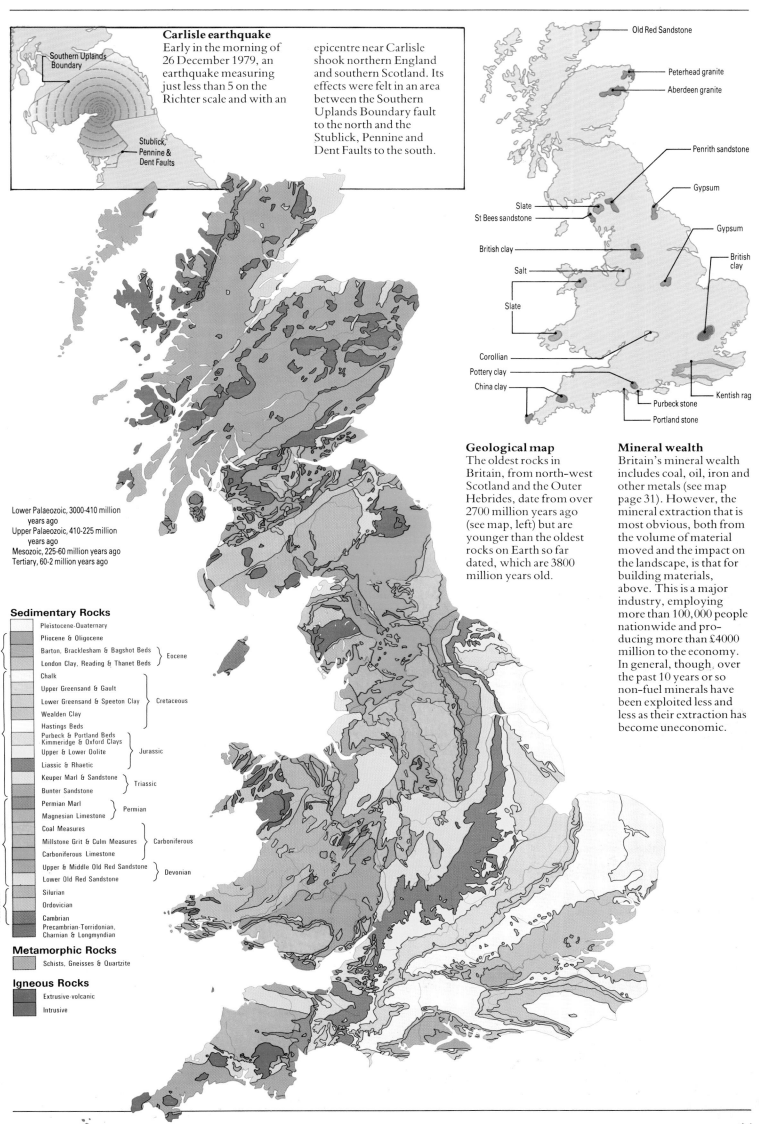

Carlisle earthquake
Early in the morning of 26 December 1979, an earthquake measuring just less than 5 on the Richter scale and with an epicentre near Carlisle shook northern England and southern Scotland. Its effects were felt in an area between the Southern Uplands Boundary fault to the north and the Stublick, Pennine and Dent Faults to the south.

Southern Uplands Boundary

Stublick, Pennine & Dent Faults

Old Red Sandstone

Peterhead granite

Aberdeen granite

Penrith sandstone

Gypsum

Slate

St Bees sandstone

Gypsum

British clay

British clay

Salt

Slate

Corollian

Kentish rag

Pottery clay

China clay

Purbeck stone

Portland stone

Lower Palaeozoic, 3000-410 million years ago
Upper Palaeozoic, 410-225 million years ago
Mesozoic, 225-60 million years ago
Tertiary, 60-2 million years ago

Geological map
The oldest rocks in Britain, from north-west Scotland and the Outer Hebrides, date from over 2700 million years ago (see map, left) but are younger than the oldest rocks on Earth so far dated, which are 3800 million years old.

Mineral wealth
Britain's mineral wealth includes coal, oil, iron and other metals (see map page 31). However, the mineral extraction that is most obvious, both from the volume of material moved and the impact on the landscape, is that for building materials, above. This is a major industry, employing more than 100,000 people nationwide and producing more than £4000 million to the economy. In general, though, over the past 10 years or so non-fuel minerals have been exploited less and less as their extraction has become uneconomic.

Sedimentary Rocks

Tertiary
- Pleistocene-Quaternary
- Pliocene & Oligocene
- Barton, Bracklesham & Bagshot Beds } Eocene
- London Clay, Reading & Thanet Beds

Mesozoic
- Chalk
- Upper Greensand & Gault
- Lower Greensand & Speeton Clay } Cretaceous
- Wealden Clay
- Hastings Beds
- Purbeck & Portland Beds
  Kimmeridge & Oxford Clays
- Upper & Lower Oolite } Jurassic
- Liassic & Rhaetic
- Keuper Marl & Sandstone } Triassic
- Bunter Sandstone

Upper Palaeozoic
- Permian Marl } Permian
- Magnesian Limestone
- Coal Measures
- Millstone Grit & Culm Measures } Carboniferous
- Carboniferous Limestone
- Upper & Middle Old Red Sandstone } Devonian
- Lower Old Red Sandstone

Lower Palaeozoic
- Silurian
- Ordovician
- Cambrian
- Precambrian-Torridonian, Charnian & Longmyndian

Metamorphic Rocks
- Schists, Gneisses & Quartzite

Igneous Rocks
- Extrusive-volcanic
- Intrusive

PHYSICAL GEOGRAPHY

The landscape of Britain is determined primarily by the geology of the area. The different types of underlying rock, laid down during the great Earth movements of the past, produce different kinds of countryside. Hard granites form high moorland dotted with crumbling castle-like tors, as in Exmoor and Dartmoor. Chalk gives rise to undulating downs cut by dry valleys, scenery so typical of Hampshire, Sussex and Kent. Clay produces flat poorly drained grassland, for which East Anglia is renowned.

Some Earth movements and their effects on Britain's physical geography are still going on today. For example, it is only about 10,000 years ago that the glaciers of the last Ice Age retreated. Once a great weight, such as that of ice, is removed, the Earth's crust springs up again. This rebound is still happening in the north of the country, lifting Scotland slowly out of the ocean, and is balanced by a general subsidence in the south, where flooded river valleys along England's south coast are becoming inlets of the sea.

Superimposed on all this are the effects on the landscape of the weather and the ocean. Rain, wind and frost are gradually breaking down all exposed rocks, especially in hilly and mountainous areas, and the rivers are transporting the debris down towards the lowland plains and the sea. The waves and winds of the ocean are attacking and breaking up the rocks and headlands, and transporting the broken material away to form new beaches. The landscape is constantly changing.

The scenery of glaciation

For most of the past two million years Britain was subjected to the effects of an Ice Age. At times, the average annual temperature fell to −9°C and ice sheets more than 1000 m thick extended southwards as far as London in the east and to the Channel in the south. Movements of the ice sheets and the valley glaciers ripped great volumes of rocky material from the uplands, producing scoured surfaces and deep U-shaped valleys, as in the Welsh and Cumbrian mountains. When the glaciers melted all this transported material was left as sandy mounds, gravelly banks and thick layers of boulder clay on the lower land. Huge boulders torn from their outcrops were left stranded tens of kilometres away.

At Ingleborough in the Pennines a large block of rock lies stranded in a curious position. Such 'erratics' indicate glacial action – wind and water cannot move such large masses.

The work of rivers

In its youthful stage, near its source in the mountains, a river erodes the underlying rock, forming a V-shaped valley. In its mature stage, it is moving fast enough to transport rock debris and gently erode its bed. It cuts a winding valley across the land. Where river bends get silted up, it changes course. In its old age, the river deposits the material it has carried from the uplands. Round Britain, most rivers eventually enter estuaries with strong tides that carry the debris seawards.

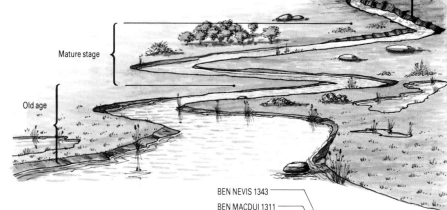

Youthful stage

Mature stage

Old age

Highest, largest, longest

In Britain, the term mountain is used only for land which rises above 600 m. The rugged topography of the Grampians, Welsh and Cumbrian mountains produces not only the highest peaks – the diagram, right, shows the four or five highest for Scotland, Wales and England – but also the largest lakes and the sources of the longest rivers.

MOUNTAINS (HEIGHT m)

BEN NEVIS 1343
BEN MACDUI 1311
BRAERIACH 1294
CAIRN TOUL 1292
CAIRN GORM 1244
SNOWDON 1085
CARNEDD LLEWELYN 1062
CARNEDD DAFYDD 1066
GLYDER FAWR 999
GLYDER FÀCH 994
SCAFELL PIKES 969
SCA FELL 963
HELVELLYN 950
SKIDDAW 930
BOW FELL 902

LAKES (AREA km²/DEPTH m)

LOCH LOMOND 71·2/189
LOCH NESS 56·2/228
LOCH AWE 38·7/93
LOCH MAREE 28·4/111
LOCH MORAR 26·6/309
WINDERMERE 14·7/66
ULLSWATER 8·9/62
BASSENTHWAITE/DERWENT WATER 5·3/21
CONISTON 4·8/56
LAKE VYRNWY 4·5/62
BALA LAKE 4·3/38

RIVERS (LENGTH km)

SPEY 157
CLYDE 158
NENE 161
TAY 188
WYE 215
GREAT OUSE 230
AIRE-HUMBER 260
TRENT 300
THAMES 346
SEVERN 354

Highland and lowland zones

A section N–S through Britain, below (see main map for position of the section line), shows that the older deformed rocks in the centre of the ancient Caledonian mountain chain have survived as rugged uplands and the younger relatively undisturbed rocks of south-east England have produced flat plains or, at most, gentle downlands.

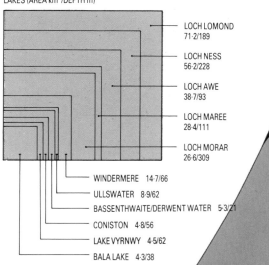

m
1350
900
450
0

N

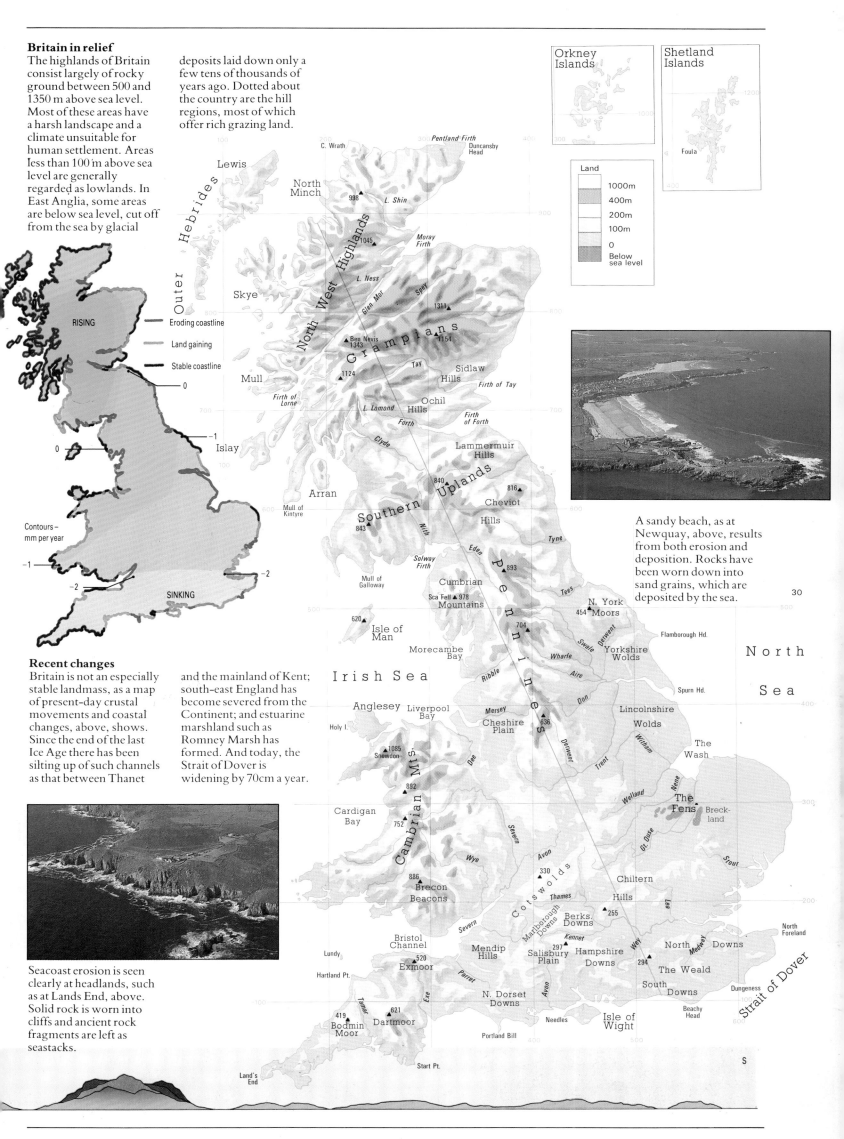

Britain in relief

The highlands of Britain consist largely of rocky ground between 500 and 1350 m above sea level. Most of these areas have a harsh landscape and a climate unsuitable for human settlement. Areas less than 100 m above sea level are generally regarded as lowlands. In East Anglia, some areas are below sea level, cut off from the sea by glacial deposits laid down only a few tens of thousands of years ago. Dotted about the country are the hill regions, most of which offer rich grazing land.

Recent changes

Britain is not an especially stable landmass, as a map of present-day crustal movements and coastal changes, above, shows. Since the end of the last Ice Age there has been silting up of such channels as that between Thanet and the mainland of Kent; south-east England has become severed from the Continent; and estuarine marshland such as Romney Marsh has formed. And today, the Strait of Dover is widening by 70cm a year.

RISING

Eroding coastline
Land gaining
Stable coastline

Contours – mm per year

SINKING

Seacoast erosion is seen clearly at headlands, such as at Lands End, above. Solid rock is worn into cliffs and ancient rock fragments are left as seastacks.

A sandy beach, as at Newquay, above, results from both erosion and deposition. Rocks have been worn down into sand grains, which are deposited by the sea.

Orkney Islands

Shetland Islands

Foula

Land
1000m
400m
200m
100m
0
Below sea level

C. Wrath
Pentland Firth
Duncansby Head
Lewis
North Minch
Hebrides
Outer
998
L. Shin
Skye
1045
Moray Firth
L. Ness
Glen Mor
Spey
North West Highlands
Grampians
1311
Ben Nevis 1343
1154
1124
Tay
Sidlaw Hills
Firth of Tay
Mull
Firth of Lorne
L. Lomond
Ochil Hills
Forth
Firth of Forth
Arran
Clyde
Lammermuir Hills
Mull of Kintyre
840
Southern Uplands
816
Cheviot Hills
843
Nith
Eden
Tyne
Solway Firth
893
Pennines
Cumbrian Mountains
Tees
Sca Fell 978
N. York Moors
454
620
Isle of Man
Derwent
Flamborough Hd.
Morecambe Bay
Swale
Wharfe
Yorkshire Wolds
Irish Sea
Ribble
Aire
Spurn Hd.
Anglesey
Liverpool Bay
Mersey
704
Don
Lincolnshire Wolds
Holy I.
636
Cheshire Plain
Witham
The Wash
1085
Snowdon
Dee
Derwent
Trent
Nene
Welland
The Fens
Breckland
892
Cardigan Bay
Cambrian Mts.
752
Severn
Gt. Ouse
Stour
886
Wye
Avon
330
Cotswolds
Chiltern Hills
Brecon Beacons
Thames
255
Severn
Marlborough Downs
Berks. Downs
Kennet
Bristol Channel
297
North Downs
Medway
Lundy
Mendip Hills
Salisbury Plain
Hampshire Downs
Wey
North Foreland
Hartland Pt.
520
Exmoor
Avon
294
The Weald
South Downs
Beachy Head
Dungeness
N. Dorset Downs
Needles
Isle of Wight
Exe
Parret
419
Bodmin Moor
621
Dartmoor
Portland Bill
Strait of Dover
Tamar
Land's End
Start Pt.

North Sea

S

30

13

CLIMATE

Britain has a temperate climate. The reason for this is twofold. First, the surrounding sea acts as a temperature buffer. Water tends to take longer to heat up and to cool down than does both land and air so that in general the sea is cooler than the land in summer and warmer in winter, and coastal areas can experience cool conditions when inland it is warm and vice versa. Second, Britain lies in the latitudes that come under the influences of both the warm air moving northwards from the tropics and the cold air sweeping down from the North Pole. The prevailing winds resulting from the interaction of these two air masses are either warm south-westerlies or cold north-easterlies. The Gulf Stream, which carries warm water from the tropics to the Arctic, has a moderating effect along Britain's west coast but its overall influence is minor.

The turbulence between the polar and tropical air masses produces 'frontal systems'. A front is a boundary between two distinct and opposing masses of air. As a front passes over a particular place it brings with it constantly changing conditions of temperature, cloud cover and rainfall. These fluctuating conditions, so typical in Britain, constitute 'the weather'.

In general terms, in winter the west of Britain is warmer than the east, and in summer the south is warmer than the north. The south-east shows the greatest contrasts in temperature. The west has more rainfall than the south, while in some parts of the east most of the annual rainfall occurs during the summer months.

Global air circulation

Warm air is constantly rising at the equator. It then moves north and south at high altitudes. When this air becomes cool, it descends. This is near the tropics. In the Northern Hemisphere, some of the air then spreads southwards and some moves further northwards. Cold air from the North Pole is spreading outwards, and the two air masses meet over Britain. However, the turning of the Earth deflects northerly and southerly winds east and west respectively.

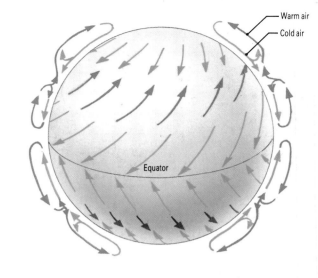

Warm air
Cold air

Equator

Frontal systems

Cold and warm air masses do not mix but slide past each other, producing fronts. The friction between the air masses creates eddies, with the opposing fronts swirling around and competing against each other. As each eddy develops (see diagram), successive cold and warm fronts pass over the land.

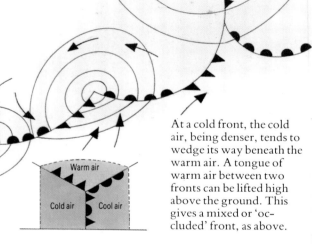

▲▲▲ Cold front
◖▲◖▲ Occluded front
◖◖◖ Warm front

Warm air

Cold air   Cool air

At a cold front, the cold air, being denser, tends to wedge its way beneath the warm air. A tongue of warm air between two fronts can be lifted high above the ground. This gives a mixed or 'occluded' front, as above.

Depressions or rain areas

Frontal systems passing over Britain tend to have a common history. The cold north-east and warm south-west winds meet over the Atlantic Ocean. As they slide past one another they begin to curl round, the north-easterlies turning southwards forming a cold front and the south-westerlies turning northwards forming a warm front. The winds spiral inwards towards a low-pressure area at the apex of the two fronts. This whole system drifts eastwards over Britain as the Earth turns on its axis. From the ground, the approach of a warm front can be seen by a sequence of high-, medium-, then low-altitude clouds coming from the west. As the warm front itself passes over, there is usually rainfall. This is followed by a settled warm spell as the warm air mass moves over. The cold front then passes, bringing with it rain and a drop in temperature.

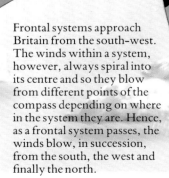

Frontal systems approach Britain from the south-west. The winds within a system, however, always spiral into its centre and so they blow from different points of the compass depending on where in the system they are. Hence, as a frontal system passes, the winds blow, in succession, from the south, the west and finally the north.

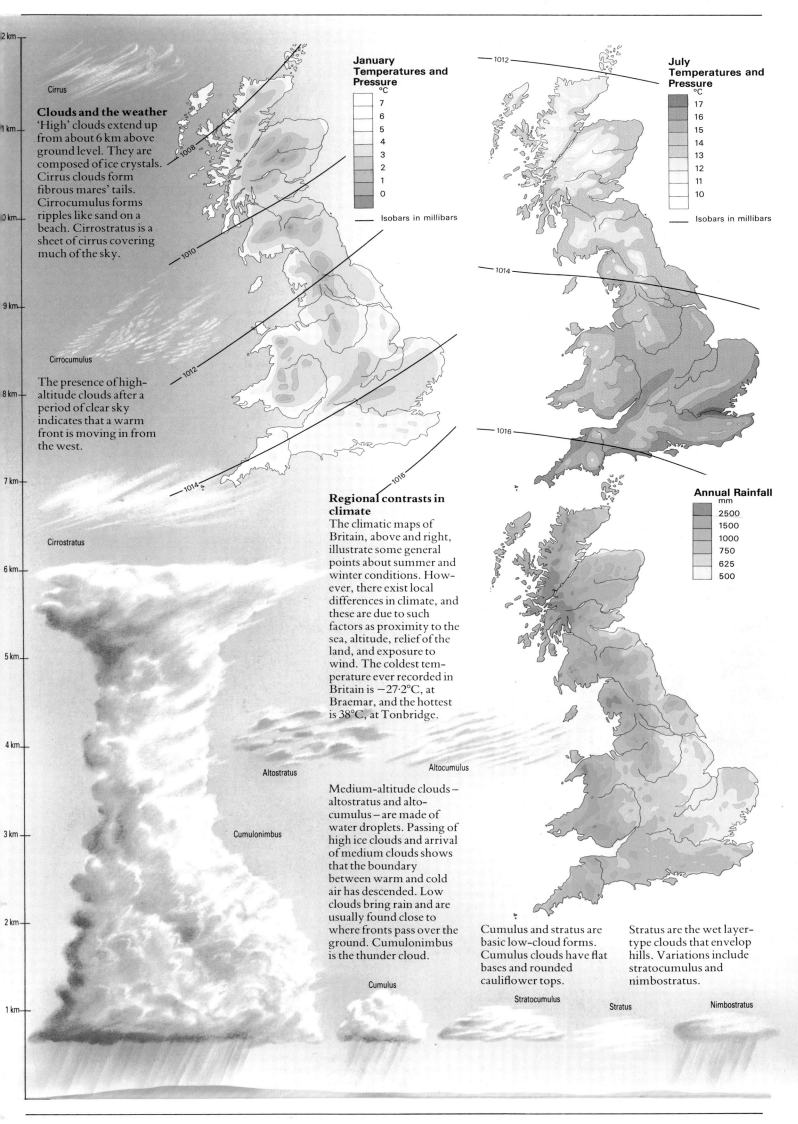

Clouds and the weather
'High' clouds extend up from about 6 km above ground level. They are composed of ice crystals. Cirrus clouds form fibrous mares' tails. Cirrocumulus forms ripples like sand on a beach. Cirrostratus is a sheet of cirrus covering much of the sky.

The presence of high-altitude clouds after a period of clear sky indicates that a warm front is moving in from the west.

Cirrus

Cirrocumulus

Cirrostratus

Cumulonimbus

Altostratus

Altocumulus

Cumulus

Stratocumulus

Stratus

Nimbostratus

January Temperatures and Pressure
°C
7
6
5
4
3
2
1
0

Isobars in millibars

1008
1010
1012
1014

July Temperatures and Pressure
°C
17
16
15
14
13
12
11
10

Isobars in millibars

1012
1014
1016

Annual Rainfall
mm
2500
1500
1000
750
625
500

Regional contrasts in climate
The climatic maps of Britain, above and right, illustrate some general points about summer and winter conditions. However, there exist local differences in climate, and these are due to such factors as proximity to the sea, altitude, relief of the land, and exposure to wind. The coldest temperature ever recorded in Britain is −27·2°C, at Braemar, and the hottest is 38°C, at Tonbridge.

Medium-altitude clouds – altostratus and alto-cumulus – are made of water droplets. Passing of high ice clouds and arrival of medium clouds shows that the boundary between warm and cold air has descended. Low clouds bring rain and are usually found close to where fronts pass over the ground. Cumulonimbus is the thunder cloud.

Cumulus and stratus are basic low-cloud forms. Cumulus clouds have flat bases and rounded cauliflower tops.

Stratus are the wet layer-type clouds that envelop hills. Variations include stratocumulus and nimbostratus.

NATURAL HABITATS

The geological evolution of Britain, its rock structure, physical geography and climate have all worked together to produce its natural habitats. Soils have been formed by breakdown of the rocks by ice, water and wind and the addition of organic material from living creatures. The nature of the soil and the climate determine which plants can grow in a particular area. The vegetation then gives rise to the animal life.

In every habitat, each living creature depends upon another. The plants use the energy of sunlight to build up foodstuffs from carbon dioxide in the air and water and nutrients drawn up from the soil. A plant's food is for its own use, but inevitably plant-eating animals come and take it. These animals are chased and eaten by predators which may, in turn, be eaten by other predators. Every plant that is not grazed and animal that is not hunted to death eventually dies. When it does, its remains are eaten by scavenging creatures and broken down by decomposing organisms such as fungi and bacteria. This results in carbon dioxide being returned to the atmosphere and nutrients to the soil, and so the cycle of life continues.

Although not a stable condition, as animals and plants struggle for survival, it is the natural one. However, human beings disrupt the simple cycle. Ever since large-scale farming started in Britain, some 4500 years ago, the natural vegetation of the land has been gradually transformed. Today, open landscape continues to be turned into farmland or given over to urban development.

Mixed habitats
Britain has a very wide variety of natural environments. In many places, such as here at Wicken Fen, different habitats can be found close to one another.

Food chains
Food chains – living systems in which energy is passed around by one creature eating another – are found in every habitat. In each example of habitat shown opposite some of the representative creatures are illustrated, colour-coded to indicate their position on the generalized food chain shown left.

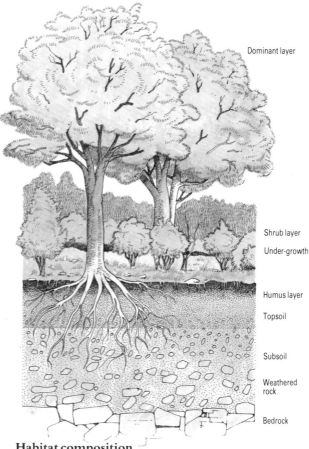

Habitat composition
Taking as an example a forest, trees form the dominant layer. Then come varying amounts of lower shrub and undergrowth. Humus, on the surface of the soil, consists of organic material. Plant roots and soil animals lie in the topsoil layer. Pebbles and stones lie on the bedrock.

Dominant layer

Shrub layer

Under-growth

Humus layer

Topsoil

Subsoil

Weathered rock

Bedrock

Soil types
Soil – the loose substance that covers rocks – consists of a complex mixture of rocky and biological materials, worked on by weather and burrowing organisms. In Britain many different types are to be found. Cambisol is little altered from the original rock. Rendzina is a thin soil found over limestone. Gleysol is a grey, wet muddy soil formed from unconsolidated sediments. Fluvisol is found in river valleys and has an organic-rich surface. Luvisol is wet and clayey. Histosol is mostly peat. Podsol has a cemented layer and is found on hills. Arenosol is pale and sandy. Ranker is a dark soil on hard rocky slopes. The names are mostly Russian in origin, a legacy of where most pioneering soil study was done.

Sun

Nutrients in the soil

Plants

Primary consumers (herbivores)

Secondary consumers (1st order predators)

Tertiary consumers (2nd order predators)

Scavengers and decomposers

Cambisol
Rendzina
Gleysol
Fluvisol
Luvisol
Histosol
Podsol
Arenosol
Ranker

Birch scrub

The rocky northern isles of Scotland support only scrubby woodlands of birch and mountain ash, with an undergrowth of bracken and heather. The open nature of the habitat encourages birds of prey, giving them a clear view of the ground and its inhabitants.

Potential vegetation

The map below gives an idea of the type of vegetation expected across Britain if the land was relatively free of human interference. This is very theoretical since all natural habitats have been broken up and in places completely destroyed; they are now impossible to map accurately.

Oak & beech forest
Mountain vegetation (not illustrated)

Proportion of each natural habitat type

In the Middle Ages, forests occupied more than 35% of the land. Today they account for less than 10% and only a few isolated ancient forest areas remain; Epping Forest, Essex, is a good example.

Pine and mixed conifer forest

The acid soils and the cool climates of north-east Scotland support hardy coniferous trees. The fall of needles from such trees produces a deep ground-litter that decomposes only slowly; the lack of humus sometimes yields little undergrowth.

Deciduous forest

The traditional woodland of most of Britain consists of oak, ash and, in the south, beech. Such forests produce a vigorous shrub layer and undergrowth. The rich variety of plants supports many different animals.

Heath

Heathland and moorland are open habitats, found on sandy and peaty soil respectively. Heather and bracken are typical large plants, with mosses and lichens providing the undergrowth. The sunny aspect of these open lands encourages reptiles.

Alder woodland

Along the banks of rivers the main trees are water-loving types such as alder and willow. Rushes and sedges grow in wet areas. Aquatic birds, like herons and ducks, feed on the animals and plants that are found in still and flowing water.

Salt marshes

Tidal areas support hardy plants that can survive immersion both in salt water and fresh, and also frequent drying. Tough grasses colonize salty mudbanks, and wading birds probe for burrowing invertebrates in the open mudflats.

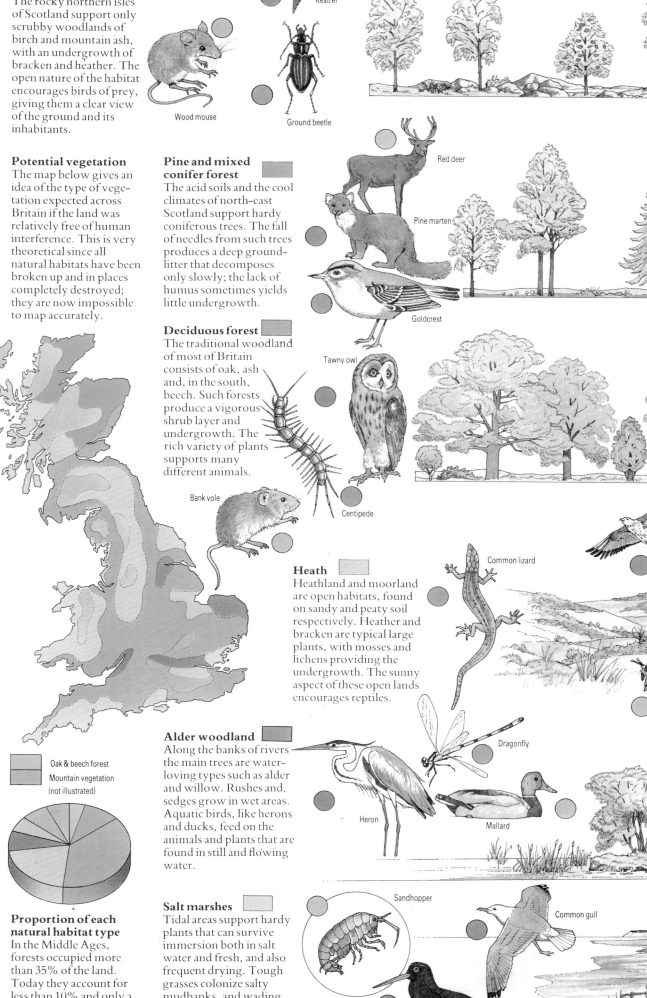

Kestrel

Wood mouse

Ground beetle

Red deer

Pine marten

Goldcrest

Tawny owl

Bank vole

Centipede

Common lizard

Buzzard

Bumble bee

Dragonfly

Heron

Mallard

Sandhopper

Common gull

Oystercatcher

BRITAIN IN THE MID-18TH CENTURY

In 1750 Britain was still a traditional, agrarian society, as yet untouched by the upheavals of industrialisation. The great majority of people were poor and lived and worked on the land, like their ancestors before them. Only about one-tenth of the population lived in towns or cities, of which London with its 750,000 or so inhabitants was by far the largest. Since the Civil War of the 17th century, power rested no longer with the monarchy, but with a government dominated by aristocratic landowners, whose interests determined policy at home and abroad.

Aggressive imperial expansion abroad gave Britain a lead in international trade, opened up new markets and stimulated the growth of the navy. In the New World, sugar and cotton plantations worked by slaves yielded huge profits for their British owners, as did the slave trade itself.

At home, where slavery was illegal, the number of impoverished rural labourers increased as larger, more productive, landholdings were created, backed by the force of law. The Enclosure Acts cleared wasteland, common pasture and woodland, and deprived villagers of their traditional rights to collect wood, graze animals and set traps. Severe trespass and game laws were passed to protect private property. Slowly, the British peasantry began to disappear as the smaller landowners were squeezed out of the market.

This was a period that saw the traditional self-sufficiency and barter of rural life replaced by a cash economy and widespread distribution of basic commodities. Artisans and traders of all kinds found an expanding market for their goods, and the growth of transportation gradually led to improvements in the roads and waterways.

At home and abroad, the pursuit of profit brought with it a steady accumulation of capital. In trade and commerce a new middle class was developing, while changes on the land created a labour surplus. These were the preconditions for the industrial revolution that was soon to transform British society.

Parliament

Parliament consisted of a small, powerful House of Lords and a House of Commons elected by a tiny fraction of the adult male population. As members were not paid, both chambers were run by rich merchants, bankers and landowners, whose interests predominated. Many towns, including Birmingham, Manchester, Sheffield and Leeds, were not represented at all. Scotland had only one more MP than Cornwall. Some of the rural boroughs represented had only a handful of voters. They became known as rotten boroughs. Each county returned two MPs, irrespective of size. Voting was not secret, and bribery and intimidation were rife.

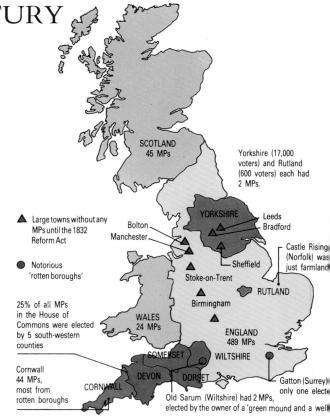

SCOTLAND 45 MPs

Yorkshire (17,000 voters) and Rutland (600 voters) each had 2 MPs.

YORKSHIRE
Leeds
Bradford
Bolton
Manchester
Sheffield
Stoke-on-Trent
Birmingham
RUTLAND
Castle Rising (Norfolk) was just farmland

▲ Large towns without any MPs until the 1832 Reform Act

● Notorious 'rotten boroughs'

25% of all MPs in the House of Commons were elected by 5 south-western counties

WALES 24 MPs
ENGLAND 489 MPs
SOMERSET
WILTSHIRE
DEVON
DORSET
CORNWALL

Cornwall 44 MPs, most from rotten boroughs

Gatton (Surrey) only one elected

Old Sarum (Wiltshire) had 2 MPs, elected by the owner of a 'green mound and a well'

The urban and rural poor

Food, mainly cereals, absorbed much of the income of the poor. They hardly ever ate meat, and their clothes were home-made or cast offs from the local gentry. When bad harvests pushed up the price of bread, people took to the streets (left).

A third of the population lived in villages or small market towns in the agricultural belt across the middle of Britain. For landless labourers (below) the seasonal nature of the work kept them and their families in great poverty.

Overseas trade

The Navigation Acts of the 17th century ensured that all trade between Britain and its colonies was carried on by British ships. The colonies could buy their manufactured goods only from Britain, and they were forbidden to sell outside the Empire. Consequently, goods that arrived at British ports from the colonies were often re-exported to Europe at a great profit. Newcastle, like other small ports, also imported a variety of goods from Europe, in return exporting cloth and sometimes coal. Complicated trade regulations and high customs duties led to widespread smuggling.

Imports to Newcastle upon Tyne 1744

	Belgium	Holland	Germany	France	Jersey	Italy	Spain	Portugal	Sweden	Norway	Russia	Denmark	Turkey	Africa	East Indies	USA	S. America	Canada
No. ships	7	64	178	37	5	20	9	8	28	77	60	109	4	8	4	1	3	46
Apples and pears																		
Oranges																		
Currants, grapes																		
Onions																		
Nuts																		
Grain																		
Wine																		
Spirits																		
Sugar																		
Beef, pork																		
Cheese																		
Bones																		
Hides, horses, hoofs																		
Sealskins																		
Guano																		
Timber																		
Bark																		
Flax, hemp																		
Rope																		
Mats																		
Oil cake																		
Linseed																		
Grease																		

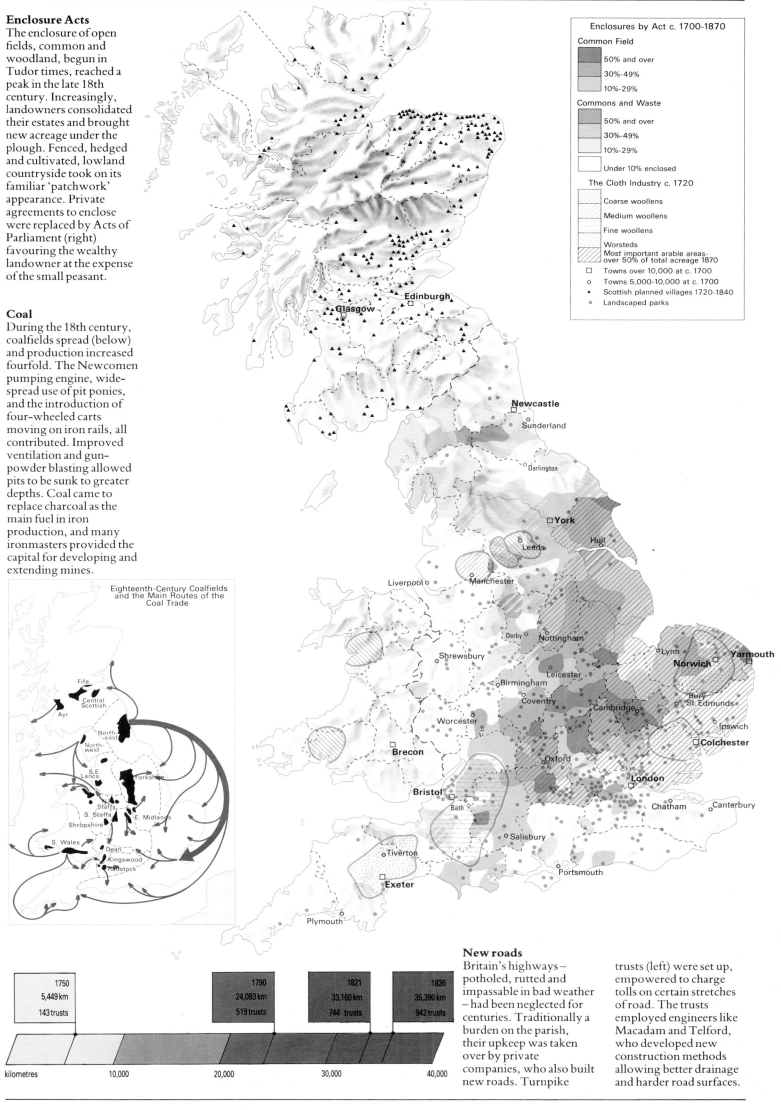

Enclosure Acts

The enclosure of open fields, common and woodland, begun in Tudor times, reached a peak in the late 18th century. Increasingly, landowners consolidated their estates and brought new acreage under the plough. Fenced, hedged and cultivated, lowland countryside took on its familiar 'patchwork' appearance. Private agreements to enclose were replaced by Acts of Parliament (right) favouring the wealthy landowner at the expense of the small peasant.

Coal

During the 18th century, coalfields spread (below) and production increased fourfold. The Newcomen pumping engine, widespread use of pit ponies, and the introduction of four-wheeled carts moving on iron rails, all contributed. Improved ventilation and gunpowder blasting allowed pits to be sunk to greater depths. Coal came to replace charcoal as the main fuel in iron production, and many ironmasters provided the capital for developing and extending mines.

Enclosures by Act c. 1700-1870

Common Field
- 50% and over
- 30%-49%
- 10%-29%

Commons and Waste
- 50% and over
- 30%-49%
- 10%-29%
- Under 10% enclosed

The Cloth Industry c. 1720
- Coarse woollens
- Medium woollens
- Fine woollens
- Worsteds
- Most important arable areas – over 50% of total acreage 1870
- □ Towns over 10,000 at c. 1700
- ○ Towns 5,000-10,000 at c. 1700
- ▲ Scottish planned villages 1720-1840
- • Landscaped parks

Eighteenth-Century Coalfields and the Main Routes of the Coal Trade

New roads

Britain's highways – potholed, rutted and impassable in bad weather – had been neglected for centuries. Traditionally a burden on the parish, their upkeep was taken over by private companies, who also built new roads. Turnpike trusts (left) were set up, empowered to charge tolls on certain stretches of road. The trusts employed engineers like Macadam and Telford, who developed new construction methods allowing better drainage and harder road surfaces.

1750	1790	1821	1836
5,449 km	24,083 km	33,160 km	35,390 km
143 trusts	519 trusts	744 trusts	942 trusts

kilometres   10,000   20,000   30,000   40,000

THE INDUSTRIAL REVOLUTION

In 1829 Thomas Carlyle characterised his age as 'the Age of Machinery'. He was describing the world's first industrial revolution. From the 1780s Britain was transformed by mechanical innovation, multiplying the productive power of human society. Economic growth was accompanied by a population explosion, providing labour and domestic markets for finished goods. The dramatic rise in supply and demand, imports and exports, investment and profit, set in motion forces that continued to accelerate the process of change.

Initially the Industrial Revolution was based on cotton, coal and steam power, but from the 1830s the railway boom stimulated iron and steel production. Industrial landscapes mushroomed across the coalfields and textile regions: factories, mines, workshops, blast furnaces, railways and steam engines surrounded by the cramped terraces that housed the first generation of industrial workers – and their successors.

The power to make things, and to move goods and people faster than ever before instilled confidence in those who turned 'muck into brass'.

'Progress' became a byword for the men who made fortunes from commerce and industry – the new middle class – and they were quick to claim political power. The 1832 Reform Act enfranchised the £10-householder and ended the old regime of landed wealth. Industrial society would henceforth be directed by the beliefs, values and aspirations of the middle class, not the aristocracy.

For the men, women and children who were driven in search of work to the new factory towns, industrialisation brought new levels of exploitation and hardship. The upheaval, and the bitterness and misery it caused, found expression in Luddite machine-breaking and, more positively, in early trade unionism.

After the 1830s, new forms of social control evolved – the Poor Law, factory legislation and improvements in urban conditions. The old moral and economic order of rural society had gone for ever, replaced by the political economy of industrial capitalism and the spectacle, in William Blake's words, of 'dark satanic mills' in 'England's green and pleasant land'.

The cotton trade
Between 1800 and 1840 the mechanisation of the textile industry brought about a huge rise in cotton imports and exports and revenue increased fourfold. Inventions such as the spinning jenny, flying shuttle and, later, power loom, revolutionised production in the Lancashire cotton mills – Britain's first factories.

Total value
1840
£50,000,000

Columns
×1,000,000 lbs

Total value
1800
£13,000,000

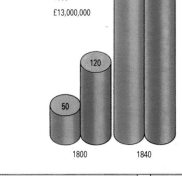

Imports
Exports

Parliamentary reform
The 1832 Reform Act had two main objectives: a more just and rational distribution of seats, and the extension of voting rights to the new middle classes. New urban seats were created to even out major discrepancies in constituency size. Most of the rotten boroughs, controlled by local landowners, were abolished. After 1832, a man qualified to vote who owned or rented a house worth £10 or more a year. This added about 300,000 new voters to the previous half-million – altogether, about 7% of the adult population. Later reforms (1867 and 1884) enfranchised male ratepayers, but even by 1914 only one third of the adult population could vote, with women still excluded.

New boroughs with 2 seats
1. Manchester
2. Birmingham
3. Leeds
4. Greenwich
5. Sheffield
6. Sunderland
7. Devonport
8. Wolverhampton
9. Finsbury
10. Marylebone
11. Lambeth
12. Bolton
13. Bradford
14. Blackburn
15. Oldham
16. Brighton
17. Halifax
18. Stockport
19. Stoke-on-Trent
20. Stroud

New boroughs with 1 seat
21. Ashton-under-Lyne
22. Bury
23. Chatham
24. Cheltenham
25. Dudley
26. Frome
27. Gateshead
28. Huddersfield
29. Kidderminster
30. Kendal
31. Rochdale
32. Salford
33. South Shields
34. Tynemouth
35. Wakefield
36. Walsall
37. Warrington
38. Whitby
39. Whitehaven
40. Merthyr Tydfil

▲ Boroughs abolished

● New boroughs with 1 seat

• New boroughs with 2 seats

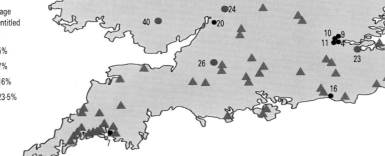

Percentage adults entitled to vote:

1831 5%
1832 7%
1867 16%
1884 23·5%

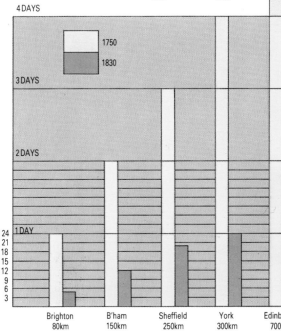

4 DAYS

1750
1830

3 DAYS

2 DAYS

1 DAY

HOURS

24
21
18
15
12
9
6
3

Brighton 80km
B'ham 150km
Sheffield 250km
York 300km
Edinburgh 700km

Faster travel
Even before the railways, great progress was made in reducing travelling time and costs. Between 1750 and 1830, journey times between some major cities were cut by 80% (above). A network of canals linking industrial centres was built, to speed up the movement of freight. The harder, more durable road surfaces developed by the turnpike trusts encouraged the building of faster, more comfortable carriages. During the great coaching age, speeds of 20 km/h were maintained, with stops at coaching stations for fresh horses and for passengers. Daily newspapers were delivered by stagecoach, and the Royal Mail developed as a regular national postal service.

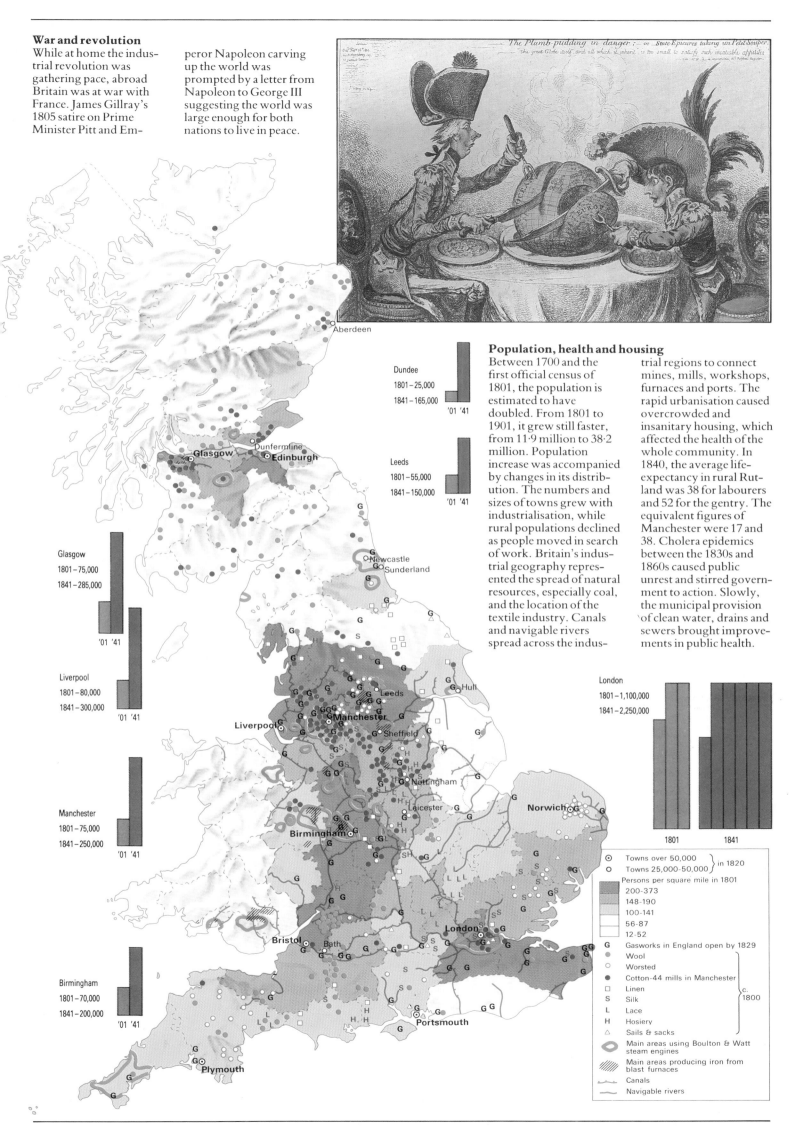

War and revolution

While at home the industrial revolution was gathering pace, abroad Britain was at war with France. James Gillray's 1805 satire on Prime Minister Pitt and Emperor Napoleon carving up the world was prompted by a letter from Napoleon to George III suggesting the world was large enough for both nations to live in peace.

The Plumb-pudding in danger; — or State Epicures taking un Petit Souper

Population, health and housing

Between 1700 and the first official census of 1801, the population is estimated to have doubled. From 1801 to 1901, it grew still faster, from 11·9 million to 38·2 million. Population increase was accompanied by changes in its distribution. The numbers and sizes of towns grew with industrialisation, while rural populations declined as people moved in search of work. Britain's industrial geography represented the spread of natural resources, especially coal, and the location of the textile industry. Canals and navigable rivers spread across the industrial regions to connect mines, mills, workshops, furnaces and ports. The rapid urbanisation caused overcrowded and insanitary housing, which affected the health of the whole community. In 1840, the average life-expectancy in rural Rutland was 38 for labourers and 52 for the gentry. The equivalent figures of Manchester were 17 and 38. Cholera epidemics between the 1830s and 1860s caused public unrest and stirred government to action. Slowly, the municipal provision of clean water, drains and sewers brought improvements in public health.

Dundee
1801 – 25,000
1841 – 165,000
'01 '41

Leeds
1801 – 55,000
1841 – 150,000
'01 '41

Glasgow
1801 – 75,000
1841 – 285,000
'01 '41

Liverpool
1801 – 80,000
1841 – 300,000
'01 '41

Manchester
1801 – 75,000
1841 – 250,000
'01 '41

Birmingham
1801 – 70,000
1841 – 200,000
'01 '41

London
1801 – 1,100,000
1841 – 2,250,000
1801   1841

Aberdeen
Dunfermline
Glasgow   Edinburgh
Newcastle
Sunderland
Leeds   Hull
Liverpool   Manchester
Sheffield
Nottingham
Leicester   Norwich
Birmingham
Bristol   Bath
London
Portsmouth
Plymouth

| | Towns over 50,000 | } in 1820 |
| | Towns 25,000–50,000 | |

Persons per square mile in 1801
200-373
148-190
100-141
56-87
12-52

G   Gasworks in England open by 1829
Wool
Worsted
Cotton–44 mills in Manchester
Linen
S   Silk
L   Lace
H   Hosiery
Sails & sacks
} c. 1800

Main areas using Boulton & Watt steam engines
Main areas producing iron from blast furnaces
Canals
Navigable rivers

WORKSHOP OF THE WORLD

The Great Exhibition of 1851 announced to the world that Britain was an industrial nation second to none. Although German and North American competitors were later to take the lead, for the time being Britain's world dominance was assured. The Victorian and Edwardian eras were years of peace, stability and prosperity, which laid the foundations of modern urban society. 'Of all decades in our history', wrote the contemporary historian G.M. Young, 'a wise man would choose the 1850s to be young in.'

But 19th-century Britain was also a very divided society, and many did not share in the prosperity. While skilled workers who were in regular employment benefited from rising wages and 'self-help' forms of association such as co-operative stores and friendly societies, millions of unskilled and casual labourers led a precarious existence, with only the punitive deterrent of the workhouse to underwrite the risks of near-starvation wages, bad food, overcrowding and disease. To make matters worse, the vast reserves of cheap labour upon whom the new 'free-market' economy depended were constantly swollen by immigrants from Ireland and eastern Europe. One in four of

the population lived below a very meagre poverty line.

As well as class differences, society was also divided very rigidly according to gender. In an age that upheld the virtues of family life, married women could expect to see their health ruined by excessive child-bearing and inadequate medical care. Working-class women were especially disadvantaged, poorly paid in the labour market and overburdened – and without means – in the home.

The extremes of wealth and want generated great Victorian social movements for improvement and reform. Philanthropists, radicals and socialists all devoted their energies to making a less needy, more democratic, more egalitarian society. By the end of this period, the government had accepted, at least in principle, that the state had some duty to care for the well-being of its people.

A powerful unifying force in Britain at this time, which lasted up to World War I and beyond, was the Empire and all that it stood for. Jubilee celebrations for the Queen Empress, Boer War jingoism and popular music-hall songs invited the humblest subject to identify with nationhood and take pride in a empire on which 'the sun never set'.

£6079 (0·5%)

UPPER CLASS

MIDDLE CLASS

WORKING CLASS

(1867 figures)

Victorian women
The Victorian middle classes perfected an ideal of separate spheres for men and women. The public world of trade and commerce was essentially a male preserve. Women were confined to the home – 'the angel of the hearth' (right) and guardian of the family's moral well-being. A woman was always expected to place her family's needs above her own. Lower down the social scale, the National Federation of Women Workers (below), formed in 1906, unionised many thousands of unskilled women workers.

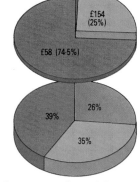

£154 (25%)

£58 (74·5%)

39%   26%

35%

Income and wealth
The upper class, whose annual income of £6000 plus was 26% of the national income, was still very rich compared with the much larger middle class (above). The working-class masses were by far the poorest.

Domestic service
By 1914, there were about 1·5 million domestic servants in Britain, men and women of all ages (right). Life was hard and the hours were long. Some families had just one servant, while the wealthier ones had as many as 30.

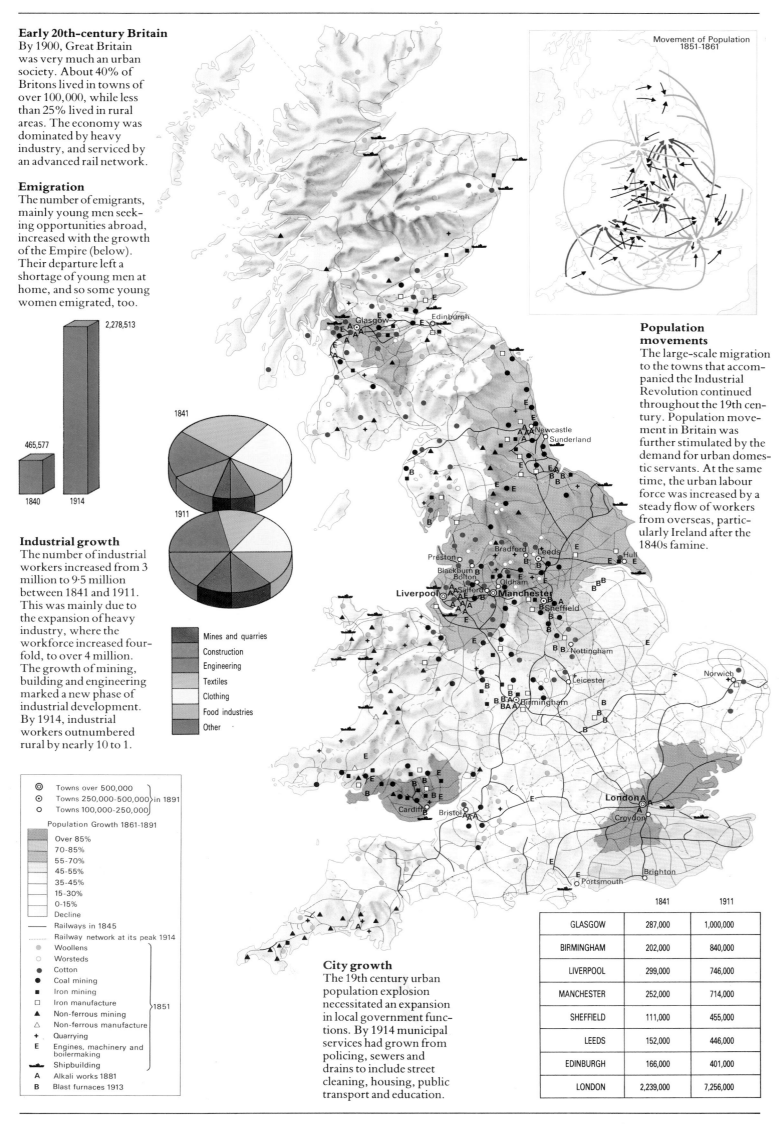

Early 20th-century Britain

By 1900, Great Britain was very much an urban society. About 40% of Britons lived in towns of over 100,000, while less than 25% lived in rural areas. The economy was dominated by heavy industry, and serviced by an advanced rail network.

Emigration

The number of emigrants, mainly young men seeking opportunities abroad, increased with the growth of the Empire (below). Their departure left a shortage of young men at home, and so some young women emigrated, too.

2,278,513

465,577

1840   1914

Industrial growth

The number of industrial workers increased from 3 million to 9·5 million between 1841 and 1911. This was mainly due to the expansion of heavy industry, where the workforce increased fourfold, to over 4 million. The growth of mining, building and engineering marked a new phase of industrial development. By 1914, industrial workers outnumbered rural by nearly 10 to 1.

1841

1911

Mines and quarries
Construction
Engineering
Textiles
Clothing
Food industries
Other

Movement of Population
1851-1861

Population movements

The large-scale migration to the towns that accompanied the Industrial Revolution continued throughout the 19th century. Population movement in Britain was further stimulated by the demand for urban domestic servants. At the same time, the urban labour force was increased by a steady flow of workers from overseas, particularly Ireland after the 1840s famine.

⊚	Towns over 500,000	
⊙	Towns 250,000-500,000	in 1891
○	Towns 100,000-250,000	

Population Growth 1861-1891

Over 85%
70-85%
55-70%
45-55%
35-45%
15-30%
0-15%
Decline

─── Railways in 1845
········ Railway network at its peak 1914

●	Woollens
○	Worsteds
●	Cotton
●	Coal mining
■	Iron mining
□	Iron manufacture
▲	Non-ferrous mining
△	Non-ferrous manufacture
+	Quarrying
E	Engines, machinery and boilermaking
⚓	Shipbuilding
A	Alkali works 1881
B	Blast furnaces 1913

1851

City growth

The 19th century urban population explosion necessitated an expansion in local government functions. By 1914 municipal services had grown from policing, sewers and drains to include street cleaning, housing, public transport and education.

	1841	1911
GLASGOW	287,000	1,000,000
BIRMINGHAM	202,000	840,000
LIVERPOOL	299,000	746,000
MANCHESTER	252,000	714,000
SHEFFIELD	111,000	455,000
LEEDS	152,000	446,000
EDINBURGH	166,000	401,000
LONDON	2,239,000	7,256,000

TWO WORLD WARS

World War I (1914-18) brought with it the dislocation of British society. The loss of life on a hitherto unprecedented scale shattered Edwardian complacency, while the accumulated war debts strained Britain's economy and hastened its decline relative to the USA. Overseas, British imperial supremacy was rocked by Irish republicanism and Indian nationalism, and at home labour discontent once again raised its head. The bitter defeat of the General Strike of 1926 represented a major setback for the labour movement.

Soon after the war, in 1918, women gained the vote after half a century of campaigning: first, just those over 30, together with all men over 21 years of age, and later, in 1928, women over 21, too. Labour replaced the Liberals as the party of opposition, while outside Parliament disillusion with old values gave expression to the growth of the new ideologies of communism and fascism. However, they neither achieved mass support nor took root as they did in Continental Europe.

The collapse of the New York stockmarket, the 'Wall Street crash' of 1929, signalled world wide economic slump. In Britain, where successive Conservative and Labour governments had been struggling to restore the balance of payments, a coalition National government was formed to deal with the crisis. It cut back public expenditure and began to run down the traditional heavy industries, with fearful consequences for employment.

There were now two Britains: in the north and north-west whole communities lost their livelihoods and had to rely on means-tested poor relief for subsistence; in the south-east and the midlands new light manufacturing and consumer goods industries flourished and living standards improved.

There was gradual economic improvement in the late 1930s, but it was war, which had been feared for some time, that eventually brought about full employment and formed the basis of a new social consensus. World War II (1939-45) was fought as a 'just war': democracy and freedom against fascism and tyranny. The war effort rested on the morale of the whole nation, as aerial bombardment directly involved the civilian population. Winston Churchill emerged as the popular wartime leader whose rhetoric reinforced the collective will to win and left the people of post-war Britain determined never to return to the poverty and waste of the 1930s.

War and class-war
When World War I broke out in August 1914, nationalist fervour swung the Labour party and the TUC behind the government's recruitment drive. Unions co-operated with employers in a war that claimed the lives of 750,000 Britons, with more than 1·5 million injured or missing (below). After the 1918 armistice, prices rose steeply and labour disputes returned. Unemployment soared, and in 1921 miners, railway and transport workers formed an ill-fated triple alliance in an unsuccessful bid to prevent their wages being cut. The *Punch* cartoon (centre) shows what the employers thought of it.

Government spending
After the Liberals introduced pensions and national insurance in 1909-11, government spending rose steeply to nearly £70 million by 1920. Almost half the government's revenue was from duties on sugar, beer and tobacco. The 1920s saw government attempting to reduce its expenditure, with cutbacks in civil service pay following in 1931. During the 1930s the government spent more on encouraging business than on welfare provision. By 1939, the government's largest source of revenue, about 40%, came from direct taxes.

PUNCH, OR THE LONDON CHARIVARI—April 20, 1921.

THE PROBLEM-PICTURE OF 1921.
HOW TO MAKE THE TAIL WAG.

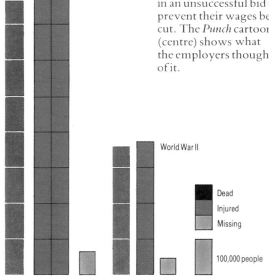

World War I

World War II

- Dead
- Injured
- Missing

☐ 100,000 people

——— Education
- - - - Unemployment
· · · · Health
–·–·– Old age pensions

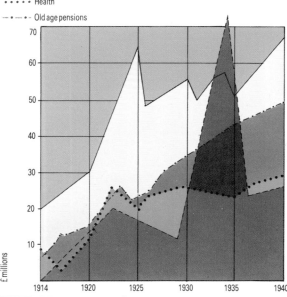

£ millions

Crisis in the 1930s

The depression of the 1930s was exacerbated by the dependence of many towns on a single industry. When, in 1930, unemployment first reached 3 million and the Labour government failed to balance its budget, foreign creditors, fearful of an economic collapse, began to withdraw their gold from the Bank of England. That autumn, the gold standard was abandoned, and a National government, made up of all parties, was elected to solve the crisis. Under this government, unemployment fell to 1·7 million by 1937, but was rising again when war intervened in 1939.

Smaller families

The average number of children in a family fell from 6·16 in the 1860s to as low as 2·07 in the 1930s. This resulted from better education and understanding of family economics, the rise of the status of women from that of mere child-bearer, and the use of contraception. Also, a modicum of social welfare reduced the need for large, self-supporting families.

| 1861 | 1899 | 1915 | 1934 |

▓ Individual in family

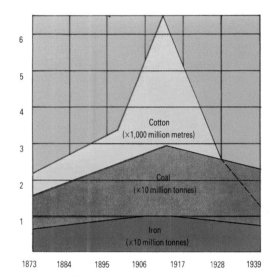

Industries in decline

The neglect of foreign markets at the expense of military requirements during World War I accelerated Britain's already declining share of world trade in the interwar period. The older industries – cotton, coal, and iron and steel – suffered most. By the mid-1930s Japan had replaced Britain as the world's major supplier of cotton. Demand for coal fell and coal exporters faced stiff competition from Germany and Poland. In the iron and steel industries, imports began to outstrip exports.

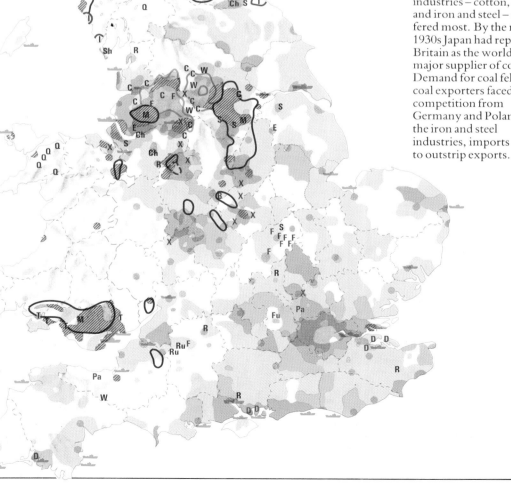

Changes in Population 1931-1938

☐	Decrease
▓	0-10% increase
▓	10-20% increase
▓	Over 20% increase
⚓	Major ports
⚓	Other ports

Ill-balanced Industry (more than 30% of workers in a single industry)

—M—	Mining
—I—	Iron ore
—W—	Wool
—C—	Cotton
– – –	Pottery
Q	Quarrying
S	Iron & steel
T	Steel & tinplate
E	Engineering
Sh	Shipbuilding
R	Railway works
Ru	Rubber
Ch	Chemicals
D	Naval dockyards
X	Other textiles & clothing
F	Footwear
B	Bricks
Pa	Paper
G	Glass
Fu	Furniture
Fo	Food

Major areas of unemployment

▨	Over 15%
▨	Under 15%

New industries

During the 1930s industries based on car-making (opposite) and other mass-production consumer goods thrived on the edge of towns such as Oxford, Luton, Coventry and London.

RECONSTRUCTION AND GROWTH

Post-war Britain promised a better deal for everyone, based on consensus politics and full employment. The 1942 Beveridge Report had outlined measures to eliminate the five evil giants – Want, Disease, Ignorance, Idleness and Squalor – and in the first post-war general election of 1945, the Labour party, with its commitment to wholesale social reform, won a landslide victory. The new government founded the welfare state, based on the universal provision of health, education and social insurance. For the next 30 years, Labour and Conservative governments pledged to maintain it, but failed to achieve the standards found elsewhere in Europe.

The 1945 Labour government's immediate problem was to stabilise an economy crippled by war debts to the United States. Rationing of foodstuffs and other essentials was introduced, but the measure proved unpopular and, in 1951, was ended by the Conservatives. By the late 1950s the austerity was past, and a huge expansion in the production of consumer goods ushered in the 'affluent society'.

A new youth market emerged. 'Pop' music – epitomised by the Beatles – became a major industry, and youth culture – from 'mods and rockers' to 'hippies' and, later, 'punks' – was seized on by advertising and the media. The all-round boom economy created labour shortages and attracted immigrant workers from Asia, the Caribbean and southern Europe, who took many of the least-inviting and worst-paid jobs.

Despite this apparent prosperity, Britain's position was in decline as the USA and USSR emerged as 'superpowers' and the nuclear age dawned. In the wake of colonial conflicts, from Cyprus to Malaya, Britain lost an empire but emerged as the leader of a pluralistic, multi-racial commonwealth. This and French opposition deflected Britain from an early involvement in the European Economic Community, which it eventually joined in 1973 as a lesser European power.

During the post-war boom, living standards improved as never before. Consumer expenditure in the 1950s nearly doubled, as a new range of electrical and other durable goods, such as those shown here, became commonplace in British homes.

Inflation and unemployment

Post-war reconstruction of industry and transport, with expanding world trade, helped government to keep down unemployment. In the 1950s and 1960s, with inflation at 3-4%, jobs were plentiful, especially in the public services. However, in the next 10 years, the value of the £ fell first by half, and then again by a third. In 1973, the price of oil trebled, and in 1975 inflation reached 27%, as production slowed and unemployment levels not seen since the 1930s became widespread. Since 1980, inflation has fallen, but there has been a steep rise in unemployment.

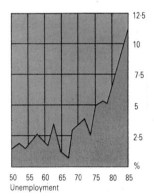

Unemployment

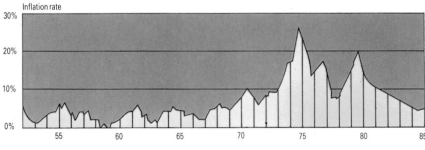

Inflation rate

Occupational change

Between 1921 and 1951, heavy industry declined, but the growth of light engineering kept up the employment levels in engineering as a whole. Some coalmines were closed, reducing the numbers of miners, while service-sector employment expanded dramatically. White-collar workers increased by a half. Post-war rebuilding stimulated employment in the building trade, but the number of transport workers was reduced after the nationalisation of the railways.

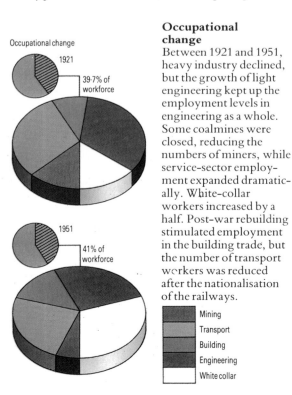

Occupational change

1921

39·7% of workforce

1951

41% of workforce

- ▨ Mining
- ▨ Transport
- ▨ Building
- ▨ Engineering
- ▢ White collar

Working population

Since the war, traditional opposition to women working outside the home has declined. The share of the workforce accounted for by women has grown steadily, with a sharp increase in 1964–79. By 1974, immigrant workers, male and female, made up 7·5% of Britain's workforce, many of whom have settled and made their home in Britain.

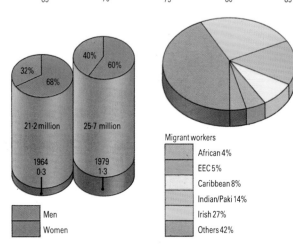

32% 68%

40% 60%

21·2 million

25·7 million

1964
0·3

1979
1·3

- ▨ Men
- ▨ Women

Migrant workers

- ▨ African 4%
- ▨ EEC 5%
- ▢ Caribbean 8%
- ▨ Indian/Paki 14%
- ▨ Irish 27%
- ▨ Others 42%

Britain's post-war economic miracle could not last, for successive governments had failed to establish the economy on a sound footing. As early as 1967, Harold Wilson's Labour government was forced to devalue the pound. Ten years later, another Labour government was reduced to borrowing money from the International Monetary Fund. The conditions of the loan included major cuts in public spending, which took place against a background of rising unemployment.

Growing disillusion with the welfare state, and the apparent failure of consensus politics, strengthened the appeal of the new right. In the general election of 1979, Margaret Thatcher, who exemplified this break with the post-war tradition, led the Tories to victory. She introduced 'monetarism' as the solution to Britain's economic ills, and invoked the 'Victorian values' of self-help and a free market economy. Under her government, inflation was brought under control. Unemployment, on the other hand, fuelled by a world recession, continued to rise.

Black Britons
Between 1966 and 1978 Britain's black population almost doubled, to about 3·5% of the total population. About 40% were Afro-Caribbean, the others mainly Asian. Most settled in low-paid jobs in the inner-city areas of Greater London, the West Midlands and Yorkshire. In the late 1970s, as the economy declined, a relatively high proportion of them became unemployed. Tighter immigration controls have since reduced the number of immigrants.

Black population

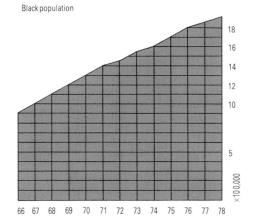

Population trends
Up to the 1960s Great Britain's population grew quite quickly, with a high birth rate and falling death rate. By the mid-1970s the growth rate had slowed almost to a stop. In 1977 there were 35% fewer births per year than in 1964. Couples were marrying later and having smaller families. Regional population changes in the 1970s and early 1980s reflected not so much the falling birth rate as the decline of the older industrial cities relative to the new industries and new towns.

Type of area	Population 1981 × 1,000,000	% Growth 1978-81
Inner London	2·5	−17·7
Outer London	4·2	−5·0
Large cities	2·2	−5·1
New towns	2·2	+15·1
Resorts	3·3	+4·9

Mortality patterns
From 1950 to 1975 life expectancy in Great Britain increased by about three years for men, to 70, and by over four years for women, to 75. Today, people die less from water- and food-borne diseases than from diseases of the heart and circulation and cancers. The major causes of death for Britons aged between 1 and 24, and for men up to 44, are accidents, poisoning and violence. For women 24-64, cancers are the main cause, and for men over 45 and women over 65, circulatory diseases.

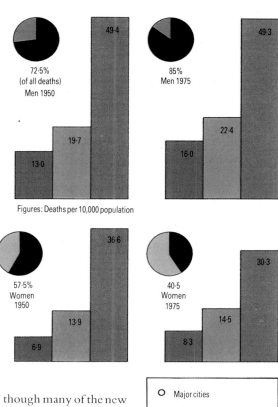

Figures: Deaths per 10,000 population

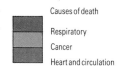

Causes of death

Respiratory

Cancer

Heart and circulation

New towns
After the war, the government took control of building, directing labour and materials into solving the desperate housing shortage. By 1952, 1,200,000 new flats and houses had been built, mostly by local councils. The New Towns Act of 1946 was aimed chiefly at reducing overcrowding in the main cities. By 1950, work had begun on the first 12 new towns: 7 were to take population from London, 4 were to serve the densely populated coalmining communities of Durham, South Wales and Scotland, and one was for the Corby steel industry. The government also passed legislation concerning the location of industry, though many of the new towns north of the Mersey-Humber line failed to attract major new industries.

○ Major cities
● New towns
● Expanding towns
● Towns with planned expansion

1 Birmingham
2 Coventry
3 Aldridge-Brownhills
4 Milton Keynes
5 Luton
6 Welwyn
7 Wellingborough
8 St Neots

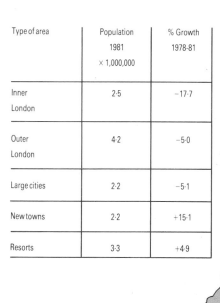

BRITAIN IN THE 1980s

Britain in the 1980s has its share of social contradictions, with widening gaps between rich and poor, employed and unemployed, and prospering and depressed regions. The impact of the economic recession and cuts in public spending have been uneven, affecting some groups much more than others. Living standards, education and work opportunities today very much depend on where people live and on their class, gender, and ethnic background.

New affluence

For many in work the 1980s have brought affluence, especially in the southern shires where the sunrise industries – particularly computers and electronics – have grown up. Technological innovation has created a new range of consumer goods and opened up new cultural possibilities. Home computers, video-tape recorders, personal cassette-radios and cable TV are becoming increasingly common in the British home.

Consumer spending has also reflected a growing public concern with diet and health and fitness in general. In particular, the interest in jogging, aerobics and health foods has expanded consumer markets. So too has youth culture, with its emphasis on new styles mixed with nostalgia, seen in many of today's hair styles and clothes designs.

Population

In 1951 the population of Great Britain was 48,854,000. It grew by 5% between 1951 and 1961, and then by another 5%, to 53,979,000, over the next decade. By 1981 the rate of increase had fallen to about 0.5%. The population figure itself fell slightly between 1982 and 1983 despite an increase in life expectancy and fall in infant mortality over the previous decade.

	1973	1983
Live births (×1,000)	779	721
Deaths (×1,000)	669	662
Life expectancy (years)		
Men	69	71
Women	75	77
Infant mortality (per 1,000)	17	10

Standard of living

Though average earnings rose between 1973 and 1983, nearly 5 million households continued to live in overcrowded conditions. Moreover, 5% of households, mostly in privately rented property, still shared the basic amenities of hot water, a bath and outside wc. The proportion of households having the use of a car rose, but access was not evenly distributed: 70% in the south-west and East Anglia, compared with 51% in the north and 52% in Scotland.

(1975=100)	1973	1983
Average weekly earnings	35.9	146.1
Retail price index (1980=100)	69.4	248.6
Households having use of:	%	%
Car	53.9	62.1
TV set	93.4	96.9
Telephone	43.4	77.3
Central heating	38.5	63.9
Refrigerator	77.6	97.0
Deep freeze	NA	34.2
Washing machine	66.6	81.3

Education

Between 1973 and 1983 the proportion of pupils and students in full-time education increased. There was also a slight drop in the pupil-to-teacher ratios, as the number of children of school age fell faster than the number of teachers. In Scotland, more than 40% of children stay on at school after 16, compared with Devon, Norfolk and Lancashire, where the figure is less than 25%. Some inner cities spend up to twice as much per child on education as some rural boroughs.

	1973	1983
Pupils in state schools		
Primary (no. per teacher)	26	22
Secondary (no. per teacher)	17	16
% in comprehensives	50.7	91.1
Participation in full-time education (as % of age group)	%	%
2-4 school	15.7	29.2
16-17 school	28.9	26.3
further education	7.4	15.4
18-20 school	2.3	1.0
further education	4.8	7.9
Universities	5.5	6.2
No. in full-time higher education (×1,000)	482.2	568

Marriage

Between 1973 and 1983 there was an increase in the ratio of civil to religious marriages, occasioned partly by the proportional increase in second marriages. In 1984 the median age for a first marriage was 24.7 for men and 22.6 for women, in both cases the highest it had been for 30 years. The median age for remarriage of both divorced men and women has also increased in recent years, and the divorce rate has now slowed up considerably since 1980.

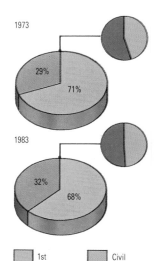

1973

1983

1st / 2nd+ Civil / Religious

Young and old

Britain's pensioners (women aged 60 and over and men aged 65 and over) have increased in number since 1951. The 1960s saw a 17% rise over the previous decade, while in the 1970s the number rose by a further 10%. About 30% of today's pensioners live alone, with less than 5% looked after in old people's homes. From 1951 the number of children under 16 also grew. At the height of the 'bulge', in 1971, it reached 13 million, but since has fallen back to 1960s levels.

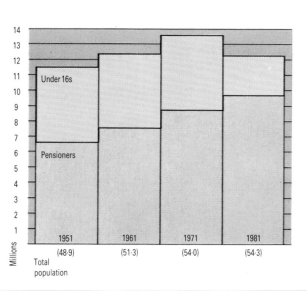

Under 16s

Pensioners

| 1951 | 1961 | 1971 | 1981 |
| (48.9) | (51.3) | (54.0) | (54.3) |

Millions / Total population

Smoking and health

In 1982, for the first time, smokers were a minority in every social group. The reduction has been greatest among professional men and women and least among manual workers, and overall greater among men than women. Still, smoking remains the largest single cause of preventable death. In 1985, 1 in 7 of deaths were from smoking-related diseases, and the death toll since 1945 is 3 million. A further 1½ million deaths from smoking are expected by the year 2000.

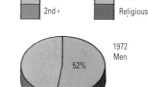
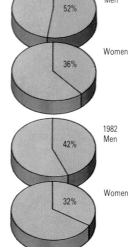

1972 Men 52%
Women 36%
1982 Men 42%
Women 32%

Population patterns

Social and economic planning depends on knowing how the population will change. Death rates are much easier to predict than birth rates, which fluctuate in response to short-term social and economic changes. Present projections suggest that Britain's population will increase by about 4% by the year 2000. There will also be an increase in the average age of the population, the group showing the fastest rate of growth being the over 60s, in particular the over-75s.

Positive and negative effects

At the opposite extreme, for those sections of Britain's population living in a marginal economy of dole queues or irregular – and sometimes undeclared – income, life is a struggle. Public spending cuts in social services, health care and housing have reduced the living standards, in particular, of many low-paid and casual workers, single parents, and the elderly and infirm. In the inner cities and those regions dependent on declining industries, hardship is increasing. The mounting frustration and discontent has sometimes expressed itself in emotional scenes on industrial picket lines, and in more extreme cases, in outbreaks of urban rioting.

However, alongside these conflicts, the 1980s have also seen the growth of constructive social movements, with an emphasis on peace, women's rights, and concern for the environment. While these movements and the methods they employ are not always supported by the public at large, they have succeeded in focusing attention on problems of crucial importance to the modern age. How those problems are resolved will play a large part in determining what Britain will be like in the 1990s and beyond.

Ethnic minorities

Since 1951 the proportion of non-whites resident in Britain but who were born overseas has increased from 2% to 6%. Their distribution has been uneven. By the 1980s the highest concentration (1 in 20) was in the south-east, followed by the West Midlands (just under 1 in 25), the East Midlands and Yorkshire and Humberside (both 1 in 50) and the north-west (just under 1 in 50). For all other regions – including Scotland – the figure is about 1 in 100.

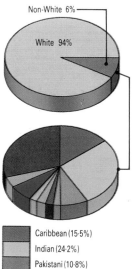

Non-White 6%

White 94%

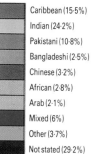

Caribbean (15·5%)
Indian (24·2%)
Pakistani (10·8%)
Bangladeshi (2·5%)
Chinese (3·2%)
African (2·8%)
Arab (2·1%)
Mixed (6%)
Other (3·7%)
Not stated (29·2%)

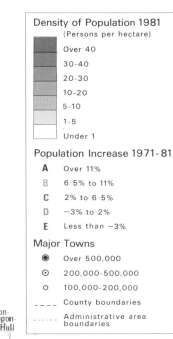

Density of Population 1981
(Persons per hectare)
Over 40
30-40
20-30
10-20
5-10
1-5
Under 1

Population Increase 1971-81
A   Over 11%
B   6·5% to 11%
C   2% to 6·5%
D   −3% to 2%
E   Less than −3%

Major Towns
⊚   Over 500,000
⊙   200,000-500,000
○   100,000-200,000
- - -   County boundaries
·····   Administrative area boundaries

COAL, OIL AND GAS

Britain has the largest energy resources of any country in western Europe, and since 1980 it has been almost self-sufficient in national energy supply. Almost 95% of its energy needs are met by coal, oil and gas. The remainder comes from nuclear and hydroelectric power.

Britain accounts for 15% of total western European primary energy consumption (second only to West Germany), but national energy consumption has fallen by 10% in the past 10 years. This has been the result mainly of industrial recession. This period has also seen a continuing shift away from use of coal, which has been increasingly replaced by North Sea gas and oil, and to a lesser extent by nuclear power.

Coal

Coal is still Britain's richest natural energy resource. At current rates of consumption, there are sufficient reserves to last 300 years. Coalmining is the exclusive right of the National Coal Board (NCB), which was set up in 1947 to manage the industry as all coal mines passed into public ownership following the Coal Nationalisation Act 1946.

The bulk of the nation's coal (72%) is used to generate electricity. But demand for coal is falling steadily – by 19% since 1973 – and is expected to continue falling. A combination of plans by the government to expand nuclear power, the opening in 1986 of a cross-Channel electricity supply link providing cheap French electricity, and the loss of markets to imported coal during the 1984 miners' strike suggest that demand for home-produced coal will continue to fall. In the 20 months to September 1985, 34 (out of a total of more than 150) pits were closed or faced with closure for economic reasons.

Oil

In 1979 annual world oil consumption peaked at nearly 24 billion barrels. Since then it has fallen by 14%. No major industrial country has cut its consumption more dramatically than Britain. Since the peak year of 1973, British oil consumption has fallen by 27%, in line with the decline of industry. However, during the same period, the country's petrol consumption has increased by more than 20%. More than half the growth in national energy demand between 1959 and 1978 was due to increased needs of transport, and half of that from private transport. The number of private cars has grown by more than 400% since the early 1950s.

Currently, annual oil consumption is around 880 million barrels. Proven reserves of oil in the North Sea amount to over 3100 million barrels but total remaining reserves may be more than five times as much as this. Offshore oil production and oil refining are carried out almost exclusively by privately owned companies of which British Petroleum (BP) and Shell Transport and Trading are the two largest British companies.

Gas

Over the past 10 years natural gas production in Britain has remained fairly steady, while consumption has risen by 42%. The proportion contributed by gas to the national energy budget has almost doubled since the early 1970s. It now provides more than a third of British energy. At the current rates of consumption, natural gas resources in the North Sea are projected to run out in the next decade, when an increasing proportion will be piped in from Norwegian gas fields.

Privately owned companies predominate in gas production while the publically owned British Gas Corporation is responsible for gas distribution.

Sources of energy   1984-85

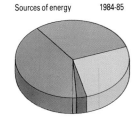

Energy supplied

Consumers

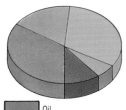

- Oil
- Coal
- Gas
- Nuclear
- Hydroelectric
- Electricity
- Energy lost during conversion

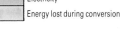

- Industry–power
- Road transport
- Domestic–heating
- Other transport
- Other (lighting, electrical appliances etc.)

Energy flow

The diagram, right, shows the energy flow pattern for Britain: the sources of energy, the proportion used in generating electricity, and the end uses. Conversion losses and low efficiency mean that, ultimately, more energy is wasted than is put to work.

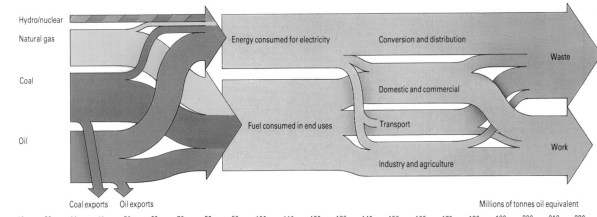

Energy use

Britain is better supplied with energy than many other industrialised countries. But a major change in fortune is likely in the next 30 years as oil and gas particularly become less available and more expensive. To date, there has been little investment in alternative sources of energy, other than nuclear power. In the short term, the Department of Energy is encouraging greater energy-use efficiency.

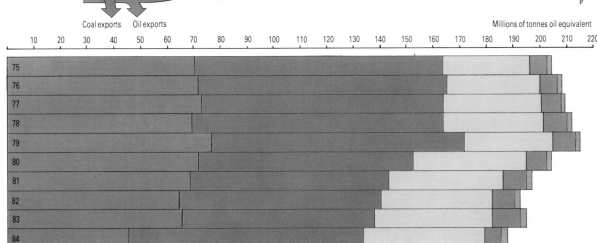

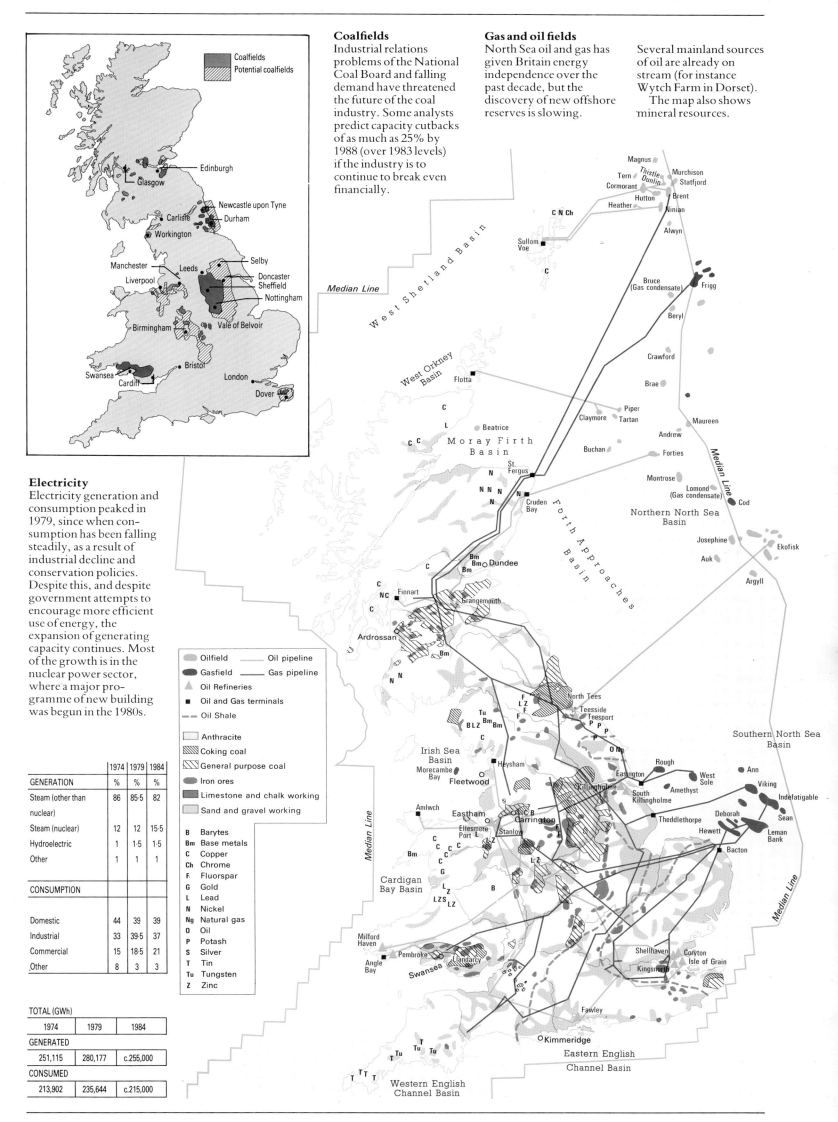

Coalfields

Industrial relations problems of the National Coal Board and falling demand have threatened the future of the coal industry. Some analysts predict capacity cutbacks of as much as 25% by 1988 (over 1983 levels) if the industry is to continue to break even financially.

Gas and oil fields

North Sea oil and gas has given Britain energy independence over the past decade, but the discovery of new offshore reserves is slowing.

Several mainland sources of oil are already on stream (for instance Wytch Farm in Dorset). The map also shows mineral resources.

Electricity

Electricity generation and consumption peaked in 1979, since when consumption has been falling steadily, as a result of industrial decline and conservation policies. Despite this, and despite government attempts to encourage more efficient use of energy, the expansion of generating capacity continues. Most of the growth is in the nuclear power sector, where a major programme of new building was begun in the 1980s.

Map legend (inset)

- Coalfields
- Potential coalfields

Edinburgh, Glasgow, Newcastle upon Tyne, Carlisle, Durham, Workington, Selby, Manchester, Leeds, Doncaster, Liverpool, Sheffield, Nottingham, Birmingham, Vale of Belvoir, Bristol, Swansea, Cardiff, London, Dover

Symbols

- ⬤ Oilfield — Oil pipeline
- ⬤ Gasfield — Gas pipeline
- ▲ Oil Refineries
- ■ Oil and Gas terminals
- -- Oil Shale

- Anthracite
- Coking coal
- General purpose coal
- Iron ores
- Limestone and chalk working
- Sand and gravel working

- B Barytes
- Bm Base metals
- C Copper
- Ch Chrome
- F. Fluorspar
- G Gold
- L Lead
- N Nickel
- Ng Natural gas
- O Oil
- P Potash
- S Silver
- T Tin
- Tu Tungsten
- Z Zinc

	1974	1979	1984
GENERATION	%	%	%
Steam (other than nuclear)	86	85·5	82
Steam (nuclear)	12	12	15·5
Hydroelectric	1	1·5	1·5
Other	1	1	1
CONSUMPTION			
Domestic	44	39	39
Industrial	33	39·5	37
Commercial	15	18·5	21
Other	8	3	3

TOTAL (GWh)

	1974	1979	1984
GENERATED	251,115	280,177	c.255,000
CONSUMED	213,902	235,644	c.215,000

NUCLEAR AND HYDROELECTRIC POWER

Nuclear power

Nuclear power has not become the popular energy source once predicted. Its problems have been many and controversial: doubts about capital costs and productivity, about reactor safety, and about the safety of transporting nuclear fuel and depositing of nuclear waste. There is also concern about the generation of increasing amounts of plutonium, a product of uranium fission, and how this could lead to nuclear weapons proliferation.

Nuclear power currently supplies 16% of Britain's electricity, but the proportion is planned to rise to 25% by 1995. There are 10 nuclear power plants in operation, with 6 more planned or under construction. The Central Electricity Generating Board (CEGB) power stations are serviced by British Nuclear Fuels (BNFL), which in 1984 became a public limited company. The United Kingdom Atomic Energy Authority (UKAEA) is responsible for the economic, safety and environmental aspects of the nuclear power industry.

The future of the nuclear power building programme depends largely on the outcome of the lengthy public enquiry held in 1984–85 into the planned installation of a new station at Sizewell on the Suffolk coast. The Sizewell B station is to be an American-designed Pressurized Water Reactor (PWR).

Hydroelectric power

Hydroelectric power provides nearly a quarter of the world's electricity but makes only a fractional contribution to British energy needs – currently less than 1·5%.

There is thought to be limited potential for further substantial development of this natural energy resource in Britain, although Dinorwig power station in North Wales shows what is possible. Dinorwig – the biggest power station of its kind in Europe – can meet total Welsh needs.

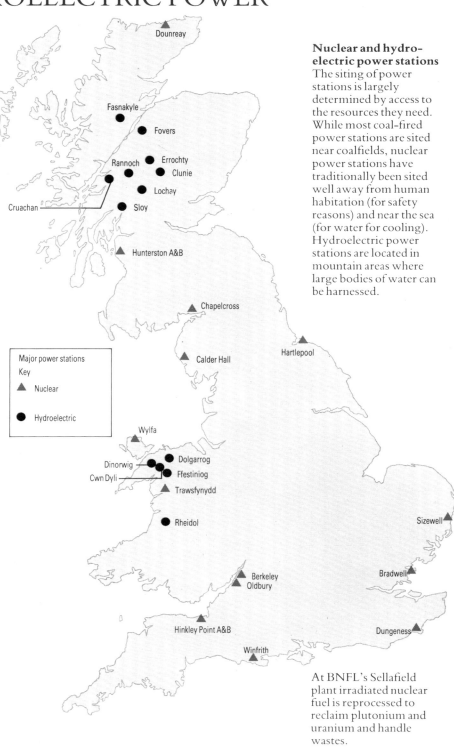

Nuclear and hydro-electric power stations
The siting of power stations is largely determined by access to the resources they need. While most coal-fired power stations are sited near coalfields, nuclear power stations have traditionally been sited well away from human habitation (for safety reasons) and near the sea (for water for cooling). Hydroelectric power stations are located in mountain areas where large bodies of water can be harnessed.

At BNFL's Sellafield plant irradiated nuclear fuel is reprocessed to reclaim plutonium and uranium and handle wastes.

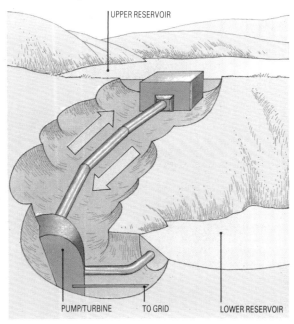

Pumped storage schemes

Power stations like Dinorwig exploit the difference in water levels between two reservoirs. Water falling from an upper reservoir turns the turbines that produce the electricity. The water is pumped back using electricity generated in off-peak periods.

ALTERNATIVE ENERGY SOURCES

Coal, oil, gas and nuclear fuels are non-renewable resources. The government is now spending more than £10 million a year in support of its renewable, or alternative, energy programme. Alternative energy sources currently make a negligible contribution to national energy needs, but the prospect of increasingly expensive and scarce oil in particular has encouraged steady research into the possibilities of tapping the energy of solar radiation, tides and sea waves, wind, and heat from hot, dry rocks beneath the Earth's surface.

The potential of these different sources is still at an early stage of investigation, but there seem to be good prospects in Britain for harnessing wind, tidal and geothermal power.

The biggest 'alternative' source of energy (with current technology), however, is energy conservation, that is using the country's existing energy supply more efficiently.

Energy conservation

About 60% of the energy supplied in Britain is wasted – during conversion, distribution and consumption. Research has shown that with more efficient use, Britain could cut its energy needs by half at no cost to its standard of living. This could be achieved in several ways.

First, the heat produced by electricity generation at power stations is often treated as waste. In coal-fired stations, for example, two-thirds of the heat generated is lost through the cooling towers. This energy could instead be harnessed and used. Such 'combined heat and power' schemes could be used to provide district heating.

Second, many buildings lack adequate insulation. Heat dissipation through walls, windows and roofs can be greatly reduced with even simple 'do-it-yourself' measures.

Third, in a well-insulated home or office, 'free heat gain' – the heat given off by lights, machines and human bodies – can be exploited.

Fourth, motor vehicles could be made more fuel-efficient. As little as 12% of the petrol put into the least efficient cars is converted into useful motive power at the wheels; the rest is given off as heat or lost through drag.

The government, through the Department of Energy, is encouraging cost-effective energy conservation measures, investigating improved methods of energy utilisation, and discouraging wasteful use of energy. In 1983 it set up an Energy Efficiency Office which, as one of its functions, is developing home energy audits.

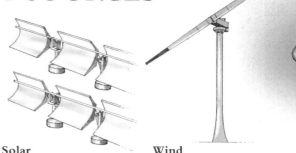

Solar
The price of solar systems has yet to fall enough to make them attractive for use on a large scale in Britain, although about 20,000 homes do have solar-heated water.

Tidal/wave
The Severn estuary provides a potential site for tidal power. Exploitation of energy generated by the waves is likely to be limited due to expense and complexity.

Wind
Some 10,000 windmills were used in Britain in the 19th century. Only a few hundred are now in use. Parts of Scotland and south-east England hold the greatest potential.

Geothermal
Geothermal energy uses the heat of rocks at great depth to heat water and uses the resultant steam to generate electricity. Experiments in Cornwall have been promising.

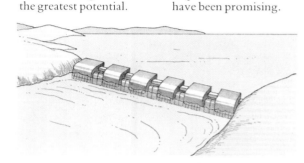

Domestic energy conservation
Many British homes use central heating without adequate insulation, so much of the heat is wasted and fuel bills are higher than they need be.

Homes can be made more energy efficient with double glazing, roof insulation, lagged pipes and hot water tanks, cavity wall insulation, and draught excluders. Together these can reduce heat losses by up to as much as 40%.

1 Lagged pipe work etc
2 Roof space insulation
3 Double glazing
4 Cavity wall insulation
5 Residual heat from occupants and cooker etc.
6 Efficient draft exclusion
7 Improved car design

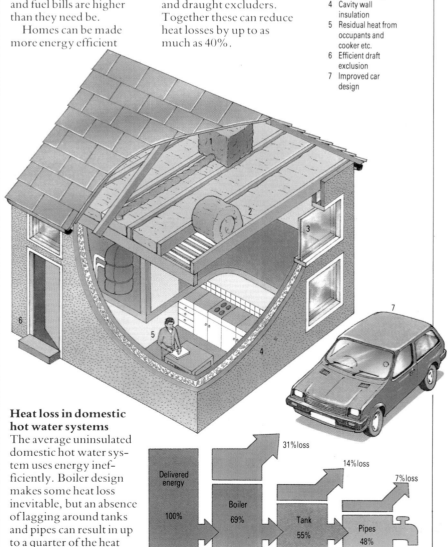

Heat loss in domestic hot water systems
The average uninsulated domestic hot water system uses energy inefficiently. Boiler design makes some heat loss inevitable, but an absence of lagging around tanks and pipes can result in up to a quarter of the heat generated being lost.

Delivered energy 100% | Boiler 69% | 31% loss | Tank 55% | 14% loss | Pipes 48% | 7% loss

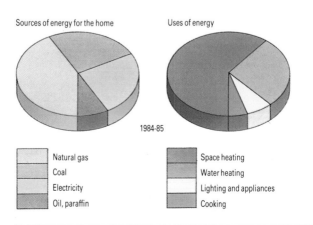

Sources of energy for the home

Uses of energy

1984-85

Natural gas
Coal
Electricity
Oil, paraffin

Space heating
Water heating
Lighting and appliances
Cooking

THE CONTROL OF POLLUTION

Pollution is not a new problem. Smoke from coal-burning was a health hazard in Britain as early as the 14th century. In 1952, an estimated 4000 Londoners died from the effects of a particularly virulent winter smog.

The attention given to pollution in the last 20 years has resulted in the imposition of increasingly strict controls on industry, with many positive results. But the problem is by no means solved. Acid pollution, contamination of air and water by heavy metals, and the disposal of nuclear waste remain major issues.

Acid pollution

Acid pollution is one of the most harmful and pervasive forms of air pollution. In the last decade it has become a major international political issue as the pollution produced by one country can be carried to others, where its full effects are felt.

When oil and coal are burned, they give off sulphur dioxide (SO_2) and nitrogen oxides (NO_x). Some of these chemicals are 'dry deposited' as gas and particles near the sources. Others react with moisture in the atmosphere, turning to acid and returning to Earth as 'wet deposited' pollution – acid rain, snow, fog and sleet.

Britain is the fourth largest source of SO_2 in the world, and a major source of NO_x. Most SO_2 and NO_x are by-products of electricity generation by coal-fired power stations. Petrol-driven road vehicles are also a major source of NO_x.

While the effects of acid pollution in Britain are not yet thoroughly researched, forest damage is suspected, lake and river acidification is reported, and building corrosion is common – £20 million is being spent on the restoration of Westminster Abbey alone.

Carbon dioxide

The burning of oil, coal and natural gas gives off carbon dioxide (CO_2), which accumulates in the atmosphere and reduces the amount of solar radiation reflected back into space from the Earth. This creates a 'greenhouse effect'. A doubling of CO_2 concentrations could increase global temperatures by 2–3°C, altering weather patterns, disrupting ecosystems and moving crop-growing regions further north. As a major coal consumer (accounting for 18% of the western European total), Britain is a major source of carbon dioxide.

Lead

One of the most controversial pollution issues of recent years has been that of the effects of lead on health. The toxic effects of lead are well known. Less certain is how harmful it is at the levels to which people are routinely exposed, from contaminated food and water, and from motor vehicle exhaust fumes. The effects of lead on the mental development of children have come under particular scrutiny. Several European countries are now following the example of the USA in introducing lead-free petrol.

Nuclear waste

Spent fuel from a nuclear power station contains uranium and plutonium that can be used again,

and a small quantity of radioactive waste. Reprocessing (of the kind carried out at Sellafield, for example) separates the reusable material from the waste, which must then be disposed of safely. The disposal of radioactive waste has caused considerable public concern.

Until stopped by public opposition, Britain dumped liquid wastes of low radiation levels into the sea. Such dumping may eventually be permanently banned. High-level wastes present a different problem. Liquid wastes of this type are generally kept in special concrete storage tanks, which must be scrupulously maintained while the wastes are solidified for more permanent disposal. Solid high-level wastes will take thousands of years to de-activate; Britain is now researching the best rock formations in which to bury the waste.

Acid in the atmosphere
The burning of fossil fuels for energy production and to drive industry is the largest source of acid pollution (and of carbon dioxide).

There are several ways of cleaning emissions. Coal can be washed before it is used to remove sulphurous deposits; sulphur can be removed from coal during burning; or exhaust gases – from power stations and cars alike – can be filtered. Many of these processes are expensive, but the repair of damage to soils, forests and lakes will be more expensive in the long term.

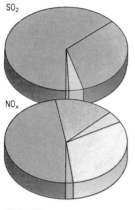
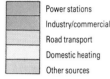

Power stations
Industry/commercial
Road transport
Domestic heating
Other sources

Didcot power station in Oxfordshire is one of the largest coal-fired power stations in Britain.

Spread of air pollution
When the local effects of sulphur pollution were first noticed in Britain, the solution used was to build higher chimneys to disperse the pollutants to the winds; many existing coal- and oil-fired power stations,

for example, bear chimneys that are 200m or more tall. But constructing tall outlet chimneys had the effect of carrying the pollutants further afield.

1 50% dry deposited

2 30% in local rain

3 20% forms acid in clouds that can travel over 1500km from the source

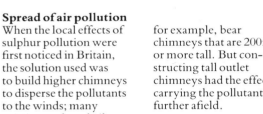

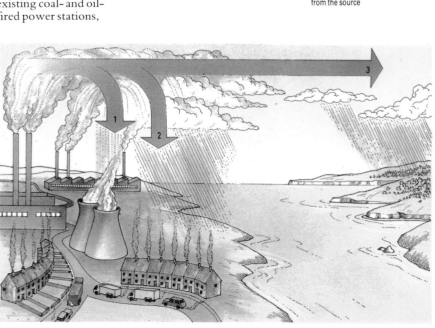
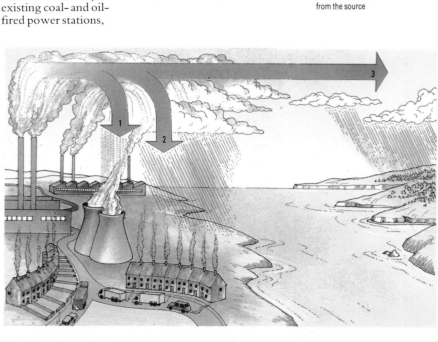

Water pollution

Despite recent progress, many British rivers and lakes are still polluted. The sources are both direct (industrial discharge and sewage) and indirect (the run-off from the soil of groundwater acidified by acid pollution).

Fertilisers washed off farmland can produce a massive overgrowth of algae and a reduction in oxygen levels in water, killing fish and plants. Nitrates from sewage and fertilisers could pose a particular health threat if they were to get into drinking water. Pesticide run-off can kill wildlife and in extreme cases could threaten public health. Heavy metals such as cadmium (from fertilisers and smelting) and mercury (from industrial effluent and sewage) can find their way into drinking and coastal water. The chemicals are highly poisonous and their ill-effects are cumulative. Cadmium levels in some especially heavily polluted estuaries have encouraged recommendations that no-one should regularly eat shellfish from the waters.

Polluted rivers and coasts

Parts of Britain's coast are subject to pollution from industrial waste and untreated domestic sewage and more than 2800 km of rivers are too polluted to support animal life. Organic pollution changes the oxygen content of river water and the sensitivity of different invertebrates to this change gives a relatively simple means of visually estimating the amount of pollution.

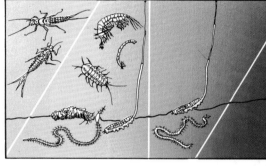

A Stonefly nymph   B Caddis fly larva   C Sludge worm   D No life
    Mayfly nymph   Freshwater shrimp   Rat-tailed maggot
                Sludge worm
                Rat-tailed maggot
                Water louse
                Bloodworm

Animals shown at A will only be found in clean water while those at B will indicate some pollution. If only animals shown at C are found, fairly serious pollution can be expected; these creatures are protected from the effects of pollution, the former by its ability to store oxygen in its bloodstream, the latter because it breathes oxygen from the surface of the water by means of its breathing tube. If no life is found, the water is obviously seriously polluted.

Control measures

Pollution control legislation in Britain is not yet wide-ranging and is often variable in effect. There is no national toxic waste management policy; controls on pesticides are voluntary; and only recently has the 1974 Control of Pollution Act started to become fully enforced on a nationwide basis. The only statutory obligations regarding water quality are contained in the 1973 Water Act, which calls for a general 'national policy' for maintaining inland water quality. Air pollution, though, has been markedly reduced since the 1956 Clean Air Act. Since 1960, the average concentration of smoke in the atmosphere has fallen by 80%.

In the mid-19th century, the lower Thames was an open sewer. Thousands of people died from recurring epidemics of Asiatic cholera. Attempts to clean up the river paid off in the 1970s, when mercury levels fell following controls on industrial discharges. Fish have now returned.

NATURE CONSERVATION

Unlike many other countries, Britain has little true wilderness left. The need to support a large population on a small land area has radically remodelled the British landscape, reducing the area left for wildlife and natural habitat. Agricultural intensification during and since World War II has wrought particularly marked changes. Wetland, moorland, heathland and downland have been 'reclaimed'; hedgerows and woodland have been cleared to make bigger fields that are easier to plough and crop; and increasing quantities of chemical fertilizer have been applied to the land. The resulting increase in yields has been remarkable, but the natural environment has suffered proportionately.

Two Countryside Commissions (one for England and Wales, one for Scotland) and the Nature Conservancy Council are primarily responsible for statutory nature conservation. Working in conjunction with local authorities, they are, under the Wildlife and Countryside Act of 1981, empowered to preserve and enhance the environment by, for example, restricting development, acquiring and reclaiming derelict land, and instigating amenity schemes. The Commissions are also responsible for maintaining the integrity of the country's 'green belts', the areas designated around large cities and towns where it is intended the land should be left open and free from further development of roads, industry or housing.

Britain's statutory protected areas offer great, but not complete, relief from development. Nearly three-quarters of national park land is privately owned, and much of it is actively farmed; a fifth of Exmoor's moorland was lost to farming between 1947 and 1976. Then there is confusion over what Areas of Outstanding Natural Beauty are supposed to achieve – they are not protected from development by farming, forestry or industry. And Sites of Special Scientific Interest are often maintained only through voluntary agreements between local authorities and farmers to keep the land out of intense agricultural production – farming using traditional methods is permitted.

Buttermere, a glacial valley lake in the heart of the Lake District National Park. Britain's national parks cover some 13,600 sq km, or 9% of the area of England and Wales. The public are encouraged to visit these areas while still protecting the environment by the provision of free car parks, camping and caravan areas, nature trails and information centres.

Urban spread

In the last 30 years, the population of Britain's big urban areas has been falling, and that of towns and rural areas growing. One result is that 15,000 hectares of land a year are being covered by new development. Inner city renewal has meanwhile not always taken place – millions of houses need major repairs, and 46,000 hectares of land have been left derelict in England alone.

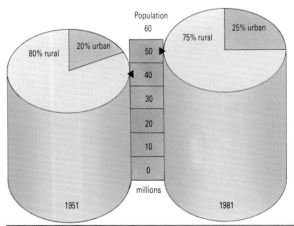

Population
millions

1951		1981
80% rural	20% urban	75% rural 25% urban

Forestry

Deciduous woodland is the natural vegetation of Britain which was once almost entirely covered in forest. Today, Britain has less forest cover by proportion than any other European country except Ireland – a sparse 9%. Half of this is coniferous woodland planted since 1895. Ancient woodlands and broadleaf forests of oak, beech and other native species make up less than one-third of Britain's forest cover. The biggest changes have been wrought by clearance for agriculture or conversion to conifer plantations. Conifers are grown for timber and as raw material for the paper industry.

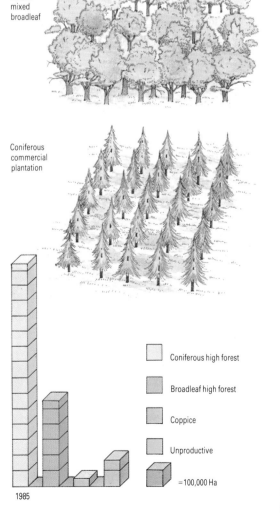

Natural mixed broadleaf

Coniferous commercial plantation

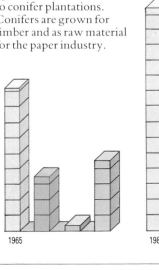

□ Coniferous high forest

□ Broadleaf high forest

□ Coppice

□ Unproductive

□ =100,000 Ha

1965   1985

Habitat loss and threatened wildlife

Between 1945 and 1972, 80% of hedgerow trees – once one of Britain's richest reservoirs of flora and fauna – died through disease or were removed. Hedgerows were removed at a rate of 7250 km per year, and nearly a third of Britain's ancient woodlands were cleared. Since then removal of hedgerows has slowed but today wetlands, meadows, moorland and grassland are similarly at risk. Habitat loss such as this is the main threat to wildlife. Britain has about 1400 flowering plant species, 420 native mammal, bird, reptile, amphibian and fish species, and 50,000 species of insects and other invertebrates. But nearly one-fifth of the plants, and many of the mammals, birds and reptiles, are threatened.

WETLANDS   About 100,000 hectares of wetland are drained every year, threatening the plants, birds and fish that depend on them.

OTTERS   Throughout Europe otters are on the decline. Pesticides and the removal of river vegetation are the main causes.

ORCHIDS   These are among the rarest of British plants. Many species have been pushed to the edge of extinction as a result of habitat loss from urban development.

BADGERS   These woodland creatures are thought to spread tuberculosis to cattle. Thousands have been gassed in the past seven years.

THE NORFOLK BROADS   Although man-made, these are an important site for wildlife and recreation. Yet all but three of the Broads are now seriously polluted.

Changing land use and conservation

With over 54 million people packed into a small area of land, conflict over differing land use priorities is hard to avoid. One result is that Britain's land use questions have an environmental dimension, and vice versa. But with more than four-fifths of the land area given over to farming, agriculture is the major factor. Unlike urban land, rural land is subject to little legislative control.

80·3%

10·2%

9·5%

×1,000,000 Ha

Urban
Forestry
Agriculture

National Parks
National Park Direction Areas (Scotland)
Areas of Outstanding Natural Beauty
National Scenic Areas (Scotland)
Heritage Coast and Coastal Conservation Zones (Scotland)
Green Belt
Proposed Green Belt
Areas of Special Scientific, Landscape or Historic Interest

Protected areas

Britain's protected areas range from the 10 national parks (the Lake District is the biggest) to the 3900 Sites of Special Scientific Interest (which can be as small as a copse or roadside verge). There are also 33 Areas of Outstanding Natural Beauty in all parts of the country, and 1195 km of heritage coast. Many of these areas are protected as much for recreation as for conservation.

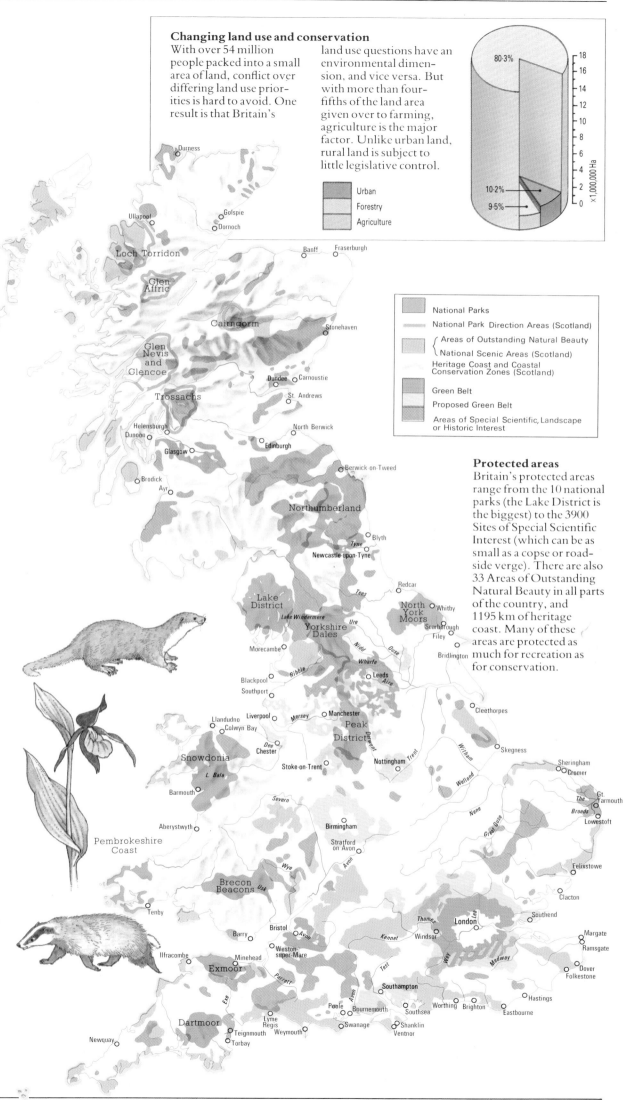

OLD AND NEW NETWORKS

Traditional means of communication such as the letter post, radio and newspapers are still with us, but in the last five years or so they have been joined by new computer-based methods of information transfer such as teletext and electronic mail.

In telecommunications, the trend is towards transmitting information in the form of a rapid series of electrical pulses, because these 'digital' signals are less vulnerable to electrical interference than the wavelike (analogue) signals they are replacing. Computers also process information in digital form. The convergence of computer and communication technologies gave rise to Information Technology (IT) and sparked off the communications explosion. Today, telephone calls, TV pictures and computer data can be transmitted in digital form via common links that include, nationwide, underground cables and microwave relays and, internationally, undersea cables and satellite systems.

Dish aerials at the London Teleport receive from satellites microwaves carrying TV signals. Microwaves are radio waves with wavelengths of less than 30 cm.

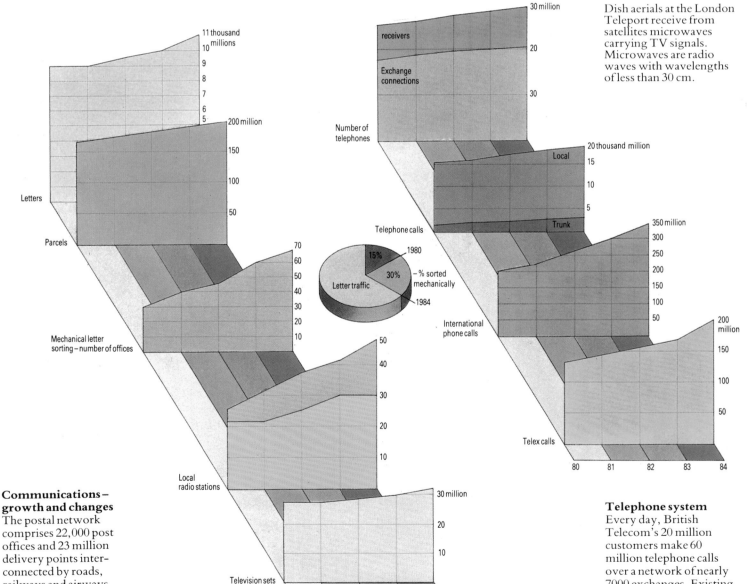

Communications – growth and changes
The postal network comprises 22,000 post offices and 23 million delivery points inter-connected by roads, railways and airways. Inland letter service is the monopoly of the Royal Mail but electronic mail services now provide competition in this area. Private couriers provide competing services for parcel and document exchanges.

Telephone system
Every day, British Telecom's 20 million customers make 60 million telephone calls over a network of nearly 7000 exchanges. Existing exchanges are steadily being replaced by new System X exchanges that use the latest digital technology. A national digital telephone network overlaying the existing one should be completed by 1988.

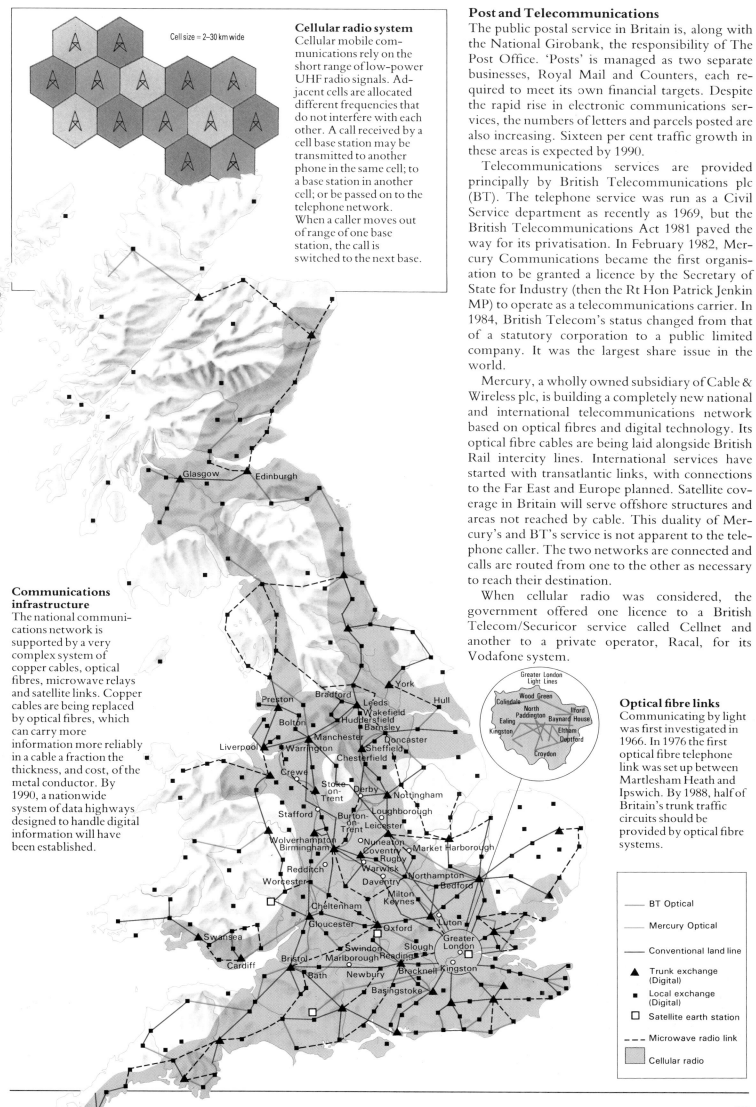

Cellular radio system

Cellular mobile communications rely on the short range of low-power UHF radio signals. Adjacent cells are allocated different frequencies that do not interfere with each other. A call received by a cell base station may be transmitted to another phone in the same cell; to a base station in another cell; or be passed on to the telephone network. When a caller moves out of range of one base station, the call is switched to the next base.

Cell size = 2–30 km wide

Communications infrastructure

The national communications network is supported by a very complex system of copper cables, optical fibres, microwave relays and satellite links. Copper cables are being replaced by optical fibres, which can carry more information more reliably in a cable a fraction the thickness, and cost, of the metal conductor. By 1990, a nationwide system of data highways designed to handle digital information will have been established.

Post and Telecommunications

The public postal service in Britain is, along with the National Girobank, the responsibility of The Post Office. 'Posts' is managed as two separate businesses, Royal Mail and Counters, each required to meet its own financial targets. Despite the rapid rise in electronic communications services, the numbers of letters and parcels posted are also increasing. Sixteen per cent traffic growth in these areas is expected by 1990.

Telecommunications services are provided principally by British Telecommunications plc (BT). The telephone service was run as a Civil Service department as recently as 1969, but the British Telecommunications Act 1981 paved the way for its privatisation. In February 1982, Mercury Communications became the first organisation to be granted a licence by the Secretary of State for Industry (then the Rt Hon Patrick Jenkin MP) to operate as a telecommunications carrier. In 1984, British Telecom's status changed from that of a statutory corporation to a public limited company. It was the largest share issue in the world.

Mercury, a wholly owned subsidiary of Cable & Wireless plc, is building a completely new national and international telecommunications network based on optical fibres and digital technology. Its optical fibre cables are being laid alongside British Rail intercity lines. International services have started with transatlantic links, with connections to the Far East and Europe planned. Satellite coverage in Britain will serve offshore structures and areas not reached by cable. This duality of Mercury's and BT's service is not apparent to the telephone caller. The two networks are connected and calls are routed from one to the other as necessary to reach their destination.

When cellular radio was considered, the government offered one licence to a British Telecom/Securicor service called Cellnet and another to a private operator, Racal, for its Vodafone system.

Optical fibre links

Communicating by light was first investigated in 1966. In 1976 the first optical fibre telephone link was set up between Martlesham Heath and Ipswich. By 1988, half of Britain's trunk traffic circuits should be provided by optical fibre systems.

Greater London Light Lines
Wood Green
Colindale
North Paddington
Ealing
Kingston
Ilford
Baynard House
Eltham
Deptford
Croydon

BT Optical

Mercury Optical

Conventional land line

▲ Trunk exchange (Digital)

■ Local exchange (Digital)

□ Satellite earth station

- - - Microwave radio link

Cellular radio

BROADCASTING AND THE PRESS

Television

Two organisations are authorised by the government to provide national public television and radio broadcasts, the British Broadcasting Corporation (BBC) and the Independent Broadcasting Authority (IBA). The British Broadcasting Company began broadcasting in this country in 1922. In 1926 it became the British Broadcasting Corporation (BBC). The BBC, whose second television channel opened in 1964, operates under the terms of a licence from the Home Secretary. It derives most of its income from licence fee receipts.

The Television Act, 1954, created the Independent Television Authority (ITA) to select and take responsibility for the activities of the new independent television (ITV) companies that the Act made possible. The first ITV transmission was in September 1955. Now, 16 ITV companies (15 area contractors plus TV-am) provide 99% of the population with local and networked programmes. ITV's second channel, Channel 4, opened in 1982. The service is financed by subscriptions from the 15 ITV area contractors. ITV generates income from selling advertising time.

In January 1983, the BBC launched Britain's first early morning television programme, 'Breakfast Time'. This was followed a month later by independent television's early morning breakfast-time service, provided by TV-am.

British television viewers now watch about 30 million television sets, more than one per household. But today, the television set is a vehicle not only for watching broadcast and cable television programmes, but also for viewing videotape films and gaining access to computer-based information systems. These are the teletext and viewdata services.

Teletext

Television signals contain brief blank periods between frames, originally inserted to allow the receiver to 'recover' before the next picture began. Television receivers no longer need this recovery period, which is now used for the transmission of extra data. Pages of information are transmitted in digital code. When the page number selected by the viewer coincides with the page number transmitted, the page appears on the screen instead of, or superimposed on, the live picture. This is teletext. The BBC's teletext service is called CEEFAX and ITV's is called ORACLE.

TV systems

Television programming can now reach the home from transmitters fed by land-line, microwave or satellite; directly from satellites using roof-top dish aerials; or by underground cable from a central TV station.

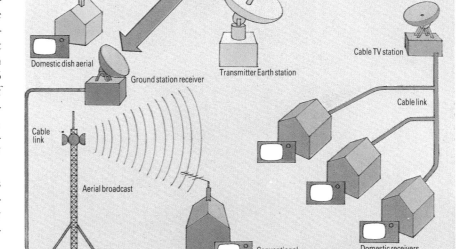

Domestic dish aerial

Ground station receiver

Transmitter Earth station

Cable TV station

Cable link

Cable link

Cable link

Aerial broadcast

Conventional domestic receivers

Domestic receivers

A typical viewdata screen shot

Viewdata

British Telecom's Prestel, the world's first public viewdata service, was introduced to Britain in 1979. Users can access over 310,000 pages (screens) of information on their own computer terminals. Prestel is used by businesses to distribute information. Users are charged for the phone call and the use of each page.

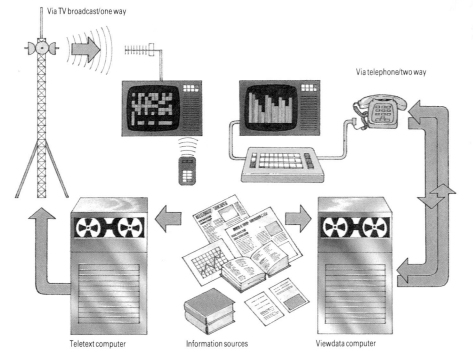

Via TV broadcast/one way

Via telephone/two way

Teletext computer

Information sources

Viewdata computer

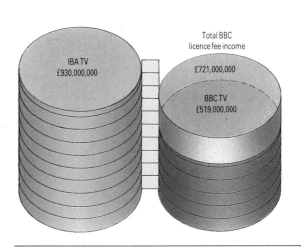

IBA TV
£930,000,000

Total BBC licence fee income

£721,000,000

BBC TV
£519,000,000

Radio

In 1971, the government transformed the ITA into the Independent *Broadcasting* Authority (IBA) and made it responsible for the establishment of Independent Local Radio (ILR). The first 3 stations opened in 1973 and now there are over 50. About 17.5 million people listen to their local ILR station every week. ILR has a 28% share of all radio listening. The BBC also operates local radio stations (currently 30) to complement its 4 network and national regional services. In 1985, the Home Secretary invited applications for licences to operate community radio stations. Twenty were selected to begin the experimental service in 1986. Stations must offer programming not offered by local radio.

The press

National and regional morning and national Sunday newspaper circulations have shown little change in recent years, but free newspapers have experienced rapid growth. Free papers began as classified advertising sheets with little or no editorial content. Their advertising revenue and economical production methods allow publishers to give them away and still show a profit. Editorial content has been increased and free papers now compete with established 'paid-for' newspapers.

Fleet Street, the centre of Britain's newspaper industry, continues to suffer from out-of-date production methods and poor management–union relations. There has been considerable resistance to the introduction of new technology, but the growth of the free press, the adoption of some new technology in the regional press, and the advent of News (UK), publishing a national daily newspaper, *Today*, by the most advanced production methods available, all challenge traditional production methods in the national press.

New technology

The production of newspapers (and magazines and books) was a labour-intensive and therefore costly task until the information-handling capacity of current computer and communications technology bypassed some of the traditional production stages. Trade unions have resisted new technology where it threatens the jobs of their members. However, one of its advantages is that editorial and printing centres need not be physically close to one another. They can be linked by telephone or satellite. Reduced production costs have also made 'free' newspapers possible.

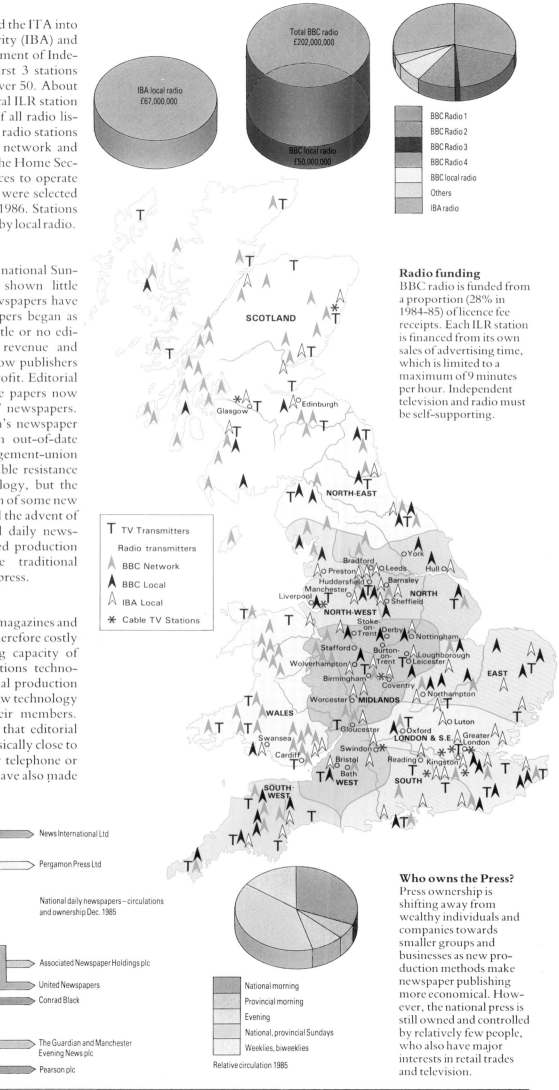

Radio funding
BBC radio is funded from a proportion (28% in 1984–85) of licence fee receipts. Each ILR station is financed from its own sales of advertising time, which is limited to a maximum of 9 minutes per hour. Independent television and radio must be self-supporting.

T TV Transmitters
　Radio transmitters
　BBC Network
　BBC Local
　IBA Local
* Cable TV Stations

Who owns the Press?
Press ownership is shifting away from wealthy individuals and companies towards smaller groups and businesses as new production methods make newspaper publishing more economical. However, the national press is still owned and controlled by relatively few people, who also have major interests in retail trades and television.

National morning
Provincial morning
Evening
National, provincial Sundays
Weeklies, biweeklies

Relative circulation 1985

BBC Radio 1
BBC Radio 2
BBC Radio 3
BBC Radio 4
BBC local radio
Others
IBA radio

IBA local radio £67,000,000

Total BBC radio £202,000,000

BBC local radio £50,000,000

The Sun
Daily Mirror
Daily Express
Daily Mail
Daily Star
Daily Telegraph
Guardian
Times
Financial Times

News International Ltd
Pergamon Press Ltd

National daily newspapers – circulations and ownership Dec. 1985

Associated Newspaper Holdings plc
United Newspapers
Conrad Black
The Guardian and Manchester Evening News plc
Pearson plc

AGRICULTURE AND FISHING

Agriculture

With respect to climate and soil type, less than 20% of Britain's land is of high farming quality and more than 30% is of low quality. Furthermore, each year agriculture loses some 10,000 hectares of arable land to meet the needs of housing, industry and transport. However, farming is one of Britain's success stories in terms of output, efficiency and self-sufficiency. The agricultural industry produces over 60% of the country's food requirements with less than 3% of its working population. Currently, the number of agricultural workers represents less than a third of the post-war (1946) farming workforce and is the smallest proportion of the population engaged in agriculture of any western European country.

In general, farming patterns in Britain represent a sophisticated adjustment to physical conditions, to market demands, and to changing agricultural technology. Overall, Britain is a country of mixed farming. The main arable areas are mostly in the east and some parts of the Midlands and southern England. In the west, where rainfall and relief make arable cropping difficult, grassland for livestock production predominates.

Technology has made a considerable contribution to agricultural efficiency. Today there are more than 500,000 tractors and some 57,000 combine harvesters in use, and a million tonnes of nitrogen fertilisers are applied to the land each year. State support to farmers has also played a major part. Following the 1948 Agriculture Act, the Ministry of Agriculture provided farmers with deficiency payments, grants and subsidies of various kinds. Subsidy and support for agriculture was increased further when in 1973 Britain joined the European Economic Community (EEC) and became subject to its Common Agricultural Policy (CAP). The basis of the CAP is the intervention of guaranteed prices set for agricultural products and the levy of duties on agricultural imports from outside the EEC, together with other subsidies, payments and assistance to farmers. Britain's greater efficiency in agriculture, the small proportion of its resources devoted to it, and its high level of food imports relative to the Community member states, has put it at a disadvantage under the CAP. Farmers receive poor rewards for their high productivity, and imported foods carry particularly high prices. This has led to pressure for reform of the CAP, which commands nearly two-thirds of the total Community budget, and for increased reimbursement on Britain's membership contribution – in 1984-85 Britain contributed some £1700m to the EEC, of which just over £1000m was reimbursed.

Common Agricultural Policy

Support for Agriculture dominates the EEC Annual Budget. Levels of price support are determined annually by the Council of Ministers on the basis of proposals presented by the European Commission. They consist of a minimum price at which the member states are willing to purchase excess production which cannot be marketed profitably. It is this arrangement that has led to the surplus stocks, or mountains, of agricultural produce generated but not sold – except at below-cost prices to, for instance, the USSR.

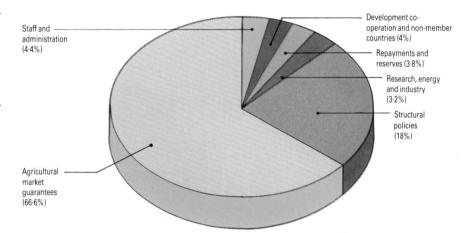

Development co-operation and non-member countries (4%)

Repayments and reserves (3·8%)

Research, energy and industry (3·2%)

Structural policies (18%)

Staff and administration (4·4%)

Agricultural market guarantees (66·6%)

Agricultural produce self-sufficiency

While the value of home-produced food related to total food consumed in Britain has increased over the years, so too has the cost of processing and distributing this food. However, home production of some principal foods has increased dramatically over the past 10 years (% by weight of total supplies): meat (78 to 89%), cheese (60 to 70%), butter (18 to 66%), wheat (59 to 100%).

Home production as % of total consumed

Home production as % of indigenous types

Food processing and distribution costs as % of total expenditure

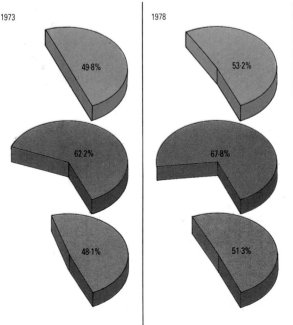

1973

49·8%

62·2%

48·1%

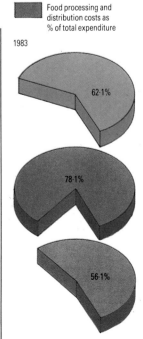

1978

53·2%

67·8%

51·3%

1983

62·1%

78·1%

56·1%

Size of farms, numbers of workers

The size of agricultural holdings in Britain ranges from less than 2 hectares to well over 200. The smallest employ only 1 or 2 people, and the largest rarely employ more than 10. The total agriculture workforce is around 700,000, of which 25% are women, 20% are part-time, and 30% are seasonal or casual workers. Of the total of 243,000 holdings, some 31,000 large farms account for about half of total output, and half of all farms account for some 90% of total output. Therefore the remaining half of all farms account for less than 10% of output. This unexpected situation (see graph) is a result primarily of the high mechanisation and productivity of many large farms but also of changes in working conditions of farm labourers and in the types of crops being cultivated.

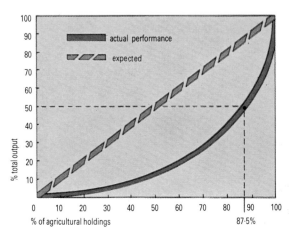

actual performance
expected

% total output

% of agricultural holdings

87·5%

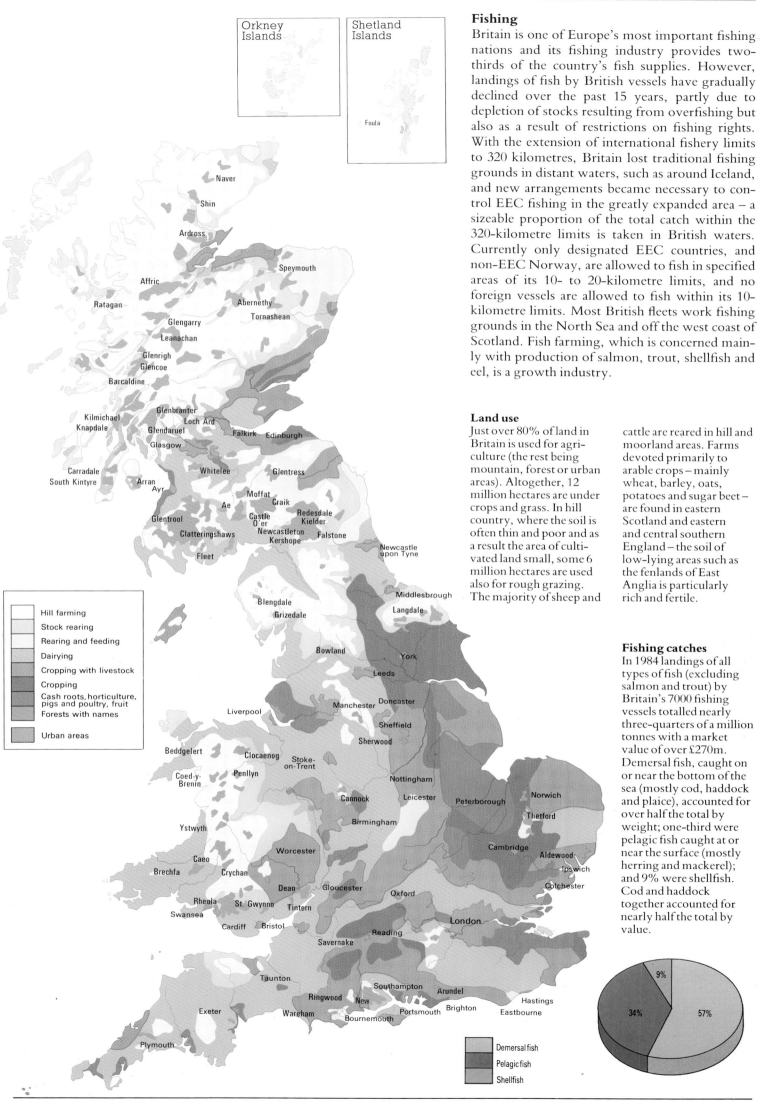

Orkney
Islands

Shetland
Islands

Foula

Fishing

Britain is one of Europe's most important fishing nations and its fishing industry provides two-thirds of the country's fish supplies. However, landings of fish by British vessels have gradually declined over the past 15 years, partly due to depletion of stocks resulting from overfishing but also as a result of restrictions on fishing rights. With the extension of international fishery limits to 320 kilometres, Britain lost traditional fishing grounds in distant waters, such as around Iceland, and new arrangements became necessary to control EEC fishing in the greatly expanded area – a sizeable proportion of the total catch within the 320-kilometre limits is taken in British waters. Currently only designated EEC countries, and non-EEC Norway, are allowed to fish in specified areas of its 10- to 20-kilometre limits, and no foreign vessels are allowed to fish within its 10-kilometre limits. Most British fleets work fishing grounds in the North Sea and off the west coast of Scotland. Fish farming, which is concerned mainly with production of salmon, trout, shellfish and eel, is a growth industry.

Land use

Just over 80% of land in Britain is used for agriculture (the rest being mountain, forest or urban areas). Altogether, 12 million hectares are under crops and grass. In hill country, where the soil is often thin and poor and as a result the area of cultivated land small, some 6 million hectares are used also for rough grazing. The majority of sheep and cattle are reared in hill and moorland areas. Farms devoted primarily to arable crops – mainly wheat, barley, oats, potatoes and sugar beet – are found in eastern Scotland and eastern and central southern England – the soil of low-lying areas such as the fenlands of East Anglia is particularly rich and fertile.

Fishing catches

In 1984 landings of all types of fish (excluding salmon and trout) by Britain's 7000 fishing vessels totalled nearly three-quarters of a million tonnes with a market value of over £270m. Demersal fish, caught on or near the bottom of the sea (mostly cod, haddock and plaice), accounted for over half the total by weight; one-third were pelagic fish caught at or near the surface (mostly herring and mackerel); and 9% were shellfish. Cod and haddock together accounted for nearly half the total by value.

Map labels:

Naver, Shin, Ardross, Speymouth, Affric, Abernethy, Tornashean, Ratagan, Glengarry, Leanachan, Glenrigh, Glencoe, Barcaldine, Glenbranter, Loch Ard, Kilmichael, Knapdale, Glendaruel, Falkirk, Edinburgh, Glasgow, Carradale, South Kintyre, Whitelee, Glentress, Arran, Ayr, Moffat, Craik, Ae, Castle O'er, Redesdale, Kielder, Glentrool, Clatteringshaws, Newcastleton, Kershope, Falstone, Fleet, Newcastle upon Tyne, Middlesbrough, Blengdale, Langdale, Grizedale, Bowland, York, Leeds, Liverpool, Manchester, Doncaster, Sheffield, Sherwood, Beddgelert, Clocaenog, Stoke-on-Trent, Coed-y-Brenin, Penllyn, Nottingham, Cannock, Leicester, Peterborough, Norwich, Thetford, Birmingham, Ystwyth, Cambridge, Aldewood, Caeo, Worcester, Ipswich, Brechfa, Crychan, Colchester, Rheola, Dean, Gloucester, Oxford, St. Gwynno, Tintern, Swansea, Cardiff, Bristol, London, Savernake, Reading, Taunton, Southampton, Arundel, Ringwood, New, Hastings, Wareham, Portsmouth, Brighton, Eastbourne, Bournemouth, Exeter, Plymouth

Legend:
- Hill farming
- Stock rearing
- Rearing and feeding
- Dairying
- Cropping with livestock
- Cropping
- Cash roots, horticulture, pigs and poultry, fruit
- Forests with names
- Urban areas

Pie chart:
9%
34%
57%

- Demersal fish
- Pelagic fish
- Shellfish

INDUSTRY AND INVESTMENT

The main characteristic of recent trends in Britain's industrial structure has been the decline in its manufacturing industries as producers, investors and employers. The nature of the decline is, on the one hand, competitive, on the other, technological.

Falling competitiveness

Britain's share of world trade in manufactures – a key measure of competitiveness – fell from over 20% of the total to less than 9% from 1939 to 1985. The decline may be attributed not only to price factors but also to poor quality, design, delivery dates, after-sales service and marketing. It has not merely been the result of entry into foreign markets of newly industrialised countries, such as Hong Kong and Taiwan, since Britain's recent performance has been well below that of its established industrial competitors, the United States, West Germany and Japan. At a time when patterns of international trade are increasingly influenced by the decisions of multinational companies on location, investment, choice of technology and products, a significant proportion of Britain's companies seem to have been wasting their energies on the wrong goods and trying to sell them in the wrong markets.

Investment and technology

Manufacturing is becoming an increasingly capital- as opposed to labour-intensive production activity. Its success depends on investment in technologies which reduce the requirement for labour. In Britain over the past decade, total investment in the industrial sector has increased, mainly as a result of oil exploration, retrieval and processing, but investment in manufacturing has

gradually declined and, like output, now stands at a level lower than in 1979 (currently some 10% of total investment). The country is faced with the problem of investing either in traditional manufacturing to enhance competitiveness by utilising the latest technologies, or in alternative industries that will form a new base of output, exports and employment. On a world basis, future economic activity in industrialised countries is likely to be in the fields of microelectronics, robotics and information technology.

After the oil runs out

Currently, Britain's North Sea oil revenues are sheltering it from its balance of payments problems arising from the decline of manufacturing. This will continue only for as long as the oil is accessible, recoverable and marketable at ruling prices – proven reserves indicate that this is no more than ten years. The service sector is providing alternative production and employment opportunities, but not at the same rate as manufacturing's decline and with much less contribution to exports. It is hoped that the microelectronics industry will prove a major growth area but to date Britain has experienced a net deficit in foreign trade in this field. Britain must seriously consider how far its traditional manufacturing can apply the latest technologies to win back lost export and domestic markets. Only by sacrificing employment opportunities in the short-term can long-term employment in manufacturing become more assured. With its manufacturing trade balance in the red for the first time since the Industrial Revolution, Britain needs robust long-term alternative industries before the oil runs out.

National employment

Dominating the picture is the increasing concentration of jobs in the South-east. There are two reasons for this. First, the decline in primary and manufacturing industries (top half of table below) has affected this region less than others. Second, the South-east benefits from a large presence of expanding service industries (bottom half of table). Population densities and movements, and membership of the European Economic Community, have reinforced these trends.

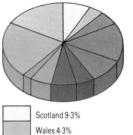

Scotland 9·3%
Wales 4·3%
North 4·9%
North-west 11·4%
Yorks & Humber 8·4%
E. Midlands 6·8%
W. Midlands 9·3%
South-west 7·4%
East Anglia 3·4%
Greater London 16·6%
S. East (exc GL) 18·2%

Industries employing above national average

Industries employing highest regional proportion

Regional distribution of employees and employment (mid-1985)

Manufacturing accounts nationally for just over 25% of jobs, yet the West Midlands employs 36·2% of workers in its various manufacturing industries while in the South-east almost 50% of jobs are in the service sector. A study in 1979 by the National Economic Development Office (NEDO) found that the contribution of the fastest-growing industries (energy; chemicals; electrical engineering; finance; transport and communications) to both output and employment of a region meant that the South-east was highly favoured.

	TOTAL GB	S.E. (exc GL)	S.E. (GL only)	East Anglia	South-west	West Midlands	East Midlands	Yorks and Humber	North-west	North	Wales	Scot-land
INDUSTRIAL SECTOR % of regional employment accounted for by each industrial sector: (rounded figures)												
Agriculture, forestry, fishing	1·6	1·8	0·1	4·8	2·9	1·5	2·2	1·5	0·7	1·3	2·6	2·1
Energy and water supply	2·9	1·7	1·3	1·6	1·7	2·4	5·1	5·4	2·5	5·1	5·3	4·0
Metal manufacturing and chemicals	3·7	2·8	1·8	2·7	2·9	5·5	4·1	5·9	4·5	6·7	6·3	2·4
Metal goods, engineering and vehicles	12·2	15·0	7·3	11·2	11·7	22·3	13·1	10·1	12·5	11·7	9·1	9·3
Other manufacturing	9·8	7·8	7·4	11·3	9·1	8·4	17·3	13·0	11·4	9·2	7·2	10·6
Construction	4·4	4·3	4·1	4·7	4·9	3·8	4·2	4·5	4·1	4·6	4·9	5·9
Wholesale distributors, hotels, catering	10·6	10·3	11·0	11·8	13·4	10·5	8·9	11·0	10·3	9·5	9·3	10·7
Retail distribution	10·3	11·3	9·4	11·3	10·1	9·8	9·2	10·1	10·7	10·7	10·3	11·0
Transport and communications	6·1	5·7	9·5	6·2	5·3	4·4	5·2	5·1	5·8	5·4	5·3	5·7
Banking, insurance and finance	9·3	8·5	18·1	7·4	8·2	7·4	6·3	6·9	8·1	6·0	5·9	7·4
Public administration and defence	8·7	7·8	10·8	7·1	7·7	8·2	7·3	7·3	9·4	8·1	11·9	8·0
Education, health and other services	20·3	22·9	19·4	19·9	22·2	15·8	17·0	19·3	20·1	21·6	22·0	22·0

Employment trends

In 19th century Britain, the agricultural industry declined in the wake of mechanisation, and manufacturing and energy industries grew. This century has seen a continuation of this trend, but increasingly the picture is one of manufacturing's own decline in favour of service sector employment. A hundred years ago it would have been hard to imagine the country producing half its temperate food needs with 3% of its labour force, and 40 years ago to picture an economy in which no more than 20% of workers are in manufacturing. Moreover, a sizeable proportion of these workers would be performing non-manual functions. Yet for Britain this is what present trends suggest by the end of the century.

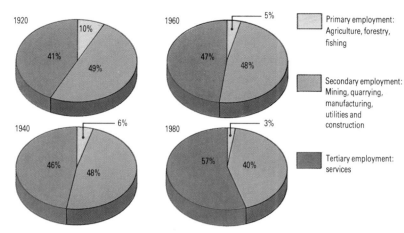

Primary employment: Agriculture, forestry, fishing

Secondary employment: Mining, quarrying, manufacturing, utilities and construction

Tertiary employment: services

Decline in manufacturing activity

The British economy has traditionally relied heavily upon manufacturing to provide jobs. However, the loss of nearly 3 million jobs in manufacturing since 1970 has been partly offset by a growth in other sectors of industry, such as in the service sector, where almost 500,000 jobs have been created. Yet employment growth outside manufacturing has been erratic; in some periods there have even been job losses in the service sector as a result of Britain's stagnant economy. Jobs disappearing in manufacturing are typically those of full-time, manual, male workers, while new jobs emerging in the service sector are typically part-time, non-manual, and filled by female workers.

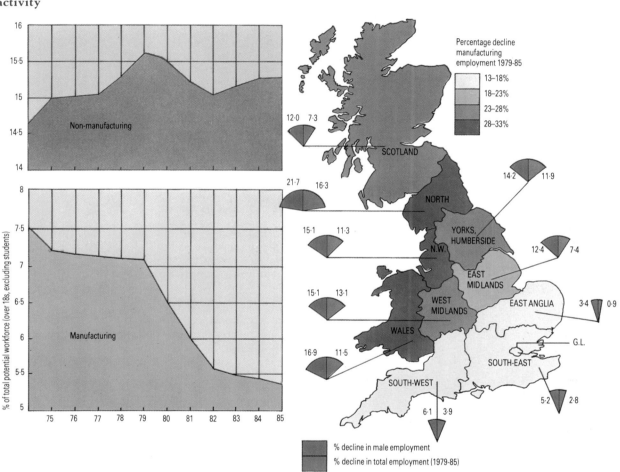

Percentage decline manufacturing employment 1979–85

13–18%
18–23%
23–28%
28–33%

% decline in male employment

% decline in total employment (1979-85)

The North: a case history

The North of England is currently experiencing the worst combined and cumulative problems of regional economic disadvantage. In the first half of 1984, the region had the highest redundancy rate (2·8%), and the highest unemployment rate (nearly 19%) of any region in 1984 and 1985. Alongside this, output in the North fell from 91·1% to 89·6% of the national average between 1974 and 1983, and government spending on social security and other state benefits has in recent years been higher than for any other region except Wales. Explanations are not hard to find. In 1974 manufacturing accounted for 35·6% of the region's output; by 1983 it had fallen to 28·6%. Also there was a decline in construction employment of 39%; a fall of 25% in jobs in the energy industries (mainly coal); and even a drop of 4·5% in service sector employment. Surprisingly, though, the NEDO report (see table caption opposite) showed the North is well placed for fast-growing industries.

Right: A new pharmaceutical plant near Newcastle. Large companies can receive from the state financial inducements to create employment in economically depressed areas.

EMPLOYMENT AND UNEMPLOYMENT

For some 20 years after World War II Britain's economy was run with no more than 2% of the workforce unemployed – less than half a million people. Throughout 1985 unemployment remained above the three million mark (13·5%). There are several reasons why the country has slipped so far away from full employment.

Deflationary policies

First, adjustments made since the early 1970s to meet fluctuations in the country's economy have all contributed to the rise in unemployment. Measures taken in budgets and public spending reviews have increasingly been responses to rises in inflation, balance of payments deficits, and oil price shocks. The adoption of a tight monetary policy has reduced inflation. However, associated increases in interest rates and the resulting higher exchange value for the pound have posed problems for the economy. Consumer spending has decreased, as has investment in plant and equipment, and the higher exchange rate has made exports less competitive. Thus demand for goods and sevices in the economy has been increasingly inadequate to support jobs.

The supply side

Apart from the management of demand, there is the quality of production. Here the two factors referred to on pages 44-45 are again significant. The competitive factor means that Britain's falling share of world trade in manufactures has reduced the ability of its manufacturing industries to offer jobs, while the technological factor has meant that fewer workers are required to produce the same level of output, let alone a lower one.

Finally, there is the 'structural' dimension. Industry's reduced ability to offer employment has coincided with a period in which the numbers seeking work – the labour supply – have risen. The rise is due to the sharp increase in both the number of young people entering the labour market – a legacy of the post-war birth bulge – and the number of women seeking work.

What can be done?

Economists have identified three main solutions to the problem. First, matters can be left to market forces and international competition. However, this puts manufacturing under more pressure, which might lead to increased unemployment. While special measures such as Youth Training Schemes can cushion the blow of unemployment for particular age groups, job losses in manufacturing fall most heavily on already disadvantaged regions and categories of workers. Second, economic demand can be boosted through internationally co-ordinated reflation. Increased public investment on, say, railways and roads, would run less risk of increasing imports than would tax reductions that left consumers free to buy British or not. Finally, consideration can be given to reducing hours of work, to earlier retirement, to training and study leave, and to job sharing, so that the work is spread among a larger number of people. The increased use of microelectronics technology may reinforce such policy redirection.

Working population and employed labour force

The rise in Britain's unemployment has not been a smooth one. From 1945 to 1967 unemployment was held at an average level of ⅓ million. It was not until 1971 that it crept above ¾ million. By 1980 it stood at 1½ million. The first half of the 1980s saw it pass the 3 million mark. There has been a progressively shorter period between each doubling. This is the result of the reduced capacity of the economy to provide and sustain jobs (the lower line on the graph), together with the increased numbers looking for work as the labour force increases (upper line).

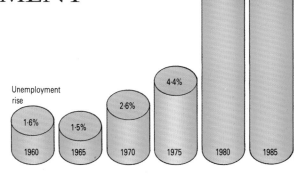

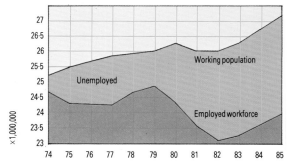

Regional unemployment

Such aggregate unemployment figures conceal the problems faced by certain regions of the country. The table, right, compares the South-east, the least affected region, with the five worst affected regions. In the latter, over half the male unemployment has occurred since 1979. Regional inequalities are even more marked for long-term unemployment (for more than one year).

Male unemployment (selected regions) 1984-85	% of total workforce	Additional % unempl. compared with '79	Long-term male unemployed as % rate of total unemployed	Long-term male unemployment rate
South-east	11·6	+7·3	38·31	4·4
Yorkshire and Humberside	17·2	+10·7	43·7	7·5
West Midlands	17·8	+11·7	50·9	9·2
North-west	19·7	+11·6	48·9	9·6
Wales	20·0	+11·5	44·6	8·9
North	22·4	+12·5	47·5	10·5

Total workforce = all over-18s excluding students

The flexible firm

Apart from any pressure from rising unemployment upon traditional employment and work-time patterns, many British employers are now looking to introduce more flexibility into the numbers they employ, the form of their employment contracts, the jobs workers do, and the way in which they are paid. They are seeking to achieve this by reorganising their labour force into a small core group of professional and skilled key workers, surrounded by groups of semi-skilled, part-time and contract employees – the end of the hierarchical structure of the firm.

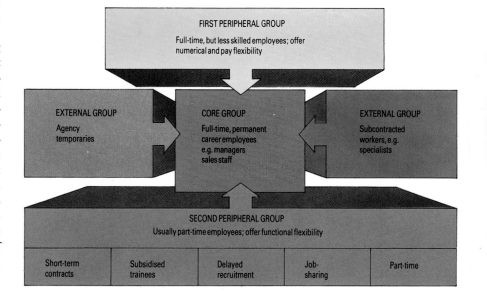

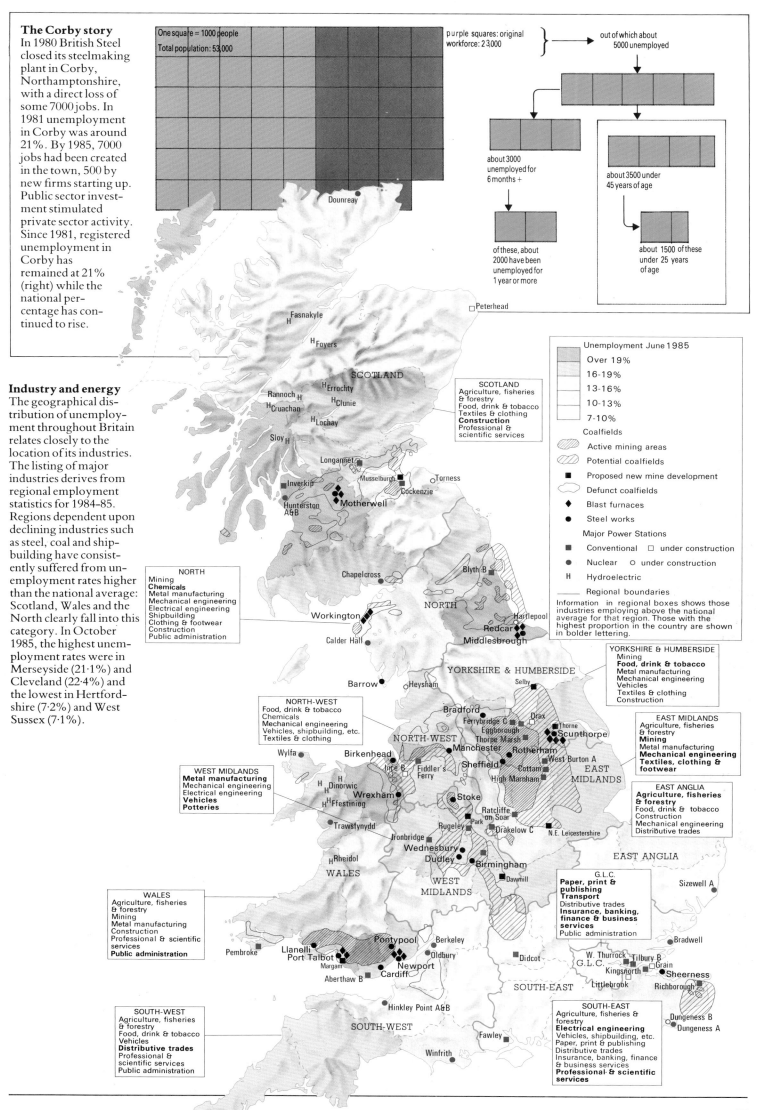

The Corby story

In 1980 British Steel closed its steelmaking plant in Corby, Northamptonshire, with a direct loss of some 7000 jobs. In 1981 unemployment in Corby was around 21%. By 1985, 7000 jobs had been created in the town, 500 by new firms starting up. Public sector investment stimulated private sector activity. Since 1981, registered unemployment in Corby has remained at 21% (right) while the national percentage has continued to rise.

One square = 1000 people
Total population: 53,000

purple squares: original workforce 23,000

out of which about 5000 unemployed

about 3000 unemployed for 6 months +

about 3500 under 45 years of age

of these, about 2000 have been unemployed for 1 year or more

about 1500 of these under 25 years of age

Industry and energy

The geographical distribution of unemployment throughout Britain relates closely to the location of its industries. The listing of major industries derives from regional employment statistics for 1984–85. Regions dependent upon declining industries such as steel, coal and shipbuilding have consistently suffered from unemployment rates higher than the national average: Scotland, Wales and the North clearly fall into this category. In October 1985, the highest unemployment rates were in Merseyside (21·1%) and Cleveland (22·4%) and the lowest in Hertfordshire (7·2%) and West Sussex (7·1%).

SCOTLAND
Agriculture, fisheries & forestry
Food, drink & tobacco
Textiles & clothing
Construction
Professional & scientific services

NORTH
Mining
Chemicals
Metal manufacturing
Mechanical engineering
Electrical engineering
Shipbuilding
Clothing & footwear
Construction
Public administration

Unemployment June 1985
Over 19%
16–19%
13–16%
10–13%
7–10%

Coalfields
Active mining areas
Potential coalfields
Proposed new mine development
Defunct coalfields
Blast furnaces
Steel works

Major Power Stations
Conventional   under construction
Nuclear   under construction
Hydroelectric
Regional boundaries

Information in regional boxes shows those industries employing above the national average for that region. Those with the highest proportion in the country are shown in bolder lettering.

YORKSHIRE & HUMBERSIDE
Mining
Food, drink & tobacco
Metal manufacturing
Mechanical engineering
Vehicles
Textiles & clothing
Construction

NORTH-WEST
Food, drink & tobacco
Chemicals
Mechanical engineering
Vehicles, shipbuilding, etc.
Textiles & clothing

EAST MIDLANDS
Agriculture, fisheries & forestry
Mining
Metal manufacturing
Mechanical engineering
Textiles, clothing & footwear

WEST MIDLANDS
Metal manufacturing
Mechanical engineering
Electrical engineering
Vehicles
Potteries

EAST ANGLIA
Agriculture, fisheries & forestry
Food, drink & tobacco
Construction
Mechanical engineering
Distributive trades

WALES
Agriculture, fisheries & forestry
Mining
Metal manufacturing
Construction
Professional & scientific services
Public administration

G.L.C.
Paper, print & publishing
Transport
Distributive trades
Insurance, banking, finance & business services
Public administration

SOUTH-WEST
Agriculture, fisheries & forestry
Food, drink & tobacco
Vehicles
Distributive trades
Professional & scientific services
Public administration

SOUTH-EAST
Agriculture, fisheries & forestry
Electrical engineering
Vehicles, shipbuilding, etc.
Paper, print & publishing
Distributive trades
Insurance, banking, finance & business services
Professional & scientific services

SCOTLAND · Dounreay · Fasnakyle H · Foyers H · Errochty H · Rannoch H · Clunie H · Cruachan H · Lochay H · Sloy H · Longannet · Inverkip · Musselburgh · Torness · Cockenzie · Hunterston A&B · Motherwell · Peterhead · NORTH · Chapelcross · Blyth B · Workington · Hartlepool · Calder Hall · Redcar · Middlesbrough · Barrow · Heysham · YORKSHIRE & HUMBERSIDE · Selby · Bradford · Drax · Ferrybridge C · Thorne · Eggborough · Thorpe Marsh · Scunthorpe · NORTH-WEST · Manchester · Rotherham · West Burton A · Wylfa · Birkenhead · Sheffield · Cottam · EAST MIDLANDS · Ince B · Fiddler's Ferry · High Marnham · Dinorwic H · Wrexham · Stoke · Ratcliffe on Soar · EAST ANGLIA · Trawsfynydd · Park · Drakelow C · N.E. Leicestershire · Ffestiniog H · Ironbridge · Rugeley · Rheidol H · Wednesbury · Dudley · Birmingham · WALES · WEST MIDLANDS · Dawmill · Sizewell A · Pontypool · Berkeley · Bradwell · Pembroke · Llanelli · Port Talbot · Oldbury · W. Thurrock · Tilbury B · Margam · Newport · Didcot · G.L.C. · Kingsnorth · Sheerness · Cardiff · Grain · Aberthaw B · Littlebrook · Richborough · SOUTH-EAST · Hinkley Point A&B · Dungeness B · SOUTH-WEST · Dungeness A · Fawley · Winfrith

47

FOREIGN TRADE

Britain has traditionally been, and remains, a trading nation. Currently, it exports some 30% of production in order to cover the equally high percentage of expenditure on imports. However, the relationship between exports and imports has altered over the years, swinging from deficit to surplus and back again, and altering in relative composition, destinations and origins.

There are four main reasons for the country's trading role. First, Britain lacks certain raw materials and as a result of its climate is unable to produce certain foodstuffs, which it must import. Second, it is superior in producing certain goods and services, such as electronics and merchant banking, which other countries need. Third, Britain has to compete with other countries' products in its home market and abroad. Lastly, it has become an oil-producing nation.

Changes in trading patterns

Britain's Industrial Revolution made it the world leader in iron and steel, textiles and railways. Deposits of iron ore and coal, the development of spinning and weaving machinery, the exploitation of crude steelmaking technology, and steam-engine power, gave the country a head start. This advantage was lost soon after World War II. Japan developed a steel industry based on high-quality raw materials and exploiting large-scale production and advanced technology, while many foreign companies exploited the low wages, poor labour organisation and lack of social provision in developing countries in order to undercut prices for textile and clothing production. Furthermore, changing consumer tastes and greater affluence meant that the motor car and aeroplane superseded rail as a means of transport.

International trade shares

Britain's share of world trade in manufactures has fallen by over 50% since World War II and continues to fall. The prime cause is a long-term deep-rooted decline in its international competitiveness.

1980	1983	
17	17·5	U.S.A.
14·2	13·5	W. Germany
9·5	11	Japan
	8·4	UK/France (equal %)
6·2	6·2	Italy

6 countries together = 65% of 1983 total trade

Goods traded

The composition of Britain's visible exports and imports reflects both its natural advantages and disadvantages and, increasingly, its competitiveness. The need to import certain raw materials and foodstuffs remains unavoidable, but the change from surplus to deficit in foreign trade in manufactured and semi-manufactured goods has caused successive governments great alarm. The country is losing ground, both in terms of traditional specialisation and its domestic markets. Imports have reached very high levels: two-thirds of all vehicles and one-half and one-third respectively of electrical and mechanical engineering products are foreign. Some British industries have disappeared in the face of foreign competition.

Food, beverages, tobacco
Basic materials
Oil
Other mineral fuels and lubricants
Semi-manufactured goods
Finished manufactured goods
Commodities, transactions not classified by type

£21,745m £16,394m } deficit

Imports   Exports
1974

£74,510m £70,400m deficit } deficit

Imports   Exports
1984

Britain's trading partners

Nearly half the country's exports and imports are now accounted for by the European Economic Community (EEC). However, in the decade since Britain's entry, the trade deficit with the EEC has increased tenfold.

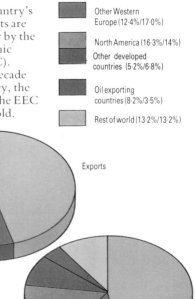

EEC (44·7%/45·5%)
Other Western Europe (12·4%/17·0%)
North America (16·3%/14%)
Other developed countries (5·2%/6·8%)
Oil exporting countries (8·2%/3·5%)
Rest of world (13·2%/13·2%)

Exports

Imports

Invisible trade

Since 1974 Britain has earned a surplus from its invisible transactions. These fall into three main groups: receipts from payments arising from services, such as tourism, sea and air transport, and the commercial and financial activities of the City of London; interest, profits and dividends on past British investments overseas; and 'transfers', which are both government and private financial movements. Within transfers, the present net outflow of some £2 billion cancels out the surplus on interest, profits and dividends, partly as a result of government contribution to the EEC.

Current account

Combining visible and invisible trade figures provides the overall 'current account' of the balance of payments. This has improved from a deficit of £3 bn in 1974 to a surplus of £6·5 bn in 1981 but has since reduced to £0·9 bn.

Invisible trade
1984 figures: £bn (£1,000m)

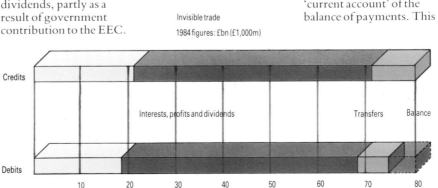

Credits

Interests, profits and dividends   Transfers   Balance

Debits

10   20   30   40   50   60   70   80

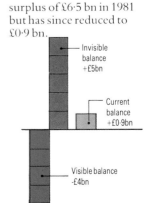

Invisible balance +£5bn

Current balance +£0·9bn

Visible balance -£4bn

Balance of payments

This has three components: visible trade, invisible trade and capital movements. Visible trade comprises raw materials, fuels, food and manufactured goods. Britain has traditionally covered its import bill for the first three items by exporting manufactures. In the past 15 years, though, there have been two key changes. First, after being faced with massive increases in its import bill as a result of oil price rises, North Sea oil production started and generated revenues that created a balance of payments surplus. Second, hidden by this change in oil fortunes, British manufacturing saw its balance of payments surplus turn to deficit in 1983.

Invisible trade is an additional source of foreign currency, and includes transport, tourism, insurance and the returns from investment abroad. 'Invisibles' have always made a positive contribution to the balance of payments but they amount to only a fraction of visible trade figures. The imbalance of payments will become greater still as North Sea oil production declines and if manufacturing continues to slide into deficit. Also, the main item of benefit on the invisibles account, interest, profits and dividends, is tied in with capital movements, the third component.

Capital movements represent the outflow and inflow of funds to set up production or purchase assets overseas. Since the abolition of exchange controls in 1979, there has been a large movement of British funds overseas by companies and by financial institutions. Without investing abroad, Britain's foreign currency income generated under 'invisibles' would not be realised. However, high levels of overseas investment deprive the country's manufacturing industry of much needed capital.

Britain as an oil-producing nation

Between 1974 and 1984 Britain experienced a complete turnaround from deficit to surplus on its oil account. But in the same period manufacturing moved from surplus to deficit. For oil to continue to support the balance of payments, either improved oil exploration techniques must lead to new resources being discovered, or new industrial products and processes must be developed to supplement oil and manufacturing's export contribution.

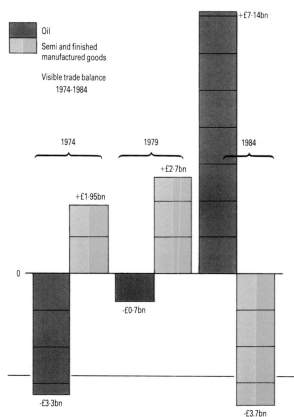

Oil

Semi and finished manufactured goods

Visible trade balance 1974-1984

1974   1979   1984

+£7·14bn

+£2·7bn

+£1·95bn

-£0·7bn

-£3·3bn

-£3·7bn

Influence of the multinationals

Multinational companies (MNCs) are characterised by having production facilities in more than one country. They can therefore influence patterns of foreign trade by their own strategic business decisions. So large proportions of a country's exports, while leaving the country physically, merely pass from one location of an MNC's production chain to another. In Britain, the influence of MNCs is illustrated by their contribution to the decline of manufacturing in the West Midlands. In 10 major companies within the region recent years have seen one-third of their workforce being made redundant and large-scale disinvestment in Britain. The consequences for employment, production and exports for their British operations are illustrated below.

The companies: GEC, GKN, Cadbury, Dunlop, Lucas, Tube Investments, IMI, Delta, Glynwed and BSR

1 % of global workforce in Britain
2 % of world production in Britain
3 British exports as % of total overseas sales

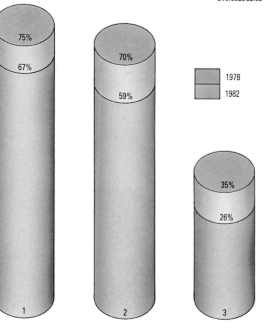

1978
1982

75%
67%

70%
59%

35%
26%

1   2   3

British Petroleum's Magnus oil production platform in the North Sea. In the 1970s, at the time of the Middle East oil crisis and anticipated North Sea oil bonanza, some politicians suggested using Britain's revenues and benefits from oil to finance the regeneration of industry through increased investment in the private and public sectors. Today part of oil revenues are used to cover the costs of unemployment.

THE PUBLIC SECTOR

The public sector is concerned with taxation, borrowing and expenditure by central and local government. The government reviews its expenditure plans each year in the Budget and from this sets taxation and borrowing levels.

As public expenditure in Britain approached 50% of all spending in the mid-1970s, economists and politicians became concerned with the prospects of the government spending more of the taxpayers' money than the taxpayers themselves. Yet the scale and use of public spending are inevitable responses to economic and social circumstances. Total public spending includes both direct spending on goods and services such as hospitals and teachers' pay, and 'transfer payments' such as unemployment benefit, social security, and retirement pensions. Currently, nearly half of all public spending is transfer payments, so that the government's direct command over economic resources is no more than a quarter of total spending in the economy. The rise in unemployment and the increased proportion of older people make increasing demands on the public purse. These changes in employment and population structures leave the government with less revenue from taxes on those in work to finance the increased expenditure.

Control of public expenditure
Arguments supporting the strict control and, if possible, reduction of public expenditure include the virtues of market forces, the inflationary consequences of a high rate of public spending, and

the importance of a flourishing wealth-creating private sector. A high priority for the government recently has been to hold down the level of funding needed to run the state sector. By reducing the call on private sector resources, through tax cuts and other concessions, it has sought to provoke the private sector into creating services (such as health care) which were the traditional preserve of the state. It has also looked to greater profitability in manufacturing industry as the first step towards creating better long-term employment prospects.

There are, however, counter-arguments for financing certain economic activities, especially health and education, from government funds. Evidence is put forward that the free availability of these services at the point of consumption is good for the economy and not merely convenient for the recipient. Failure to spend on such provision creates disadvantages and costs for the community more generally. Similarly, reasons are advanced for taking advantage of the contribution that public spending can make to the level of demand – and therefore the level of economic activity and employment – in an economy. If demand is low, public spending can compensate for this, especially through public capital investment such as road building, in ways that need not lead to accelerated inflation or increase in imports. In addition, the contributions of government spending to the quality of housing, training and education, transport and so on in the economy can contribute to the effectiveness of the private sector.

Public expenditure and GDP
Currently, public expenditure represents some 40% of total national spending (the Gross Domestic Product or GDP). Governments have sought to reduce this amount by cuts in actual and planned spending and reductions in benefits. Recently, the figures have been kept down by the inclusion of revenue from sales of assets – privatisation of companies such as British Telecom – as 'negative' public spending.

Ratio of expenditure to GDP YEAR	Planning total plus net debt interest	Percentage of total expenditure on goods and services
80-81	42·5%	24%
81-82	44%	24%
82-83	43·5%	24%
83-84	42·5%	24%
84-85	42·5%	23%

Managing the economy
Public spending is a major component of demand in the economy, along with consumer spending, private investment and exports. Each component of demand can be lowered or raised by government economic measures and policies in order to either curb inflation or to boost demand and sustain a higher level of output and employment. Public expenditure can even be financed by borrowing, provided it boosts economic activity and leads to higher tax revenues. The diagram below shows four possible policies (lower taxes etc.) that together may create full use of all resources.

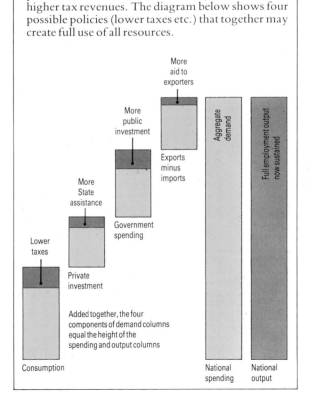

More aid to exporters

More public investment

More State assistance

Lower taxes

Private investment

Government spending

Exports minus imports

Aggregate demand

Full employment output now sustained

Added together, the four components of demand columns equal the height of the spending and output columns

Consumption

National spending

National output

Planned public spending in real terms
There are three ways of looking at the composition of public expenditure: by programmes, by spending authorities, and by economic categories. Programmes broadly reflect government departments. They are dominated by social security (30% of total spending). Spending authorities are bodies that control actual expenditure. These are dominated by central government. Public corporations, or nationalised industries, make relatively minor demands on the public purse as they raise most of their own finance through pricing policies. Economic categories illustrate how the money is spent within the various departments.

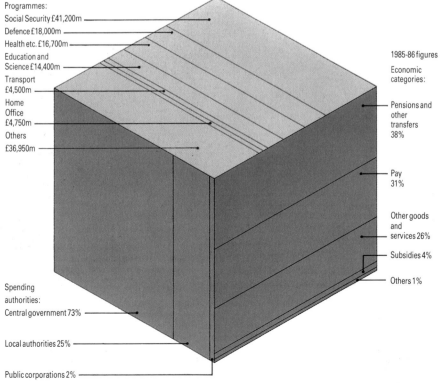

Programmes:
Social Security £41,200m
Defence £18,000m
Health etc. £16,700m
Education and Science £14,400m
Transport £4,500m
Home Office £4,750m
Others £36,950m

1985-86 figures

Economic categories:

Pensions and other transfers 38%

Pay 31%

Other goods and services 26%

Subsidies 4%

Others 1%

Spending authorities:
Central government 73%
Local authorities 25%
Public corporations 2%

Government departments

Although Health and Social Security accounts for more public expenditure than any other government department, Defence (including Royal Ordnance Factories) has the greatest number of civil servants (over 200,000). The highest concentration of civil servants is in the South-east, with more than 1 in 3 of the total. However, the past 10 years have seen an increasing number of civil service departments being moved out of London to decentralise the system – Vehicle Licence to Swansea, Overseas Development to East Kilbride, Income Tax to Shipley, Customs and Excise to Southend. In the same period there has been a 20% reduction in staffing levels.

Public spending 1983-87

Changes in expenditure over recent years show social security (currently some £42 bn) top of the 'league table' of gains and losses and spending on trade and industry, employment and energy (£6 bn) at the bottom. Housing (£6·1 bn), which used to rank high in the table, has been the second biggest loser of funds. (In real terms, the planning total increased by less than 1%.)

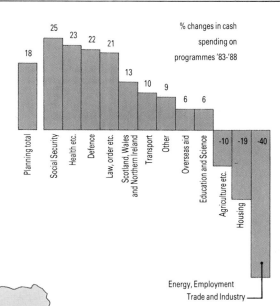

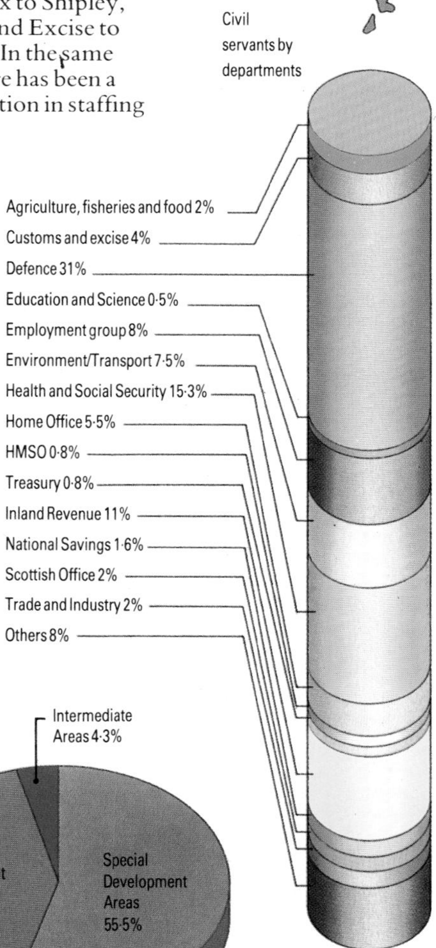

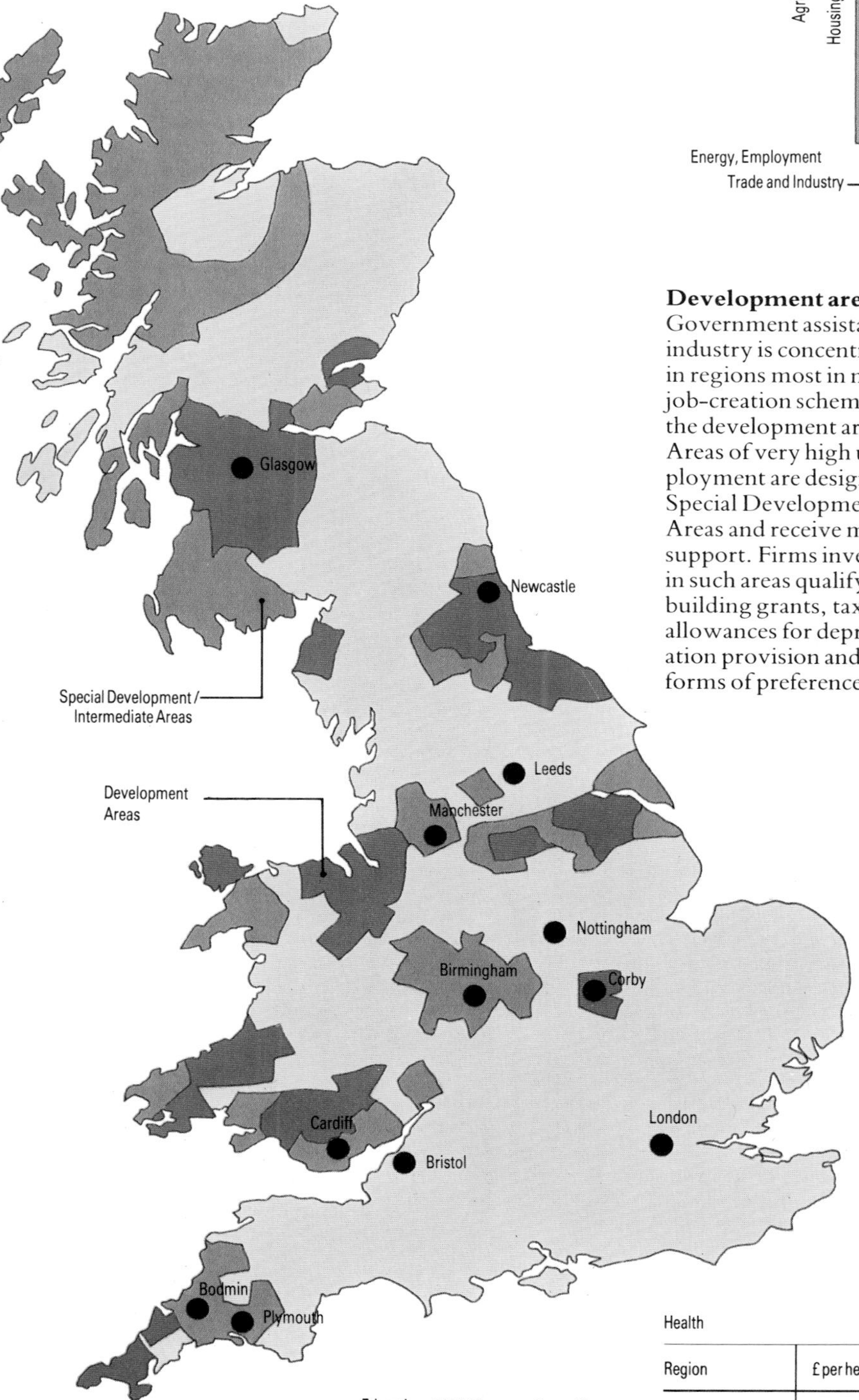

% changes in cash spending on programmes '83-'88

- Planning total 18
- Social Security 25
- Health etc. 23
- Defence 22
- Law, order etc. 21
- Scotland, Wales and Northern Ireland 13
- Transport 10
- Other 9
- Overseas aid 6
- Education and Science 6
- Agriculture etc. -10
- Housing -19
- Energy, Employment Trade and Industry -40

Development areas

Government assistance to industry is concentrated in regions most in need of job-creation schemes – the development areas. Areas of very high unemployment are designated Special Development Areas and receive most support. Firms investing in such areas qualify for building grants, tax allowances for depreciation provision and other forms of preference.

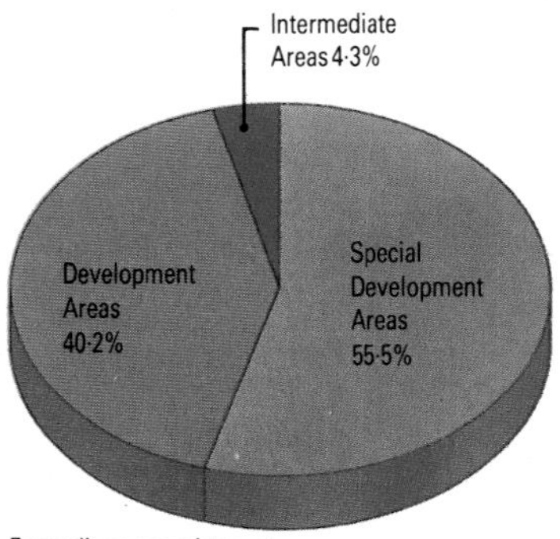

Civil servants by departments

- Agriculture, fisheries and food 2%
- Customs and excise 4%
- Defence 31%
- Education and Science 0·5%
- Employment group 8%
- Environment/Transport 7·5%
- Health and Social Security 15·3%
- Home Office 5·5%
- HMSO 0·8%
- Treasury 0·8%
- Inland Revenue 11%
- National Savings 1·6%
- Scottish Office 2%
- Trade and Industry 2%
- Others 8%

Expenditure on assistance to industry 1984-85 – total £630m

- Intermediate Areas 4·3%
- Development Areas 40·2%
- Special Development Areas 55·5%

Special Development / Intermediate Areas

Development Areas

Map labels: Glasgow, Newcastle, Leeds, Manchester, Nottingham, Birmingham, Corby, Cardiff, Bristol, London, Bodmin, Plymouth

Regional capital expenditure

Currently, the greatest item of capital expenditure (investment to create or maintain productivity and services for future output) is economic services, including employment, agriculture, trade and industry, road building and water supply. In 1982-83 this totalled nearly £2bn. Health and Social Services, and General Administration and Defence each accounted for just under £1bn investment, while Education, as well as Housing and Community Development accounted for some £½bn each. The South-east was the region attracting the greatest share of capital spending in each of the first three categories listed, while in the last category Scotland accounted for 50% of the total.

Education and Health

In recent years, total expenditure by health authorities and education authorities has been greatest in Scotland on a per head of population basis. Figures for selected regions, right, illustrate the wide range of expenditure levels.

Education 1984-85	Annual figures
Region	£ per head
North	£220
Yorks & Humbs	£220
East Anglia	£185
South-east	£230
Wales	£265
Scotland	£330

Health	
Region	£ per head
West Midlands	£225
Northern	£245
Yorkshire	£230
East Anglian	£230
N.E. Thames	£280
Oxford	£210
Wales	£270
Scotland	£310

INCOME AND WEALTH

Three main factors determine a family's standard of living: first, the number of individuals in the family that are actively working and earning an income; second, the individuals' jobs and levels of pay; and, third, any other sources of income available to the family. Other factors are government taxation on income; any benefits provided by the state; and any assets, either inherited or saved, owned by members of the family that bestow economic advantages.

Similar criteria are used to determine the levels of income and wealth of a locality, a region or the country as a whole. The general principles of how these factors influence the distribution of wealth are considered in the text below and opposite, while the British picture is highlighted in the diagrams and captions.

Consider two families living next door to each other. The first comprises two working parents and two older working children. The second consists of an unemployed father, a non-working mother, a school-leaver yet to find a job and a grandmother living in. In each case the family unit comprises four people, but the activity rates – the balance between working population and dependents – are very different. The first family is putting more into the national economy in tax, the second is drawing more in state benefits. The influence of family structure upon the total incomes of the two households is considerable, even before actual levels of pay and income are considered. The income of the first family could be eight times greater than that of the second.

Pay levels are nevertheless important. Salaries of non-manual workers tend to be higher than those of their manual counterparts, while men's pay generally remains higher than women's. Industry, occupation and age also account for pay differences, as does the sector – private or public – and the mechanism for pay determination that applies. Unearned income from various sources – interest, dividends and rent – varies according to the nature of the family's investment and ownership of assets. Also, entitlements to certain state benefits are directly related to unearned income as well as earned income. Proportions of unemployed and retired members in the family are of particular significance in this respect.

Sources of household income

The main source of household income in Britain is wages and salaries (currently about 66%). The greatest regional dependence upon wages and salaries is in the East Midlands (70%). Social security benefits and pensions feature most prominently in the North (11% and 12·2% respectively), and self-employment in East Anglia (8·6%).

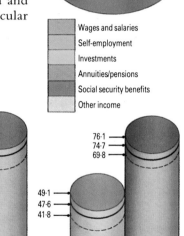

- Wages and salaries
- Self-employment
- Investments
- Annuities/pensions
- Social security benefits
- Other income

Activity rates

Activity rates are measured as the percentage of the adult population (aged 16 and over) in the civilian labour force – those in or seeking employment. They are an important factor reflecting population structure and the level of economic activity, and influencing overall income levels. Activity rates for men are considerably higher than for women, but they have been decreasing steadily while those for women increased in the 1970s and have been flattening out in the 1980s. For both men and women, the highest regional activity rates are to be found in the South-east and the lowest in Wales.

- Women
- Men

— Maximum
— Overall figure for GB
------ Minimum

% of over 16s in the labour force

Personal income

The table below compares the 1982-83 average gross weekly income for currently the most well-off region of Britain (the South-east) with the four poorest. Comparison of the data with that for 1979-80 shows that in recent years the difference in per capita income between the South-east and the other regions has widened – 40% up in the South-east and only 31% up in Wales and the West Midlands, for example. With the retail price index (a measure of the cost of living) going up by 34·5% between 1980 and 1983, real income per capita rose by over 5% in the South-east but elsewhere in the country fell by an almost equal amount.

The map, right, reflects how this pattern of inequality is altered by taxation. It shows annual personal income after income tax and national insurance contributions deductions for the regions. Wales still has the lowest average income level (£3231), with the West Midlands, the North, and Yorkshire and Humberside only slightly better placed. At the top, the South-east is ahead again (£4188, with Greater London £4567). In fact, the South-east is the only region with a figure higher than the national average (£3697).

Household income in £ – selected regions	Average income per week 1982-83		Income derived from social security benefits
	Per person	Per household	
North	66·8	158·5	17·3
Yorkshire, H'side	65·7	163·2	15·7
South-east	89·4	210·5	10·9
W. Midlands	69·5	174·1	15·3
Wales	64·6	166·4	17·6

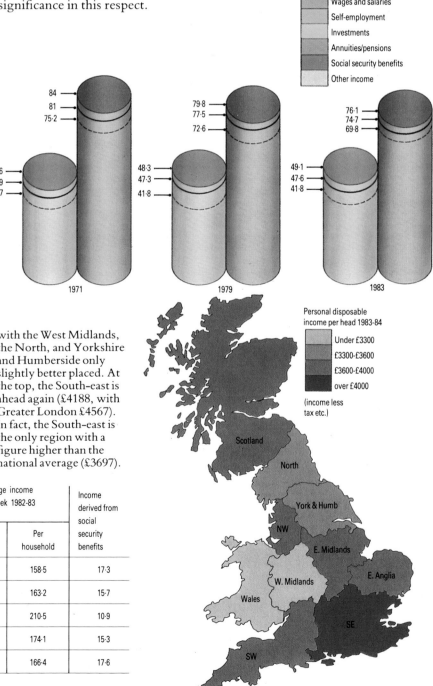

Personal disposable income per head 1983-84

- Under £3300
- £3300-£3600
- £3600-£4000
- over £4000

(income less tax etc.)

Social wage, assets and non-financial factors

Standards of living are not determined by gross income levels alone, since these are subject to deductions for taxation and national insurance. Moreover, tax liability does not relate solely to income level; mortgage interest for the home owner-occupier is an important qualification for reduced liability at any income level. Personal disposable income (net take-home pay after stoppages) is therefore more important than gross income as a determinant of an individual's standard of living. Every individual also derives benefits from public expenditure (see pages 50–51). The benefit from the collective provision of services and facilities by the state, without a direct charge for such transactions, is known as the social wage.

The distribution of wealth is also determined by savings, by assets owned such as land, dwellings, stocks and shares, and by the economic advantages their ownership bestows beyond the income derived from them. Under the British tax system only the income yielded from wealth attracts taxation and not the ownership of the wealth itself, except where it is transferred at death. Finally, knowledge of rights, access to facilities and familiarity with entitlements and procedures are also important in the distribution of income and wealth.

The prosperity map

A prosperity index, developed by Newcastle University's Centre for Urban and Regional Development Studies, shows that prosperity in the south of England is 30% higher than that of Scotland or Wales. At the top is Winchester, Hamp-shire, with very low unemployment (5·3%), job expansion and many two-car families, while at the other extreme is Consett, Co. Durham, where a steelworks closure has pushed unemployment up to 25%.

Distribution of wealth

Variations in income are far less extreme than variations in wealth, which is concentrated in the hands of a tiny minority. For the very richest, stocks and shares represent a substantial element, while middle-class wealth is tied up more in property and savings. If occupational and state pension rights are classed as wealth, the concentrations become less pronounced – the shares of the richest 1% and 10% fall from that shown below to 12% and 35% respectively.

Earnings and working hours

The highest average earnings for men and women – both manual and non-manual workers – are to be found in the South-east. The lowest average earnings for men are those for workers in the South-west (manual) and East Midlands (non-manual), and for women in the East Midlands (manual) and Yorkshire and Humberside (non-manual). The average full-time working week, excluding overtime, is around 38 hours for men and 36 hours for women.

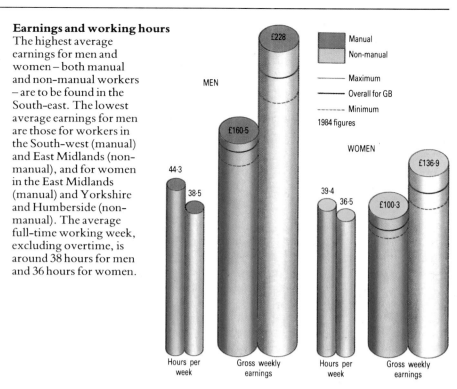

Manual
Non-manual
— Maximum
— Overall for GB
--- Minimum
1984 figures

MEN
£228
£160·5
44·3
38·5
Hours per week
Gross weekly earnings

WOMEN
39·4
36·5
£100·3
£136·9
Hours per week
Gross weekly earnings

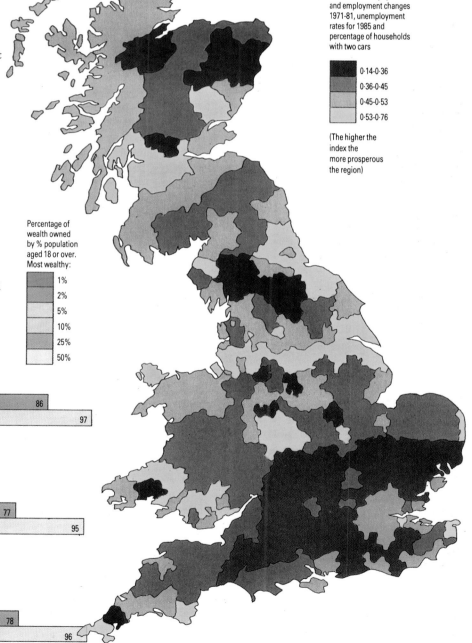

Index based on population and employment changes 1971-81, unemployment rates for 1985 and percentage of households with two cars

- 0·14-0·36
- 0·36-0·45
- 0·45-0·53
- 0·53-0·76

(The higher the index the more prosperous the region)

Percentage of wealth owned by % population aged 18 or over. Most wealthy:

- 1%
- 2%
- 5%
- 10%
- 25%
- 50%

1971
31
39
52
65
86
97

1979
22
28
40
54
77
95

1983
20
27
40
54
78
96

THE NATIONAL ECONOMY

An overview of the recent picture

As far as manufacturing is concerned, the last few years have been characterised by a contraction of economic activity. Jobs have been lost, output has fallen and, if North Sea oil exploration and retrieval are discounted, there has been a decrease in investment and a surplus in the balance of foreign trade has become a deficit. Britain's lack of competitiveness internationally is all the more serious given the unique, though temporary, advantages of the 'oil effect'. In this sense, the economy could only get better; it may be that the rates of growth and the productivity improvements achieved in the mid-1980s owe more to the low starting base of the economy created by recession than to the strength of subsequent performance.

Post-war Britain has suffered from an economic vicious circle. Arising from low output, low productivity and high unit costs have come low exports, high imports, low investment, inflation and low profits. Inevitably, this had led to continued low economic growth. This would have mattered less if Britain's key competitors had not been enjoying a contrasting economic virtuous circle, with investment, output and productivity leading to international competitiveness, profitability and growth. This contrast may not be solely an economic distinction. Social structures, political policies and the absence of an institutional machinery for directing investment and innovation contribute to the difference in effectiveness of the British economy compared to countries such as Sweden and West Germany.

Tackling the problem

Undoubtedly, the decline of manufacturing is the main cause of Britain's economic problems. With output falling and foreign trade in deficit for the first time, with investment reduced in real terms, and with more than three million unemployed as evidence of decline, the engine of the British economy is in need of overhaul. However, for the economy to grow, not only must manufacturing be boosted but disparities within the economy must also be resolved. Three of these are particularly significant. First, the private and public sectors are seen as competitors for limited government funds, yet they are interdependent and can benefit from economic encouragement. Second, regional fortunes have in recent years been allowed to diverge more and more although the economic problems of regions such as the North are to some extent a consequence of the increasing prosperity of the South-east. Third, a dual economy has started to emerge, with a thriving financial sector based in London co-existing with economic and social decline elsewhere, and this makes it difficult to achieve a nationwide democratic consensus.

Currently, the government is seeking to boost the economy by lowering income tax rates and public expenditure levels. It is also seeking to reduce inflation, create jobs by setting up training schemes, encourage investment in new technology and offering financial assistance to companies wishing to set up new plants. Furthermore, it is striving for better trading terms within the European Economic Community.

Circular flow of income

There are three key processes in an economy, which lead to the three approaches to measuring its value – the national income. Each process, with appropriate definitions and adjustments for foreign trade, leads to the same figure, but each has a different emphasis. All income is derived from economic activity: pay, profits or rent. This income is all spent on consumption, savings or investment. The proceeds of this expenditure go on the products and services generated by the economy. Income from output completes and restarts the economic cycle.

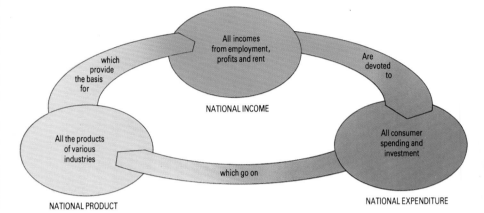

Britain's comparative performance

The overall level of activity in an economy can be defined as the total value added in the production of goods and services in a year – the annual Gross Domestic Product (GDP). A comparison of GDP per head of population between Britain and its major industrial competitors (below) shows that in recent years other countries have continued to do better. A comparison of the total sizes of GDPs (lower chart below), shows Britain had the slowest growth of all countries in all the periods, although recently its performance has matched that of other European countries.

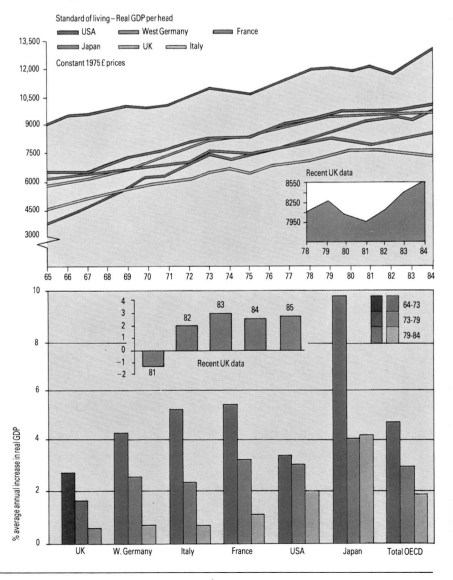

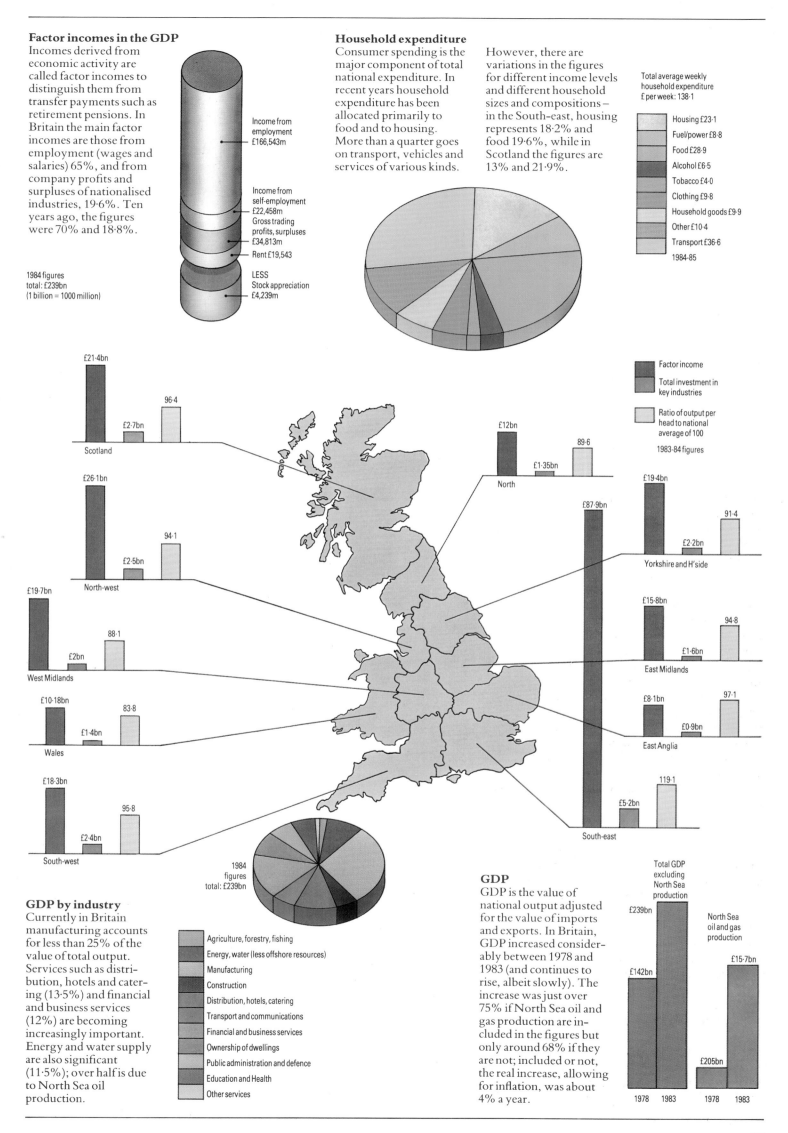

Factor incomes in the GDP
Incomes derived from economic activity are called factor incomes to distinguish them from transfer payments such as retirement pensions. In Britain the main factor incomes are those from employment (wages and salaries) 65%, and from company profits and surpluses of nationalised industries, 19·6%. Ten years ago, the figures were 70% and 18·8%.

1984 figures
total: £239bn
(1 billion = 1000 million)

Income from employment £166,543m

Income from self-employment £22,458m
Gross trading profits, surpluses £34,813m
Rent £19,543

LESS Stock appreciation £4,239m

Household expenditure
Consumer spending is the major component of total national expenditure. In recent years household expenditure has been allocated primarily to food and to housing. More than a quarter goes on transport, vehicles and services of various kinds.

However, there are variations in the figures for different income levels and different household sizes and compositions – in the South-east, housing represents 18·2% and food 19·6%, while in Scotland the figures are 13% and 21·9%.

Total average weekly household expenditure £ per week: 138·1

Housing £23·1
Fuel/power £8·8
Food £28·9
Alcohol £6·5
Tobacco £4·0
Clothing £9·8
Household goods £9·9
Other £10·4
Transport £36·6
1984-85

Factor income
Total investment in key industries
Ratio of output per head to national average of 100
1983-84 figures

Scotland
£21·4bn
£2·7bn
96·4

North-west
£26·1bn
£2·5bn
94·1

West Midlands
£19·7bn
£2bn
88·1

Wales
£10·18bn
£1·4bn
83·8

South-west
£18·3bn
£2·4bn
95·8

North
£12bn
£1·35bn
89·6

Yorkshire and H'side
£19·4bn
£2·2bn
91·4

East Midlands
£15·8bn
£1·6bn
94·8

East Anglia
£8·1bn
£0·9bn
97·1

South-east
£87·9bn
£5·2bn
119·1

GDP by industry
Currently in Britain manufacturing accounts for less than 25% of the value of total output. Services such as distribution, hotels and catering (13·5%) and financial and business services (12%) are becoming increasingly important. Energy and water supply are also significant (11·5%); over half is due to North Sea oil production.

1984 figures
total: £239bn

Agriculture, forestry, fishing
Energy, water (less offshore resources)
Manufacturing
Construction
Distribution, hotels, catering
Transport and communications
Financial and business services
Ownership of dwellings
Public administration and defence
Education and Health
Other services

GDP
GDP is the value of national output adjusted for the value of imports and exports. In Britain, GDP increased considerably between 1978 and 1983 (and continues to rise, albeit slowly). The increase was just over 75% if North Sea oil and gas production are included in the figures but only around 68% if they are not; included or not, the real increase, allowing for inflation, was about 4% a year.

Total GDP excluding North Sea production
£239bn
£142bn
North Sea oil and gas production
£15·7bn
£205bn
1978 1983 1978 1983

ROAD AND RAIL

Over the last 25 years or so, the most spectacular change in ·Great Britain's transport system has been the building of motorways and the closure of many railway lines.

Between 1950 and 1959 the number of vehicles on British roads doubled, to 8·7 million, of which 5·2 million were cars. This was due partly to a rise in people's income, after a period of post-war austerity, but more importantly to the end of petrol rationing in 1953. The government responded by building new, faster roads. In December 1958, Britain's first motorway was opened, the 13-kilometre Preston bypass, followed in 1959 by the first stretch, 116 kilometres, of the M1. Since then, the motorway network has grown to over 2,700 kilometres and is still growing.

The boom in road traffic begun in the 1950s was bad for the newly nationalised railways, who, with worsening finances, were ill-equipped to face competition. A modernisation plan started in the late 1950s had to be scrapped because of mounting losses. By the early 1960s the railways were losing more than £100 million a year.

The government, unwilling to subsidise them further, responded with a plan to close one-third of the railway network and thereby make the railways more profitable. Of nearly 29,000 kilometres of track open in 1961, less than 17,000 kilometres survive today.

During the 1960s British Rail (BR) rose to the challenge of competition from roads and air travel by electrifying the London–Birmingham–Glasgow line to run faster trains and cut passengers' journey times. Since then, BR has introduced faster trains on other lines, including 'high-speed' trains, which, with a top speed of over 200km/h, are the fastest diesel trains in the world. The line from London's King's Cross to Edinburgh is being electrified and, by 1990, will carry passengers at speeds of up to 225km/h. Freight, too, is now being moved much faster by rail, with modern wagons capable of running at 145km/h.

Nearly two-thirds of all freight moved in Great Britain is transported by lorry. Lorries are now bigger and heavier (up to 38 tonnes including the load), with a maximum permitted speed .limit of 80km/h (50 mph). There are more than 100,000 road haulage firms in Great Britain, most of them very small with only one or two lorries. The largest, the National Freight Company, passed from the public sector into private hands in 1982. Its counterpart in passenger transport, the National Bus Company, which runs a fleet of long-distance coaches, is also likely to be privatised.

Investment, public and private, has been concentrated on the major routes linking the big cities. The journey from London to Glasgow, whether by road or rail, is much faster today than it was 20 or 30 years ago. Yet, over the same period, local passenger services have declined steadily. Partly because of a lack of investment, partly because of an increase in car ownership, the number of local buses on Britain's roads went down from 42,000 in 1961 to 26,000 in 1984. The brunt of both bus and rail cuts has been borne by the rural areas, many of which are less accessible by public transport today than they were in the 1950s.

The interchange between the M6 and the M38 at Gravelly Hill near Birmingham, popularly known as 'Spaghetti junction', is the centre-piece of Britain's motorways. Each of its three arms carries more than 50,000 vehicles every day. However, the increase in traffic, particularly heavy lorries, has caused cracks to appear, and the junction is often closed for repairs.

How people travel
The results of a 1979 survey on forms of travel in Britain (below) show that the most common methods of making everyday journeys (any distance over 50m) are the car (including van or lorry) and walking. The importance of walking shows how short everyday journeys often are: many are less than 1km. It also shows that Britons, unlike Americans, find it quickest, and often most convenient, to cover short distances on foot.

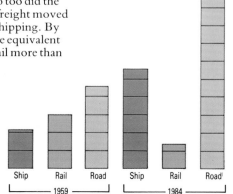

- Car (43%)
- Walking (39%)
- Bus (11%)
- Bicycle (3%)
- Train (2%)
- Motorcycle (1%)
- Other (1%)

Passenger transport
Since World War II, there has been a significant shift from public to private transport. Between 1959 and 1984 car and motorcycle travel, measured in passenger kilometres (number of travellers × distance they travel), increased threefold, from 13bn to 42bn, while bus travel nearly halved. Train travel, apparently, declined only slightly, but the figures conceal a substantial drop in the overall number of rail users.

  Passenger km × 1 billion

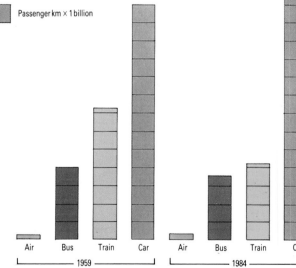

Air	Bus	Train	Car	Air	Bus	Train	Ca

— 1959 —   — 1984 —

Freight transport
Between 1959 and 1984 the volume of freight moved by road, measured in tonne kilometres (weight × distance moved) more than doubled. So too did the volume of freight moved by coastal shipping. By contrast, the equivalent figure for rail more than halved.

  tonne km × 1 billion

Ship	Rail	Road	Ship	Rail	Road

— 1959 —   — 1984 —

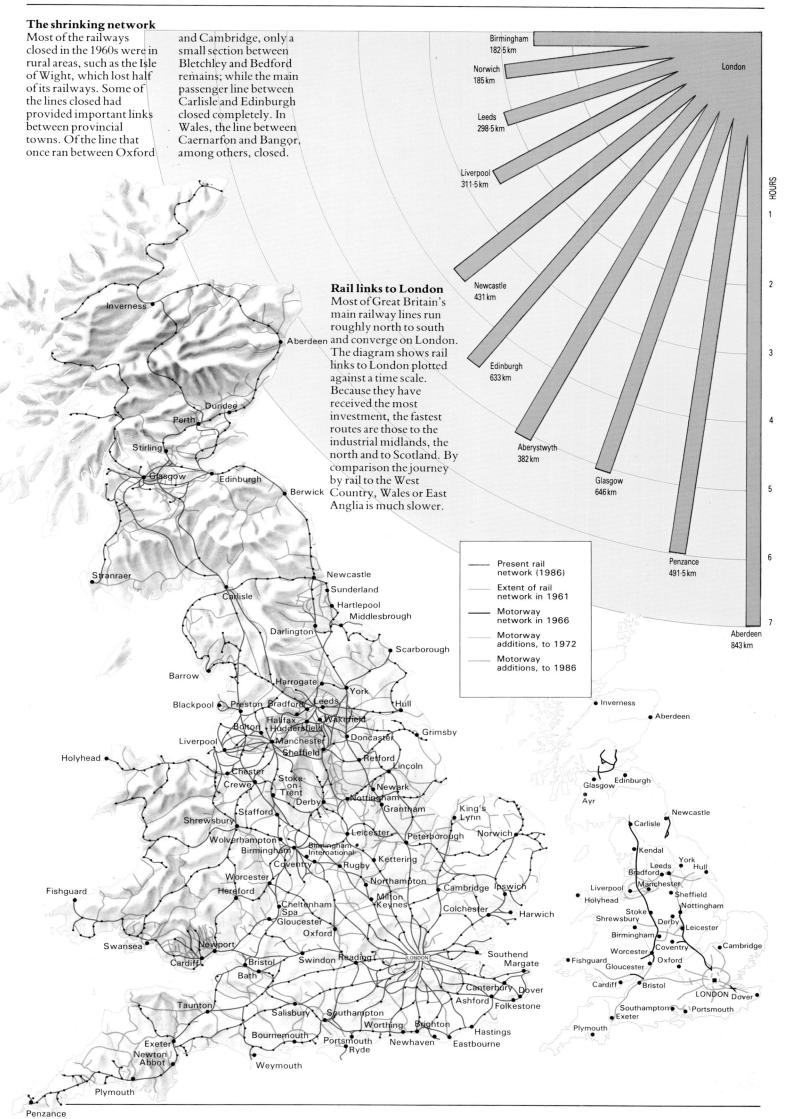

The shrinking network

Most of the railways closed in the 1960s were in rural areas, such as the Isle of Wight, which lost half of its railways. Some of the lines closed had provided important links between provincial towns. Of the line that once ran between Oxford and Cambridge, only a small section between Bletchley and Bedford remains; while the main passenger line between Carlisle and Edinburgh closed completely. In Wales, the line between Caernarfon and Bangor, among others, closed.

Rail links to London

Most of Great Britain's main railway lines run roughly north to south and converge on London. The diagram shows rail links to London plotted against a time scale. Because they have received the most investment, the fastest routes are those to the industrial midlands, the north and to Scotland. By comparison the journey by rail to the West Country, Wales or East Anglia is much slower.

Birmingham 182·5 km
Norwich 185 km
Leeds 298·5 km
Liverpool 311·5 km
London
Newcastle 431 km
Edinburgh 633 km
Aberystwyth 382 km
Glasgow 646 km
Penzance 491·5 km
Aberdeen 843 km

HOURS
1
2
3
4
5
6
7

Present rail network (1986)
Extent of rail network in 1961
Motorway network in 1966
Motorway additions, to 1972
Motorway additions, to 1986

57

PORTS, AIRPORTS AND TRUNK ROADS

Just as travel within Great Britain has seen a shift from rail to road over the past quarter-century, so too patterns in travel to and from Great Britain have changed.

Once the great ocean-going liners, such as the *Queen Elizabeth* and *Queen Mary*, ran a weekly service from Southampton to New York. In 1961, around 250,000 passengers crossed the Atlantic to North America by sea. By 1983, the number had dropped to 30,000, and most of the liners were serving as pleasure-cruise ships or had been scrapped. Only the *QEII*, the last great liner to be built, still sails regularly across the Atlantic, catering for the richer package tourists.

By the early 1950s an airliner could cross the Atlantic, without refuelling, in 15 hours, compared with the fastest ocean liner, which took five days. In 1962, for the first time, more people flew into Britain than arrived by sea. That lead was increased during the 1960s by the widespread use of jet aircraft, with cruising speeds of 880 km/h, more than twice as fast as the old propeller planes they replaced. In the early 1970s the first wide-bodied jets were introduced, which, with their much greater carrying capacity, made long-distance flying far cheaper and brought about substantial reductions in air fares.

However, for short crossings to Europe, it is still cheaper and often more convenient to go by sea. Since the 1960s the volume of passenger and freight transport crossing the Channel by this route has increased considerably. There has been a large expansion in cross-Channel heavy lorry traffic, encouraged by the growth of Britain's motorways and the raising of the weight limit on British roads to accommodate the larger European lorries.

However, the future of the cross-Channel ferries is uncertain, now that Britain and France have agreed to build the Channel Tunnel. The tunnel is scheduled to open to the public in 1993, running shuttle trains from near Folkestone to carry cars and lorries to near Calais. There will also be passenger trains from London to Paris direct,

which will cut the average journey time by half, to about three hours.

Britain's improvements in international transport over the past few decades have not been altogether painless. Residents living near London's Heathrow airport, which already handles around 250,000 aircraft every year, are opposed to the building of a fifth terminal at Heathrow because of the extra noise it will create. Likewise, a long-standing proposal to expand Stansted to provide a third London airport is very much out of favour with the local townspeople. There has also been opposition to the increase in heavy lorries, which, protesters say, pollute the air with diesel fumes and noise, damage the roads and are a menace to other road users.

International passengers
Today, long-distance sea travel has been largely superseded by long-distance air travel. The sharp increase, between 1961 and 1984, in the number of passengers flying in or out of Britain was due partly to the introduction of wide-bodied jet airliners and cheap package holidays. Over the same period, passenger arrivals and departures at sea ports more than trebled, largely because of the increase in cross-Channel passengers to and from France and the Low Countries.

British Caledonian aircraft at Gatwick airport. With a fleet of 40 planes and 7 on order in 1986, 'B Cal' is Britain's largest private airline. State-owned British Airways operates 138 aircraft, 31 helicopters, and has another 7 planes on order.

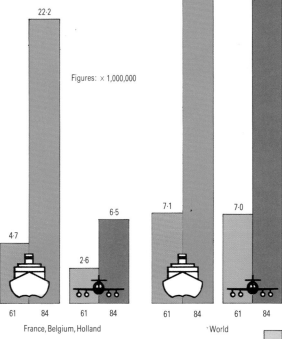

Figures: × 1,000,000

49·9

26·1

22·2

7·1 7·0

6·5

4·7

2·6

61 84   61 84   61 84   61 84

France, Belgium, Holland   World

Major ports
Sullom Voe, in the Shetland Islands, became Britain's busiest port, because of North Sea oil. Until 1977 it was insignificant, but in 1978 it first handled more than 1 million tonnes of oil, and in 1983 overtook London as Britain's busiest port. Most of Sullom Voe's cargo is oil destined for refineries at ports such as Milford Haven. The North Sea ports of Tees and Hartlepool also owe much of their importance to oil. The port of London declined as container ships became too large for the Thames.

= 2,000,000 tonnes

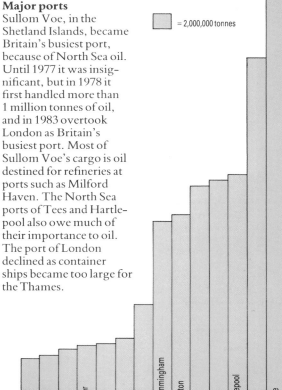

Dover | Felixstowe | Clyde | Manchester | Liverpool | Medway | Orkneys | Grimsby/Immingham | Southampton | Forth | Milford | Tees/Hartlepool | London | Sullom Voe

The transport system

The trunk roads are Great Britain's main traffic arteries. The government maintains the motorway system, which carries nearly 13% of the nation's traffic, and 12,000 km of other trunk roads. These roads are the responsibility of the Department of Transport, in England, or the Scottish and Welsh Offices. BR, with a turnover in 1983 of £3·2 bn, controls all the main railways. Sea ports are mostly in the hands of trusts, such as the Dover Harbour Board, or local councils.

Air passengers

Heathrow is Britain's busiest airport, handling 29 million passengers in 1984 (about half of all Britain's air passengers). The opening of a fourth terminal in 1986 increased its capacity to 38 million. Gatwick is the second busiest airport, with about 14 million a year. Heathrow and Gatwick are owned by the British Airways Authority. BAA also own Aberdeen and Glasgow airports. Many airports are in the hands of local councils, including Manchester airport, Britain's third largest.

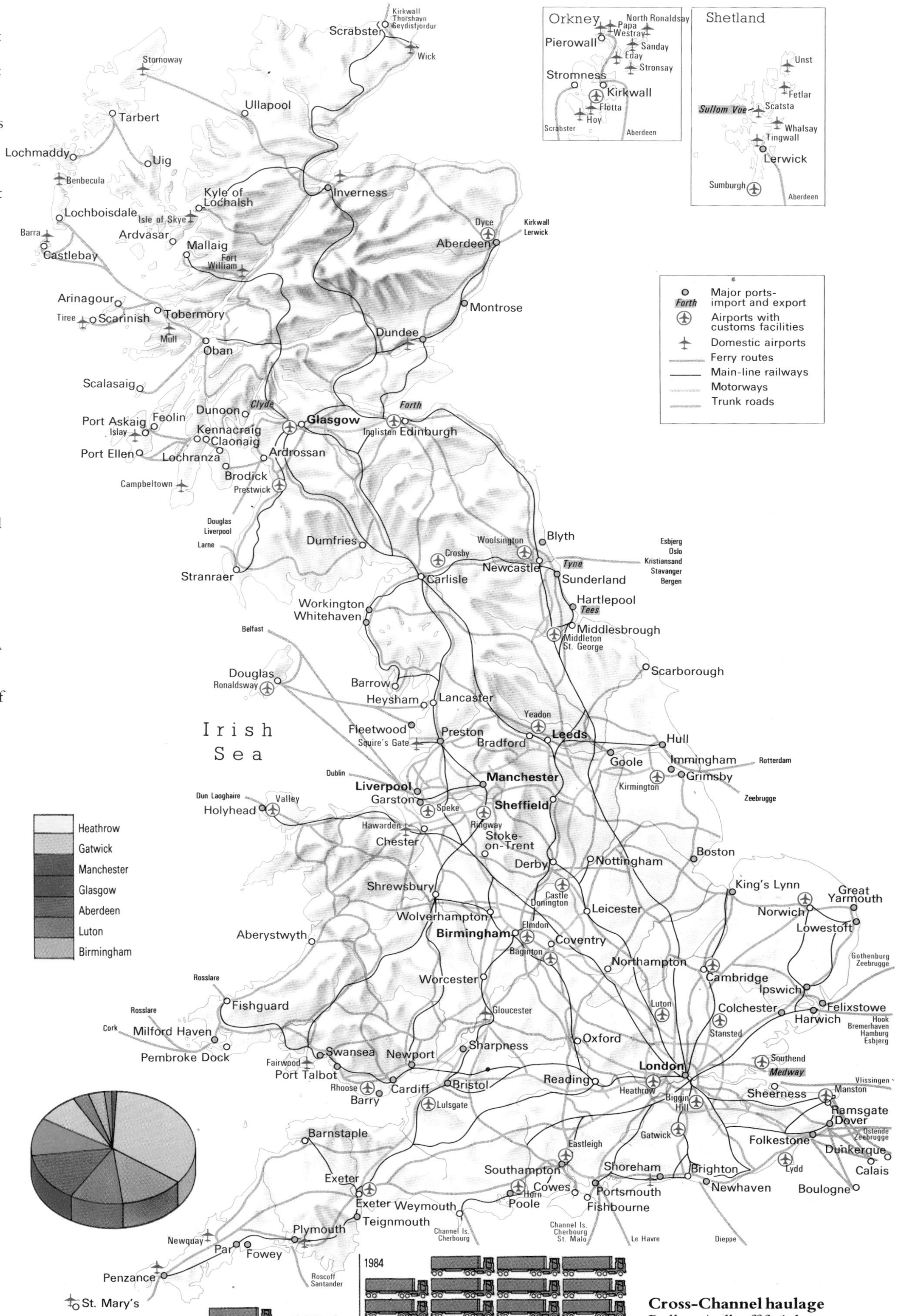

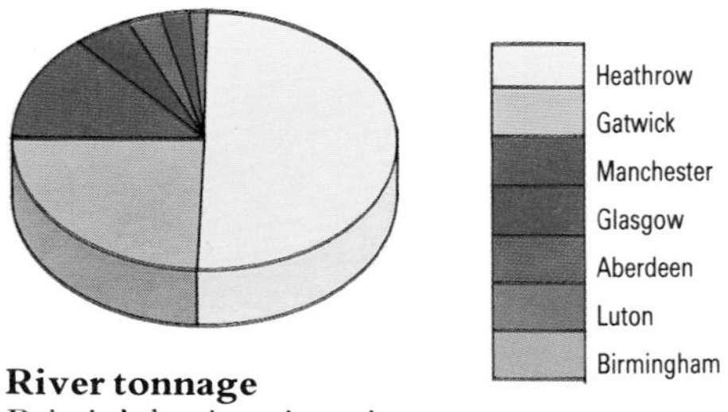

Heathrow
Gatwick
Manchester
Glasgow
Aberdeen
Luton
Birmingham

River tonnage

Britain's busiest river, in terms of its share of freight, is the Thames. Nearly 20 million tonnes of goods are picked up every year by sea-going ships from ports on the River Thames like Tilbury, while a further 4 million tonnes are internal to the river, such as oil carried from Canvey Island to distribution points upstream. The Humber, Britain's next busiest river, accounts for the movement of nearly 9 million tonnes of freight every year.

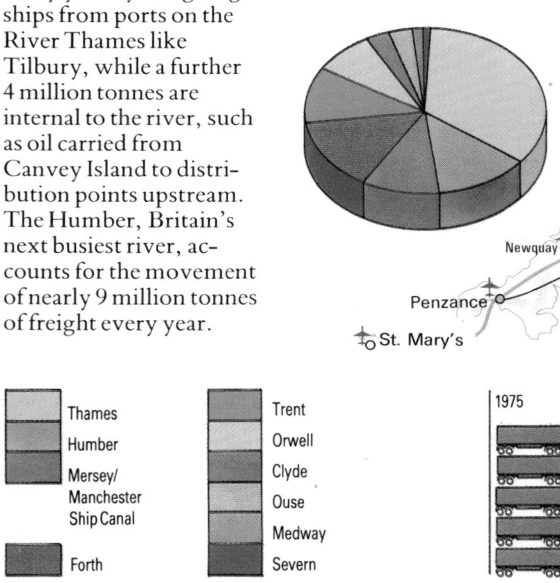

Thames
Humber
Mersey/ Manchester Ship Canal
Forth
Trent
Orwell
Clyde
Ouse
Medway
Severn

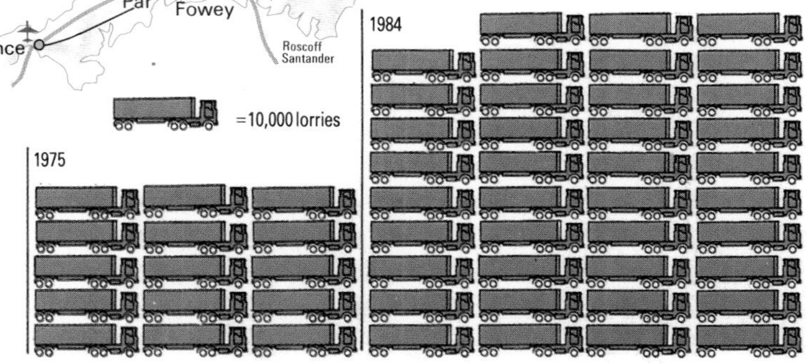

Legend

○ Major ports- import and export
Forth
⊕ Airports with customs facilities
⊥ Domestic airports
Ferry routes
Main-line railways
Motorways
Trunk roads

Cross-Channel haulage

Roll-on/roll-off freight traffic across the Dover Straits is growing fast. In nine years the number of heavy lorries (over 30 tonnes) crossing by ferry in either direction increased from around 151,000 to 392,000.

= 10,000 lorries

1984

1975

INNER CITIES

Today many of the great cities of the Industrial Revolution are in decline, with falling employment, rising crime, poor housing and movement of population away from the inner cities out to the suburbs, commuter belts or beyond.

Most of today's inner city areas were themselves once suburbs, built on the edges of cities in Victorian times. The Great Exhibition of 1851 was held in London's Hyde Park, then on the western edge of the city. By 1906 that edge had moved five kilometres further west, to White City, where the Imperial Exhibition of that year was held. As London's suburbs began to sprawl, encouraged by subsidised housing and the development of bus and tram routes into open country, they gradually enveloped villages such as Highgate and Chiswick. At the same time, the overcrowded City of London population started falling.

For the first time, in the 1950s, the population of many major cities started to fall. London's total population peaked at 8.5 million in 1939 and has been falling ever since. Nowadays, only towns of fewer than 200,000 inhabitants – mostly the newer towns – have static or increasing populations.

Often inner city depopulation was the result of an official policy to relieve overcrowding. Some London councils, for example, built 'overspill' estates, as far away as Bodmin in Cornwall. The development of new towns, such as Harlow and Milton Keynes, was also intended to attract people out of London and to encourage employers to relocate.

From the 1960s London, in common with other major cities, also began to lose jobs. The old industries around which the cities had grown up, and which supported the economy of the inner cities, were in decline, and the newer growth industries could not make up the job losses. They were, in any case, often developed in the new towns or on greenfield sites away from the city, where building and land were less expensive.

With most investment in building – whether homes, factories or offices – going outside the city, many inner city buildings fell into disrepair. To make matters worse, some of the investment that did go to the inner cities was misguided. The 1960s housing boom produced a rash of redevelopment schemes in which many a sound Victorian house was pulled down to make way for a modern tower block. Many of the tower blocks are themselves now being demolished, either because of structural problems or because councils recognise the failure of this vast social experiment.

The problems the inner cities face today pose a challenge to government now and in the future. If the more affluent continue to move away, and the inner cities fail to attract investment, the cost of basic amenities, such as street lighting, will increasingly be borne by fewer and fewer people. Moreover, those who remain will be the socially disadvantaged who cannot afford to move – the old, the one-parent families, the poorly paid and the unemployed. So far, attempts at reviving the inner cities by means of new housing, development schemes, and, in London, housing co-operatives, have generally failed to arrest the decline.

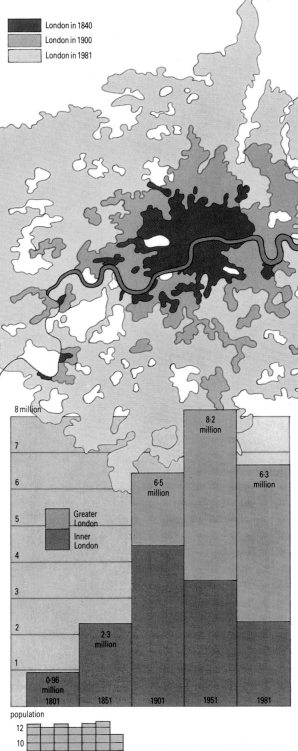

London in 1840
London in 1900
London in 1981

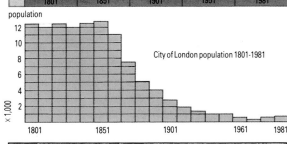

City of London population 1801-1981

London's spread
The ancient core of London is the City, an area known as the 'square mile'. Since the 1800s London has spread, mostly to the west, upwind of the smells from the city. Today the Greater London area, which until 1986 was administered by the Greater London Council, occupies 1,600 km² from Hayes in the west to Bexley in the east.

Population losses
As London expanded, the population first of the City, and eventually of the whole of London, began to fall. From a peak of 128,000 on the 1851 census, the population of the City fell to 27,000 by the turn of the century, as offices began to replace homes, and people moved out to suburbs such as Hackney. By 1971 the resident population had fallen to 4,000, many of whom were caretakers. Since then, a new housing estate in the Barbican has slightly increased the City's population.

Dockland revival
Some disused docks, like St Katharine's, in London, are being redeveloped. New buildings such as Tower Hotel and a trade/conference centre stand alongside busy shops that have been converted from old warehouses.

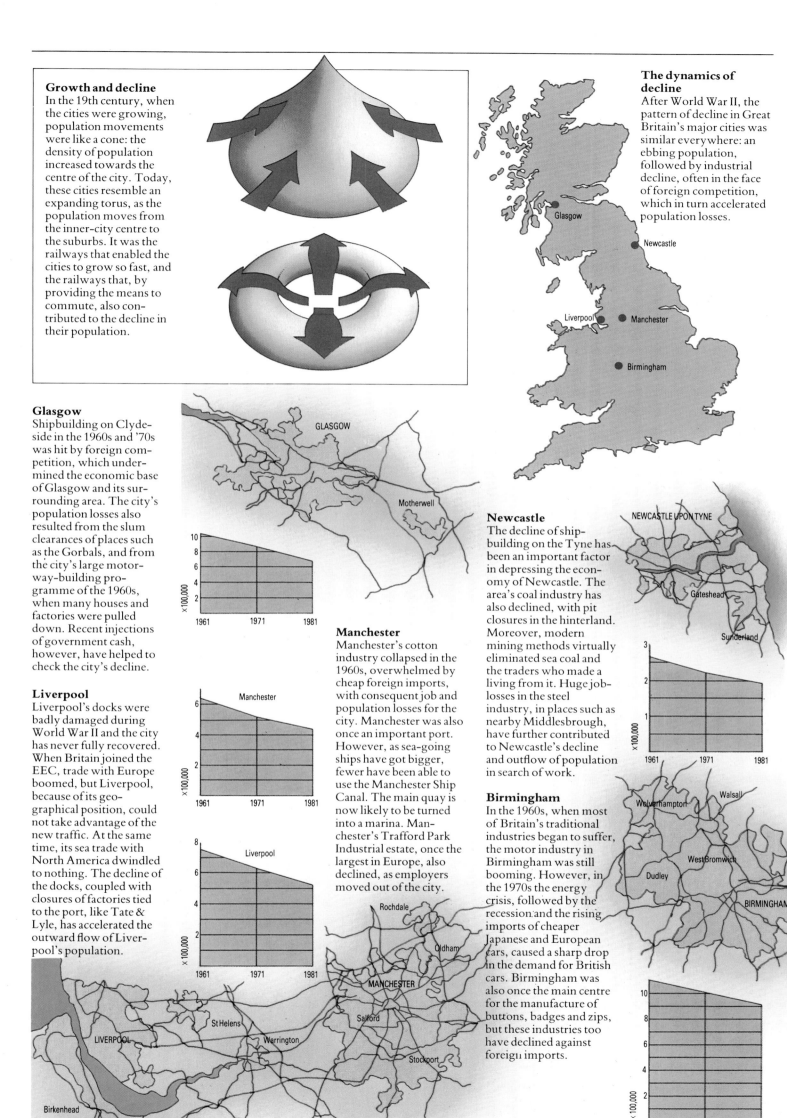

Growth and decline

In the 19th century, when the cities were growing, population movements were like a cone: the density of population increased towards the centre of the city. Today, these cities resemble an expanding torus, as the population moves from the inner-city centre to the suburbs. It was the railways that enabled the cities to grow so fast, and the railways that, by providing the means to commute, also contributed to the decline in their population.

The dynamics of decline

After World War II, the pattern of decline in Great Britain's major cities was similar everywhere: an ebbing population, followed by industrial decline, often in the face of foreign competition, which in turn accelerated population losses.

Glasgow

Shipbuilding on Clydeside in the 1960s and '70s was hit by foreign competition, which undermined the economic base of Glasgow and its surrounding area. The city's population losses also resulted from the slum clearances of places such as the Gorbals, and from the city's large motorway-building programme of the 1960s, when many houses and factories were pulled down. Recent injections of government cash, however, have helped to check the city's decline.

Liverpool

Liverpool's docks were badly damaged during World War II and the city has never fully recovered. When Britain joined the EEC, trade with Europe boomed, but Liverpool, because of its geographical position, could not take advantage of the new traffic. At the same time, its sea trade with North America dwindled to nothing. The decline of the docks, coupled with closures of factories tied to the port, like Tate & Lyle, has accelerated the outward flow of Liverpool's population.

Manchester

Manchester's cotton industry collapsed in the 1960s, overwhelmed by cheap foreign imports, with consequent job and population losses for the city. Manchester was also once an important port. However, as sea-going ships have got bigger, fewer have been able to use the Manchester Ship Canal. The main quay is now likely to be turned into a marina. Manchester's Trafford Park Industrial estate, once the largest in Europe, also declined, as employers moved out of the city.

Newcastle

The decline of shipbuilding on the Tyne has been an important factor in depressing the economy of Newcastle. The area's coal industry has also declined, with pit closures in the hinterland. Moreover, modern mining methods virtually eliminated sea coal and the traders who made a living from it. Huge job-losses in the steel industry, in places such as nearby Middlesbrough, have further contributed to Newcastle's decline and outflow of population in search of work.

Birmingham

In the 1960s, when most of Britain's traditional industries began to suffer, the motor industry in Birmingham was still booming. However, in the 1970s the energy crisis, followed by the recession and the rising imports of cheaper Japanese and European cars, caused a sharp drop in the demand for British cars. Birmingham was also once the main centre for the manufacture of buttons, badges and zips, but these industries too have declined against foreign imports.

61

STATE AND CONSTITUTION

The United Kingdom does not have a written constitution. Instead, formal and informal procedures and practices have become established, which determine how the government and Parliament operate together. The British constitution is thus a system of laws, customs and conventions which have developed between the Crown, Parliament and people over more than 500 years. These define the composition and powers of state organisations, and regulate them in their dealings with one another, and with the private citizen.

Power and legislation

In the British state, power flows from the monarchy – known constitutionally as the Crown. Members of the civil service, police forces and the armed sevices are all servants of the Crown. However, Parliament is the supreme legislative body. All legislation must have the assent of the two parliamentary chambers, the House of Commons and the House of Lords, and the Crown. The powers that government departments and other organisations have are normally delegated to them by Parliament. If Parliament has not legislated in a particular area, the Crown is held to have prerogative powers, and the Crown and its servants may do as they wish. If Parliament has legislated, then administrative and legal arrangements are controlled by statute law, expressed in Acts of Parliament or regulations made under statute.

The British constitution

The powers of Parliament and those of the Crown overlap as shown. Immediately below the Crown is the Privy Council, which includes the Prime Minister and members of past and present cabinets, the leader of the Opposition in Parliament, and important members of opposition parties, as well as a small number of senior serving or retired civil servants or diplomats. Members of the Privy Council take the title 'Right Honourable', and are addressed as such during debates in the House of Commons. The Privy Council is summoned to meet from time to time at Buckingham Palace. The Crown can rule directly, through the Privy Council, by making Orders-in-Council. An Order-in-Council using statutory powers has to be laid before both Houses of Parliament, who must give their consent if the Order is to become law. An Order that uses prerogative powers of the monarchy, for example in the interests of the defence of the realm, is not subject to Parliament's approval.

Public spending

Public expenditure includes spending by local authorities, as well as central government organisations and agencies. Most is spent by central government on social security, including pensions and other payments from the National Insurance system. The next biggest item is defence and the armed forces, which, as a share of public spending, rose by nearly 2% over seven years. In 1978/9 more was spent on education than on defence, but this has since been reversed.

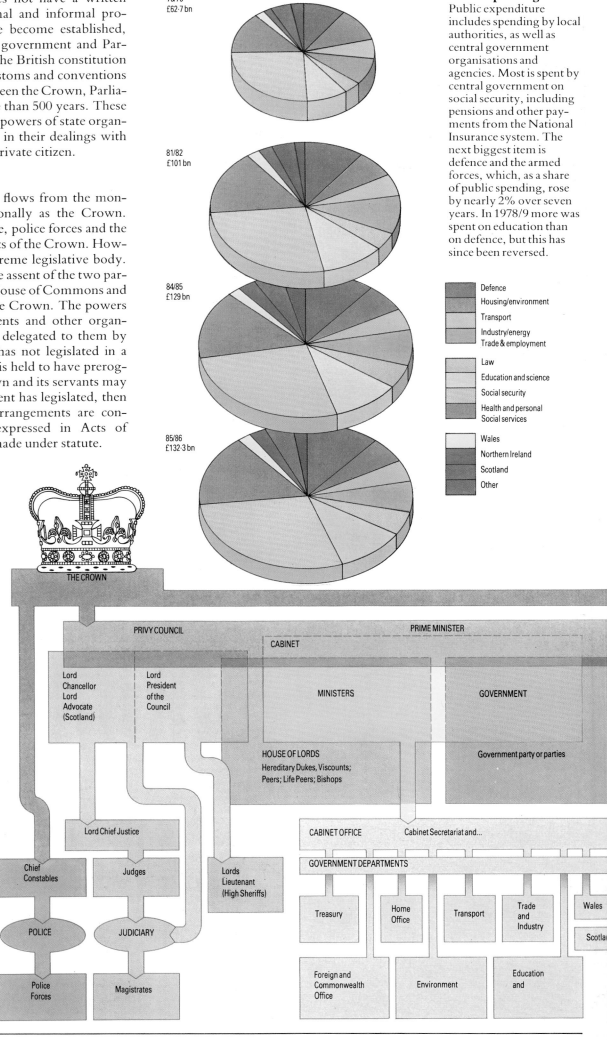

78/79
£62·7 bn

81/82
£101 bn

84/85
£129 bn

85/86
£132·3 bn

Defence
Housing/environment
Transport
Industry/energy
Trade & employment

Law
Education and science
Social security
Health and personal
Social services

Wales
Northern Ireland
Scotland
Other

THE CROWN

PRIVY COUNCIL

PRIME MINISTER

CABINET

Lord Chancellor
Lord Advocate (Scotland)

Lord President of the Council

MINISTERS

GOVERNMENT

HOUSE OF LORDS
Hereditary Dukes, Viscounts; Peers; Life Peers; Bishops

Government party or parties

Lord Chief Justice

CABINET OFFICE

Cabinet Secretariat and...

GOVERNMENT DEPARTMENTS

Chief Constables

Judges

Lords Lieutenant (High Sheriffs)

Treasury

Home Office

Transport

Trade and Industry

Wales

Scotla...

POLICE

JUDICIARY

Foreign and Commonwealth Office

Environment

Education and

Police Forces

Magistrates

The Queen at the Palace of Westminster for the State Opening of Parliament. Each year, on this occasion, members of both Houses go to the House of Lords to hear the Queen's Speech. This is a statement, read aloud by the Queen and written by the government, which announces its plans for legislation during the coming session of Parliament and its major policy objectives.

Government

The head of government is the Prime Minister, who is appointed and invited to form a government by the Crown. The Prime Minister is selected on the basis that he or she can command the support of a majority of Members of Parliament in the House of Commons. The constitutional convention is that the Prime Minister will be the leader of the majority party (the party holding most seats) in the Commons. There is no clear precedent for whom the Crown should choose if there is no one party in the House of Commons whose leader can command the support of a majority of MPs.

The Prime Minister appoints all the other members of the government from the ranks of the majority-party Members of Parliament or their supporters in the House of Lords. Up to 24 key ministers are appointed to be members of the Cabinet. Major government decisions are usually taken or endorsed by the Cabinet as a whole. The decisions of the Cabinet then become the formal decisions of Her (or His) Majesty's Government.

Members of the Cabinet always include the Chancellor of the Exchequer, and the Secretaries of State who head the larger government departments. Ministers in charge of smaller ministries, or working inside the larger departments, do not necessarily belong to the Cabinet. Junior members of the government are appointed as Parliamentary Under-Secretaries or Parliamentary Private Secretaries to Ministers and Secretaries of State. In all, about 100 MPs and peers (House of Lords members) are usually appointed to government posts.

Cabinet committees

Cabinet government is central to the British government system. Important government decisions are taken, not by individual ministers and departments, but by cabinet committees of ministers, officials, or both. Some of the committees are permanent, while others may be brought together to consider a single issue, and are then dissolved. These are called MISC (for Miscellaneous) or GEN (for General) committees. The Cabinet is the highest administrative body in the elected executive system. The Prime Minister and other ministers are in charge of the executive departments of state, and are expected to account to Parliament for their expenditure and activities. Individual MPs do not have an absolute right to information from government ministers or departments, but may pursue inquiries by asking questions in Parliament or through the work of special parliamentary committees.

Major Cabinet Committees

Cabinet (C)
Run by Prime Minister

Overseas and Defence Affairs (OD)
Run by Prime Minister

European Economic Community (OD [E])
Run by the Foreign Secretary

Home Defence of Britain (OD [HD])
Run by the Home Secretary

South Atlantic (Falklands) (OD [SA])
Run by the Prime Minister

Economic affairs (E)
Run by the Prime Minister

Nationalised industries (E[NI])
Run by the Prime Minister

Civil Service (E[CS])
Run by the Minister for the Civil Service

Pay policy for public sector (E[PSP])
Run by the Chancellor of the Exchequer

Home affairs, education, social policy (H)
Run by the Home Secretary

Environmental affairs (EN)
Run by the Secretary of State for the Environment

Joint Intelligence Committee (JIC)
Run by the Cabinet Office Co-ordinator of Intelligence

British Security and Intelligence services (PSIS)
Run by the Cabinet Secretary

Government publicity plans (MIO)
Run by the Press Secretary to the Prime Minister

Public Records Policy (MISC 3)
Run by the Attorney General's Department

Nuclear weapons (Trident) (MISC 7)
Run by the Prime Minister

Grants to local authorities (MISC 21)
Run by the Home Secretary

The Queen's Speech and future legislation (QL)
Run by the Leader of the House

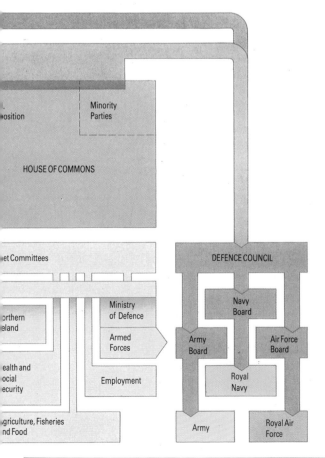

HOUSE OF COMMONS

Minority Parties

osition

et Committees

DEFENCE COUNCIL

orthern eland

Ministry of Defence

Navy Board

Armed Forces

Army Board

Air Force Board

ealth and ocial ecurity

Employment

Royal Navy

griculture, Fisheries nd Food

Army

Royal Air Force

PARLIAMENT

Members of Parliament in the House of Commons are elected to their seats for the lifetime of a Parliament, normally a maximum of five years. Voting takes place at either a General Election (for all seats in the House of Commons) or a by-election (when a seat falls vacant). Election is by a simple majority vote of those eligible to vote in their constituency (electoral area). Since the enactment of the Representation of the People Acts (1918 and 1928), Britain has had universal adult suffrage.

The House of Commons has 650 seats, made up of 523 for England, 38 for Wales, 72 for Scotland and 17 for Northern Ireland. The other parliamentary chamber, the House of Lords, seats the Lords Spiritual (Archbishops and senior Bishops of the Church of England) and the Lords Temporal (hereditary and life peers). Members of the House of Lords are not elected.

All-party committees

Any draft law, or 'Bill', presented before Parliament must have the majority support of both Houses at each of its three readings before it can become an Act of Parliament. In the process, the Bill often undergoes amendments. Between the second and third readings, the Bill will normally be referred to an all-party committee, known as a standing committee, for closer scrutiny. The committee stage is followed by a report stage, when further amendments may be considered.

The House of Commons

The present chamber was designed and built in 1950, replacing an older chamber destroyed by German bombing in 1941. The Commons' business is directed and controlled by the Speaker or his or her deputy. While the Speaker is presiding, the Commons' mace, a symbol of parliamentary authority, is placed in the centre of the chamber. In Parliament, members of both Houses have certain unique privileges, including immunity from prosecution for anything they may say.

Sometimes a select committee will also consider the detailed terms of a Bill. The main work of the better-known select committees, however, is to hold major investigations into issues of public interest. In 1979, changes were made in the select committee system to enable MPs to conduct a closer examination of the expenditure, administration and policies of the major government departments.

The political parties

The major national political parties represented in the House of Commons since 1945 have been the Conservative Party and the Labour Party, with the Liberal Party in third place. For the 1983 election, the Liberal Party formed an electoral Alliance with the newly founded Social Democratic Party (SDP). Since 1970, nationalist parties in Scotland and Wales have also been permanently represented in the House of Commons.

Broadly, the Conservative Party favours reduced government regulation of economic and industrial activity, and diminished public expenditure. Its main sources of income are private donations, mostly from business. By contrast, the Labour Party is traditionally in favour of the redistribution of wealth and greater governmental contol of economic affairs in order to create a more egalitarian society. Eighty per cent of Labour Party funds are provided by trade unions, and the balance by members' subscriptions.

The popular vote

In every General Election since 1945, more than 90% of parliamentary seats have been held by the Labour and Conservative parties. There has been one minority government, between February and October 1974, when Labour had only 301 out of 635 seats. In 1950, Labour polled the largest number of votes but held a minority of seats. In 1945, Labour under Clement Attlee gained an overall majority of 146 seats, the largest-ever postwar majority. In 1983, Conservative PM Margaret Thatcher held an overall majority of 144 (the second largest). The 1970s saw the arrival of new parties: the Scottish National Party (SNP) and the Welsh National Party (Plaid Cymru). The Social Democratic Party, led by disaffected former Labour ministers, made its electoral debut in 1983.

Taxation

Each year, the Chancellor of the Exchequer asks Parliament to approve his Budget, including the government plans for taxation. Taxes are collected by two government departments: the Inland Revenue and Customs and Excise.

Key (£bn)
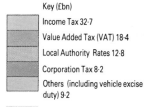

Income Tax 32·7
Value Added Tax (VAT) 18·4
Local Authority Rates 12·8
Corporation Tax 8·2
Others (including vehicle excise duty) 9·2

Oil duties/ Petroleum Revenue 13·3

Spirits, beer, wine, tobacco duties 7·9

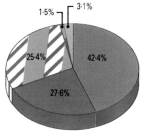

1·5%   3·1%
25·4%   42·4%
27·6%

Share of vote 1983 election

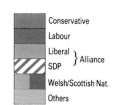

Conservative
Labour
Liberal }
SDP   } Alliance
Welsh/Scottish Nat.
Others

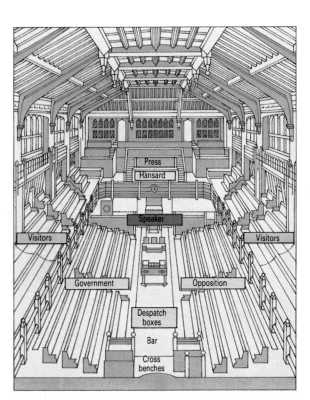

Press
Hansard
Speaker
Visitors
Visitors
Government
Opposition
Despatch boxes
Bar
Cross benches

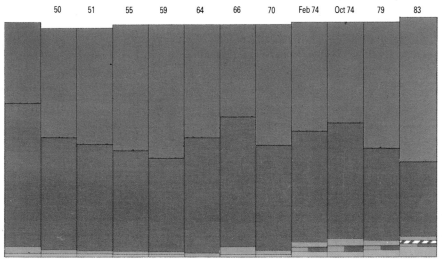

50   51   55   59   64   66   70   Feb 74   Oct 74   79   83

Constituencies

The 1983 General Election returned a Conservative government with an enhanced majority. The safest Conservative seats are in the country areas of England and the richer metropolitan districts. Labour draws its main support from inner-city industrial areas, the north of England, Scotland and Wales. Support for the Liberal/SDP Alliance is more evenly spread. As the 1983 election showed, the numbers of eligible voters can vary considerably between constituencies: 94,000 in the Isle of Wight, as compared with 22,000 in the Western Isles of Scotland. Most constituencies, however, have between 52,000 and 75,000 electors. The proportion of electors using their vote also varied, from about 50%

to 90%. The highest turnouts were in rural areas, whereas low voter turnouts were recorded in the inner-city areas of London, Manchester, Birmingham and Glasgow. British constituencies are also grouped into larger 'Euro-constituencies', each of which elects a Member of the European Parliament (MEP).

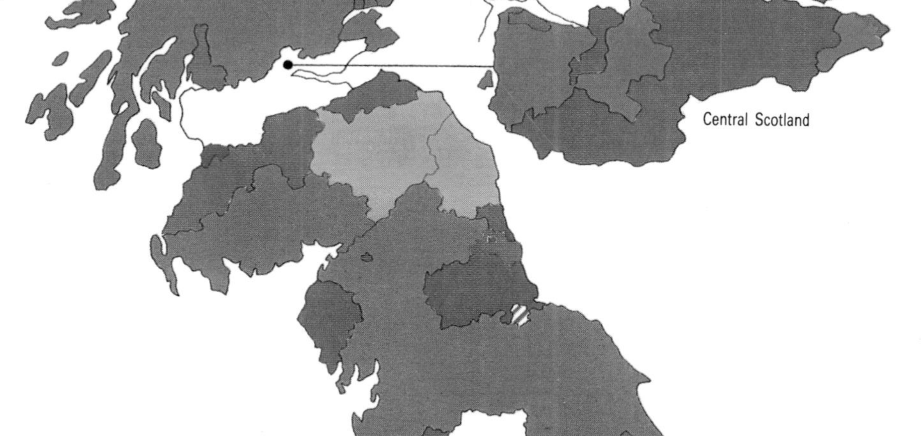

| Conservative |
| Labour |
| Liberal |
| SDP |
| Plaid Cymru |
| SNP |

Shetland Islands

Orkney Islands

Central Scotland

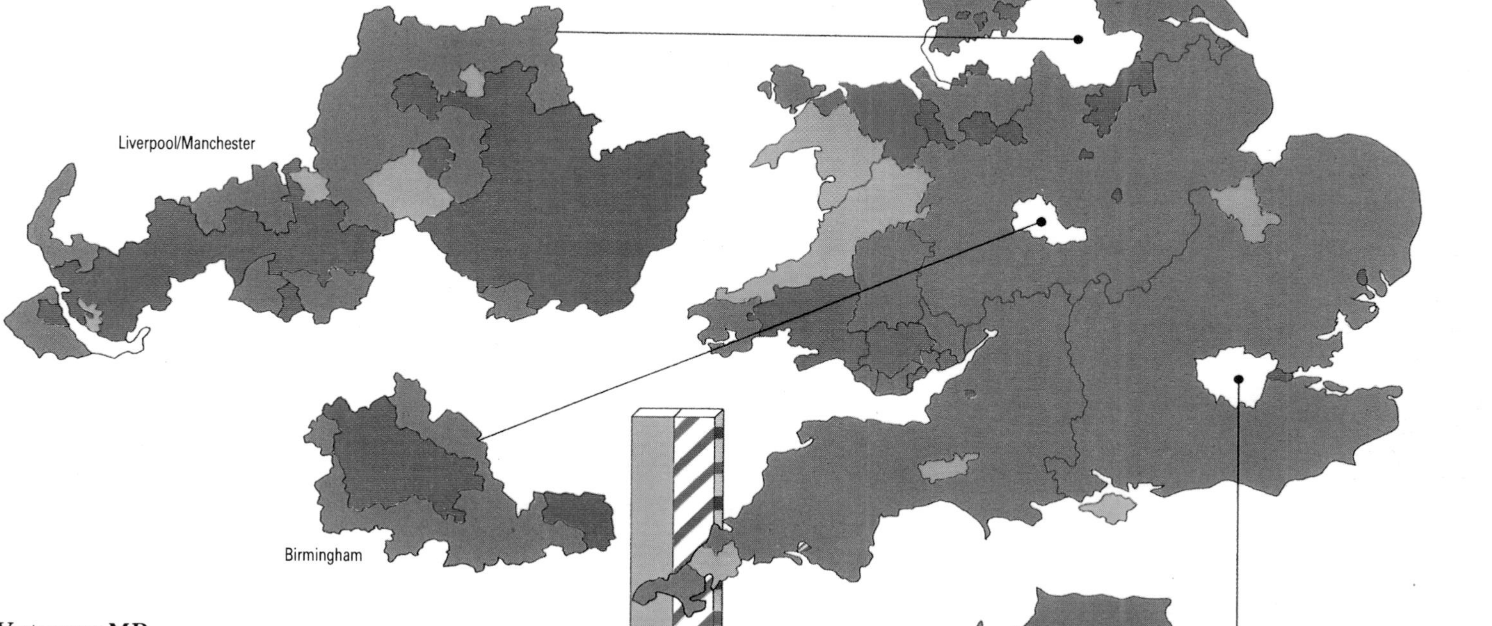

Liverpool/Manchester

Birmingham

Greater London

Votes per MP

Under Britain's present electoral system the number of seats held by a party in Parliament does not reflect the total number of votes polled by that party in a General Election. On the basis of the 1983 General Election results the Conservatives benefited most from the system and the SDP/Liberal Alliance came off worst. The election results (right) showed that the Alliance needed, on average, more than 10 times as many votes per MP as the victorious Conservatives. Proportional representation (PR), a system used in other democratic countries, would have produced different

results. With PR, the number of MPs elected is, as far as possible, proportional to the share of the national vote each party obtains. In Britain, however, some MPs are elected not so much because of their party but because they are considered to be good representatives of their constituents' interests.

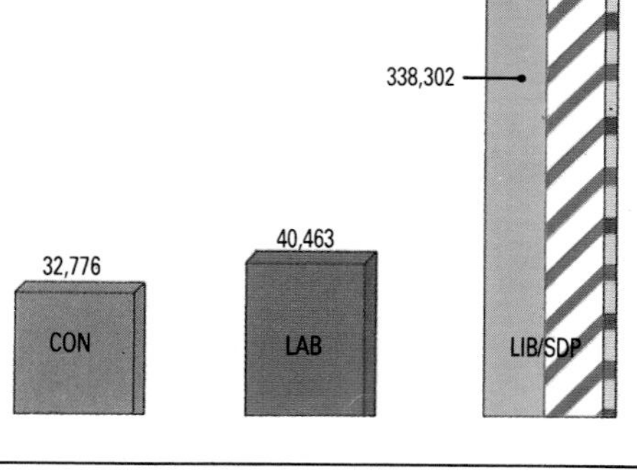

338,302

32,776
CON

40,463
LAB

LIB/SDP

LOCAL GOVERNMENT AND ADMINISTRATION

Compared to many western countries, the British government system is highly centralised. Central government appoints all members of many public bodies, including those responsible for health, water, sewerage, gas and electricity distribution. Local government authorities have only such functions and powers as have been granted them by Parliament, and even then they may have only minimal discretion as to how to carry out their duties within the context of central-government policy decisions. In matters of education, social services, housing, fire protection, planning policy and road maintenance, central government determines national policy, leaving local authorities responsible for its detailed execution.

All judiciary functions are centrally controlled, and elected local authorities have only limited powers in respect of local police forces. Many government activities, such as the provision of social security or employment services, or the regulation of trade and industry, have no local government component, elected or otherwise.

Local government reform

Since local government reform of the 1960s and 1970s, there has generally been in England and Wales a two-tiered system of district and county (or Metropolitan County) councils. In 1963 the London County Council was extended to become the Greater London Council (GLC) in the first of three major reforms. Complete restructuring of local authority functions, and the formation of further Metropolitan Counties, followed the Local Government Act of 1972, and similar reforms took place in Scotland two years later. Subsequently, the GLC and Metropolitan Counties were abolished, in 1986. Representatives of the government and district councils were appointed to joint boards and agencies to take over the responsibilities of the Metropolitan Councils.

The division between county and district council is much longer established in Scotland, having begun when Royal Charters were first granted to independent 'burghs' during the early middle ages. Today, Scotland has 9 regional councils, 53 district councils and 3 islands councils. Regional and district councils work together on industrial development, local amenities and tourism.

Local authority elections

Throughout Britain, local authority elections are held every four years. Traditionally candidates have not always represented nationally-organised political parties, and many 'independent' members still sit on parish, district and county councils. However, by 1973, more than half of councils in England and Wales, and one-third of those in Scotland, were controlled by a single national political party. Five years later, four out of five English and Welsh councils, and three out of five councils in Scotland, were controlled by one party, including Scottish and Welsh national parties.

County councils

In England and Wales, county councils are responsible for education, fire, consumer protection, major roads, overall structure planning, passenger transport, and refuse disposal. District councils deal with housing, local roads, building and development control, local amenities (such as parks) and refuse collection. In Scotland, regional councils have functions akin to those of an English county though they usually cover larger geographical areas, with special arrangements for the Scottish Highlands and islands.

Local government income

Local authorities are financed primarily by rates – the tax levied each year on property owners, according to the value of the house or other premises they own. Evaluation of the property is made by the Inland Revenue. Rate income to local authorities is supplemented by direct grants from central government. Rate support grants can be used as a means of redistributing resources between wealthier and poorer areas, or to control local authority spending.

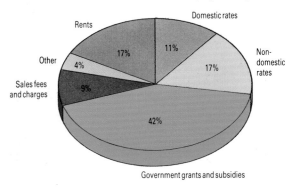

Domestic rates 11%
Non-domestic rates 17%
Rents 17%
Other 4%
Sales fees and charges 9%
Government grants and subsidies 42%

1 TYNE AND WEAR
2 CLEVELAND
3 WEST YORKSHIRE
4 SOUTH YORKSHIRE
5 GREATER MANCHESTER
6 MERSEYSIDE

7 WEST MIDLANDS
8 BEDFORDSHIRE
9 BERKSHIRE
10 WEST GLAMORGAN
11 MID GLAMORGAN
12 SOUTH GLAMORGAN

Local authority employees

In 1985, over 1·9 million people were employed by local authorities in Great Britain, including administrative, professional and technical staff, policemen, firemen, teachers and manual workers. Nearly half of all local government workers are employed in the education service. Pay and conditions for local authority staff are set by individual councils, but often within the framework of a wider trade union agreement.

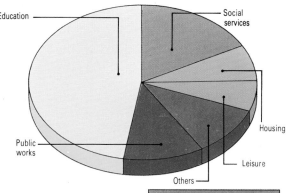

Education
Social services
Public works
Housing
Others
Leisure

Carving up the capital

Before it was abolished in 1986, along with five other Metropolitan County councils, the Greater London Council was responsible for strategic planning, large-scale housing provision, major roads and traffic management schemes, arts and recreation, London Transport, and many other public functions. A directly-related authority, ILEA (Inner London Education Authority) which runs schools and polytechnics in central London, continued to operate but is now a directly elected body. London boroughs continue to deal with local planning, housing, local roads and parks, libraries and amenities, social services and (in outer London boroughs) education. Further legislation introduced in the 1980s has reduced local authorities' powers to determine the level of rates they may levy, or the purposes for which they plan their expenditure, and replaced parts of the 'rate support' system with more stringent government controls.

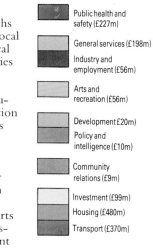

Public health and safety (£227m)
General services (£198m)
Industry and employment (£56m)
Arts and recreation (£56m)
Development £20m)
Policy and intelligence (£10m)
Community relations (£9m)
Investment (£99m)
Housing (£480m)
Transport (£370m)

Service discontinued

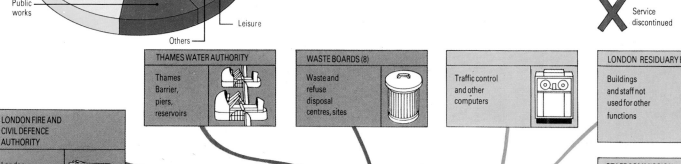

THAMES WATER AUTHORITY
Thames Barrier, piers, reservoirs

WASTE BOARDS (8)
Waste and refuse disposal centres, sites

Traffic control and other computers

LONDON RESIDUARY BODY
Buildings and staff not used for other functions

LONDON FIRE AND CIVIL DEFENCE AUTHORITY
London Fire Brigade

STAFF COMMISSION
Provision of jobs for former GLC staff

Traffic planning
Cycle routes

14·9%
13%
3·7%
3·7%
1·3%
0·7%
0·5%
24·2%
6·5%
31·5%

GREATER LONDON ENTERPRISE BOARD
Employment schemes and industrial development

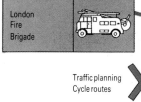

LONDON REGIONAL TRANSPORT
Underground and bus services

Employment grants
Unemployment centres
Greater London
Training Board

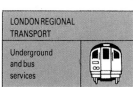

LONDON BOROUGHS (32)
GLC housing and estates

ARTS COUNCIL
Grants to opera, ballet and theatre

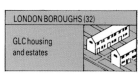

THAMESMEAD TRUST
Housing in Thamesmead

SPORT
Sports grounds and other facilities

LONDON BOROUGHS GRANTS UNIT
Grants to charitable and other regional bodies

Police committees
Ethnic communities

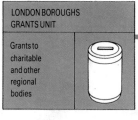

INNER LONDON EDUCATION AUTHORITY
Inner London schools

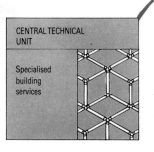

CENTRAL TECHNICAL UNIT
Specialised building services

LONDON PLANNING ADVISORY SERVICE
Greater London area planning

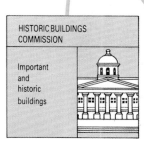

HISTORIC BUILDINGS COMMISSION
Important and historic buildings

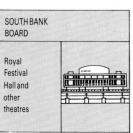

SOUTH BANK BOARD
Royal Festival Hall and other theatres

DEFENCE AND ARMED FORCES

Today, most British overseas commitments, except in Europe and the Falkland Islands, have been withdrawn, substantially altering both the pattern and extent of British military activity since World War II. Britain's military resources are now concentrated in the United Kingdom and West Germany, with the armed forces equipped and organised primarily for operations in central Europe.

Broadly, British defence forces are organised to carry out two long-established policies: participation in the North Atlantic Treaty Organisation (NATO) military alliance, and the maintenance and operation of strategic nuclear weapons.

Some full-time units in Britain form part of the special NATO Allied Mobile Force, and can operate in outlying NATO regions such as Turkey or Norway. Mobile and airborne troops could also be used in British 'rapid deployment force' operations outside the normal NATO area, in accordance with plans developed with the United States.

A large part of the British defence budget is spent on the research and development, operation and maintenance of nuclear weapons. These include both strategic long-range nuclear missiles carried by Polaris submarines, and nuclear bombs with which to arm Royal Air Force aircraft and Royal Navy helicopters. The Polaris system, which forms the basis of Britain's policy of nuclear deterrence, may in the future be replaced by the still more powerful Trident.

Britain in NATO

The NATO treaty was signed in Washington in April 1947. Britain, the United States, Canada and nine other European countries formed the NATO alliance to oppose the growing military might of the Soviet Union. Today 16 countries belong to NATO. The Eastern European defence treaty organisation, the Warsaw Pact, was set up in opposition to NATO in 1955.

NATO and the Warsaw Pact both operate collective security systems, in which the United States and the Soviet Union respectively take a leading role. NATO is controlled by the North Atlantic Council, which normally meets in Brussels. Britain participates through a Permanent Representative and a civil and military staff. NATO countries can be represented at meetings of the Council by their heads of state, or by foreign or defence ministers. Such meetings are usually held two or three times annually.

There are three major NATO Commanders, one of whom is always a British admiral based in Britain. He is known as Commander-in-Chief, Channel, and has his headquarters at Northwood in north-west London. The other two major NATO commanders, who are always US officers, are the Supreme Allied Commander, Atlantic (SACLANT), based in North Virginia, and the Supreme Allied Commander, Europe, based in Brussels.

Armed forces
From a defence budget of £17 billion (1985), £500 million was spent on Polaris submarines, and a further £2·5 billion on the Royal Navy as a whole. Most of the Army's expenditure of £2·8 billion went on maintaining British forces in West Germany; £800 million is spent on home land forces. At a cost of £3·7 billion, the Royal Air Force was the most expensive service, while the direct costs of the Territorial Army and other reserve forces were £300 million. Defence support functions are also costly, and include £2·3 billion on research and development, £1·3 billion on training and £3 billion on the administration and maintenance of headquarters and defence bases in Britain.

Polaris submarine HMS *Revenge* leaves the Clyde estuary on 'deterrent patrol'. *Revenge* is one of four Polaris submarines, each of which carries 16 missiles armed with nuclear warheads. One submarine leaves before the previous one has returned, so that the Polaris deterrent is present at sea at all times. Each patrol lasts two months.

Armed Forces (1985)		
Front line units	Unit	No.
Royal Navy		
Submarines	Vessels	24
Carriers and assault ships	Vessels	4
Other craft (Destroyers; frigates; anti-mine; patrol)	Vessels	107
Airborne	Squadrons	17
Royal Marines	Commandos	4
Regular Army		
Armoured corps	Regiments	9
Artillery	Regiments	22
Engineers	Regiments	13
Infantry	Battalions★	56
Special Air Services (SAS)	Regiments	1
Army Air Corps	Regiments	4
Territorial Army	Regiments	20
Infantry	Battalions	35
Royal Air Force		
Strike/attack	Squadrons	11
Offensive support	Squadrons	5
Air defence	Squadrons	9
Maritime patrol	Squadrons	4
Reconnaissance/early warning	Squadrons	4
Transport/tankers	Squadrons	14
Search and rescue	Squadrons	2
Surface to air missiles	Squadrons	8
Ground defence	Squadrons	5
Auxiliary Air Force	Squadrons	6

★A battalion is part of a regiment, the largest army unit. Infantry figures are commonly given in battalions.

Intelligence-gathering is vital to Britain's defence. Radar stations such as the one shown, right, belong to a nation-wide radar network which monitors the movements of both civil and military aircraft.

Many military bases are linked to satellites, which are used for communication, navigation, and photographic and electronic reconaissance, and would warn of any missile strike against Britain.

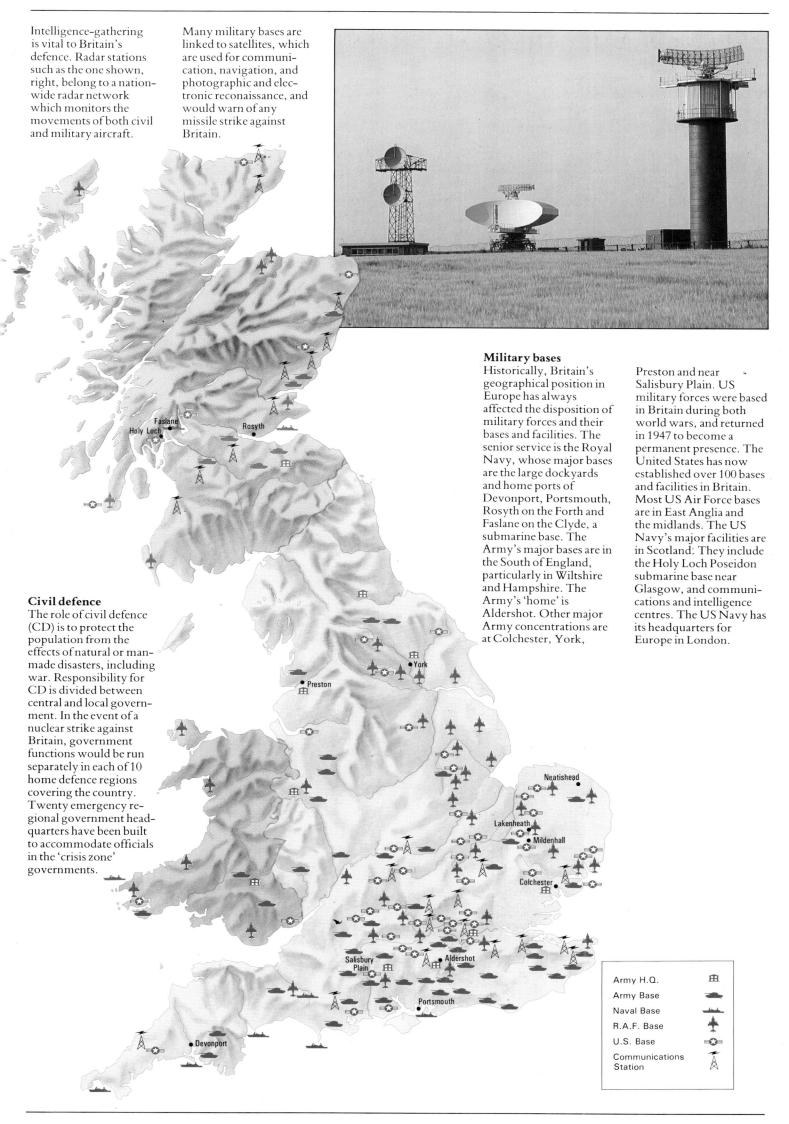

Military bases

Historically, Britain's geographical position in Europe has always affected the disposition of military forces and their bases and facilities. The senior service is the Royal Navy, whose major bases are the large dockyards and home ports of Devonport, Portsmouth, Rosyth on the Forth and Faslane on the Clyde, a submarine base. The Army's major bases are in the South of England, particularly in Wiltshire and Hampshire. The Army's 'home' is Aldershot. Other major Army concentrations are at Colchester, York,

Preston and near Salisbury Plain. US military forces were based in Britain during both world wars, and returned in 1947 to become a permanent presence. The United States has now established over 100 bases and facilities in Britain. Most US Air Force bases are in East Anglia and the midlands. The US Navy's major facilities are in Scotland: They include the Holy Loch Poseidon submarine base near Glasgow, and communications and intelligence centres. The US Navy has its headquarters for Europe in London.

Civil defence

The role of civil defence (CD) is to protect the population from the effects of natural or man-made disasters, including war. Responsibility for CD is divided between central and local government. In the event of a nuclear strike against Britain, government functions would be run separately in each of 10 home defence regions covering the country. Twenty emergency regional government headquarters have been built to accommodate officials in the 'crisis zone' governments.

Faslane
Holy Loch
Rosyth

York
Preston

Neatishead
Lakenheath
Mildenhall
Colchester

Salisbury Plain
Aldershot

Portsmouth

Devonport

Army H.Q.	
Army Base	
Naval Base	
R.A.F. Base	
U.S. Base	
Communications Station	

AIRSPACE AND SEASPACE

Every day, thousands of civil and military aircraft operate over Britain, at heights ranging from ground level to 10,000 metres and above. To enable them to do so safely, sophisticated rules, navigational arrangements and monitoring systems are necessary. The procedures used by civil aircraft are administered and controlled by the National Air Traffic Services (NATS) of the Civil Aviation Authority, who have established a series of airways. Major British and international airports are connected by these airways, which are known by such titles as Green One (Birmingham to Dublin) or Amber Two (London to Paris).

Royal Air Force units protect British airspace by detecting, investigating and, if need be, engaging with unidentified aerial activity in the NATO-agreed UK Air Defence Region. This region can extend as far as 320 kilometres from the coast, and as high as 25,000 metres. Information from radar stations and other surveillance systems is co-ordinated with aircraft and missile units by the control centres in the UK Air Defence Ground Environment (UKADGE) system.

The key components of Britain's UKADGE are a network of civil and military radar stations, whose information is shared between NATS and military radar controllers. NATS and the RAF co-ordinate the tracking of civil aircraft from two joint civil–military control centres: London Air Traffic Control Centre, at West Drayton, near Heathrow airport, and the Scottish Air Traffic Control Centre at Prestwick, near Ayr. Flight plans for civil aircraft are filed at these control centres and immediately become available for military air defence controllers to check. West Drayton and Prestwick also supervise search and rescue services provided by the RAF.

To co-ordinate transatlantic flights to and from Europe, a joint British–Irish civil air traffic control organisation, the Shanwick Oceanic Control, has been established. Information about civil aircraft movement is shared between its two control centres, at Prestwick and Shannon Airport, Eire.

Airspace

Besides operating the main airways, NATS also has an 'upper ATS (Air Traffic Services)' route system, used by aircraft flying at 27,500 metres and above. These routes are for longer-distance flights, and for international flights crossing Britain. When aircraft cross from one nationally controlled airspace to another, the flight is 'handed over' to the new country's control system. The first information on an unidentified flight crossing into British airspace would probably come from the NATO radar system NADGE (NATO Air Defence Ground Environment). The airspace above certain places in Britain may be designated as a 'danger area', or as 'prohibited' or 'restricted'. Civil aircraft are warned not to enter these areas at prescribed times, if at all. Danger areas are often declared above military firing ranges or exercise areas. Nuclear power plants are usually surrounded by prohibited airspace.

Legend:
- Fisheries
- Oil/gas exploration

Boeing 747 over the houses at Heathrow. The United Kingdom low-flying system was reviewed in the 1970s after crashes between low-flying civil and military aircraft. Civil low flying is concentrated around major airports.

Military low flying is restricted near cities, but is more in evidence in remote countryside areas. A special low-flying zone, the Highlands Restricted Area, is used by RAF and US Air Force pilots to practise low-level flying at night.

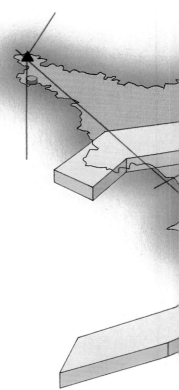

North Sea tapestry

Policing Britain's 'offshore tapestry' of fisheries and energy resources (oil and gas fields in the North Sea) is undertaken by the Royal Navy's Fisheries Protection Squadron, and RAF Nimrod maritime aircraft. The air/sea patrols are also responsible for reporting oil spillages around the UK, or any infringement of British fishing limits. To counter any attack on an oil rig or other resources, a Royal Marine response force is based at Arbroath, Scotland.

Early warning

The Royal Air Force has nine air defence squadrons patrolling British airspace. These include both Phantom and Tornado aircraft. At selected airfields, such as Leuchars in Scotland, the service maintains an Interceptor Alert Force, with pairs of aircraft ready to take off at short notice to identify any unknown aircraft in the region.

Northern waters are patrolled by RAF Shackleton airborne early-warning aircraft, equipped with long-range radar. The Shackletons, whose design dates from World War II, are supplemented by AWACS, a more modern NATO and US Air Force early-warning aircraft. Maritime surveillance is carried out jointly by the RAF and the Royal Navy. The RAF provides Nimrod maritime surveillance aircraft which are normally based at St Mawgan, Cornwall, and at Kinloss, on the Moray Firth.

If Britain were ever attacked from the air, the RAF's principle task would be to defend major British and American airbases, using interceptor aircraft and missiles. Long-range surface-to-air Bloodhound missile batteries are already installed in the East Anglia and Lincolnshire areas, and shorter-range Rapier missile units could be positioned around some key military airfields. Civil and industrial targets would be less defensible and more vulnerable to attack.

RAF operators at a UKADGE long-range radar station. Each of four main radar control centres and six smaller reporting posts co-ordinate the activities of defending aircraft and missiles.

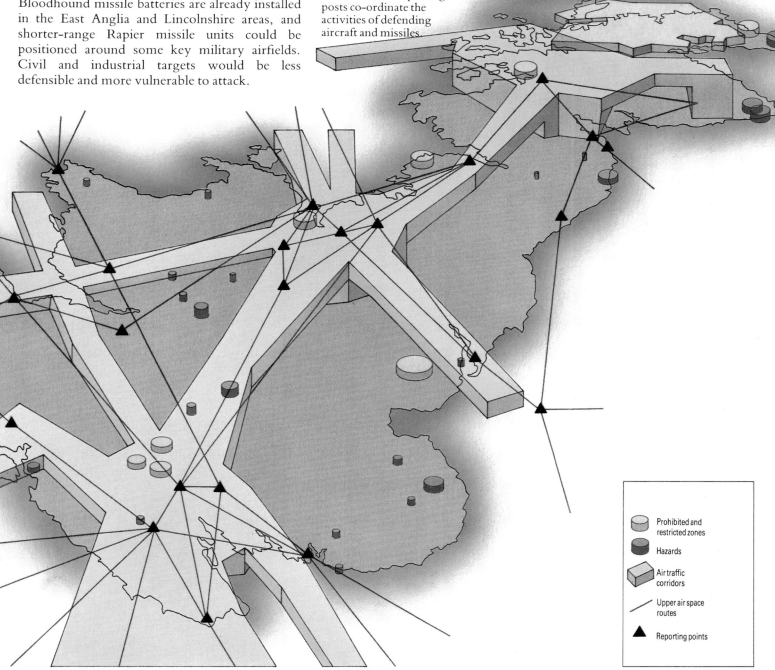

▬	Prohibited and restricted zones
▬	Hazards
▱	Air traffic corridors
╱	Upper air space routes
▲	Reporting points

POLICE, CRIME AND THE JUDICIARY

Britain has no national police force as such, though the Home Office co-ordinates training, research and development and mutual support between individual forces. The Home Office also runs a variety of central support services, including the maintenance of police communications, a forensic science service, and the operation of the Police National Computer (PNC) system, which is linked to all police forces in the country.

Except in London and Northern Ireland, police forces are financed and supervised by police authorities, composed partly of nominated councillors, and partly of magistrates. Most police forces cover the same area as a single county council (or, in Scotland, a regional council). There are also ten indirectly appointed joint police authorities, each serving two or more counties. Elected local government representatives may approve or disapprove police budgets, but are not permitted to consider 'operational' aspects of police work.

In London, where there is no local police authority, the Home Secretary is answerable to Parliament for the work of the Metropolitan Police. As well as policing London, the Metropolitan Police provides all or most of the members of some nationally organised police functions, such as the Fraud Squad, the National Drugs Intelligence Unit, the National Identification Bureau (formerly the Criminal Records Office), the Flying Squad, the Royalty and Diplomatic Protection Squads, and the Special Branch. There are also nine Regional Crime Squads in England and Wales and nine Regional Criminal Intelligence offices.

Crime and the judiciary

Crimes are divided into 'recordable' offences and lesser breaches of the law. Only recordable offences result in a personal record being created on the Police National Computer and at the Scotland Yard National Identification Bureau. Although minor traffic offences such as illegal parking may be tried in a magistrate's court together with much more serious breaches of the law, they are not usually regarded as recordable offences.

Judges and magistrates are normally appointed by the Lord Chancellor, who is a member of the government and Cabinet. However, constitutionally, party politics should not affect these appointments. The executive head of the judiciary is the Lord Chief Justice, a senior full-time judge.

Since 1945, Britain has taken a number of steps allowing international legal bodies to intervene in British legal decisions. As a member of the European Economic Community, Britain is subject to EEC law, which primarily affects industrial, employment and social matters. Britain has also ratified the European Convention on Human Rights, and is consequently subject to the judgements of the Court of Human Rights, in Strasbourg, France.

The courts

Most criminal offences are dealt with by magistrates' courts. But cases can be referred, on appeal or review, or for sentencing, to a crown court. Crown court judges may be barristers who sit as part-time recorders, or they may be senior High Court judges. High Court and Circuit judges periodically visit the major regional courts to deal with civil or criminal cases. Civil cases will often start in 'county' courts. From both crown and county courts, appeals may be taken to the High Court, or the Court of Appeal. After the Court of Appeal, a case may go the House of Lords for further review. Cases involving human rights or EEC law may go to the European Court of Human Rights or European Court of Justice.

Victims' survey

Many more crimes are known to be committed than are reported to the police, as these results of a 1981 Home Office survey show. The levels of reported crime vary widely as a proportion of the type of crime committed. For instance, because police 'clear-up' rates of burglaries and similar crimes tend to be very low, they are often reported only if the victim can make an insurance claim. Rape is also under-reported because of the fears and anxieties of some of the victims. Vandalism, the survey showed, accounted for more than a third of crimes experienced by those interviewed, yet only 8% of such crimes were reported.

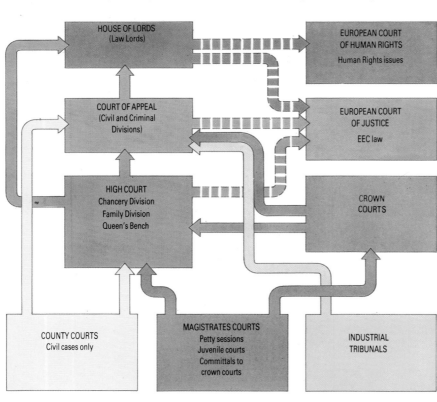

Police force boundaries

Following the 1964 Police Act, British police forces were extensively merged. There are now 43 police areas in England and Wales, and 8 in Scotland. (A single police force, the Royal Ulster Constabulary (RUC) covers Northern Ireland.) The highest courts in Britain, the Court of Appeal and the High Court are all located in London. In Scotland, there is a separate system of Sheriff and District Courts. The final Court of Criminal Appeal is the High Court of Justiciary, which meets in Edinburgh.

Police National Computer

Police officers can use the Police National Computer (PNC) to call up more than 47 million national records on people, vehicles and property. Computer records are consulted more than 70 million times a year. Terminals to PNC are located at all police force headquarters.

Types of crime

In 1983, more than 3 million criminal offences were notified to the police. They are shown below broken down by percentage. The average number of crimes recorded by the police per million population rose from 12,000 in the early 1950s to more than five times this level by the mid-1980s. There are major variations in crime levels between police force areas, especially between the metropolitan and non-metropolitan areas. In urban areas, for example, robbery and burglary are much more common than in rural districts. But this is not the case for serious offences of violence, or for sexual offences.

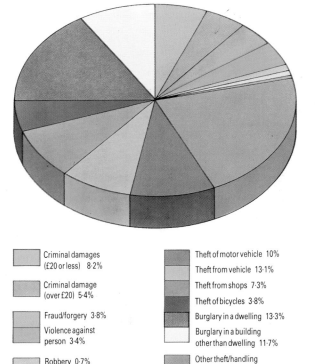

- Criminal damages (£20 or less) 8·2%
- Criminal damage (over £20) 5·4%
- Fraud/forgery 3·8%
- Violence against person 3·4%
- Robbery 0·7%
- Sexual offences 0·6%
- Theft of motor vehicle 10%
- Theft from vehicle 13·1%
- Theft from shops 7·3%
- Theft of bicycles 3·8%
- Burglary in a dwelling 13·3%
- Burglary in a building other than dwelling 11·7%
- Other theft/handling stolen goods 18·4%
- Other 0·3%

Circuits

District Courts

The 'Met'

The Metropolitan Police is responsible for policing Greater London and parts of Essex, Surrey and Hertfordshire. In 1985, it was reorganised into 8 separate area commands.

- Area HQs

1 Chigwell
2 Hackney City Road
3 Eltham
4 East Dulwich
5 Kingston
6 Notting Dale
7 Paddington Green
8 Cannon Row

POWER OUTSIDE THE GOVERNMENT

Apart from the formal power of the state, there are many other influences at work in Britain, as in other modern societies. These include business, the press, professional and industrial groups and other pressure groups. Some pressure groups are 'sectional': they represent people or organisations who share similar social or economic interests. The two most prominent and powerful of this type are the employers' organisation, the Confederation of British Industry (CBI) and the Trades Union Congress (TUC). Others include the Law Society, the British Medical Association (BMA) and the National Farmers' Union (NFU).

A second type of pressure group is the 'cause' organisation, whose members have common beliefs or aims but whose backgrounds and other interests may vary widely. Some of these groups, such as locally based campaigns on planning issues, are often transitory, but others, like the international aid charity Oxfam, the housing charity Shelter and the National Council for Civil Liberties (NCCL), have campaigned for decades.

Cause organisations achieve influence by publicity and by activities that might include lobbying councillors and MPs, holding demonstrations or exerting pressure on government departments by other means. Such campaigns may be particularly effective in the period before an election.

Confederation of British Industry

Many industrial firms belong to employers' organisations, often representing a single industry or section of an industry. Employers' organisations may negotiate collectively with trade unions on wages and conditions, as well as representing members' views to the government. Collectively, these employers' federations and other companies in the public and private sectors form the Confederation of British Industry, which is consulted by government departments.

The CBI's formal influence on government policy was consolidated in the 1960s when, with the TUC, its members were appointed to a new National Economic Development Council (NEDC). This tripartite government-union-industry body has many subsidiary development committees, all of which are charged with planning jointly for economic growth in a particular sector.

The Stock Exchange in the City of London has become a powerful institution and a major influence on national economic affairs.

The Church

About one in five Britons is a member of an established religion or faith, including Hinduism, Islam and other faiths. One in six people is a member of a Christian faith, though membership varies widely by region: in England 13% of the population, in Wales 23% and in Scotland 37%.

The Church of England is the main established church, having a formal place in the British state system. The monarch must be a member of the church, and appoints all its high officials – deans, bishops and archbishops – on the advice of the Prime Minister. Two Archbishops (York and Canterbury) and 24 bishops are members of the House of Lords. The governing body of the Church of England, the General Synod, includes the bishops, clergy and lay members of the Church, representing its 13,500 parishes. In Scotland, the presbyterian Church of Scotland is the established church. Its 1,765 churches are governed locally by Kirk Sessions, and nationally by a Scottish General Assembly.

Members of the Synod, seen here in session, are drawn from the clergy and laity. They consider both spiritual and administrative matters.

Trades Union Congress

The original Trades Union Congress of 1868 was little more than a debating shop. Today, about 10 million working people are members of the 93 trade unions affiliated to the TUC. Altogether, half of British workers belong to a trade union, a high proportion compared to other advanced industrial countries. The United States is 20% unionised, Japan 22% and West Germany 26%. A trade union's major function is collectively to represent workers in negotiating agreements on rates of pay and working conditions. In addition, many unions conduct research into health and safety at the workplace, organise industrial and professional education and training for their members and lobby government and other bodies.

During the 1980s, union membership declined as a consequence of increasing unemployment, and the trend by managers towards decentralised bargaining with workers and their representatives. However, the two largest unions still each represent more than a million members. These are the Transport and General Workers Union (TGWU), with 1·5 million members, and the Amalgamated Union of Engineering Workers (AUEW), with 1·2 million members. In Scotland, trade unions are represented by the Scottish TUC.

Members of the National Union of Mineworkers (NUM) demonstrate during the bitter, year-long miners' strike.

Non-aligned groups

The role of voluntary groups, unrelated to other established bodies or authorities, is widely recognised in Britain. The government both accepts voluntary groups and expects them to carry out functions ranging from running Citizens' Advice Bureaux (which are funded by the Department of Trade and Industry) to providing charitable services to assist the disabled, the elderly, or other disadvantaged groups. Many organisations of this kind are supported by local authority grants.

'Cause' organisations mount educational and publicity campaigns related to both charitable and political objectives. The non-aligned pressure groups that have received most publicity during the 1980s are those associated with campaigns on behalf of the environment, or against nuclear weapons. In Britain, the most prominent campaigns have been led by the Campaign for Nuclear Disarmament (CND), a movement calling for Britain to scrap its nuclear weapons, and the Greenpeace and Friends of the Earth (FoE) environmental groups. Recently, organisations raising funds to help feed the hungry in the Third World, such as Live Aid and Sport Aid, have attracted much public support.

Formed in the 1950s, CND was reborn as a mass peace movement in the 1980s with the appearance of a new generation of nuclear weapons.

SPORT

Many of the world's most popular sports originated in Britain. Golf, for example, began in Scotland in the 15th century, while the modern form of Association Football took shape in England in the 19th century.

Today, enthusiasm for sport remains strong, but assessing the degree of participation can present problems as many sports take place on an informal basis. However, there is a growing awareness of the benefits of sport in terms of health and as a social activity. As a result, successive governments have followed policies of supporting sport. A Parliamentary Under-Secretary in the Department of the Environment has the task of co-ordinating government policy on sport in England while the Secretaries of State for Wales and Scotland fulfil a similar role in their respective regions.

Government assistance to sport is the responsibility of three independent bodies – the Sports Council, the Sports Council for Wales and the Scottish Sports Council. The activities of the Welsh and Scottish Councils are restricted to their own countries, while the Sports Council deals both with England and with sporting matters that affect Britain as a whole.

Gambling
Betting and commercial gaming organisations together estimate that the British spend in excess of £6000 million annually on gambling. Horse and greyhound racing attract considerably more of this money than casinos, lotteries and licensed bingo and, apart from some cricket matches, are the only two sporting events where betting is allowed at the venue. However, most racing bets are placed at off-course and off-track betting offices, of which there are about 11,000.

'Doing the pools' is one of the most popular forms of gambling, though with average stakes of less than £1·20 a person, it is likely that few participants think of it as gambling at all. Between them, the two largest pools companies, Littlewoods and Vernons, accept about 10 million coupons a week in the football season, which suggests that about 15 million people are taking part. At the height of the season, pay-outs to prize winners amount to about £3 million a week.

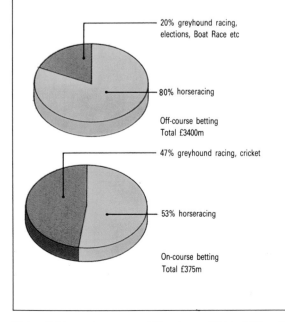

20% greyhound racing, elections, Boat Race etc

80% horseracing

Off-course betting
Total £3400m

47% greyhound racing, cricket

53% horseracing

On-course betting
Total £375m

Most popular sports on television
Sports coverage on television amounts to about 2500 hours a year. The relative sizes of audiences provide an indication of each sport's popularity. A snooker tournament, for example, may in its entirety attract up to 23 million viewers and a darts tournament may be watched by more than 12 million. Despite (or because of) falling attendances at matches, Association Football remains popular on television, with the BBC's Match of the Day having an average audience of about 8·5 million.

TOP TEN SPORTS –				
of people that watch sport on television,				
percentage interested (based on household survey 1984)				
Men	%		Women	%
1 Snooker	76		1 Tennis	56
2 Football	69		Skating	56
3 Athletics	52		3 Snooker	52
Boxing	52		4 Athletics	47
5 Motor car racing	49		5 Show jumping	46
Tennis	49		6 Swimming	36
7 Cricket	47		7 Snow sports	35
Darts	47		8 Darts	34
9 Golf	42		9 Football	33
10 Rugby Union	40		10 Golf	23

Participation
About 4 out of every 10 adults claim they take physical exercise at least once a month in summer. This figure is highest among young people – 6 out of 10 in the 16–24 age group. More men than women claim to take part in sport regularly.

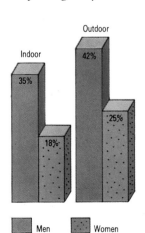

Indoor
35%
18%

Outdoor
42%
25%

Men   Women

Of all the outdoor sports, fishing is by far the most popular. There are about 4 million sea and freshwater anglers in Britain. Of the latter, many fish for salmon and trout to eat, but in England and Wales some are competitive fish anglers, seeking coarse fish such as pike, carp and tench.

Funding and sponsorship

The Sports Councils' aims include encouraging wider participation, providing better facilities and raising standards of performance. Between them the three councils allocated about £36 million of government funds in 1984–85. This included grants to the governing bodies of various sports, and loans and grants to voluntary bodies and local authorities. In addition, they finance the National Sports Centres (see map).

Sports facilities are mainly run by local authorities, whose total expenditure on recreation and sport in 1984–85 was about £800 million. This level of funding may change in future as a result of government reorganisation of local authorities, which came into effect in 1986. Local authorities provide facilities such as swimming baths, sports centres, playing fields, athletics stadia, tennis courts and parks. Schools and colleges also provide sports facilities, mainly to their own students.

Finance for sport is also found in the private sector. Sponsorship is playing an increasing role, with some £120 million in 1985 going mainly to sporting organisations and specific events.

Horseracing

Horseracing takes two main forms – flat racing and National Hunt (steeplechasing and hurdling). The most important races of the flat season (March to November) are the classics: the Derby and the Oaks at Epsom, the 2000 and the 1000 Guineas at Newmarket, and the St Leger at Doncaster. The highlight of the National Hunt season (end July to beginning of June) is the steeplechase Festival meeting at Cheltenham in March.

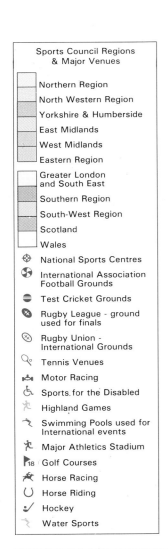

Run every summer, the London Marathon first took place in 1981, with 8000 entrants. Ten times the number applied in 1986, for 22,000 places. Anyone over 18 may enter. Marathons are also held in Southampton and Manchester.

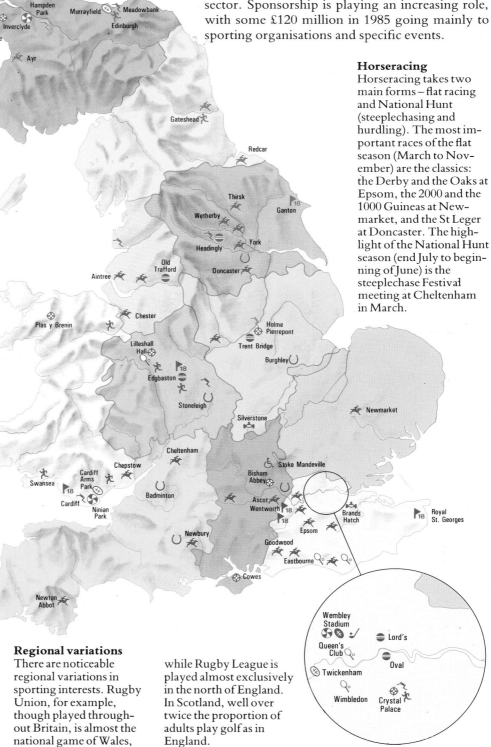

Sports Council Regions & Major Venues

- Northern Region
- North Western Region
- Yorkshire & Humberside
- East Midlands
- West Midlands
- Eastern Region
- Greater London and South East
- Southern Region
- South-West Region
- Scotland
- Wales

- ⊕ National Sports Centres
- ◍ International Association Football Grounds
- ⊖ Test Cricket Grounds
- ⊗ Rugby League – ground used for finals
- ⊗ Rugby Union – International Grounds
- ◍ Tennis Venues
- ⊷ Motor Racing
- ⅋ Sports for the Disabled
- 🏃 Highland Games
- ⌇ Swimming Pools used for International events
- 🏃 Major Athletics Stadium
- ⚑18 Golf Courses
- 🏇 Horse Racing
- ∪ Horse Riding
- ✓ Hockey
- ⌇ Water Sports

Regional variations

There are noticeable regional variations in sporting interests. Rugby Union, for example, though played throughout Britain, is almost the national game of Wales, while Rugby League is played almost exclusively in the north of England. In Scotland, well over twice the proportion of adults play golf as in England.

TOURISM

In Britain, tourism is a major industry and an important part of the economy. Incorporating travel agents, tour operators, the hotel and catering trades, it employs more than one and a half million people. In financial terms, it has a vast turnover, with foreign currency earnings reaching over £4000 million in 1984. Income from tourism has for several years made up more than a tenth of all foreign currency earnings from invisible exports, which also include insurance and other financial services, and sea and air travel.

There is considerable government support for the industry. This is administered by the British Tourist Authority (BTA) and three tourist boards, the English, Welsh and Scottish. These, like the BTA, are statutory bodies. The BTA is responsible for overseas promotion of British tourism, while the boards work within Britain. (The Scottish Tourist Board also does some promotion abroad, but it is the only national board to do so.)

As well as promoting tourism, tourist boards are responsible for developing and improving tourist accommodation and amenities, and administering grants and loans to help with this. The boards' work includes publishing accommodation guides for tourists and listing establishments that have taken part in a voluntary registration scheme. Information for tourists is given through information centres located in major towns and tourist areas, and via the Prestel information service.

Top 20 sites
The term 'tourist attraction' embraces everything from amusement parks to museums and galleries. There are 3000 such attractions open to the public in England alone – below are Britain's top 20 (1984).

1 Blackpool Pleasure Beach
   6,700,000
2 Tower of London
   4,087,000
3 British Museum (Lon)
   3,236,700
4 Science Museum (Lon)
   3,019,900
5 National Gallery (Lon)
   2,936,900
6 Natural History Museum (Lon)
   2,318,000
7 Madame Tussaud's (Lon)
   2,118,400
8 Alton Towers pleasure park
   1,956,000
9 Victoria & Albert Museum (Lon)
   1,692,800
10 Tate Gallery (Lon)
   1,265,600
11 London Zoo
   1,224,690
12 Bradgate Park pleasure park
   1,200,000
   Wicksteed Park pleasure park
   1,200,000
14 Burrell Collection (Glasgow)
   1,109,000
15 Kew Botanic Gardens
   1,084,290
16 Thorpe Park pleasure park
   1,020,000
17 Royal Academy of Arts (Lon)
   1,004,000
18 Camelot (Lancs)
   1,000,000
19 Roman Baths (Bath)
   931,170
20 National Railway Museum (York)
   889,500

In the past 10 years wildlife attractions such as Windsor Safari Park (above) have become increasingly popular with British tourists.

Tourist economy
Although tourism brings in a large amount of foreign exchange, this is usually more than offset by British tourists' spending overseas. In the 1980s, almost every year has seen a deficit in what is known as the 'travel account' – usually around £300 million. Overseas tourists' spending in Britain is concentrated in England. Scottish receipts represent about 6% of the total, Welsh about 2%.

British expenditure overseas

Foreign

Home

Tourism income

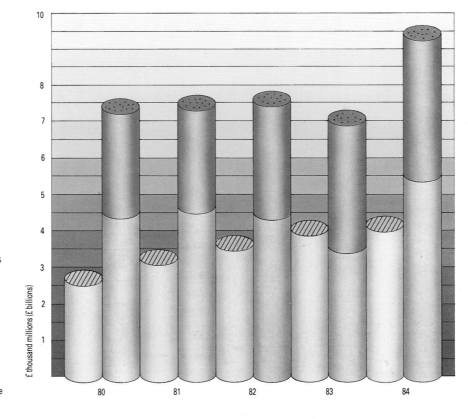

£ thousand millions (£ billions)

80   81   82   83   84

Numbers of visitors
The largest number of visitors to Britain from a single country is the 2·8 million from the United States. Recent years have seen a continual rise in visitors from North America as a whole, encouraged by favourable exchange rates.

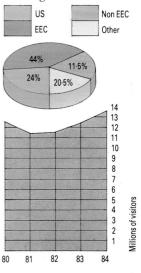

US   Non EEC
EEC   Other

44%   11·5%
24%   20·5%

14
13
12
11
10
9
8
7
6
5
4
3
2
1

Millions of visitors

80 81 82 83 84

The tourists

Currently, Britain attracts in a year about 14 million tourists from overseas, mainly from western Europe. For example, in 1984 the EEC group of countries provided 7·5 million tourists. Important as overseas tourism is, however, it is only part of the industry's concern. In the same year, tourist trips within Great Britain by British residents numbered some 140 million.

Most visitors to Britain choose to travel in summer, with August as the peak month. London, with some 40 million visits a year to its various tourist attractions, is more than twice as popular as any region in Britain. All historic towns seem to be especially popular with people from overseas. In both Winchester and Chester, for example, this group of tourists usually make up about a third of the total.

Tourist boards

The Welsh and Scottish Tourist Boards operate as two single bodies, but the English Tourist Board (ETB) sponsors and aids 12 regional boards (their boundaries are shown on the map). These work in partnership with the ETB, local trade interests and local government in promoting tourism in their areas.

Independent organisations such as the Automobile Association (AA) and Royal Automobile Club (RAC) supplement the work of the boards, providing tourists with sightseeing and accommodation information.

Tourism map

Britain's rich heritage comprises not only historic buildings, museums and art galleries but also nature reserves, National Parks and areas of natural beauty. Tourist sites of all kinds are managed by government-financed bodies such as English Heritage or by independent organisations, of which the National Trust, a charity with a million members, is the largest.

UK tourist trips

Tourism within Britain by British residents is far from restricted to holiday-making. In summer, the population makes about 600 million leisure day trips, only 15% of which are made while on holiday away from home. Most British holidaymakers stay with friends or relatives rather than rent holiday accommodation.

Map legend

- National Parks
- National Park Direction Areas (Scotland)
- Areas of Outstanding Natural Beauty / National Scenic Areas (Scotland)
- Heritage Coast and Coastal Conservation Zones (Scotland)
- Long Distance Footpaths
- Navigable rivers
- Canals
- Tourist Board Area boundaries
- Urban areas
- Regional proportion of total tourist nights spent in Britain 10mm=10%.
- British visitors
- Overseas visitors

Map labels

Durness, Ullapool, Golspie, Dornoch, Loch Torridon, Glen Affric, Banff, Fraserburgh, Speyside Way, Caledonian Canal, Cairngorm, Stonehaven, Glen Nevis and Glencoe, SCOTLAND, West Highland Way, Carnoustie, Trossachs, St. Andrews, Helensburgh, Dunoon, Forth and Clyde Canal, North Berwick, Proposed Southern Upland Way, Union Canal, Brodick, Ayr, Berwick-on-Tweed, Northumberland, NORTHUMBRIA, Blyth, Tyne, Pennine Way, CUMBRIA, Redcar, Cleveland Way, Tees, Whitby, Lake District, North York Moors, Scarborough, Millennium Way, Lake Windermere, Ure, YORKSHIRE AND HUMBERSIDE, Filey, Yorkshire Dales, Nidd, Bridlington, Douglas, Morecambe, Wharfe, Ouse, Leeds and Liverpool Canal, Ribble, Aire, Wolds Way, Blackpool, Southport, NORTH WEST, Mersey, Peak District, Cleethorpes, Llandudno, Colwyn Bay, Weaver Navig., Derwent, Dee, Trent Navigation, Skegness, Witham Navigation, Snowdonia, EAST MIDLANDS, Sheringham, Cromer, L. Bala, Shropshire Union Canal, Welland, The Broads, Barmouth, Offa's Dyke, Severn, Trent & Mersey Canal, Nene, Gt. Yarmouth, WALES, HEART OF ENGLAND, Lowestoft, Aberystwyth, Path, Stratford on Avon, EAST ANGLIA, Felixstowe, Pembrokeshire Coast, Wye, Avon, Oxford Canal, Grand Union Canal, Clacton, Pembrokeshire Coast Path, Brecon Beacons, Usk, THAMES AND CHILTERNS, Lee Navigation, LONDON, Southend, Tenby, Monmouth & Brecon Canal, Ridgeway, Thames, Windsor, Margate, Barry, Avon, Kennet & Avon Canal, Kennet, North Downs Way, Ramsgate, Ilfracombe, Minehead, Weston-super-Mare, Test, Medway, Dover, Folkestone, Exmoor, Parrett, South Downs Way, SOUTH-EAST, Hastings, WEST COUNTRY, SOUTHERN, Worthing, Brighton, Eastbourne, Exe, South-West Peninsula Path, Poole, Bournemouth, Southsea, Dartmoor, Lyme Regis, Swanage, Shanklin, Ventnor, Newquay, Teignmouth, Weymouth, Torbay, South-West Peninsula Path

Visits by British residents chart

Visits by British residents — □ =1 million trips

Cumbria
Northumbria
North West
Yorkshire & Humbs
Heart of England
East Midlands
Thames/Chiltern
East Anglia
London
West Country
Southern
South East
Scotland
Wales

ARCHITECTURE

Britain's architectural heritage is among the richest in the world. It dates back at least to Roman times, though little remains of that period other than archeological sites. Of the buildings of the 4th to the 15th centuries, the most dramatic, and best-surviving, are the country's castles and cathedrals. Many of the castles were built soon after the Norman conquest of 1066 and most of the cathedrals were built during the latter part of the Middle Ages, when the Church (then Catholic) was most wealthy and powerful. However, over the centuries both have been modified and extended.

Later examples of architectural splendour are the stately homes of the aristocracy. Various styles are evident, from the detailed brick and timber work of the Elizabethan era to the graceful simplicity of Georgian times. Some of the styles reflect strong influences from France, Italy and Spain. The 19th century saw the rapid and extensive development of civic and industrial architecture – town halls, railway stations, factories – as the newly rich industrialists of the era put their mark on the cities they helped build and develop.

Today in Britain, buildings of special architectural or historical interest are protected by law. In England they are the responsibility of the Department of the Environment, through English Heritage. Similar bodies operate in both Scotland and Wales, through the Secretaries of State for Scotland and Wales respectively.

Churches and cathedrals

To build these, stone was frequently carried great distances – and occasionally imported from mainland Europe – to ensure that the very best materials were always used. Skilled stonemasons and glaziers were employed, and these are still to be found in many cathedral towns as restoration and repair work of ancient buildings is constantly needed.

Stately homes

Britain has several hundred stately homes. The original owners were usually rich enough to indulge in great splendour, and often eccentricity too. Some have magnificent landscaped gardens like Blenheim. Many stately homes have recently been opened to the public to help the present owners cover the high running costs.

Industrial towns

The 19th century saw an enormous amount of house-building in the industrial centres of Britain to accommodate the large numbers of factory and mine workers. Long rows of the typical terraced houses, built of stone or brick, can still be seen in many parts of Britain.

Georgian houses

The simple well-proportioned style of Georgian town houses (around 1720) was designed to appeal to the wealthy of the day. The best remaining examples are in Bath, Avon

Changing styles of architecture

In Britain, many styles of building have developed over the centuries in response to such influences as the availability of materials, the purpose of the building and, of course, fashion. The drawings below show a range of examples from around the country. Housing, in particular, displays 'vernacular architecture' – the native or regionally indigenous style of building.

Castles

These served as homes for nobles and soldiers, but the main criterion in their design was defensibility. Over the centuries, construction improved until they were virtually impregnable. The Norman motte and bailey style gradually gave way to a curtain wall and inner keep or tower design. Political changes eventually made castles unnecessary and after about 1500 very few were built simply as fortresses.

Traditional homes

These have often been made of locally available materials, of which stone has been the most commonly used. In the Highlands of Scotland, subsistence farmers, or crofters, used rough stone to make their simple homes. In the north of England, limestone, flint and cob have been used. In parts of southern England, timber and thatch houses are still to be seen. Thatch is one of the oldest roofing materials used. It is made from straw or reeds, tied in bundles.

Industrial buildings

From about 1815, industry gradually replaced craftsmanship as the basis for building. Even early examples of industrial architecture, such as the first road and rail bridges and dockland sites, were constructed from mass-produced building parts rather than being built by large gangs of labourers using traditional methods.

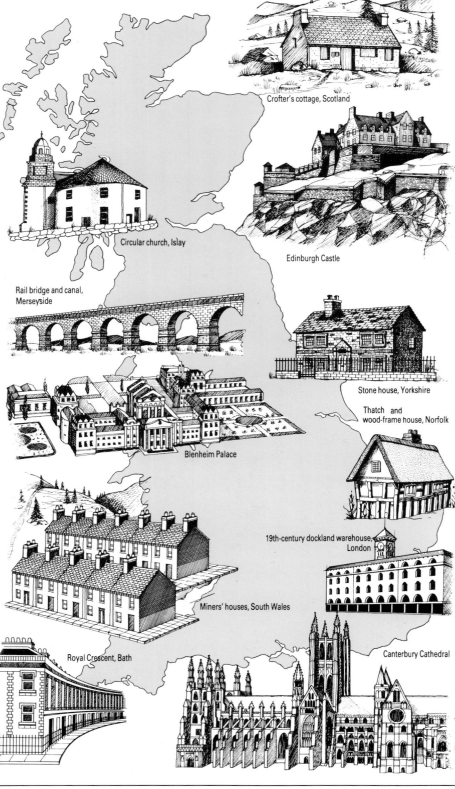

Crofter's cottage, Scotland

Circular church, Islay

Edinburgh Castle

Rail bridge and canal, Merseyside

Blenheim Palace

Stone house, Yorkshire

Thatch and wood-frame house, Norfolk

19th-century dockland warehouse, London

Miners' houses, South Wales

Royal Crescent, Bath

Canterbury Cathedral

Modern architecture

In Britain, the 20th century has seen great developments in building and architecture, especially in house building and town planning. Following World War I, whole new suburban housing estates and new towns were built, particularly in the then economically thriving Midlands and the south of England. They were to cope with the increasing population and to satisfy people's greater expectations of life in peacetime.

More new towns were established soon after World War II, and in the 1950s and 1960s slum clearance and the development of derelict and bombed areas took place on a large scale. The new approach to the housing problem was to build tower blocks of flats. However, high-rise housing has not worn well, and in recent years several tower blocks have been demolished as a result of being too costly to repair and for sociological reasons. Today's municipal housing is low-rise.

The 1980s have seen a further move in style towards 'post modernism', which combines both historical and modern references. Some modern British architects have adopted a 'high tech' approach, often creating a decoration that stems solely from expression of structure and services. The public, however, has often shown itself to be unimpressed by the architecture of the Modern Movement, and has more readily accepted the sympathetic planning of more traditionally designed buildings.

Organisation and standards

An independent body, the Royal Institute of British Architects (RIBA), and the Royal Incorporation of Architects in Scotland, with which it is allied, exercise controls over standards in architecture education. The Department of the Environment and the Royal Fine Art Commission exercise aesthetic control by means of planning laws. Finally, the British Standards Institute sets out performance and safety criteria.

Housing

In the mid-1970s the building of tower blocks, involving extensive use of prefabricated concrete and glass, gave way to low-rise housing exploiting more traditional materials such as brick and tile. This housing estate near Evesham, designed by British architects Darbourne and Darke, was built in the early 1980s. Many modern estates like this incorporate shops, libraries and schools built with the same materials and to the same style to create harmony.

Post modernism

The post modernist movement began in the early 1980s. British architects of this school include Jeremy Dickson, who has designed housing schemes based on the classical villa, and Terry Farrell, who designed the TV-am building in London (above). This is a renovated warehouse set alongside the Grand Union Canal. Colour and 'art deco' features are widely used.

High-tech buildings

The Renault Centre, Swindon, designed by architect Norman Foster, displays an undulating roof suspended from tubular steel poles by tension rods. Built as a warehouse, exhibition hall and offices, it has been described as 'humane high-tech'.

THE ARTS

The arts form one of Britain's most important tourist attractions. London is regarded as a major world centre for theatre, classical and popular music, opera, dance and fine art, and in recent years, as a result of government policy, the arts have become more available to the regions.

General arts policy is the responsibility of the Minister for the Arts, and government expenditure on national museums and art galleries is administered by the Office of Arts and Libraries in England and the Secretaries of State for Wales and Scotland in their respective countries. In 1984–85 this amounted to some £260 million. Additional funding comes from local authorities – in 1984–85 over £400 million was spent on public libraries, local museums and art galleries – and from sponsorship and patronage by industrial and commercial concerns – currently about £14·5 million a year. However, with the Arts Council and local authorities undergoing substantial change, support for the arts from private sources is likely to become an increasingly significant factor in the next two or three years. Consumer expenditure on the arts and entertainment amounts to about 5% of total annual household income.

Government funding
The largest portion of this – currently about 40% or some £100 million – goes to the Arts Council. This is an independent body, established in 1946, which gives financial help and advice to a large number of arts organisations, ranging from major opera and theatre companies to small dance and music groups. It also supports, together with local authorities, 15 regional arts associations in England and Wales, and subsidises the separate Scottish and Welsh Arts Councils.

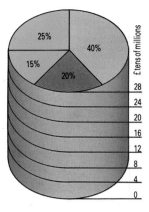

Arts Council
British Library
Others
National galleries and museums

£ tens of millions
28
24
20
16
12
8
4
0

25%
40%
15%
20%

Calendar of events
Many of the events shown here are held annually, often attracting both participants and audiences from all over the world. In addition, each year there are several hundred local events all over the country.

Festivals and exhibitions
There are some 240 professional arts festivals in Britain each year. The largest is the month-long Edinburgh International Festival, which annually stages about 200 performances of world-class theatre, opera and dance, and numerous 'fringe' events, in which amateur performers of all kinds take part. Important regional and cultural events include London's Notting Hill West Indian Carnival, and the Welsh Eisteddfods, of which the Royal National (below) is the largest.

Consumer spending on the arts
Despite government subsidies and continued support from overseas visitors, theatres and concert halls in Britain struggle to survive as people spend increasingly more on home entertainment and less on live performances of the arts.

1984-85

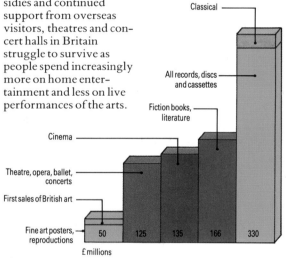

Classical

All records, discs and cassettes

Fiction books, literature

Cinema

Theatre, opera, ballet, concerts

First sales of British art

Fine art posters, reproductions

50   125   135   166   330

£ millions

Arts Calendar – selected major events
JANUARY
Viking festival, York (starts)
FEBRUARY
Hallé Orchestra concerts, Manchester
MARCH
Shakespeare season, Stratford (starts)
Southampton Open Brass Band Contest
Harrogate Youth Music Festival
APRIL
Sunday Times Student Festival, Swansea
Newport Drama Festival
MAY
Newbury Spring Festival
Chichester Festival theatre season (starts)
Southern Counties Craft Market, Farnham
Perth Festival of Arts, Tayside
Bath Festival (starts)
Glyndebourne Festival Opera Season (starts)
JUNE
Open Air Theatre Season, Regent's Park, Lon.
Dundee Festival
Aldeburgh Festival of Music and Arts
Royal Academy Summer Exhibition, Lon.
JULY
York Mystery Plays
Cheltenham International Music Festival
Promenade Concerts, Lon. (start)
Shrewsbury International Music Festival
AUGUST
Royal National Eisteddfod
Edinburgh International Festival
Three Choirs Festival
SEPTEMBER
Annual Festival of Light Music, Bexhill
OCTOBER
Antique Dealers' Fair, Whalley, Lancs
NOVEMBER/DECEMBER
Lord Mayor's Show, London
Cardiff Festival of Music

Theatres

Of a total of 310 major theatres (those seating more than 200 people), 60 house resident theatre companies that receive state support. Arts Council funding of regional theatre is now being given priority over London's.

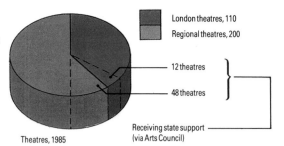

London theatres, 110
Regional theatres, 200

12 theatres
48 theatres

Receiving state support (via Arts Council)

Theatres, 1985

Covent Garden (above) once London's wholesale fruit and vegetable market, is now a major tourist attraction. It has become a focal point for street entertainers of all kinds.

Fine art

Interest and financial support for fine art is found throughout the country. The Burrell Collection in Glasgow is the newest major museum, featuring tapestries, paintings and *objets d'art*. The Third Eye Centre (right), also in Glasgow, is one of the many new small galleries that exhibit the work of young artists.

Cinema and television

There are some 1300 cinema screens in Britain. Attendances have declined drastically over the past 30 years, probably as a result of increased television viewing – the BBC and ITV together broadcast more than 60 hours of arts programmes on television each week – but also because of the way in which public funding for the film industry was until recently related to cinema attendances. Patterns of cinema-going in the last few years have been affected by the growth of the video market, which enables people to watch feature films in their homes.

Arts centres and performing groups

There are more than 200 arts centres and over 100 major museums and art galleries around Britain. Annually these attract more than 20 million visitors. The majority are in and around London, although the past five years have seen the establishment of important museums outside the capital – the National Railway Museum and Jorvik Viking Museum (York), the Ironbridge Gorge Museum, the Mary Rose Museum (Portsmouth) and the Open Air Museum (Durham).

In cinema and theatre, London's West End is the hub, although its Barbican Centre and South Bank arts complex are major sites, the Royal Shakespeare Company is based at Stratford upon Avon, and the National Museum of Photography, Film and Television is now well established in Bradford.

Britain has several international-class opera companies, including the English National, Welsh National, Royal Opera (at Covent Garden), Opera North (based in Leeds), and the Scottish Opera; symphony orchestras such as the London Symphony, Hallé (in Manchester) and the City of Birmingham; and dance companies, of which Sadler's Wells, the Royal Ballet, London Festival Ballet, Ballet Rambert, and London Contemporary Dance Theatre are best known.

Music and dance

In Britain, symphony orchestras, chamber orchestras and choral groups together number several hundred. A highlight of annual classical-music events is the season of Henry Wood Promenade Concerts, the Proms, in London's Albert Hall (below). Throughout the country, jazz, popular and folk music, ballet and other forms of dance are also popular, and there is a growing number of music events by ethnic groups, in particular Indian and West Indian.

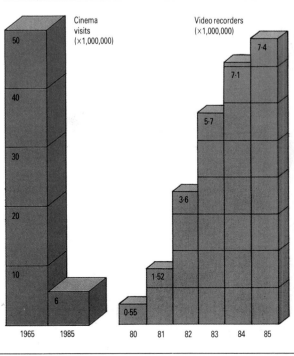

Cinema visits (×1,000,000)

Video recorders (×1,000,000)

50
40
30
20
10
6

7·4
7·1
5·7
3·6
1·52
0·55

1965 1985

80 81 82 83 84 85

ACKNOWLEDGEMENTS AND BIBLIOGRAPHY

The major thematic maps in the reference section were compiled by Peter Furtado, Lionel Bender, Mike March and Patrick Nugent from material provided by the authors. The maps were made and drawn by Clyde Surveys Ltd. of Maidenhead.

The editors and publishers would like to acknowledge the following as some major sources for these maps:

p11 Geology: Tectonic Map of Great Britain, the Institute of Geological Sciences 1966; and Oxford University Press.

p15 Climate: *The Climate of the British Isles* T J Chandler and S Gregory, Longman 1976.

p19 18th-century Britain: *An Historical Geography of England and Wales* ed R A Dodgshon and R A Butler, Academic Press 1978. *Man Made the Land* Alan R H Baker and J B Harley, David & Charles 1973.

p21 Industrial Revolution: *The Early Industrial Revolution* E Pawson, Batsford 1979.

p23 Workshop of the World: *The Movement of Population* C T Smith, Geographical Journal vol 117, 1951.

p30 Mineral Resources: *The Mineral Resources of Britain* John Blunden, Hutchinson 1975. *A Geography of Energy in the UK* John Fernie, Longman 1981.

p37 Nature Conservation: Countryside Commission, various official maps 1985.

p39, 41 Communications: BBC, IBA, Post Office and British Telecom Official Handbooks 1984-85.

p43 Agriculture: *Types of Farming in Britain* K Buchanan and D J Sinclair, Association of Agriculture 1966.

p47 Industry: *The Containment of Urban England* Peter Hall, George Allen & Unwin, 1974. *Britain 1985*, HMSO. *Regional Trends 1985* HMSO.

p57,59 Transport: British Rail and Ministry of Transport Official Maps 1961, 1985.

p69 Defence: *Defence Land Reviews*, HMSO 1973. Civil Aviation Authority published charts 1985; *Army, Navy and Air Force Lists* HMSO 1985.

p79 Tourism: English, Wales and Scottish Tourist Boards and the Nature Conservancy Council published data 1984-85.

Countless books have been written about the history, geography and countryside of Britain. The following titles (as well as those mentioned above) might be of interest about the geography of Britain:

The Personality of Britain Sir Cyril Fox and L F Chitty, National Museum of Wales 1932.

The UK Space ed J W House, Weidenfeld and Nicolson 1977.

The British Isles: A Systematic Geography J W Watson and J B Sissons, Nelson 1964.

Countryside Conservation Bryn Green, George Allen & Unwin 1985.

National Parks: Conservation or Cosmetics Ann and Malcolm McEwen. George Allen & Unwin 1982.

Britain's Structure and Scenery L D Stamp, Collins 1984.

Urban and Regional Planning Peter Hall, Penguin 1974.

Airport Strategy and Planning K R Sealy, Oxford University Press 1976.

Land Use and Living Space R H Best, Methuen 1981.

A Living History of the British Isles ed W G V Balchin, Country Life 1981.

A Natural History of the British Isles ed Pat Morris, Country Life 1979.

The Making of the English Landscape W G Hoskins, Penguin 1970.

Wales F V Emery, Longman 1969.

The Making of the Scottish Landscape R N Millman, Batsford 1975.

Editors Lionel Bender, Mike March, assisted by Madeleine Bender

Designer Patrick Nugent

Picture Researcher Juliet Brightmore

Typesetting Peter Furtado

ILLUSTRATORS

Alan Suttie: pages 10, 11, 12, 13, 20, 21, 26, 27, 28, 29, 50, 51, 52, 53, 56, 57, 64, 65, 70, 71, 81, 82

Bill Donohoe: pages 8, 9, 16, 17, 32, 33, 34, 35, 36, 37, 38, 39, 42, 43, 44, 45, 46, 47, 48, 49

Hayward Art Group: pages 18, 19, 22, 23, 24, 25, 30, 31, 54, 55, 58, 59, 62, 63, 66, 67, 72, 73, 76, 77, 78, 79, 83, 84

Chris Forsey: pages 14, 15

Make-up: Mike Pilley, Radius

PICTURE CREDITS

10 top and inset Institute of Geological Sciences, London; 12 British Geological Survey; 13 The Photo Source; 16 Dr John Mason; 18 top Mansell Collection; 18 bottom University of Reading, Institute of Agricultural History and Museum of English Rural Life; 21 Mansell Collection; 22 centre William Powell Frith *Many Happy Returns of the Day*, 1856. Harrogate Museums and Art Gallery; 22 bottom left Trades Union Congress Library; 22 bottom right BBC Hulton Picture Library; 24 centre *Punch*, April 20th, 1921; 24 bottom right Austin Rover; 26 Topham Picture Library; 32 British Nuclear Fuels, PLC; 34–35 top John McCormick; 35 bottom Thames Water; 36 The Photo Source; 38 British Telecom Photo Library; 40 Prestel, British Telecommunications PLC; 45 Haigh and Ringrose Ltd (part of Costain Group PLC); 49 Photograph by British Petroleum; 56 Aerofilms Ltd; 58 Flight International/Quadrant Picture Library; 60 Aerofilms Ltd; 63, 68 Illustrated London News Picture Library; 69 Jerry Mason; 70 Flight International/Quadrant Picture Library; 71 *Jane's Defence Weekly*/Hughes; 73 Central Office of Information. Crown copyright; 74 top The Stock Exchange; 74 bottom Robert Miles; 75 top Raissa Page/Format Photographers Picture Agency; 75 bottom Camera Press; 76 top–77 Frank Spooner Pictures; 76 bottom, 78 Britain on View Photographic Library; 81 top and centre Arcaid Photographic Library. Photo Richard Bryant; 81 bottom Foster Associates; 82 Wales Tourist Board Photographic Library; 83 top left Britain on View Photographic Library; 83 centre Scottish Tourist Board Photographic Library; 83 bottom right The Photo Source.

ORDNANCE SURVEY 1:250 000 Maps

Legend

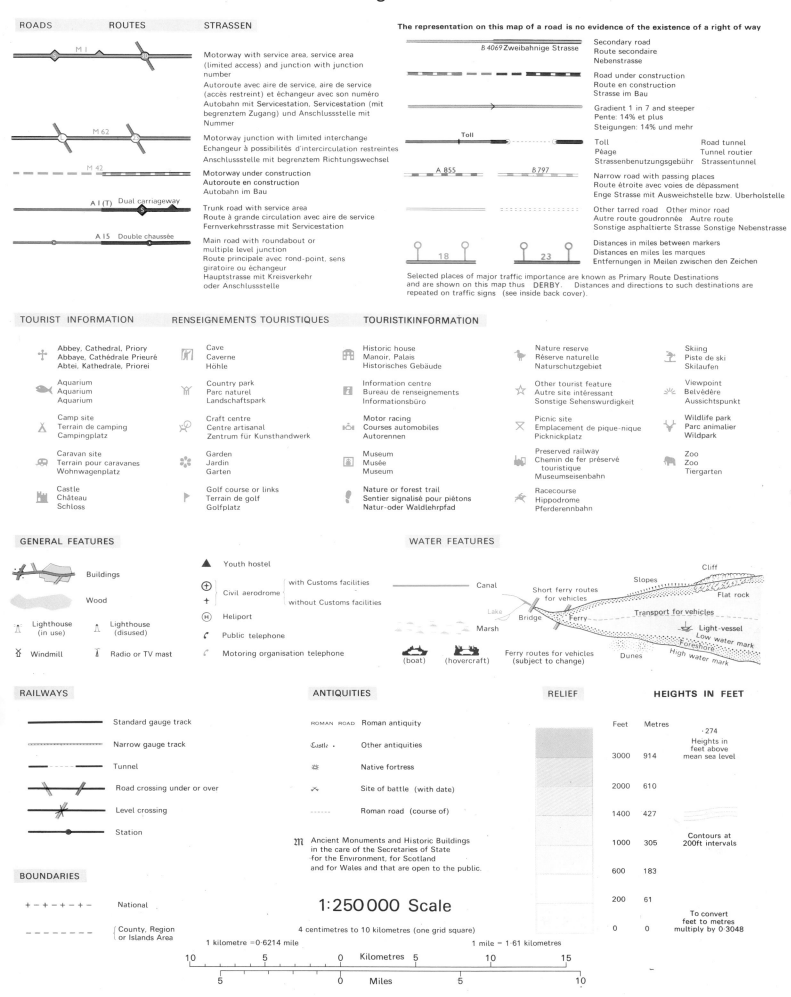

ROADS   ROUTES   STRASSEN

The representation on this map of a road is no evidence of the existence of a right of way

Motorway with service area, service area (limited access) and junction with junction number
Autoroute avec aire de service, aire de service (accès restreint) et échangeur avec son numéro
Autobahn mit Servicestation, Servicestation (mit begrenztem Zugang) und Anschlussstelle mit Nummer

Motorway junction with limited interchange
Echangeur à possibilités d'intercirculation restreintes
Anschlussstelle mit begrenztem Richtungswechsel

Motorway under construction
Autoroute en construction
Autobahn im Bau

Trunk road with service area
Route à grande circulation avec aire de service
Fernverkehrsstrasse mit Servicestation

Main road with roundabout or multiple level junction
Route principale avec rond-point, sens giratoire ou échangeur
Hauptstrasse mit Kreisverkehr oder Anschlussstelle

B 4069 Zweibahnige Strasse

Secondary road
Route secondaire
Nebenstrasse

Road under construction
Route en construction
Strasse im Bau

Gradient 1 in 7 and steeper
Pente: 14% et plus
Steigungen: 14% und mehr

Toll — Road tunnel
Péage — Tunnel routier
Strassenbenutzungsgebühr — Strassentunnel

A 855   B 797
Narrow road with passing places
Route étroite avec voies de dépassment
Enge Strasse mit Ausweichstelle bzw. Uberholstelle

Other tarred road   Other minor road
Autre route goudronnée   Autre route
Sonstige asphaltierte Strasse Sonstige Nebenstrasse

18   23
Distances in miles between markers
Distances en miles les marques
Entfernungen in Meilen zwischen den Zeichen

Selected places of major traffic importance are known as Primary Route Destinations and are shown on this map thus DERBY.   Distances and directions to such destinations are repeated on traffic signs (see inside back cover).

TOURIST INFORMATION   RENSEIGNEMENTS TOURISTIQUES   TOURISTIKINFORMATION

Abbey, Cathedral, Priory
Abbaye, Cathédrale Prieuré
Abtei, Kathedrale, Priorei

Aquarium
Aquarium
Aquarium

Camp site
Terrain de camping
Campingplatz

Caravan site
Terrain pour caravanes
Wohnwagenplatz

Castle
Château
Schloss

Cave
Caverne
Höhle

Country park
Parc naturel
Landschaftspark

Craft centre
Centre artisanal
Zentrum für Kunsthandwerk

Garden
Jardin
Garten

Golf course or links
Terrain de golf
Golfplatz

Historic house
Manoir, Palais
Historisches Gebäude

Information centre
Bureau de renseignements
Informationsbüro

Motor racing
Courses automobiles
Autorennen

Museum
Musée
Museum

Nature or forest trail
Sentier signalisé pour piétons
Natur-oder Waldlehrpfad

Nature reserve
Réserve naturelle
Naturschutzgebiet

Other tourist feature
Autre site intéressant
Sonstige Sehenswurdigkeit

Picnic site
Emplacement de pique-nique
Picknickplatz

Preserved railway
Chemin de fer préservé touristique
Museumseisenbahn

Racecourse
Hippodrome
Pferderennbahn

Skiing
Piste de ski
Skilaufen

Viewpoint
Belvédère
Aussichtspunkt

Wildlife park
Parc animalier
Wildpark

Zoo
Zoo
Tiergarten

GENERAL FEATURES

Buildings

Wood

Lighthouse (in use)

Lighthouse (disused)

Windmill

Radio or TV mast

▲ Youth hostel

⊕ Civil aerodrome { with Customs facilities
✛ { without Customs facilities

Ⓗ Heliport

☏ Public telephone

☏ Motoring organisation telephone

WATER FEATURES

Canal

Lake

Bridge   Ferry

Marsh

Short ferry routes for vehicles

Transport for vehicles

Cliff
Slopes
Flat rock

Light-vessel
Low water mark
Foreshore
High water mark
Dunes

(boat)   (hovercraft)
Ferry routes for vehicles (subject to change)

RAILWAYS

Standard gauge track

Narrow gauge track

Tunnel

Road crossing under or over

Level crossing

Station

ANTIQUITIES

ROMAN ROAD Roman antiquity

Castle · Other antiquities

※ Native fortress

⚔ Site of battle (with date)

------ Roman road (course of)

ₘ Ancient Monuments and Historic Buildings in the care of the Secretaries of State for the Environment, for Scotland and for Wales and that are open to the public.

BOUNDARIES

+ − + − + − + National

− − − − − − − { County, Region or Islands Area

RELIEF   HEIGHTS IN FEET

Feet	Metres	
		·274
		Heights in feet above mean sea level
3000	914	
2000	610	
1400	427	
1000	305	Contours at 200ft intervals
600	183	
200	61	
0	0	To convert feet to metres multiply by 0·3048

1:250 000 Scale

4 centimetres to 10 kilometres (one grid square)

1 kilometre = 0·6214 mile   1 mile = 1·61 kilometres

10   5   0   Kilometres 5   10   15

5   0   Miles   5   10

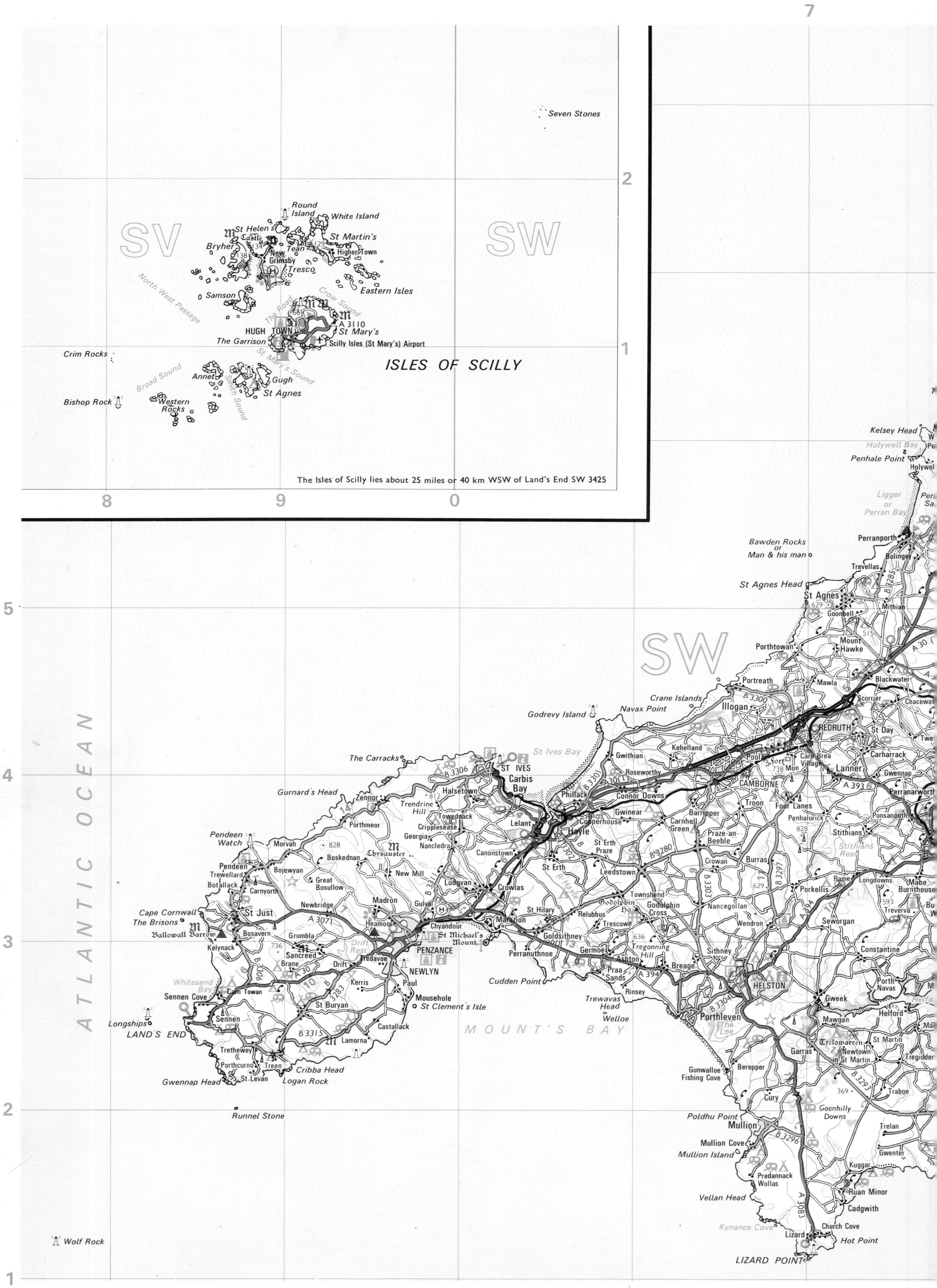

ISLES OF SCILLY (inset map)

Seven Stones

SV

SW

Round Island
White Island
St Helen's
Castle
Bryher
New
Grimsby
Teän
Tresco
St Martin's
Higher Town
Eastern Isles
North West Passage
Samson
Crow Sound
The Road
HUGH TOWN
A 3110
St Mary's
The Garrison
Scilly Isles (St Mary's) Airport
St Mary's Sound
Crim Rocks
Broad Sound
Annet
Gugh
St Agnes
South Sound
Bishop Rock
Western
Rocks

ISLES OF SCILLY

The Isles of Scilly lies about 25 miles or 40 km WSW of Land's End SW 3425

Kelsey Head
Holywell Bay
Penhale Point
Holywel
Ligger
or
Perran Bay
Per
Sa
Bawden Rocks
or
Man & his man
Perranporth
Bolingey
Trevellas
St Agnes Head
St Agnes
Mithian
Goonbell
Porthtowan
Mount
Hawke
SW
Portreath
Mawla
Blackwater
Crane Islands
Navax Point
Godrevy Island
Illogan
Scorrier
Chacewat
REDRUTH
St Day
Twe
Gwithian
Keheland
Pool
Carn Brea
Village
Carharrack
St Ives Bay
Phillack
Roseworthy
CAMBORNE
Lanner
Gwennap
The Carracks
ST IVES
Carbis
Bay
Connor Downs
Barripper
Troon
Four Lanes
Penhalurick
Perranarworth
Gurnard's Head
Zennor
Halsetown
Gwinear
Carnhell
Green
Praze-an-
Beeble
Ponsanooth
Trendrine
Hill
Towednack
Copperhouse
Stithians
Porthmeor
Cripplesease
Lelant
Hayle
Townshend
Crowan
Burras
Stithians
Resr
Pendeen
Watch
Morvah
Georgia
Nancledra
Canonstown
St Erth
Praze
Leedstown
Porkellis
Rame
Longdowns
Mabe
Burnthouse
Chysauster
Boskednan
828
New Mill
St Erth
Godolphin
Cross
Nancegollan
Treverva
Pendeen
Trewellard
Botallack
Bojewyan
Great
Bosullow
Ludgvan
Relubbus
Wendron
Seworgan
Carnyorth
Newbridge
Madron
Gulval
Crowlas
Townshend
Dolphin
Cross
Constantine
Cape Cornwall
St Just
A 3071
Heamoor
Chyandour
St Hilary
Goldsithney
Tregonning
Hill
Sithney
The Brisons
Bosavern
Grumbla
Marazion
Germoe
Breage
Porth
Navas
Ballowall Barrow
Kelynack
736
Sancreed
Drift
Tredavoe
PENZANCE
St Michael's
Mount
Perranuthnoe
HELSTON
Gweek
Helford
Brane
Drift
NEWLYN
Ashton
Praa
Sands
Garras
Trelowarren
Newtown-
in-St Martin
St Martin
Whitesand
Bay
Carn Towan
Kerris
Paul
Cudden Point
Rinsey
Porthleven
The
Loe
Mawgan
Tregidden
Sennen Cove
Mousehole
St Clement's Isle
Trewavas
Head
Welloe
Longships
Sennen
St Buryan
Castallack
MOUNT'S BAY
Gunwalloe
Fishing Cove
Berepper
Cury
Traboe
LAND'S END
B 3315
Lamorna
Poldhu Point
Goonhilly
Downs
Trethewey
Treen
Cribba Head
Mullion
Trelan
Porthcurno
St Levan
Logan Rock
Gwennap Head
Runnel Stone
Mullion Cove
Mullion Island
Gwenter
Kuggar
Predannack
Wollas
Ruan Minor
Cadgwith
Vellan Head
Kynance Cove
Church Cove
Wolf Rock
Lizard
Hot Point
LIZARD POINT

ATLANTIC OCEAN

86

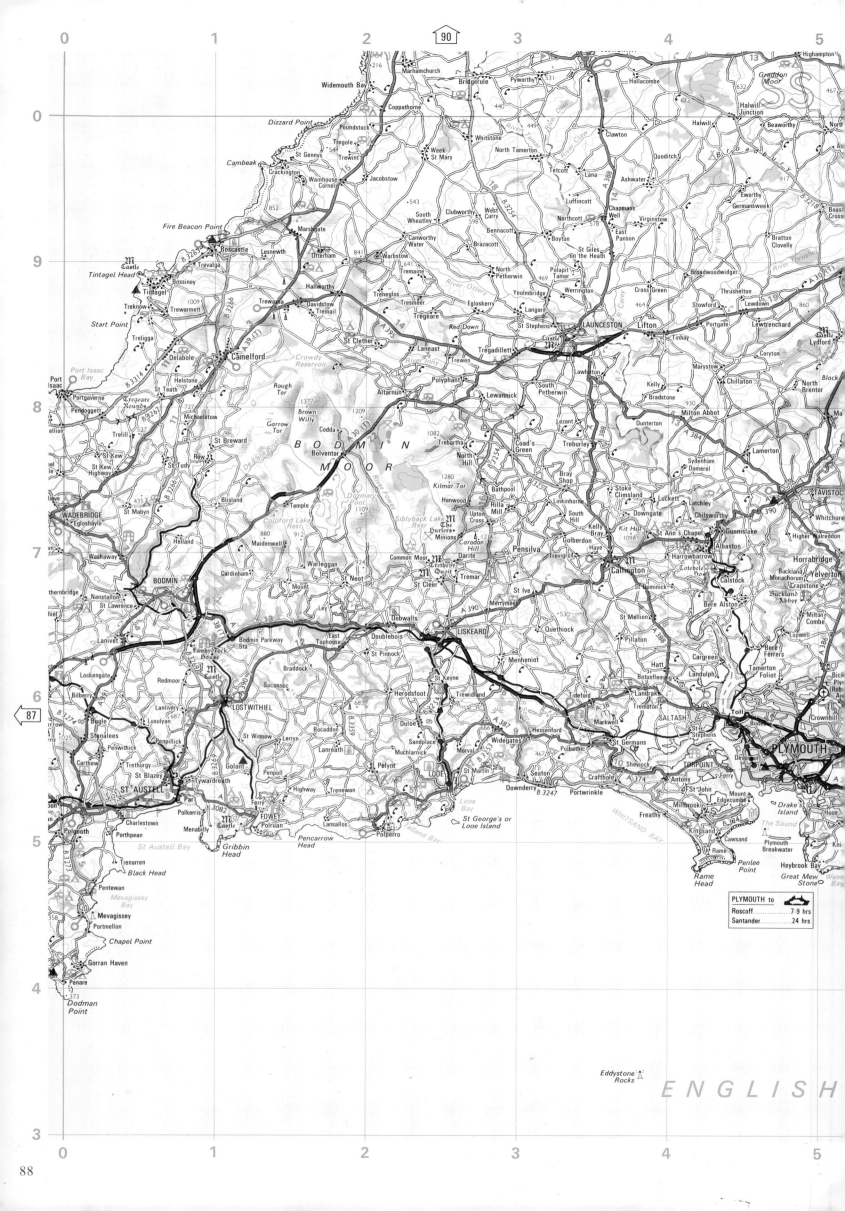

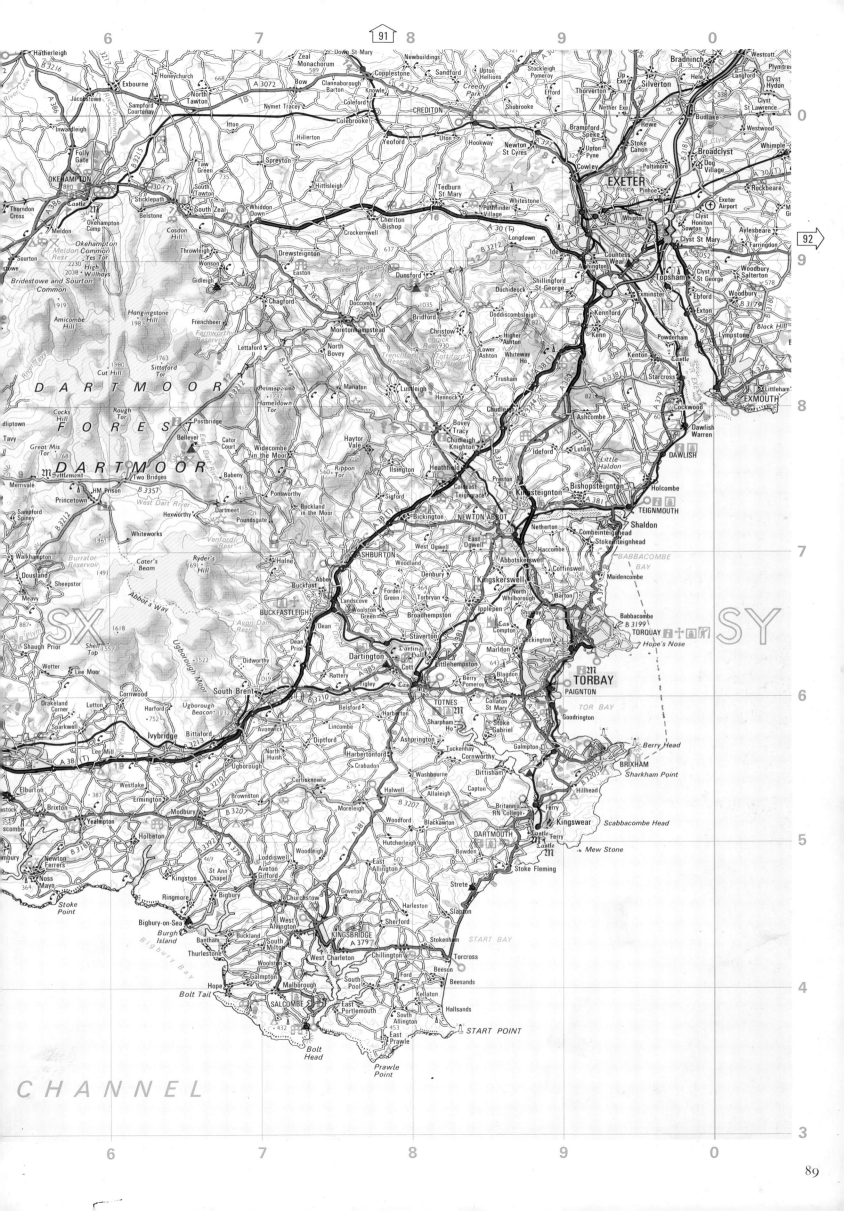

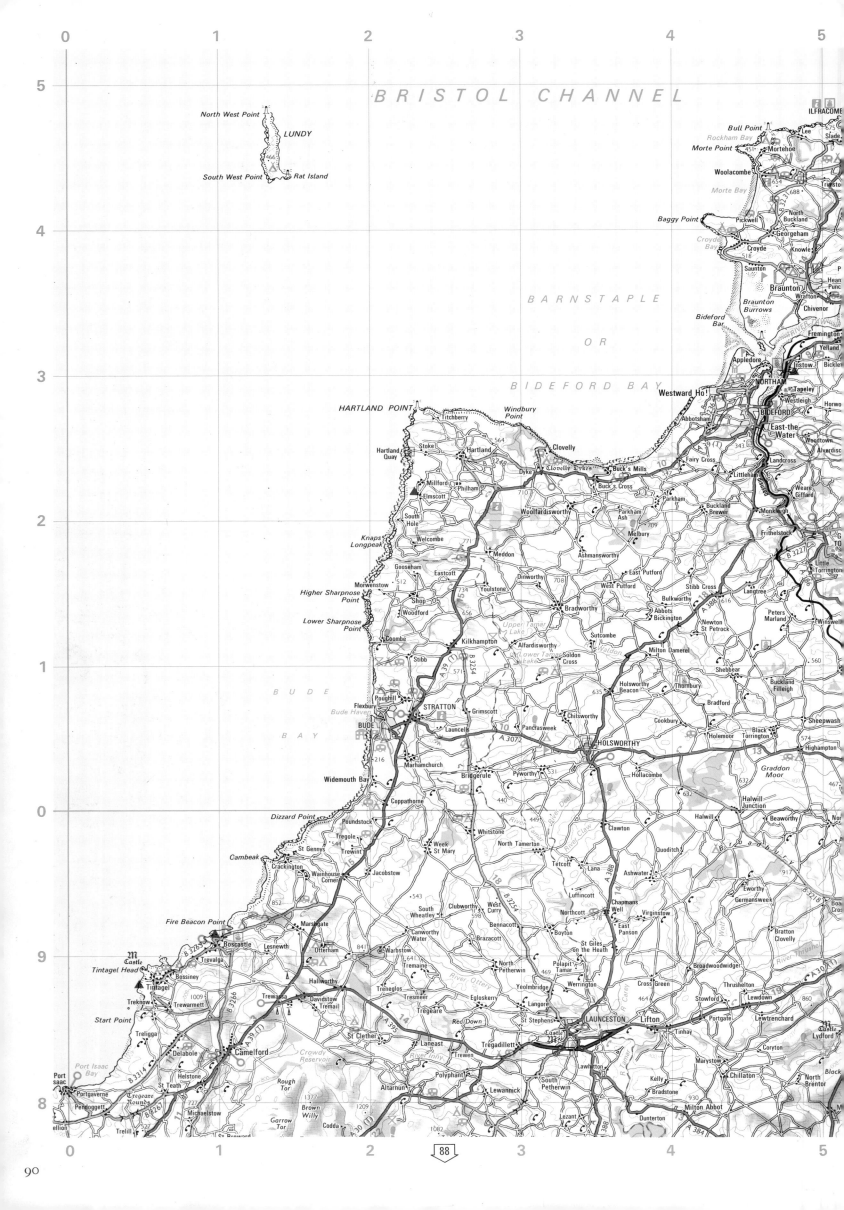

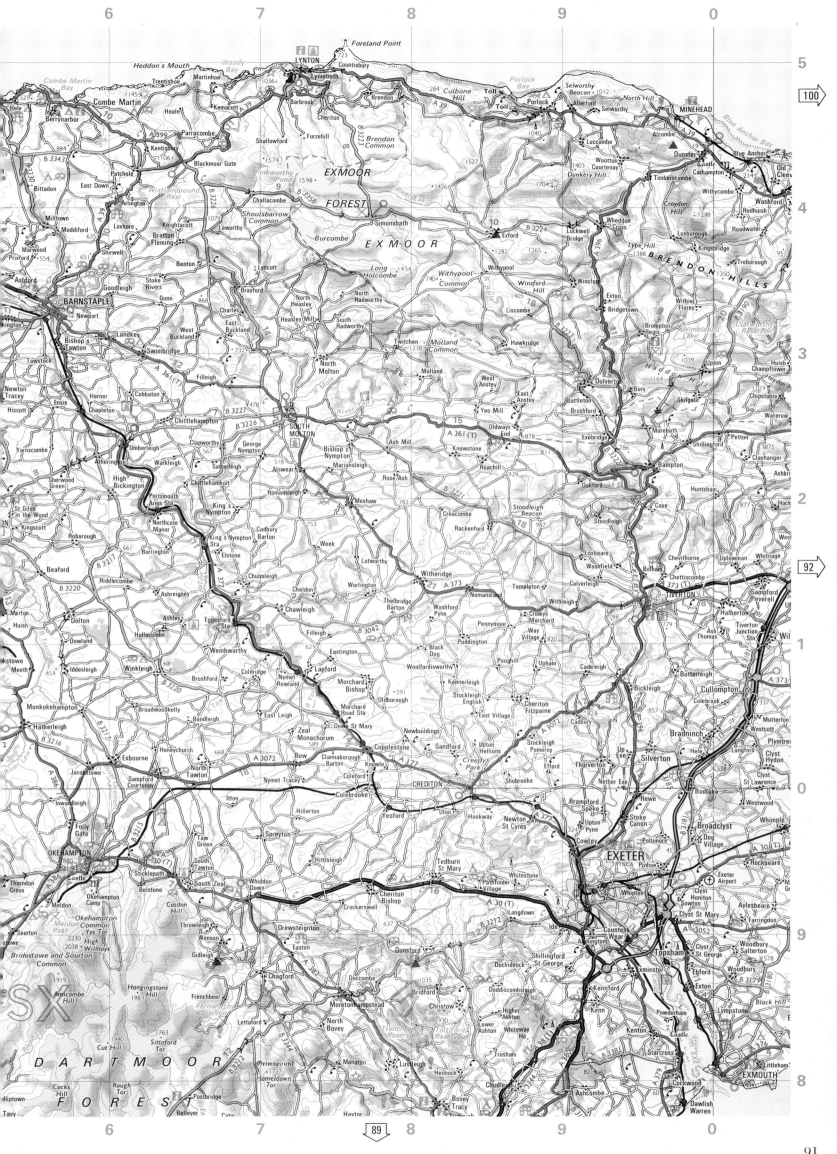

96

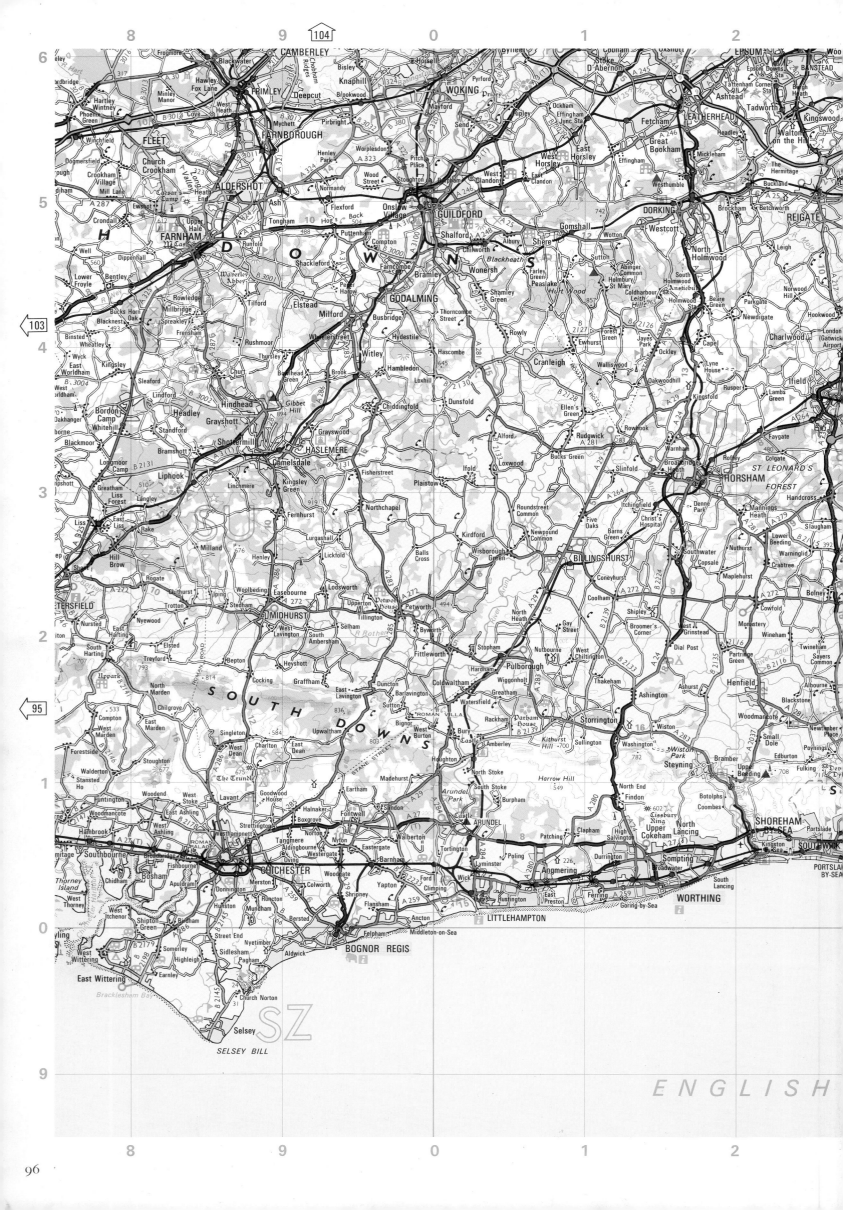

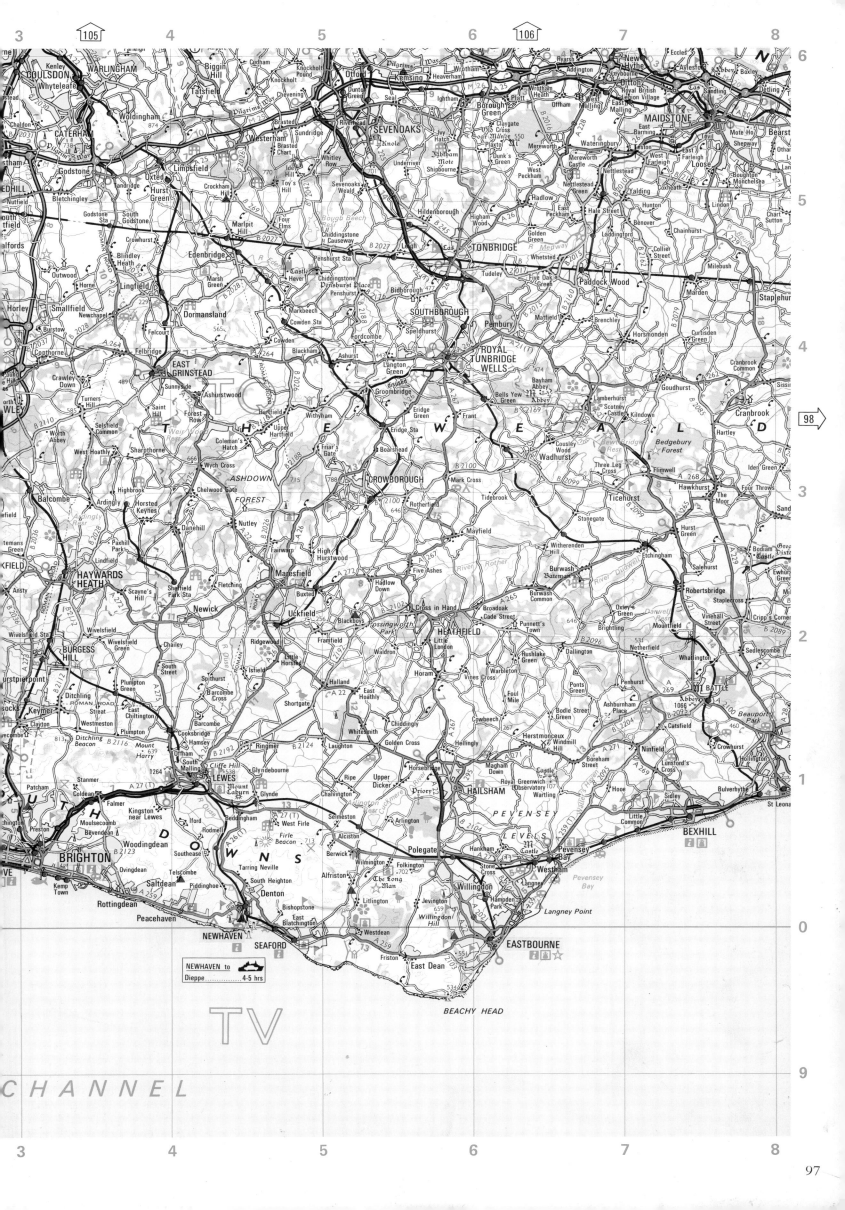

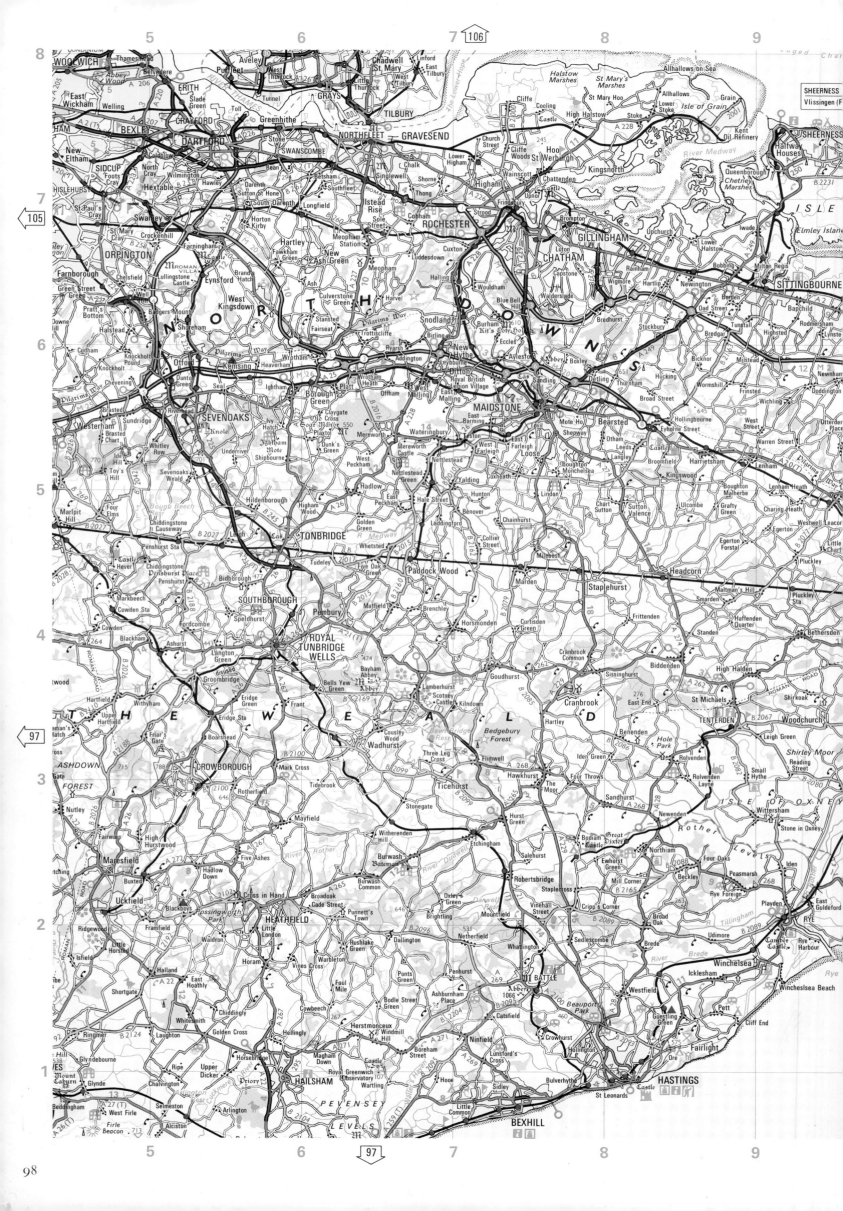

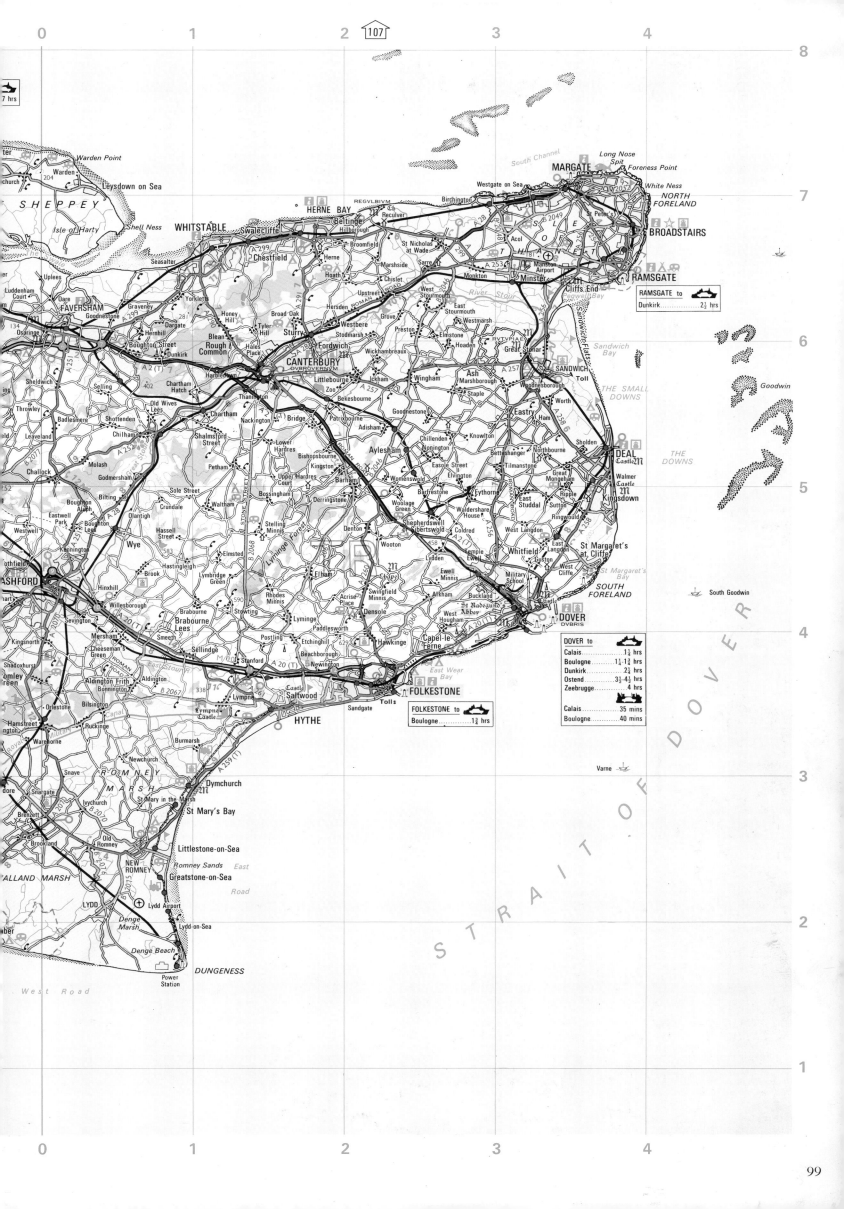

SHEPPEY

Warden Point
Warden
Leysdown on Sea
Isle of Harty
Shell Ness
Seasalter

South Channel
Long Nose Spit
Foreness Point
MARGATE
White Ness
NORTH FORELAND

WHITSTABLE
HERNE BAY
Beltinge
Hillborough
Reculver
Birchington
Westgate on Sea
St Peter's
BROADSTAIRS
Swalecliffe
Chestfield
Broomfield
Herne
Hoath
St Nicholas at Wade
Marshside
Chislet
Acol
Manston Airport
Minster
RAMSGATE

Uplees
Luddenham Court
Oare
FAVERSHAM
Graveney
Goodnestone
Honey Hill
Broad Oak
Upstreet
West Stourmouth
East Stourmouth
Westmarsh
Cliffs End
Pegwell Bay

Ospringe
Sheldwich
Selling
Hernhill
Boughton Street
Dunkirk
Dargate
Yorkletts
Tyler Hill
Sturry
Westbere
Stodmarsh
Preston
Elmstone
Hoaden
Great Stonar
Sandwich Bay

REGVLBIVM
RVTVPIAE
SANDWICH
Toll
THE SMALL DOWNS
Goodwin

Throwley
Badlesmere
Leaveland
Shottenden
Chilham
Old Wives Lees
Chartham Hatch
Harbledown
CANTERBURY
DVBROVERNVM
Littlebourne
Zoo
Ickham
Wingham
Marshborough
Staple
Woodnesborough
Worth

Challock
Molash
Godmersham
Chartham
Nackington
Bridge
Patrixbourne
Bekesbourne
Goodnestone
Eastry
Ham
Sholden
DEAL
Castle
THE DOWNS

Boughton Aluph
Bilting
Shalmsford Street
Lower Hardres
Bishopsbourne
Kingston
Adisham
Chillenden
Nonington
Knowlton
Betteshanger
Northbourne
Walmer Castle
Kingsdown

Westwell
Eastwell Park
Boughton Lees
Olantigh
Crundale
Waltham
Petham
Upper Hardres Court
Barham
Aylesham
Easole Street
Elvington
Great Mongeham
Ripple
Sutton
Ringwould

Kennington
Wye
Hassell Street
Sole Street
Bossingham
Derringstone
Womenswold
Woolage Green
Barfrestone
Eythorne
East Studdal
East Langdon

ASHFORD
Hinxhill
Willesborough
Brook
Hastingleigh
Elmsted
Stelling Minnis
Denton
Wooton
Shepherdswell
Sibertswold
Coldred
Waldershare House
West Langdon
Whitfield
Guston
St Margaret's at Cliffe
St Margaret's Bay
SOUTH FORELAND

Kingsnorth
Sevington
Mersham
Brabourne
Brabourne Lees
Smeeth
Lymbridge Green
Rhodes Minnis
Lyminge Forest
Elham
Lydden
Ewell Minnis
Temple Ewell
Military School
West Cliffe
Castle
South Goodwin

Shadoxhurst
Cheeseman's Green
Sellindge
Stowting
Lyminge
Paddlesworth
Postling
Etchinghill
Acrise Place
Swingfield Minnis
Densole
Alkham
West Hougham
St Radegund Abbey
Buckland
DOVER
DVBRIS

Bromley Green
Aldington Frith
Bonnington
Aldington
Smeeth
Stanford
Newington
Beachborough
Hawkinge
Capel-le-Ferne
East Wear Bay

Hamstreet
Warehorne
Orlestone
Bilsington
Lympne
Lympne Castle
FOLKESTONE
Sandgate
HYTHE
Tolls

Ruckinge
Newchurch
Burmarsh
Dymchurch
Snave
ROMNEY MARSH
St Mary in the Marsh
St Mary's Bay

Snargate
Ivychurch
St Mary's Bay
Littlestone-on-Sea
Romney Sands
East Road
Greatstone-on-Sea

Brenzett
Brookland
Old Romney
NEW ROMNEY
WALLAND MARSH
LYDD
Denge Marsh
Lydd Airport
Lydd-on-Sea

DUNGENESS
Denge Beach
Power Station
West Road

STRAIT OF DOVER

South Channel
Varne

RAMSGATE to
Dunkirk............2½ hrs

FOLKESTONE to
Boulogne............1¾ hrs

DOVER to
Calais............1¼ hrs
Boulogne............1¼-1¾ hrs
Dunkirk............2¼ hrs
Ostend............3½-4½ hrs
Zeebrugge............4 hrs

Calais............35 mins
Boulogne............40 mins

7 hrs

A 2 (T)
A 251
A 299
A 28
A 290
A 291
A 257
A 258
A 256
A 253
A 2049
A 2055
A 20 (T)
M 20
A 259 (T)
B 2067
B 2068
B 2046
B 2011
B 2015

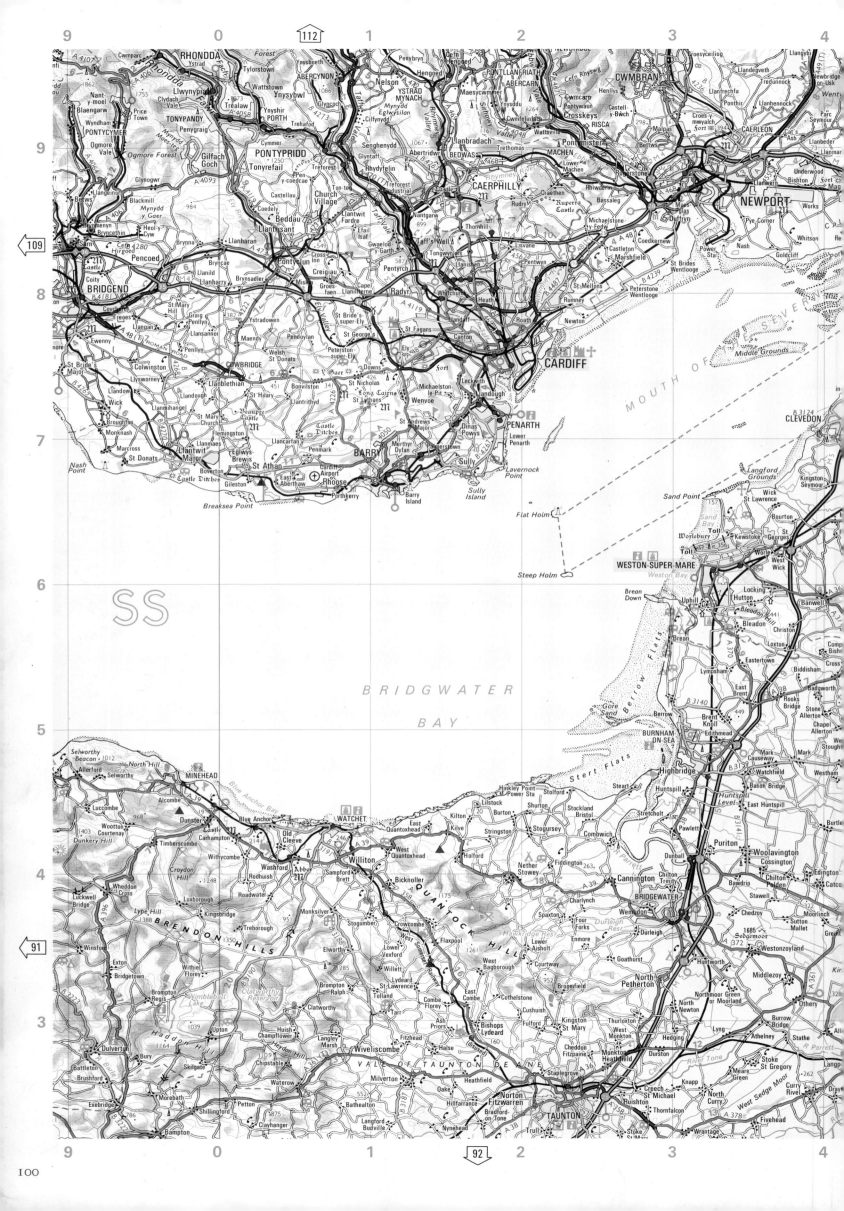

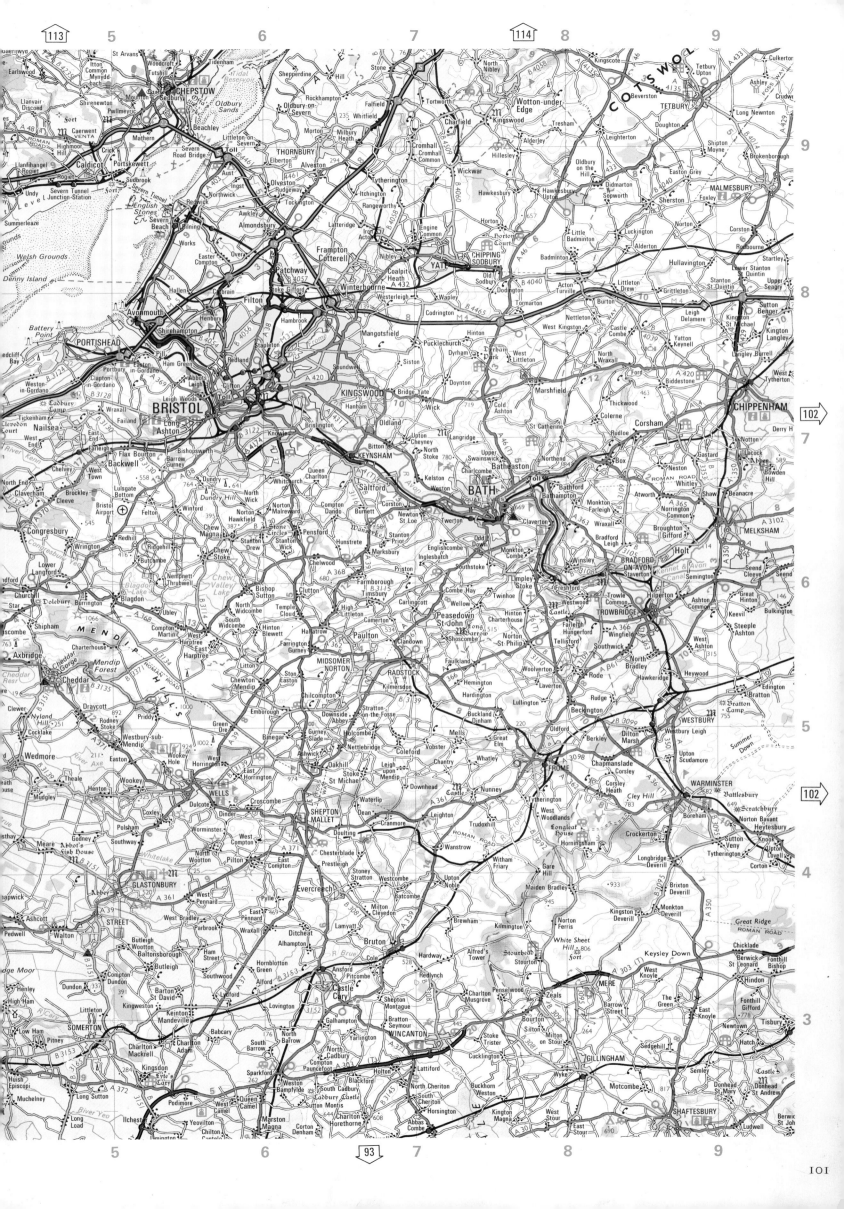

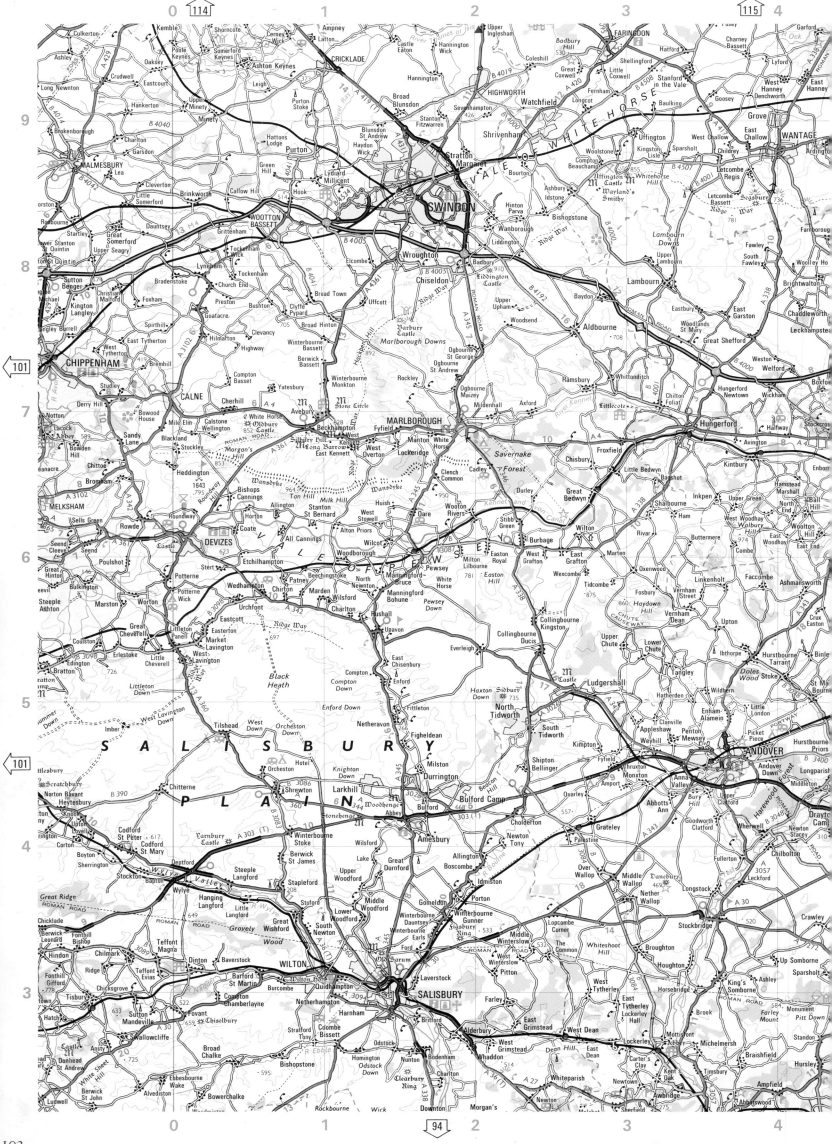

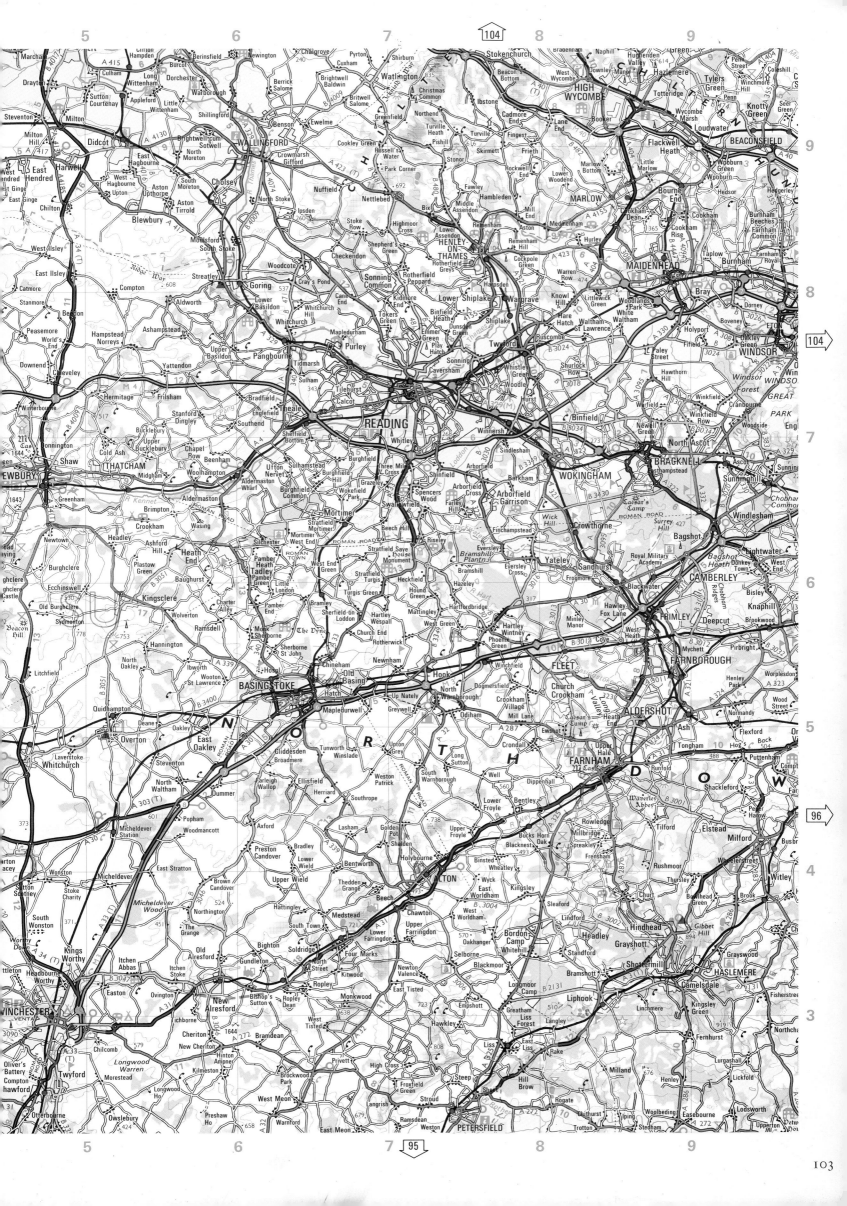

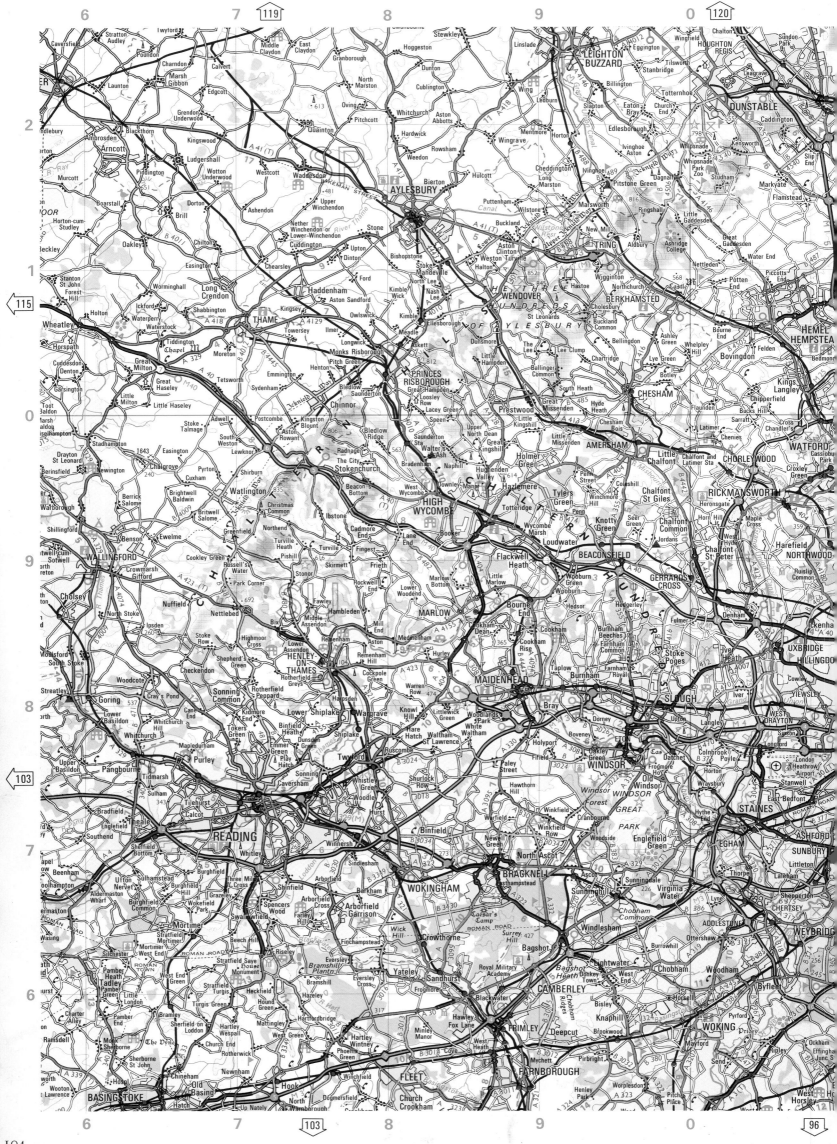

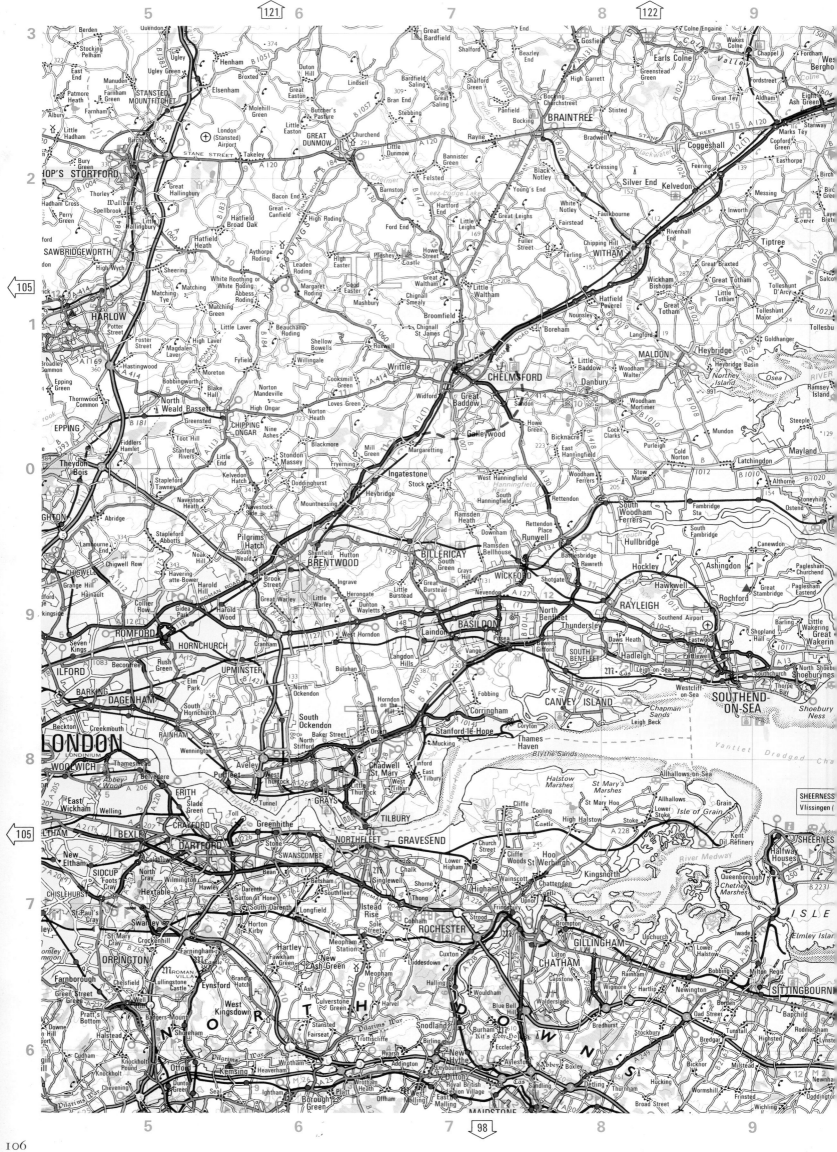

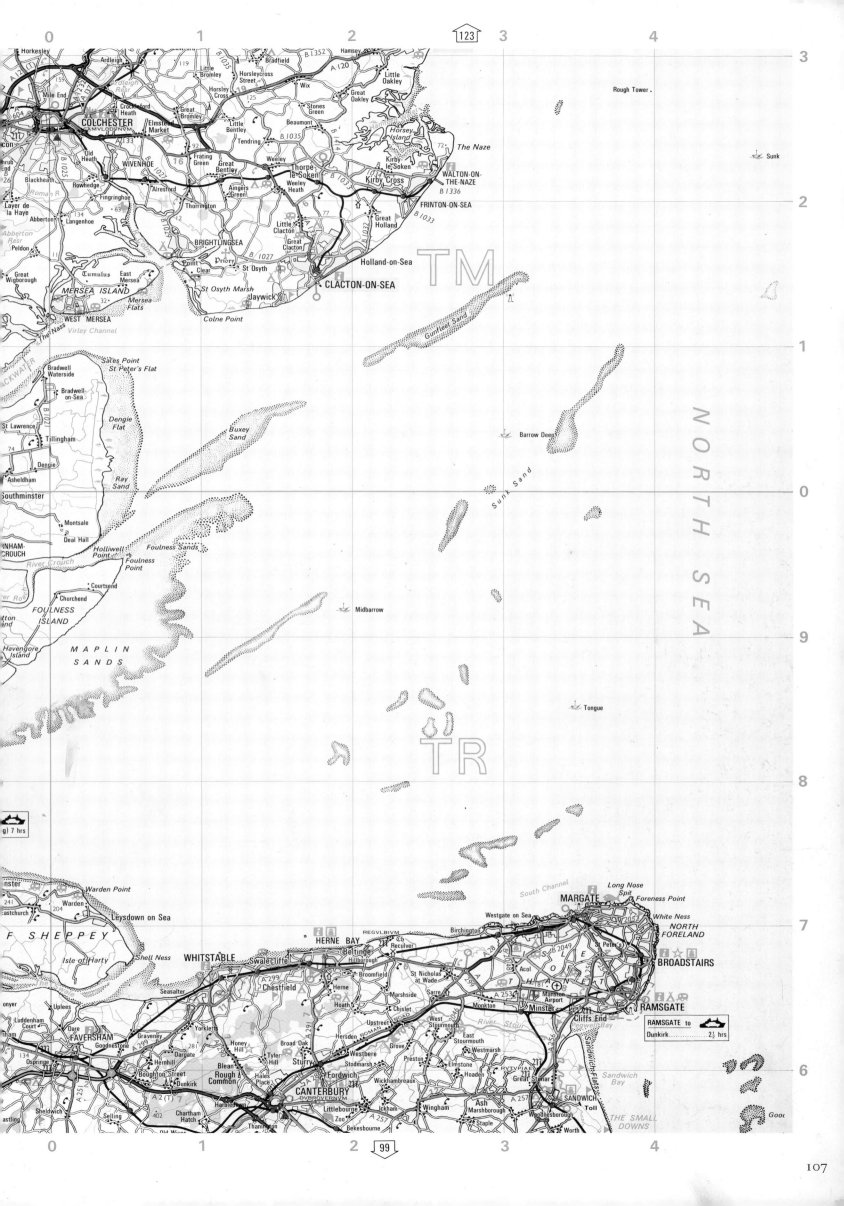

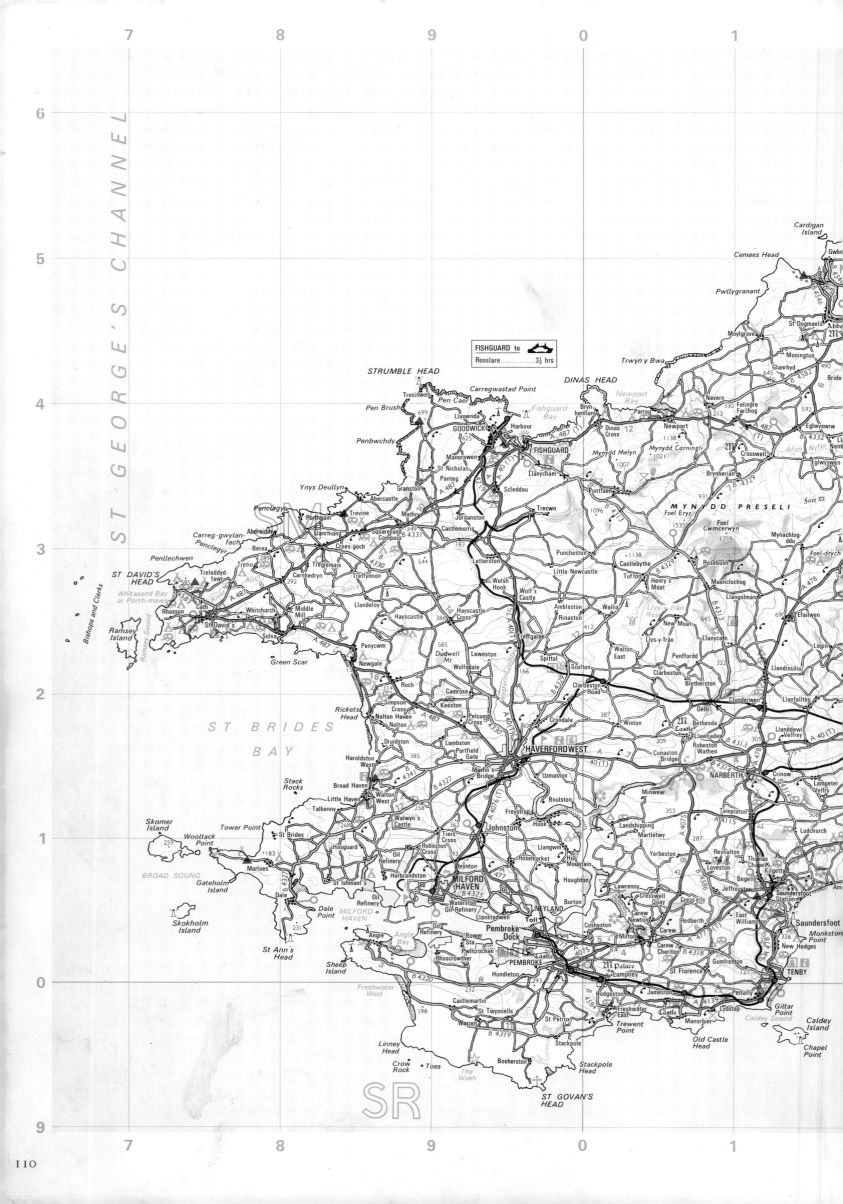

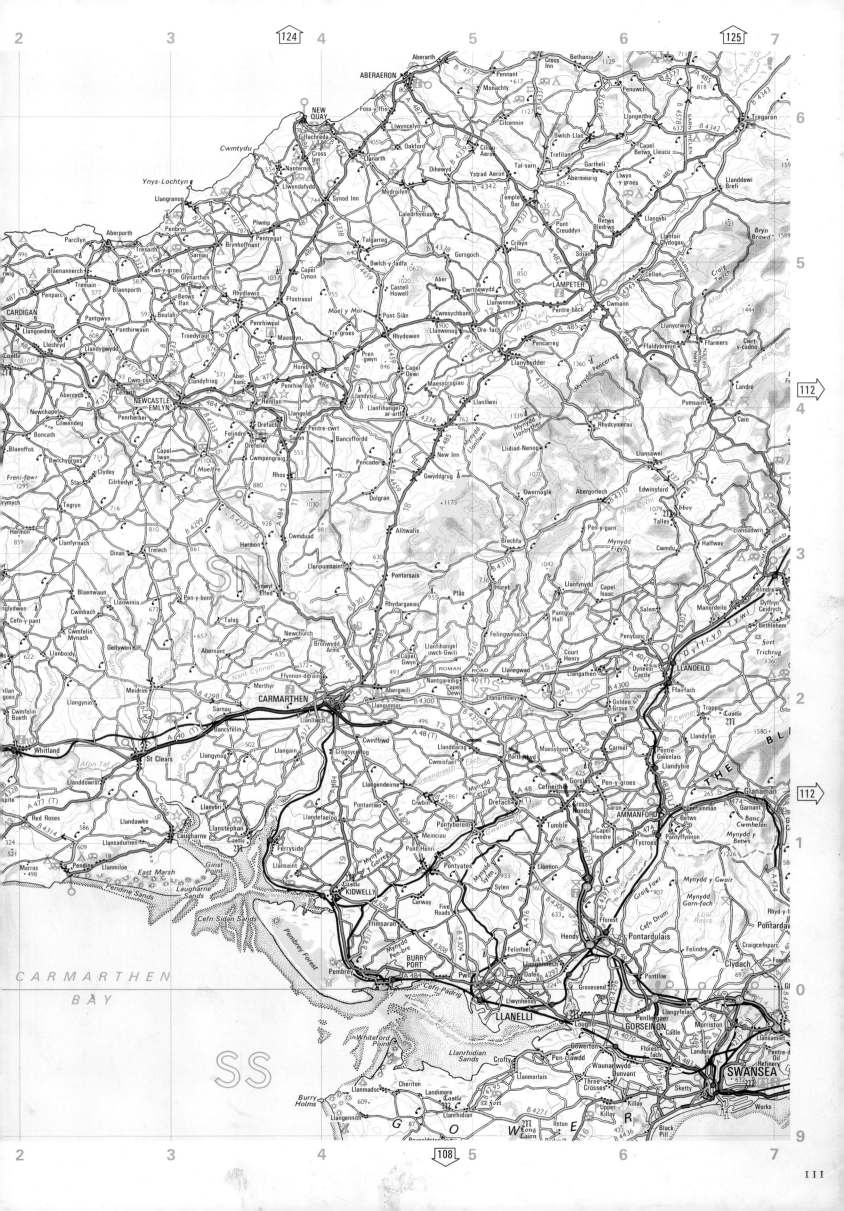

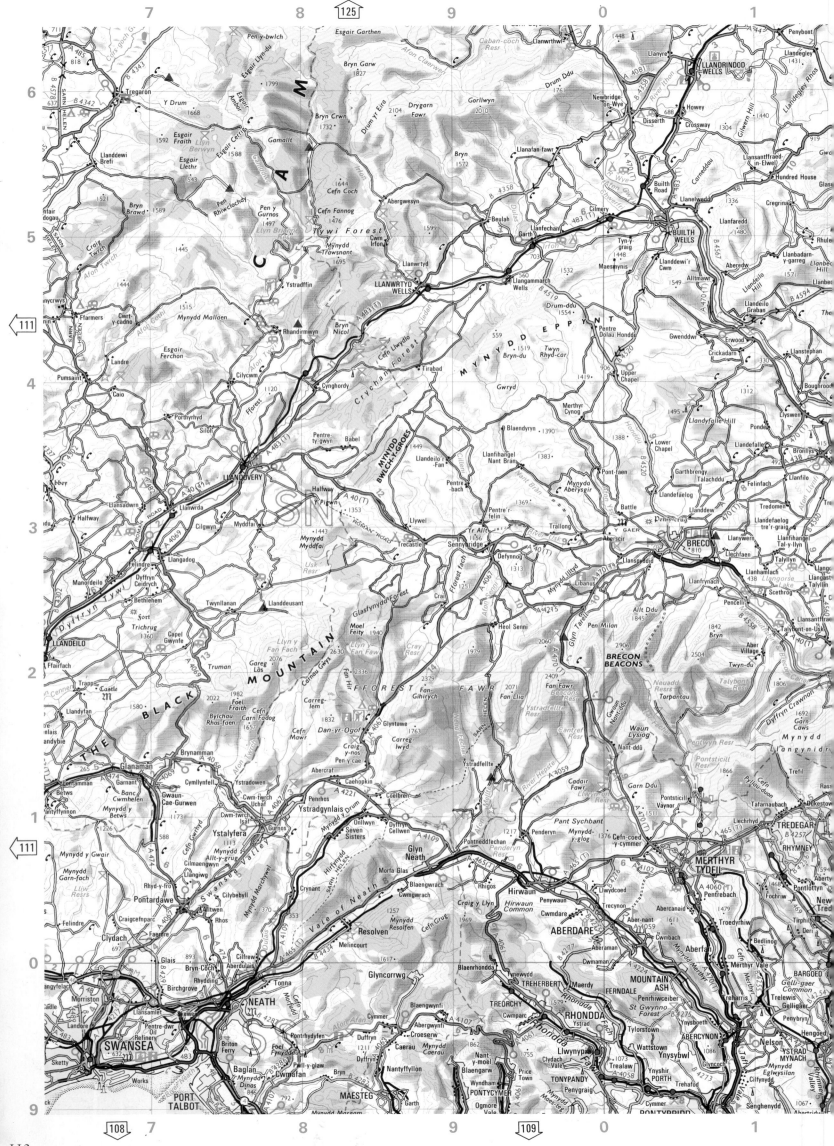

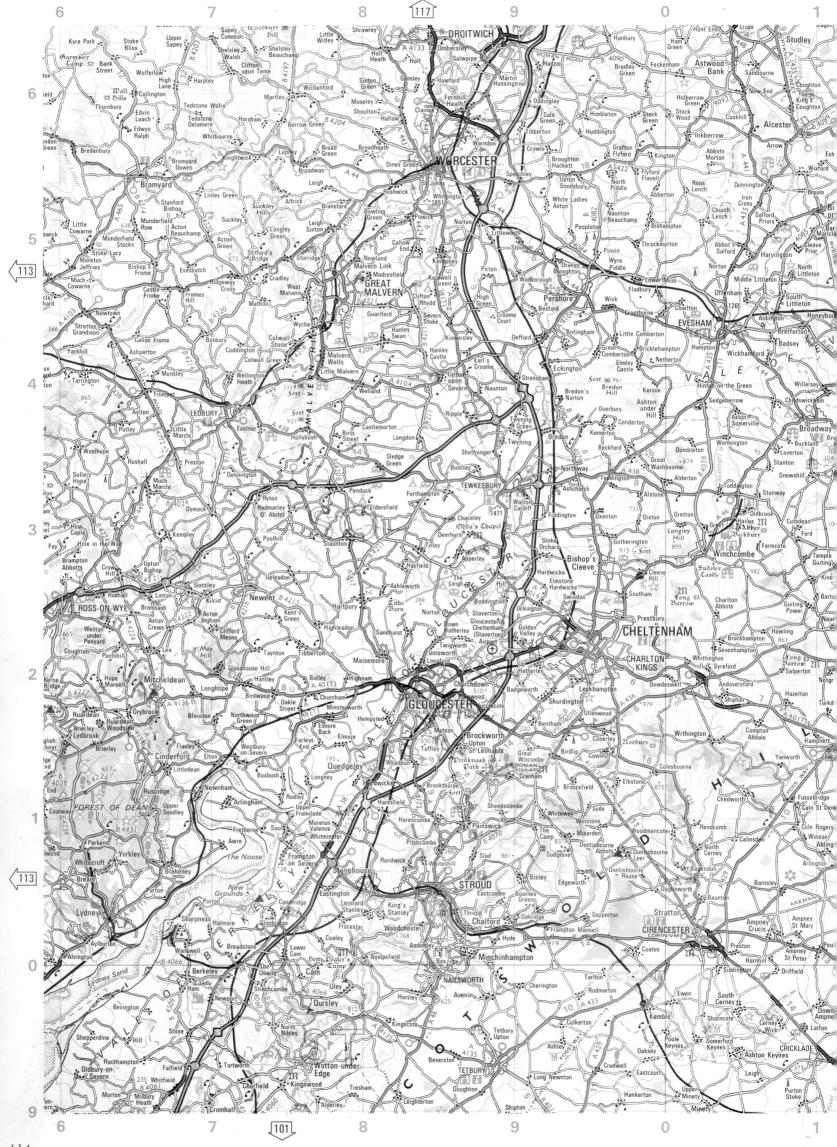

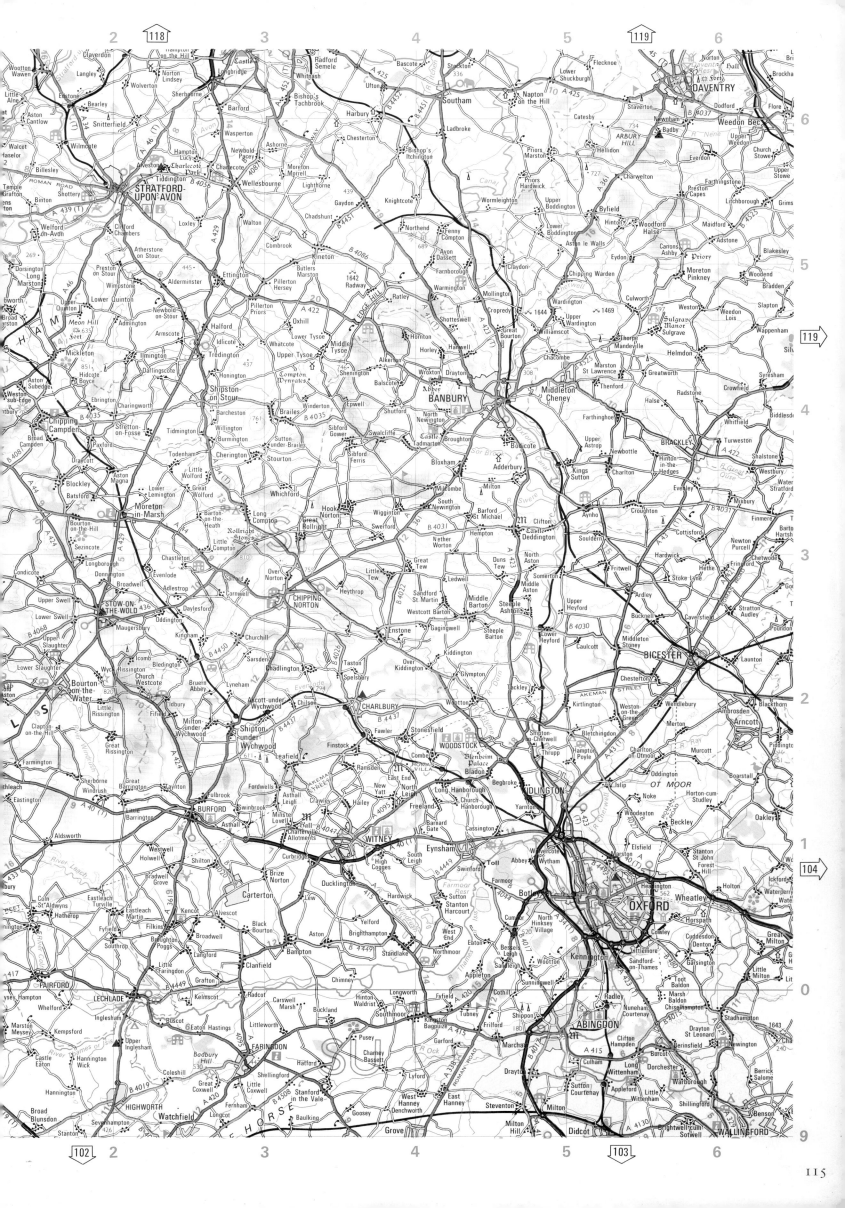

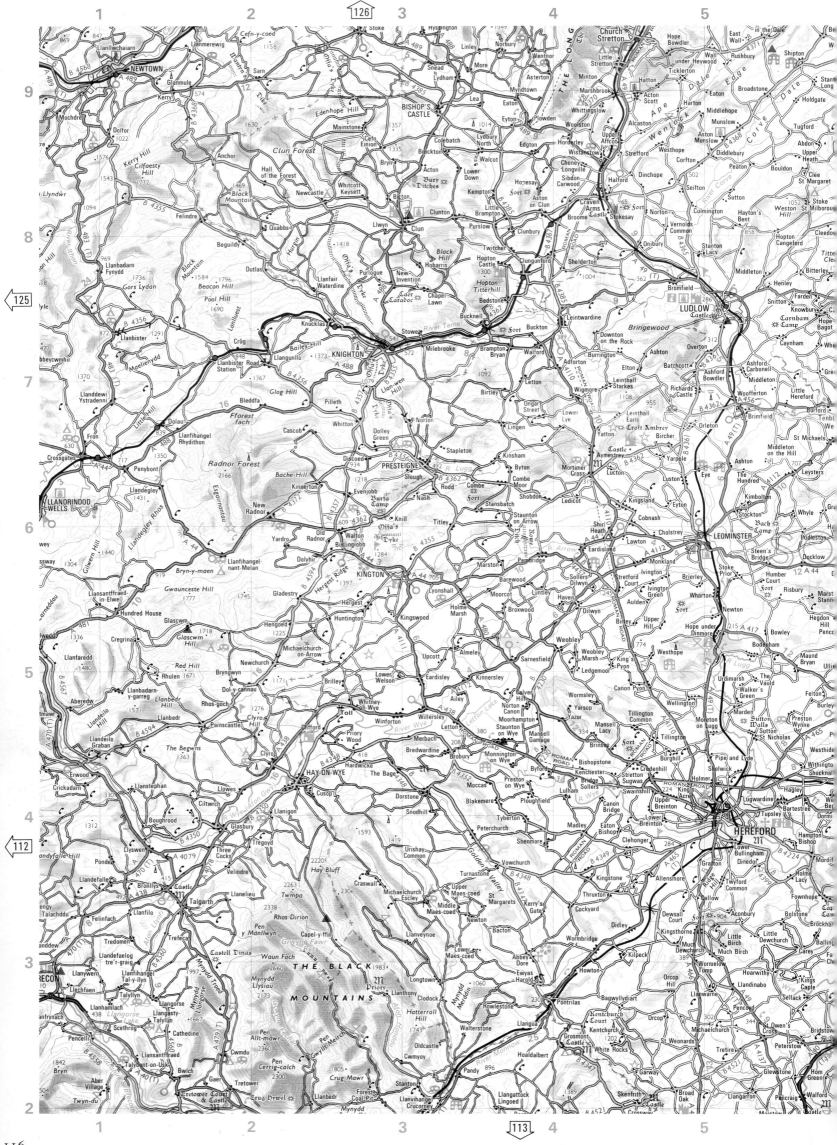

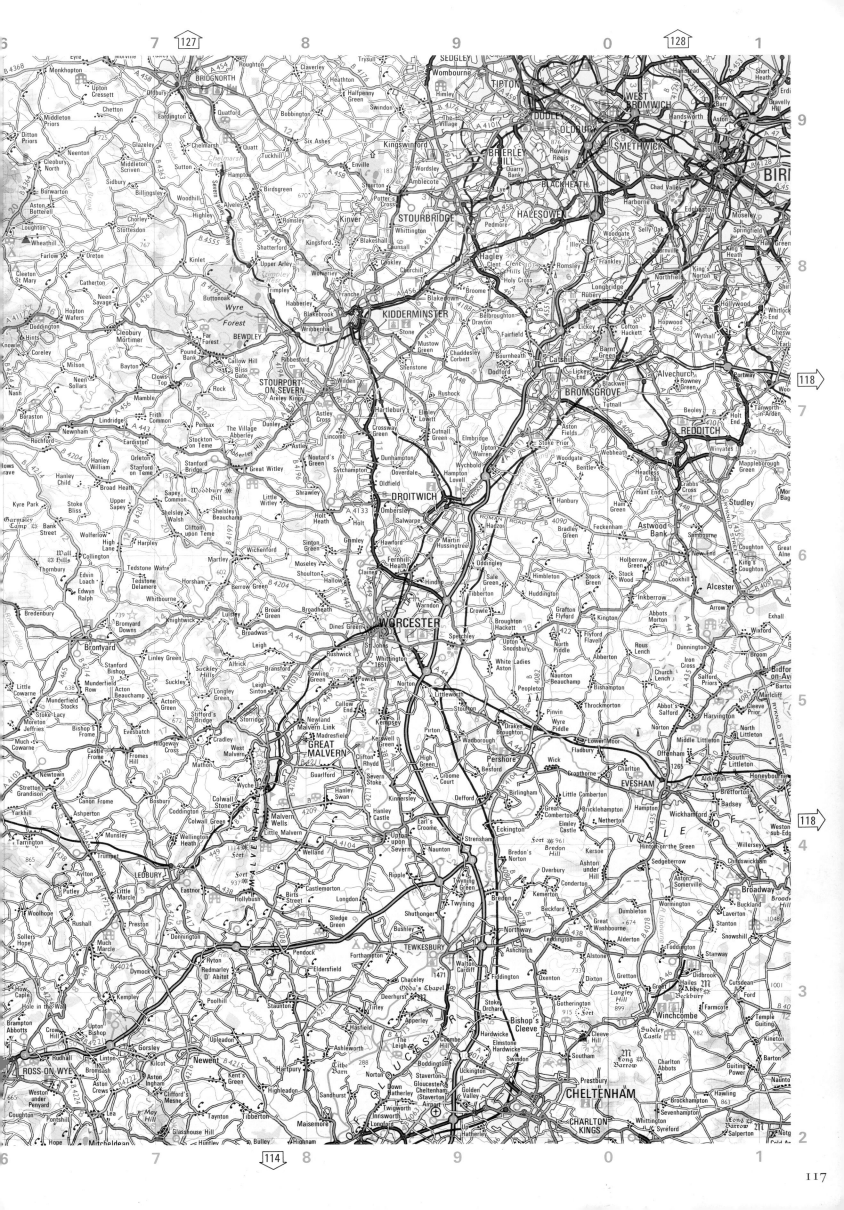

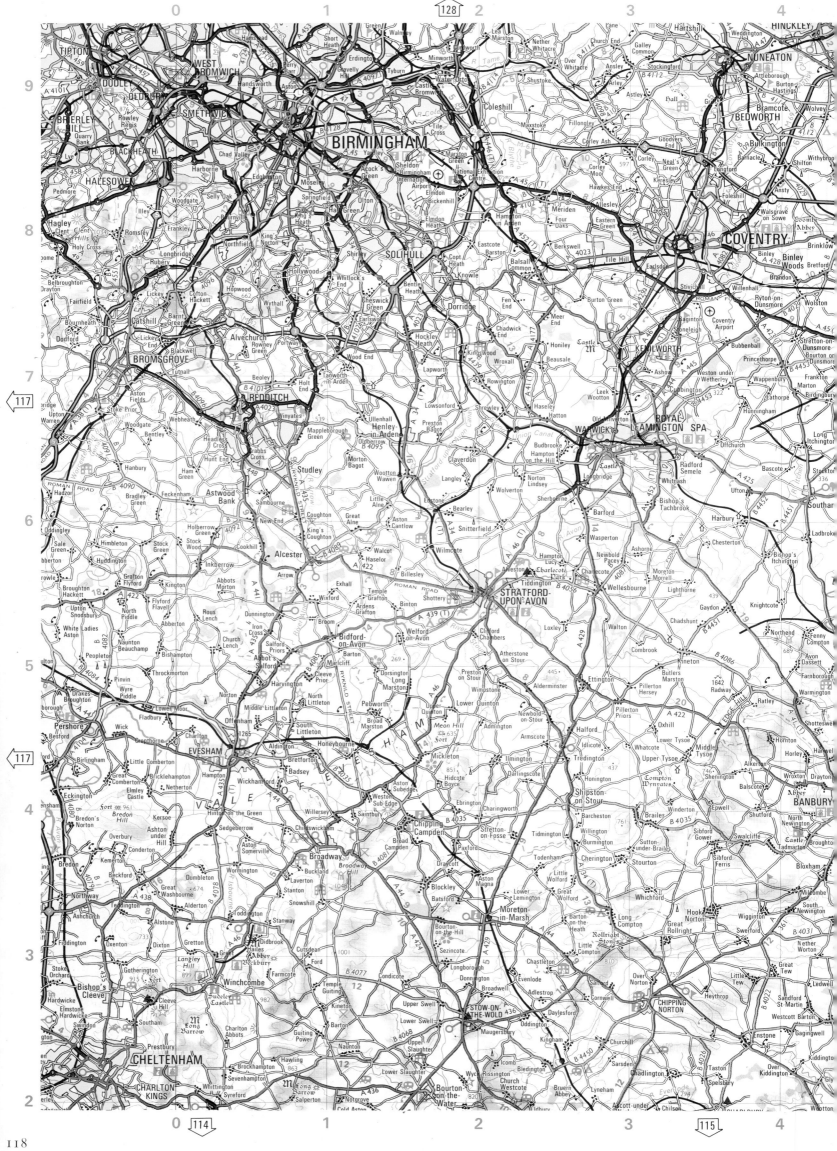

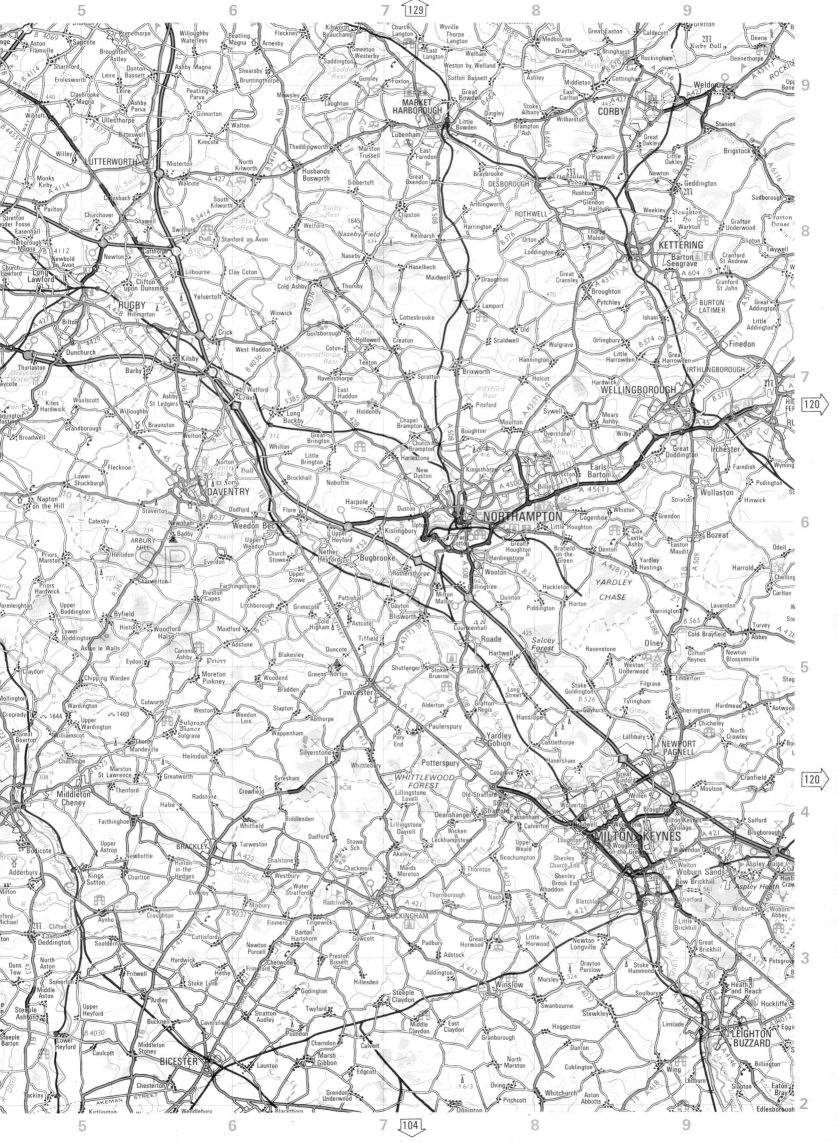

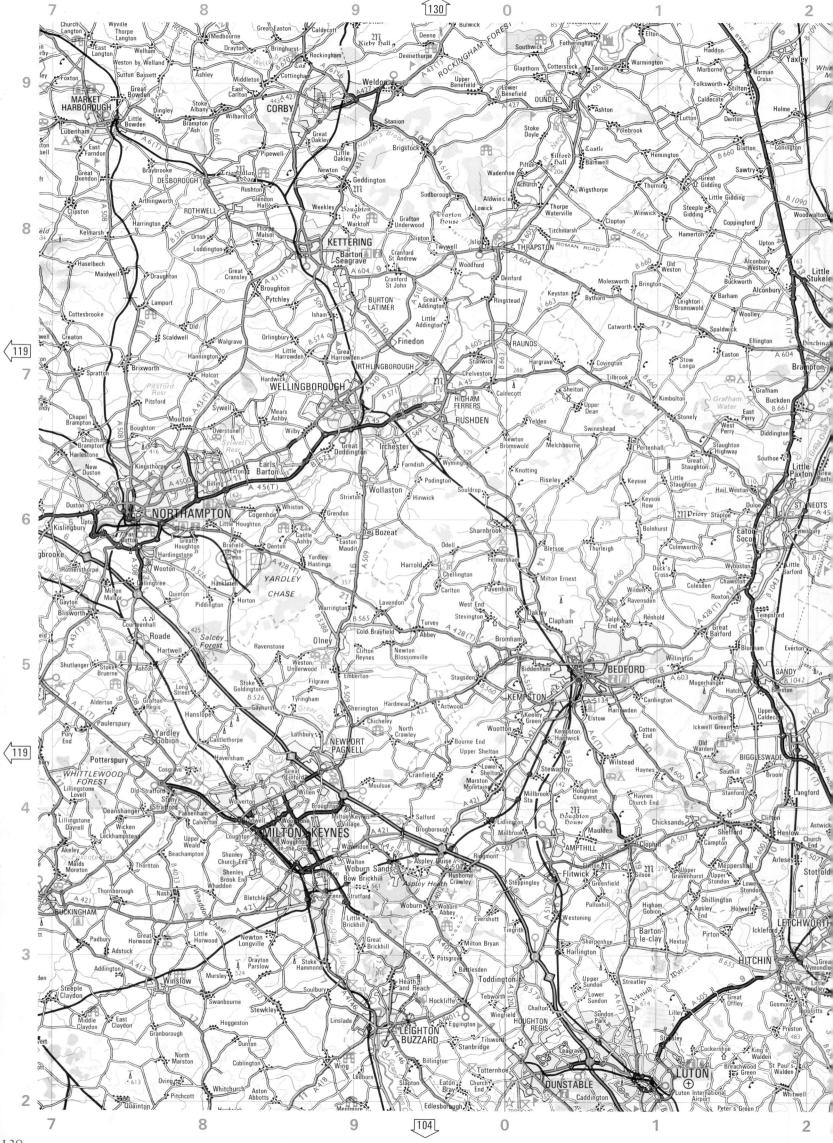

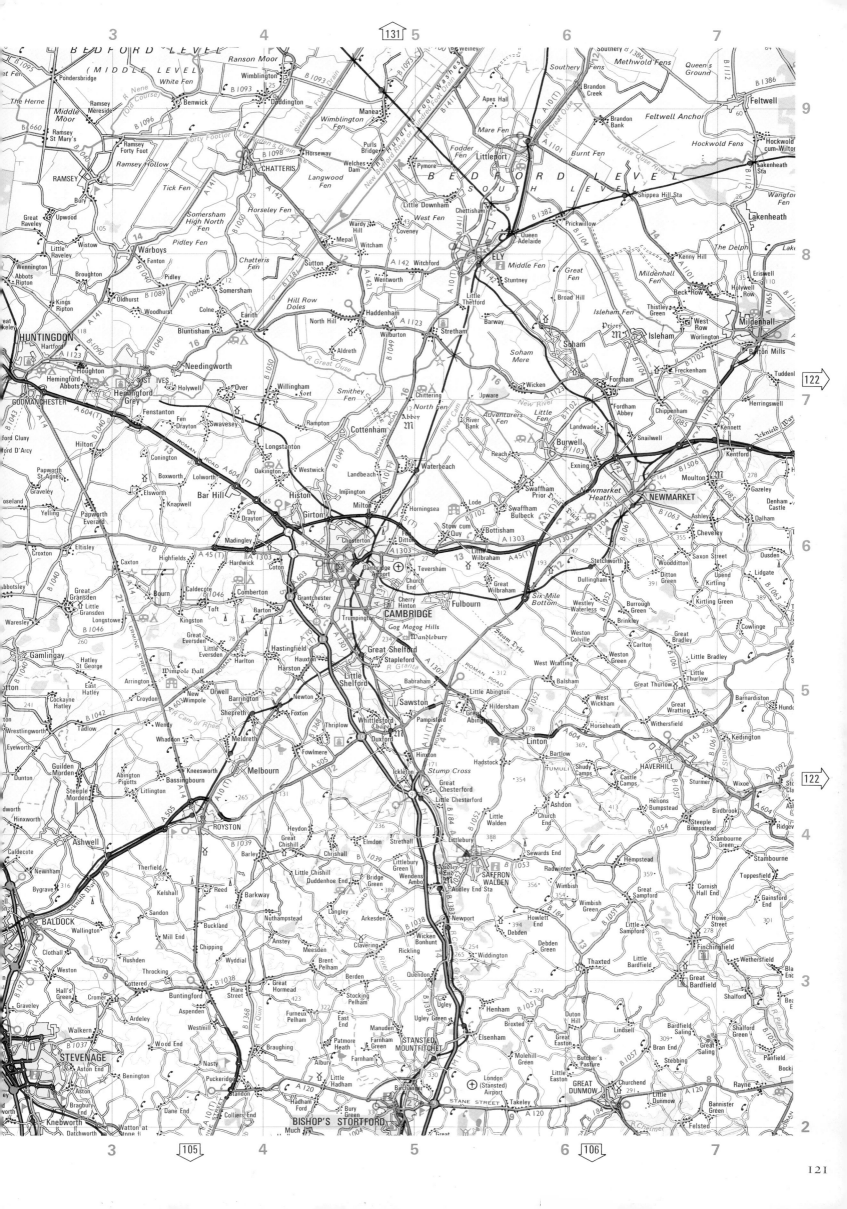

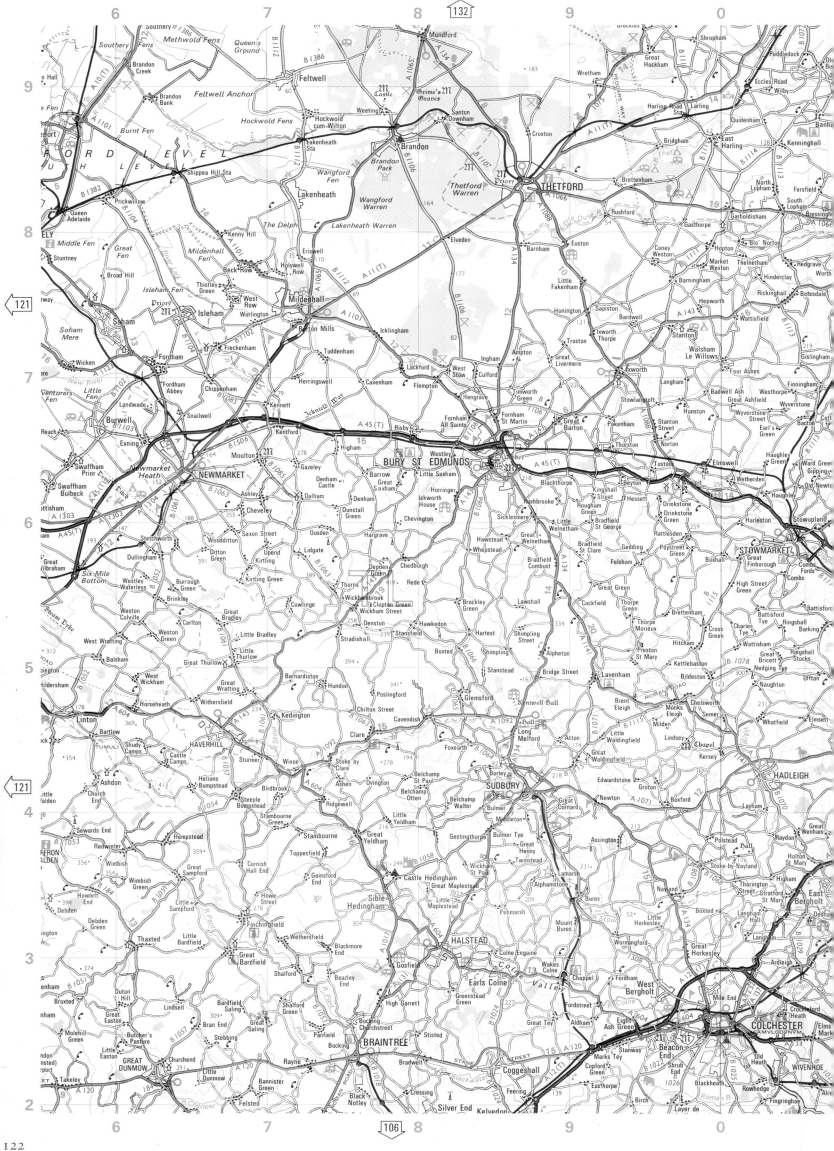

SH

Porthor

Penrhyn Mawr
Ty-hen
Bryncroes
Botwnnog
Rhedyn
Llanbedrog
Rhydlios
Rhoshirwaun
Llanbedrog
Nanhoron
Trwyn
Llanbedrog
Capel
Carmel
Castell
Llawr Dref
Llangian
St Tudwal's
Road
Braich Anelog
Rhiw
Llanengan
Llwchmynydd
Aberdaron
Sarn Bach
Braich y Pwll
Uwchmynydd
Bwlchtocyn
St Tudwal's
Islands
Pen y Cil
Ynys Gwylan-fawr
Cilan Uchaf
Trwyn yr Wylfa

Bardsey Sound
Trwyn Cilan

Bardsey Island
(Ynys Enlli)

Harlech
Llanfair
Pen-sarn
Llandanwg
Llanbedr
Coed Ystumgwern
Burial Cham
Dyffryn Ardud
Tal-y-bont
Llana
BARMOUTH
The Bar
Barmouth Bay
Fairbourne

C A R D I G A N

B A Y

Llwyngwril
Llangelynnin
Rhoslefain
Llanfendigaid
Aber Dysynni
TYWYN
Caethle
Aberdy
Aberdovey Bar
Ynyslas
Borth
Upper Borth
Llangorwen
ABERYSTWYTH
Llanbadar
The Bar
Pen Dinas
Penparcau
Rhydyfelin

SN

Llanfarian
Blaenplwyf
Rhadmad
Llanddeiniol
Carreg Ti-pw
Llanrhystud
Trefe
Llansantffraed
Rhyd-Rosser
Llanon
Nebo
Aberarth
Bethania
Cross Inn
Aberaeron
Pennant
Monachty
Penuwch
NEW QUAY
Foss-y-ffin
Llwyncelyn
Cilcennin
Bwlch-Llan
Gilfachreda
Oakford
Cilia
Cwmtydu

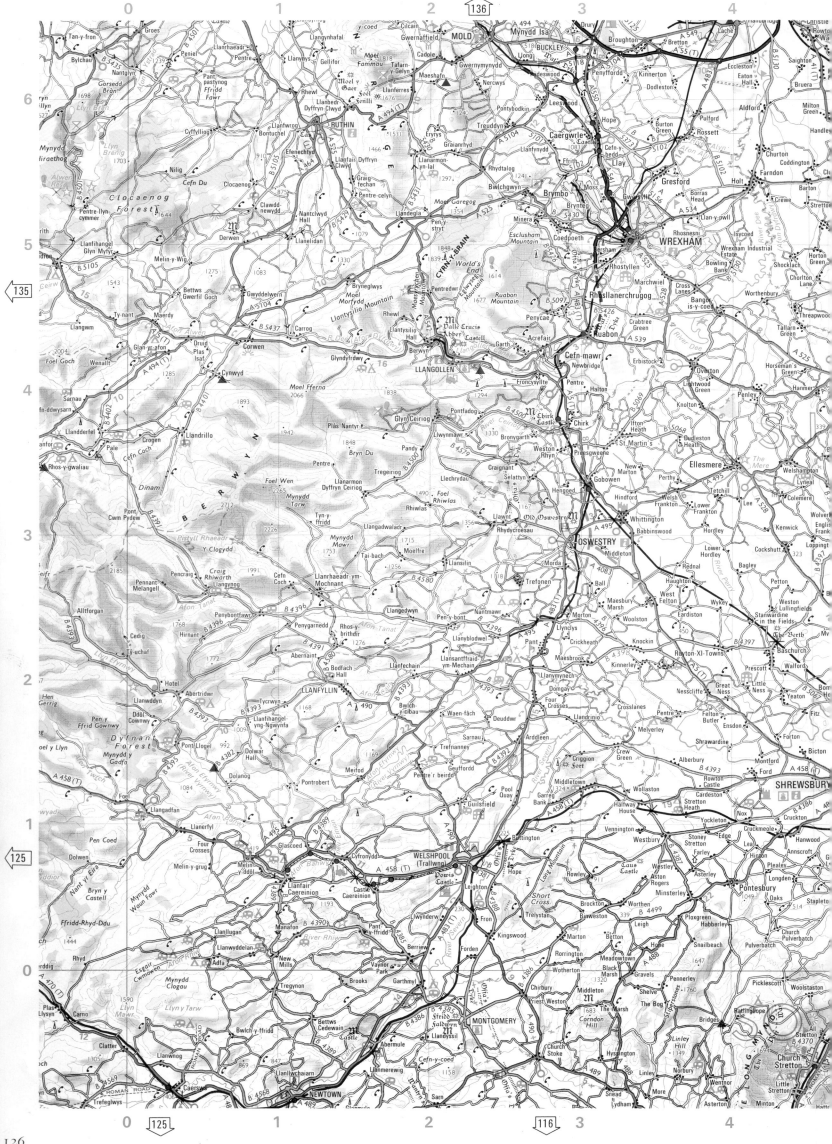

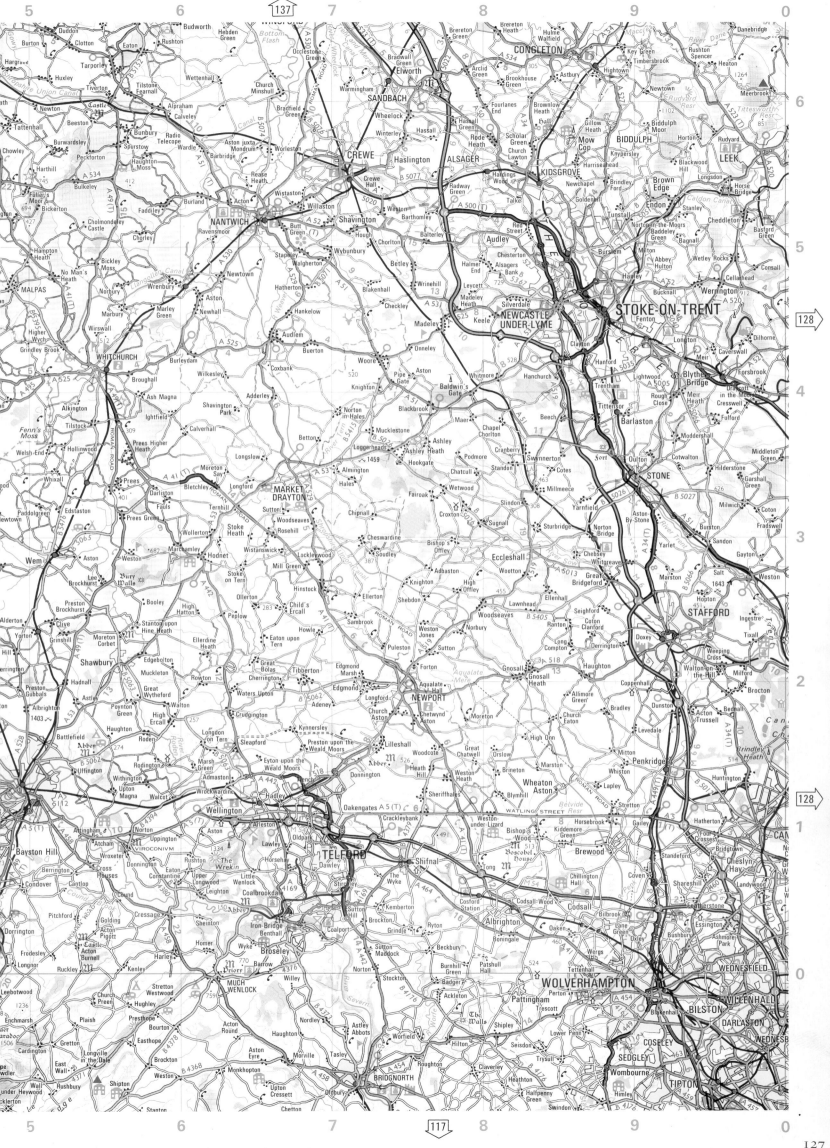

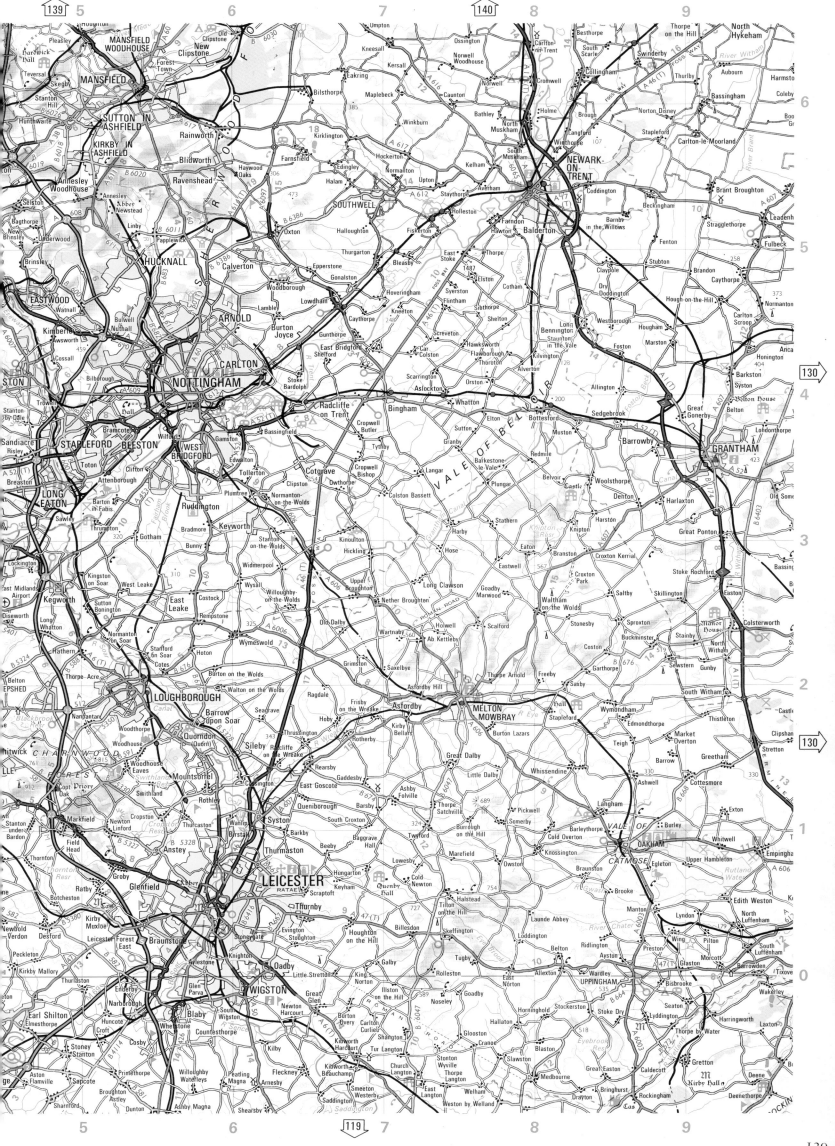

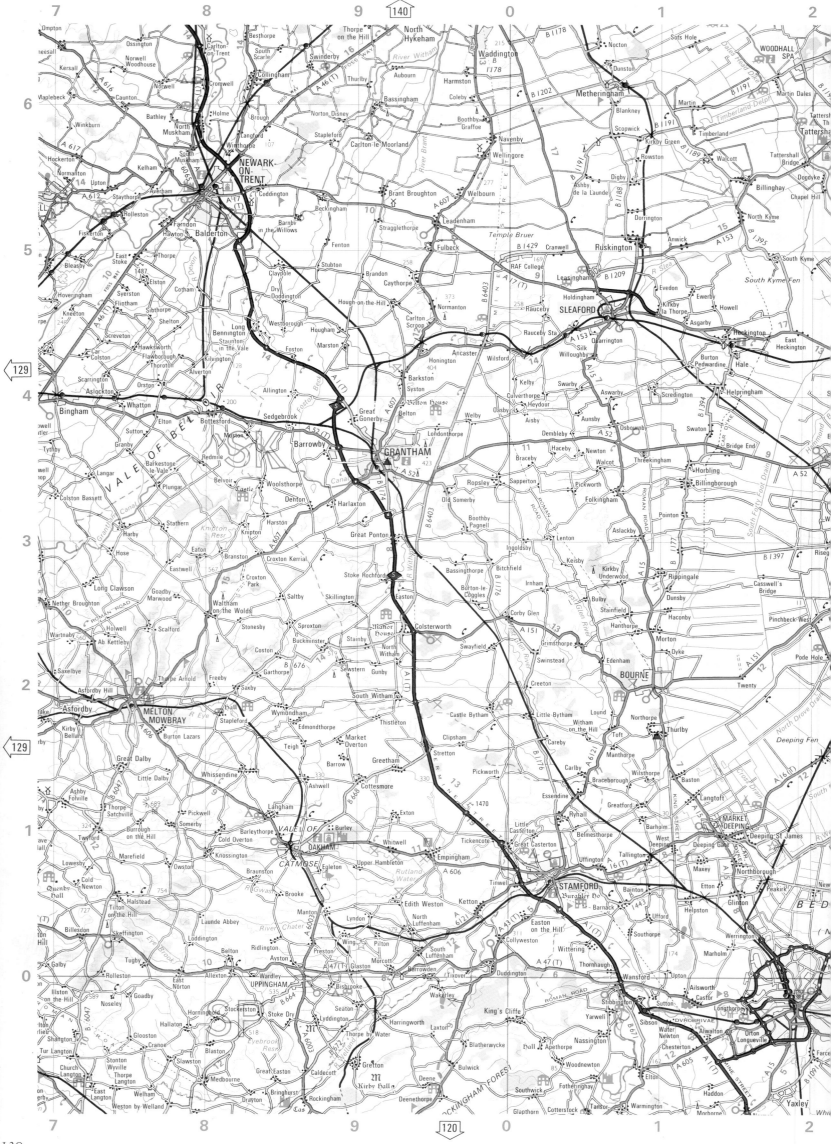

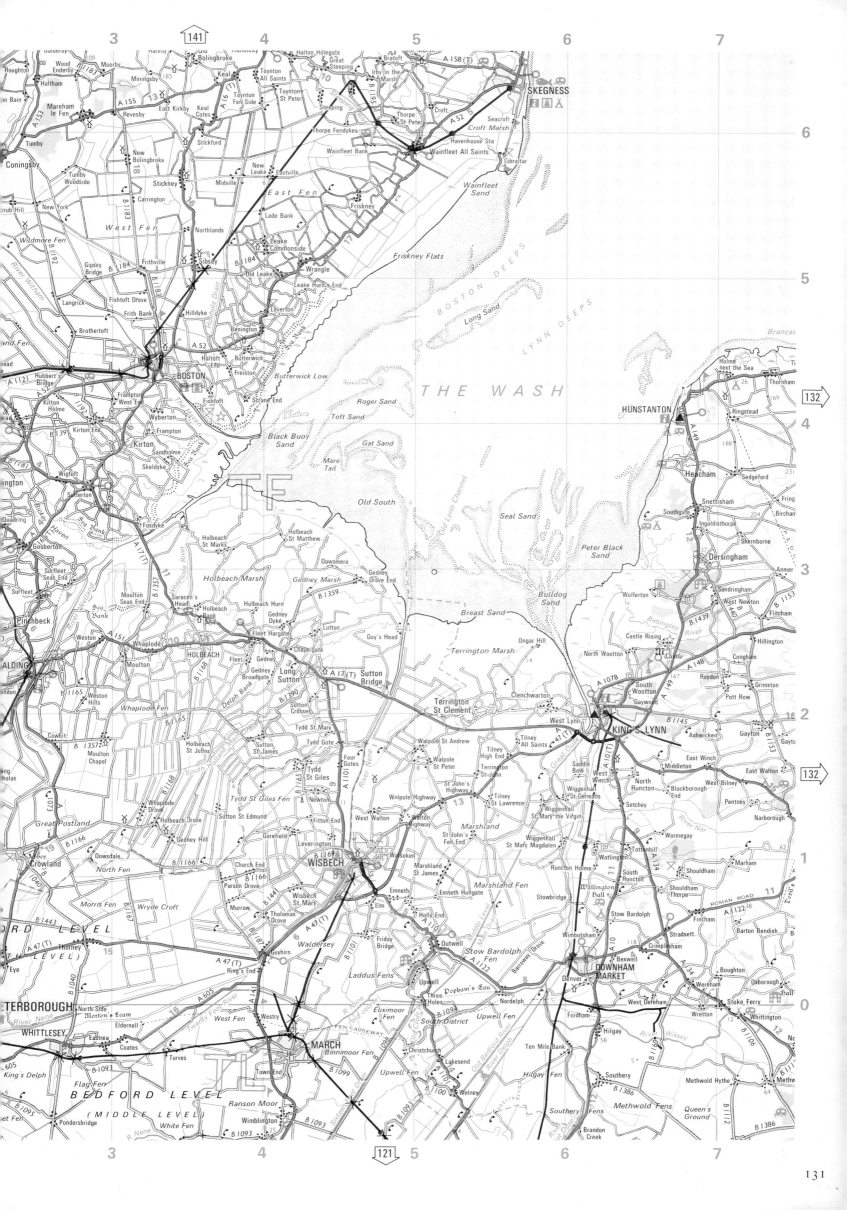

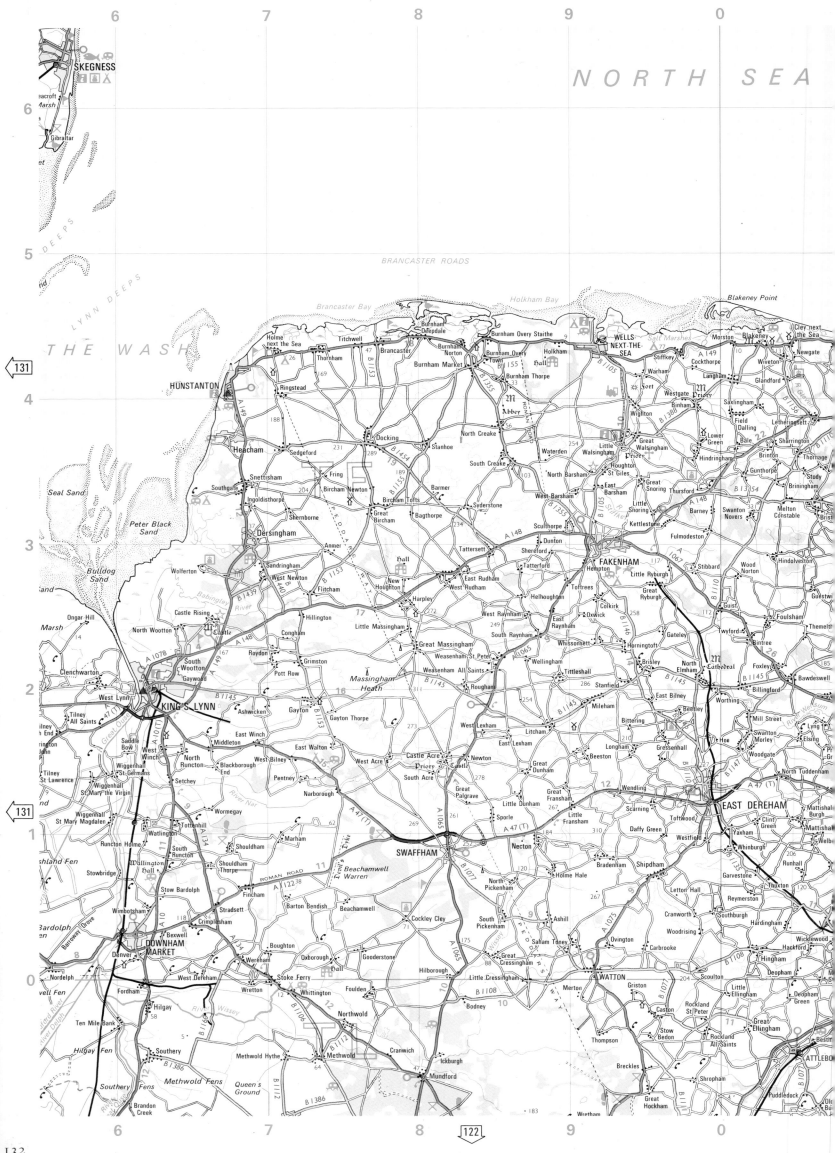

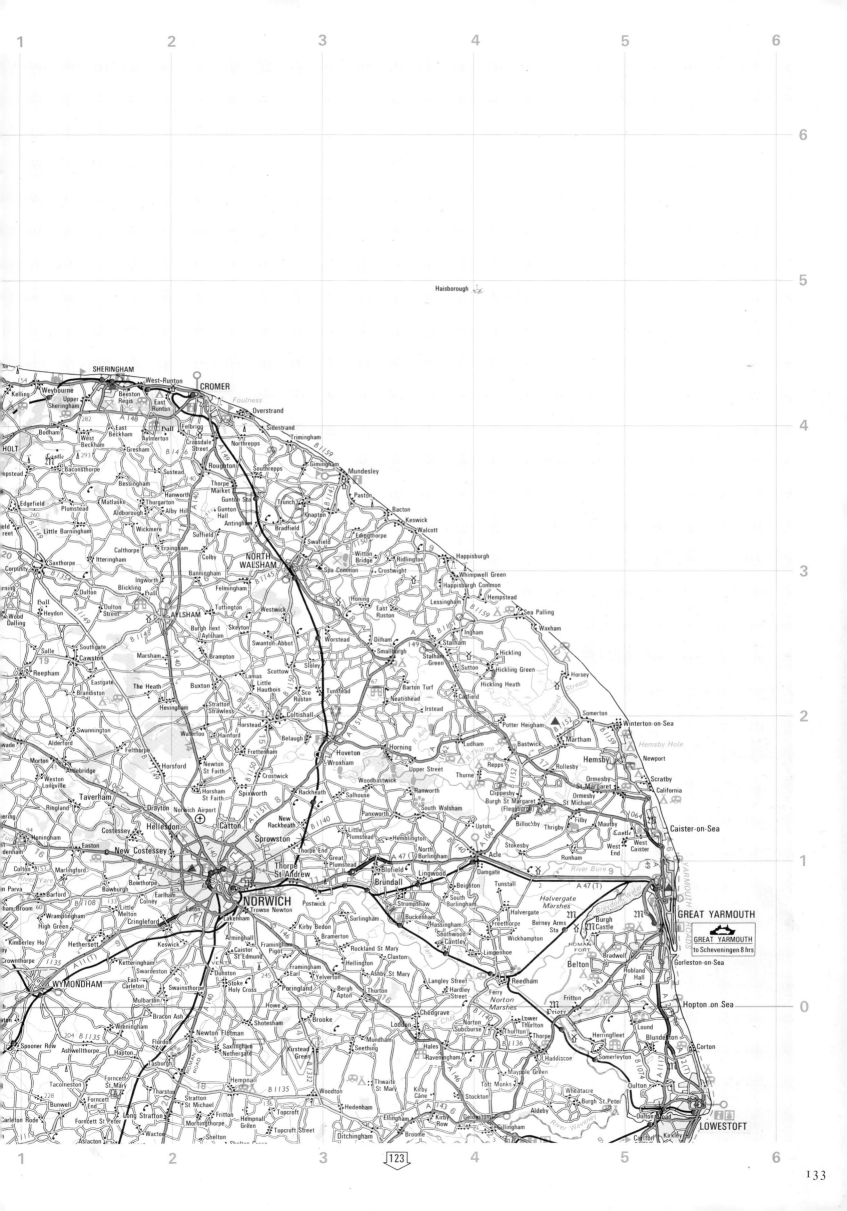

SC

LIVERPOOL
BAY

LIVERPOOL to 🚢	
Dublin	7-8¾ hrs
Belfast	9 hrs
Douglas	4 hrs
	(seasonal)

Great
Bank

Great
Bank

Hundred
End

Bank

Beccon

Tarleton

Marshside
Sands

Angry Brow

Crossens

Banks

Marshside

SOUTHPORT

Churchtown

Mere
Brow

A 565 (T)

Sollom

Holmeswood

Birkdale

Bescar Lane
Station

Rufford

Scarisbrick

Tarlscough

Ainsdale

Shirdley
Hill

New
Lane

Burscough
Bridge

Pinfold

Burscough

Halsall

ORMSKIRK

Westhead

Freshfield

FORMBY

Haskayne

Great Altcar

Aughton
Park

Scarth
Hill

Hightown

Ince
Blundell

Aughton

Bickersta

Lydiate

Lunt

Thornton

Sefton

Melling

MAGHULL

RAINFC

Hall Road
Sta

Netherton

Great
Crosby

Ford

KIRKBY

Kirkby
Industrial Esta

Blundellsands

Waterloo

Crosby

CROSBY

LITHERLAND

Aintree

Knowsley

Seaforth

West
Derby

Knowsley
Hall

BOOTLE

New Brighton

Toll

WALLASEY

Seacombe

Tunnel

LIVERPOOL

Childwall

HUYTON-WITH-
ROBY

East
Hoyle Bank

Mockbeggar

Moreton

Toll

Woolton

West Hoyle Bank

HOYLAKE

Greasby

Upton

Rock
Ferry

New Ferry
Port Sunlight

Allerton

Hunt's
Cross

Halewoo

Point of Ayr

West
Kirby

Grange

Frankby

BIRKENHEAD

Prenton

Storeton

Grassendale

Garston

Speke

Talacre

Caldy

Irby

Barnston

Bromborough

Liverpool
Airport

Hale

Mostyn Bank

Thurstaston

Pensby

BEBINGTON

Eastham
Sands

PRESTATYN

Gronant

Gwespyr

Ffynnongroyw

HESWALL

Thornton
Hough

Raby

Eastham

Dungeo
Banks

RHYL

Meliden

Gwaenysgor

Llanasa

Glan-y-don

Dawpool
Bank

Gayton

Parkgate

Willaston

Ince Bank

Kinmel Bay

Towyn

Gop Hill

Mostyn

Holywell
Bank

Gayton
Sands

Childer
Thornton

ELLESMERE
PORT

ABERGELE

Rhuddlan

Trelawnyd

Trelogan

Holywell

NESTON

Ness

Whitby
Little
Stanney

Oil
Refinery

Ince

St George

Bodelwyddan

Dyserth

Moel Hiraddug

Whitford

Downing

Greenfield

Bagillt Bank

Burton

Thornton-
le-Moors

Moelfre
Isaf

Glascoed

Cwm

Carmel

Abbey

Bagillt

Puddington

Capenhurst

Stoak

Lowther
College

Rhualt

Pen-y-cefn

Brynford

Milwr

White
Sands

Ledsham

A 5117 (T)

Wervin

St Asaph
(Lanelwy)

Tremeirchion

Babell

Pentre
Halkyn

Castle

FLINT

Shotwick

Backford

Mollington

Picto

Bridge
Traffo

Llannerch
Hall

Caerwys

Holkyn Mountain

Flint
Mountain

Works

Mickle
Trafford

Graig

Afon-
wen

Ysceifiog

Lixwm

Halkyn

Saughall

Guilde
Suttor

Bont-newydd

Trefnant

Bodfari

Rhes-
y-cae

CONNAH'S
QUAY

Shotton

Sealand

Upton

Hoole

Littleton

Henllan

Nannerch

Rhosesmor

Hendre

Northop
Hall

Queensferry

Mancot

Blacon

CHESTER
DEVA

Christleto

DENBIGH

Llangwyfan

Pen-y-
cloddiau

Rhydymwyn

Northop

Soughton
(Sychdyn)

Hawarden

Sandycroft

Handbridge

Rowto

Castle

Moel Llys-
y-coed

Cilcain

Ewloe

Broughton

Cache

Llangynhafal

Gwernaffield

MOLD

Mynydd Isa

Bretton

Llanrhaeadr

Pentre

Moel
Fammau

Tafarn-
y-Gelyn

Cadole

BUCKLEY

Penyffordd

Kinnerton

Eaton
Hall

Bruera

Nantglyn

Peniel

Gellifor

Maeshafn

Gwernymynydd

Padeswood

Dodleston

Gorsedd
Bron

Pant-
pastynog

Ffridd
Fawr

Rhewl

Llanbedr-
Dyffryn-Clwyd

Moel y
Gaer

Llanferres

Nercwys

Leeswood

Hope

Pulford

Aldford

Milton
Green

Bylchau

Cyffylliog

Bontuchel

RUTHIN

Treuddyn

Pontybodkin

Caergwrle

Cefn-y-
bedd

Rossett

Handley

Efenechtyd

Llanfair Dyffryn
Clwyd

Eryrys

Llanarmon-
yn-Ial

Llay

Churton

Coddington

Mynydd
Hiraethog

Nilig

Graig
fechan

Pentre-celyn

Rhydtalog

Llanelidan

Ffrith

Gresford

Borras
Head

Holt

Farndon

Clocaenog
Forest

Clawdd-
newydd

Moel Garegog

Llandegla

Bwlchgwyn

Brymbo

Moss
Llan-y-pwll

Gwersyllt

Derwen

Pen-y-
stryt

Minera

Brynteg

Isycoed

Pentre-llyn-
cymmer

Coedpoeth

WREXHAM

Esclusham
Mountain

Rhosnesni

Wrexham Industrial

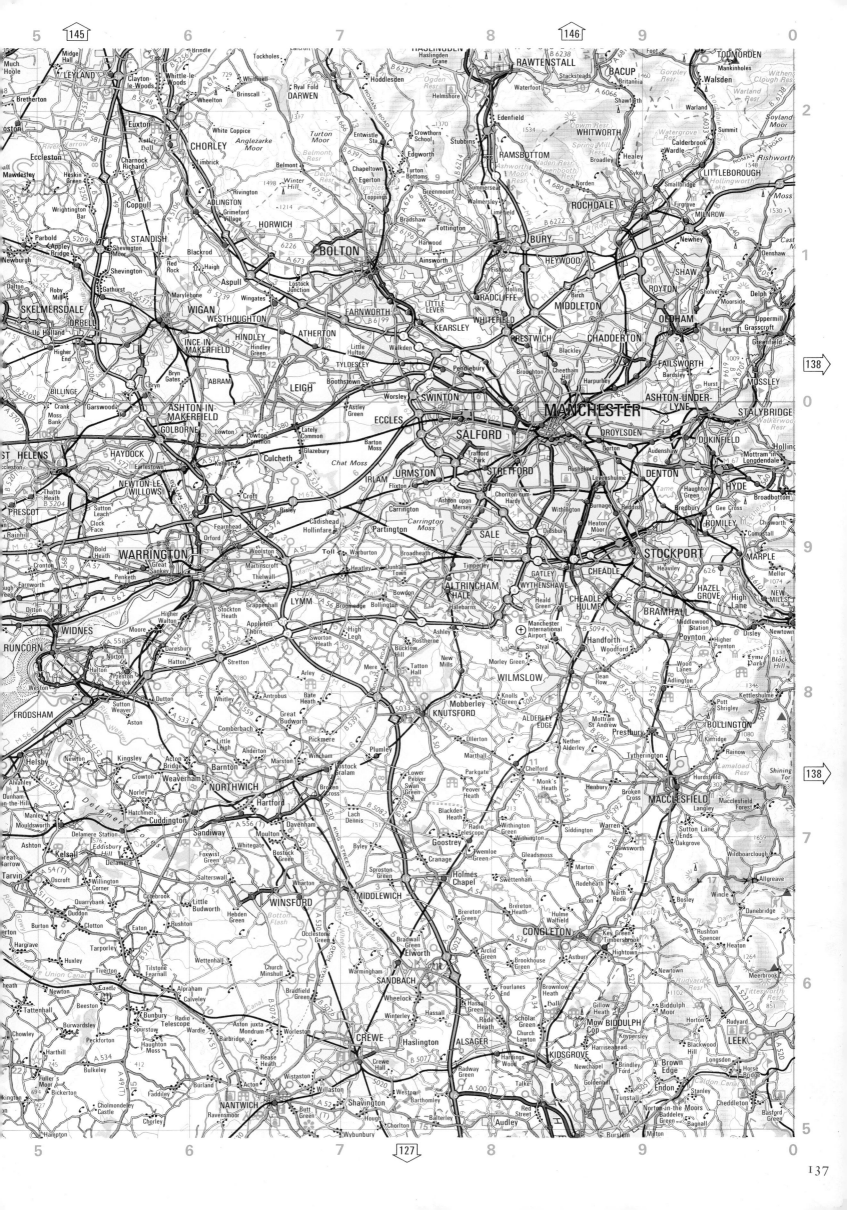

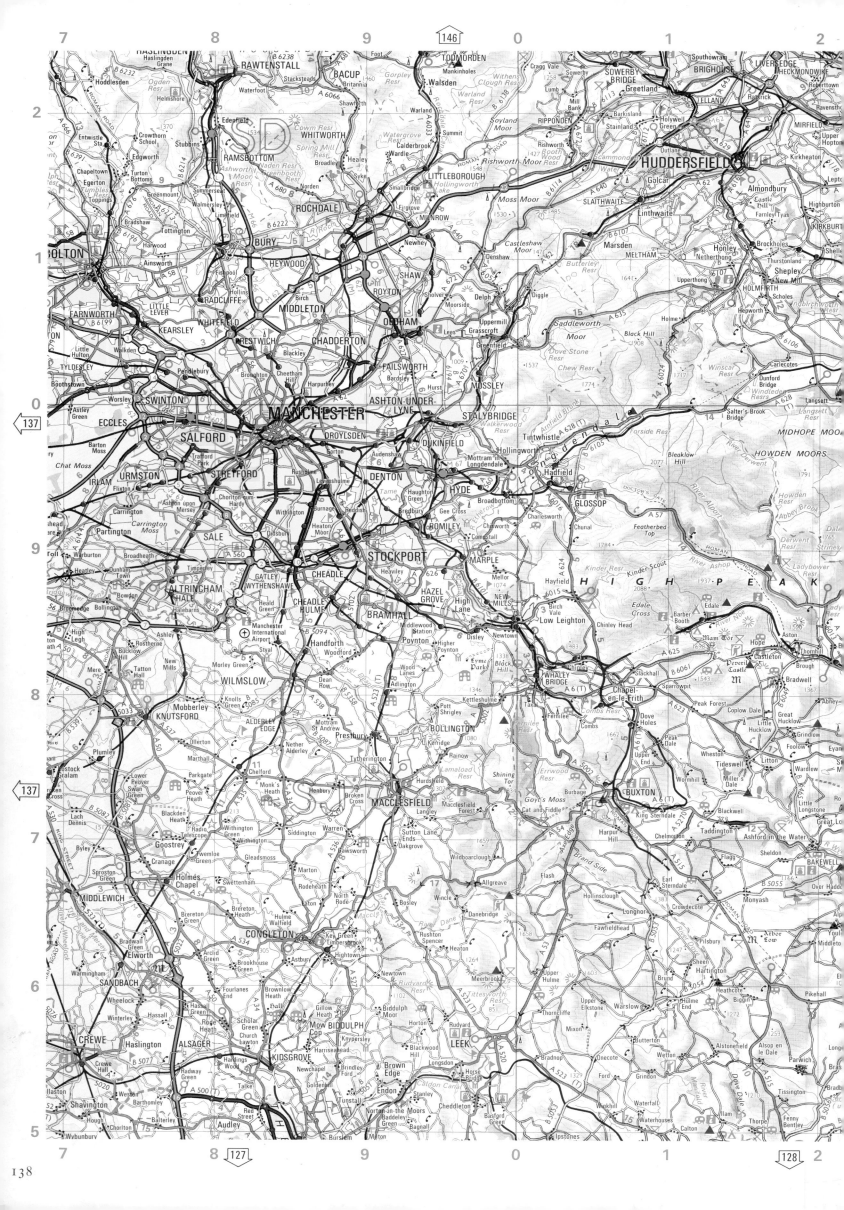

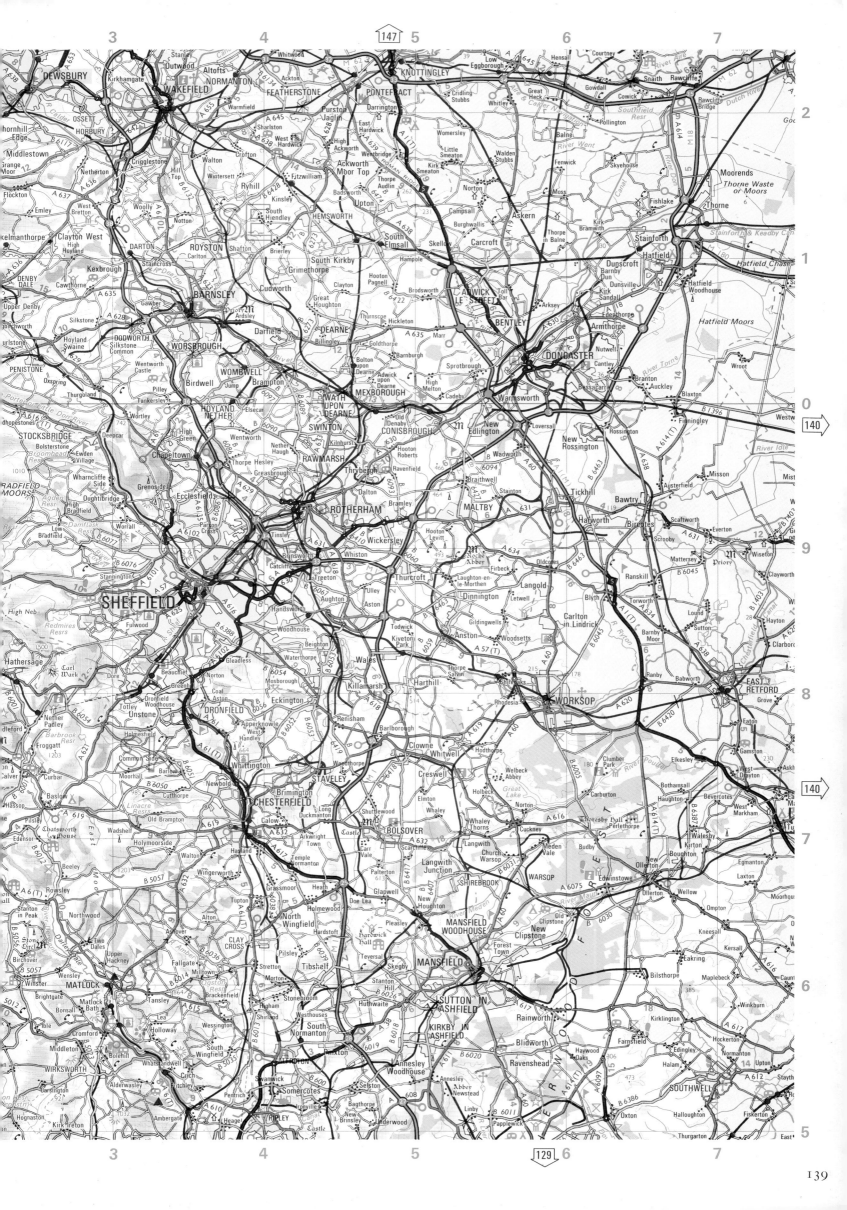

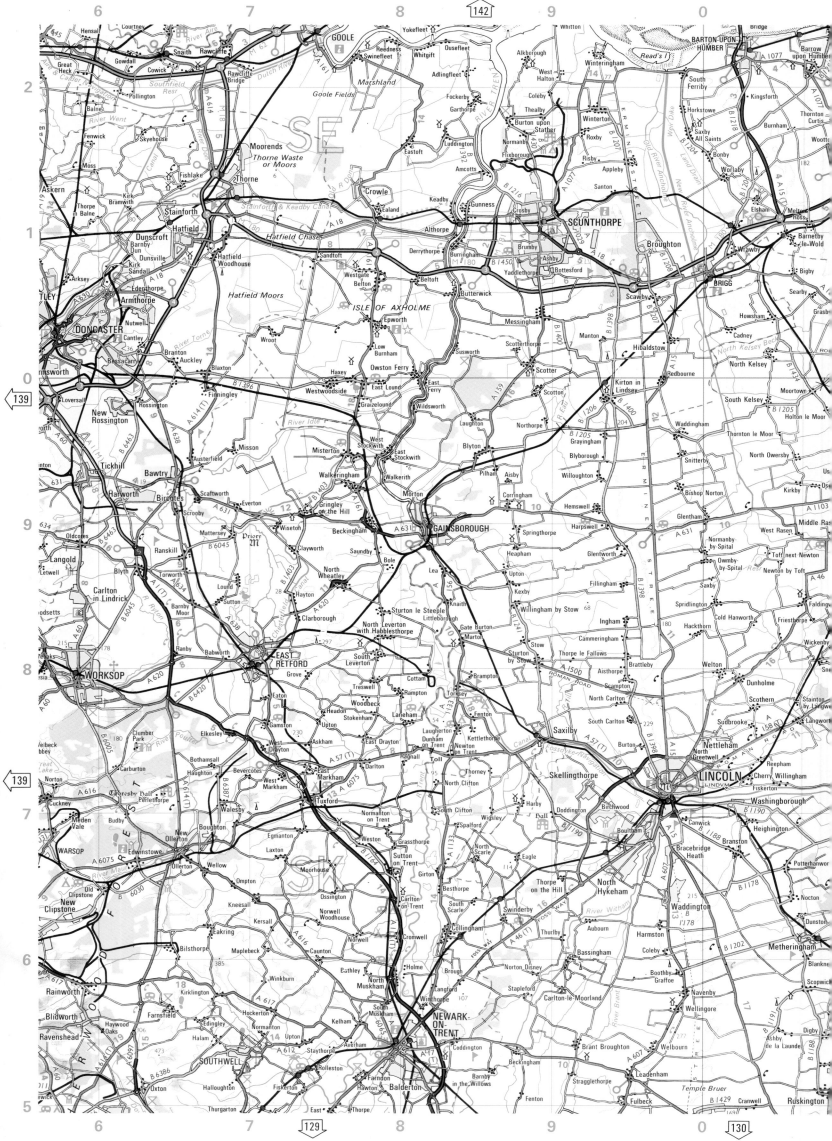

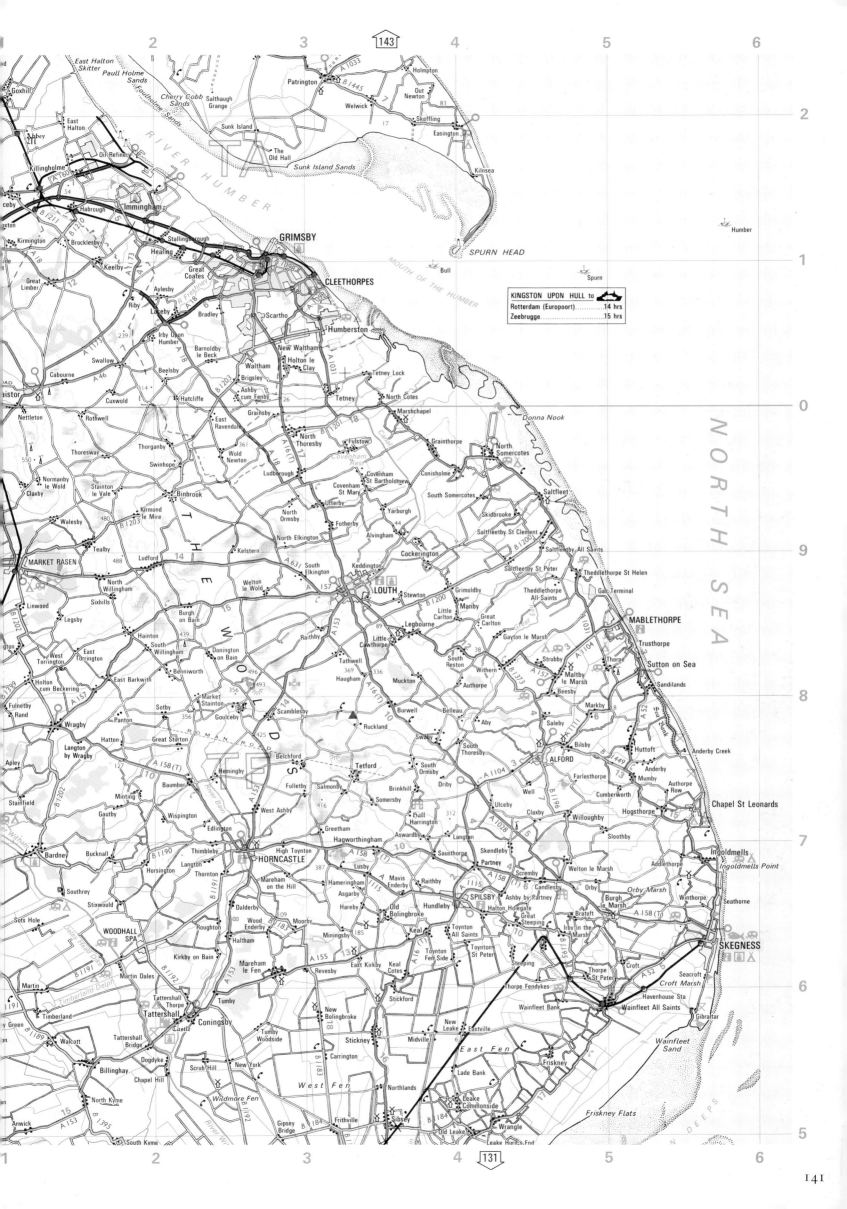

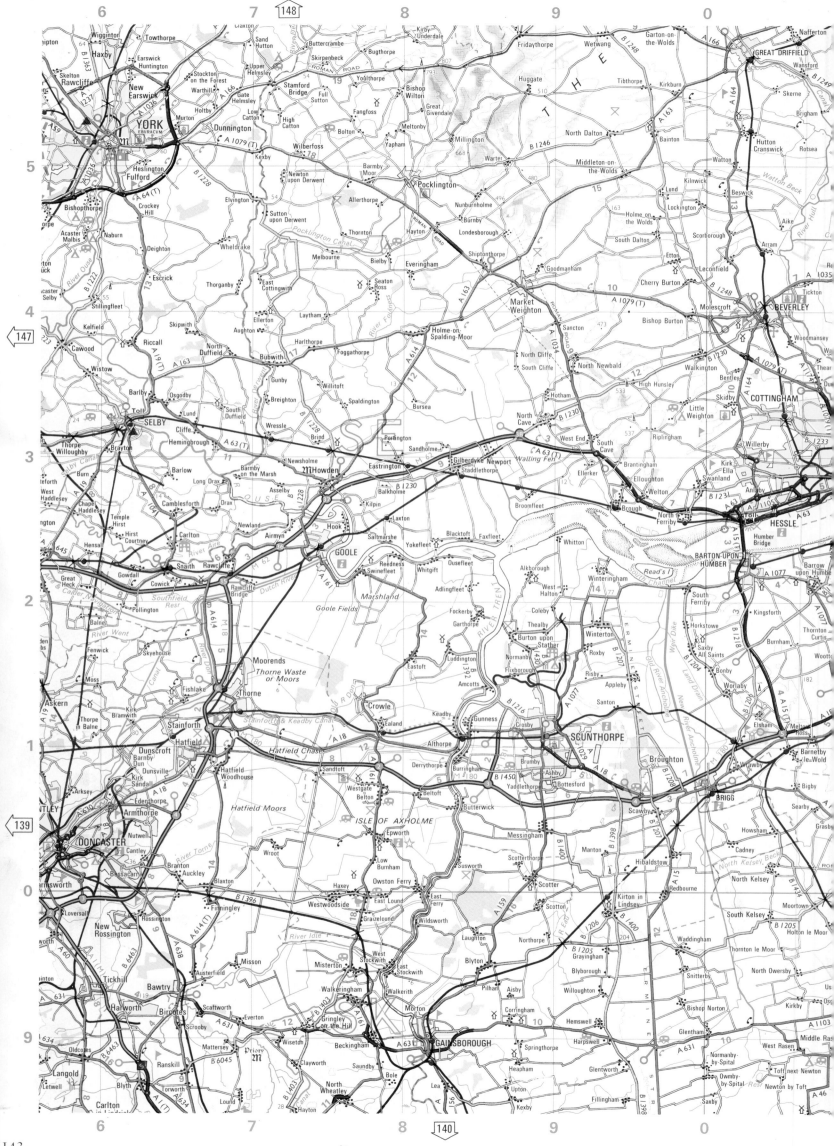

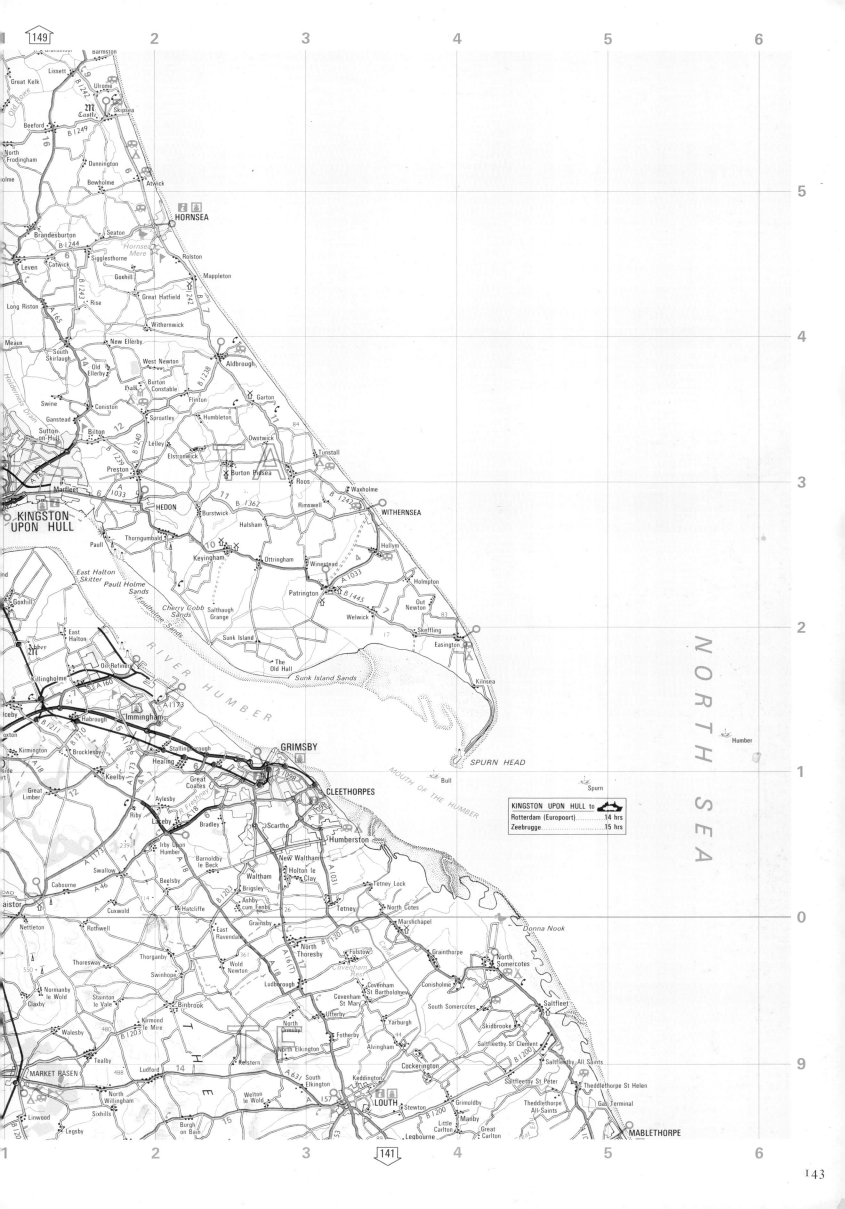

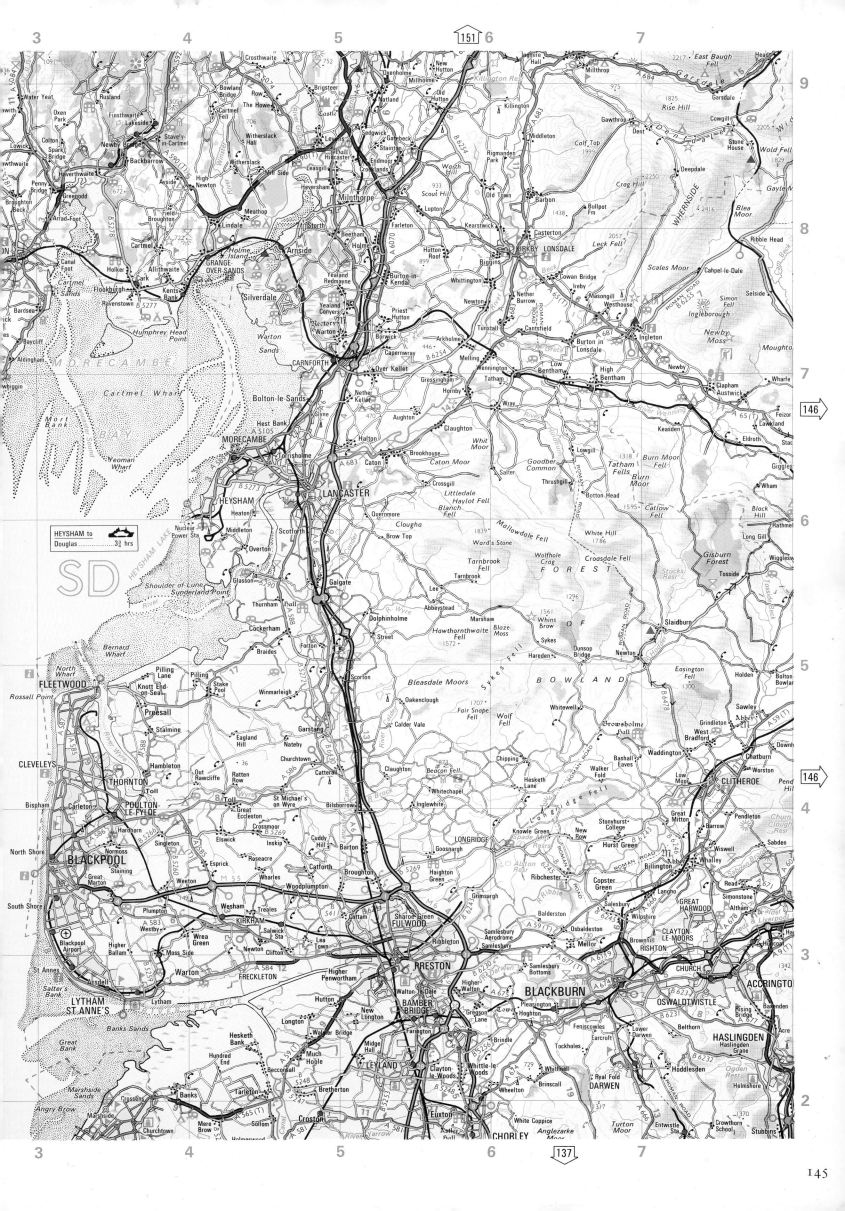

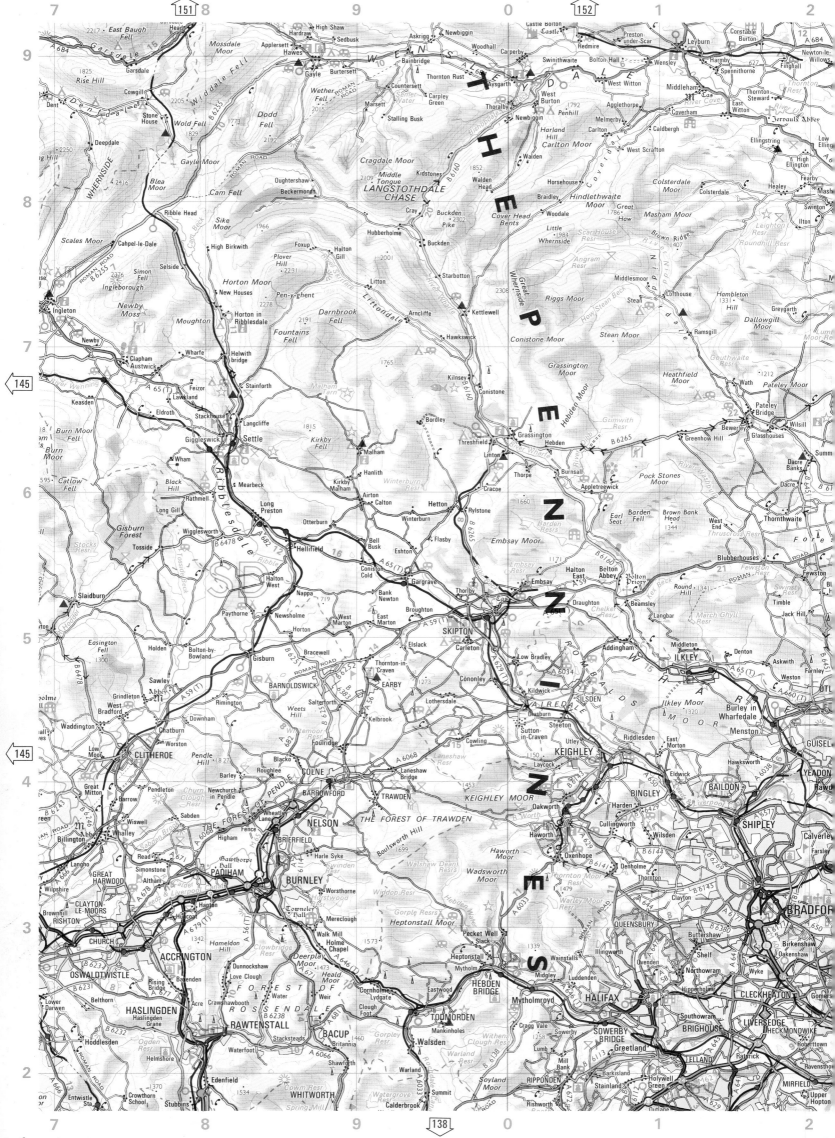

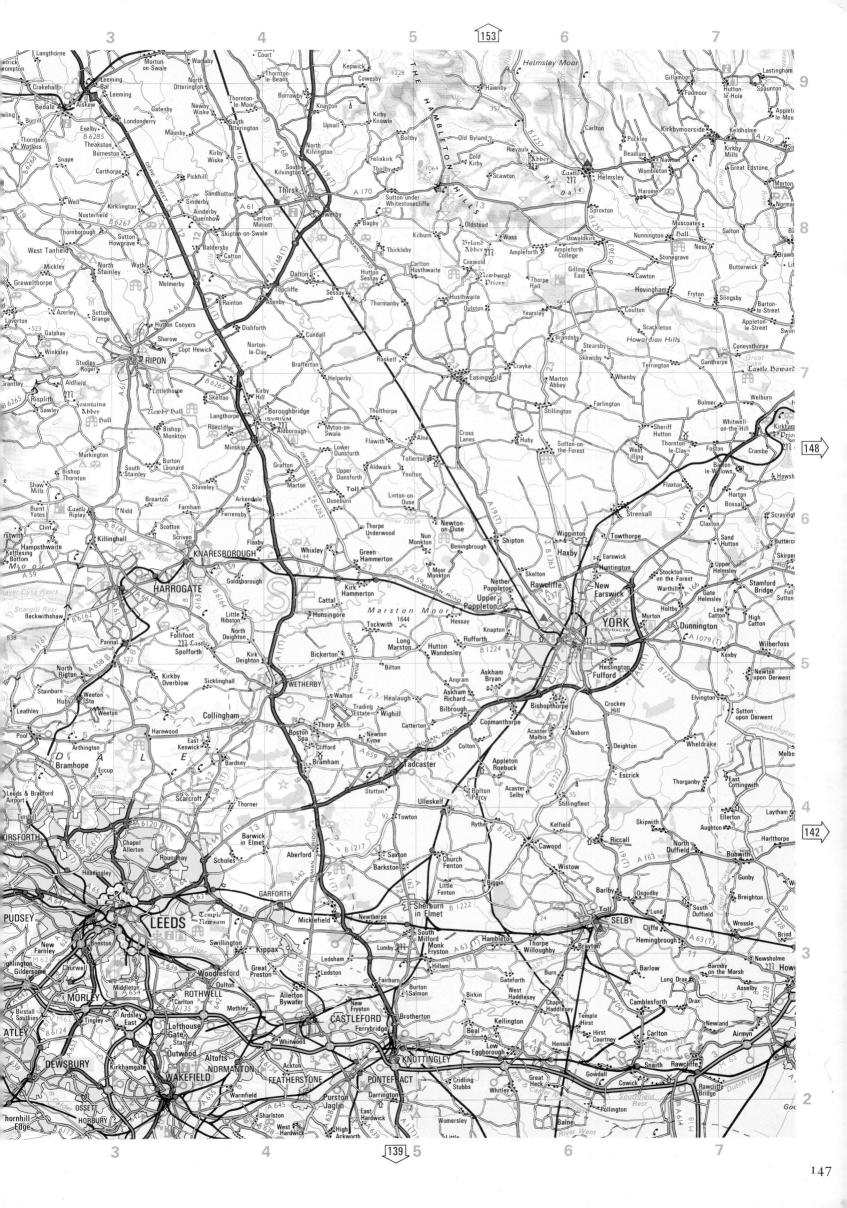

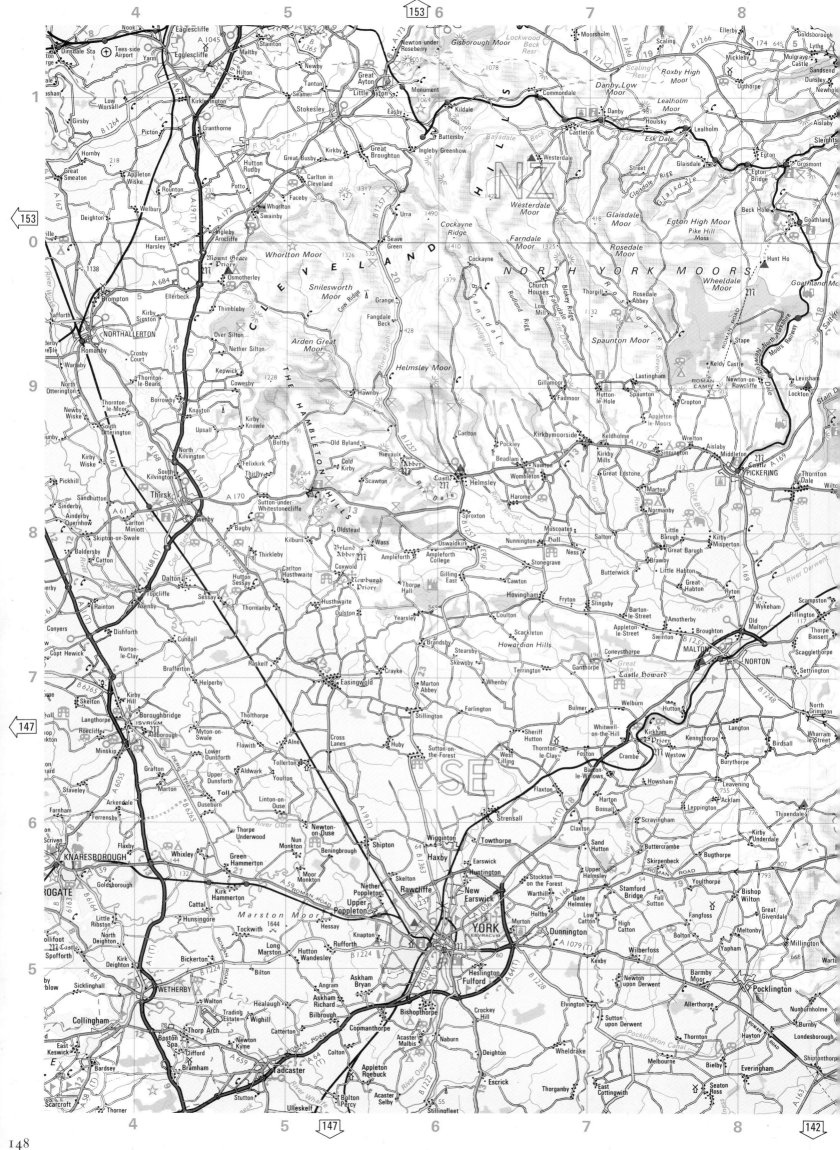

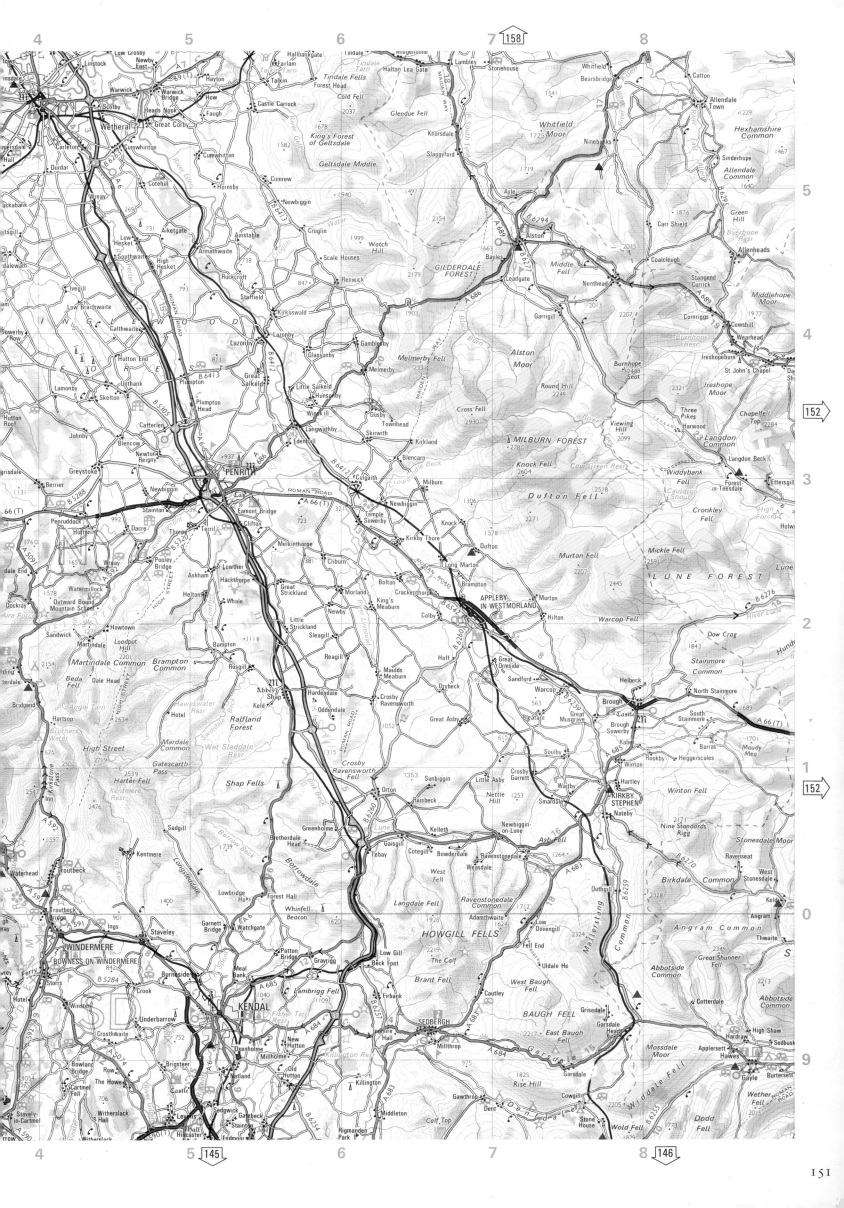

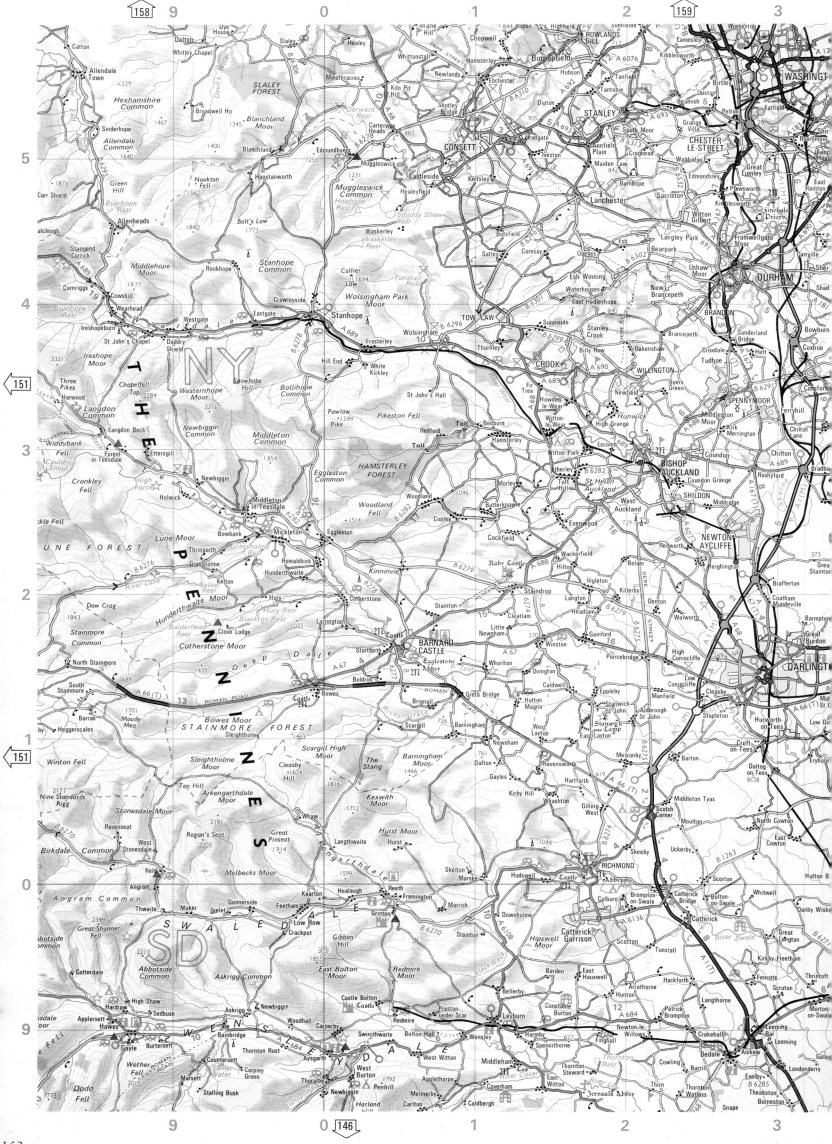

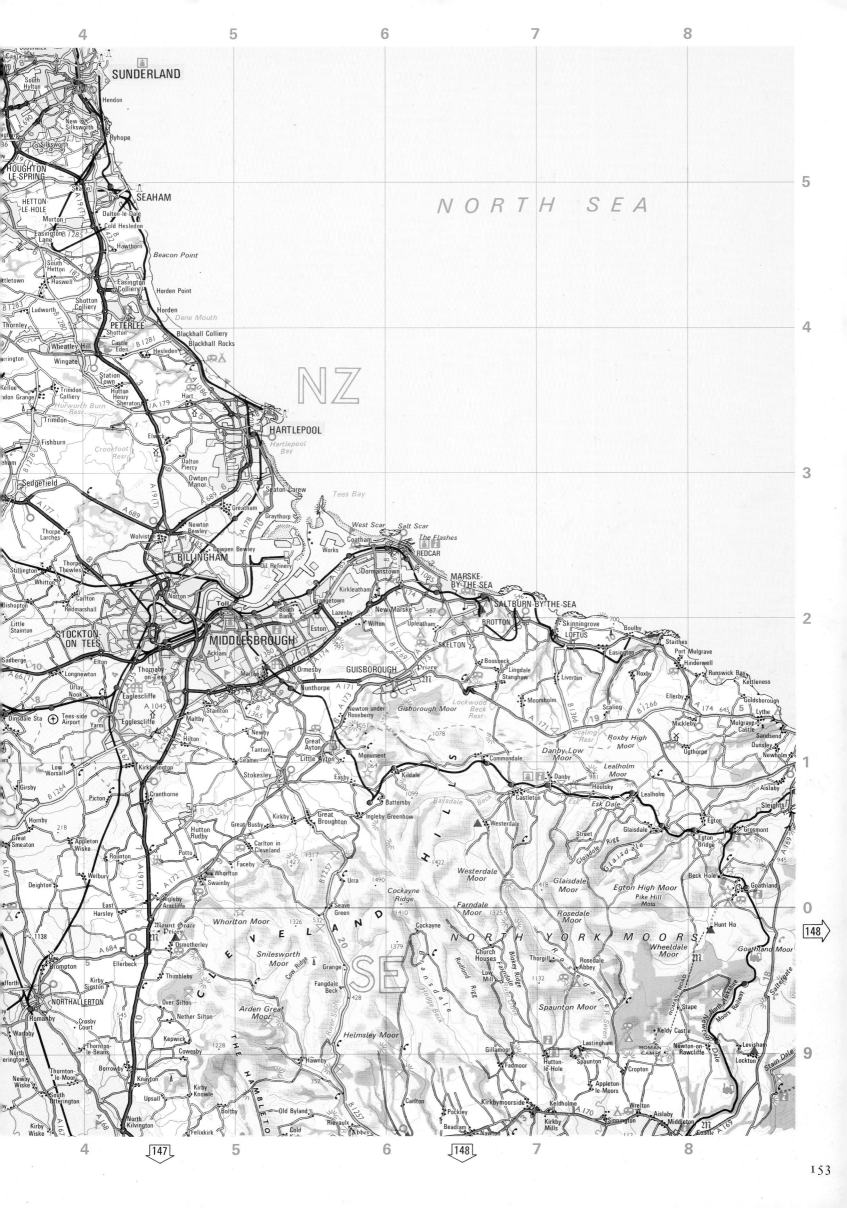

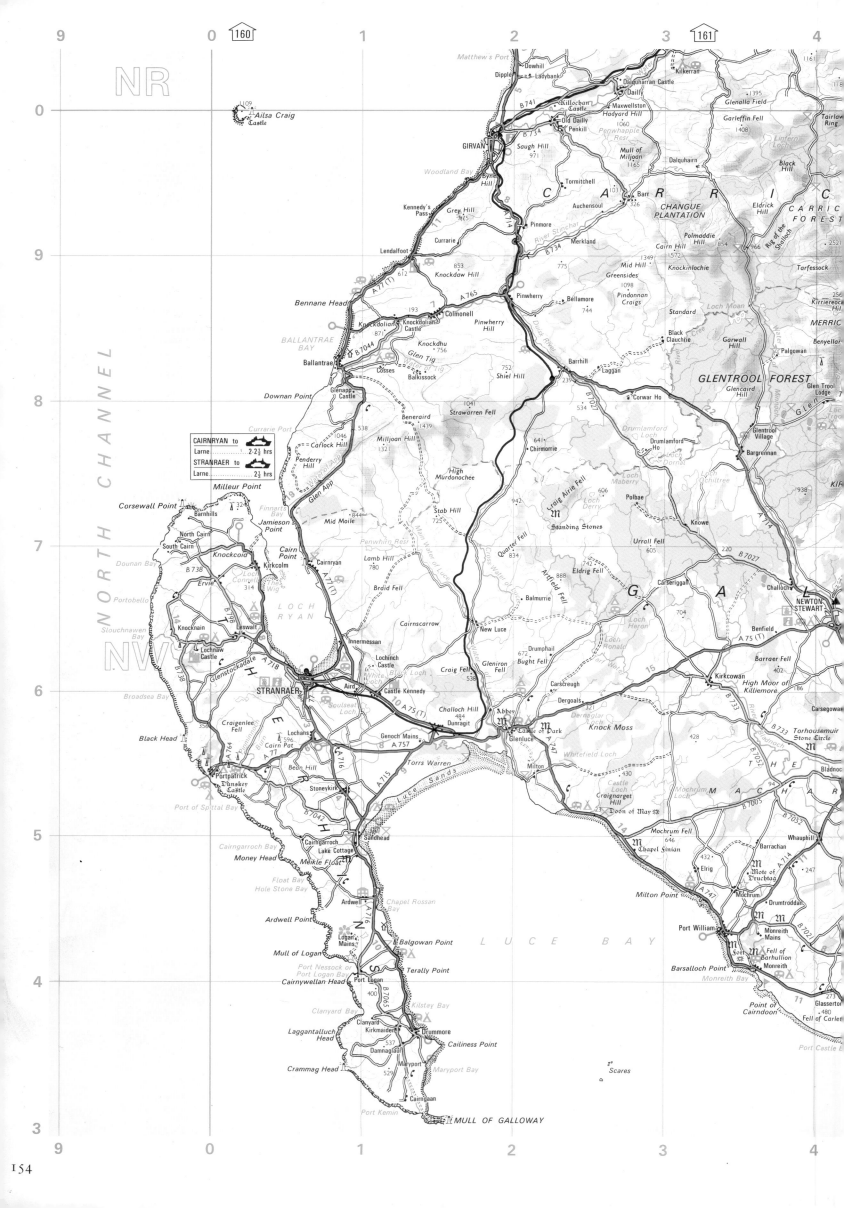

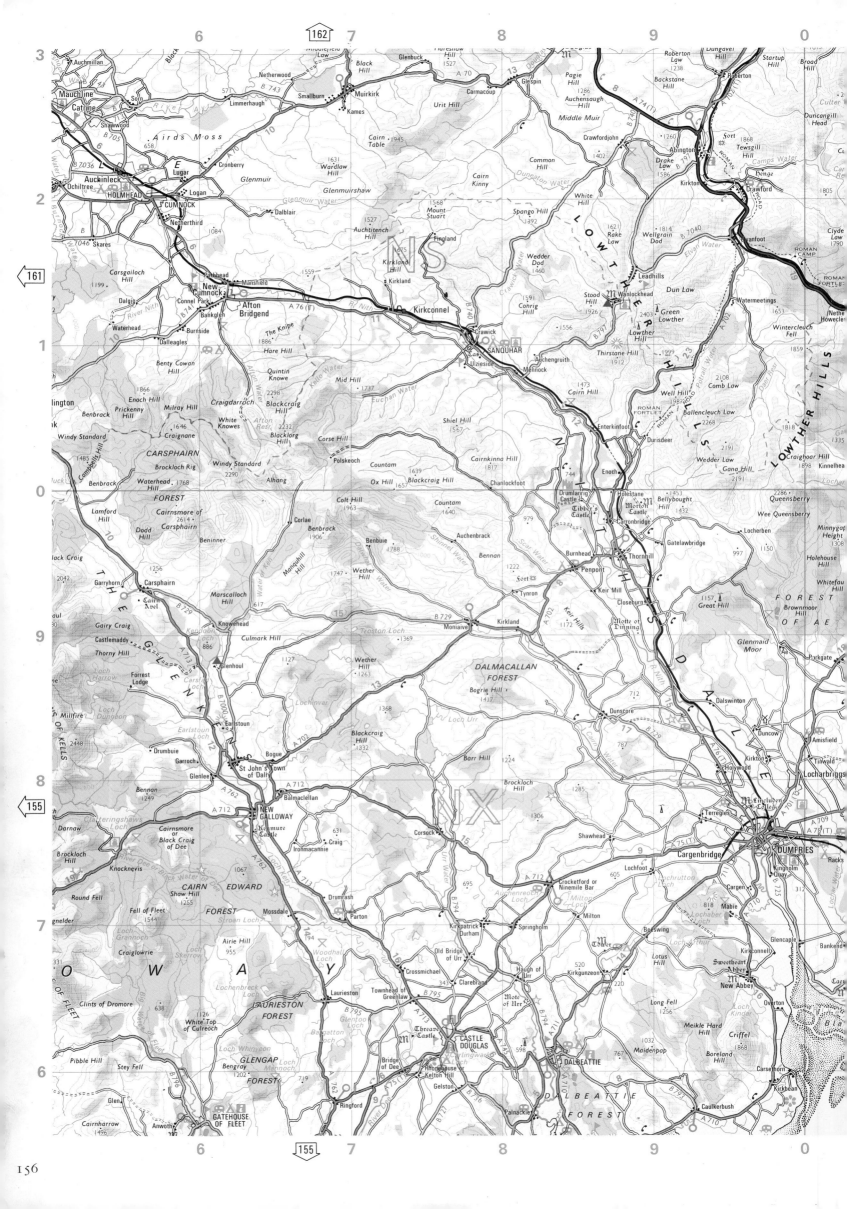

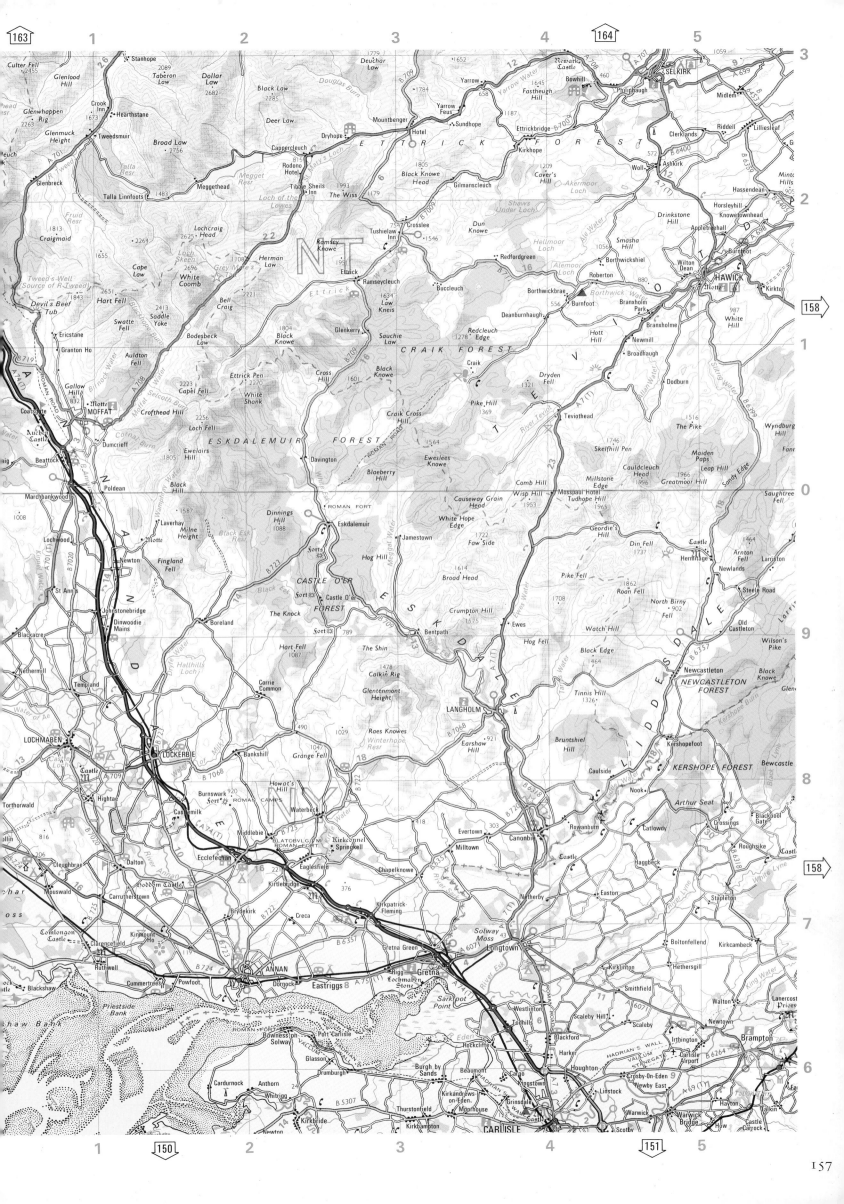

NEWCASTLE UPON TYNE to ⛴
Seasonal
Bergen............................20-25 hrs
Esbjerg..........................18½-21 hrs
Stavanger.......................17-18½ hrs
Gothenburg.....................25-27½ hrs

NORTH SEA

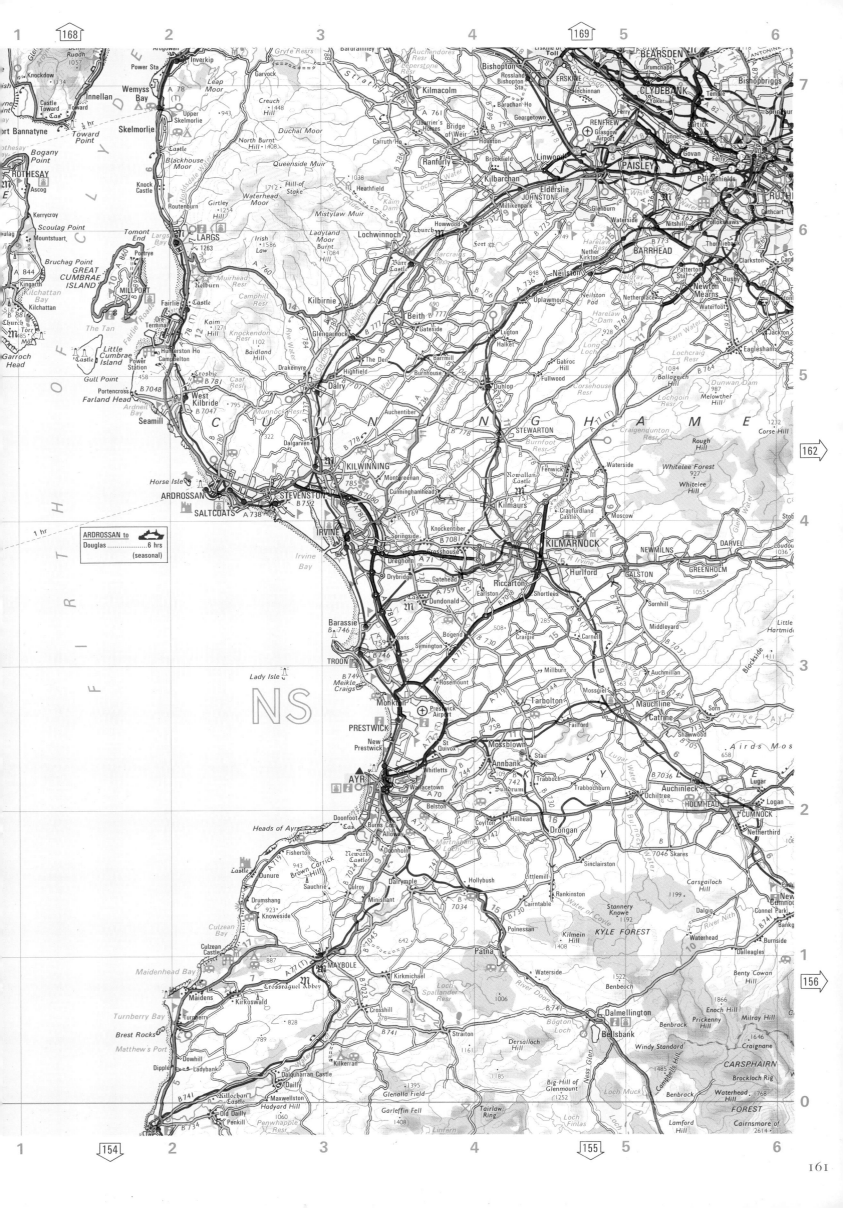

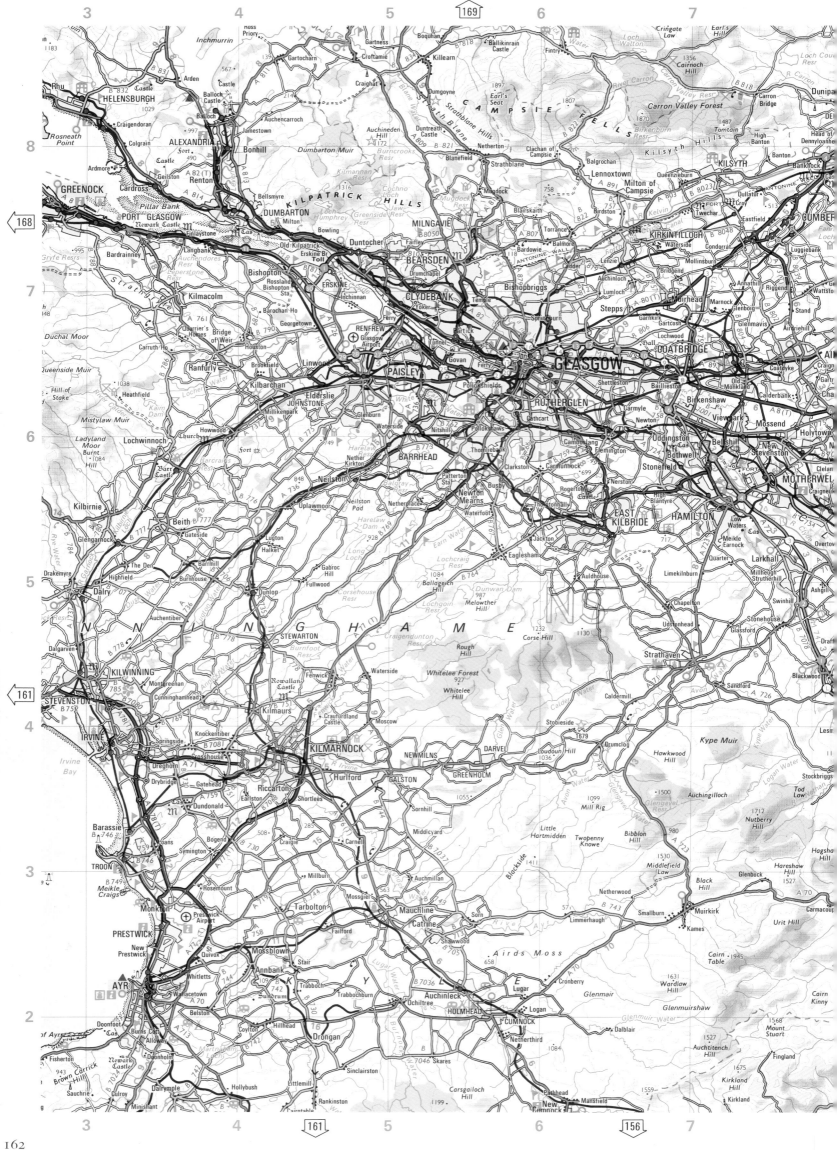

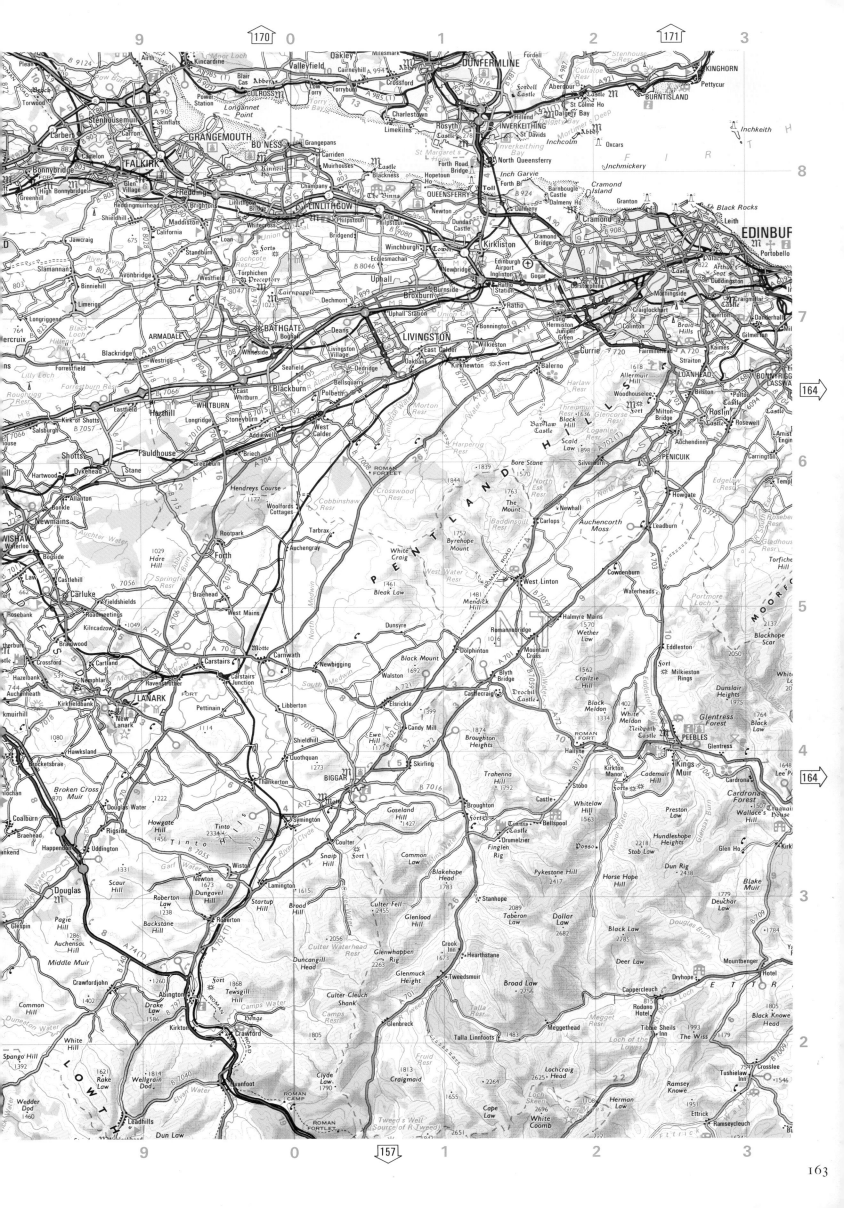

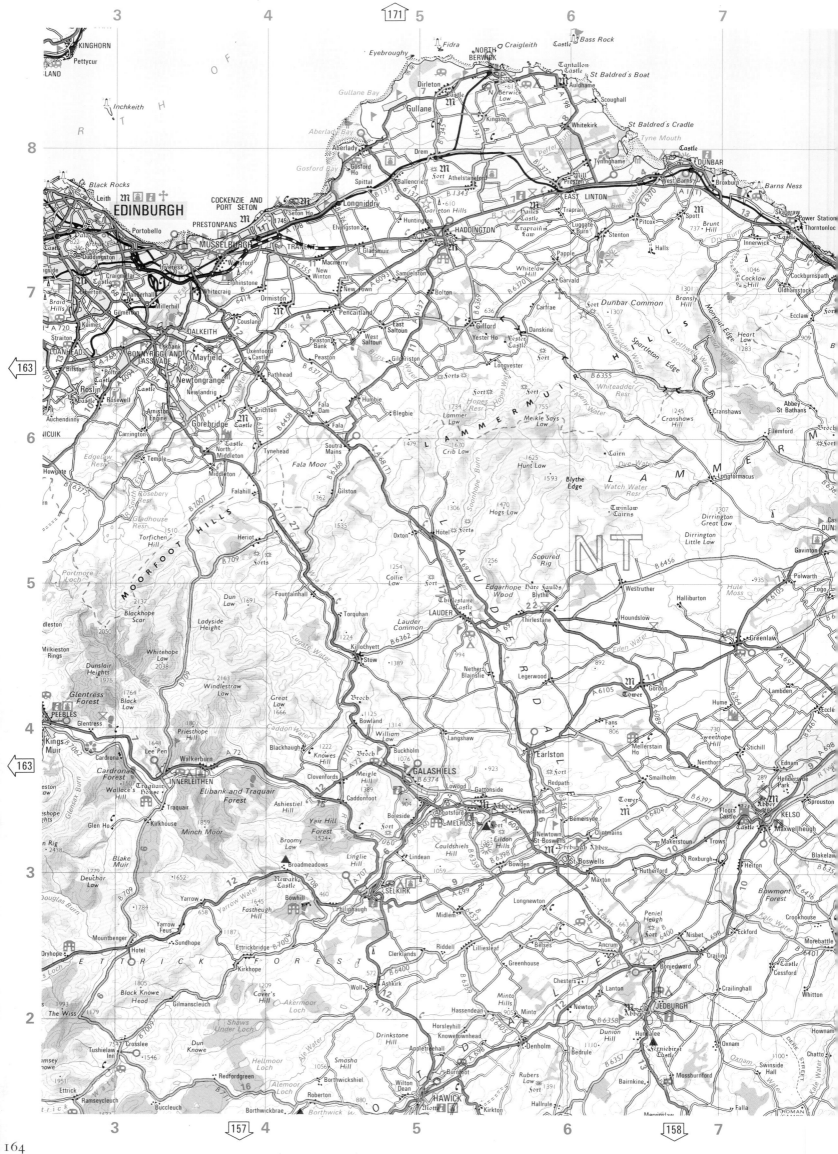

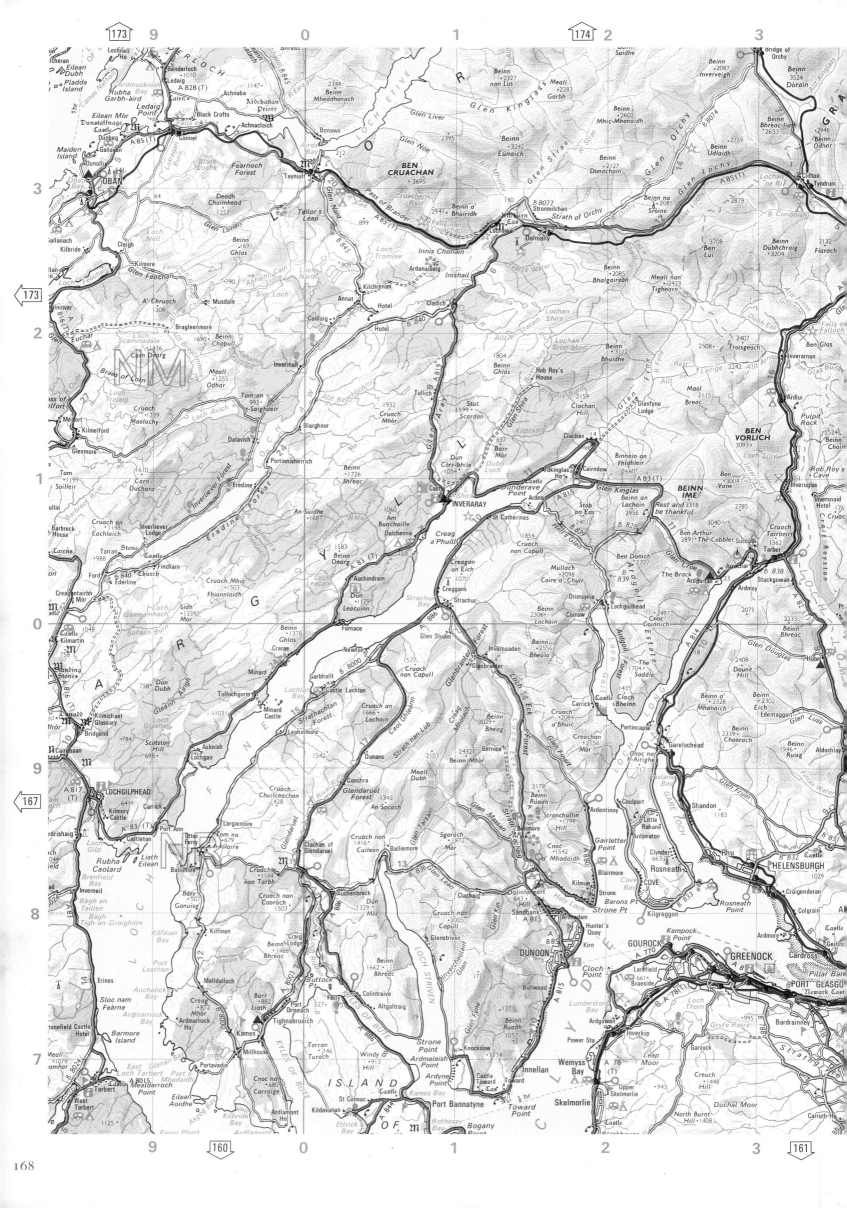

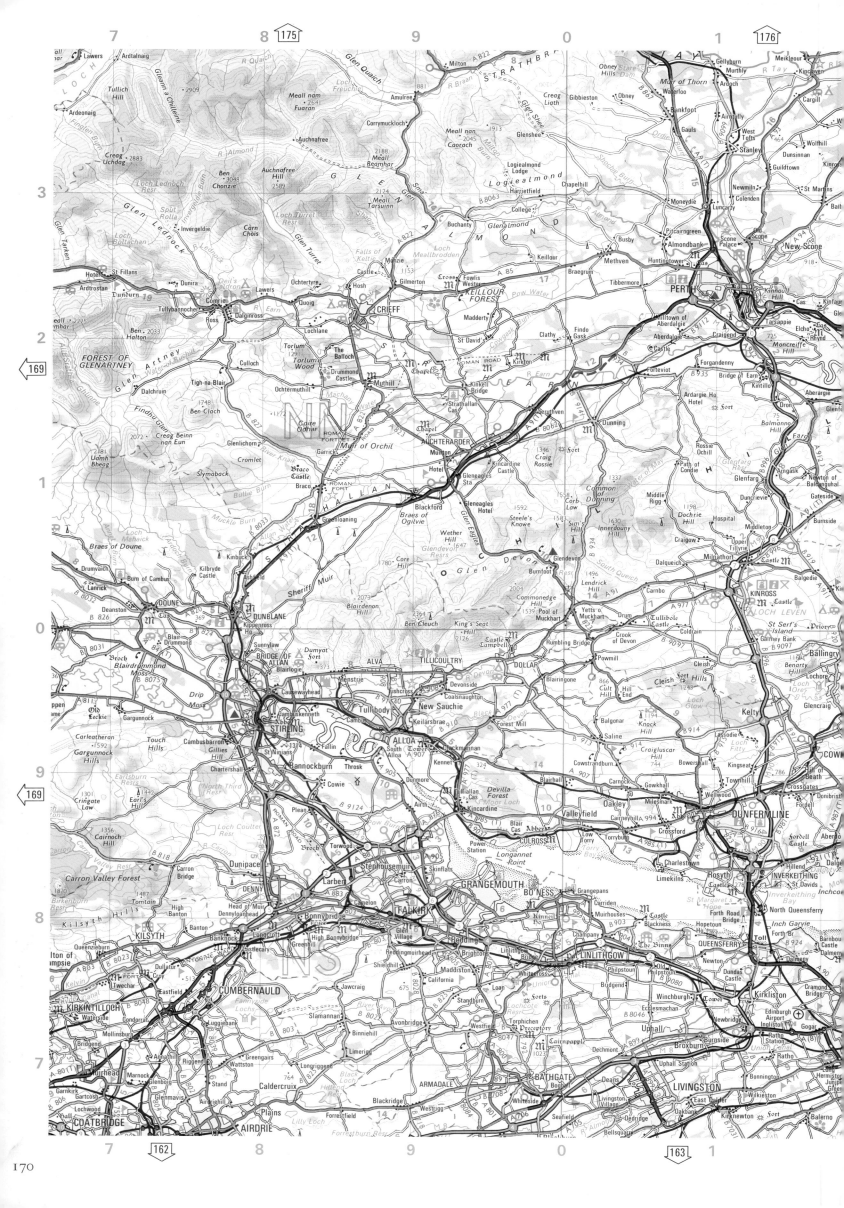

INNER HEBRIDES

Point of
Ardnamurchan

An A

Cairns of Coll

Eag na Maoile
Eilean Mór

Rubha Mór
Rubh' a
Bhinnein
B 8072
Bousd
Sorisdale
5
155

Cliad Bay
Gallanach
Grishipoll
Arnabost
Rubha Hogh
B 8071
Ballyhaugh
·239
Bagh Feisdlum
Ben
Hogh
Loch
Cliad
1 hr
Hogh Bay
·340
Arinagour
COLL
Quinish Point

Rubha a'
Ghraineig
Totronald
B 8070
Acha
Loch Eatharna
Rubha
an Aird
Aileodr
Port Mine
Castle
Eilean
Ornsay
Caliach Point
Monish

Breachacha
Castle
Friesland
Rubha
na h-Eathar
Port nam
Partan
544
Calgary
Rubha
nan Oirean

Calgary Point
Crossapol
Bay
Port na
h-Eathar
Rubha Fàsachd
Calgary Bay

Gunna
Port a'
Mhurain
Soa
Loch Breachacha
Treshnish
Point
Ensay
Carn
Mór
·1122

Urvaig
Haunn
708
Cruachan
Odhar
31
839
Kilnini

Rubha
Port Bhiosd
Vaul
Bay
Salum
Rubha Dubh
Rubh'
a' Chaoil
Burg
Fanmo

Hough
Skerries
Clachan Mór
Vaul
B 8069
Ruaig
Caolas
Cairn na
Burgh Beg
Rubh' an
t-Suibhein
LOCH
TUA

Balevullin
Rubha
Nead a' Gheòidh
Fladda
Rubha na
Sròine

Hough
Bay
Kenovay
Gott Bay
Soa
Eilean
Dioghlum
Rubha
Chràiginis
389
Tiree
Airport
B 8068
B 8065
337
Lunga
Gometra
509
Beinne
Creagach
·1026

Kilkenneth
Moss
Scarinish
Rubha na
Seann Charraige
Maisgeir
Eilean
na Creiche
ULV

Middleton
Heylipol
Heanish
TIREE
Bac Mór or
Dutchman's Cap
Little
Colonsay
·201

Port Mór
Barrapol
Crossapol
Rubha
Tràigh an Dùin
Bac Beag

Port Bharrapol
B 8065
Balemartine
HYNISH
BAY
Staffa
Fingal's Cave

Rinn
Thorbhais
Balephuil
B 8067
Càrnan
Mór
462
Mannal
Erisgeir
Sgeir
Faoilin

Balephuil
Bay
Hynish

Port Snoig
NL

Réidh
Eilean
Rubha nan
Cearc
Rubha na
h-Uamha

Eilean
Annraidh
Garbh Phort
C
B

IONA
Baile
Mór
333
Aridhglas
265
Eorabus

Stac an Aoineidh
Fionnphort
Loch Poit
na h-I
Loch
Làthaich
Arun

Eilean na h-
Aon Chaorach
Fidden
Beinn a'
369
Ghlinne Mhòir
Bunessan

Greave
Eilean
nam Muc
Erraid
246
ROSS
OF
M

Soa
Island
Eilean
a' Chalmain
Ardalanish
Beinn a'
Chool-airigh
411
Uisken
Ardchiavaig
AC
Dur

Rubha nam
Maol Móra
Rubh'
Ardalanish
Ardalanish
Bay

West Reef
Torran Rocks

·Sgeir Dhoirbh

Dubh

172

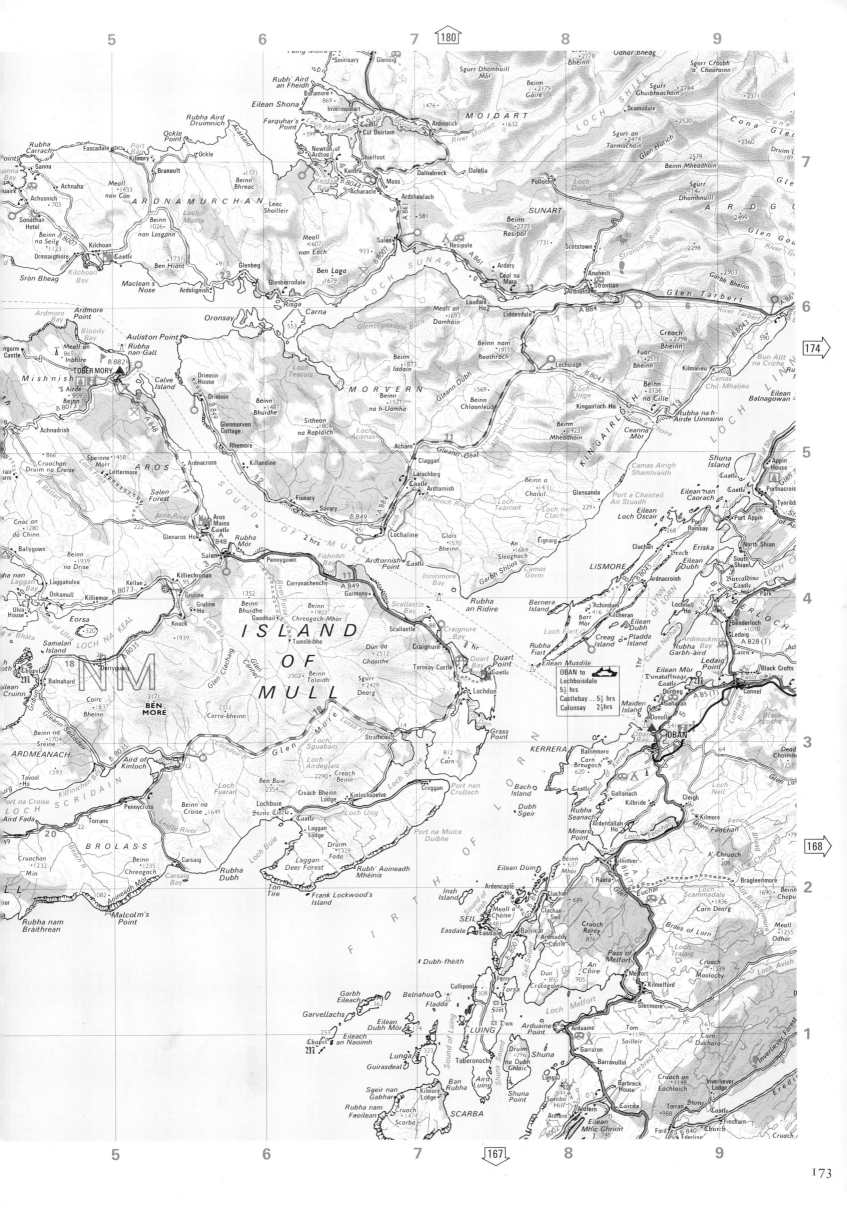

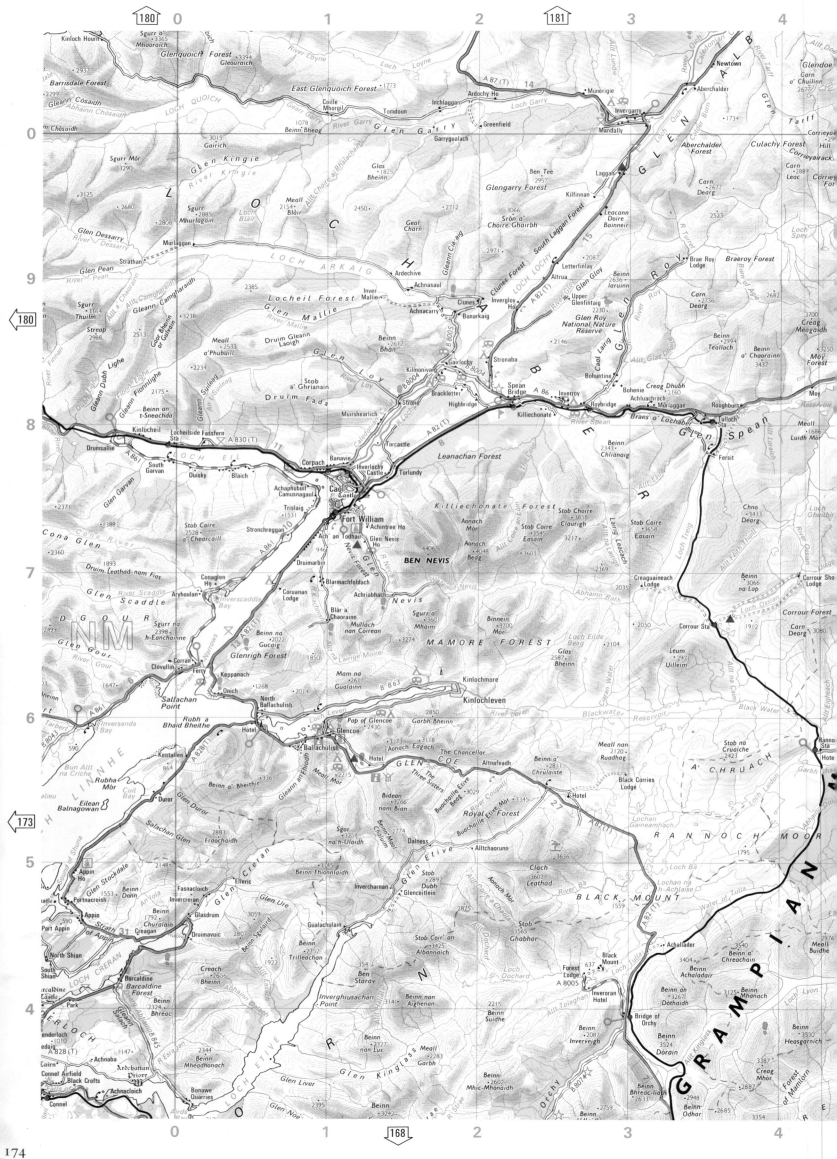

0   1   2   3   4

14

15

L   O   C   H

9

8

7

6

5

4

BEN NEVIS

Fort William

Kinloch Hourn
Sgurr a'
Mhaoraich · 3365
Glenquoich Forest
Gleouraich · 3394
Barrisdale Forest
· 2937
· 2299
Gleann Còsaidh
Gleann Abhainn Chòsaidh
m Chòsaidh
· 3125
Sgurr Mòr
3290
Glen Dessarry
River Dessarry
· 2808
Sgurr
Mhurlagain · 2885
Strathan
Glen Pean
River Pean
Sgurr
Thuilm · 3164
Streap
2988
Glen Dubh
Lighe
Gleann Camgharaidh
· 3238
Gleann Camgharaidh
Gearr Bheinn
or Gulvain
Sgùrr na
h-Eanchainne
Beinn an
t-Sneachda
Kinlocheil
Drumsallie
South
Garvan
Duisky
Blaich
Corpach
Banavie
Caol
Trislaig
Stronchreggan
Achintree Ho
Ach' an Todhair
Cona River
· 2360
Druim Leathad nam Fias
1893
Glen Scaddle
Conaglen
Ho
Aryhoulan
Inverscaddle
Bay
Corran
Clovullin
Ferry
Keppanach
Onich
North
Ballachulish
Kentallen
Duror
Glen Stockdale
Appin Ho
Portnacroish
Appin
North Shian
South
Shian
Park
Achnaba
Barcaldine
Barcaldine
Forest
Connel Airfield
Black Crofts
Connel
East Glenquoich Forest
· 1773
River Loyne
Coille
Mhorgil
Tomdoun
Glen Garry
River Garry
Beinn Bheag
1078
Gairich
3015
Glen Kingie
River Kingie
Loch
Blair
Meall Blàir
2154
Loch Arkaig
Murlaggan
2385
Locheil Forest
Glen Mallie
River Mallie
Meall
a'Phubuill
2533
Druim Gleann
Laoigh
Stob
a' Ghrianan
Druim Fada
Muirshearlich
Inver
Mallie
Achnasaul
Achnacarry
Bunarkaig
Kilmonivaig
Strone
Loch
Loyne
A 87 (T)
Garrygualach
Greenfield
Glas
Bheinn · 1825
2450
Geal
Charn
Gleann Cia-aig
Loch Garry
Ben Tee
2957
Glengarry Forest
Sròn a'
Choire Ghairbh
2971
Clunes
Invergloy
Ho
2612
Beinn
Bhàn
Gairlochy
2146
Spean
Bridge
High bridge
Killiechonate
Ardochy Ho
Inchlaggan
Munerigie
Invergarry
Mandally
Laggan
Kilfinnan
3066
Leacann
Doire
Bainneir
Letterfinlay
Altrua
Upper
Glenfintaig
Glen Roy
National Nature
Reserve
Stronaba
Bohuntine
Inverroy
Roybridge
Braes o' Lochaber
Murlaggan
Aberchalder
Newtown
Aberchalder
Forest
Corrieyairack
1734
Carn
Dearg · 2677
Culachy Forest
Corrieyairack
Carn
Leac · 2889
Corrie
2523
Brae Roy
Lodge
Braeroy Forest
Beinn
Iaruinn · 2636
Carn
Dearg · 2736
2682
Creag Dhubh
Achluachrach
Roughburn
Tulloch
Sta
Fersit
3700
Beinn
Teallach · 2994
Creag
Meagaidh
3250
Moy
Forest
Beinn
a' Chaorainn
3437
Moy
Moy
Reservoir
Meall
Luidh Mòr
1686
Beinn
Chlianaig
2343
Glen Spean
Caledonian
Torcastle
Inverlochy
Castle
Torlundy
Leanachan Forest
Killiechonate Forest
Aonach
Mòr
Stob Choire
3858
Stob Coire
Easain · 3545
Aonach
Beag · 4048
3603
4406
Glen Nevis
Ben Nevis
Nevis Forest
Druimarbin
Blarmachfoldach
Achriabhach
Coruanan
Lodge
Blàr a'
Chaorainn
Mullach
nan Coirean
3274
Sgurr a'
Mhaim · 3601
Binnein
Mòr · 3700
Glas
Bheinn · 2587
MAMORE FOREST
Stob Choire
Clanrigh · 3858
Stob Coire
Easain · 3658
Lairig Leacach
Creaguaineach
Lodge
2035
Abhainn Rath
Beinn
na Lap · 3066
Chno
Dearg · 3433
Loch Treig
Corrour Sho
Lodge
Corrour Forest
Carn
Dearg · 3080
Corrour Sta
1912
Loch Ossian
Loch Eilde
Beag
Leum
Uileim · 2971
DGOUR
NM
Glen Gour
River Gour
Sgurr na
h-Eanchainne
2398
Beinn na
Gucaig · 2022
Glenrigh Forest
Mam na
Gualainn · 2611
Kinlochmore
Kinlochleven
Pap of Glencoe
2430
Glencoe
Garbh Bheinn
2850
Ballachulish
Hotel
Beinn a' Bheithir
3361
Meall Mòr
2215
Bidean
nam Bian · 3766
GLEN COE
Aonach Eagach
3173
The Three Sisters
Altnafeadh
Buachaille Etive
Beag · 3029
Buachaille Etive
Mòr · 3345
Royal Forest
River Coupall
Beinn a'
Chrulaiste · 2811
The Chancellor
Hotel
Black Corries
Lodge
Meall nan
Ruadhag · 2120
Stob na
Cruaiche · 2423
Ranno
Sta
Hote
A' CHRUACH
Blackwater Reservoir
Black Water
RANNOCH MOOR
Garbh Gha
Lochan
Gaineamhach
Loch Bà
1795
Rubh a
Bhaid Bheithe
Inversanda
Bay
Sallachan
Point
Cuil Bay
Rubha
Mòr
Bun Allt
na Criche
Eilean
Balnagowan
Glen Creran
Elleric
Fasnacloich
Invercreran
Glasdrum
Druimavuic
Creagan
Beinn
Donn · 1792
Churalain
Salachan Glen
Beinn
Fraochaidh · 2883
Glen Ure
Gualachulain
Beinn
Sgulaird · 3059
Glen Creran
Beinn Ehionnlaidh
Invercharnan
Glen Etive
Sgor
na h-Ulaidh · 3258
3145
Stob
Dubh · 2897
Glenceitlein
Dalness
2774
Beinn Maol
Chalum
Alltchaorunn
Clach
Leathad · 3602
Loch Bà
3636
Aonach Mòr
2875
Stob Coir' an
Albannaich · 3425
BLACK MOUNT
1559
Achallader
3540
Beinn a'
Chreachain · 3267
Beinn
Achaladair · 3404
Creach
Bheinn · 2656
Beinn
Trilleachan · 2752
1922
Ben Starav
3541
Stob
Ghabhar · 3565
354
Loch Dochard
Black
Mount
637
Forest
Lodge
Inveroran
Hotel
Bridge
of Orchy
Inveen
Beinn
Inverveigh · 2087
Beinn an
Dòthaidh · 3267
Beinn
Dòrain · 3524
3125
Beinn
Mhanach · 3125
Beinn
Heasgarnich
3530
Meall
Buidhe · 2976
Forest
of Mamlorn
Barcaldine
Castle
Inverghiusachan
Point
3141
Glen Kinglass
Beinn nan
Aighenan
2215
Beinn
Suidhe
Beinn
nan Lus · 2327
Meall
Garbh · 2283
Beinn
Mheadhonach · 2344
Bonawe Quarries
Glen Liver
Glen Noe
2395
Beinn
3242
Beinn
Mhic-Mhonaidh · 2602
Ardb
Orchy
2759
Beinn
2685
Creag
Mhòr · 3387
2948
2887
Beinn
Bhreac-liath · 2633
Beinn
Odhar · 2948
3354

0   1   2   3   4

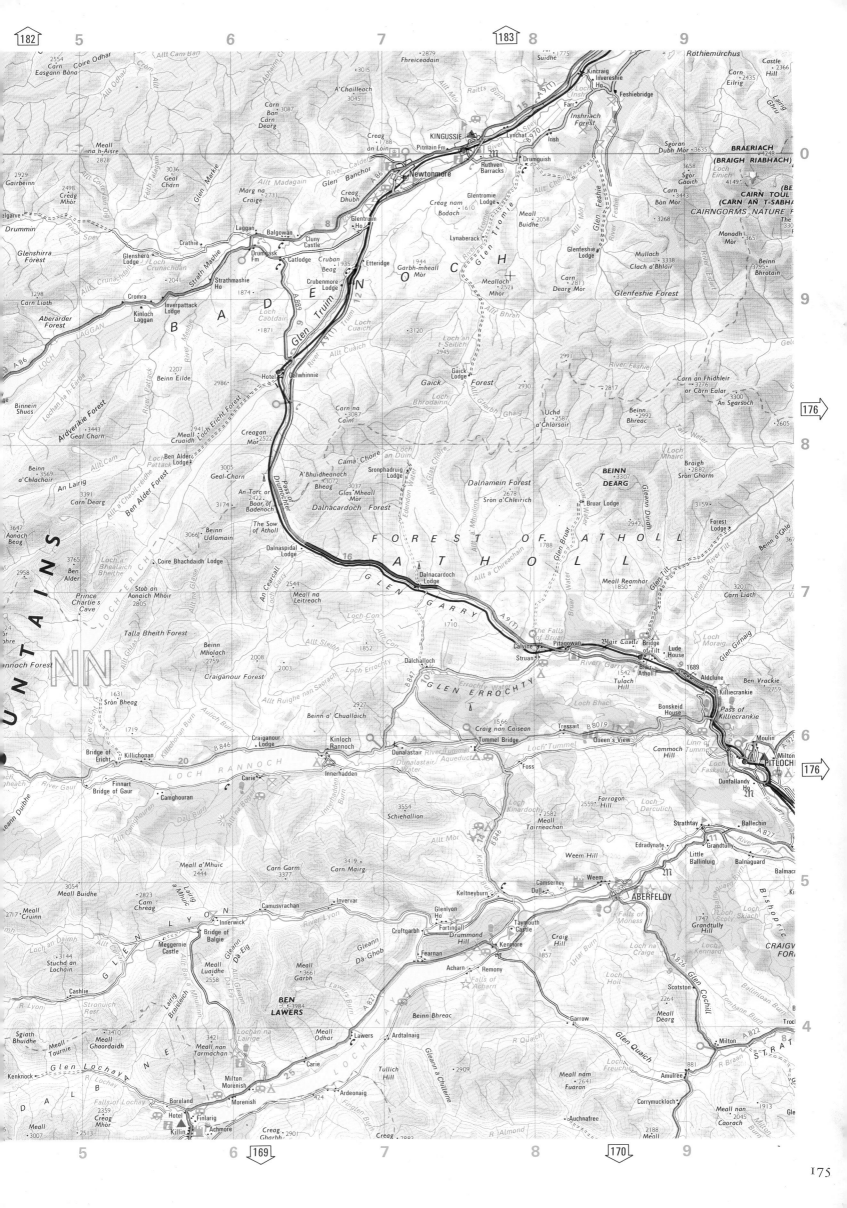

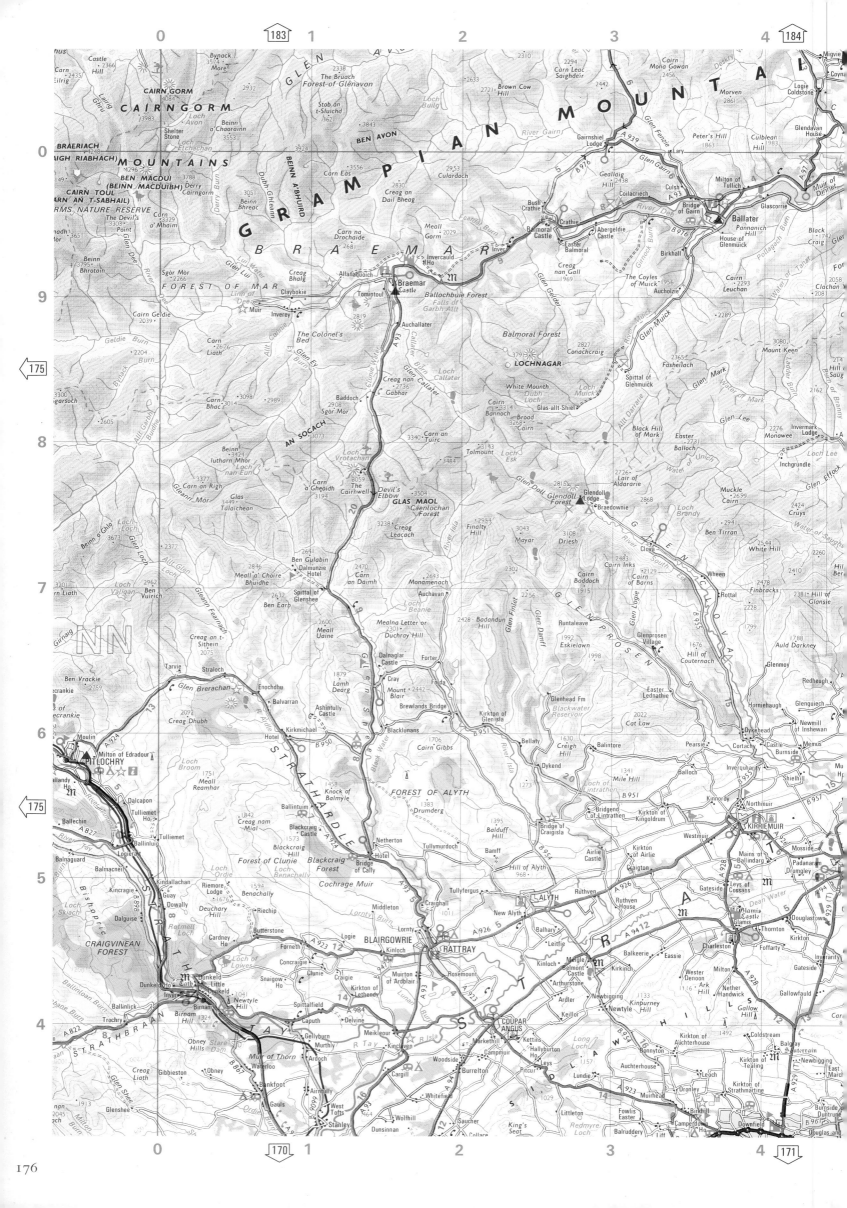

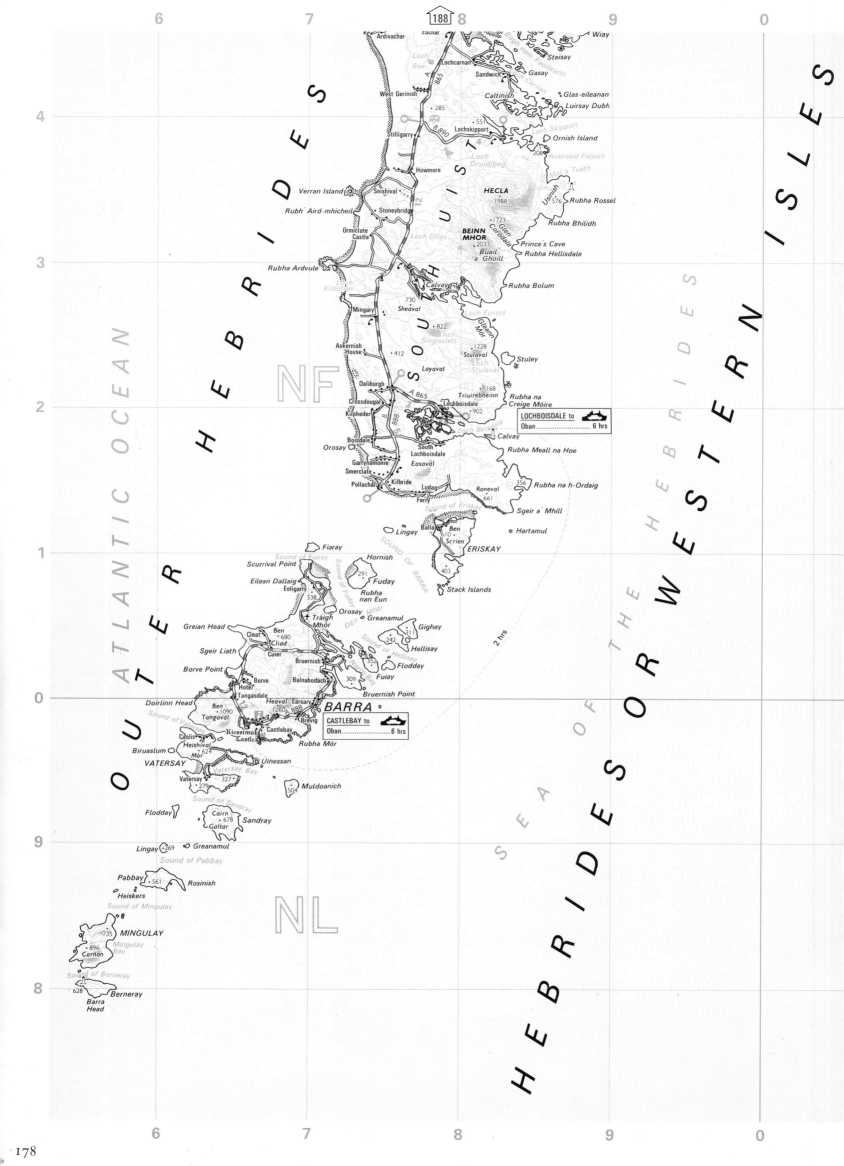

Wiay

Steisay

Loch
Bee
Ardivachar
Euchar
Lochcarnan
Gasay
Sandwick
Bagh nam Faoileann
West Gerinish
Caltinish
Glas-eileanan
Luirsay Dubh

285

551
Lochskipport
Loch Skipport

Tilligarry
B 890
Ornish Island
Loch Druidibeg
208
Acairseid Falaich

Howmore
Mol a' Tuath

Verran Island
Snishival
HECLA
1988
Usinish
576
Rubha Rossel

Rubh Aird-mhicheil
Stoneybridge
Rubha Bhilidh

Ormiclate
Castle
1723
Glen
Corodale
Prince's Cave

BEINN
MHOR
Buail
a' Ghoill
Rubha Hellisdale

Rubha Ardvule
2033

Loch
Kildonan
Calvay
Rubha Bolum

Loch Ollay

Mingary
730
Sheaval

SOUTH
822
Loch
Snigisclett
Loch Eynort
Gleann
Mor

Askernish
House
412
1228
Stulaval
Loch
Stulaval
Stuley

Daliburgh
Layaval
UIST

Crossdougal
A 865
1168
Triuirebheinn
Rubha na
Creige Móire

Kilpheder
B 888
Lochboisdale
902

Boisdale
LOCHBOISDALE to
Oban..........6 hrs

Orosay
South
Lochboisdale
Calvay

Garrynamonie
Easaval
Rubha Meall na Hoe

Smerclate
Kilbride
Rubha na h-Ordaig
356

Pollachar
Ludag
Ferry
Roneval
661

Sgeir a' Mhill

Sound of Eriskay

Lingay
Balla
Ben
610
Scrien
Hartamul

Fiaray
ERISKAY

Sound of Fiaray
Hornish

Scurrival Point
291
Fuday

Eilean Dallaig
Rubha
nan Eun

Eoligarry
338
403
Stack Islands

Orosay
Oitir Mhór

Greian Head
Tràigh
Mhór
Greanamul
Gighay

Cleat
Ben
680
Cliad
242
311

Sgeir Liath
Cuier
Hellisay

Borve Point
Bruernish
352
Flodday

Borve
Balnabodach
Fuiay

Hotel
Tangasdale
309

Doirlinn Head
Heaval
Earsary
Bruernish Point

Ben
1090
Tangaval
1260
B 888
Brevig
BARRA

Sound of Vatersay
Kiessimul
Castle
Castlebay
CASTLEBAY to
Oban..........6 hrs

Caolis
Rubha Mór

Biruaslum
Heishival
Mór
624
Uinessan

VATERSAY
Vatersay
279
327
504
Muldoanich

Vatersay Bay

Flodday
Cairn
678
Galtar
Sandray

Sound of Sandray

Lingay
269
Greanamul

Sound of Pabbay

Pabbay
561
Rosinish

Heiskers

Sound of Mingulay
NL

735
MINGULAY
Mingulay
Bay

896
Carnan

Sound of Berneray

628
Berneray
Barra
Head

ATLANTIC OCEAN

OUTER

HEBRIDES

NF

SEA OF THE HEBRIDES OR WESTERN ISLES

HEBRIDES

2 hrs

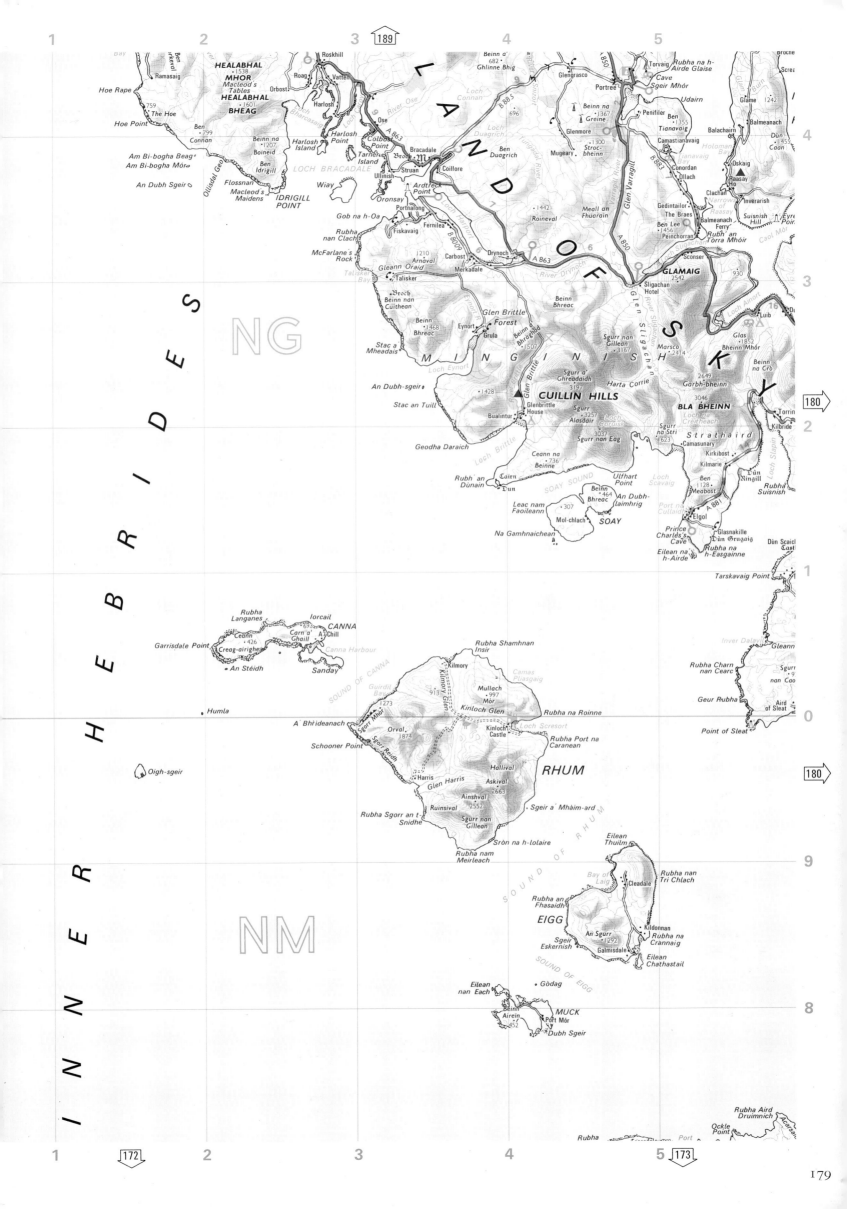

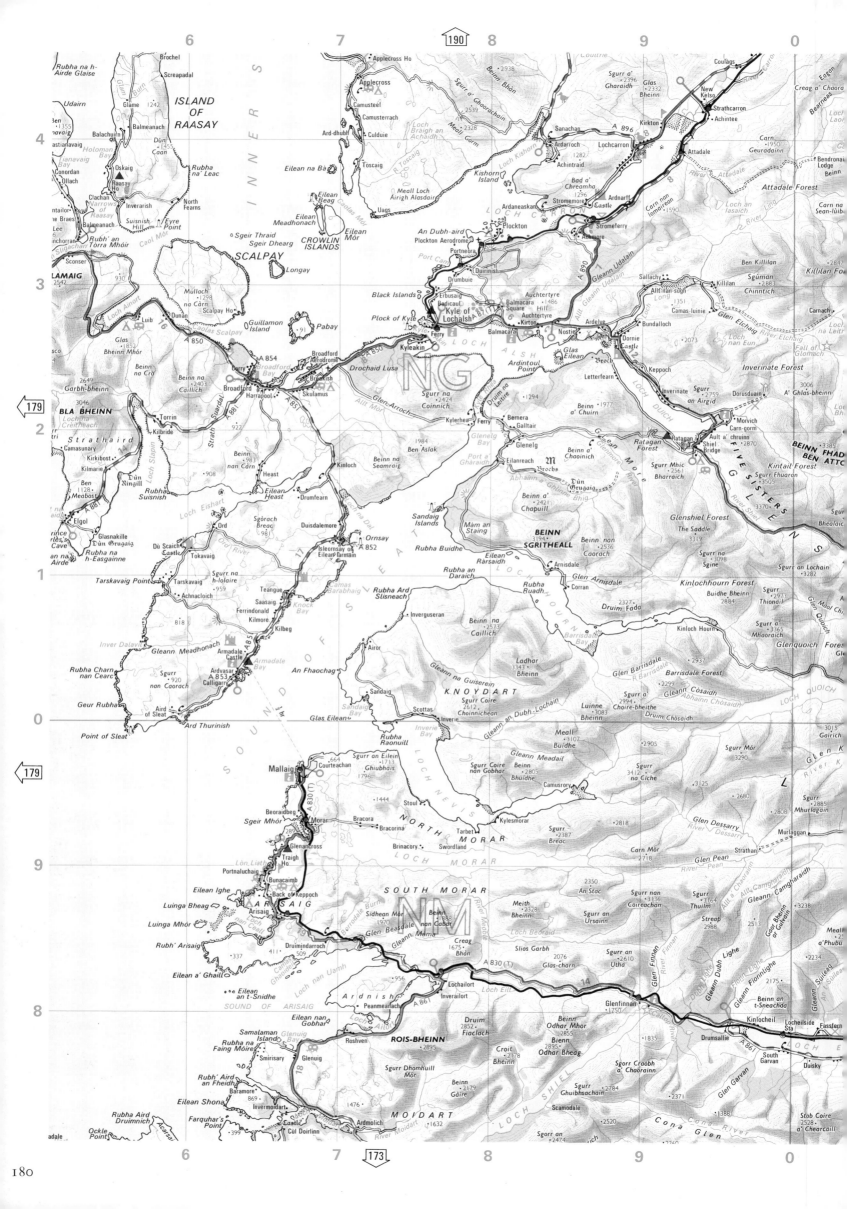

179
179

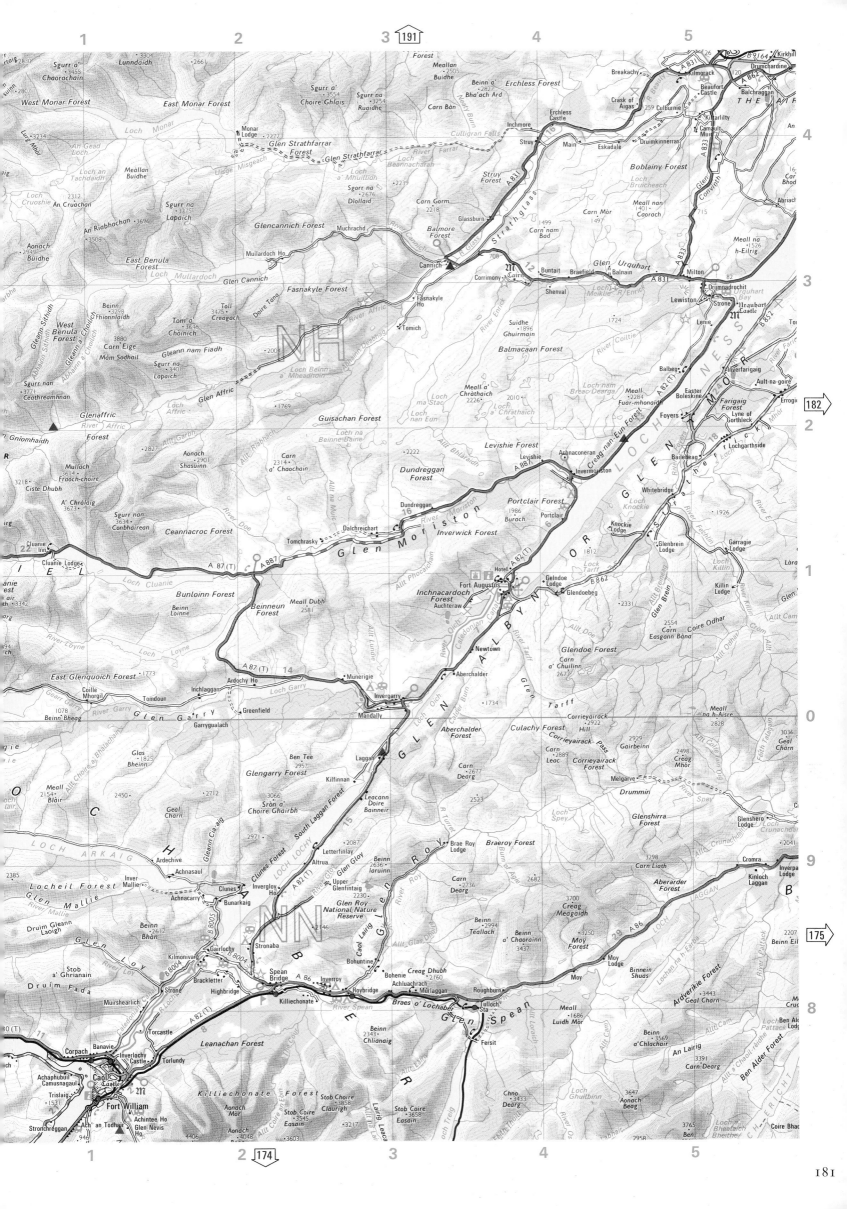

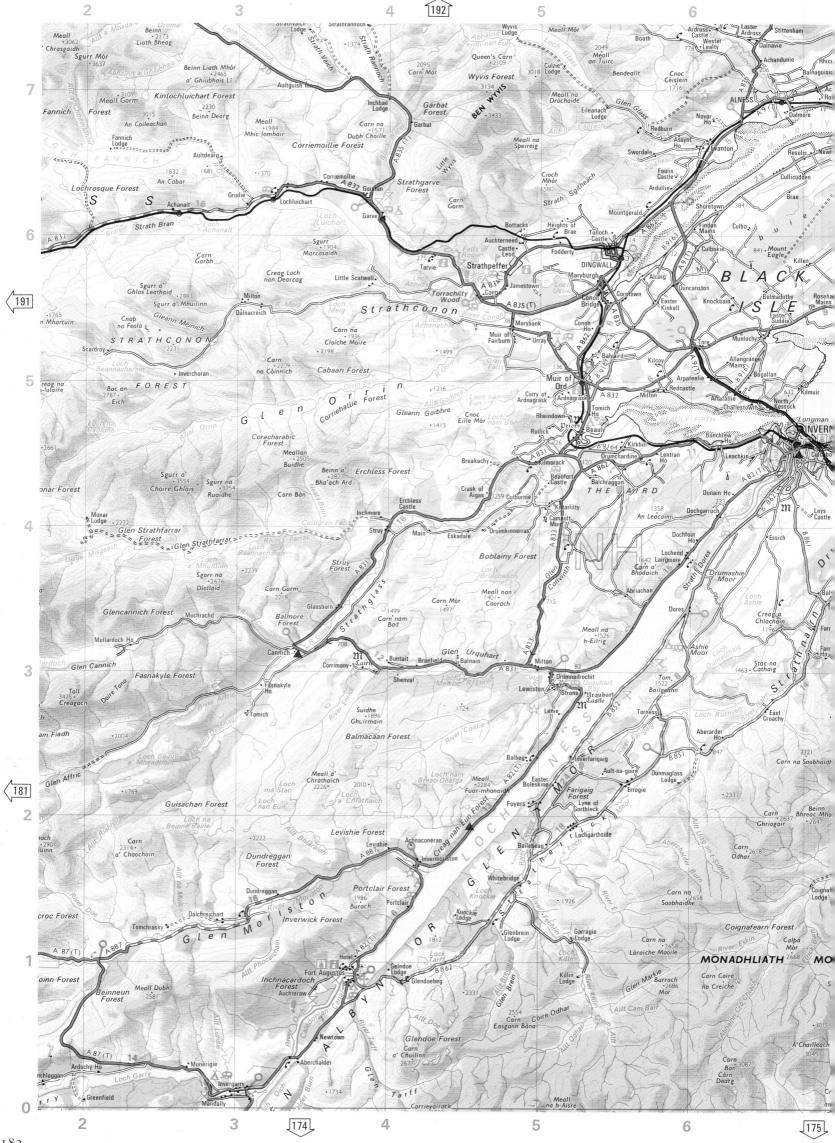

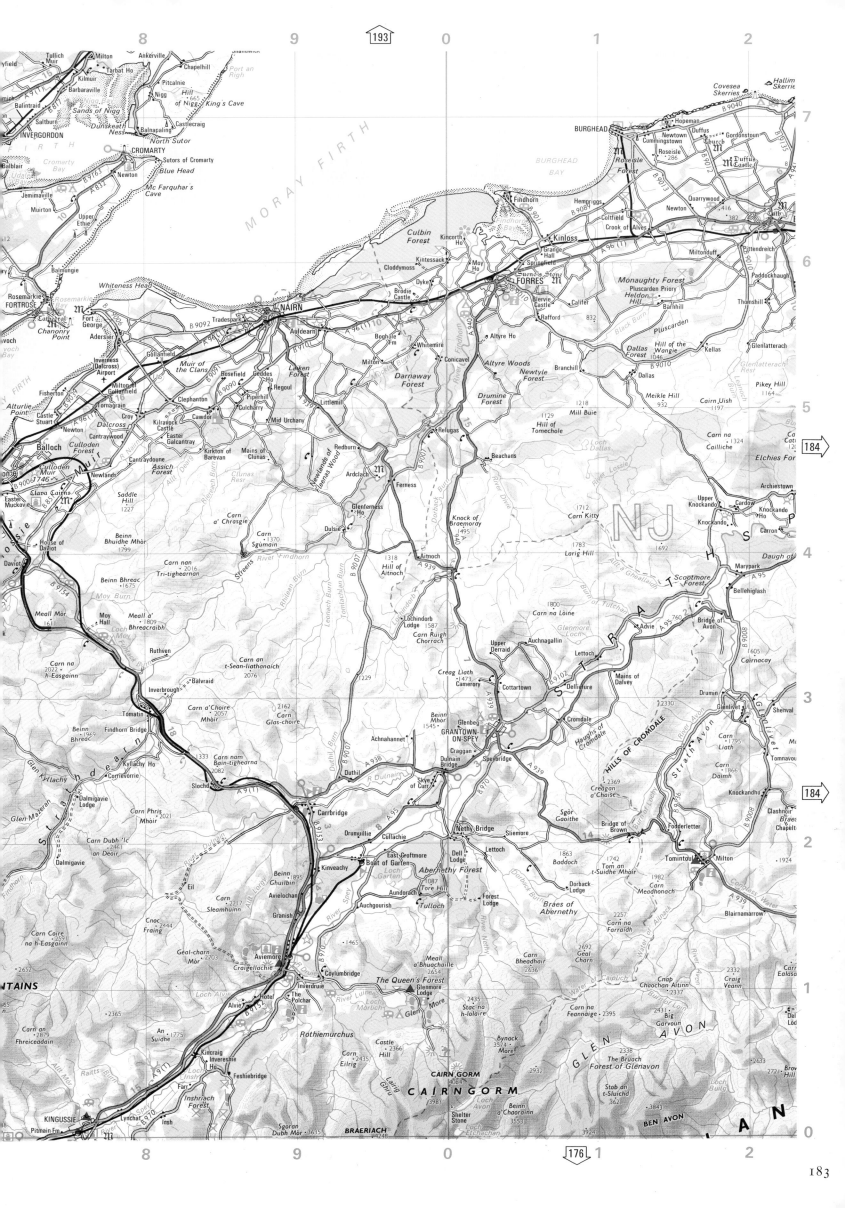

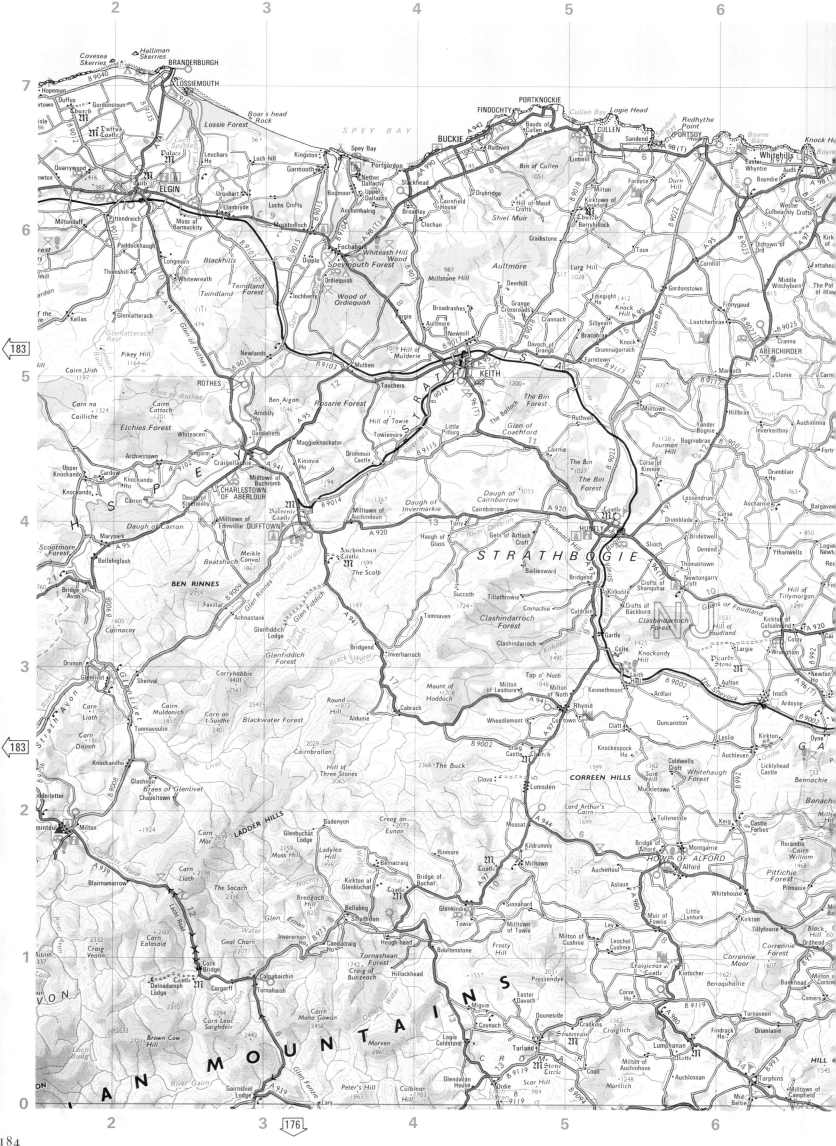

OUTER HEBRIDES OR WESTERN ISLES

INNER HEBRIDES

HEBRIDES

THE HEBRIDES OR

THE LITTLE MINCH

NF

North Uist area (upper left)

Rubha
Bhoisnis
Vaitam
Sound of Berneray
Torogay
Groay
Gilsay
Sgeir a'
Chàil
Lingay
Scaravay
Newtonferry
Newton
B.893
Aird
Thormaid
Sursay
Opsay
Beinn
·624
Mhòr
Trumisgarry
Tahay
Crogary
Mór ·588
Crogary
na Hoe
504
Hermetray
Groatay
Rubha
an Dùine
Loch
Fada Loch
Skealtar
Lochmaddy
Weaver's Point
Hotel
Loch
Maddy
Rubha nam Plèac
B.867
·824
North Lee
Madadh Gruamach
·920
South Lee
An t-Aigeach
Loch Eport
Sidinish
Rubha Mhic
Gille-mhìcheil
Eigneig Mhór
1139
EAVAL
Eigneig Bheag
Liernish
Floddaybeg
Floddaymore
Eimsay
·379
Ronay
·325
Rubha na Rodagrich
Rossinish
Maragay Mór
Maaey Riabhach
Greanamul Deas
Rubha Cam
nan Gall
·334
Wiay
·Glas-eileanan
Luirsay Dubh
Skipport
Ornish Island
Acairseid Falaich
Mol a' Tuath
·576
Rubha Rossel
Rubha Bhilidh

188
178

Ferry boxes

LOCHMADDY to [ferry] Tarbert .... 2½ hrs

2 hrs

UIG to [ferry] Tarbert .... 2 hrs

Skye area (right)

An t-Iasg
Camas
Mór
Cairidh nan Ob
Balgown
Kilbride Point
Totsca
Idrigill
WATERNISH
POINT
Uig Bay
An Càmastac
Healaval
Eilean Iosal
Eilean Creagach
Ascrib Islands
Ru Chorachan
LOCH SNIZORT
Poll na
h-Ealaidh
Ben
·931
Geary
Geary
Ard Beag
Trumpan
WATERNISH
Loch
Losait
Ardmore Point
Halistra
Gillen
Score
Horan
Biod nan
Laog
Eilean
Mór
Lyndale
Point
DUNVEGAN
HEAD
Hallin
Isay
Island
Mingay
Beinn
Charnach Bheag
Lusta
Greshornish
Point
Greshornish
Lyndale
Ho
Sgeir nam
Biast
Loch
Bay
Flashader
Tre
Geodha nan Each
Galtrigill
Gob
na Hoe
Claigan
·1074
Beinn
Chreagach
A.850
Edinbane
Borreraig
Ben
Ettow
Uig
B.886
Bay River
Be
An Ceannaich
Feriniquarrie
Totaig
·866
Ben
·806
Uigshader
Milovaig
Oisgill
Bay
Lephin
Colbost
Dunvegan
Skinidin
Kilmuir
Cruachan Beinn a'
Chearcaill
Neist
Waterstein
Head
Glen Dale
Hamara River
Broch
B.884
A.863
Lonmore
·872
Moonen
Bay
Ben
Corkeval
Roskhill
Hoe Rape
Ramasaig
HEALABHAL
1538
MHOR
Macleod's
Tables
HEALABHAL
1601
BHEAG
Roag
Vatten
Loch
Connan
·759
The Hoe
Orbost
Harlosh
ISLAND
Hoe Point
Ben
·799
Connan
Loch
Bharcasaig
Ose
River Ose
A.863
Am Bi-bogha Beag
Am Bi-bogha Mór
Beinn na
·1207
Boineid
Harlosh
Island
Harlosh
Point
Colbost
Point
Bracadale
Broch
Coillore
An Dubh Sgeir
Ben
Idrigill
Tarner
Island
Ullinish
Struan
Ollisdal Geo
Flossnan
Macleod's
Maidens
Wiay
LOCH BRACADALE
Wiay
Ardtreck
Point
Oronsay
Coillore
IDRIGILL
POINT
Gob na h-Oa
Portnalong
Rubha
nan Clach
Fiskavaig
Fernilea
McFarlane's
Rock
·1210
Arnaval
B.8009
Carbost
Gleann Oraid
Merkadale
Talisker
Bay
Talisker
Broch
Beinn nan
Cùithean
Beinn
·1468
Bhreac
Eynort
Stac a
Mheadais
An Dubh-sgeir
MI
Loch Eynort
Stac an Tuill
Geodha Daraich
Rubh' an
Dùnain
Rubha
Langanes
Iorcail
CANNA

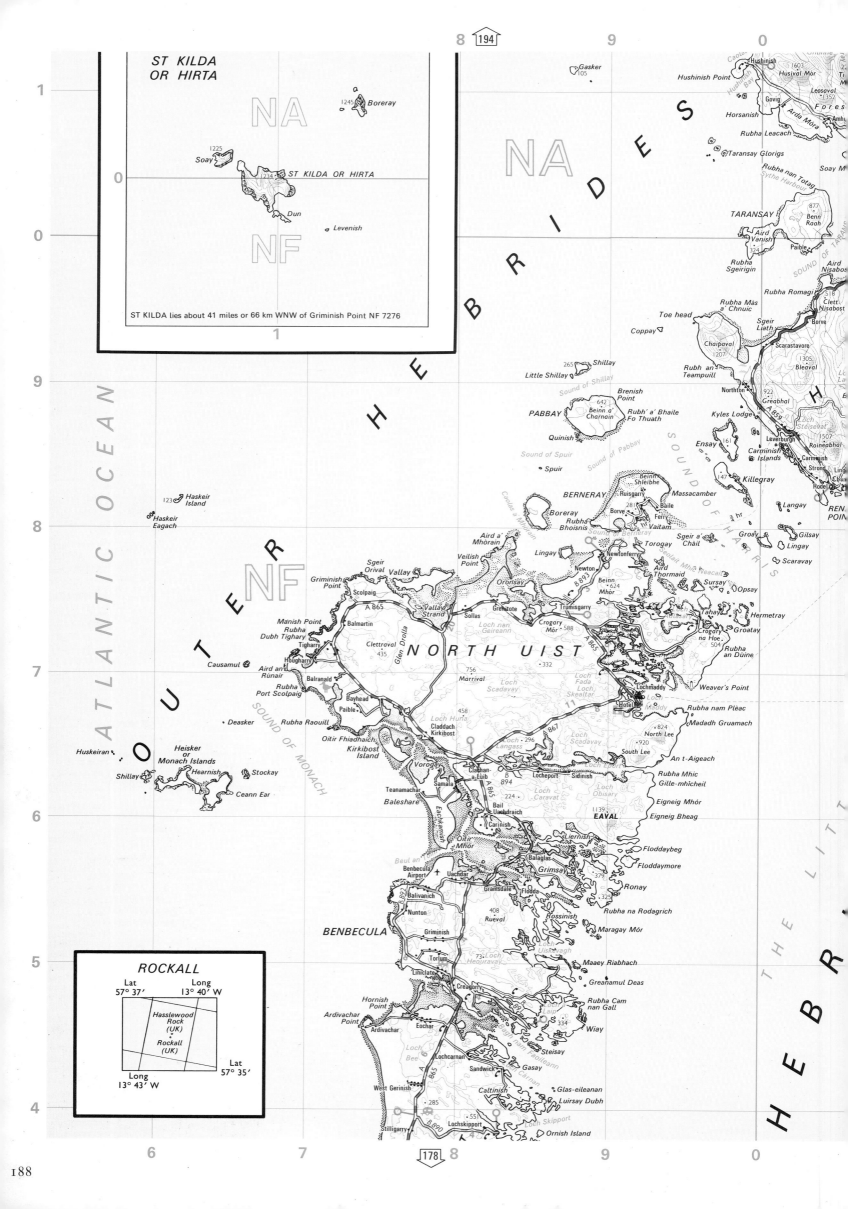

ST KILDA OR HIRTA

NA

Gasker
105

Boreray
1245

NA

NA

Soay
1225

1234
ST KILDA OR HIRTA

Dun

NF

Levenish

ST KILDA lies about 41 miles or 66 km WNW of Griminish Point NF 7276

Hushinish
Husival Mòr
1603

Hushinish Point
Leosaval
1352

Horsanish
Forest

Rubha Leacach

Govig
Arda Mòra

Taransay Glorigs

Rubha nan Totag
Sythe Harbour

Soay

TARANSAY

Benn
Raah
877

Aird
Vanish
Aird
Nisabost

Rubha
Sgeirigin

Paible

Rubha Màs
a' Chnuic

Rubha Romagi

Člett
Nisabost
518

Toe head

Sgeir
Liath

Borve

Scarastavore

H E B R I D E S

Coppay

Chaipaval
1207

Bleaval
1305

Shillay
265

Rubh an
Teampuill

Northton

Greabhal
922

Little Shillay

Sound of Shillay

Brenish
Point

A 859

Bleaval
1507

PABBAY

Beinn a'
Charnain
642

Rubh' a' Bhaile
Fo Thuath

Kyles Lodge

Loch
Steisevat

Quinish

Ensay

Leverburgh

Carminish
Islands

Roineabhal

Sound of Spuir

Sound of Pabbay

161

Killegray

Carminish
Strond

Spuir

Sound of Harris

Rodel

Beinn
Shleibhe

Langay

H E B R I D E S

BERNERAY

Ruisgarry
281

Massacamber

147

Lingay

Boreray

Borve

Baile

Groay

Gilsay

Haskeir
Island
123

Rubha
Bhoisnis

Ferry

Vaitam

Scaravay

Aird a'
Mhòrain

Sound of Berneray

Torogay

Sgeir a'
Chàil

Sursay

Opsay

Haskeir
Eagach

Seoltad Mhòr Neacail

Lingay

Veilish
Point

Lingay

Newtonferry

Aird
Thormaid

O U T E R

Sgeir
Orival

Valley

Oronsay

Newton

Beinn
Mhòr
624

Hermetray

Griminish
Point

Scolpaig

Vallay
Strand

Sollas

Grenitote

Trumisgarry

Tahay

NF

A 865

Balmartin

Loch nan
Geireann

Crogary
Mòr
588

Crogary
na Hoe
504

Groatay

Manish Point
Rubha
Dubh Tighary

Tigharry

N O R T H   U I S T

Rubha
an Dùine

Causamul

Hougharry

Aird an
Rùnair

Balranald

756
Marrival

332

Loch
Scadavay

Loch
Fada
Loch
Skealtar

Lochmaddy

Weaver's Point

Rubha
Port Scolpaig

Bayhead

Paible

Claddach
Kirkibost

Loch Huna
458

296
Loch
Langass

867

Loch
Scadavay
920

Hotel

North Lee
824

Rubha nam Plèac

Madadh Gruamach

Deasker

Rubha Raouill

Oitir Fhiadhaich

Kirkibost
Island

Vorogay

Clachan-
a'-luib

B
894

Lochport

Sidinish

South Lee

An t-Aigeach

Huskeiran

Heisker
or
Monach Islands

Hearnish

Stockay

Teanamachar

Samala

Bail
Uachdraich

224

Loch
Caravat

Loch
Obisary

Rubha Mhic
Gille-mhìcheil

Eigneig Mhòr

Shillay

Ceann Ear

Baleshare

Carinish

EAVAL
1139

Eigneig Bheag

Oitir
Mhòr

Liernish

Floddaybeg

Floddaymore

Benbecula
Airport

Uachdar

Balaglas

Grimsay

Flodda

Ronay

Balivanich

Gramsdale

379

Rubha na Rodagrich

Nunton

Rueval
408

Rossinish

Maragay Mòr

Griminish

BENBECULA

Uiskevagh

Maaey Riabhach

Torlum

Loch
Heouravay
73

Greanamul Deas

Liniclate

Rubha Cam
nan Gall

Creagorry

Hornish
Point

334

Wiay

Ardivachar
Point

Eochar

Steisay

Ardivachar

Loch
Bee

Lochcarnan

Gasay

Glas-eileanan

West Gerinish

Sandwick

Luirsay Dubh

285

Caltinish

Stilligarry

Lochskipport
55

Loch Skipport

Ornish Island

ROCKALL

A T L A N T I C   O C E A N

SOUND OF MONACH

H E B R

T H E   L I T T

THE MINCH

NB

DES OR WESTERN ISLES

NG

NORTH HARRIS

2153
Stulaval
191
Aline Lodge
2165
Oreval
f Harris
2392
Uisgnaval Mòr
713
Ardvourlie
Seaforth Island
Scaladale River
1874
Beinn Mhor
Eishken
Lemreway
Gob na Milaid
747
Srianach
Eilean Iubhard
Camas Allt nam Bearnach

1069
Clisham
Clett Ard
1532
Maaruig
1473
Caiteshal
1542
Crionaig
1217
Uisenis
Mol Truisg
Gob Rubh Uisenis

Meavig
B 887
Bunavoneadar
1829
Sgaoth Aird
Loch Seaforth
1733
Toddun
Rhenigidale
Ard Caol
Geo Dubh
Eilean Mòr a Bhàigh
Gob Rubh Uisenis
Rubha Bhrollum
Rubh' a'Bhaird

Gob Aird an Tolmachain
Isay
Ardhasaig
1547
Gillaval Glas
Urgha
Loch Trollamarig
Leac Eskadale
SOUND OF SHIANT

Beinn Dhubh
1661
Ben Luskentyre
Tarbert
A 859
Carragreich
Kyles Scalpay
Garbh Eilean
Galtachean
528
Cadha na Gaoidhsich
Eilean Mhuire

Luskentyre
1532
Aird Mheadhonach
1096
Carnach
Rubha Crago
Shiant Islands
Eilean an Tighe

South Harris Forest
Loch Ceann Dibig
Scotasay
Ferry
Aird Riabhach

Seilebost
Drinishader
Meavag
961
341
SCALPAY
Eilean Glas

1267
An Coileach
Ceann-na-Cleithe
Grosebay
Plocrapool Point
Plocrapool
Rubha Bhocaig

Ardvey
Likisto
Lackalee
Scadabay
Beacravik
Geocrab
Kyles Stockinish
Cluer

h-nam-bàgh
Manish
Aird Mhànais
Stockinish Island

Flodabay
Ardvey
Quidnish
Rubha Quidnish

Lingarabay Island

Loch Finsbay

2½ hrs

Fladda-chùain
83
Sgeir nam Maol

2 hrs

Eilean Trodday

RUBHA HUNISH
Loch Hunish
Rubha na h-Aiseig

An t-Iasgair
Tulm Bay
The Aird
Kilmaluag Bay
Bàgh nan Gunnaichean

WATERNISH POINT
An Càmastac
Healaval
Eilean Iosal
Eilean Creagach
Ascrib Islands
Lub Score
Monument
Kilmaluag
Sgeir na Eireann
Eilean Flodigarry

Ard Beag
Ben Geary
931
Geary
Cairidh nan Ò b
Bornesketaig
Kilmuir
Kilvaxter
Meall na Suiramach
1781
Flodigarry
Staffin Bay
Staffin Island

Ardmore Point
Trumpan
Gillen
Halistra
Hallin
Score Horan
Biod nan Laog
Balgown
Suidh' a' Mhinn
Linicro
Totscore
Kilbride Point
Staffin
A 855
Kilt Rock
Elishader
Valtos

DUNVEGAN HEAD
Mingay
Benn Charnach Bheag
Lusta
Greshornish Point
Eilean Mòr
Idrigill
Uig Bay
Uig
Earlish
Balnaknock
Bioda Buidhe
1523
Marishader
Garros
Rubha nam Brathairean
Breakrey

Isay Island
Sgeir nam Biast
Loch Bay
Ru Chorachan
Beinn Edra
2006
Peinlich
Creag a' Lain
1995
Leac Tressirnish
Lealt

Geodha nan Each
Galtrigill
Gob na Hoe
Claigan
Greshornish
Lyndale Point
Lyndale Ho
Kingsburgh
Beinn a' Sgà
Tote

Ben Ettow
Borreraig
Uig
Beinn Bhreac
1074
Flashader
Treaslane
The Aird
Eyre
THE STORR
2358
Old Man of Storr
TROTTERNISH

An Ceannaich
Feriniquarrie
Fotaig
Edinbane
Bernisdale
Kensaleyre
Beinn a' Chearcaill
1812
Holm Island

Milovaig
Lephin
Colbost
866
Ben Uigshader
682
Glen Bernisdale
Tote
Carbost
Borve
Loch Fada
Prince Charles's Cave

Neist
Waterstein Head
Ben Corkeval
Skinidin
Dunvegan
Kilmuir
Lonmore
Roskhill
872
Cruachan Beinn a' Chearcaill
Skeabost
Uigshader
Drumuie
Achachork
1288
Rubha na h-Airde Glaise

Hoe Rape
HEALABHAL MHOR
1538
Macleod's Tables
HEALABHAL BHEAG
1601
Roag
Vatten
Orbost
Harlosh
Beinn a' Ghlinne Bhig
Uigshader
Glengrasco
Portree
Cave
Sgeir Mhór
Udairn

The Hoe
759
Ben
799
Ben Connan
Harlosh Island
Harlosh Point
Colbost Point
696
Beinn na Greine
1367
Glenmore
1300
Stroc-bheinn
Penifiler
Ben Tianavaig
1355
Torrin

Hoe Point
Am Bi-bogha Beag
Am Bi bogha Mòr
Beinn na Boineid
1207
Tarner Island
Bracadale
211
Ben Duagrich
Mugeary
Camastianavaig
Dùn Caan
1455

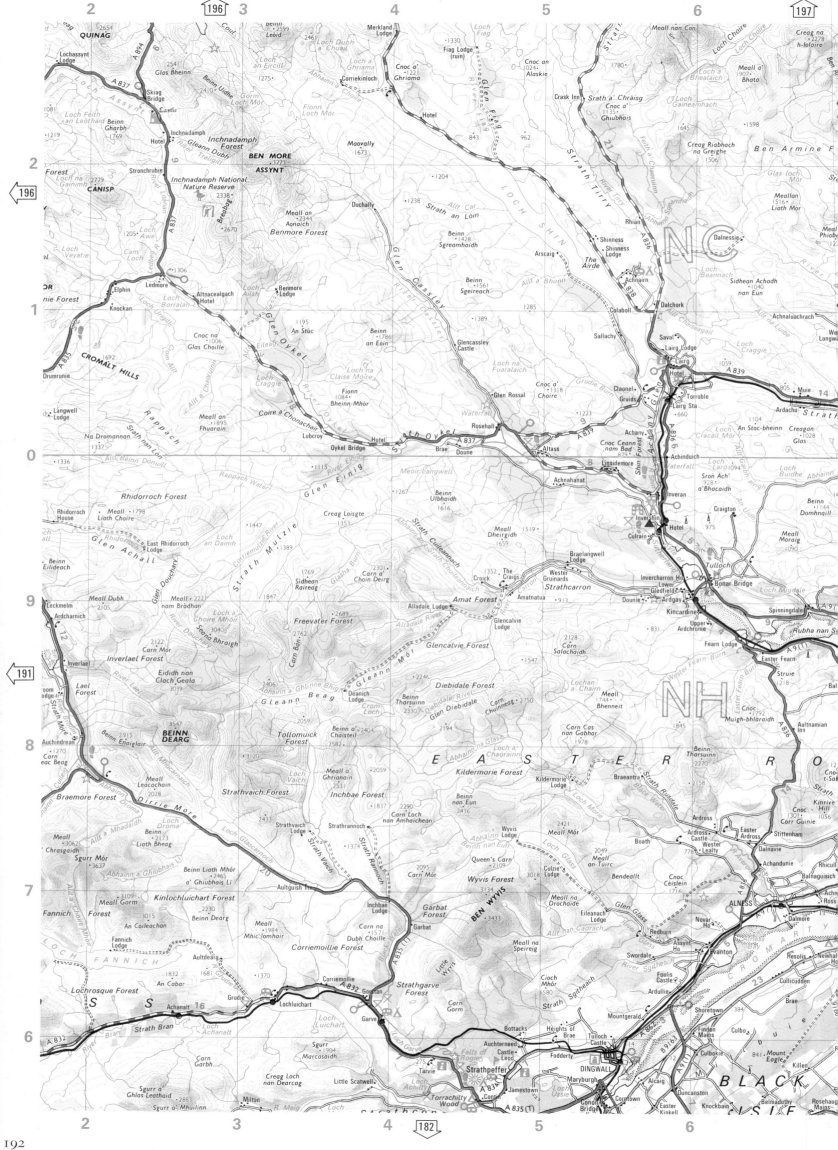

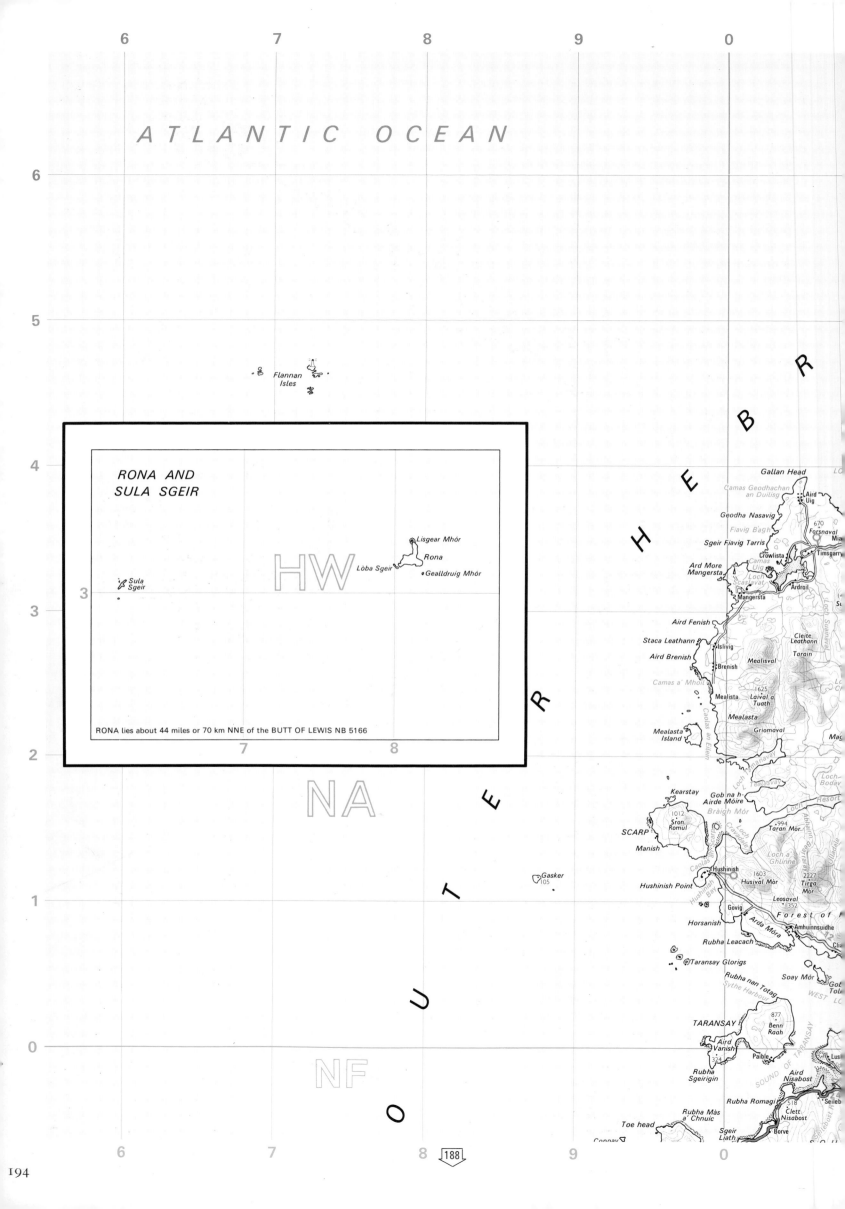

ATLANTIC OCEAN

H E B R

RONA AND
SULA SGEIR

HW

Lisgear Mhór

Rona

Lòba Sgeir

Gealldruig Mhór

Sula
Sgeir

RONA lies about 44 miles or 70 km NNE of the BUTT OF LEWIS NB 5166

Flannan
Isles

Gallan Head

Camas Geodhachan
an Duilisg

Aird
Uig

Geodha Nasavig

670
Forsnaval
Mia

Sgeir Fiavig Tarris

Fiavig Bàgh

Crowlista

Timsgarry

Ard More
Mangersta

Camas
Uig

Loch
Suainaval

Loch
Suainaval

Ardroil

Mangersta

Aird Fenish

Cleite
Leathann

Staca Leathann

Islivig

Tarain

Aird Brenish

Mealisval

Brenish

Mealista

1625
Laival a
Tuath

Camas a' Mhoil

Mealasta

Mealasta
Island

Griomaval

Caolas an Eilean

Mag

Loch
Bodav

Loch
Resort

Kearstay

Gob na h-
Airde Mòire

Bràigh Mór

1012
Sron
Romul

994
Taran Mór

SCARP

Loch a'
Ghlinne

Manish

Loch
Crannda

Caolas Scarp

Hushinish

1603
Husival Mòr

2227
Tirga
Mór

Hushinish Point

Hushinish
Bay

Leosaval
1352

Forest of

Govig

Aird Mhòr

Amhuinnsuidhe

Horsanish

Cli

Rubha Leacach

Taransay Glorigs

Soay Mór

Rubha nan Totag

Got
Tol

Sythe Harbour

WEST
LO

TARANSAY

877
Benn
Raah

Aird
Vanish

Lus

Paible

324

Rubha
Sgeirigin

Aird
Nisabost

SOUND OF TARANSAY

Rubha Romagi

Rubha Màs
a' Chnuic

518
Clett
Nisabost

Seileb

Toe head

Sgeir
Liath

Borve

Connav

SOU

HW

NA

NF

R

E

T

U

O

Gasker
105

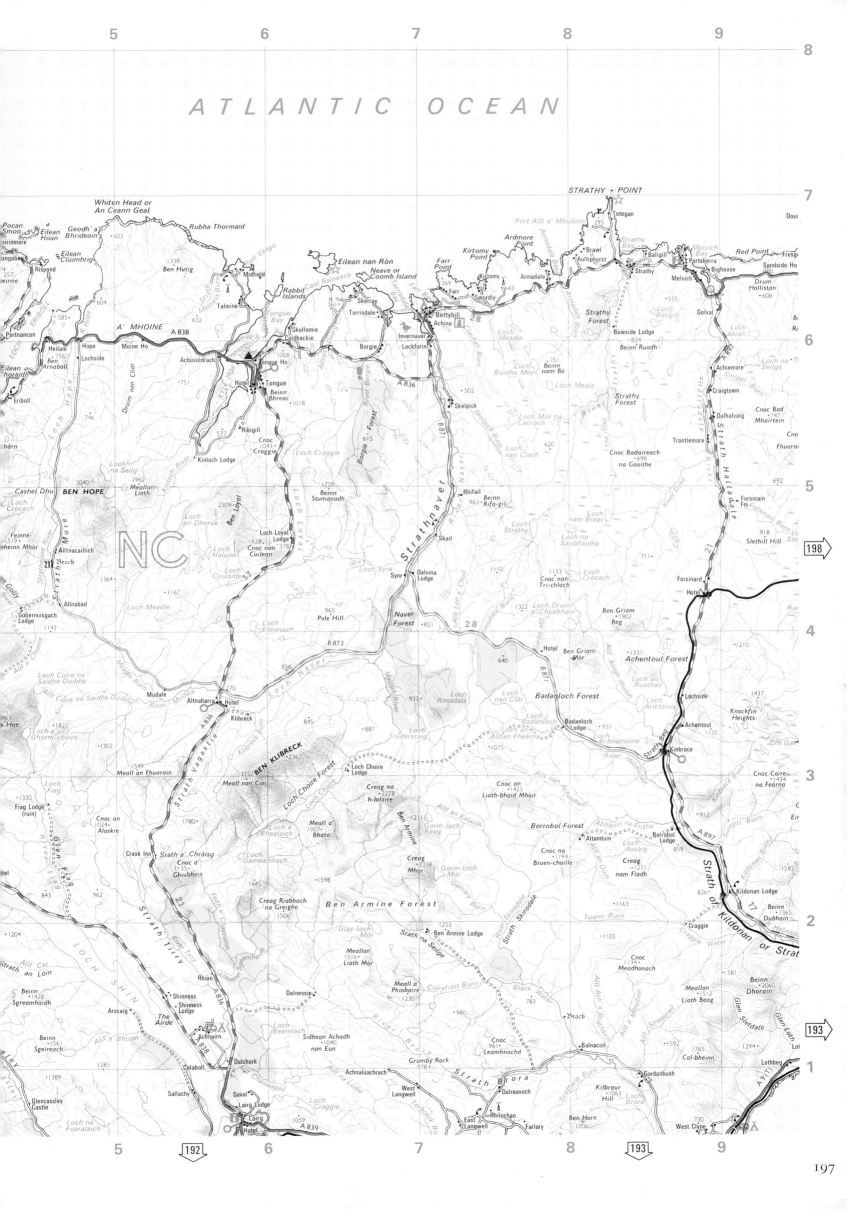

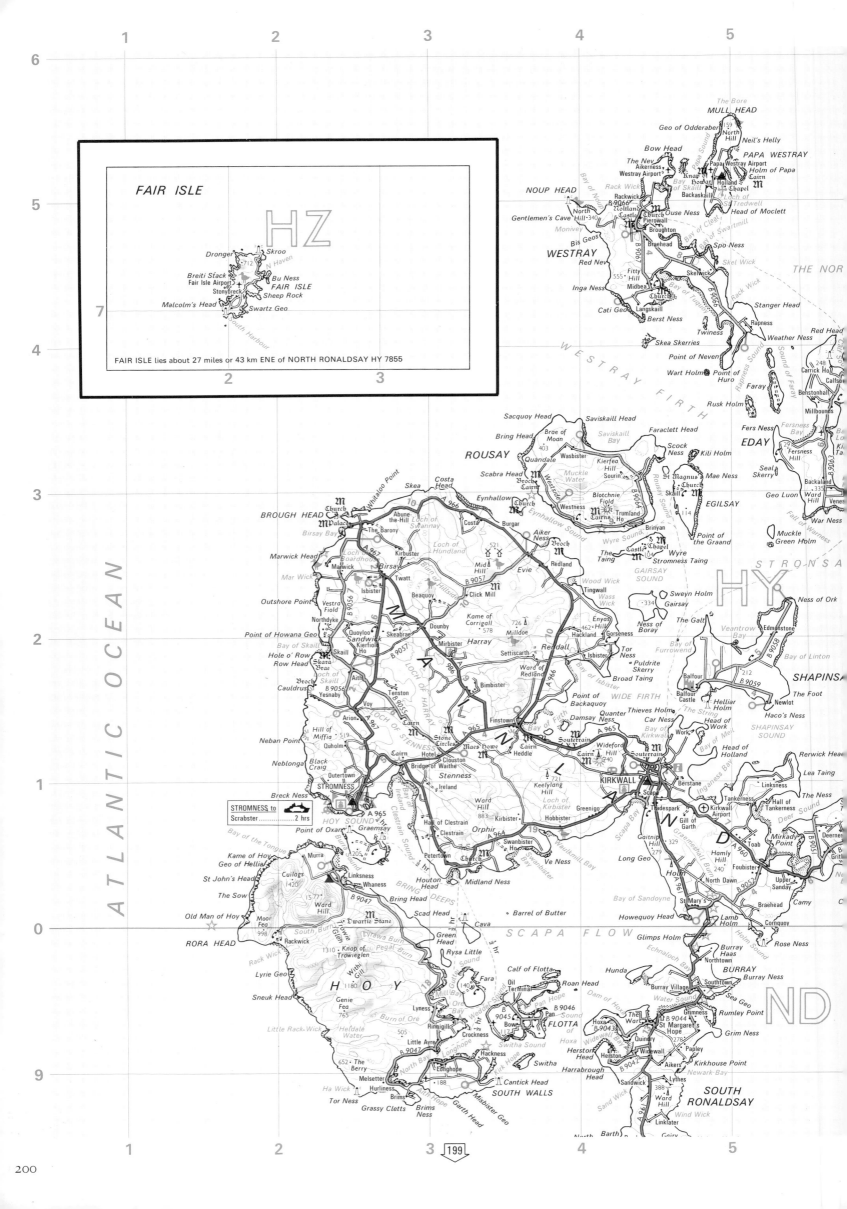

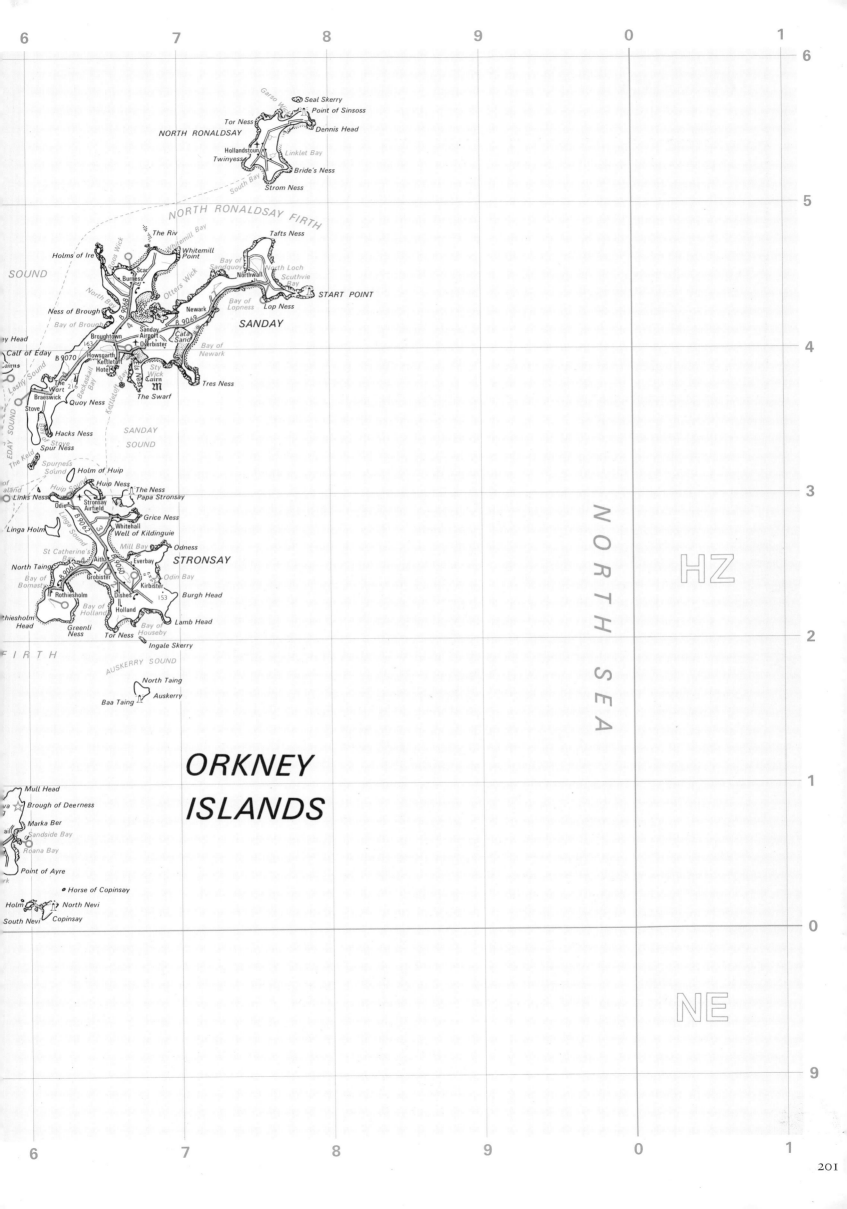

6

Seal Skerry
Point of Sinsoss
Garso Wick
Tor Ness
Dennis Head
NORTH RONALDSAY
Hollandstoun
Twinyess
Linklet Bay
Bride's Ness
South Bay
Strom Ness

5

NORTH RONALDSAY FIRTH

The Riv
Whitemill Bay
Tafts Ness
Holms of Ire
Roos Wick
Whitemill
Point
SOUND
Scar
Burness
Bay of
Sandquoy
North Loch
Scuthvie
Bay
Northwall
START POINT
North Bay
B.9068
Otters Wick
Ness of Brough
Bay of
Lopness
Lop Ness
Newark
Bay of Brough
B.9069
Calf of Eday
ey Head
Broughtown
Sanday
Airport
SANDAY
163
Overbister
Cata
Sand
Bay of
Newark

4

B.9070
Howsgarth
Kettletoft
Hotel
Sty
Wick
Cairn
Cairns
The
Wart
216
Braeswick
Tres Ness
Lashy Sound
Stove
Quoy Ness
The Swarf

Hacks Ness
SANDAY
Stove
Spur Ness
SOUND

3

Spurness
Sound
Holm of Huip
of
aland
Huip Ness
The Ness
Links Ness
Huip Sound
Papa Stronsay
Odie
Stronsay
Airfield
Grice Ness
B.9062
Whitehall
Linga Holm
Well of Kildinguie
Linga Sound
Mill Bay
Odness
St Catherine's
Bay
Everbay
STRONSAY
North Taing
Aithy
B.9060
Grobister
Odin Bay
Bay of
Bomasty
Kirbister
Rothiesholm
Dishes
153
Burgh Head
thiesholm
Head
Holland
Bay of
Holland
Greenli
Ness
Tor Ness
Bay of
Houseby
Lamb Head

2

FIRTH
Ingale Skerry
AUSKERRY SOUND
North Taing
Auskerry
Baa Taing

ORKNEY
ISLANDS

1

Mull Head
Brough of Deerness
va
Marka Ber
Sandside Bay
Roana Bay
Point of Ayre
rk
Horse of Copinsay
Holm
North Nevi
South Nevi
Copinsay

NORTH SEA

HZ

NE

SHETLAND ISLANDS

ATLANTIC OCEAN

ST MAGNUS BAY

Esha Ness area (top right):
Grind of the Navir
Scraada
ESHA NESS
The Bruddans
Isle of Stenness
Skerry of Eshaness
Stenness
Dore Holm
The Drongs
Baa Taing
Ure
Sae Breck
Braehoulland
Tangwick
Scarff
Burnside
Hillswick
Ness of Hillswick
Isle of Nibo
Lang He
Erne S
Strom Ness
MUCKLE ROE
Murbie Stac
Swarbacks Head
Vementry
Gruna

Ve Skerries

Cribbie
North Ness
Fogla Skerry
Virda Field
Biggings
PAPA STOUR
Holm of Melby
Sound of Papa
Isle of West Burrafirth
West Burrafirth
Brindisteel
Noonsbrou
Melby Ho
Garth
Quilva Taing
Sandness
Pund Head
Sandness Hill
Bay of Deepdale
Burga Water
Sulma Water
Loch of Voxterb
Mu Ness
Dale
Stourbrough Hill
Bridge of Walls
Voe of Dale
Burn of Dale
Wats Ness
Mid Walls
Sta
Browland
Skarpigarth
Burraland
Walls
Gruting
Braga Ness
Vaila Sound
Ward of Culswick
Uskie Geo
Vaila Hall
Culswick
Vaila
Strom Ness
Brock
Housa Water
The Nev
Westerwick
Giltarump
Wester Wick
Sil Wick
West Moulie Ge

Foula (centre):
Da Logat
Strem Ness
The Kame
Da Scrodhurdins
Harrier
Wester Hoevdi
The Sneug
Head o' da Taing
Ham
FOULA
Wick of Mucklabrek
Hametoun
Hellabrick's Wick
Hesti Geo
South Ness

HO

ATLANTIC OCEAN

HT

Isle of Fetha
Garmus Taing
Uyea ·231
Burrier Wick
The Breck
Fugla Ness
South Wick
564
North
Roe ·
Hevdadale Head
Egga Field
Lang Clodie Wick
644 Beorgs of
Skelberry
Gruna Stack
North Roe
Turls Head
Roer
The Faither
Watir
Muckle Ossa
·351 Ketligill
Heillia Head
Stonga
Banks
Housetter
740
Ockran Head
Burries
Man
Ness
o' Scord
1475·
Ronas
Collafirth
Hill
Colla
South Head
Gluss
The Clifts
Voe ·
Ollaber
Whalwick Taing
Water
Hamnavoe
Faan
Head of Stanshi
Heylor
·567
Hill
Grind of the Navir
Ure
Scarff
Braehoulland
Burnside
Urafirth
Eela
Scraada
Water
ESHA NESS
Sae
Tangwick
A 9078
B 9079
Breck
205·
Gluss
The Bruddans
Brae Wick
Hillswick
Bardist
Isle of Stenness
Stenness
Ness of
Ness of Olnesfirth
Skerry of Eshaness
Dore Holm
Hillswick
Burraland
The Drongs
·389
Baa Taing
Sullom
Isle of Nibon
Cairn
ST MAGNUS
·396
Mangaster
Lang Head
BAY
Egilsay
Islesburgh
Mavis
Turvalds Head
·315
Grind
Erne Stack
Busta
Ve Skerries
Strom Ness
Roesound
555
MUCKLE ROE
South
Ward
Linga
Murbie Stacks
Little-ayre
Cribbie
·285
North Ness
Swarbacks Head
Swarbacks Minn
Fogla Skerry
Virda
Field
PAPA STOUR
Vementry
Papa
272·
Biggings
Cairn
Little
·298
Isle of
Gruna
West Burrafirth
SHETLAND
Sound of Papa
Holm of Melby
West
Burrafirth
Melby Ho
Garth
Brindister
Clousta
ISLANDS
Quilva Taing
Noonsbrough
Sandness
A 971
Unifirth
Aith
·817
Pund Head
Sandness
·313
Bay of Deepdale
Hill
Burga
Aithsting
Water
Dale
Twatt
Mu Ness
Burn of Dale
·567
Bixter
Voe of Dale
Stourbrough
·246
West
Hill
Bridge of Walls
Effirth
Wats Ness
Mid Walls
Stanydale
Tresta
Skarpigarth
Walls
Browland
Semblister
Rus
650·
Braga Ness
Burraland
Gruting
·437
Sand
Garderhouse
Uskie Geo
Vaila
Ward of
Gossa
Hall
Flate

SHETLAND
ISLANDS

Content

The index lists all the definitive names shown in the map section of the Atlas. For each entry the Atlas page number is listed and the National Grid map reference is given to the nearest kilometre of the feature to which the name applies.

For long linear features, such as the River Thames, more than one reference is given. For these multiple entries and where a name applies to more than one feature the County, Region or Island Area name is also given.

Abbreviations used in the index to identify the nature of certain named features and abbreviations for Counties used in the Index are listed here.

Method of Listing Names

Names are listed alphabetically in the index as they appear on the map. For example, 'Ashdown Forest' appears under 'A', while 'Forest of Bere' is under 'F'. Similarly, 'Beaulieu River' appers under 'B' but 'River Thames' is under 'R'. When the definite article precedes a name, the name appears first. Thus, 'The Wash' becomes 'Wash, The' and is listed under 'W'. An exception to this rule is made in the case of Gaelic and Welsh place names. These are listed under the initial letter of the Gaelic or Welsh definite article. For example, 'An Ceannaich' is listed under 'A' and 'Y Llethr' is listed under 'Y'.

How to use this Index   Example:

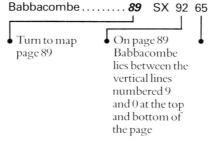

Babbacombe .... **89** SX 92 65

- Turn to map page 89
- On page 89 Babbacombe lies between the vertical lines numbered 9 and 0 at the top and bottom of the page
- Babbacombe lies between the horizontal lines numbered 6 and 7 at left or right of the page

This reference system is a simplification of the National Grid system which allows one to pinpoint a place very accurately on the map and to find the same place on any other map of any scale using the same system. A full explanation is given with the National Grid map of Great Britain on the last endpaper.

List of County Names showing Abbreviations used in this Index

England

Avon	Avon
Bedfordshire	Beds
Berkshire	Berks
Buckinghamshire	Bucks
Cambridgeshire	Cambs
Cheshire	Ches
Cleveland	Cleve
Cornwall	Corn
Cumbria	Cumbr
Derbyshire	Derby
Devon	Devon
Dorset	Dorset
Durham	Durham
East Sussex	E. Susx
Essex	Essex
Gloucestershire	Glos
Greater London	G. Lon
Greater Manchester	G. Man
Hampshire	Hants
Hereford & Worcester	H & W
Hertfordshire	Herts
Humberside	Humbs
Isle of Wight	I. of W
Kent	Kent
Lancashire	Lancs
Leicestershire	Leic
Lincolnshire	Lincs
Merseyside	Mers
Norfolk	Norf

North Yorkshire	N. Yks
Northamptonshire	Northnts
Northumberland	Northum
Nottinghamshire	Notts
Oxfordshire	Oxon
Shropshire	Shrops
Somerset	Somer
South Yorkshire	S. Yks
Staffordshire	Staffs
Suffolk	Suff
Surrey	Surrey
Tyne and Wear	T. & W
Warwickshire	Warw
West Midlands	W. Mids
West Sussex	W. Susx
West Yorkshire	W. Yks
Wiltshire	Wilts

Other Areas

Isle of Man	I. of M
Isles of Scilly	I. Scilly

Wales

Clwyd	Clwyd
Dyfed	Dyfed
Gwent	Gwent
Gwynedd	Gwyn
Mid Glamorgan	M. Glam
Powys	Powys
South Glamorgan	S. Glam
West Glamorgan	W. Glam

Region & Island Area Names
Scotland

Regions

Borders	Border
Central	Central
Dumfries & Galloway	D & G
Fife	Fife
Grampian	Grampn
Highland	Highl
Lothian	Lothn
Strathclyde	Strath
Tayside	Tays

Island Areas

Orkney	Orkney
Shetland	Shetld
Western Isles	W. Isles

Feature codes

H = Hill, mountain
F = Forest, wood
W = Water
T = City, town, village
R = Roman antiquity
A = Non-Roman antiquity
P = Town on Primary Route
Q = Landmark on Primary Route

Abbas Combe | | | | | **Adstock**

A

Adstock Anstiebury

Adstock *T* 119 SP 7330
Adstone *T* 119 SP 5951
Adventurers Fen 121 TL 5568
Advie *T* 183 NJ 1234
Adwell *T* 104 SU 6999
Adwick le Street *T* 139 SE 5308
Adwick upon Dearne *T* 139 SE 4701
Adziel 185 NJ 9553
Ae *T* 156 NX 9889
Affleck *T* 185 NJ 8623
Affleck Castle *A* 177 NO 4938
Affpuddle *T* 93 SY 8093
Afon Aeron *W* 111 SN 5158
Afon Afan *W* 109 SS 8295
Afon Aled *W* 135 SH 9570
Afon Alun or River Alyn *W* 126 SJ 3756
Afon Alwen *W* 135 SJ 0343
Afon Banwy *W* 125 SJ 0510
Afon Banwy neu Einion *W* 126 SJ 1308
Afon Bidno *W* 125 SN 8783
Afon Biga *W* 125 SN 8689
Afon Cain *W* 126 SJ 1618
Afon Cefni *W* 134 SH 4572
Afon Ceirw *W* 135 SH 9447
Afon Cennen *W* 111 SN 6418
Afon Cerist *W* 125 SH 8416
Afon Claerwen *W* 125 SN 8862
Afon Cledwen *W* 135 SH 8964
Afon Clwyd or River Clwyd *W* 135 SJ 0376
Afon Clywedog, Clwyd *W* 135 SJ 0962
Afon Clywedog, Powys *W* 125 SN 9386
Afon Conwy *W* 135 SH 7768
Afon Cothi *W* 111 SN 6134
Afon Cynin *W* 111 SN 2718
Afon Cywyn *W* 111 SN 3115
Afon Ddu *W* 135 SH 7564
Afon Dewi Fawr *W* 111 SN 3023
Afon Duad *W* 111 SN 3729
Afon Dugoed, Gwyn *W* 125 SH 9012
Afon Dugoed, Powys *W* 125 SH 9012
Afon Dulas, Gwyn *W* 125 SH 7608
Afon Dulas, Powys *W* 125 SN 7898
Afon Dulyn *W* 135 SH 7267
Afon Dwyfach *W* 134 SH 4746
Afon Dwyfor *W* 134 SH 4941
Afon Dyfi *W* 125 SH 8816
Afon Dyfi or River Dovey *W* 125 SN 6696
Afon Dyfrdwy or River Dee, Ches *W* 126 SJ 4056
Afon Dyfrdwy or River Dee, Clwyd *W* 136 SJ 2380
Afon Dyfrdwy or River Dee, Clwyd *W* 126 SJ 3743
Afon Dyfrdwy or River Dee, Mers *W* 136 SJ 2380
Afon Dysynni *W* 125 SH 6407
Afon Eden *W* 135 SH 7129
Afon Efyrnwy or River Vyrnwy *W* 126 SJ 1714
Afon Gamlan *W* 125 SH 7124
Afon Glaslyn *W* 134 SH 5943
Afon Gronw *W* 111 SN 2221
Afon Gwydderig *W* 109 SN 8531
Afon Gwy or River Wye, Glos *W* 127 SO 5398
Afon Gwy or River Wye, Gwent *W* 127 SO 5398
Afon Gwy or River Wye, Powys *W* 112 SO 0153
Afon Honddu *W* 113 SO 2926
Afon Leri *W* 125 SN 6689
Afon Llafar *W* 135 SH 8734
Afon Lliw *W* 108 SS 5999
Afon Llugwy *W* 135 SH 7059
Afon Llwchwr or River Loughor *W* 108 SS 4897
Afon Llynfi *W* 109 SO 1432
Afon Lwyd *W* 125 SN 8690
Afon Machno *W* 135 SH 7849
Afon Marteg *W* 125 SO 0075
Afon Mawddach *W* 125 SH 7322
Afon Mellte *W* 109 SN 9211
Afon Mynwy or River Monnow, Gwent *W* 113 SO 4717
Afon Mynwy or River Monnow, H. & W *W* 113 SO 4717
Afon Nyfer *W* 110 SN 1237
Afrn Porth-llwyd *W* 135 SH 7466
Afon Rheidol *W* 125 SN 6778
Afon Rhiw *W* 125 SJ 0401
Afon Senni *W* 109 SN 9225
Afon Taf *W* 111 SN 2515
Afon Tanat, Clwyd *W* 126 SJ 1524
Afon Tanat, Powys *W* 125 SJ 0425
Afon Teifi *W* 111 SN 5446
Afon Trannon *W* 125 SN 9491
Afon Troddi or River Trothy *W* 113 SO 4512
Afon Tryweryn *W* 135 SH 9138
Afon Twrch, Dyfed *W* 111 SN 6648
Afon Twrch, Dyfed *W* 109 SN 7715
Afon Twrch, Powys *W* 125 SH 9714
Afon Twrch, Powys *W* 109 SN 7715
Afon Twymyn *W* 125 SH 8801
Afon Tywi *W* 111 SN 5720
Afon-wen *T* 136 SJ 1371
Afon Wnion *W* 125 SH 8021
Afon Ysgir *W* 109 SO 0031
Afon Ystrad *W* 135 SJ 0163
Afon Ystwth *W* 125 SN 6275
Afton Bridgend *T* 156 NS 6212
Afton Reservoir *W* 156 NS 6304
Afton Water *W* 156 NS 6308
Agden Resr *W* 139 SK 2692
Agglethorpe *T* 146 SE 0886
A' Ghairbhe *W* 180 NH 0259
A' Ghlas-bheinn *H* 180 NH 0023
A' Ghoil 196 NC 3571
Aignish *T* 195 NB 4832
Aike *T* 142 TA 0545
Aiker Ness, Orkney 200 HY 3826
Aikerness, Orkney *T* 200 HY 4552
Aikers *T* 200 ND 4590
Aiketgate *T* 151 NY 4846
Aikton *T* 150 NY 2753
Ailey *T* 113 SO 3448
Ailsa Craig 154 NX 0199
Ailworth *T* 130 TL 1198
Ainderby Quernhow *T* 147 SE 3481
Ainderby Steeple *T* 152 SE 3392
Aingers Green *T* 107 TM 1120
Ainsdale *T* 136 SD 3112
Ainshval *H* 179 NM 3794
Ainstable *T* 151 NY 5346
Ainsworth *T* 137 SD 7610
Aintree *T* 136 SJ 3798
Aira Force *W* 151 NY 3920
Aird, D. & G *T* 154 NX 0960
Aird, Strath *T* 167 NM 7600
Aird, W. Isles *T* 195 NB 5635
Aird a' Mhòrain 188 NF 8379
Aird an Rùnair 188 NF 6970
Aird an Troim 195 NB 2316
Aird Barvas 195 NB 3553
Aird Brenish 194 NA 9727
Aird Dell *T* 195 NB 4761
Aird-dhubh, Highld 180 NG 7040
Aird Dhubh, Highld 190 NG 9382
Airde, The 197 NC 5313
Aird Fada 173 NM 4424
Aird Fenish 194 NA 9929
Aird Luing 167 NM 7406
Aird Mhànais *T* 189 NG 1188
Aird Mheadhonach *T* 189 NG 1898
Aird Nisabost 188 NG 0497
Aird of Coigach 196 NC 0811
Aird of Kinloch 173 NM 5228
Aird of Sleat *T* 180 NG 5900
Aird Riabhach *T* 189 NG 2396
Airdrie *T* 162 NS 7665
Airdriehill *T* 162 NS 7867
Airds Bay *W* 168 NN 0032
Airds Moss 162 NS 6024
Aird, The, Highld *T* 187 NG 4052
Aird, The, Highld 187 NG 4376
Aird, The, Highld 182 NH 5642
Aird Thormaid 188 NF 9376
Aird Tong *T* 195 NB 4636
Aird Uig *T* 194 NB 0438
Aird Vanish 188 NF 9999
Aire & Calder Navigation, Humbs *W* 139 SE 5920
Aire & Calder Navigation, N. Yks *W* 139 SE 5920
Airedale 146 SE 0345
Airie Hill *H* 156 NX 6268
Airlie Castle 176 NO 2952
Airmyn *T* 142 SE 7225
Airntully *T* 170 NO 0935
Airor *T* 180 NG 7105
Airth *T* 170 NS 8987
Airton *T* 146 SD 9059
Aisby, Lincs *T* 130 SK 8792
Aisby, Lincs *T* 130 TF 0138
Aiskew *T* 147 SE 2788
Aislaby, N. Yks *T* 148 NZ 8608
Aislaby, N. Yks *T* 148 SE 7785
Aisthorpe *T* 140 SK 9480
Aith, Orkney 200 HY 2417
Aith, Orkney *T* 201 HY 6525
Aith, Shetld *T* 203 HU 3455
Aith, Shetld 205 HU 6390
Aith Hope *W* 200 ND 2988
Aith Ness 203 HU 5144
Aithsetter *T* 203 HU 4430
Aithsting 203 HU 3455
Aith Voe, Shetld *W* 203 HU 3458
Aith Voe, Shetld *W* 203 HU 4328
Aith Wick *W* 203 HU 4429
Aitnoch 183 NH 9839
Akeld *T* 165 NT 9529
Akeley *T* 119 SP 7037
Akeman Street, Bucks *R* 104 SP 7715
Akeman Street, Glos *R* 114 SP 0904
Akeman Street, Oxon *R* 115 SP 3314
Akenham *T* 123 TM 1448
Akermoor Loch *W* 164 NT 4021
Alavna Roman Fort *R* 150 NY 0337
Albaston *T* 88 SX 4270
Alberbury *T* 126 SJ 3614
Albourne *T* 96 TQ 2616
Albrighton, Shrops *T* 127 SJ 4918
Albrighton, Shrops *T* 127 SJ 8104
Alburgh *T* 123 TM 2687
Albury, Herts *T* 105 TL 4324
Albury, Surrey *T* 96 TQ 0447
Alby Hill *T* 133 TG 1934
Alcaig *T* 182 NH 5657
Alcaston *T* 116 SO 4587
Alcester *T* 118 SP 0857
Alciston *T* 97 TQ 5005
Alcombe *T* 91 SS 9745
Alconbury *T* 120 TL 1876
Alconbury Weston *T* 120 TL 1776
Aldbar Castle 177 NO 5757
Aldborough, Norf *T* 133 TG 1834
Aldborough, N. Yks *T* 147 SE 4066
Aldbourne *T* 102 SU 2675
Aldbrough *T* 143 TA 2438
Aldbrough St John *T* 152 NZ 2011
Aldbury *T* 104 SP 9612
Aldclune *T* 175 NN 8963
Aldeburgh *T* 123 TM 4656
Aldeburgh Bay *W* 123 TM 4755
Aldeby *T* 133 TM 4593
Aldenham *T* 105 TQ 1398
Alderbury *T* 94 SU 1827
Alderford *T* 133 TG 1218
Alderholt *T* 94 SU 1212
Alderley *T* 101 ST 7690
Alderley Edge *T* 137 SJ 8478
Aldermaston *T* 103 SU 5965
Aldermaston Wharf 103 SU 6067
Alderminster *T* 118 SP 2348
Aldershot *T* 103 SU 8650
Alderton, Glos *T* 114 SP 0033
Alderton, Northnts *T* 119 SP 7446
Alderton, Shrops *T* 127 SJ 4924
Alderton, Suff *T* 123 TM 3441
Alderton, Wilts *T* 101 ST 8483
Alderwasley *T* 128 SK 3153
Aldfield *T* 147 SE 2669
Aldford *T* 136 SJ 4259
Aldham *T* 122 TL 9125
Aldingbourne *T* 96 SU 9205
Aldingham *T* 145 SD 2871
Aldington, H. & W *T* 118 SP 0644
Aldington, Kent *T* 99 TR 0636
Aldington Frith *T* 99 TR 0436
Aldochlay *T* 168 NS 3591
Aldreth *T* 121 TL 4473
Aldridge *T* 128 SK 0500
Aldringham *T* 123 TM 4461
Aldsworth *T* 115 SP 1510
Aldunie *T* 184 NJ 3626
Aldwark, Derby *T* 139 SK 2257
Aldwark, N. Yks *T* 147 SE 4663
Aldwick *T* 96 SZ 9198
Aldwincle *T* 120 TL 0081
Aldworth *T* 103 SU 5579
Aled Isaf Reservoir *W* 135 SH 9159
Alemoor Loch *W* 157 NT 3914
Ale Water, Border *W* 157 NT 4318
Ale Water, Border *W* 165 NT 9064
Alexandria *T* 169 NS 3880
Alfardisworthy *T* 90 SS 2911
Alfington *T* 92 SY 1197
Alfold *T* 96 TQ 0334
Alford, Grampn *T* 184 NJ 5716
Alford, Lincs *T* 141 TF 4575
Alford, Somer *T* 93 ST 6032
Alfred's Tower 93 ST 7435
Alfreton *T* 128 SK 4155
Alfrick *T* 117 SO 7553
Alfriston *T* 97 TQ 5103
Alhampton *T* 93 ST 6234
Alhang, D. & G *H* 156 NS 6401
Alhang, Strath *H* 156 NS 6401
Aline Lodge 195 NB 1911
Alkborough *T* 142 SE 8821
Alkerton *T* 118 SP 3742
Alkham *T* 99 TR 2542
Alkington *T* 127 SJ 5339
Alkmonton *T* 128 SK 1838
Alladale Lodge 192 NH 4389
Alladale River *W* 191 NH 4088
Allaleigh *T* 89 SX 8153
Allanaquoich *T* 176 NO 1291
Allangrange Mains 182 NH 6251
Allanton, Border *T* 165 NT 8654
Allanton, Strath *T* 163 NS 8557
Allan Water, Border *W* 157 NT 4707
Allan Water, Central *W* 169 NN 8006
Allan Water, Tays *W* 169 NN 8006
Allardice *T* 177 NO 8174
All Cannings *T* 102 SU 1660
Allendale Common 151 NY 8345
Allendale Town *T* 151 NY 8355
Allenheads *T* 151 NY 8545
Allensmore *T* 113 SO 4636
Aller *T* 92 ST 4029
Allerby *T* 150 NY 0839
Aller Dean 165 NT 9947
Allerford *T* 91 SS 9045
Allermuir Hill *H* 163 NT 2266
Allerston *T* 149 SE 8782
Allerthorpe *T* 142 SE 7847
Allerton *T* 136 SJ 4085
Allerton Bywater *T* 147 SE 4227
Allesley *T* 118 SP 2981
Allestree *T* 128 SK 3439
Allexton *T* 130 SK 8100
Allgreave *T* 138 SJ 9767
Allhallow-on-Sea *T* 106 TQ 8478
Allhallows *T* 98 TQ 8377
Alligin Shuas *T* 190 NG 8357
Allimore Green *T* 127 SJ 8519
Allington, Lincs *T* 130 SK 8540
Allington, Wilts *T* 102 SU 0663
Allington, Wilts *T* 102 SU 2039
Allithwaite *T* 145 SD 3876
Allnabad 197 NC 4642
Alloa *T* 170 NS 8892
Allonby *T* 150 NY 0843
Allonby Bay *W* 150 NY 0742
Alloway *T* 161 NS 3318
All Saints South Elmham *T* 123 TM 3482
All Stretton *T* 126 SO 4695
Allt *H* 113 SO 2917
Allt a' Bhunn *W* 197 NC 5012
Allt Ach' a' Bhàthaich *W* 193 NC 8114
Allt a' Chaoil-rèidhe *W* 175 NN 5276
Allt a' Chaorainn *W* 174 NN 9688
Allt a' Chaoruinn *W* 191 NC 2704
Allt a' Chireachain *W* 175 NN 7772
Allt a' Choire Mhòir *W* 191 NH 1968
Allt a' Chonais *W* 191 NH 0747
Allt a' Choromaig *W* 168 NM 9221
Allt a' Chraois *W* 197 NC 4439
Allt à Ghealladh, Grampn *W* 183 NJ 1238
Allt à Ghealladh, Highld *W* 183 NJ 1238
Allt a' Ghiubhais *W* 190 NG 7968
Allt Airigh-dhamh *W* 198 NC 8237
Allt a' Mhadaidh *W* 191 NH 2374
Allt a' Mhuilinn, Highld *W* 193 NC 8313
Allt a' Mhuilinn, Tays *W* 175 NN 7675
Alltan Dearg *W* 197 NC 6460
Allt an Dùin *W* 198 NC 8124
Allt an Ealaidh *W* 198 NC 7227
Allt an Stacain *W* 168 NN 1320
Allt an Tairbh *W* 166 NR 5588
Allt an Tiaghaich *W* 196 NC 1523
Allt an t-Srathain *W* 190 NG 7156
Allt Arnan, Central *W* 168 NN 3018
Allt Arnan, Strath *W* 168 NN 3018
Allt Bail a' Mhuilinn *W* 175 NN 5743
Allt Beinn Dònuill *W* 191 NH 2299
Allt Beitheach *W* 173 NM 7552
Allt Beochlich *W* 168 NN 0315
Allt Bhlàraidh *W* 182 NH 3518
Allt Bhran *W* 175 NN 7889
Allt Braglenmore *W* 168 NM 9218
Allt Breineag *W* 182 NH 4708
Allt Cam, Highld *W* 175 NN 4477
Allt Cam, Highld *W* 175 NN 5178
Allt Cam Ban *W* 182 NH 5606
Allt Camgharaidh *W* 174 NM 9888
Allt Camghouran *W* 175 NN 5354
Allt Car *W* 197 NC 4417
Allt Chaiseagail *W* 197 NC 5909
Alltchaorunn 174 NN 1951
Allt Choire a' Bhalachain *W* 174 NN 1198
Allt Chomhraig *W* 175 NN 8197
Allt Cinn-locha *W* 167 NR 7879
Allt Coire a' Chaolain *W* 174 NN 2147
Allt Coire an Eòin *W* 174 NN 2273
Allt Coire Iain Oig *W* 175 NN 5197
Allt Coire na Saidhe Duibh *W* 197 NC 4835
Allt Con *W* 175 NN 6967
Allt Conait *W* 175 NN 5245
Allt Connie *W* 176 NO 0786
Allt Crunachdain *W* 175 NN 5291
Allt Cuaich *W* 175 NN 6786
Allt Darrarie *W* 176 NO 3283
Allt Ddu *H* 109 SO 0224
Allt Dearg *W* 183 NH 8246
Allt Dochard *W* 174 NN 2044
Allt Doe *W* 182 NH 4107
Allt Easach *W* 174 NN 0642
Allt Eigheach *W* 174 NN 4361
Allt Eileag *W* 191 NC 3007
Allt Fearna *W* 168 NN 1222
Allt Fèith Thuill *W* 174 NN 3771
Allt Fionn Ghlinne *W* 168 NN 3222
Alltforgan *T* 125 SH 9624
Allt Forsiescye *W* 199 ND 0258
Allt Garbh *W* 181 NH 1719
Allt Garbh-airigh *W* 192 NH 6398
Allt Garbh Buidhe *W* 176 NN 9981
Allt Gharbh Ghaig *W* 175 NN 7782
Allt Ghlas *W* 175 NN 5366
Allt Glas Choire *W* 175 NN 7376
Allt Glas Dhoire *W* 174 NN 3285
Allt Gleann Da-Eig *W* 175 NN 6042
Allt Gleann nam Meann *W* 169 NN 5212
Allt Gleann Udalain *W* 180 NG 8528
Allt Glen Loch *W* 176 NO 0171
Allt Goibhre *W* 182 NH 4348
Allt Hallater *W* 174 NN 1340
Allt Kinglass *W* 174 NN 3437
Allt Làire *W* 174 NN 3276
Allt Lon a' Chuil *W* 198 NC 7242
Allt Loraich *W* 174 NN 3978
Allt Lorgy *W* 183 NH 8716
Allt Lundie *W* 182 NH 2905
Allt Madagain *W* 175 NN 6398
Alltmawr *T* 112 SO 0746
Allt Mhoille *W* 168 NN 1231
Allt Mhucarnaich *W* 191 NH 2579
Allt Mòr, Highld *W* 180 NG 7221
Allt Mòr, Highld *W* 183 NH 7404
Allt Mòr, Highld *W* 175 NN 8295
Allt Mòr, Tays *W* 175 NN 7353
Allt na Bogair *W* 175 NN 6055
Alltnacaillich 197 NC 4545
Allt na Caim *W* 174 NN 3762
Allt na Doire Garbhe *W* 181 NH 0429
Allt na Gile *W* 166 NR 4877
Allt na Glaise *W* 175 NN 5769
Allt na h-Airbhe *T* 191 NH 1193
Allt na h-Eirigh *W* 190 NG 7053
Allt na Lairige, Highld *W* 174 NN 2872
Allt na Lairige, Strath *W* 168 NN 2517
Allt na Lairige Moire *W* 174 NN 1163
Allt na Lùibe *W* 192 NC 6608
Allt na Muic *W* 182 NH 2515
Allt nan Achaidhean *W* 198 NC 7928
Allt nan Airighean *W* 166 NR 3650
Allt nan Caorach *W* 182 NH 5267
Allt nan Ramh *W* 196 NC 2237
Allt-nan-Sugh *T* 180 NG 9029
Allt Odhar *W* 182 NH 5205
Allt Phocaichain *W* 182 NH 3211
Allt Riabhach *W* 182 NH 2118
Allt Riobain *W* 169 NN 4529
Allt Ruighe nan Saorach *W* 175 NN 6463
Allt Sleibh *W* 175 NN 6566
Allt Smeòrail *W* 193 NC 8512
Allt Srath à' Ghlinne *W* 169 NN 6717
Allt Tolaghan *W* 174 NN 2640
Allt Uisg an t-Sidhein *W* 182 NH 6117
Alltwalis *T* 111 SN 4431
Alltwen *T* 108 SN 7203
Almeley *T* 113 SO 3351
Almer *T* 93 SY 9199
Almington *T* 127 SJ 7034
Almondbank *T* 170 NO 0626
Almondbury *T* 138 SE 1615
Almondsbury *T* 101 ST 6084
Alne *T* 147 SE 4965
Alness *T* 182 NH 6569
Alness Bay *W* 182 NH 6467
Alnham *T* 159 NT 9910
Alnmouth *T* 159 NU 2410
Alnmouth Bay *W* 159 NU 2510
Alnwick *P* 159 NU 1813
Alphamstone *T* 122 TL 8735
Alpheton *T* 122 TL 8850
Alphington *T* 89 SX 9189
Alport *T* 139 SK 2264
Alpraham *T* 137 SJ 5859
Alresford *T* 107 TM 0621
Alrewas *T* 128 SK 1715
Alsager *T* 127 SJ 7955
Alsagers Bank *T* 127 SJ 8048
Alsop en le Dale *T* 128 SK 1655
Alston *T* 151 NY 7146
Alstone *T* 114 SO 9832
Alstonefield *T* 128 SK 1355
Alston Moor 151 NY 7240
Alston Reservoir *W* 145 SD 6136
Alswear *T* 91 SS 7222
Altandhu *T* 196 NB 9812
Altanduin 198 NC 8126
Altarnun *T* 87 SX 2281
Altass *T* 192 NC 5000
Alterwall *T* 199 ND 2865
Altgaltraig 168 NS 0473
Altham *T* 146 SD 7732
Althorne *T* 106 TQ 9199
Althorpe *T* 142 SE 8309
Altnabreac Station 198 ND 0045
Altnacealgach Hotel 196 NC 2610
Altnafeadh 174 NN 2256
Altnaharra *T* 197 NC 5635
Altofts *T* 147 SE 3723
Alton, Derby *T* 139 SK 3664
Alton, Hants *T* 103 SU 7239
Alton, Staffs *T* 128 SK 0742
Alton Pancras *T* 93 ST 6902
Alton Priors *T* 102 SU 1162
Alton Water Reservoir *W* 123 TM 1436
Altrincham *T* 137 SJ 7688
Altrua *T* 174 NN 2490
Alturlie Point 183 NH 7149
Altyre House 183 NJ 0254
Altyre Woods *F* 183 NJ 0253
Alum Bay *W* 94 SZ 3085
Alva *T* 170 NS 8897
Alvanley *T* 137 SJ 4974
Alvaston *T* 128 SK 3833
Alvechurch *T* 118 SP 0272
Alvecote *T* 128 SK 2404
Alvediston *T* 94 ST 9723
Alveley *T* 117 SO 7684
Alverdiscott *T* 90 SS 5125
Alverstoke *T* 95 SZ 6099
Alverstone *T* 95 SZ 5785
Alverton *T* 129 SK 7942
Alvescot *T* 115 SP 2704
Alveston, Avon *T* 101 ST 6388
Alveston, Warw *T* 118 SP 2356
Alvie *T* 183 NH 8609
Alvingham *T* 141 TF 3691
Alvington *T* 113 SO 6000
Alwalton *T* 130 TL 1395
Alwen Reservoir *W* 135 SH 9453
Alweston *T* 93 ST 6614
Alwinton *T* 158 NT 9206
Alyth *T* 176 NO 2448
Amat Forest 192 NH 4690
Amatnatua *T* 192 NH 4790
Am Balg 196 NC 1866
Ambergate *T* 128 SK 3551
Amber Hill *T* 131 TF 2346
Amberley, Glos *T* 114 SO 8501
Amberley, W. Susx *T* 96 TQ 0213
Am Bi-bogha Beag 186 NG 1938
Am Bi-bogha Mòr 186 NG 1838
Amble-by-the Sea *T* 159 NU 2604
Amblecote *T* 117 SO 8985
Ambleside *T* 151 NY 3704
Ambleston *T* 110 SN 0025
Ambrosden *T* 115 SP 6019
Am Buachaille *H* 168 NN 0507
Amcotts *T* 142 SE 8514
Amersham *P* 104 SU 9798
Amesbury *T* 102 SU 1641
Am Fraoch Eilean 166 NR 4762
A' Mhoine 197 NC 5261
Amhuinnsuidhe *T* 188 NB 0408
Amicombe Hill *H* 89 SX 5687
Amington *T* 128 SK 2304
Amisfield *T* 156 NY 0082
Amlwch *T* 134 SH 4493
Amlwch Port *T* 134 SH 4593
Ammanford *T* 111 SN 6312
Amotherby *T* 148 SE 7473
Ampfield *T* 94 SU 4023
Ampleforth *T* 147 SE 5878
Ampleforth College 147 SE 5978
Ampney Crucis *T* 114 SP 0702
Ampney St Mary *T* 114 SP 0802
Ampney St Peter *T* 114 SP 0801
Amport *T* 102 SU 3044
Ampthill *T* 120 TL 0337
Ampton *T* 122 TL 8671
Amroth *T* 110 SN 1607
Amulree *T* 175 NN 9036
An Acairseid *W* 173 NM 4363
Anaheilt *T* 173 NM 8162
Anancaun *T* 190 NH 0262
An Ard *T* 190 NG 8075
An Cabar *H* 182 NH 2564
An Càmastac 186 NG 2365
An Caol *T* 190 NG 6152
Ancaster *T* 130 SK 9843
An Ceannaich 186 NG 1350
An Ceann Geal or Whiten Head 197 NC 5068
An Cearcall 175 NN 6270
Anchachork *T* 187 NG 4845
Anchor *T* 116 SO 1785
An Clachan 166 NR 2171
An Coileach *H* 189 NG 0892
An Coileachan *H* 182 NH 2468
An Coire 173 NM 8114
Ancroft *T* 165 NU 0045
An Cruachan, Highld *H* 181 NH 0935
An Cruachan, Strath *H* 167 NM 6900
Ancrum *T* 164 NT 6224
Ancton *T* 96 SU 9800
An Cuaidh *H* 190 NG 7689
Anderby *T* 141 TF 5275
Anderby Creek *T* 141 TF 5576
Anderson *T* 93 SY 8897
Anderton *T* 137 SJ 6475
Andover *P* 102 SU 3645
Andover Down *T* 102 SU 3946
Andoversford *T* 114 SP 0219
Andreas *T* 144 SC 4199
An Dubh-aird 180 NG 7833
An Dubh-laimhrig 187 NG 4715
An Dubh Sgeir, Highld 186 NG 1936
An Dubh Sgeir, Highld 186 NG 3422
An Dubh-sgeir, Strath 160 NR 6655
An Dùn 199 ND 1425
An Dùnan 166 NR 5773
An Fhaochag 180 NG 6903
An Garbh-eilean 196 NC 3373
An Gead Loch *W* 181 NH 1038
Angersleigh *T* 92 ST 1919
Angle *T* 110 SM 8603
Angle Bay *W* 110 SM 8803
Anglesey 134 SH 4179
Angle Tarn *W* 151 NY 4114
Anglezarke Moor 137 SD 6417
Angmering *T* 96 TQ 0704
Angram, N. Yks *T* 152 SD 8899
Angram, N. Yks *T* 147 SE 5248
Angram Common 151 SD 8499
Angram Resr *W* 146 SE 0476
An Grianan *H* 196 NC 2662
Angry Brow 136 SD 3019
Anie 169 NN 5810
An Iola *W* 174 NM 9847
Ankerville *T* 193 NH 8174
Anlaby *T* 142 TA 0328
An Lairig 175 NN 4977
An Leacainn *H* 182 NH 5741
An Lèan-chàrn *H* 197 NC 4252
An Liathanach *H* 191 NH 1357
Anmer *T* 132 TF 7429
Annan *T* 157 NY 1966
Annandale 157 NY 1294
Annaside *T* 144 SD 0986
Annat, Highld *T* 190 NG 8954
Annat, Strath *T* 168 NN 0322
Annat Bay *W* 190 NH 0396
Annathill *T* 169 NS 7270
Anna Valley *T* 102 SU 3444
Annbank *T* 161 NS 4022
Annesley *T* 129 SK 5053
Annesley Woodhouse *T* 129 SK 4953
Annet 86 SV 8608
Annet Burn *W* 169 NN 6906
Annfield Plain *T* 152 NZ 1651
Annick Water *W* 161 NS 3843
Annochie *T* 185 NJ 9342
Annscroft *T* 126 SJ 4508
An Riabhachan *H* 181 NH 1234
An Rubha 166 NR 3595
Ansdell *T* 145 SD 3428
Ansford *T* 93 ST 6433
An Sgarsoch, Grampn *H* 175 NN 9383
An Sgarsoch, Tays *H* 175 NN 9383
An Sgurr *H* 179 NM 4684
An Sleaghach *H* 173 NM 7643
Ansley *T* 118 SP 3091
Anslow *T* 128 SK 2125
Anslow Gate *T* 128 SK 1925
An Socach, Grampn *H* 176 NO 0980
An Socach, Highld *H* 196 NC 2658
An Socach, Strath *H* 168 NS 0587
An Stac *H* 180 NM 8688
An Stèidh 179 NG 2103
Anstey, Herts *T* 121 TL 4032
Anstey, Leic *T* 129 SK 5408
Anstiebury *A* 96 TQ 1544

Aylesham Bay of Laig

Aylesham *T* 99 TR 2352
Aylestone *T* 129 SK 5700
Aylmerton *T* 133 TG 1839
Aylsham *T* 133 TG 1926
Aylton *T* 117 SO 6637
Aymestrey *T* 116 SO 4265
Aynho *T* 115 SP 5133
Ayot St Lawrence *T* 105 TL 1916
Ayot St Peter *T* 105 TL 2115
Ayr *P* 161 NS 3320
Ayres, The 144 NX 4303
Aysgarth *T* 146 SE 0188
Ayside *T* 145 SD 3983
Ayston *T* 130 SK 8601
Aythorpe Roding *T* 106 TL 5915
Ayton, Border *T* 165 NT 9261
Ayton, N. Yks *T* 149 SE 9985
Aywick, Shetld *T* 205 HU 5386
Ay Wick, Shetld *W* 205 HU 5386
Azerley *T* 147 SE 2574

B

Baa Taing, Orkney 201 HY 6715
Baa Taing, Shetld 204 HU 2774
Babbacombe *T* 89 SX 9265
Babbacombe Bay *W* 89 SX 9568
Babbet Ness 171 NO 5914
Babbinswood *T* 126 SJ 3330
Babcary *T* 93 ST 5628
Babel *T* 109 SN 8335
Babell *T* 136 SJ 1573
Babeny 89 SX 6775
Babingley River *W* 132 TF 6725
Babraham *T* 121 TL 5150
Babworth *T* 140 SK 6880
Bac an Eich *H* 182 NH 2248
Bac Beag 172 NM 2337
Bach Camp *A* 113 SO 5460
Bache Hill *H* 116 SO 2163
Bach Island 173 NM 7726
Bachlaig 166 NR 4175
Back *T* 195 NB 4840
Backaland *T* 200 HY 5630
Backaskail Bay *W* 201 HY 6438
Backaskaill 200 HY 4850
Backbarrow *T* 145 SD 3584
Backburn *T* 177 NO 8592
Backfolds *T* 185 NK 0252
Backford *T* 136 SJ 3971
Backhill, Grampn *T* 185 NJ 7939
Backhill, Grampn *T* 185 NK 0039
Backhill of Clackriach *T* 185 NJ 9246
Backhill of Trustach *T* 177 NO 6397
Backies *T* 193 NC 8302
Backlass *T* 199 ND 2053
Backmuir of New Gilston *T* 171 NO 4308
Back of Keppoch *T* 180 NM 6588
Backstane Hill *H* 163 NS 9128
Backwell *T* 101 ST 4868
Backworth *T* 159 NZ 3072
Bac Mór or Dutchman's Cap 172 NM 2438
Bacon End *T* 106 TL 6018
Baconsthorpe *T* 133 TG 1237
Bacton, H. & W *T* 113 SO 3732
Bacton, Norf *T* 133 TG 3433
Bacton, Suff *T* 122 TM 0567
Bacup *T* 146 SD 8623
Bad a' Chreamha *H* 180 NG 8536
Badachro *T* 190 NG 7873
Badandun Hill *H* 176 NO 2067
Badanloch Forest 198 NC 8035
Badanloch Lodge 198 NC 7933
Badavanich 191 NH 1058
Bad Bog 190 NG 9281
Badbury *T* 102 SU 1980
Badbury Hill *H* 115 SU 2694
Badbury Rings *A* 94 ST 9503
Badby *T* 119 SP 5659
Badcall, Highld *T* 196 NC 1542
Badcall, Highld *T* 196 NC 2455
Badcall Bay *W* 196 NC 1641
Badcaul *T* 190 NH 0191
Baddeley Green *T* 127 SJ 9051
Baddesley Ensor *T* 128 SP 2798
Baddidarach *T* 196 NC 0823
Baddinsgill Reservoir *W* 163 NT 1255
Baddoch, Grampn 176 NO 1382
Baddoch, Highld *H* 183 NJ 0819
Badenoch 175 NN 7091
Badenscoth *T* 185 NJ 7038
Badentarbat Bay *W* 190 NC 0108
Badenyon 184 NJ 3419
Badger *T* 127 SO 7699
Badgers Mount *T* 105 TQ 4961
Badgeworth *T* 114 SO 9019
Badgworth *T* 100 ST 3952
Badicaul *T* 180 NG 7529
Badingham *T* 123 TM 3068
Badlesmere *T* 99 TR 0054
Badlipster 199 ND 2449
Badluarach *T* 190 NG 9994
Badminton *T* 101 ST 8082
Badninish *T* 193 NH 7694
Badrallach *T* 191 NH 0691
Badsey *T* 118 SP 0743
Badsworth *T* 139 SE 4614
Badwell Ash *T* 122 TL 9969
Bagby *T* 147 SE 4680
Bagendon *T* 114 SP 0106
Bage, The *T* 113 SO 2943
Baggrave Hall 129 SK 6908
Baggy Point 90 SS 4140
Bàgh an Tailleir *W* 168 NR 8580
Bagh Feisdlum *W* 172 NM 2558
Bàgh Loch an Ròin *W* 196 NC 1954
Bàgh na Doide *W* 167 NR 7076
Bagh nam Faoilean *W* 188 NF 8345
Bàgh nan Gunnaichean *W* 187 NG 4574
Bàgh Tigh-an-Droighinn *W* 168 NR 8579
Bagillt *T* 136 SJ 2275
Bagillt Bank 136 SJ 2276
Baginton *T* 118 SP 3475
Baglan *T* 109 SS 7592
Bagley *T* 126 SJ 4027
Bagnall *T* 127 SJ 9251
Bagshot, Surrey *T* 104 SU 9163
Bagshot, Wilts *T* 102 SU 3165
Bagshot Heath *F* 104 SU 9161
Bagthorpe, Norf *T* 132 TF 7932
Bagthorpe, Notts *T* 129 SK 4751
Bagworth *T* 129 SK 4408
Bagwyllydiart *T* 113 SO 4426
Baidland Hill *H* 161 NS 2552
Baildon *T* 146 SE 1539
Baile *T* 188 NF 9381
Bailebeag *T* 182 NH 5018
Baile Boidheach *T* 167 NR 7473
Baile Mór *T* 172 NM 2824
Bailey Hill *H* 116 SO 2472
Bailiesward 184 NJ 4737
Baillieston *T* 162 NS 6763
Bail Uachdraich *T* 188 NF 8160
Bainbridge *T* 152 SD 9390
Bainton, Cambs *T* 130 TF 0906
Bainton, Humbs *T* 149 SE 9652
Bairnkine *T* 158 NT 6515
Bait or St Mary's Island 159 NZ 3575
Bakers End *T* 105 TL 3917
Baker Street *T* 106 TQ 6381
Bakethin Reservoir *W* 158 NY 6391
Bakewell *T* 138 SK 2168
Bala *P* 135 SH 9236
Balachuirn *T* 180 NG 5540
Balaglas *T* 188 NF 8457
Bala Lake or Llyn Tegid *W* 135 SH 9133
Balallan *T* 195 NB 2920
Balbeg *T* 182 NH 4224
Balbeggie *T* 170 NO 1629
Balbegno Castle 177 NO 6473
Balbithan *T* 185 NJ 7917
Balbithan House 185 NJ 8118
Balblair *T* 183 NH 7066
Balcary Point 155 NX 8249
Balcherry *T* 193 NH 8182
Balchladich *T* 196 NC 0330
Balchraggan *T* 182 NH 5343
Balchrick *T* 196 NC 1960
Balcombe *T* 97 TQ 3130
Balcomie 171 NO 6209
Balcurvie *T* 171 NO 3401
Balderhead Reservoir *W* 152 NY 9218
Baldersby *T* 147 SE 3578
Balderstone *T* 145 SD 6332
Balderton *T* 130 SK 8251
Baldhu *T* 86 SW 7743
Baldinnie *T* 171 NO 4211
Baldock *T* 121 TL 2433
Baldoon Sands 155 NX 4653
Baldrine *T* 144 SC 4281
Balduff Hill *H* 176 NO 2253
Baldwin *T* 144 SC 3581
Baldwinholme *T* 150 NY 3352
Baldwin's Gate *T* 127 SJ 7940
Bale *T* 132 TG 0136
Balemartine *T* 172 NL 9841
Balephetrish Bay *W* 172 NM 0047
Balephuil *T* 172 NL 9640
Balephuil Bay *W* 172 NL 9440
Balerno *T* 163 NT 1666
Baleshare 188 NF 7861
Balevullin *T* 172 NL 9546
Balfield *T* 177 NO 5468
Balfour *T* 200 HY 4716
Balfour Castle 200 HY 4716
Balfron *T* 169 NS 5488
Balgaveny *T* 184 NJ 6640
Balgavies 177 NO 5351
Balgedie *T* 170 NO 1604
Balgonar *T* 170 NT 0293
Balgove *T* 185 NJ 8133
Balgowan *T* 175 NN 6394
Balgowan Point 154 NX 1242
Balgown *T* 186 NG 3868
Balgray *T* 176 NO 4038
Balgray Reservoir *W* 161 NS 5157
Balgrochan *T* 169 NS 6278
Balgy *T* 190 NG 8454
Balhalgardy *T* 185 NJ 7623
Balhary 176 NO 2646
Baliasta *T* 205 HP 6009
Baligill *T* 198 NC 8566
Balintore, Highld *T* 193 NH 8675
Balintore, Tays 176 NO 2859
Balintraid *T* 183 NH 7370
Balivanich *T* 188 NF 7755
Balkeerie 176 NO 3244
Balkholme *T* 142 SE 7928
Balkissock *T* 154 NX 1381
Ball *T* 126 SJ 3026
Balla *T* 178 NF 7811
Ballabeg *T* 144 SC 2470
Ballacannell *T* 144 SC 4382
Ballacarnane Beg *T* 144 SC 3088
Ballachulish *T* 174 NN 0858
Ballageich Hill *H* 161 NS 5350
Ballagyr *T* 144 SC 2684
Ballajora *T* 144 SC 4790
Ballamodha *T* 144 SC 2773
Ballantrae *T* 154 NX 0882
Ballantrae Bay *W* 154 NX 0783
Ballantrushal *T* 195 NB 3753
Ballard Point 94 SZ 0481
Ballasalla, I. of M *T* 144 SC 2769
Ballasalla, I. of M *T* 144 SC 3497
Ballater *T* 176 NO 3695
Ballaugh *T* 144 SC 3493
Ballechin 175 NN 9353
Balleigh *T* 193 NH 7084
Ballencleuch Law *H* 156 NS 9304
Ballencreiff *T* 171 NT 4878
Ball Hill *T* 102 SU 4263
Balliekine *T* 160 NR 8739
Balliemore, Strath 173 NM 8328
Balliemore, Strath 168 NS 0584
Ballig *T* 144 SC 2882
Ballikinrain Castle 169 NS 5687
Ballimore, Central 169 NN 5317
Ballimore, Strath 168 NR 9283
Ballinaby *T* 166 NR 2267
Ballindean 171 NO 2529
Ballinger Common *T* 104 SP 9103
Ballingham *T* 113 SO 5731
Ballingry *T* 170 NT 1797
Ballinlick 176 NN 9840
Ballinloan Burn *W* 176 NN 9542
Ballinluig *T* 176 NN 9752
Ballintuim *T* 176 NO 1054
Balloch, Highld *T* 183 NH 7347
Balloch, Strath *T* 169 NS 3982
Balloch, Tays 176 NO 3557
Ballochan *T* 177 NO 5290
Ballochbuie Forest *F* 176 NO 1990
Balloch Castle 169 NS 3983
Ballochroy 160 NR 7252
Balloch, The *H* 184 NJ 4748
Ballo Reservoir *W* 171 NO 2204
Ballowall Barrow *A* 86 SW 3531
Balls Cross *T* 96 SU 9826
Ballygown *T* 173 NM 4343
Ballygrant *T* 166 NR 3966
Ballyhaugh 172 NM 1758
Ballymichael *T* 160 NR 9231
Balmacaan Forest 182 NH 4025
Balmacara *T* 180 NG 8127
Balmacara Square *T* 180 NG 8028
Balmaclellan *T* 156 NX 6579
Balmacneil 176 NN 9750
Balmae *T* 155 NX 6845
Balmaha *T* 169 NS 4290
Balmalcolm 171 NO 3108
Balmanno Hill *H* 170 NO 1414
Balmartin *T* 188 NF 7273
Balmeanach, Highld 187 NG 5234
Balmeanach, Highld 180 NG 5540
Balmedie *T* 185 NJ 9617
Balmerino *T* 171 NO 3524
Balmer Lawn *T* 94 SU 3003
Balmoral Castle 176 NO 2595
Balmoral Forest 176 NO 2487
Balmore *T* 169 NS 6073
Balmore Forest 182 NH 3333
Balmullo *T* 171 NO 4220
Balmungie 183 NH 7459
Balmurrie 154 NX 2066
Balnabodach *T* 178 NF 7101
Balnacoil *T* 193 NC 8011
Balnacra *T* 190 NG 9846
Balnafoich 183 NH 6835
Balnagown Castle 193 NH 7675
Balnaguard *T* 175 NN 9451
Balnaguard Burn *W* 175 NN 9249
Balnaguisich *T* 192 NH 6771
Balnahard, Strath *T* 173 NM 4534
Balnahard, Strath 166 NR 4199
Balnain *T* 182 NH 4430
Balnakeil *T* 196 NC 3968
Balnakeil Bay *W* 196 NC 3869
Balnaknock *T* 187 NG 4162
Balnamoon 177 NO 5563
Balnapaling *T* 183 NH 7969
Balne *T* 139 SE 5919
Balquhidder *T* 169 NN 5320
Balranald *T* 188 NF 7169
Balruddery Farm 171 NO 3132
Balsall Common *T* 118 SP 2377
Balscote *T* 118 SP 3941
Balsham *T* 121 TL 5850
Balta 205 HP 6608
Baltasound, Shetld *T* 205 HP 6208
Balta Sound, Shetld *W* 205 HP 6508
Balterley *T* 127 SJ 7450
Balthangie *T* 185 NJ 8351
Baltonsborough *T* 93 ST 5434
Balvaird *T* 182 NH 5351
Balvarran 176 NO 0762
Balvenie Castle *A* 184 NJ 3240
Balvicar *T* 173 NM 7616
Balvraid *T* 183 NH 8331
Bamber Bridge *T* 145 SD 5626
Bamburgh *T* 165 NU 1834
Bamff 176 NO 2251
Bamford *T* 138 SK 2083
Bampton, Cumbr *T* 151 NY 5118
Bampton, Devon *T* 91 SS 9522
Bampton, Oxon *T* 115 SP 3103
Bampton Common 151 NY 4716
Banavie *T* 174 NN 1177
Banbury *P* 119 SP 4540
Banc Cwmhelen *H* 108 SN 6811
Banchory *T* 177 NO 7095
Banchory-Devenick *T* 177 NJ 9002
Banc Nant-rhys *H* 125 SN 8279
Bancyfelin *T* 111 SN 3218
Bancyffordd *T* 111 SN 4037
Bandirran House 171 NO 1930
Banff *T* 185 NJ 6864
Bangor *P* 134 SH 5771
Bangor-is-y-coed *T* 126 SJ 3945
Banham *T* 122 TM 0687
Bank *T* 94 SU 2807
Bankend, D. & G *T* 156 NY 0268
Bankend, Strath *T* 163 NS 8033
Bankfoot *T* 170 NO 0635
Bankglen *T* 156 NS 5912
Bankhead, Grampn *T* 184 NJ 6608
Bankhead, Grampn *T* 185 NJ 8910
Bank Newton *T* 146 SD 9153
Banknock *T* 169 NS 7879
Banks, Cumbr *T* 158 NY 5664
Banks, Lancs *T* 136 SD 3920
Bankshill *T* 157 NY 1982
Banks Sands 145 SD 3624
Bank Street *T* 117 SO 6362
Banningham *T* 133 TG 2129
Banniskirk House 199 ND 1657
Bannister Green *T* 106 TL 6920
Bannockburn *T* 169 NS 8190
Ban Rubha 167 NM 7106
Banstead *T* 105 TQ 2559
Bantham *T* 89 SX 6643
Banton *T* 169 NS 7579
Banwell *T* 100 ST 3959
Baosbheinn *H* 190 NG 8665
Bapchild *T* 98 TQ 9262
Bapton *T* 102 ST 9938
Baramore *T* 173 NM 6474
Barassie *T* 161 NS 3232
Barbaraville *T* 193 NH 7472
Barber Booth *T* 138 SK 1184
Barbon *T* 145 SD 6282
Barbreck House 167 NM 8306
Barbreck River *W* 173 NM 8407
Barbridge *T* 137 SJ 6165
Barbrook *T* 91 SS 7147
Barbrook Resr *W* 139 SK 2877
Barbury Castle *A* 102 SU 1576
Barby *T* 119 SP 5470
Barcaldine *T* 174 NM 9641
Barcaldine Castle *A* 173 NM 9040
Barcaldine Forest *F* 174 NM 9640
Barcheston *T* 118 SP 2639
Barcloy Hill *H* 155 NX 7552
Barcombe *T* 97 TQ 4114
Barcombe Cross *T* 97 TQ 4215
Barcraigs Reservoir *W* 161 NS 3957
Barden *T* 152 SE 1493
Barden Fell 146 SE 0858
Barden Reservoirs *W* 146 SE 0257
Bardfield Saling *T* 122 TL 6828
Bard Head 203 HU 5135
Bardister 204 HU 3577
Bardney *T* 141 TF 1169
Bardon Mill 158 NY 7764
Bardowie *T* 169 NS 5873
Bardrainney *T* 168 NS 3473
Bardsea *T* 145 SD 3074
Bardsey *T* 147 SE 3643
Bardsey Island or Ynys Enlli 124 SH 1222
Bardsey Sound *W* 124 SH 1324
Bardsley *T* 137 SD 9201
Bardwell *T* 122 TL 9473
Barewood *T* 113 SO 3856
Barford, Norf *T* 133 TG 1107
Barford, Warw *T* 118 SP 2761
Barford St Martin *T* 94 SU 0531
Barford St Michael *T* 115 SP 4332
Barfrestone *T* 99 TR 2650
Bargatton Loch *W* 156 NX 6961
Bargoed *T* 109 ST 1599
Bargrennan *T* 154 NX 3576
Barham, Cambs *T* 120 TL 1375
Barham, Kent *T* 99 TR 2050
Barham, Suff *T* 123 TM 1451
Bar Hill *T* 121 TL 3863
Barholm *T* 130 TF 0810
Barkby *T* 129 SK 6309
Barkestone-le-Vale *T* 129 SK 7835
Barkham *T* 104 SU 7867
Barking, G. Lon *T* 105 TQ 4785
Barking, Suff *T* 122 TM 0753
Barkingside *T* 105 TQ 4489
Barkin Isles 195 NB 4023
Barkisland *T* 138 SE 0519
Barkston, Lincs *T* 130 SK 9241
Barkston, N. Yks *T* 147 SE 4936
Barkway *T* 121 TL 3835
Barkwith *T* 141 TF 1681
Barlaston *T* 127 SJ 8938
Barlavington *T* 96 SU 9716
Barlborough *T* 139 SK 4777
Barlby *T* 147 SE 6334
Barlestone *T* 128 SK 4205
Barley, Herts *T* 121 TL 3938
Barley, Lancs *T* 146 SD 8240
Barleythorpe *T* 130 SK 8409
Barling *T* 106 TQ 9289
Barlow, Derby *T* 139 SK 3474
Barlow, N. Yks *T* 147 SE 6428
Barlow, T. & W *T* 159 NZ 1560
Barmby Moor *T* 148 SE 7848
Barmby on the Marsh *T* 142 SE 6928
Barmekin Hill *H* 185 NJ 7207
Barmer *T* 132 TF 8133
Barmoor Castle 165 NT 9939
Barmore Island 168 NR 8771
Barmouth *T* 124 SH 6116
Barmouth Bay *W* 124 SH 5913
Barmpton *T* 152 NZ 3118
Barmston *T* 149 TA 1659
Barnack *T* 130 TF 0704
Barnacle *T* 118 SP 3884
Barnard Castle *T* 152 NZ 0516
Barnard Gate *T* 115 SP 4010
Barnardiston *T* 122 TL 7148
Barnbougle Castle 170 NT 1678
Barnburgh *T* 139 SE 4803
Barnby *T* 123 TM 4789
Barnby Dun *T* 139 SE 6109
Barnby in the Willows *T* 130 SK 8652
Barnby Moor *T* 139 SK 6684
Barnes *T* 105 TQ 2276
Barnet *T* 105 TQ 2496
Barnetby le Wold *T* 142 TA 0509
Barney *T* 132 TF 9932
Barnham, Suff *T* 122 TL 8779
Barnham, W. Susx *T* 96 SU 9604
Barnham Broom *T* 133 TG 0807
Barnhead *T* 177 NO 6657
Barnhill *T* 183 NJ 1457
Barnhills 154 NW 9871
Barningham, Durham *T* 152 NZ 0810
Barningham, Suff *T* 122 TL 9676
Barningham Moor 152 NZ 0608
Barnoldby le Beck *T* 143 TA 2303
Barnoldswick *T* 146 SD 8746
Barns Green *T* 96 TQ 1226
Barnsley, Glos *T* 114 SP 0705
Barnsley, S. Yks *P* 139 SE 3406
Barns Ness 164 NT 7277
Barnstaple *P* 91 SS 5533
Barnstaple or Bideford Bay *W* 90 SS 3432
Barnston, Essex *T* 106 TL 6419
Barnston, Mers *T* 136 SJ 2883
Barnt Green *T* 118 SP 0073
Barnton *T* 137 SJ 6375
Barnwell *T* 120 TL 0484
Barnwood *T* 114 SO 8618
Barochan House 161 NS 4168
Barons Point 168 NS 2281
Barony, The *T* 200 HY 2627
Barr *T* 154 NX 2794
Barra 178 NF 6801
Barra Castle 185 NJ 7925
Barrachan *T* 154 NX 3649
Barrack *T* 185 NJ 8942
Barraer Fell *H* 154 NX 3761
Barraglom *T* 195 NB 1634
Barra Head 178 NL 5579
Barrahormid *T* 167 NR 7183
Barrapol *T* 172 NL 9543
Barras, Cumbr *T* 151 NY 8411
Barras, Grampn *T* 177 NO 8480
Barrasford *T* 158 NY 9173
Barravullin *T* 173 NM 8207
Barr Castle *A* 161 NS 3458
Barregarrow *T* 144 SC 3288
Barrel of Butter 200 HY 3500
Barr Ganuisg *H* 168 NR 9280
Barr Glen 160 NR 6937
Barrhead *T* 161 NS 5058
Barr Hill, D. & G *H* 156 NX 7881
Barrhill, Strath *T* 154 NX 2382
Barrington, Cambs *T* 121 TL 3949
Barrington, Somer *T* 92 ST 3918
Barripper *T* 86 SW 6238
Barrisdale Bay *W* 180 NG 8605
Barr Liath *H* 168 NR 9773
Barrmill *T* 161 NS 3651
Barr Mór, Strath *H* 173 NM 8138
Barr Mór, Strath *H* 168 NN 1312
Barrock *T* 199 ND 2571
Barrock House 199 ND 2862
Barrow, Lancs *T* 145 SD 7338
Barrow, Leic *T* 130 SK 8915
Barrow, Shrops *T* 127 SJ 6500
Barrow, Suff *T* 122 TL 7663
Barroway Drove *T* 131 TF 5703
Barrowby *T* 130 SK 8836
Barrow Deep (lightship) 107 TM 3003
Barrowden *T* 130 SK 9400
Barrowford *T* 146 SD 8539
Barrow Gurney *T* 101 ST 5367
Barrow-in-Furness *P* 144 SD 1969
Barrow Street *T* 93 ST 8330
Barrow upon Humber *T* 142 TA 0721
Barrow upon Soar *T* 129 SK 5717
Barrow upon Trent *T* 128 SK 3528
Barr Water *W* 160 NR 6937
Barry, S. Glam *T* 109 ST 1167
Barry, Tays *T* 171 NO 5334
Barry Island *T* 109 ST 1166
Barry Links 171 NO 5432
Barry Links Station 171 NO 5433
Barsalloch Point 154 NX 3441
Barsby *T* 129 SK 6911
Barsham *T* 123 TM 3989
Barston *T* 118 SP 2078
Bartestree *T* 113 SO 5641
Bartford St Martin *T* 94 SU 0531
Bar, The, Dyfed 124 SN 5781
Bar, The, Gwyn 134 SH 4160
Bar, The, Gwyn 124 SH 6014
Barth Head 199 ND 4285
Barthol Chapel *T* 185 NJ 8134
Barthomley *T* 127 SJ 7652
Bartley *T* 94 SU 3112
Bartlow *T* 121 TL 5845
Barton, Cambs *T* 121 TL 4055
Barton, Ches *T* 126 SJ 4454
Barton, Devon *T* 89 SX 9067
Barton, Glos *T* 114 SP 1025
Barton, Lancs *T* 145 SD 5137
Barton, N. Yks *T* 152 NZ 2308
Barton, Warw *T* 118 SP 1051
Barton Bendish *T* 132 TF 7105
Barton Hartshorn *T* 119 SP 6430
Barton in Fabis *T* 129 SK 5232
Barton in the Beans *T* 128 SK 3906
Barton-le-Clay *T* 120 TL 0831
Barton-le-Street *T* 148 SE 7274
Barton-le-Willows *T* 148 SE 7163
Barton Mills *T* 122 TL 7173
Barton Moss *T* 137 SJ 7397
Barton on Sea *T* 94 SZ 2393
Barton-on-the-Heath *T* 115 SP 2532
Barton Seagrave *T* 120 SP 8977
Barton Stacey *T* 102 SU 4341
Barton St David *T* 93 ST 5431
Barton Turf *T* 133 TG 3522
Barton-under-Needwood *T* 128 SK 1818
Barton-upon-Humber *T* 142 TA 0322
Barvas *T* 195 NB 3649
Barway *T* 121 TL 5475
Barwell *T* 129 SP 4496
Barwick *T* 93 ST 5613
Barwick in Elmet *T* 147 SE 4037
Baschurch *T* 126 SJ 4222
Bascote *T* 118 SP 4063
Basford Green *T* 128 SJ 9951
Bashall Eaves *T* 145 SD 7043
Bashley *T* 94 SZ 2497
Basildon *P* 106 TQ 7088
Basingstoke *P* 103 SU 6352
Basingstoke Canal *W* 103 SU 8453
Baslow *T* 139 SK 2572
Bason Bridge *T* 100 ST 3445
Bassaleg *T* 100 ST 2787
Bassenthwaite *T* 150 NY 2332
Bassenthwaite Lake *W* 150 NY 2129
Bassett *T* 94 SU 4216
Bassingbourn *T* 121 TL 3344
Bassingfield *T* 129 SK 6137
Bassingham *T* 140 SK 9159
Bassingthorpe *T* 130 SK 9628
Bass Rock 171 NT 6087
Basta *T* 205 HU 5294
Basta Voe *W* 205 HU 5296
Baston *T* 130 TF 1114
Bastwick *T* 133 TG 4217
Batchcott *T* 116 SO 4971
Batcombe, Dorset *T* 93 ST 6104
Batcombe, Somer *T* 101 ST 6939
Bate Heath *T* 137 SJ 6879
Bateman's *A* 97 TQ 6723
Bath *P* 101 ST 7464
Bathampton *T* 101 ST 7766
Bathealton *T* 92 ST 0724
Batheaston *T* 101 ST 7867
Bathford *T* 101 ST 7966
Bathgate *T* 163 NS 9768
Bathley *T* 140 SK 7759
Bathpool *T* 88 SX 2874
Batley *T* 147 SE 2424
Batsford *T* 115 SP 1834
Battersby *T* 153 NZ 5907
Battersea *T* 105 TQ 2876
Battery Point 101 ST 4677
Battisford *T* 122 TM 0554
Battisford Tye *T* 122 TM 0254
Battle, E. Susx *T* 97 TQ 7416
Battle, Powys *T* 109 SO 0131
Battlefield *T* 127 SJ 5116
Battlesbridge *T* 106 TQ 7794
Battlesbury *A* 101 ST 8945
Battlesden *T* 120 SP 9628
Battleton *T* 91 SS 9127
Battramsley *T* 94 SZ 3098
Bauds of Cullen *T* 184 NJ 4867
Baugh Fell 151 SD 7393
Baughurst *T* 103 SU 5861
Baulking *T* 102 SU 3191
Baumber *T* 141 TF 2274
Baunton *T* 114 SP 0204
Bavelaw Castle *A* 163 NT 1662
Baverstock *T* 94 SU 0232
Bawburgh *T* 133 TG 1508
Bawden Rocks or Man & his man 86 SW 7053
Bawdeswell *T* 132 TG 0420
Bawdrip *T* 100 ST 3439
Bawdsey *T* 123 TM 3440
Bawtry *P* 139 SK 6593
Baxenden *T* 146 SD 7726
Baxterley *T* 128 SP 2897
Bayble Bay *W* 195 NB 5330
Bayble Hill *H* 195 NB 5030
Baycliff *T* 145 SD 2872
Baydon *T* 102 SU 2878
Bayford *T* 105 TL 3008
Bayham Abbey *T* 97 TQ 6436
Bayhead *T* 188 NF 7468
Bayles *T* 151 NY 7045
Baylham *T* 123 TM 1051
Bay of Backaland *W* 200 HY 5730
Bay of Bomasty *W* 201 HY 6123
Bay of Brough *W* 201 HY 6541
Bay of Cleat *W* 200 HY 4646
Bay of Cruden *W* 185 NK 0935
Bay of Deepdale *W* 202 HU 1754
Bay of Firth *W* 200 HY 3814
Bay of Fladdabister *W* 203 HU 4432
Bay of Furrowend *W* 200 HY 4719
Bay of Holland *W* 201 HY 6423
Bay of Houseby *W* 201 HY 6821
Bay of Ireland *W* 200 HY 2809
Bay of Isbister *W* 200 HY 3918
Bay of Keisgaig *W* 196 NC 2469
Bay of Kirkwall *W* 200 HY 4413
Bay of Laig *W* 179 NM 4688

Bermondsey   Bloxworth

Bermondsey T 105 TQ 3579
Bernard Wharf 145 SD 3451
Bernera T 180 NG 8020
Bernera Island 173 NM 7939
Berneray, W. Isles 188 NF 9181
Berneray, W. Isles 178 NL 5580
Berney Arms Station 133 TG 4605
Bernice 168 NS 1391
Bernisdale T 187 NG 4050
Berrick Salome T 104 SU 6293
Berriedale T 193 ND 1222
Berriedale Water W 199 ND 0730
Berrier T 151 NY 4029
Berriew T 126 SJ 1800
Berrington, Northum T 165 NU 0043
Berrington, Shrops T 127 SJ 5307
Berrow T 100 ST 2952
Berrow Flats 100 ST 2854
Berrow Green T 117 SO 7458
Berry Head 89 SX 9456
Berry Hill T 113 SO 5712
Berryhillock T 184 NJ 5060
Berryl's Point 87 SW 8467
Berrynarbor T 91 SS 5646
Berry Pomeroy T 89 SX 8261
Berry, The H 200 ND 2490
Berry Top H 177 NO 8696
Bersham T 126 SJ 3049
Berstane 200 HY 4610
Bersted T 96 SU 9200
Berst Ness 200 HY 4441
Berth, The A 126 SJ 4323
Bervie Bay W 177 NO 8372
Bervie Water W 177 NO 8074
Berwick T 97 TQ 5105
Berwick Bassett T 102 SU 1073
Berwick Hill T 159 NZ 1775
Berwick St James T 102 SU 0739
Berwick St John T 94 ST 9422
Berwick St Leonard T 93 ST 9233
Berwick-upon-Tweed P 165 NT 9953
Berwyn, Clwyd H 135 SJ 0431
Berwyn, Clwyd T 126 SJ 1943
Berwyn, Gwyn H 135 SJ 0431
Berwyn, Powys H 135 SJ 0431
Bescar Lane Station 136 SD 3914
Besford T 117 SO 9145
Bessacarr T 139 SE 6101
Bessels Leigh T 115 SP 4501
Bessingham T 133 TG 1636
Besthorpe, Norf T 132 TM 0695
Besthorpe, Notts T 140 SK 8264
Beswick T 149 TA 0148
Betchworth T 96 TQ 2150
Bethania, Dyfed T 124 SN 5763
Bethania, Gwyn T 135 SH 6250
Bethel T 134 SH 5265
Bethersden T 98 TQ 9240
Bethesda, Dyfed T 110 SN 0918
Bethesda, Gwyn T 135 SH 6266
Bethlehem T 108 SN 6825
Bethnal Green T 105 TQ 3482
Betley T 127 SJ 7548
Betsham T 98 TQ 6071
Betteshanger T 99 TR 3152
Bettiscombe T 92 SY 3999
Bettisfield T 126 SJ 4635
Betton, Shrops T 126 SJ 3102
Betton, Shrops T 127 SJ 6937
Bettws, Gwent T 113 SO 2919
Bettws, Gwent T 100 ST 2990
Bettws Cedewain T 126 SO 1296
Bettws Gwerfil Goch T 135 SJ 0346
Bettws Newydd T 113 SO 3606
Bettyhill T 197 NC 7062
Betws, Dyfed T 111 SN 6311
Betws, M. Glam T 109 SS 9087
Betws Bledrws T 111 SN 5951
Betws Garmon T 134 SH 5357
Betws Ifan T 111 SN 3047
Betws-y-Coed P 135 SH 7956
Betws-yn-Rhos T 135 SH 9073
Beulah, Dyfed T 111 SN 2946
Beulah, Powys T 112 SN 9251
Beul an Toim W 188 NF 7857
Bevendean T 97 TQ 3406
Bevercotes T 140 SK 6972
Beverley T 142 TA 0339
Beverston T 114 ST 8693
Bevington T 114 ST 6697
Bewaldeth T 150 NY 2134
Bewcastle T 158 NY 5674
Bewcastle Fells H 158 NY 5681
Bewdley T 117 SO 7875
Bewerley T 146 SE 1564
Bewholme T 149 TA 1650
Bewl Bridge Reservoir W 97 TQ 6832
Bexhill T 97 TQ 7407
Bexley T 105 TQ 4775
Bexwell T 132 TF 6303
Beyton T 122 TL 9362
Biargar 203 HU 3635
Bibblon Hill H 162 NS 6632
Bibury T 114 SP 1106
Bicester T 115 SP 5822
Bickenhall T 92 ST 2818
Bickenhill T 118 SP 1882
Bicker T 131 TF 2237
Bicker Haven 131 TF 2533
Bickerstaffe T 136 SD 4404
Bickerton, Ches T 127 SJ 5052
Bickerton, N. Yks T 147 SE 4550
Bickington, Devon T 91 SS 5332
Bickington, Devon T 89 SX 7972
Bickleigh, Devon T 91 SS 9407
Bickleigh, Devon T 89 SX 5262
Bickleton T 90 SS 5031
Bickley T 105 TQ 4268
Bickley Moss T 127 SJ 5449
Bicknacre T 106 TL 7802
Bicknoller T 100 ST 1139
Bicknor T 98 TQ 8658
Bickton T 94 SU 1412
Bicton, Shrops T 126 SJ 4415
Bicton, Shrops T 116 SO 2982
Bidborough T 97 TQ 5643
Biddenden T 98 TQ 8438
Biddenham T 120 TL 0250
Biddestone T 101 ST 8673
Biddisham T 100 ST 3853
Biddlesden T 119 SP 6340
Biddlestone T 158 NT 9608
Biddulph T 137 SJ 8857
Biddulph Moor T 137 SJ 9058
Bidean nam Bian H 174 NN 1454
Bideford P 90 SS 4526
Bideford Bar 90 SS 4333
Bideford or Barnstaple Bay W 90 SS 3432
Bidford-on-Avon T 118 SP 1052
Bielby T 142 SE 7843
Bieldside T 177 NJ 8802
Biel Water W 171 NT 6375
Bierley T 95 SZ 5178
Bierton T 104 SP 8315
Bigbury T 89 SX 6646
Bigbury Bay W 89 SX 6342
Bigbury-on-Sea T 89 SX 6544
Bigby T 142 TA 0507
Bigga 205 HU 4479
Biggar, Cumbr T 144 SD 1966
Biggar, Strath T 163 NT 0437
Big Garvoun H 183 NJ 1408
Bigges's Pillar H 159 NU 1207
Biggin, Derby T 138 SK 1559
Biggin, Derby T 128 SK 2648
Biggin, N. Yks T 147 SE 5434
Biggings T 202 HU 1760
Biggin Hill T 105 TQ 4158
Biggin Hill Airport 105 TQ 4160
Biggins T 145 SD 6078
Biggleswade T 120 TL 1944
Big Hill of Glenmount H 155 NS 4500
Bighouse 198 NC 8964
Bighton T 95 SU 6134
Bignor T 96 SU 9814
Big Sand T 190 NG 7579
Bigton T 203 HU 3721
Big Water of Fleet W 156 NX 5662
Bilberry T 87 SX 0160
Bilborough T 129 SK 5141
Bilbrook T 127 SJ 8803
Bilbrough T 147 SE 5346
Bilbster T 199 ND 2853
Bildeston T 122 TL 9949
Billericay T 106 TQ 6794
Billesdon T 129 SK 7102
Billesley T 118 SP 1456
Billia Field H 205 HU 3786
Billing T 119 SP 8062
Billingborough T 130 TF 1134
Billinge T 137 SD 5300
Billingford, Norf T 132 TG 0120
Billingford, Suff T 123 TM 1678
Billingham T 153 NZ 4623
Billinghay T 130 TF 1555
Billingley T 139 SE 4304
Billingshurst T 96 TQ 0825
Billingsley T 117 SO 7085
Billington, Beds T 104 SP 9422
Billington, Lancs T 145 SD 7235
Billockby T 133 TG 4213
Bill of Portland 93 SY 6768
Billsmoor Park 158 NY 9496
Billy Row T 152 NZ 1637
Bilsborrow T 145 SD 5140
Bilsby T 141 TF 4776
Bilsington T 99 TR 0434
Bilsthorpe T 139 SK 6460
Bilston, Lothn T 163 NT 2664
Bilston, W. Mids T 128 SO 9597
Bilstone T 128 SK 3605
Bilting T 99 TR 0549
Bilton, Humbs T 143 TA 1633
Bilton, Northum T 159 NU 2210
Bilton, N. Yks T 147 SE 4750
Bilton, Warw T 119 SP 4873
Bimbister T 200 HY 3216
Binbrook T 141 TF 2193
Bincombe T 93 SY 6884
Binegar T 101 ST 6149
Binfield T 104 SU 8471
Binfield Heath T 104 SU 7478
Bin Forest, The F 184 NJ 5143
Bingfield T 159 NY 9772
Bingham T 129 SK 7039
Bingham's Melcombe A 93 ST 7702
Bingley T 146 SE 1139
Binham T 132 TF 9839
Binley, Hants T 102 SU 4253
Binley, W. Mids T 118 SP 3777
Binley Woods T 118 SP 3977
Binnein an Fhidhleir H 168 NN 2110
Binnein Mór H 174 NN 2166
Binnein Shuas H 175 NN 4682
Binniehill T 170 NS 8572
Binnimoor Fen 131 TL 4497
Binns, The A 170 NT 0578
Bin of Cullen H 184 NJ 4864
Binsey H 150 NY 2235
Binstead T 95 SZ 5791
Binsted T 103 SU 7740
Bin, The H 184 NJ 5043
Binton T 118 SP 1454
Bintree T 132 TG 0123
Binweston T 126 SJ 3004
Bioda Buidhe H 187 NG 4366
Biod an Athair H 186 NG 1554
Biod nan Laog 186 NG 2958
Birch, Essex T 106 TL 9419
Birch, G. Man T 137 SD 8507
Bircham Newton T 132 TF 7633
Bircham Tofts T 132 TF 7732
Birchanger T 105 TL 5122
Bircher T 116 SO 4765
Birch Green T 106 TL 9419
Birchgrove T 108 SS 7098
Birchington T 99 TR 2969
Birchover T 139 SK 2462
Birch Vale T 138 SK 0286
Birchwood T 140 SK 9369
Bircotes T 139 SK 6391
Birdbrook T 122 TL 7041
Birdham T 95 SU 8200
Birdingbury T 118 SP 4368
Birdlip T 114 SO 9214
Birdsall T 148 SE 8165
Birdsgreen T 117 SO 7685
Birdston T 169 NS 6575
Birdwell T 139 SE 3401
Birdwood T 114 SO 7418
Birgham T 165 NT 7839
Birk Beck W 151 NY 5907
Birkdale T 136 SD 3215
Birkdale Common 151 NY 8302
Birkenburn Reservoir W 169 NS 6780
Birkenhead P 136 SJ 3288
Birkenhills T 185 NJ 7445
Birkenshaw, Strath T 162 NS 6961
Birkenshaw, W. Yks T 146 SE 2028
Birker Force W 150 SD 1899
Birkhall T 176 NO 3493
Birkhill T 171 NO 3534
Birkin T 147 SE 5327
Birley T 113 SO 4553
Birling, Kent T 98 TQ 6860
Birling, Northum T 159 NU 2406
Birlingham T 117 SO 9343
Birmingham P 118 SP 0787
Birmingham International Airport 118 SP 1784
Birnam T 176 NO 0341
Birnam Hill H 176 NO 0340
Birness T 185 NJ 9933
Birnock Water W 157 NT 1008
Birns Water W 164 NT 4865
Birrier 205 HU 5488
Birsay 200 HY 2825
Birsay Bay W 200 HY 2427
Birse T 177 NO 5597
Birsemore T 177 NO 5297
Birstall T 129 SK 5909
Birstall Smithies T 147 SE 2225
Birstwith T 147 SE 2359
Birtley, H. & W T 116 SO 3669
Birtley, Northum T 158 NY 8778
Birtley, T. & W T 152 NZ 2756
Birts Street T 117 SO 7836
Biruaslum 178 NL 6096
Bisbrooke T 130 SP 8899
Bis Geos 200 HY 4147
Bishampton T 118 SO 9951
Bishop Auckland P 152 NZ 2029
Bishopbriggs T 169 NS 6170
Bishop Burton T 142 SE 9839
Bishopdale Beck W 146 SD 9885
Bishop Hill H 170 NO 1804
Bishop Middleham T 152 NZ 3331
Bishop Monkton T 147 SE 3266
Bishop Norton T 140 SK 9892
Bishopric 176 NN 9647
Bishop Rock 86 SV 8006
Bishops and Clerks 110 SM 6625
Bishopsbourne T 99 TR 1852
Bishops Cannings T 102 SU 0364
Bishop's Castle T 116 SO 3288
Bishop's Caundle T 93 ST 6913
Bishop's Cleeve T 114 SO 9527
Bishop's Frome T 117 SO 6648
Bishop's Itchington T 118 SP 3957
Bishops Lydeard T 92 ST 1629
Bishop's Nympton T 91 SS 7523
Bishop's Offley T 127 SJ 7829
Bishop's Stortford P 105 TL 4821
Bishop's Sutton T 95 SU 6131
Bishop's Tachbrook T 118 SP 3161
Bishop's Tawton T 91 SS 5630
Bishopsteignton T 89 SX 9073
Bishopstoke T 95 SU 4719
Bishopston T 108 SS 5889
Bishopstone, Bucks T 104 SP 8010
Bishopstone, E. Susx T 97 TQ 4701
Bishopstone, H. & W T 113 SO 4143
Bishopstone, Wilts T 94 SU 0725
Bishopstone, Wilts T 102 SU 2483
Bishop Sutton T 101 ST 5859
Bishop's Waltham T 95 SU 5517
Bishopswood, Somer T 92 ST 2512
Bishop's Wood, Staffs T 127 SJ 8309
Bishopsworth T 101 ST 5768
Bishop Thornton T 147 SE 2663
Bishopthorpe T 147 SE 5947
Bishopton, Durham T 153 NZ 3621
Bishopton, Strath T 169 NS 4371
Bishopton Station 169 NS 4370
Bishop Wilton T 148 SE 7955
Bishton T 100 ST 3987
Bisley, Glos T 114 SO 9006
Bisley, Surrey T 104 SU 9559
Bispham T 145 SD 3040
Bissoe T 86 SW 7741
Bisterne Close T 94 SU 2302
Bitchfield T 130 SK 9828
Bittadon T 91 SS 5441
Bittaford T 89 SX 6657
Bittering T 132 TF 9317
Bitterley T 116 SO 5677
Bitterne T 95 SU 4413
Bitteswell T 119 SP 5385
Bitteswell Aerodrome 119 SP 5184
Bitton T 101 ST 6869
Bix T 104 SU 7285
Bixter T 203 HU 3352
Bla Bheinn H 187 NG 5221
Blaby T 129 SP 5697
Blacka Burn W 158 NY 7878
Blackacre T 157 NY 0490
Blackadder T 165 NT 8552
Blackadder Water W 165 NT 8252
Blackawton T 89 SX 8051
Black Bay W 160 NR 7726
Black Beck W 152 SE 1093
Blackborough T 92 ST 0909
Blackborough End T 132 TF 6613
Black Bourton T 115 SP 2804
Blackboys T 97 TQ 5120
Blackbrook T 127 SJ 7639
Blackbrook Reservoir W 129 SK 4517
Black Buoy Sand 131 TF 4139
Black Burn, Cumbr W 151 NY 6940
Black Burn, Grampn W 183 NJ 1256
Blackburn, Grampn T 185 NJ 8212
Blackburn, Lancs P 145 SD 6828
Blackburn, Lothn T 163 NS 9865
Blackburn Common 158 NY 8092
Blackburn Rig 165 NT 7966
Blackbury Castle A 92 SY 1892
Black Callerton T 159 NZ 1769
Black Clauchrie T 154 NX 2984
Black Combe 144 SD 1486
Black Corries Lodge 174 NN 2956
Black Craig, D. & G H 155 NX 5095
Black Craig, Grampn H 176 NO 4394
Black Craig, Orkney 200 HY 2111
Blackcraig Castle 176 NO 1053
Blackcraig Forest F 176 NO 1151
Blackcraig Hill, D. & G H 156 NS 7401
Blackcraig Hill, D. & G H 156 NX 7082
Blackcraig Hill, Strath H 156 NS 6406
Blackcraig Hill, Tays H 176 NO 0952
Black Craig of Dee or Cairnsmore H 156 NX 5875
Black Crofts T 168 NM 9234
Blackden Heath T 137 SJ 7871
Black Devon, Central W 170 NS 9693
Black Devon, Fife W 170 NS 9693
Black Dog, Devon T 91 SS 8009
Blackdog, Grampn T 185 NJ 9514
Blackdog Rock 185 NJ 9613
Black Down, Devon H 92 ST 0906
Black Down, Devon 88 SX 5081
Black Down, Dorset H 93 SY 6187
Black Down Hills H 92 ST 1616
Black Edge, Border H 157 NY 4288
Black Edge, D. & G H 157 NY 4288
Black Esk W 157 NY 2293
Black Esk Reservoir W 157 NY 2096
Black Fell H 158 NY 7173
Blackfield T 95 SU 4401
Blackford, Cumbr T 157 NY 3962
Blackford, Somer T 100 ST 4147
Blackford, Somer T 93 ST 6526
Blackford, Tays T 170 NN 8909
Blackfordby T 128 SK 3318
Blackgang T 95 SZ 4876
Blackgang Chine 95 SZ 4876
Blackhall T 177 NO 6795
Blackhall Colliery 153 NZ 4539
Blackhall Forest F 177 NO 6695
Blackhall Rocks T 153 NZ 4638
Blackham T 97 TQ 5039
Blackhaugh T 164 NT 4238
Black Head, Corn 86 SW 7716
Black Head, Corn 87 SX 0348
Black Head, D. & G 154 NW 9856
Blackheath, Essex T 107 TM 0021
Blackheath, Surrey 96 TQ 0446
Black Heath, Wilts 102 SU 0751
Blackheath, W. Mids T 118 SO 9786
Black Hill, Ches H 138 SJ 9982
Black Hill, Derby H 138 SE 0704
Black Hill, Devon H 92 SY 0285
Black Hill, D. & G H 157 NT 1500
Black Hill, Grampn H 184 NJ 6712
Blackhill, Grampn T 185 NK 0755
Blackhill, Grampn T 185 NK 0843
Black Hill, Lothn H 163 NT 1863
Black Hill, N. Yks H 146 SD 7760
Black Hill, Shrops H 116 SO 3279
Black Hill, Strath H 162 NS 7029
Black Hill, Strath H 154 NX 3896
Black Hill, W. Yks H 138 SE 0704
Black Hill of Mark, Grampn H 176 NO 3281
Black Hill of Mark, Tays H 176 NO 3281
Blackhills 184 NJ 2758
Blackhope Burn W 157 NT 1311
Blackhope Scar H 164 NT 3148
Blackhouse Moor 161 NS 2064
Black Islands 180 NG 7529
Black Isle 182 NH 6556
Black Knowe, Border H 157 NT 2210
Black Knowe, Border H 157 NT 2807
Black Knowe, Border H 158 NY 5487
Black Knowe, D. & G H 157 NT 2807
Black Knowe, Northum H 158 NY 5891
Black Knowe, Northum H 158 NY 6481
Black Knowe Head H 164 NT 3122
Blackland T 102 SU 0168
Black Law, Border H 163 NT 2127
Black Law, Border H 164 NT 3042
Blackley T 137 SD 8602
Black Loch, Central W 170 NS 8670
Black Loch, D. & G W 154 NX 1161
Black Loch, Strath W 170 NS 8670
Black Lochs W 168 NM 9231
Blacklorg Hill H 156 NS 6504
Blacklunans T 176 NO 1460
Black Lyne W 158 NY 5481
Blackman's Law H 158 NY 7498
Black Marsh T 126 SO 3299
Black Meldon H 163 NT 2042
Blackmill T 109 SS 9386
Blackmoor T 95 SU 7733
Blackmoor Gate 91 SS 6443
Blackmoor Vale 93 ST 7315
Blackmore T 106 TL 6001
Blackmore End T 122 TL 7330
Black Mount, Highld 174 NN 2947
Black Mount, Strath T 174 NN 2842
Black Mount, Strath 174 NN 2947
Black Mount, Strath H 163 NT 0846
Black Mountain, Powys H 116 SO 1677
Black Mountain, Shrops H 116 SO 1983
Black Mountains, The, Gwent H 113 SO 2427
Black Mountains, The, H. & W H 113 SO 2427
Black Mountains, The, Powys H 113 SO 2427
Black Mountain, The, Dyfed H 109 SN 7618
Black Mountain, The, Powys H 109 SN 7618
Blackness T 170 NT 0579
Blacknest T 103 SU 7941
Black Notley T 106 TL 7620
Blacko T 146 SD 8641
Black Pill T 108 SS 6190
Black Point 160 NR 7104
Blackpool P 145 SD 3035
Blackpool Airport 145 SD 3231
Blackpool Gate T 158 NY 5377
Blackridge T 163 NS 8967
Blackrock, Gwent T 109 SO 2112
Blackrock, Strath T 166 NR 3063
Black Rocks, Lothn 171 NT 2777
Black Rocks, N. Yks T 149 TA 0486
Blackrod T 137 SD 6110
Black Sail Pass 150 NY 1811
Blackshaw T 157 NY 0465
Blackshaw Bank 157 NY 0462
Blackside H 162 NS 5930
Blackstone T 96 TQ 2316
Blackthorn T 104 SP 6219
Blackthorpe T 122 TL 9063
Blacktoft T 142 SE 8424
Blackton Reservoir W 152 NY 9418
Blacktop T 185 NJ 8604
Black Torrington T 90 SS 4605
Blackwater, Corn T 86 SW 7346
Black Water, Grampn W 184 NJ 3530
Blackwater, Hants T 104 SU 8460
Black Water, Highld W 193 NC 7815
Black Water, Highld W 182 NH 4066
Black Water, Highld W 192 NH 5776
Black Water, Highld W 174 NN 3861
Blackwater, I. of W T 95 SZ 5086
Black Water, Tays W 176 NO 1459
Blackwaterfoot T 160 NR 8928
Blackwater Forest 184 NJ 3126
Black Water of Dee or River Dee W 156 NX 5973
Blackwater Reservoir, Highld W 174 NN 3060
Blackwater Reservoir, Tays W 176 NO 2560
Blackwater River W 104 SU 7364
Blackwell, Derby T 138 SK 1272
Blackwell, H. & W T 118 SO 9972
Blackwood, Gwent T 109 ST 1797
Blackwood, Strath T 162 NS 7943
Blackwood Hill T 127 SJ 9255
Blacon T 136 SJ 3868
Bladerstone T 145 SD 6232
Bladnoch T 155 NX 4254
Bladon T 115 SP 4414
Blaeberry Hill H 157 NT 2801
Blaenannerch T 111 SN 2549
Blaenau Ffestiniog T 135 SH 7045
Blaenavon T 113 SO 2509
Blaendyryn T 112 SN 9337
Blaenffos T 111 SN 1937
Blaengarw T 109 SS 9092
Blaengwrach T 109 SN 8705
Blaengwynfi T 109 SS 8996
Blaenpennal T 125 SN 6364
Blaenplwyf T 124 SN 5775
Blaenporth T 111 SN 2648
Blaenrhondda T 109 SS 9299
Blaenwaun T 111 SN 2327
Blagdon, Avon T 101 ST 5058
Blagdon, Devon T 89 SX 8560
Blagdon Hill T 92 ST 2118
Blagdon Lake W 101 ST 5159
Blaich T 174 NN 0377
Blaina T 109 SO 2008
Blair Atholl T 175 NN 8765
Blair Castle, Fife 170 NS 9685
Blair Castle, Tays A 175 NN 8666
Blairdaff T 185 NJ 6917
Blairdenon Hill, Central H 170 NN 8601
Blairdenon Hill, Tays H 170 NN 8601
Blair Drummond 169 NS 7398
Blairdrummond Moss 169 NS 7197
Blairgowrie T 176 NO 1745
Blairhall T 170 NT 0089
Blairingone T 170 NS 9896
Blairlogie T 169 NS 8296
Blairmore T 168 NS 1982
Blairnamarrow 184 NJ 2115
Blairskaith T 169 NS 5975
Blaisdon T 114 SO 7017
Blakebrook T 117 SO 8176
Blakedown T 117 SO 8878
Blake Hall 105 TL 5305
Blakehope Fell H 158 NY 8494
Blakehope Head H 163 NT 1030
Blakelaw T 164 NT 7730
Blakeman's Law H 158 NY 8795
Blakemere T 113 SO 3641
Blake Muir 164 NT 3030
Blakeney, Glos T 114 SO 6707
Blakeney, Norf T 132 TG 0243
Blakeney Point 132 TG 0046
Blakenhall, Ches T 127 SJ 7247
Blakenhall, W. Mids T 127 SO 9197
Blakeshall T 117 SO 8381
Blakesley T 119 SP 6250
Blakey Ridge H 148 SE 6897
Blanch Fell 145 SD 5760
Blanchland T 152 NY 9650
Blanchland Moor 152 NY 9553
Blandford Camp T 93 ST 9108
Blandford Forum P 93 ST 8806
Blandford St Mary T 93 ST 8805
Bland Hill T 146 SE 2053
Blanefield T 169 NS 5579
Blane Water W 169 NS 5183
Blankney T 140 TF 0760
Blàr a' Chaorainn 174 NN 1066
Blàr Dearg 199 ND 0454
Blarghour 168 NM 9913
Blarmachfoldach T 174 NN 0969
Blarnalearoch T 191 NH 1490
Blary Hill H 160 NR 7136
Blashford T 94 SU 1506
Blaston T 129 SP 8095
Blatherwycke T 130 SP 9795
Blatobulgium R 157 NY 2175
Blawith T 145 SD 2888
Blaxhall T 123 TM 3657
Blaxton T 139 SE 6700
Blaydon T 159 NZ 1762
Blaze Moss H 145 SD 6153
Bleadon T 100 ST 3456
Bleadon Hill H 100 ST 3557
Bleak Law H 163 NT 0651
Bleaklow Hill H 138 SK 1096
Blea Moor 146 SD 7782
Blean T 99 TR 1261
Bleasby T 129 SK 7149
Bleasdale Moors 145 SD 5648
Blea Tarn, Cumbr W 150 NY 2914
Bleatarn, Cumbr T 151 NY 7313
Bleaval H 188 NG 0391
Blebocraigs T 171 NO 4315
Bleddfa T 116 SO 2068
Bledington T 115 SP 2422
Bledlow T 104 SP 7702
Bledlow Ridge T 104 SU 7997
Blegbie T 164 NT 4761
Blencarn T 151 NY 6331
Blencathra or Saddleback H 150 NY 3127
Blencogo T 150 NY 1948
Blencow T 151 NY 4532
Blendworth T 95 SU 7013
Blenheim Palace A 115 SP 4416
Blennerhasset T 150 NY 1741
Blervie Castle 183 NJ 0757
Bletchingdon T 115 SP 5017
Bletchingley T 97 TQ 3250
Bletchley, Bucks T 120 SP 8634
Bletchley, Shrops T 127 SJ 6233
Bletherston T 110 SN 0721
Bletsoe T 120 TL 0258
Blewbury T 103 SU 5385
Blickling T 133 TG 1728
Blidworth T 129 SK 5956
Blindburn 158 NT 8210
Blindcrake T 150 NY 1434
Blindley Heath T 97 TQ 3646
Blisland T 87 SX 1073
Blissford T 94 SU 1713
Bliss Gate T 117 SO 7472
Blisworth T 119 SP 7253
Blithfield Reservoir W 128 SK 0524
Blockley T 115 SP 1635
Blofield T 133 TG 3309
Blo' Norton T 122 TM 0179
Bloody Bay W 173 NM 4858
Bloodybush Edge H 158 NT 9014
Blore T 128 SK 1349
Blorenge H 113 SO 2712
Blotchnie Fiold H 200 HY 4128
Blovid 203 HU 4119
Bloxham T 115 SP 4235
Bloxwich T 128 SK 0002
Bloxworth T 93 SY 8894

Blubberhouses Bretherdale Head

Blubberhouses *T* 146 SE 1755
Blue Anchor *T* 100 ST 0243
Blue Anchor Bay *W* 100 ST 0145
Blue Bell Hill *T* 98 TQ 7462
Blue Head 183 NH 8166
Bluemull Sound *W* 205 HP 5502
Blundellsands *T* 136 SJ 3099
Blundeston *T* 133 TM 5197
Blunham *T* 120 TL 1551
Blunsdon St Andrew *T* 102 SU 1389
Bluntisham *T* 121 TL 3674
Blyborough *T* 140 SK 9394
Blyford *T* 123 TM 4276
Blymhill *T* 127 SJ 8112
Blyth, Northum *T* 159 NZ 3181
Blyth, Notts *T* 139 SK 6286
Blyth Bridge *T* 163 NT 1345
Blythburgh *T* 123 TM 4575
Blythe *T* 164 NT 5849
Blythe Bridge *T* 128 SJ 9541
Blythe Edge *H* 164 NT 6056
Blythe Sands 106 TQ 7580
Blyton *T* 140 SK 8594
Boarhills *T* 171 NO 5614
Boarhunt *T* 95 SU 6008
Boar of Badenoch or An Torc, Highld *H* 175 NN 6276
Boar of Badenoch or An Torc, Tays *H* 175 NN 6276
Boarshead *T* 97 TQ 5332
Boar's Head Rock 184 NJ 2968
Boars of Duncansby *W* 199 ND 3775
Boarstall *T* 104 SP 6214
Boasley Cross *T* 88 SX 5093
Boath *T* 192 NH 5774
Boat of Garten *T* 183 NH 9419
Bobbing *T* 98 TQ 8864
Bobbington *T* 117 SO 8090
Boblainy Forest *F* 182 NH 4938
Bocaddon *T* 87 SX 1758
Boch-ailean 193 ND 1020
Bochastle 169 NN 6107
Bockhampton *T* 93 SY 7291
Bocking *T* 106 TL 7523
Bocking Churchstreet *T* 122 TL 7625
Boconnoc 87 SX 1460
Boddam, Grampn *T* 185 NK 1342
Boddam, Shetld *T* 203 HU 3915
Boddington *T* 114 SO 8925
Boddin Point 177 NO 7153
Bodedern *T* 134 SH 3380
Bodelwyddan *T* 135 SJ 0075
Bodenham, H. & W *T* 113 SO 5351
Bodenham, Wilts *T* 94 SU 1626
Bodesbeck Law *H* 157 NT 1610
Bodewryd *T* 134 SH 4090
Bodfach Hall 126 SJ 1320
Bodfari *T* 135 SJ 0970
Bodffordd *T* 134 SH 4276
Bodham *T* 133 TG 1240
Bodiam *T* 98 TQ 7825
Bodicote *T* 119 SP 4638
Bodieve *T* 87 SW 9973
Bodior 134 SH 2876
Bodle Street Green *T* 97 TQ 6514
Bodmin *P* 87 SX 0767
Bodmin Moor 87 SX 1876
Bodmin Parkway Station 87 SX 1164
Bodney *T* 132 TL 8398
Bodorgan 134 SH 3867
Bodorgan Station 134 SH 3870
Boduan *T* 134 SH 3237
Bogallan *T* 182 NH 6350
Bogany Point 161 NS 1065
Bogbrae *T* 185 NK 0335
Bogend *T* 161 NS 3932
Bogh a' Chùirn 167 NR 6893
Boghall *T* 163 NS 9968
Boghole Farm 183 NH 9755
Bogmoor *T* 184 NJ 3563
Bogniebrae *T* 184 NJ 5945
Bognor Regis *P* 96 SZ 9399
Bograxie *T* 185 NJ 7119
Bogrie Hill *H* 156 NX 7885
Bogside 163 NS 8354
Bog, The *T* 126 SO 3598
Bogton *T* 184 NJ 6751
Bogton Loch *W* 161 NS 4605
Bogue 156 NX 6481
Bohenie *T* 174 NN 2982
Bohortha *T* 87 SW 8632
Bohuntine *T* 174 NN 2983
Boisdale *T* 178 NF 7417
Bojewyan *T* 86 SW 3934
Bolam *T* 152 NZ 1922
Bolam Lake *W* 159 NZ 0881
Bold Heath *T* 137 SJ 5389
Boldon *T* 159 NZ 3561
Boldon Colliery 159 NZ 3462
Boldre *T* 94 SZ 3198
Boldron *T* 152 NZ 0314
Bole *T* 140 SK 7987
Bolehill *T* 128 SK 2955
Boleside *T* 164 NT 4933
Bolham *T* 91 SS 9514
Bolham Water *T* 92 ST 1612
Bolingey *T* 86 SW 7653
Bollihope Common 152 NY 9834
Bollington, Ches *T* 137 SJ 7286
Bollington, Ches *T* 137 SJ 9377
Bolney *T* 96 TQ 2623
Bolnhurst *T* 120 TL 0859
Bolshan 177 NO 6252
Bolsover *T* 139 SK 4770
Bolsterstone *T* 139 SK 2796
Bolstone *T* 113 SO 5532
Boltby *T* 147 SE 4986
Bolt Head 89 SX 7236
Bolton, Cumbr *T* 151 NY 6323
Bolton, G. Man *P* 137 SD 7108
Bolton, Humbs *T* 148 SE 7752
Bolton, Lothn *T* 171 NT 5070
Bolton, Northum *T* 159 NU 1013
Bolton Abbey *T* 146 SE 0754
Bolton-by-Bowland *T* 146 SD 7849
Boltonfellend *T* 157 NY 4768
Boltongate *T* 150 NY 2340
Bolton Hall 152 SE 0789
Bolton-le-Sands *T* 145 SD 4868
Bolton-on-Swale *T* 152 SE 2599
Bolton Percy *T* 147 SE 5341
Bolton Priory *A* 146 SE 0754
Bolton upon Dearne *T* 139 SE 4502
Bolt's Law *H* 152 NY 9545
Bolt Tail 89 SX 6639
Bolventor *T* 87 SX 1876
Bomere Heath *T* 127 SJ 4719
Bonar Bridge *T* 192 NH 6191
Bonawe *T* 168 NN 0033
Bonby *T* 142 TA 0015
Boncath *T* 111 SN 2038
Bonchester Bridge *T* 158 NT 5812
Bondleigh *T* 91 SS 6504
Bonehill *T* 128 SK 1902
Bo'Ness *T* 170 NS 9981
Bonhill *T* 169 NS 3979
Boningale *T* 127 SJ 8102
Bonjedward *T* 164 NT 6523
Bonkle *T* 163 NS 8356
Bonnington, Kent *T* 99 TR 0535
Bonnington, Northnts *T* 170 NT 1269
Bonnington Smiddy 177 NO 5739
Bonnybank 171 NO 3503
Bonnybridge *T* 169 NS 8280
Bonnykelly *T* 185 NJ 8653
Bonnyrigg and Lasswade *T* 164 NT 3065
Bonnyton, Tays 176 NO 3338
Bonnyton, Tays *T* 177 NO 6655
Bonsall *T* 139 SK 2858
Bonskeid House 175 NN 8961
Bont *T* 113 SO 3819
Bontddu *T* 125 SH 6718
Bont Dolgadfan *T* 125 SH 8800
Bont-goch or Elerch *T* 125 SN 6886
Bont-newydd, Clwyd *T* 135 SJ 0170
Bontnewydd, Gwyn *T* 134 SH 4860
Bont Newydd, Gwyn *T* 125 SH 7720
Bontuchel *T* 135 SJ 0857
Bonvilston *T* 109 ST 0674
Booker *T* 104 SU 8491
Booley *T* 127 SJ 5725
Boosbeck *T* 153 NZ 6617
Boot *T* 150 NY 1701
Boothby Graffoe *T* 140 SK 9859
Boothby Pagnell *T* 130 SK 9730
Boothstown *T* 137 SD 7200
Booth Wood Reservoir *T* 144 SD 1088
Bootle, Cumbr *T* 144 SD 1088
Bootle, Mers *P* 136 SJ 3394
Bootle Fell 144 SD 1488
Bootle Station 150 SD 0989
Boquhan 169 NS 5387
Boraston *T* 117 SO 6170
Borcheston *T* 129 SK 4804
Borden *T* 98 TQ 8862
Bordley *T* 146 SD 9364
Bordon Camp *T* 95 SU 7936
Boreham, Essex *T* 106 TL 7509
Boreham, Wilts *T* 101 ST 8844
Boreham Street *T* 97 TQ 6611
Borehamwood *T* 105 TQ 1996
Boreland, Central 169 NN 5534
Boreland, D. & G *T* 157 NY 1791
Boreland Hill *H* 156 NX 9460
Boreray, W. Isles 188 NF 8581
Bore Stane 163 NT 1459
Bore, The *W* 200 HY 4956
Borgie *T* 197 NC 6759
Borgie Forest *F* 197 NC 6654
Borgue, D. & G *T* 155 NX 6348
Borgue, Highld *T* 199 ND 1325
Borle Brook *W* 117 SO 7088
Borley *T* 122 TL 8442
Bornesketaig *T* 186 NG 3771
Borness *T* 155 NX 6145
Borness Point 155 NX 6144
Boroughbridge *T* 147 SE 3966
Borough Green *T* 97 TQ 6057
Borras Head *T* 126 SJ 3653
Borreraig *T* 186 NG 1853
Borrobol Forest 198 NC 7925
Borrobol Lodge 198 NC 8626
Borrodale Burn *W* 180 NM 7086
Borrow Beck *W* 151 NY 5205
Borrowby *T* 153 SE 4289
Borrowdale, Cumbr 150 NY 2516
Borrowdale, Cumbr 151 NY 5603
Borrowdale Fells 150 NY 2613
Borrowfield 177 NO 8393
Borrowwash *T* 128 SK 4134
Borth *T* 124 SN 6190
Borthwickbrae *T* 157 NT 4113
Borthwickshiels *T* 157 NT 4315
Borthwick Water *W* 157 NT 4513
Borth-y-Gest *T* 134 SH 5637
Borve, Highld *T* 187 NG 4448
Borve, W. Isles *T* 178 NF 6501
Borve, W. Isles *T* 188 NF 9181
Borve, W. Isles *T* 188 NG 0394
Borve Point 178 NF 6401
Borve River *W* 195 NB 4254
Borwick *T* 145 SD 5273
Bosavern *T* 86 SW 3630
Bosbury *T* 117 SO 6943
Boscastle *T* 88 SX 0990
Boscobel House *A* 127 SJ 8308
Boscombe, Dorset *T* 94 SZ 1191
Boscombe, Wilts *T* 102 SU 2038
Bosham *T* 95 SU 8004
Bosherston *T* 110 SR 9694
Boskednan *T* 86 SW 4434
Bosley *T* 137 SJ 9165
Bossall *T* 148 SE 7160
Bossiney *T* 88 SX 0688
Bossingham *T* 99 TR 1549
Bosta *T* 195 NB 1440
Bostock Green *T* 137 SJ 6769
Boston *P* 131 TF 3244
Boston Deeps *W* 131 TF 5450
Boston Spa *T* 147 SE 4245
Boswinger *T* 87 SW 9941
Botallack *T* 86 SW 3632
Botany Bay *T* 105 TQ 2999
Botesdale *T* 122 TM 0575
Bothal *T* 159 NZ 2386
Bothamsall *T* 139 SK 6773
Bothel *T* 150 NY 1839
Bothenhampton *T* 93 SY 4691
Bothwell *T* 162 NS 7058
Bothwell Water *W* 164 NT 6865
Botley, Bucks *T* 104 SP 9802
Botley, Hants *T* 95 SU 5113
Botley, Oxon *T* 115 SP 4805
Botolphs *T* 96 TQ 1909
Bottacks *T* 182 NH 4960
Bottesford, Humbs *T* 142 SE 8907
Bottesford, Leic *T* 129 SK 8039
Bottisham *T* 121 TL 5460
Bottle Island 190 NB 9502
Bottomcraig *T* 171 NO 3624
Bottom Flash *W* 137 SJ 6665
Botton Head 145 SD 6661
Botusfleming *T* 88 SX 4061
Botwnnog *T* 134 SH 2631
Bough Beech Reservoir *W* 97 TQ 4948
Boughrood *T* 112 SO 1239
Boughspring *T* 113 ST 5597
Boughton, Norf *T* 132 TF 6902
Boughton, Northnts *T* 119 SP 7565
Boughton, Notts *T* 139 SK 6768
Boughton Aluph *T* 99 TR 0348
Boughton House *A* 120 SP 9081
Boughton Lees *T* 99 TR 0247
Boughton Malherbe *T* 98 TQ 8849
Boughton Monchelsea *T* 97 TQ 7651
Boughton Street *T* 99 TR 0659
Boulby *T* 153 NZ 7619
Bouldon *T* 116 SO 5485
Boulmer *T* 159 NU 2614
Boulmer Haven *W* 159 NU 2613
Boulston *T* 110 SM 9712
Boulsworth Hill *H* 146 SD 9336
Boultenstone 184 NJ 4111
Boultham *T* 140 SK 9669
Bourn *T* 121 TL 3256
Bourne *T* 130 TF 0920
Bourne End, Beds *T* 120 SP 9644
Bourne End, Bucks *T* 104 SU 8987
Bourne End, Herts *T* 104 TL 0206
Bournemouth (Hurn) Airport 94 SZ 1198
Bournemouth *P* 94 SZ 0991
Bournes Green *T* 114 SO 9104
Bourneville *T* 118 SP 0481
Bournheath *T* 118 SO 9574
Bournmoor *T* 152 NZ 3151
Bourton, Avon *T* 100 ST 3864
Bourton, Dorset *T* 93 ST 7730
Bourton, Oxon *T* 102 SU 2387
Bourton, Shrops *T* 127 SO 5996
Bourton on Dunsmore *T* 118 SP 4370
Bourton-on-the-Hill *T* 115 SP 1732
Bourton-on-the-Water *T* 115 SP 1620
Bousd 172 NM 2563
Boveney *T* 104 SU 9377
Boverton *T* 109 SS 9868
Bovey Tracey *T* 89 SX 8178
Bovingdon *T* 104 TL 0103
Bovington Camp *T* 93 SY 8388
Bow, Devon *T* 91 SS 7201
Bow, G. Lon *T* 105 TQ 3783
Bow, Orkney *T* 200 ND 3693
Bowbank *T* 152 NY 9423
Bow Brickhill *T* 120 SP 9034
Bowburn *T* 152 NZ 3038
Bowcombe *T* 95 SZ 4686
Bowd *T* 92 SY 1090
Bowden, Border *T* 164 NT 5530
Bowden, Devon *T* 89 SX 8449
Bowden Hill *T* 102 ST 9367
Bowderdale *T* 151 NY 6704
Bowdon *T* 137 SJ 7586
Bower 158 NY 7583
Bowerchalke *T* 94 SU 0223
Bowermadden *T* 199 ND 2464
Bowers Gifford *T* 106 TQ 7588
Bowershall *T* 170 NT 0991
Bowertower *T* 199 ND 2362
Bowes *T* 152 NY 9913
Bowes Moor 152 NY 9211
Bow Head 200 HY 4553
Bowhill *T* 164 NT 4227
Bowland *T* 164 NT 4540
Bowland Bridge *T* 151 SD 4189
Bowley *T* 113 SO 5452
Bowlhead Green *T* 96 SU 9138
Bowling *T* 169 NS 4473
Bowling Bank *T* 126 SJ 3948
Bowling Green *T* 117 SO 8251
Bowmanstead *T* 150 SD 3096
Bowmont Forest *F* 164 NT 7328
Bowmont Water *W* 165 NT 8124
Bowmore *T* 166 NR 3159
Bowness-on-Solway *T* 157 NY 2262
Bowness-on-Windermere *T* 151 SD 4096
Bow of Fife 171 NO 3212
Bowood House 102 ST 9770
Bowsden *T* 165 NT 9941
Bowside Lodge 198 NC 8361
Bow Street *T* 125 SN 6284
Bowthorpe *T* 133 TG 1709
Box, Glos *T* 114 SO 8600
Box, Wilts *T* 101 ST 8268
Boxbush *T* 114 SO 7413
Boxford, Berks *T* 102 SU 4271
Boxford, Suff *T* 122 TL 9640
Boxgrove *T* 95 SU 9007
Boxley *T* 98 TQ 7758
Boxted, Essex *T* 122 TL 9933
Boxted, Suff *T* 122 TL 8251
Boxworth *T* 121 TL 3464
Boylestone *T* 128 SK 1835
Boyndie *T* 184 NJ 6464
Boyndie Bay *W* 184 NJ 6765
Boyndlie *T* 185 NJ 9062
Boyne Bay *W* 184 NJ 6266
Boynton *T* 149 TA 1368
Boysack 177 NO 6249
Boyton, Corn *T* 88 SX 3191
Boyton, Suff *T* 123 TM 3747
Boyton, Wilts *T* 102 ST 9539
Bozeat *T* 120 SP 9059
Braaid *T* 144 SC 3276
Braal Castle 199 ND 1360
Brabling Green *T* 123 TM 2964
Brabourne *T* 99 TR 1041
Brabourne Lees *T* 99 TR 0840
Brabster *T* 199 ND 3269
Bracadale *T* 186 NG 3538
Braceborough *T* 130 TF 0813
Bracebridge Heath *T* 140 SK 9867
Braceby *T* 130 TF 0135
Bracewell *T* 146 SD 8648
Brackenfield *T* 139 SK 3759
Bracklesham Bay *W* 95 SZ 8195
Brackletter *T* 174 NN 1882
Brackley, Northnts *T* 119 SP 5837
Brackley, Strath *T* 160 NR 7942
Bracknell *T* 104 SU 8668
Brack, The *H* 168 NN 2403
Braco *T* 169 NN 8309
Bracobrae *T* 184 NJ 5053
Braco Castle 169 NN 8211
Bracon Ash *T* 133 TM 1899
Bracora *T* 180 NM 7192
Bracorina *T* 180 NM 7292
Bradbourne *T* 128 SK 2052
Bradbury *T* 152 NZ 3128
Bradda *T* 144 SC 1970
Bradda Head 144 SC 1869
Bradden *T* 119 SP 6448
Braddock *T* 87 SX 1662
Bradenham, Bucks *T* 104 SU 8297
Bradenham, Norf *T* 132 TF 9208
Bradenstoke *T* 102 SU 0079
Bradfield, Berks *T* 103 SU 6072
Bradfield, Essex *T* 123 TM 1430
Bradfield, Norf *T* 133 TG 2733
Bradfield Combust *T* 122 TL 8957
Bradfield Green *T* 137 SJ 6859
Bradfield Moors 139 SK 2392
Bradfield St Clare *T* 122 TL 9057
Bradfield St George *T* 122 TL 9160
Bradford, Devon *T* 90 SS 4207
Bradford, Northum *T* 165 NU 1532
Bradford, W. Yks *P* 146 SE 1633
Bradford Abbas *T* 93 ST 5814
Bradford Leigh *T* 101 ST 8362
Bradford-on-Avon *T* 101 ST 8260
Bradford-on-Tone *T* 92 ST 1722
Bradford Peverell *T* 93 SY 6592
Brading *T* 95 SZ 6386
Bradley, Derby *T* 128 SK 2246
Bradley, Hants *T* 103 SU 6341
Bradley, Humbs *T* 143 TA 2406
Bradley, Staffs *T* 127 SJ 8818
Bradley Green *T* 118 SO 9961
Bradley in the Moors *T* 128 SK 0641
Bradmore *T* 129 SK 5831
Bradninch *T* 91 SS 9903
Bradnop *T* 128 SK 0155
Bradpole *T* 93 SY 4794
Bradshaw *T* 137 SD 7312
Bradstone *T* 88 SX 3880
Bradwall Green *T* 137 SJ 7563
Bradwell, Bucks *T* 120 SP 8339
Bradwell, Derby *T* 138 SK 1781
Bradwell, Essex *T* 106 TL 8023
Bradwell, Norf *T* 133 TG 5003
Bradwell Grove *T* 115 SP 2408
Bradwell-on-Sea *T* 107 TM 0006
Bradwell Waterside *T* 107 TL 9907
Bradworthy *T* 90 SS 3214
Brae, Highld 192 NC 4301
Brae, Highld *T* 190 NG 8185
Brae, Highld *T* 183 NH 6663
Brae, Shetld *T* 204 HU 3568
Braeantra *T* 192 NH 5678
Braedownie 176 NO 2875
Braefield *T* 182 NH 4130
Braegrum 170 NO 0025
Braehead, D. & G *T* 155 NX 4252
Braehead, Orkney *T* 200 HY 4447
Braehead, Orkney 200 HY 5101
Braehead, Strath *T* 163 NS 8134
Braehead, Strath *T* 163 NS 9550
Braehead, Tays *T* 177 NO 6852
Braehoulland *T* 204 HU 2479
Braelangwell Lodge 192 NH 5192
Braemar *P* 176 NO 1591
Braemore *T* 199 ND 0830
Braemore Forest 191 NH 2276
Brae of Achnahaird *T* 196 NC 0013
Brae of Glenbervie 177 NO 7684
Brae of Moan *H* 200 HY 3733
Braeriach or Braigh Riabhach, Grampn *H* 175 NN 9499
Braeriach or Braigh Riabhach, Highld *H* 175 NN 9499
Braeroy Forest 174 NN 3791
Brae Roy Lodge *T* 174 NN 3391
Braeside *T* 168 NS 2375
Braes of Abernethy 183 NJ 0715
Braes of Balquhidder 169 NN 4921
Braes of Doune 169 NN 6905
Braes of Glenlivet 184 NJ 2421
Braes of Lorn 168 NM 8716
Braes of Ogilvie 170 NN 8907
Braes of the Carse 171 NO 2429
Braes o' Lochaber 174 NN 3180
Braes, The *T* 187 NG 5234
Braeswick *T* 201 HY 6137
Brae Wick *W* 204 HU 2478
Brafferton, Durham *T* 152 NZ 2921
Brafferton, N. Yks *T* 147 SE 4370
Brafield-on-the-Green *T* 120 SP 8258
Braga Ness 202 HU 1948
Bragar *T* 195 NB 2947
Bragbury End *T* 105 TL 2621
Bragleenmore 168 NM 9020
Braich Anelog 124 SH 1427
Braich y Pwll 124 SH 1325
Braides *T* 145 SD 4451
Braid Fell *H* 154 NX 1166
Braid Hills *H* 171 NT 2569
Braidley *T* 146 SE 0380
Braidon Bay *W* 177 NO 8677
Braidwood *T* 163 NS 8447
Bràigh Mòr *W* 194 NB 0016
Bràigh-nam-bàgh 189 NG 0889
Braigh Riabhach or Braeriach, Grampn *H* 175 NN 9499
Braigh Riabhach or Braeriach, Highld *H* 175 NN 9499
Bràigh Srôn Ghorm *H* 175 NN 9078
Braigo 166 NR 2369
Brailes *T* 118 SP 3139
Brailsford *T* 128 SK 2541
Braintree *T* 106 TL 7523
Braiseworth *T* 123 TM 1371
Braishfield *T* 94 SU 3723
Braithwaite *T* 150 NY 0624
Braithwell *T* 139 SK 5394
Bramber *T* 96 TQ 1910
Bramcote *T* 129 SK 5037
Bramdean *T* 95 SU 6128
Bramerton *T* 133 TG 2904
Bramfield, Herts *T* 105 TL 2915
Bramfield, Suff *T* 123 TM 4074
Bramford *T* 120 TL 1246
Bramhall *T* 137 SJ 8985
Bramham *T* 147 SE 4243
Bramhope *T* 147 SE 2543
Bramley, Hants *T* 104 SU 6559
Bramley, Surrey *T* 96 TQ 0044
Bramley, S. Yks *T* 139 SK 4992
Brampford Speke *T* 89 SX 9298
Brampton, Cambs *T* 120 TL 2070
Brampton, Cumbr *T* 158 NY 5361
Brampton, Cumbr *T* 151 NY 6723
Brampton, Lincs *T* 140 SK 8479
Brampton, Norf *T* 133 TG 2224
Brampton, Suff *T* 123 TM 4381
Brampton, S. Yks *T* 139 SE 4101
Brampton Abbots *T* 113 SO 6026
Brampton Ash *T* 119 SP 7987
Brampton Bryan *T* 116 SO 3772
Brampton Station 123 TM 4183
Bramshall *T* 128 SK 0633
Bramshaw *T* 94 SU 2615
Bramshill 104 SU 7461
Bramshill Plantation *F* 104 SU 7562
Bramshott *T* 95 SU 8432
Branault 173 NM 5269
Brancaster *T* 132 TF 7743
Brancaster Bay *W* 132 TF 7646
Brancaster Roads *W* 132 TF 8049
Brancepeth *T* 152 NZ 2238
Branchill *T* 183 NJ 0952
Branderburgh *T* 184 NJ 2371
Brandesburton *T* 143 TA 1147
Brandeston *T* 123 TM 2460
Brandiston *T* 133 TG 1321
Brandon, Durham *T* 152 NZ 2339
Brandon, Lincs *T* 130 SK 9048
Brandon, Northum *T* 159 NU 0417
Brandon, Suff *T* 122 TL 7886
Brandon, Warw *T* 118 SP 4076
Brandon Bank *T* 122 TL 6288
Brandon Creek *T* 122 TL 6091
Brandon Park 122 TL 7784
Brandon Parva *T* 132 TG 0707
Brandsby *T* 147 SE 5872
Brands Hatch 105 TQ 5764
Brand Side 138 SK 0468
Brane *T* 86 SW 4028
Bran End *T* 122 TL 6525
Branksome *T* 94 SZ 0692
Branksome Park *T* 94 SZ 0590
Brannie Burn *W* 168 NN 1616
Branscombe *T* 92 SY 1988
Bransdale 153 SE 6296
Bransford *T* 117 SO 7952
Bransgore *T* 94 SZ 1898
Bransly Hill *H* 171 NT 6770
Branston, Leic *T* 130 SK 8129
Branston, Lincs *T* 140 TF 0267
Branston, Staffs *T* 128 SK 2221
Branstone *T* 95 SZ 6583
Brant Broughton *T* 130 SK 9154
Brant Fell 151 SD 6795
Brantham *T* 120 TL 1034
Branthwaite *T* 150 NY 2937
Brantingham *T* 142 SE 9429
Branton, Northum *T* 159 NU 0416
Branton, S. Yks *T* 139 SE 6401
Branxholme *T* 157 NT 4611
Branxholm Park *T* 157 NT 4612
Branxton *T* 165 NT 8937
Brassington *T* 128 SK 2354
Brasted *T* 97 TQ 4755
Brasted Chart *T* 97 TQ 4653
Brat Bheinn *H* 166 NR 4966
Brathens *T* 177 NO 6798
Bratoft *T* 141 TF 4764
Brattleby *T* 140 SK 9480
Bratton *T* 101 ST 9152
Bratton Camp *A* 101 ST 9051
Bratton Clovelly *T* 88 SX 4691
Bratton Fleming *T* 91 SS 6437
Bratton Seymour *T* 93 ST 6729
Braughing *T* 121 TL 3925
Braunston, Leic *T* 130 SK 8306
Braunston, Northnts *T* 119 SP 5466
Braunstone *T* 129 SK 5502
Braunton *T* 90 SS 4836
Braunton Burrows 90 SS 4535
Brawby *T* 148 SE 7378
Brawl *T* 198 NC 8166
Brawlbin *T* 199 ND 0757
Bray *T* 104 SU 9079
Braybrooke *T* 119 SP 7684
Brayford *T* 91 SS 6834
Bray Shop *T* 88 SX 3374
Braystones *T* 150 NY 0005
Brayton *T* 147 SE 6030
Brazacott *T* 88 SX 2690
Breabag *H* 196 NC 2917
Breachacha Castle 172 NM 1553
Breachwood Green *T* 105 TL 1522
Breaclete *T* 195 NB 1536
Breadalbane 169 NN 4735
Breadstone *T* 114 SO 7100
Breagach Hill *H* 184 NJ 3313
Breage *T* 86 SW 6128
Breakachy *T* 182 NH 4644
Breakerie Water *W* 160 NR 6510
Breakish *T* 180 NG 6823
Breaksea Point 109 ST 0265
Bream *T* 113 SO 6005
Breamore *T* 94 SU 1519
Breamore House *A* 94 SU 1519
Brean *T* 100 ST 2955
Brean Down *H* 100 ST 2858
Brearton *T* 147 SE 3261
Breasclete *T* 195 NB 2135
Breaston *T* 129 SK 4633
Breast Sand 131 TF 5427
Brechfa *T* 111 SN 5230
Brechin *T* 177 NO 5960
Breckles *T* 132 TL 9494
Breck Ness 200 HY 2209
Breckrey *T* 187 NG 5162
Breck, The 204 HU 3292
Brecon *P* 109 SO 0428
Brecon Beacons *H* 109 SO 0121
Bredbury *T* 137 SJ 9291
Brede *T* 98 TQ 8218
Bredenbury *T* 113 SO 6156
Bredfield *T* 123 TM 2653
Bredgar *T* 98 TQ 8860
Bredhurst *T* 98 TQ 7962
Bredon *T* 117 SO 9236
Bredon Hill *H* 118 SO 9639
Bredon's Norton *T* 117 SO 9339
Bredwardine *T* 113 SO 3344
Breedon on the Hill *T* 128 SK 4022
Breich *T* 163 NS 9660
Breighton *T* 142 SE 7034
Breiti Stack 201 HZ 2072
Brei Wick *W* 203 HU 4740
Bremenium *R* 158 NY 8398
Bremhill *T* 102 ST 9873
Brenchley *T* 97 TQ 6741
Brendon *T* 91 SS 7648
Brendon Common 91 SS 7645
Brendon Hills *H* 92 ST 0135
Brenfield Bay *W* 168 NR 8582
Brenish *T* 194 NA 9926
Brenish Point 188 NF 9089
Brent Eleigh *T* 122 TL 9447
Brentford *T* 105 TQ 1778
Brent Knoll *T* 100 ST 3350
Brent Pelham *T* 121 TL 4331
Brentwood *T* 106 TQ 5993
Brenzett *T* 99 TR 0027
Brereton *T* 128 SK 0516
Brereton Green *T* 137 SJ 7764
Brereton Heath *T* 137 SJ 8164
Bressay 203 HU 5040
Bressay Sound *W* 203 HU 4841
Bressingham *T* 123 TM 0881
Brest Rocks 161 NS 1905
Bretby *T* 128 SK 2923
Bretford *T* 118 SP 4277
Bretforton *T* 118 SP 0944
Bretherdale Head *T* 151 NY 5705

Bretherton Burneside

Bretherton *T* 137 SD 4720
Brettabister *T* 203 HU 4857
Brettenham, Norf *T* 122 TL 9383
Brettenham, Suff *T* 122 TL 9653
Bretton *T* 136 SJ 3563
Brevig *T* 178 NL 6998
Brewham *T* 93 ST 7236
Brewlands Bridge *T* 176 NO 1961
Brewood *T* 127 SJ 8808
Breydon Water *W* 133 TG 4907
Briantspuddle *T* 93 SY 8193
Brickendon *T* 105 TL 3208
Bricket Wood *T* 105 TL 1202
Bricklehampton *T* 118 SO 9842
Bride *T* 144 NX 4401
Bridekirk *T* 150 NY 1133
Bridell *T* 110 SN 1742
Bride's Ness 201 HY 7752
Bridestowe *T* 88 SX 5189
Bridestowe and Sourton Common 89 SX 5588
Brideswell *T* 184 NJ 5839
Bridford *T* 89 SX 8186
Bridge *T* 99 TR 1854
Bridge End *T* 130 TF 1436
Bridgefoot *T* 150 NY 0529
Bridge Green *T* 121 TL 4637
Bridgemary *T* 95 SU 5803
Bridgend, Cumbr *T* 151 NY 3914
Bridgend, Fife *T* 171 NO 3911
Bridgend, Grampn *T* 184 NJ 3731
Bridgend, Grampn *T* 184 NJ 5135
Bridgend, Lothn *T* 170 NT 0475
Bridgend, M. Glam *T* 109 SS 9080
Bridgend, Strath *T* 166 NR 3362
Bridgend, Strath *T* 168 NR 8592
Bridgend, Strath *T* 169 NS 6870
Bridgend, Tays *T* 177 NO 5368
Bridgend of Lintrathen *T* 176 NO 2854
Bridge of Alford *T* 184 NJ 5617
Bridge of Allan *T* 169 NS 7997
Bridge of Avon *T* 184 NJ 1835
Bridge of Balgie 175 NN 5746
Bridge of Brown *T* 183 NJ 1220
Bridge of Buchat 184 NJ 4015
Bridge of Cally *T* 176 NO 1451
Bridge of Canny *T* 177 NO 6597
Bridge of Craigisla 176 NO 2553
Bridge of Dee *T* 156 NX 7360
Bridge of Don *T* 185 NJ 9410
Bridge of Dun *T* 177 NO 6658
Bridge of Dye *T* 177 NO 6586
Bridge of Earn *T* 170 NO 1318
Bridge of Ericht 175 NN 5258
Bridge of Feugh *T* 177 NO 7095
Bridge of Forss *T* 199 ND 0368
Bridge of Gairn *T* 176 NO 3597
Bridge of Gaur 175 NN 5056
Bridge of Muchalls *T* 177 NO 8991
Bridge of Orchy *T* 174 NN 2939
Bridge of Tilt 175 NN 8765
Bridge of Waithe 200 HY 2811
Bridge of Walls *T* 202 HU 2651
Bridge of Weir *T* 161 NS 3865
Bridgerule *T* 90 SS 2702
Bridges *T* 126 SO 3996
Bridge Sollers *T* 113 SO 4142
Bridge Street *T* 122 TL 8749
Bridgetown *T* 91 SS 9233
Bridge Trafford *T* 136 SJ 4571
Bridgewater Canal, Ches *W* 137 SJ 7287
Bridgewater Canal, G. Man *W* 137 SJ 7287
Bridge Yate *T* 101 ST 6873
Bridgham *T* 122 TL 9686
Bridgnorth *T* 127 SO 7193
Bridgtown *T* 128 SJ 9808
Bridgwater *P* 92 ST 3037
Bridgwater Bay *W* 100 ST 1852
Bridlington *P* 149 TA 1866
Bridlington Bay *W* 149 TA 2065
Bridport *T* 93 SY 4692
Bridstow *T* 113 SO 5824
Brierfield *T* 146 SD 8436
Brierley, Glos *T* 113 SO 6215
Brierley, H. & W *T* 113 SO 4956
Brierley, S. Yks *T* 139 SE 4110
Brierley Hill *T* 117 SO 9287
Briga Head 199 ND 1875
Brigg *T* 142 TA 0007
Brigham, Cumbr *T* 150 NY 0830
Brigham, Humbs *T* 149 TA 0753
Brighouse *T* 146 SE 1423
Brighstone *T* 94 SZ 4282
Brighstone Bay *W* 94 SZ 4380
Brightgate *T* 139 SK 2659
Brighthampton *T* 115 SP 3803
Brightling *T* 97 TQ 6821
Brightlingsea *T* 107 TM 0816
Brighton, Corn *T* 87 SW 9054
Brighton, E. Susx *P* 97 TQ 3104
Brightons *T* 170 NS 9377
Brightstone Forest *F* 94 SZ 4384
Brightwalton *T* 102 SU 4279
Brightwell *T* 123 TM 2543
Brightwell Baldwin *T* 104 SU 6595
Brightwell-cum-Sotwell *T* 103 SU 5890
Brignall *T* 152 NZ 0612
Brig o' Turk *T* 169 NN 5306
Brigsley *T* 143 TA 2501
Brigsteer *T* 151 SD 4889
Brigstock *T* 120 SP 9485
Brill *T* 104 SP 6513
Brilley *T* 113 SO 2649
Brimfield *T* 116 SO 5268
Brimington *T* 139 SK 4073
Brimmond Hill *H* 185 NJ 8509
Brimpsfield *T* 114 SO 9412
Brimpton *T* 103 SU 5564
Brims *T* 199 ND 2888
Brims Ness, Highld 199 ND 0471
Brims Ness, Orkney 199 ND 2988
Brinacory *T* 180 NM 7591
Brind *T* 142 SE 7431
Brindister, Shetld *T* 202 HU 2857
Brindister, Shetld *T* 203 HU 4336
Brindle *T* 145 SD 5924
Brindley Ford *T* 127 SJ 8854
Brindley Heath 128 SJ 9914
Brineton *T* 127 SJ 8013
Bring Deeps *W* 200 HY 2902
Bringewood, H. & W *F* 116 SO 4673
Bringewood, Shrops *F* 116 SO 4673
Bring Head, Orkney 200 HY 2702
Bring Head, Orkney 200 HY 3733
Bringhurst *T* 120 SP 8492
Brington *T* 120 TL 0875
Briningham *T* 132 TG 0334
Brinkburn Priory *A* 159 NZ 1198
Brinkhill *T* 141 TF 3773
Brinkley *T* 122 TL 6254
Brinklow *T* 118 SP 4379
Brinkworth *T* 102 SU 0184
Brinscall *T* 145 SD 6221
Brinsley *T* 129 SK 4649
Brinsop *T* 113 SO 4444
Brinsworth *T* 139 SK 4290
Brinton *T* 132 TG 0335
Brinyan *T* 200 HY 4327
Brisley *T* 132 TF 9521
Brislington *T* 101 ST 6270
Brisons, The 86 SW 3431
Bristol *P* 101 ST 5973
Bristol Airport 101 ST 5065
Bristol Channel *W* 108 SS 5167
Briston *T* 132 TG 0632
Britannia *T* 146 SD 8821
Britford *T* 94 SU 1628
Briton Ferry *T* 109 SS 7494
Britwell Salome *T* 104 SU 6793
Brixham *T* 89 SX 9255
Brixton, Devon *T* 89 SX 5552
Brixton, G. Lon *T* 105 TQ 3175
Brixton Deverill *T* 101 ST 8638
Brixworth *T* 119 SP 7470
Brize Norton *T* 115 SP 3007
Broad Bay or Loch a Tuath *W* 195 NB 5036
Broad Bench 93 SY 8978
Broad Blunsden *T* 102 SU 1590
Broadbottom *T* 138 SJ 9894
Broadbridge *T* 95 SU 8105
Broadbridge Heath *T* 96 TQ 1431
Broadbury 88 SX 4697
Broad Cairn, Grampn *H* 176 NO 2481
Broad Cairn, Tays *H* 176 NO 2481
Broad Campden *T* 118 SP 1637
Broad Chalke *T* 94 SU 0325
Broadclyst *T* 89 SX 9897
Broad Down *H* 92 SY 1793
Broadford *T* 180 NG 6423
Broadford Bay *W* 180 NG 6523
Broad Green *T* 117 SO 7756
Broadhaugh 157 NT 4509
Broad Haven *T* 110 SM 8613
Broad Head *H* 157 NY 3494
Broadheath, G. Man *T* 137 SJ 7689
Broad Heath, H. & W *T* 117 SO 6665
Broadheath, H. & W *T* 117 SO 8056
Broadhembury *T* 92 ST 1004
Broadhempston *T* 89 SX 8066
Broad Hill, Cambs *T* 122 TL 5976
Broad Hill, Strath *H* 163 NT 0029
Broad Hinton *T* 102 SU 1076
Broadlands House 94 SU 3520
Broad Law *H* 163 NT 1423
Broad Laying *T* 102 SU 4362
Broadley, Grampn *T* 184 NJ 3961
Broadley, Lancs *T* 137 SD 8816
Broadley Common *T* 105 TL 4206
Broad Marston *T* 118 SP 1446
Broadmayne *T* 93 SY 7286
Broadmeadows *T* 164 NT 4130
Broadmere *T* 103 SU 6247
Broad Oak, Dorset *T* 93 ST 7812
Broadoak, Dorset *T* 93 SY 4396
Broad Oak, E. Susx *T* 97 TQ 6022
Broad Oak, E. Susx *T* 98 TQ 8220
Broad Oak, H. & W *T* 113 SO 4821
Broad Oak, Kent *T* 99 TR 1661
Broadrashes *T* 184 NJ 4354
Broadsea Bay *W* 154 NW 9759
Broad Sound *W* 110 SM 7307
Broad Sound *W* 86 SV 8309
Broadstairs *T* 99 TR 3967
Broadstone, Dorset *T* 94 SZ 0095
Broadstone, Shrops *T* 116 SO 5489
Broad Street *T* 98 TQ 8356
Broad Taing 200 HY 4217
Broad Town *T* 102 SU 0978
Broadwas *T* 117 SO 7655
Broadwater *T* 96 TQ 1404
Broadway, H. & W *T* 118 SP 1037
Broadway, Somer *T* 92 ST 3215
Broadway Hill *H* 118 SP 1136
Broadwell, Glos *T* 113 SO 5911
Broadwell, Glos *T* 115 SP 2027
Broadwell, Oxon *T* 115 SP 2504
Broadwell, Warw *T* 119 SP 4565
Broadwell House 152 NY 9153
Broadwey *T* 93 SY 6683
Broadwindsor *T* 93 ST 4302
Broadwoodkelly *T* 91 SS 6105
Broadwoodwidger *T* 88 SX 4189
Brobury *T* 113 SO 3444
Brochel *T* 190 NG 5846
Brockbridge *T* 95 SU 6118
Brockdish *T* 123 TM 2079
Brockenhurst *T* 94 SU 2902
Brocketsbrae *T* 163 NS 8239
Brockford Street *T* 123 TM 1166
Brockhall *T* 119 SP 6362
Brockham *T* 96 TQ 1949
Brockhampton, Glos *T* 114 SP 0322
Brockhampton, H. & W *T* 113 SO 5932
Brockholes *T* 138 SE 1511
Brocklesby *T* 143 TA 1311
Brockley *T* 101 ST 4666
Brockley Green *T* 122 TL 8254
Brockloch Hill, D. & G *H* 155 NX 5173
Brockloch Hill, D. & G *H* 156 NX 8179
Brockloch Rig *H* 156 NS 5801
Brockton, Shrops *T* 126 SJ 3104
Brockton, Shrops *T* 127 SJ 7203
Brockton, Shrops *T* 116 SO 3285
Brockton, Shrops *T* 127 SO 5793
Brockweir *T* 113 SO 5401
Brockwood Park *T* 95 SU 6226
Brockworth *T* 114 SO 8916
Brocolitia *R* 158 NY 8571
Brocton *T* 128 SJ 9619
Brodick *T* 160 NS 0135
Brodick Bay *W* 160 NS 0237
Brodie Castle 183 NH 9857
Brodsworth *T* 139 SE 5007
Brogborough *T* 120 SP 9638
Brokenborough *T* 101 ST 9189
Broken Cross, Ches *T* 137 SJ 6873
Broken Cross, Ches *T* 137 SJ 8973
Broken Cross Muir 163 NS 8537
Brolass 173 NM 5023
Bromborough *T* 136 SJ 3582
Bromcote *T* 118 SP 4088
Brome *T* 123 TM 1376
Brome Street *T* 123 TM 1576
Bromeswell *T* 123 TM 3050
Bromfield, Cumbr *T* 150 NY 1747
Bromfield, Shrops *T* 116 SO 4877
Bromham, Beds *T* 120 TL 0051
Bromham, Wilts *T* 102 ST 9665
Bromley *T* 105 TQ 4069
Bromley Common 105 TQ 4266
Bromley Green *T* 99 TR 0036
Brompton, Kent *T* 98 TQ 7768
Brompton, N. Yks *T* 153 SE 3796
Brompton, N. Yks *T* 149 SE 9482
Brompton-on-Swale *T* 152 SE 2199
Brompton Ralph *T* 92 ST 0832
Brompton Regis *T* 91 SS 9531
Bromsash *T* 114 SO 6424
Bromsgrove *P* 118 SO 9670
Bromyard *T* 117 SO 6554
Bromyard Downs *T* 117 SO 6655
Bronaber *T* 135 SH 7131
Bronington *T* 127 SJ 4839
Bronllys *T* 109 SO 1435
Bronnant *T* 125 SN 6467
Bronwydd Arms *T* 111 SN 4123
Bronygarth *T* 126 SJ 2637
Brook, Hants *T* 94 SU 2714
Brook, Hants *T* 94 SU 3428
Brook, I. of W *T* 94 SZ 3883
Brook, Kent *T* 99 TR 0644
Brook, Surrey *T* 96 SU 9337
Brooke, Leic *T* 130 SK 8505
Brooke, Norf *T* 133 TM 2899
Brookfield *T* 161 NS 4164
Brookhouse *T* 145 SD 5464
Brookhouse Green *T* 137 SJ 8161
Brookland *T* 99 TQ 9825
Brookmans Park *T* 105 TL 2404
Brooks *T* 126 SO 1499
Brook Street *T* 105 TQ 5792
Brookthorpe *T* 114 SO 8312
Brookwood *T* 96 SU 9557
Broom, Beds *T* 120 TL 1743
Broom, Warw *T* 118 SP 0953
Broome, H. & W *T* 117 SO 9078
Broome, Norf *T* 123 TM 3491
Broome, Shrops *T* 116 SO 4081
Broomedge *T* 137 SJ 7086
Broome Park *T* 159 NU 1112
Broomer's Corner *T* 96 TQ 1221
Broomfield, Essex *T* 106 TL 7010
Broomfield, Grampn *T* 185 NJ 9532
Broomfield, Kent *T* 98 TQ 8352
Broomfield, Kent *T* 99 TR 1966
Broomfield, Somer *T* 92 ST 2231
Broomfleet *T* 142 SE 8827
Broomhead Reservoir *W* 139 SK 2696
Broom Hill, Dorset *T* 94 SU 0302
Broomhill, Northum *T* 159 NU 2401
Broomlee Lough *W* 158 NY 7969
Broomy Law *H* 164 NT 4131
Broomy Lodge 94 SU 2111
Brora *T* 193 NC 9004
Brosdale Island 166 NR 4962
Broseley *T* 127 SJ 6702
Brother Isle 205 HU 4281
Brothers Water *W* 151 NY 4012
Brothertoft *T* 131 TF 2746
Brotherton *T* 147 SE 4826
Brotton *T* 153 NZ 6819
Broubster *T* 199 ND 0360
Brough, Cumbr *P* 151 NY 7914
Brough, Derby *T* 138 SK 1882
Brough, Highld *T* 199 ND 2273
Brough, Humbs *T* 142 SE 9426
Brough, Notts *T* 140 SK 8358
Brough, Shetld *T* 205 HU 4377
Brough, Shetld 203 HU 5141
Brough, Shetld *T* 205 HU 5179
Brough, Shetld *T* 203 HU 5564
Broughall *T* 127 SJ 5641
Brough Head, Highld 199 ND 3763
Brough Head, Orkney 200 HY 2328
Brough Lodge 205 HU 5892
Brough Ness 199 ND 4482
Brough of Deeness 201 HY 5908
Brough Sowerby *T* 151 NY 7912
Brough Taing 205 HP 6304
Brough, The 204 HU 2982
Broughton, Border *T* 163 NT 1135
Broughton, Bucks *T* 120 SP 8940
Broughton, Cambs *T* 121 TL 2878
Broughton, Clwyd *T* 136 SJ 3463
Broughton, Cumbr *T* 150 NY 0731
Broughton, G. Man *T* 137 SD 8201
Broughton, Hants *T* 94 SU 3033
Broughton, Humbs *T* 142 SE 9608
Broughton, Lancs *T* 145 SD 5235
Broughton, M. Glam *T* 109 SS 9271
Broughton, Northnts *T* 120 SP 8375
Broughton, N. Yks *T* 146 SD 9451
Broughton, N. Yks *T* 148 SE 7673
Broughton, Orkney *T* 200 HY 4448
Broughton, Oxon *T* 118 SP 4238
Broughton Astley *T* 119 SP 5292
Broughton Beck *T* 145 SD 2882
Broughton Gifford *T* 101 ST 8763
Broughton Hackett *T* 117 SO 9254
Broughton Heights *H* 163 NT 1241
Broughton in Furness *T* 144 SD 2187
Broughton Mills *T* 150 SD 2290
Broughton Moor *T* 150 NY 0533
Broughton Poggs *T* 115 SP 2304
Broughtown *T* 201 HY 6641
Broughty Ferry *T* 171 NO 4630
Browland *T* 202 HU 2650
Brown Bank Head *H* 146 SE 1058
Brown Candover *T* 103 SU 5739
Brown Carrick Hill *H* 161 NS 2916
Brown Caterthun 177 NO 5566
Brown Clee Hill *H* 117 SO 5985
Brown Cow Hill *H* 184 NJ 2304
Brown Edge *T* 127 SJ 9053
Brown Head 160 NR 9025
Brownhill, Grampn *T* 185 NJ 8640
Brownhill, Lancs *T* 145 SD 6830
Brownhills *T* 128 SK 0505
Brownieside *T* 165 NU 1623
Brownlow Heath *T* 137 SJ 8360
Brownmoor Hill *H* 156 NX 9991
Brown Ridge *H* 146 SE 1077
Brownsea Island 94 SZ 0288
Brownston *T* 89 SX 6952
Brown Willy *H* 87 SX 1579
Browsholme Hall *A* 145 SD 6845
Brow Top *T* 145 SD 5258
Broxbourne *T* 105 TL 3607
Broxburn, Lothn *T* 170 NT 0772
Broxburn, Lothn *T* 164 NT 6977
Broxted *T* 121 TL 5727
Broxwood *T* 113 SO 3654
Bruach, The *H* 183 NJ 1105
Bruan *T* 199 ND 3139
Bruar Lodge 175 NN 8376
Bruar Water *W* 175 NN 8273
Bruchag Point 161 NS 1157
Bruddans, The 204 HU 2077
Brue *T* 195 NB 3449
Bruera *T* 136 SJ 4360
Bruern Abbey *T* 115 SP 2620
Bruernish *T* 178 NF 7202
Bruernish Point 178 NF 7300
Bruichladdich *T* 166 NR 2661
Bruisyard *T* 123 TM 3266
Brumby *T* 142 SE 8909
Brund *T* 138 SK 1061
Brundall *T* 133 TG 3208
Brundish *T* 123 TM 2669
Brundish Street *T* 123 TM 2671
Brunerican Bay *W* 160 NR 6907
Brunt Hill *H* 164 NT 6874
Brunton, Fife *T* 171 NO 3220
Brunton, Northum *T* 165 NU 2024
Bruntshiel Hill *H* 157 NY 4182
Bruray 205 HU 6972
Brushford, Devon *T* 91 SS 6707
Brushford, Somer *T* 91 SS 9225
Bruton *T* 93 ST 6834
Bruxie Hill *H* 177 NO 8280
Bryanston *T* 93 ST 8706
Brydekirk *T* 157 NY 1870
Bryher 86 SV 8714
Brymbo *T* 126 SJ 2953
Bryn, G. Man *T* 137 SD 5600
Bryn, Powys *H* 112 SN 9055
Bryn, Powys *H* 109 SO 0722
Bryn, Shrops *T* 116 SO 2985
Bryn, W. Glam *T* 109 SS 8192
Bryn Amlwg *H* 125 SN 9297
Brynamman *T* 108 SN 7114
Brynberian *T* 110 SN 1035
Bryn Brawd *H* 112 SN 6952
Bryncae *T* 109 SS 9982
Bryncethin *T* 109 SS 9184
Bryncir *T* 134 SH 4844
Bryn-côch *T* 109 SS 7499
Bryncroes *T* 134 SH 2231
Bryncrug *T* 124 SH 6103
Bryn Crwn *H* 112 SN 8258
Bryn Du, Clwyd *H* 126 SJ 1436
Bryn-du, Powys *H* 112 SN 9442
Bryneglwys *T* 126 SJ 1447
Brynford *T* 136 SJ 1774
Bryn Garw, Dyfed *H* 125 SN 8077
Bryn Garw, Powys *H* 125 SN 8361
Bryn Gates *T* 137 SD 5901
Brynglas Station 125 SH 6303
Bryngwran *T* 134 SH 3577
Bryngwyn, Gwent *T* 113 SO 3909
Bryngwyn, Powys *T* 113 SO 1849
Bryn-henllan *T* 110 SN 0039
Brynhoffnant *T* 111 SN 3351
Brynithel *T* 109 SO 2101
Bryn Llyndŵr *H* 125 SO 0683
Brynmawr *T* 109 SO 1912
Brynmenyn *T* 109 SS 9084
Brynna *T* 109 SS 9883
Bryn Nicol *H* 112 SN 8344
Brynrefail *T* 134 SH 4886
Brynsadler *T* 109 ST 0380
Brynsiencyn *T* 134 SH 4867
Brynteg, Clwyd *T* 126 SJ 3052
Brynteg, Gwyn *T* 134 SH 4982
Bryn, The *T* 113 SO 3309
Bryn Titli *H* 125 SN 9375
Bryn Trillyn *H* 135 SH 9459
Bryn y Castell *H* 125 SH 9705
Bryn y Fan *H* 125 SN 9388
Bryn-y-maen, Clwyd *T* 135 SH 8376
Bryn-y-maen, Powys *H* 113 SO 1657
Buachaille Etive Beag *H* 174 NN 1854
Buachaille Etive Mór *H* 174 NN 2153
Buail' a' Ghoill 178 NF 8130
Bualintur *T* 187 NG 4020
Bualnaluib *T* 190 NG 8690
Bubbenhall *T* 118 SP 3672
Bubwith *T* 142 SE 7136
Buccleuch *T* 157 NT 3214
Buchan 185 NJ 9749
Buchanan Smithy 169 NS 4689
Buchan Burn *W* 155 NX 4282
Buchan Hill *H* 155 NX 4281
Buchan Ness 185 NK 1342
Buchanty 170 NN 9328
Buchlyvie *T* 169 NS 5793
Buckabank *T* 151 NY 3749
Buckden, Cambs *T* 120 TL 1967
Buckden, N. Yks *T* 146 SD 9477
Buckden Pike *H* 146 SD 9678
Buckenham *T* 133 TG 3505
Buckerell *T* 92 ST 1200
Buckfast *T* 89 SX 7467
Buckfastleigh *T* 89 SX 7366
Buckhaven *T* 171 NT 3598
Buckholm *T* 164 NT 4838
Buckhorn Weston *T* 93 ST 7524
Buckhurst Hill *T* 105 TQ 4193
Buckie *T* 184 NJ 4265
Buckies *T* 199 ND 1163
Buckingham *T* 119 SP 6933
Buckland, Bucks *T* 104 SP 8812
Buckland, Devon *T* 89 SX 6743
Buckland, Glos *T* 118 SP 0836
Buckland, Herts *T* 121 TL 3533
Buckland, Kent *T* 99 TR 3042
Buckland, Oxon *T* 115 SU 3498
Buckland, Surrey *T* 96 TQ 2250
Buckland Abbey *A* 88 SX 4866
Buckland Brewer *T* 90 SS 4120
Buckland Common *T* 104 SP 9206
Buckland Dinham *T* 101 ST 7551
Buckland Filleigh *T* 90 SS 4609
Buckland in the Moor *T* 89 SX 7273
Buckland Monochorum *T* 88 SX 4868
Buckland Newton *T* 93 ST 6905
Buckland St Mary *T* 92 ST 2713
Bucklebury *T* 103 SU 5570
Bucklerheads 177 NO 4636
Bucklers Hard *T* 94 SU 4000
Bucklesham *T* 123 TM 2441
Buckley *T* 136 SJ 2864
Bucklow Hill *T* 137 SJ 7383
Buckminster *T* 130 SK 8722
Bucknall, Lincs *T* 141 TF 1769
Bucknall, Staffs *T* 127 SJ 9047
Bucknell, Oxon *T* 115 SP 5625
Bucknell, Shrops *T* 116 SO 3574
Bucksburn *T* 185 NJ 8909
Buck's Cross *T* 90 SS 3422
Bucks Green *T* 96 TQ 0732
Bucks Hill *T* 104 TL 0500
Bucks Horn Oak *T* 103 SU 8041
Buck's Mills *T* 90 SS 3523
Buck, The *H* 184 NJ 4123
Buckton, H. & W *T* 116 SO 3873
Buckton, Northum *T* 165 NU 0838
Buckworth *T* 120 TL 1576
Budbrooke *T* 118 SP 2665
Budby *T* 139 SK 6270
Buddo Ness 171 NO 5515
Buddon Ness 171 NO 5430
Bude *P* 90 SS 2106
Bude Bay *W* 90 SS 1706
Bude Haven *W* 90 SS 1906
Budlake *T* 89 SS 9800
Budle *T* 165 NU 1535
Budle Bay *W* 165 NU 1535
Budleigh Salterton *T* 92 SY 0682
Budock Water *T* 87 SW 7832
Buerton *T* 127 SJ 6843
Bugbrooke *T* 119 SP 6757
Bugeilyn *W* 125 SN 8292
Bught Fell *H* 154 NX 2062
Bugle *T* 87 SX 0159
Bugthorpe *T* 148 SE 7758
Buidhe Bheinn *H* 180 NG 9508
Builg Burn *W* 177 NO 6786
Builth Road *T* 112 SO 0253
Builth Wells *P* 112 SO 0451
Bulbarrow Hill *H* 93 ST 7705
Bulby *T* 130 TF 0526
Buldoo *T* 198 NC 9967
Bulford *T* 102 SU 1743
Bulford Camp *T* 102 SU 1843
Bulg *H* 177 NO 5476
Bulgham Bay *W* 144 SC 4585
Bulkeley *T* 127 SJ 5354
Bulkington, Warw *T* 118 SP 3986
Bulkington, Wilts *T* 102 ST 9458
Bulkworthy *T* 90 SS 3914
Bull (lightship) 143 TA 3809
Bull Bay *W* 134 SH 4394
Bulldog Sand 132 TF 6027
Bulley *T* 114 SO 7619
Bullie Burn *W* 169 NN 7909
Bull Point 90 SS 4646
Bullpot Farm 145 SD 6681
Bullwood *T* 168 NS 1674
Bulmer, Essex *T* 122 TL 8440
Bulmer, N. Yks *T* 148 SE 6967
Bulmer Tye *T* 122 TL 8438
Bulphan *T* 106 TQ 6385
Bulverhythe *T* 98 TQ 7708
Bulwark *T* 185 NJ 9345
Bulwell *T* 129 SK 5345
Bulwick *T* 130 SP 9694
Bumble's Green *T* 105 TL 4005
Bunacaimb *T* 180 NM 6588
Bun Allt na Criche *W* 173 NM 9256
Bun an Leoib *W* 172 NM 4023
Bunarkaig *T* 174 NN 1887
Bunavoneadar *T* 189 NB 1303
Bunbury *T* 137 SJ 5658
Bunchrew House 182 NH 6245
Bundalloch *T* 180 NG 8927
Buness, Shetld 205 HP 6209
Bu Ness, Shetld 201 HZ 2272
Bunessan *T* 172 NM 3821
Bungay *T* 123 TM 3389
Bunloinn Forest 181 NH 1707
Bunnahabhainn *T* 166 NR 4273
Bunny *T* 129 SK 5829
Buntait *T* 182 NH 4030
Buntingford *T* 121 TL 3629
Bunwell *T* 133 TM 1193
Burach *H* 182 NH 3814
Burbage, Derby *T* 138 SK 0472
Burbage, Leic *T* 119 SP 4492
Burbage, Wilts *T* 102 SU 2361
Burcombe, Somer 91 SS 7538
Burcombe, Wilts *T* 94 SU 0730
Burcot *T* 115 SU 5696
Burdale *T* 149 SE 8762
Bures *T* 122 TL 9034
Burfa Camp *A* 116 SO 2861
Burford, Oxon *T* 115 SP 2512
Burford, Shrops *T* 116 SO 5868
Burg *T* 172 NM 3845
Burgar 200 HY 3427
Burga Water *W* 202 HU 2354
Burgess Hill *T* 97 TQ 3119
Burgh, Strath 173 NM 4226
Burgh, Suff *T* 123 TM 2351
Burgh by Sands *T* 157 NY 3259
Burgh Castle *T* 133 TG 4804
Burghclere *T* 103 SU 4761
Burghead *T* 183 NJ 1169
Burghead Bay *W* 183 NJ 0867
Burghfield *T* 104 SU 6668
Burghfield Common *T* 104 SU 6566
Burghfield Hill *T* 104 SU 6667
Burgh Head 201 HY 6923
Burgh Heath *T* 96 TQ 2457
Burghill *T* 113 SO 4844
Burgh Island 89 SX 6443
Burgh le Marsh *T* 141 TF 5064
Burghley House *A* 130 TF 0406
Burgh next Aylsham *T* 133 TG 2125
Burgh on Bain *T* 141 TF 2286
Burgh St Margaret or Fleggburgh *T* 133 TG 4414
Burgh St Peter *T* 133 TM 4693
Burghwallis *T* 139 SE 5311
Burgi Geos 205 HP 4703
Burham *T* 98 TQ 7262
Burifa' Hill *H* 199 ND 2075
Buriton *T* 95 SU 7320
Burland *T* 127 SJ 6153
Burlawn *T* 87 SW 9970
Burlescombe *T* 92 ST 0716
Burleston *T* 93 SY 7794
Burley, Hants *T* 94 SU 2103
Burley, Leic *T* 130 SK 8810
Burleydam *T* 127 SJ 6042
Burley Gate *T* 113 SO 5947
Burley in Wharfedale *T* 146 SE 1646
Burley Lodge 94 SU 2405
Burley Street *T* 94 SU 2004
Burlingjobb *T* 113 SO 2558
Burlton *T* 126 SJ 4526
Burmarsh *T* 99 TR 1031
Burmington *T* 118 SP 2638
Burn *T* 147 SE 5928
Burnage *T* 137 SJ 8692
Burnaston *T* 128 SK 2832
Burnby *T* 142 SE 8346
Burncrooks Reservoir, Central *W* 169 NS 4879
Burncrooks Reservoir, Strath *W* 169 NS 4879
Burneside *T* 151 SD 5095

Capton Chapel Haddlesey

Capton T 89 SX 8353
Caputh T 176 NO 0840
Caradon Hill H 88 SX 2770
Cara Island 160 NR 6444
Carbis Bay T 86 SW 5238
Carbost, Highld T 186 NG 3731
Carbost, Highld T 187 NG 4248
Carbrooke T 132 TF 9402
Carburton T 139 SK 6173
Carcary 177 NO 6455
Carclew 87 SW 7838
Car Colston T 129 SK 7242
Carcroft T 139 SE 5410
Cardenden T 171 NT 2194
Cardeston T 126 SJ 3912
Cardiff P 109 ST 1876
Cardiff Airport 109 ST 0667
Cardigan P 111 SN 1846
Cardigan Bay W 124 SN 3793
Cardigan Island 110 SN 1651
Cardington, Beds T 120 TL 0847
Cardington, Shrops T 127 SO 5095
Cardinham T 87 SX 1268
Cardney House 176 NO 0545
Cardno 185 NJ 9663
Cardoness Castle A 155 NX 5855
Cardow T 184 NJ 1943
Cardrona T 164 NT 3039
Cardrona Forest F 164 NT 3036
Cardross, Strath T 168 NS 3477
Cardross, Strath 169 NS 6097
Cardurnock T 157 NY 1758
Car Dyke, Cambs R 130 TF 1508
Car Dyke, Cambs R 121 TL 4769
Car Dyke, Lincs R 130 TF 1437
Careby T 130 TF 0216
Careston 177 NO 5258
Carew T 110 SN 0403
Carew Cheriton T 110 SN 0402
Carew Newton T 110 SN 0404
Carey T 113 SO 5631
Carfrae T 171 NT 5769
Cargen T 156 NX 9672
Cargenbridge T 156 NX 9474
Cargill 176 NO 1536
Cargo T 157 NY 3659
Cargreen T 88 SX 4362
Carham T 165 NT 7938
Carhampton T 91 ST 0042
Carharrack T 86 SW 7341
Carie, Tays 175 NN 6157
Carie, Tays 175 NN 6437
Carinbulg Point 185 NK 0366
Carines 87 SW 7959
Carisbrooke T 95 SZ 4888
Carishader T 195 NB 0933
Cark T 145 SD 3676
Carland Cross 87 SW 8453
Carlby T 130 TF 0414
Carleatheran H 169 NS 6891
Carlecotes T 138 SE 1703
Carleton, Cumbr T 151 NY 4252
Carleton, Lancs T 145 SD 3440
Carleton, N. Yks T 146 SD 9749
Carleton Forehoe T 133 TG 0905
Carleton Rode T 123 TM 1192
Carlingcott T 101 ST 6958
Carlingwark Loch W 156 NX 7661
Carlin Tooth H 158 NT 6302
Carlisle P 151 NY 4055
Carlisle Airport 157 NY 4860
Carlock Hill H 154 NX 0877
Carlops T 163 NT 1655
Carloway T 195 NB 2042
Carlton, Beds T 120 SP 9555
Carlton, Cambs T 122 TL 6453
Carlton, Cleve T 153 NZ 3921
Carlton, Leic T 128 SK 3904
Carlton, Notts T 129 SK 6141
Carlton, N. Yks T 146 SE 0684
Carlton, N. Yks T 147 SE 6186
Carlton, N. Yks T 147 SE 6424
Carlton, Suff T 123 TM 3864
Carlton, S. Yks T 139 SE 3609
Carlton, W. Yks T 147 SE 3327
Carlton Colville T 123 TM 5190
Carlton Curlieu T 129 SP 6997
Carlton Husthwaite T 147 SE 4976
Carlton in Cleveland T 153 NZ 5004
Carlton in Lindrick T 139 SK 5884
Carlton-le-Moorland T 140 SK 9057
Carlton Miniott T 147 SE 4081
Carlton Moor 146 SE 0384
Carlton-on-Trent T 140 SK 7963
Carlton Scroop T 130 SK 9444
Carluke T 163 NS 8450
Carl Wark A 139 SK 2681
Carmacoup T 162 NS 7927
Carmarthen P 111 SN 4120
Carmarthen Bay W 108 SN 2500
Carmel, Clwyd T 136 SJ 1776
Carmel, Dyfed T 111 SN 5816
Carmel, Gwyn T 134 SH 3882
Carmel, Gwyn T 134 SH 4955
Carmel Head 134 SH 2993
Carminish T 188 NG 0284
Carminish Islands 188 NG 0185
Carmont 177 NO 8084
Carmunnock T 162 NS 5957
Carmyle T 162 NS 6561
Carmyllie T 177 NO 5542
Carna 173 NM 6259
Carn a' Bhiorain H 191 NH 1483
Carn a' Bhodaich H 182 NH 5737
Carnaby T 149 TA 1465
Carnach, Highld T 190 NH 0196
Carnach, Highld T 180 NH 0228
Carnach, W. Isles T 189 NG 2297
Carn a' Chaochain H 182 NH 2318
Carn a' Choin Deirg H 191 NH 3992
Carn a' Choire Mhòir H 183 NH 8429
Carn a' Chrasgie H 183 NH 8643
Carn a' Chuilinn H 182 NH 4103
Carn a' Ghaill H 179 NG 2606
Carn a' Gheòidh, Grampn H 176 NO 1076
Carn a' Gheòidh, Tays H 176 NO 1076
Carn a' Ghlinne H 191 NH 0660
Carn a' Mhaim H 176 NN 9995
Carnan H 178 NL 5582
Carn an Daimh H 176 NO 1371
Carnan Eoin H 166 NR 4098
Carn an Fhidhleir or Carn Ealar, Grampn H 175 NN 9084
Carn an Fhidhleir or Carn Ealar, Highld H 175 NN 9084
Carn an Fhidhleir or Carn Ealar, Tays H 175 NN 9084
Carn an Fhreiceadain H 183 NH 7207
Carnan Mòr H 172 NL 9640
Carn an Righ H 176 NO 0277
Carn an t-Sabhail or Cairn Toul H 176 NN 9697
Carn an t-Sean-liathanaich H 183 NH 8632
Carn an t-Suidhe H 184 NJ 2726
Carn an Tuirc H 176 NO 1780
Carnau Gŵys H 109 SN 8120
Carn Bàn, Highld H 182 NH 3341
Carn Bàn, Highld H 191 NH 3387
Carn Bàn, Highld H 182 NH 6303
Carn Bàn, Strath H 173 NM 7228
Carn Bàn Mòr H 175 NN 8997
Carn Beag H 191 NH 1055
Carnbee T 171 NO 5306
Carn Bhac, Grampn H 176 NO 0482
Carn Bhac, Tays H 176 NO 0482
Carn Bheadhair H 183 NJ 0511
Carnbo T 170 NO 0503
Carn Breac H 191 NH 0453
Carn Breac Beag H 191 NH 1779
Carn Brea Village T 86 SW 6841
Carn Breugach H 173 NM 8127
Carn Cas nan Gabhar H 192 NH 5280
Càrn Chois H 169 NN 7927
Carn Chuinneag H 192 NH 4883
Carn Coire na Creiche H 182 NH 6208
Carn Coire na h-Easgainn H 183 NH 7313
Carn Daimh H 184 NJ 1825
Carn Dearg, Highld H 175 NH 6302
Carn Dearg, Highld H 174 NN 4166
Carn Dearg, Highld H 175 NN 5076
Carn Dearg, Strath H 168 NM 8919
Carn Dearg, Tays H 174 NN 4166
Carn Dearg Mòr H 175 NN 8291
Carn Dubh 'Ic an Deòir H 183 NH 7719
Carn Duchara H 168 NM 8910
Carnduncan 166 NR 2467
Carne 87 SW 9138
Carn Ealar or Carn an Fhidhleir, Grampn H 175 NN 9084
Carn Ealar or Carn an Fhidhleir, Highld H 175 NN 9084
Carn Ealar or Carn an Fhidhleir, Tays H 175 NN 9084
Carn Ealasaid H 184 NJ 2211
Càrn Eàs H 176 NO 1198
Carn Easgainn Bàna H 182 NH 4806
Carneddau H 112 SO 0654
Carnedd Dafydd H 135 SH 6663
Carnedd Iago H 135 SH 7840
Carnedd Llewelyn H 135 SH 6864
Carnedd Moel-siabod H 135 SH 7054
Carnedd y Filiast H 135 SH 8744
Carn Eige H 181 NH 1226
Carn Eilrig H 183 NH 9305
Carnell T 161 NS 4632
Car Ness 200 HY 4614
Carn Fadrun A 134 SH 2835
Carnferg H 177 NO 5293
Carnforth T 145 SD 4970
Carn Gafallt H 125 SN 9464
Carn Garbh H 182 NH 2858
Carn Geuradainn H 180 NG 9839
Carn Ghriogair H 182 NH 6520
Carn Glas-choire H 183 NH 8929
Carn-gorm, Highld T 180 NG 9520
Carn Gorm, Highld H 191 NH 1350
Carn Gorm, Highld H 182 NH 3235
Carn Gorm, Highld H 182 NH 4362
Carn Gorm, Tays H 175 NN 6350
Carnhedryn T 110 SM 8027
Carnhell Green T 86 SW 6137
Carnie T 185 NJ 8005
Carnish T 188 NF 8160
Carn Kitty H 183 NJ 0942
Carn Leac H 174 NN 4097
Carn Leac Saighdeir H 184 NJ 2706
Carn Liath, Grampn H 184 NJ 1826
Carn Liath, Grampn H 184 NJ 2515
Carn Liath, Grampn H 176 NO 0386
Carn Liath, Highld H 175 NN 4790
Carn Liath, Tays H 175 NN 9369
Carn Loch nan Amhaichean H 192 NH 4175
Carn Mairg H 175 NN 6851
Carn Meadhonach H 183 NJ 1417
Carn Mhartuin H 191 NH 1754
Carn Mòr, Grampn H 184 NJ 2618
Carn Mòr, Highld H 191 NH 2487
Carn Mòr, Highld H 192 NH 4271
Carn Mòr, Highld H 182 NH 4334
Carn Mòr, Highld H 180 NM 9090
Carn Mòr, Strath H 172 NM 3948
Carn na Cailliche H 184 NJ 1847
Carn na Caim, Highld H 175 NN 6782
Carn na Caim, Tays H 175 NN 6782
Carn na Cloiche Mòire H 182 NH 3753
Carn na Còinnich H 182 NH 3251
Carn na Drochaide H 176 NO 1293
Carn na Dubh Choille H 182 NH 3867
Carn na Farraidh H 183 NJ 1114
Carn na Feannaige H 183 NJ 1008
Carn na h-Easgainn H 183 NH 7432
Carn na Làraiche Maoile H 182 NH 5811
Carn na Lòine H 183 NJ 0736
Carn nam Bad H 182 NH 4033
Carn nam Bain-tighearna H 183 NH 8425
Carn nam Buailtean H 190 NH 0086
Carn nan Iomairean H 180 NG 9135
Carn nan Sgeir 190 NC 0101
Carn nan Tri-tighearnan H 183 NH 8239
Carn na Saobhaidh H 183 NH 6724
Carn na Saobhaidhe H 182 NH 6014
Carn na Sean-lùibe H 180 NH 0235
Carno T 125 SN 9696
Carnock T 170 NT 0488
Carn Odhar H 182 NH 6317
Carnon Downs T 87 SW 7940
Carnousie T 184 NJ 6650
Carnoustie T 171 NO 5634
Carn Phris Mhòir H 183 NH 8021
Carn Ruigh Chorrach H 183 NH 9934
Carn Salachaidh H 192 NH 5187
Carn Sgùlain H 183 NH 6909
Carn Sgumain H 183 NH 8740
Carn Sleamhuinn H 183 NH 8516
Carn Towan T 86 SW 3626
Carnwath T 163 NS 9846
Carnyorth T 86 SW 3733
Carperby T 152 SE 0089
Carpley Green T 146 SD 9487
Carracks, The 86 SW 4640
Carradale T 160 NR 8138
Carradale Bay W 160 NR 8037
Carradale Point 160 NR 8136
Carradale Water W 160 NR 7843
Carragreich T 189 NG 1998
Carraig Bhàn W 166 NR 2572
Carraig Dubh 166 NR 3062
Carraig Fhada 166 NR 3444
Carraig Mhòr 166 NR 4656
Carrbridge T 183 NH 9022
Carr Brigs 171 NO 6411
Carreg Ddu 134 SH 2742
Carreg-gwylan-fach 110 SM 7730
Carreglefn T 134 SH 3889
Carreg-lem H 109 SN 8017
Carreg-lwyd H 109 SN 8615
Carreg Ti-pw 124 SN 5370
Carregwastad Point 110 SM 9240
Carreg yr Imbill 134 SH 3834
Carr End 165 NU 2232
Carrick, Fife 171 NO 4422
Carrick, Strath 168 NR 9087
Carrick, Strath T 168 NS 1994
Carrick, Strath 154 NX 3294
Carrick Forest F 154 NX 4093
Carrick House 200 HY 5638
Carrick Roads W 87 SW 8335
Carriden T 170 NT 1081
Carrine 160 NR 6609
Carrington, G. Man T 137 SJ 7492
Carrington, Lincs T 131 TF 3155
Carrington, Lothn T 164 NT 3160
Carrington Moss 137 SJ 7491
Carrog T 126 SJ 1143
Carron, Central T 170 NS 8882
Carron, Grampn T 184 NJ 2241
Carron Bridge, Central 169 NS 7483
Carronbridge, D. & G T 156 NX 8798
Carron Valley Forest, Central F 169 NS 6982
Carron Valley Forest, Strath F 169 NS 6982
Carron Valley Reservoir, Central W 169 NS 6983
Carron Valley Reservoir, Strath W 169 NS 6983
Carrot Hill H 176 NO 4540
Carr Shield T 151 NY 8047
Carrs, The 149 SE 9779
Carrutherstown T 157 NY 1071
Carruth House 161 NS 3566
Carr Vale T 139 SK 4669
Carrville T 152 NZ 3043
Carrycoats Hall 158 NY 9279
Carsaig T 173 NM 5421
Carsaig Bay W 173 NM 5421
Carscreugh 154 NX 2259
Carsegowan T 155 NX 4258
Carse Gray 177 NO 4653
Carse House 160 NR 7461
Carse of Gowrie 171 NO 2624
Carseriggan 154 NX 3167
Carsethorn T 156 NX 9959
Carsfad Loch W 156 NX 6086
Carsgailoch Hill H 161 NS 5514
Carshalton T 105 TQ 2764
Carsington T 128 SK 2553
Carsington Reservoir W 128 SK 2552
Carskiey T 160 NR 6508
Carsluith T 155 NX 4854
Carsphairn T 156 NX 5693
Carsphairn Forest F 156 NS 5701
Carstairs T 163 NS 9346
Carstairs Junction T 163 NS 9545
Carswell Marsh T 115 SU 3299
Carter Bar, Border 158 NT 6906
Carter Bar, Northum 158 NT 6906
Carter's Clay T 94 SU 3024
Carterton T 115 SP 2807
Carterway Heads T 152 NZ 0451
Carthagena Bank 171 NO 2722
Carthew T 87 SX 0055
Carthorpe T 147 SE 3083
Cartington T 159 NU 0304
Cartland T 163 NS 8646
Cartmel T 145 SD 3878
Cartmel Fell T 145 SD 4188
Cartmel Sands 145 SD 3376
Cartmel Wharf 145 SD 3668
Carway T 111 SN 4606
Cas T 160 NR 7064
Cascob T 116 SO 2466
Cashel Dhu 197 NC 4549
Cashlie 175 NN 4941
Cashmoor T 94 ST 9713
Cashtal yn Ard A 144 SC 4689
Cassington T 115 SP 4510
Cassiobury Park T 104 TQ 0997
Casswell's Bridge T 130 TF 1627
Castallack T 86 SW 4525
Castellau T 109 ST 0586
Castell Dinas A 109 SO 1730
Castell Howell T 111 SN 4448
Castell Odo A 124 SH 1828
Castell y Bere A 125 SH 6708
Castell-y-bŵch T 100 ST 2792
Casterton T 145 SD 6279
Castle 200 HY 2113
Castle Acre T 132 TF 8115
Castle an Dinas A 87 SW 9462
Castle Ashby T 120 SP 8659
Castlebay T 178 NL 6698
Castle Bolton T 152 SE 0391
Castle Bromwich T 118 SP 1590
Castle Bytham T 130 SK 9818
Castlebythe T 110 SN 0229
Castle Caereinion T 126 SJ 1605
Castle Campbell A 170 NS 9699
Castle Camps T 122 TL 6343
Castle Carrock T 151 NY 5455
Castle Cary, Somer T 93 ST 6332
Castlecary, Strath T 169 NS 7878
Castle Combe T 101 ST 8477
Castlecraig, Border T 163 NT 1344
Castlecraig, Highld T 183 NH 8269
Castle Ditches, Hants A 94 SU 1219
Castle Ditches, S. Glam A 109 SS 9667
Castle Ditches, S. Glam A 109 ST 0670
Castle Donington T 129 SK 4427
Castle Douglas T 156 NX 7662
Castle Eaton T 115 SU 1495
Castle Eden T 153 NZ 4237
Castle Forbes 184 NJ 6219
Castleford T 147 SE 4225
Castle Fraser 185 NJ 7212
Castle Frome T 117 SO 6645
Castle Gresley T 128 SK 2818
Castle Haven W 177 NO 8884
Castle Heaton T 165 NT 9041
Castle Hedingham T 122 TL 7835
Castlehill, Highld 199 ND 1968
Castle Hill, Highld H 183 NH 9505
Castlehill, Strath T 163 NS 8451
Castle Hill, Suff T 123 TM 1547
Castle Hill, W. Yks A 138 SE 1514
Castlehill Point 155 NX 8552
Castle Howard 148 SE 7170
Castle Huntly 171 NO 3029
Castle Kennedy T 154 NX 1059
Castle Lachlan 168 NS 0195
Castle Leod 182 NH 4859
Castell y Bere A 125 SH 6608
Castle Loch, D. & G W 154 NX 2853
Castle Loch, D. & G W 157 NY 0881
Castlemaddy 155 NX 5589
Castlemartin T 110 SR 9198
Castlemilk T 157 NY 1577
Castlemorris T 110 SM 9031
Castlemorton T 117 SO 7937
Castle O'er T 157 NY 2492
Castle O'er Forest F 157 NY 2493
Castle of Mey 199 ND 2973
Castle of Old Wick A 199 ND 3748
Castle of Park A 154 NX 1857
Castle Point 165 NU 1441
Castle Ring A 128 SK 0412
Castle Rising T 132 TF 6624
Castleshaw Moor 138 SD 9911
Castle Side T 152 NZ 0748
Castle Stuart 183 NH 7449
Castle Sween A 167 NR 7178
Castle, The 205 HU 3787
Castlethorpe T 119 SP 7944
Castleton, Derby T 138 SK 1583
Castleton, Gwent T 100 ST 2583
Castleton, N. Yks T 148 NZ 6807
Castleton, Strath T 168 NR 8884
Castle Toward 161 NS 1168
Castletown, Highld T 199 ND 1968
Castletown, I. of M T 144 SC 2667
Castletown, T. & W T 159 NZ 3558
Caston T 132 TL 9597
Castor T 130 TL 1298
Catacol T 160 NR 9149
Catacol Bay W 160 NR 9049
Cat and Fiddle 138 SK 0071
Cata Sand 201 HY 7040
Catbrain T 101 ST 5780
Catcleugh Reservoir W 158 NT 7303
Catcliffe T 139 SK 4288
Catcott T 100 ST 3939
Cateran Hill H 165 NU 1023
Caterham T 97 TQ 3455
Cater's Beam 89 SX 6369
Catesby T 119 SP 5259
Catfield T 133 TG 3821
Catfirth, Shetld T 203 HU 4354
Cat Firth, Shetld W 203 HU 4552
Catford T 105 TQ 3872
Catforth T 145 SD 4735
Cath T 110 SM 7525
Cathcart T 162 NS 5860
Cathedine T 109 SO 1425
Catherington T 95 SU 7014
Catherton T 117 SO 6578
Cati Geo 200 HY 4342
Cat Law H 176 NO 3161
Catlodge T 175 NN 6392
Catlowdy T 157 NY 4576
Catlow Fell 145 SD 7160
Catmore T 103 SU 4580
Caton T 145 SD 5364
Caton Moor 145 SD 5763
Cator Court 89 SX 6877
Catrine T 161 NS 5225
Cat's Ash T 100 ST 3790
Catsfield T 97 TQ 7213
Catshill T 118 SO 9674
Cattal T 147 SE 4454
Cattawade T 123 TM 1033
Catterall T 145 SD 4942
Catterick T 152 SE 2497
Catterick Bridge T 152 SE 2299
Catterick Garrison T 152 SE 1897
Catterlen T 151 NY 4833
Catterline T 177 NO 8678
Catterton T 147 SE 5146
Catthorpe T 119 SP 5578
Cattistock T 93 SY 5999
Catton, Norf T 133 TG 2312
Catton, Northum T 151 NY 8257
Catton, N. Yks T 147 SE 3778
Catton Hall 128 SK 2015
Catwick T 143 TA 1345
Catworth T 120 TL 0873
Caulcott T 115 SP 5024
Cauldcleuch Head H 157 NT 4500
Cauldcots 177 NO 6547
Cauldhame T 169 NS 6494
Cauldon T 128 SK 0749
Cauldron Snout W 151 NY 8228
Cauldrus 200 HY 2116
Cauldshiels Hill H 164 NT 5131
Caulkerbush T 150 NX 9257
Caulside T 157 NY 4480
Caunsall T 117 SO 8581
Caunton T 140 SK 7460
Causamul 188 NF 6670
Caus Castle A 126 SJ 3307
Causeway Grain Head, Border H 157 NY 3598
Causeway Grain Head, D. & G H 157 NY 3598
Causewayhead T 169 NS 8095
Causeyend T 185 NJ 9419
Causey Park 159 NZ 1795
Causey Park Bridge T 159 NZ 1994
Causey Pike H 150 NY 2120
Cautley T 151 SD 6995
Cava 200 ND 3299
Cavendish T 122 TL 8046
Cavenham T 122 TL 7669
Caversfield T 115 SP 5825
Caversham T 104 SU 7175
Caver's Hill H 164 NT 3921
Caversta T 195 NB 3619
Caverswall T 128 SJ 9543
Caw H 150 SD 2394
Cawdor T 183 NH 8450
Caw Fell H 150 NY 1310
Cawood T 147 SE 5737
Cawsand T 88 SX 4350
Cawston T 133 TG 1323
Cawthorne T 139 SE 2808
Cawton T 147 SE 6476
Caxton T 121 TL 3058
Caynham T 116 SO 5573
Caynham Camp A 116 SO 5473
Caythorpe, Lincs T 130 SK 9348
Caythorpe, Notts T 129 SK 6845
Cayton T 149 TA 0583
Cayton Bay W 149 TA 0684
Ceannacroc Forest 181 NH 1713
Ceanna Mòr 173 NM 8551
Ceann Creag-airighe H 179 NG 2205
Ceann Ear 188 NF 6462
Ceann Leathad nam Bò 199 ND 1324
Ceann na Beinne H 187 NG 4217
Ceann-na-Cleithe T 189 NG 1794
Ceann Riobha 166 NR 3585
Ceathramh Garbh 196 NC 2251
Cedig 125 SH 9922
Cefn Berain T 135 SH 9969
Cefn-brîth T 135 SH 9350
Cefn Bryn H 108 SS 5089
Cefn Carnedd A 125 SO 0190
Cefn Carn Fadog H 109 SN 7616
Cefn Cenarth H 125 SN 9676
Cefn Coch, Clwyd H 135 SJ 0035
Cefn Coch, Gwyn H 135 SJ 0035
Cefn Coch, Powys T 125 SJ 1026
Cefn Coch, Powys H 112 SN 8253
Cefn-coed-y-cymmer T 109 SO 0308
Cefn Cribwr T 109 SS 8582
Cefn-crin H 125 SO 0272
Cefn Cross T 109 SS 8682
Cefn Crug H 109 SN 8802
Cefn-ddwysarn 135 SH 9638
Cefndeuddwr 125 SH 7326
Cefn Drum H 111 SN 6104
Cefn Du H 135 SJ 0454
Cefn Einion T 116 SO 2886
Cefneithin T 111 SN 5513
Cefn Fannog H 112 SN 8251
Cefn Gwrhyd H 108 SN 7308
Cefn Hengoed T 109 ST 1496
Cefn Hirgoed H 109 SS 9383
Cefni Reservoir W 134 SH 4477
Cefn Llwydlo H 112 SN 8542
Cefn-mawr, Clwyd T 126 SJ 2842
Cefn Mawr, Powys H 109 SN 7915
Cefn Merthyr H 109 SO 0800
Cefn Morfudd H 109 SS 7997
Cefn Padrig 108 SN 4800
Cefn Pyllau-duon H 109 SO 1012
Cefn Rhyswg H 113 ST 2394
Cefn Sidan Sands 111 SN 3405
Cefn-y-bedd T 126 SJ 3156
Cefn-y-coed H 126 SO 1993
Cefn-y-pant T 111 SN 1925
Cefn yr Arail H 109 SO 0519
Cefnyresgair H 125 SN 7589
Ceidio 134 SH 4185
Ceint T 134 SH 4975
Cellan T 111 SN 6149
Cellarhead, Staffs T 128 SJ 9547
Cellar Head, W. Isles T 195 NB 5656
Cemaes T 134 SH 3793
Cemaes Bay W 134 SH 3694
Cemaes Head 110 SN 1350
Cemlyn Bay W 134 SH 3393
Cemmaes T 125 SH 8406
Cemmaes Road T 125 SH 8204
Cenarth T 111 SN 2741
Cennin T 134 SH 4645
Ceol na Mara 173 NM 7561
Ceres T 171 NO 4011
Cerne Abbas T 93 ST 6601
Cerney Wick T 114 SU 0796
Cerrigceinwen T 134 SH 4273
Cerrigydrudion T 135 SH 9548
Cessford T 164 NT 7323
Cessnock Water W 161 NS 5028
Chaceley T 114 SO 8530
Chacewater T 86 SW 7544
Chackmore T 119 SP 6835
Chacombe T 119 SP 4943
Chadderton T 137 SD 9005
Chaddesden T 128 SK 3737
Chaddesley Corbett T 117 SO 8973
Chaddleworth T 102 SU 4177
Chadlington T 115 SP 3322
Chadshunt T 118 SP 3453
Chad Valley T 118 SP 0485
Chadwell St Mary T 106 TQ 6478
Chadwick End T 118 SP 2073
Chaffcombe T 92 ST 3510
Chagford T 89 SX 7087
Chailey T 97 TQ 3919
Chainhurst T 97 TQ 7347
Chaipaval H 188 NF 9792
Chalbury Common T 94 SU 0206
Chaldon T 97 TQ 3255
Chaldon Down H 93 SY 7882
Chaldon Herring or East Chaldon T 93 SY 7983
Chale T 95 SZ 4877
Chale Bay W 95 SZ 4677
Chale Green T 95 SZ 4879
Chalfont and Latimer Station 104 SU 9997
Chalfont Common T 104 TQ 0091
Chalfont St Giles T 104 SU 9893
Chalfont St Peter T 104 TQ 0090
Chalford T 114 SO 8902
Chalgrove T 104 SU 6396
Chalk T 98 TQ 6772
Challacombe T 91 SS 6940
Challister Ness 203 HU 5767
Challoch T 154 NX 3867
Challoch Hill H 154 NX 1657
Challock T 99 TR 0150
Chalton, Beds T 120 TL 0326
Chalton, Hants T 95 SU 7316
Chalvington T 97 TQ 5209
Champany T 170 NT 0278
Chancellor, The H 174 NN 1658
Chandler's Cross T 104 TQ 0698
Chandler's Ford T 94 SU 4320
Changue Forest F 154 NX 3093
Chanlockfoot 156 NS 7900
Channerwick T 203 HU 4023
Chanonry Point 183 NH 7555
Chantry, Somer T 101 ST 7146
Chantry, Suff T 123 TM 1443
Chapel T 171 NT 2593
Chapel Allerton, Somer T 100 ST 4050
Chapel Allerton, W. Yks T 147 SE 3037
Chapel Amble T 87 SW 9975
Chapel Brampton T 119 SP 7266
Chapel Chorlton T 127 SJ 8138
Chapel-en-le-Frith T 138 SK 0580
Chapelfell Top H 152 NY 8734
Chapel Finian A 154 NX 2748
Chapelgate T 131 TF 4124
Chapel Haddlesey T 147 SE 5826

Chapelhall Clotton

Chapelhall T 162 NS 7862
Chapel Hill, Grampn T 185 NK 0635
Chapel Hill, Gwent T 113 SO 5300
Chapelhill, Highld 193 NH 8273
Chapel Hill, Lincs T 130 TF 2054
Chapelhill, Tays T 170 NO 0130
Chapelhill, Tays 177 NO 2021
Chapelknowe T 157 NY 3173
Chapel Lawn T 116 SO 3176
Chapel-le-Dale T 145 SD 7377
Chapel Ness 171 NT 4899
Chapel of Garioch T 185 NJ 7124
Chapel Point, Corn 87 SX 0243
Chapel Point, Dyfed 110 SS 1495
Chapel Rossan Bay W 154 NX 1145
Chapel Row T 103 SU 5769
Chapel Site T 150 NY 3205
Chapel St Leonards T 141 TF 5572
Chapelton, Devon T 91 SS 5726
Chapelton, Strath T 162 NS 6848
Chapelton, Tays T 177 NO 6247
Chapeltown, Grampn T 184 NJ 2421
Chapeltown, Lancs T 137 SD 7315
Chapeltown, S. Yks T 139 SK 3696
Chapman Sands 106 TQ 8383
Chapmanslade T 101 ST 8247
Chapmans Well T 88 SX 3593
Chappel T 122 TL 8928
Chard T 92 ST 3208
Chardstock T 92 ST 3104
Charfield T 101 ST 7292
Charing T 98 TQ 9549
Charing Cross Station 105 TQ 3080
Charing Heath T 98 TQ 9249
Charingworth T 118 SP 2039
Charlbury T 115 SP 3519
Charlcombe T 101 ST 7467
Charlecote T 118 SP 2656
Charlecote Park A 118 SP 2656
Charles T 91 SS 6832
Charleston T 176 NO 3845
Charlestown, Corn T 87 SX 0351
Charlestown, Dorset T 93 SY 6579
Charlestown, Fife T 170 NT 0683
Charlestown, Grampn T 177 NJ 9300
Charlestown, Highld T 190 NG 8174
Charlestown, Highld T 182 NH 6448
Charlestown of Aberlour T 184 NJ 2642
Charles Tye T 122 TM 0252
Charlesworth T 138 SK 0092
Charleton House 171 NO 4503
Charlton, G. Lon T 105 TQ 4278
Charlton, H. & W T 118 SP 0145
Charlton, Northnts T 115 SP 5235
Charlton, Wilts T 93 ST 9022
Charlton, Wilts T 102 ST 9689
Charlton, Wilts T 102 SU 1156
Charlton, Wilts T 94 SU 1723
Charlton, W. Susx T 95 SU 8812
Charlton Abbots T 114 SP 0324
Charlton Adam T 93 ST 5328
Charlton Down H 93 ST 8700
Charlton Horethorne T 93 ST 6623
Charlton Kings T 114 SO 9620
Charlton Mackrell T 93 ST 5228
Charlton Marshall T 93 ST 9003
Charlton Musgrove T 93 ST 7231
Charlton-on-Otmoor T 115 SP 5912
Charlwood T 96 TQ 2441
Charlynch T 92 ST 2337
Charminster T 93 SY 6892
Charmouth T 92 SY 3693
Charndon T 104 SP 6724
Charney Bassett T 115 SU 3895
Charnock Richard T 137 SD 5515
Charnwood Forest F 129 SK 4814
Charsfield T 123 TM 2556
Charter Alley T 103 SU 5957
Charterhouse T 101 ST 4955
Chartershall T 169 NS 8090
Charterville Allotments T 115 SP 3110
Chartham T 99 TR 1055
Chartham Hatch T 99 TR 1056
Chartridge T 104 SP 9303
Chart Sutton T 98 TQ 8050
Charwelton T 119 SP 5356
Chase Terrace T 128 SK 0409
Chasetown T 128 SK 0508
Chasewater W 128 SK 0307
Chastleton T 115 SP 2429
Chatburn T 146 SD 7644
Chatcull T 127 SJ 7934
Chatham T 98 TQ 7567
Chathill T 165 NU 1827
Chat Moss 137 SJ 7096
Chatsworth House A 139 SK 2870
Chattenden T 98 TQ 7572
Chatteris T 121 TL 3985
Chatteris Fen 121 TL 3980
Chattisham T 123 TM 0942
Chatto T 158 NT 7717
Chatton T 165 NU 0528
Chawleigh T 91 SS 7112
Chawston T 120 TL 1556
Chawton T 95 SU 7037
Cheadle, G. Man T 137 SJ 8688
Cheadle, Staffs T 128 SK 0143
Cheadle Hulme T 137 SJ 8786
Cheam T 105 TQ 2463
Chearsley T 104 SP 7110
Chebsey T 127 SJ 8628
Checkendon T 104 SU 6683
Checkley, Ches T 127 SJ 7346
Checkley, Staffs T 128 SK 0237
Chedburgh T 122 TL 7957
Cheddar T 101 ST 4553
Cheddar Gorge 101 ST 4754
Cheddar Reservoir W 101 ST 4453
Cheddington T 104 SP 9116
Cheddleton T 128 SJ 9752
Cheddon Fitzpaine T 92 ST 2427
Chedgrave T 133 TM 3699
Chedington T 93 ST 4805
Chediston T 123 TM 3577
Chedworth T 114 SP 0512
Chedzoy T 92 ST 3337
Cheeseman's Green T 99 TR 0238
Cheetham Hill T 137 SD 8400
Cheldon T 91 SS 7313
Chelford T 137 SJ 8174
Chelker Reservoir W 146 SE 0551
Chellaston T 128 SK 3730
Chellington T 120 SP 9555
Chelmarsh T 117 SO 7288
Chelmarsh Reservoir W 117 SO 7387
Chelmondiston T 123 TM 2037
Chelmorton T 138 SK 1170
Chelmsford P 106 TL 7007
Chelsea T 105 TQ 2778
Chelsfield T 105 TQ 4864
Chelsworth T 122 TL 9848
Cheltenham P 114 SO 9522
Chelveston T 120 SP 9969
Chelvey T 101 ST 4668
Chelwood T 101 ST 6361
Chelwood Gate T 97 TQ 4129
Cheney Longville T 116 SO 4285
Chenies T 104 TQ 0198
Chepstow P 113 ST 5393
Chepstow Park Wood F 113 ST 4997
Cherhill T 102 SU 0370
Cherington, Glos T 114 ST 9098
Cherington, Warw T 118 SP 2936
Cheriton, Devon 91 SS 7346
Cheriton, Devon T 92 ST 1001
Cheriton, Hants T 95 SU 5828
Cheriton, W. Glam T 108 SS 4593
Cheriton Bishop T 89 SX 7793
Cheriton Fitzpaine T 91 SS 8606
Cherrington T 127 SJ 6620
Cherry Burton T 142 SE 9942
Cherry Cobb Sands 143 TA 2221
Cherry Hinton T 121 TL 4856
Cherry Willingham T 140 TF 0372
Chertsey T 104 TQ 0466
Cheselbourne T 93 SY 7699
Chesham T 104 SP 9501
Chesham Bois T 104 SU 9699
Cheshunt T 105 TL 3602
Chesil Beach 93 SY 6180
Cheslyn Hay T 128 SJ 9807
Chessington T 105 TQ 1863
Chester P 136 SJ 4066
Chesterblade T 101 ST 6641
Chesterfield, Derby P 139 SK 3871
Chesterfield, Staffs T 128 SK 1005
Chesterfield Canal W 140 SK 7284
Chester-le-Street T 152 NZ 2751
Chesters, Border T 164 NT 6022
Chesters, Border T 158 NT 6210
Chesterton, Cambs T 130 TL 1295
Chesterton, Cambs T 121 TL 4660
Chesterton, Oxon T 115 SP 5521
Chesterton, Staffs T 127 SJ 8349
Chesterton, Warw T 118 SP 3558
Chestfield T 99 TR 1366
Cheswardine T 127 SJ 7229
Cheswick T 165 NU 0346
Cheswick Black Rocks 165 NU 0347
Cheswick Green T 118 SP 1376
Chetney Marshes 98 TQ 8871
Chetnole T 93 ST 6007
Chettiscombe T 91 SS 9614
Chettisham T 121 TL 5482
Chettle T 94 ST 9513
Chetton T 117 SO 6690
Chetwode T 119 SP 6429
Chetwynd Aston T 127 SJ 7517
Cheveley T 122 TL 6860
Chevening T 97 TQ 4857
Chevington T 122 TL 7859
Chevington Drift T 159 NZ 2699
Cheviot Hills, The, Border H 158 NT 8212
Cheviot Hills, The, Northum H 158 NT 8212
Cheviot, The H 158 NT 9020
Chevithorne T 91 SS 9715
Chew Magna T 101 ST 5763
Chew Resr W 138 SE 0301
Chew Stoke T 101 ST 5561
Chewton Mendip T 101 ST 5953
Chew Valley Lake W 101 ST 5659
Cheynies 203 HU 3438
Chicheley T 120 SP 9045
Chichester P 95 SU 8604
Chichester Harbour W 95 SU 7600
Chicken Head 195 NB 5029
Chicken Rock 144 SC 1463
Chickerell T 93 SY 6480
Chicklade T 93 ST 9134
Chicksands T 120 TL 1139
Chicksgrove T 94 ST 9729
Chidden T 95 SU 6517
Chiddingfold T 96 SU 9635
Chiddingly T 97 TQ 5414
Chiddingstone T 97 TQ 4945
Chiddingstone Causeway 97 TQ 5246
Chideock T 93 SY 4292
Chidham T 95 SU 7903
Chieveley T 103 SU 4773
Chignall Smealy T 106 TL 6611
Chignall St James T 106 TL 6709
Chigwell T 105 TQ 4493
Chigwell Row T 105 TQ 4693
Chilbolton T 102 SU 3939
Chilcombe T 93 SY 5291
Chilcompton T 101 ST 6451
Chilcote T 128 SK 2811
Childer Thornton T 136 SJ 3677
Child Okeford T 93 ST 8312
Childrey T 102 SU 3687
Child's Ercall T 127 SJ 6625
Childswickham T 118 SP 0738
Childwall T 136 SJ 4189
Chilfrome T 93 SY 5898
Chilgrove T 95 SU 8314
Chilham T 99 TR 0653
Chillaton T 88 SX 4381
Chillenden T 99 TR 2753
Chillerton T 95 SZ 4884
Chillesford T 123 TM 3852
Chillingham T 165 NU 0626
Chillington, Devon T 89 SX 7942
Chillington, Somer T 92 ST 3811
Chillington Hall 127 SJ 8607
Chilmark T 94 ST 9732
Chilson T 115 SP 3119
Chilsworthy, Corn T 88 SX 4172
Chilsworthy, Devon T 90 SS 3206
Chiltern Hills, Bucks H 104 SU 7799
Chiltern Hills, Oxon H 104 SU 7799
Chiltern Hundreds 104 SU 9588
Chilthorne Domer T 93 ST 5218
Chilton, Bucks T 104 SP 6811
Chilton, Durham T 152 NZ 2829
Chilton, Oxon T 103 SU 4885
Chilton Cantelo T 93 ST 5721
Chilton Chine 94 SZ 4082
Chilton Foliat T 102 SU 3270
Chilton Lane T 152 NZ 3031
Chilton Polden T 100 ST 3739
Chilton Street T 122 TL 7546
Chilton Trinity T 100 ST 2939
Chilworth, Hants T 94 SU 4118
Chilworth, Surrey T 96 TQ 0247
Chimney T 115 SP 3500
Chineham T 103 SU 6554
Chingford T 105 TQ 3893
Chinley T 138 SK 0482
Chinley Head T 138 SK 0584
Chinnor T 104 SP 7500
Chipchase Castle 158 NY 8875
Chipnall T 127 SJ 7231
Chippenham, Cambs T 122 TL 6669
Chippenham, Wilts P 101 ST 9173
Chipperfield T 104 TL 0402
Chipping, Herts T 121 TL 3531
Chipping, Lancs T 145 SD 6243
Chipping Campden T 118 SP 1539
Chipping Hill T 106 TL 8115
Chipping Norton T 115 SP 3127
Chipping Ongar T 105 TL 5503
Chipping Sodbury T 101 ST 7382
Chipping Warden T 119 SP 4948
Chipstable T 92 ST 0427
Chipstead T 96 TQ 2757
Chirbury T 126 SO 2698
Chirdon Burn W 158 NY 7683
Chirk T 126 SJ 2938
Chirk Castle A 126 SJ 2638
Chirmorie 154 NX 2076
Chirnside T 165 NT 8756
Chirnsidebridge T 165 NT 8556
Chirton T 102 SU 0757
Chisbury T 102 SU 2766
Chiselborough T 93 ST 4614
Chiselbury A 94 SU 0128
Chiseldon T 102 SU 1879
Chiselhampton T 115 SU 5998
Chislehurst T 105 TQ 4470
Chislet T 99 TR 2264
Chiswell Green T 105 TL 1304
Chiswick T 105 TQ 2077
Chisworth T 138 SJ 9891
Chitcomb T 95 SU 5020
Chithurst T 95 SU 8423
Chittering T 121 TL 4970
Chitterne T 102 ST 9944
Chittlehamholt T 91 SS 6420
Chittlehampton T 91 SS 6325
Chittoe T 102 ST 9566
Chivenor T 90 SS 5034
Chno Dearg H 174 NN 3774
Chobham T 104 SU 9762
Chobham Common 104 SU 9665
Chobham Ridges H 104 SU 9159
Cholderton T 102 SU 2342
Cholesbury T 104 SP 9306
Chollerton T 158 NY 9372
Cholmondeley Castle 127 SJ 5351
Cholsey T 103 SU 5886
Cholstrey T 113 SO 4659
Choppington T 159 NZ 2583
Chopwell T 159 NZ 1258
Chorley, Ches T 127 SJ 5751
Chorley, Lancs T 137 SD 5817
Chorley, Shrops T 117 SO 6983
Chorley, Staffs T 128 SK 0711
Chorleywood, Bucks T 104 TQ 0295
Chorleywood, Herts T 104 TQ 0295
Chorlton T 127 SJ 7250
Chorlton-cum-Hardy T 137 SJ 8193
Chorlton Lane T 126 SJ 4547
Chowley T 127 SJ 4756
Chrishall T 121 TL 4439
Christchurch, Cambs T 131 TL 4996
Christchurch, Dorset T 94 SZ 1592
Christchurch, Glos T 113 SO 5713
Christchurch Bay W 94 SZ 2292
Christian Malford T 102 ST 9678
Christleton T 136 SJ 4465
Christmas Common T 104 SU 7193
Christon T 100 ST 3757
Christon Bank T 165 NU 2122
Christow T 89 SX 8384
Christ's Hospital 96 TQ 1428
Chudleigh T 89 SX 8679
Chudleigh Knighton T 89 SX 8477
Chulmleigh T 91 SS 6814
Chunal T 138 SK 0391
Church, Lancs T 145 SD 7428
Church, N. Yks T 153 SE 6697
Churcham T 114 SO 7618
Church Aston T 127 SJ 7417
Church Bay W 134 SH 2989
Church Brampton T 119 SP 7165
Church Broughton T 128 SK 2033
Church Cove T 86 SW 7112
Church Crookham T 103 SU 8152
Churchdown T 114 SO 8820
Church Eaton T 127 SJ 8417
Church End, Beds T 104 SP 9921
Church End, Beds T 120 TL 1937
Church End, Cambs T 131 TF 3909
Church End, Cambs T 121 TL 4857
Church End, Essex T 121 TL 5841
Churchend, Essex T 106 TL 6322
Churchend, Essex T 107 TR 0092
Church End, Hants T 103 SU 6756
Church End, Warw T 118 SP 2992
Church End, Wilts T 102 SU 0278
Church Fenton T 147 SE 5136
Church Gresley T 128 SK 2918
Church Hanborough T 115 SP 4212
Churchill, Avon T 101 ST 4459
Churchill, Devon T 92 ST 2901
Churchill, H. & W T 117 SO 8879
Churchill, Oxon T 115 SP 2824
Churchinford T 92 ST 2112
Church Knowle T 94 SY 9381
Church Langton T 129 SP 7293
Church Lawford T 119 SP 4476
Church Lawton T 127 SJ 8255
Church Leigh T 128 SK 0235
Church Lench T 118 SP 0251
Church Minshull T 137 SJ 6660
Church Norton T 95 SZ 8795
Churchover T 119 SP 5180
Church Preen T 127 SO 5498
Church Pulverbatch T 126 SJ 4302
Churchstanton T 92 ST 1914
Church Stoke T 126 SO 2794
Churchstow T 89 SX 7145
Church Stowe T 119 SP 6357
Church Street T 98 TQ 7174
Church Stretton T 126 SO 4593
Churchtown, I. of M T 144 SC 4294
Churchtown, Lancs T 145 SD 4843
Churchtown, Mers T 136 SD 3518
Church Village T 109 ST 0886
Church Warsop T 139 SK 5668
Churchwell T 147 SE 2729
Church Westcote T 115 SP 2120
Churn Clough Reservoir W 146 SD 7838
Churnsike Lodge 158 NY 6677
Churt T 103 SU 8538
Churton T 126 SJ 4156
Churwell T 147 SE 2729
Chute Causeway R 102 SU 2955
Chwefri W 112 SO 0052
Chwilog T 134 SH 4338
Chyandour T 86 SW 4731
Chysauster A 86 SW 4535
Ciaran Water W 174 NN 2862
Cilan Uchaf T 124 SH 2923
Cilcain T 136 SJ 1765
Cilcennin T 111 SN 5260
Cilfaesty Hill H 116 SO 1384
Cilfor T 135 SH 6237
Cilfrew T 109 SN 7700
Cilfynydd T 109 ST 0892
Cilgerran T 111 SN 1943
Cilgwyn T 109 SN 7429
Ciliau-Aeron T 111 SN 5058
Cilleni W 109 SN 9034
Cilmaengwyn T 109 SN 7406
Cilmery T 112 SO 0051
Cilrhedyn T 111 SN 2835
Ciltwrch T 113 SO 1640
Cilurnum R 158 NY 9170
Cilwendeg T 111 SN 2238
Cilybebyll T 109 SN 7404
Cilycwm T 112 SN 7540
Cinderford T 114 SO 6514
Cioch Mhòr H 182 NH 5063
Cirean Geardail 196 NC 0134
Cirencester P 114 SP 0201
Cir Mhòr H 160 NR 9743
Cissbury Ring A 96 TQ 1308
Ciste Dhubh H 181 NH 0616
City Dulas T 134 SH 4787
City of London P 105 TQ 3281
City, The T 104 SU 7896
Clachaig T 168 NS 1181
Clachaig Water W 160 NR 7041
Clachan, Highld T 187 NG 5436
Clachan, Strath T 173 NM 7819
Clachan, Strath T 173 NM 8643
Clachan, Strath 168 NN 1812
Clachan, Strath T 160 NR 7656
Clachan-a-Luib T 188 NF 8163
Clachan Burn W 198 NC 7360
Clachan Hill H 168 NN 1815
Clachan Mór 172 NL 9747
Clachan of Campsie T 169 NS 6079
Clachan of Glendaruel T 168 NR 9984
Clachan-Seil T 173 NM 7818
Clachan Yell H 176 NO 4491
Clach Bheinn H 168 NS 2195
Clachbreck T 167 NR 7776
Clach Leathad H 174 NN 2349
Clachtoll T 196 NC 0427
Clackmannan T 170 NS 9191
Clacton-on-Sea P 107 TM 1714
Cladach an Eilein 195 NB 5365
Cladach Cuiashader 195 NB 5558
Cladach Dibadale 195 NB 5554
Claddach Kirkibost T 188 NF 7865
Cladich 168 NN 0921
Cladich River W 168 NN 1020
Claerwen Reservoir W 125 SN 8565
Claggain Bay W 166 NR 4653
Claggain River W 166 NR 4354
Claggan T 173 NM 6949
Clagh Ouyr H 144 SC 4188
Claife Heights 151 SD 3797
Claigan T 186 NG 2353
Claig Castle 166 NR 4762
Claines T 117 SO 8558
Clandown T 101 ST 6855
Clanfield, Hants T 95 SU 6916
Clanfield, Oxon T 115 SP 2802
Clannaborough Barton 91 SS 7402
Clanville T 102 SU 3149
Clanyard T 154 NX 1037
Clanyard Bay W 154 NX 0938
Claonaig T 160 NR 8756
Claonel T 192 NC 5604
Claonig Bay W 160 NR 8755
Clapgate T 94 SU 0102
Clapham, Beds T 120 TL 0253
Clapham, G. Lon T 105 TQ 2875
Clapham, N. Yks T 145 SD 7469
Clapham, W. Susx T 96 TQ 0906
Clappers T 165 NT 9455
Clappersgate T 150 NY 3603
Clapton T 92 ST 4106
Clapton-in-Gordano T 101 ST 4774
Clapton-on-the-Hill T 115 SP 1618
Clapworthy T 91 SS 6724
Clarbeston T 110 SN 0421
Clarbeston Road T 110 SN 0121
Clarborough T 140 SK 7383
Clardon T 199 ND 1568
Clardon Head 199 ND 1570
Clare T 122 TL 7745
Clarebrand T 156 NX 7666
Clarencefield T 157 NY 0968
Clarkston T 162 NS 5756
Clashindarroch 184 NJ 4831
Clashindarroch Forest F 184 NJ 4633
Clashmach Hill H 184 NJ 4938
Clashmore, Highld T 196 NC 0331
Clashmore, Highld T 193 NH 7489
Clashmore Wood F 193 NH 7491
Clashnessie T 196 NC 0530
Clashnessie Bay W 196 NC 0631
Clashnoir T 184 NJ 2222
Clathy 170 NN 9920
Clatt T 184 NJ 5426
Clatter T 125 SN 9994
Clatterin' Brig 177 NO 6678
Clatteringshaws Loch W 155 NX 5476
Clatto Hill H 171 NO 3506
Clatto Reservoir W 171 NO 3607
Clatworthy T 92 ST 0530
Clatworthy Reservoir W 92 ST 0431
Clauchlands Point 160 NS 0532
Claughton, Lancs T 145 SD 5342
Claughton, Lancs T 145 SD 5666
Clava Cairns A 183 NH 7544
Claverdon T 118 SP 1964
Claverham T 101 ST 4466
Clavering T 121 TL 4731
Claverley T 127 SO 7593
Claverton T 101 ST 7864
Clawdd-du-bach H 125 SN 8770
Clawdd-newydd T 135 SJ 0852
Clawton T 88 SX 3599
Claxby, Lincs T 141 TF 1194
Claxby, Lincs T 141 TF 4571
Claxton, Norf T 133 TG 3303
Claxton, N. Yks T 148 SE 6960
Claybokie T 176 NO 0890
Claybrooke Magna T 119 SP 4988
Clay Coton T 119 SP 5977
Clay Cross T 139 SK 3963
Claydon, Oxon T 119 SP 4550
Claydon, Suff T 123 TM 1350
Claygate T 105 TQ 1563
Claygate Cross T 97 TQ 6155
Clayhanger, Devon T 92 ST 0222
Clayhanger, W. Mids T 128 SK 0404
Clay Head 144 SC 4480
Clayhidon T 92 ST 1615
Clayock T 199 ND 1659
Clay of Allan 193 NH 8276
Claypole T 130 SK 8549
Clayton, Staffs T 127 SJ 8543
Clayton, S. Yks T 139 SE 4507
Clayton, W. Susx T 97 TQ 3014
Clayton, W. Yks T 146 SE 1231
Clayton-le-Moors T 145 SD 7431
Clayton-le-Woods T 145 SD 5622
Clayton West T 139 SE 2510
Clayworth T 140 SK 7388
Cleadale T 179 NM 4789
Cleadon T 159 NZ 3862
Clearbury Ring A 94 SU 1625
Clearwell T 113 SO 5708
Cleasby T 152 NZ 2513
Cleasby Hill H 152 NY 9707
Cleat, Orkney T 199 ND 4584
Cleat, W. Isles T 178 NF 6604
Cleatlam T 152 NZ 1118
Cleator T 150 NY 0113
Cleator Moor T 150 NY 0214
Cleckheaton T 146 SE 1825
Cledan W 112 SN 8845
Cleedownton T 116 SO 5880
Cleehill T 117 SO 5975
Clee St Margaret T 116 SO 5684
Cleethorpes T 143 TA 3008
Cleeton St Mary T 117 SO 6178
Cleeve T 101 ST 4565
Cleeve Hill T 114 SO 9826
Cleeve Prior T 118 SP 0849
Clehonger T 113 SO 4638
Cleigh T 168 NM 8725
Cleish T 170 NT 0998
Cleish Hills H 170 NT 0796
Cleite Leathann H 194 NB 0428
Cleland T 162 NS 7958
Clench Common T 102 SU 1765
Clenchwarton T 132 TF 5920
Clent T 117 SO 9379
Clent Hills H 117 SO 9479
Cleobury Mortimer T 117 SO 6776
Cleobury North T 117 SO 6287
Cleongart 160 NR 6734
Clephanton T 183 NH 8150
Clerklands T 164 NT 5024
Clestrain T 200 HY 3006
Clestrain Sound W 200 HY 2806
Clett 199 ND 1071
Clett Ard H 189 NB 1908
Clett Nisabost H 188 NG 0495
Clettraval H 190 NG 7572
Cleughbrae T 157 NY 0673
Clevancy T 102 SU 0575
Clevedon T 100 ST 4074
Clevedon Court A 101 ST 4271
Cleveland 153 NZ 6213
Cleveland Hills H 153 SE 5899
Cleveleys T 145 SD 3143
Cleverton T 102 ST 9785
Clewer T 101 ST 4351
Cley Hill H 101 ST 8344
Cley next the Sea T 132 TG 0443
Cliad Bay W 172 NM 1960
Cliasmol T 189 NB 0706
Cliburn T 151 NY 5824
Click Mill 200 HY 3222
Cliddesden T 103 SU 6349
Cliffe, Kent T 98 TQ 7376
Cliffe, N. Yks T 147 SE 6632
Cliffe Hill H 97 TQ 4310
Cliff End T 98 TQ 8813
Cliffe Woods T 98 TQ 7373
Clifford, H. & W T 113 SO 2445
Clifford, W. Yks T 147 SE 4244
Clifford Chambers T 118 SP 1952
Clifford's Mesne T 114 SO 7023
Cliffs End T 99 TR 3464
Clift Hills H 203 HU 3931
Clifton, Avon T 101 ST 5773
Clifton, Beds T 120 TL 1639
Clifton, Central T 168 NN 3230
Clifton, Cumbr T 151 NY 5326
Clifton, Derby T 128 SK 1644
Clifton, H. & W T 117 SO 8446
Clifton, Lancs T 145 SD 4630
Clifton, Northum T 159 NZ 2082
Clifton, Notts T 129 SK 5534
Clifton, Oxon T 115 SP 4831
Clifton Campville T 128 SK 2510
Clifton Hampden T 115 SU 5495
Clifton Reynes T 120 SP 9051
Clifton upon Dunsmore T 119 SP 5376
Clifton upon Teme T 117 SO 7161
Clift Sound W 203 HU 3933
Clifts, The 204 HU 3281
Climping T 96 SU 9902
Clint T 147 SE 2559
Clintburn 158 NY 7179
Clinterty 185 NJ 8311
Clint Green T 132 TG 0210
Clintmains T 164 NT 6132
Clints Dod H 164 NT 6268
Clints of Dromore H 155 NX 5464
Clippesby T 133 TG 4214
Clipsham T 130 SK 9716
Clipston, Northnts T 119 SP 7181
Clipston, Notts T 129 SK 6334
Clisham H 189 NB 1507
Clitheroe T 145 SD 7441
Clive T 127 SJ 5124
Clivocast T 205 HP 6000
Clocaenog T 135 SJ 0854
Clocaenog Forest F 135 SJ 0153
Clochan T 184 NJ 4061
Cloch Point 168 NS 2076
Clock Face T 137 SJ 5291
Cloddymoss T 183 NH 9860
Clodock T 113 SO 3227
Clola T 185 NK 0043
Clophill T 120 TL 0838
Clopton, Northnts T 120 TL 0680
Clopton, Suff T 123 TM 2252
Clopton Green T 122 TL 7654
Closeburn T 156 NX 8992
Close Clark T 144 SC 2775
Clothall T 121 TL 2731
Clothan 205 HU 4581
Clotton T 137 SJ 5263

Cruach Scarba

Disley

Cruach Scarba *H* 167 NM 6904
Cruach Tairbeirt *H* 168 NN 3105
Cruban Beag *H* 175 NN 6692
Crubenmore Lodge 175 NN 6791
Cruckmeole *T* 126 SJ 4309
Cruckton *T* 126 SJ 4310
Cruden Bay *T* 185 NK 0936
Crudgington *T* 127 SJ 6318
Crudwell *T* 102 ST 9592
Crûg *T* 116 SO 1972
Crug Hywel *A* 109 SO 2220
Crug Mawr *H* 113 SO 2622
Crugmeer *T* 87 SW 9076
Cruib *H* 166 NR 5684
Cruick Water *W* 177 NO 5964
Cruinn a' Bheinn *H* 169 NN 3605
Cruinn Bheinn *H* 169 NN 4312
Cruivie Castle *A* 171 NO 4122
Crulivig *T* 195 NB 1733
Crumlin *T* 109 ST 2198
Crummock Water *W* 150 NY 1519
Crumpton Hill *H* 157 NY 3491
Crundale, Dyfed *T* 110 SM 9718
Crundale, Kent *T* 99 TR 0749
Cruwys Morchard *T* 91 SS 8712
Crux Easton *T* 102 SU 4256
Cruys *H* 176 NO 4275
Crwbin *T* 111 SN 4713
Crychan Forest, Dyfed *F* 112 SN 8440
Crychan Forest, Powys *F* 112 SN 8440
Crymych *T* 111 SN 1834
Crynant *T* 109 SN 7905
Crystal Palace 105 TQ 3470
Cuaig *T* 190 NG 7057
Cubbington *T* 118 SP 3468
Cubert *T* 87 SW 7857
Cublington *T* 104 SP 8322
Cuckfield *T* 97 TQ 3024
Cucklington *T* 93 ST 7527
Cuckmere River *W* 97 TQ 5408
Cuckney *T* 139 SK 5671
Cudden Point 86 SW 5427
Cuddesdon *T* 115 SP 5903
Cuddington, Bucks *T* 104 SP 7310
Cuddington, Ches *T* 137 SJ 5971
Cuddington Heath *T* 127 SJ 4746
Cuddy Hill *T* 145 SD 4937
Cudham *T* 105 TQ 4459
Cudliptown *T* 89 SX 5279
Cudworth, Somer *T* 92 ST 3710
Cudworth, S. Yks *T* 139 SE 3808
Cuffley *T* 105 TL 3003
Cuiashader 195 NB 5458
Cuier 178 NF 6703
Cuilags *H* 200 HY 2003
Cuil Bay *W* 174 NM 9754
Cuillin Hills *H* 187 NG 4422
Culachy Forest 174 NN 3999
Culardoch *H* 176 NO 1998
Cùl Beag *H* 191 NC 1408
Culbin Forest *F* 183 NH 9962
Culblean Hill *H* 176 NJ 4001
Culbo *T* 182 NH 6360
Culbokie *T* 182 NH 6059
Culbone Hill *H* 91 SS 8247
Culburnie *T* 182 NH 4941
Culcabock *T* 183 NH 6844
Culcharry *T* 183 NH 8650
Culcheth *T* 137 SJ 6595
Cùl Doirlinn *T* 173 NM 6672
Culdrain *T* 184 NJ 5233
Culduie *T* 180 NG 7140
Culford *T* 122 TL 8370
Culgaith *T* 151 NY 6129
Culham *T* 115 SU 5095
Culkein *T* 196 NC 0333
Culkerton *T* 114 ST 9396
Cullachie *T* 183 NH 9720
Cullaloe Reservoir *W* 171 NT 1987
Cullen *T* 184 NJ 5167
Cullen Bay *W* 184 NJ 5068
Cullercoats *T* 159 NZ 3670
Cullicudden *T* 182 NH 6564
Culligran Falls *W* 182 NH 3740
Cullingworth *T* 146 SE 0636
Cullipool *T* 173 NM 7313
Cullisse 193 NH 8275
Cullivoe *T* 205 HP 5402
Culloch 169 NN 7817
Culloden Forest *F* 183 NH 7647
Culloden Muir 183 NH 7345
Cullompton *T* 92 ST 0107
Culmaily 193 NH 8099
Culmark Hill *H* 156 NX 6489
Culmington *T* 116 SO 4982
Cul Mòr *H* 196 NC 1611
Culmstock *T* 92 ST 1013
Culm Valley 92 ST 1013
Culnacraig *T* 191 NC 0603
Culnaknock *T* 187 NG 5162
Culrain *T* 192 NH 5794
Culross *T* 170 NS 9886
Culroy *T* 161 NS 3114
Culsh, Grampn *T* 185 NJ 8848
Culsh, Grampn 176 NO 3497
Culswick *T* 202 HU 2745
Culter Cleuch Shank *H* 163 NT 0322
Cultercullen *T* 185 NJ 9224
Culter Fell *H* 163 NT 0529
Culter Water *W* 163 NT 0329
Culter Waterhead Reservoir *W* 163 NT 0327
Cult Hill *H* 170 NT 0296
Cults, Grampn *T* 184 NJ 5331
Cults, Grampn *T* 185 NJ 8903
Culver Cliff 95 SZ 6385
Culverstone Green *T* 98 TQ 6363
Culverthorpe *T* 130 TF 0240
Culworth *T* 119 SP 5446
Culzean Bay *W* 161 NS 2411
Culzean Castle 161 NS 2310
Culzie Lodge 192 NH 5171
Cumbernauld *T* 169 NS 7574
Cumberworth *T* 141 TF 5073
Cumbrian Mountains *H* 150 NY 2716
Cuminestown *T* 185 NJ 8050
Cummersdale *T* 151 NY 3953
Cummertrees *T* 157 NY 1466
Cummingstown *T* 183 NJ 1369
Cumnock *T* 156 NS 5720
Cumnor *T* 115 SP 4604
Cumrew *T* 151 NY 5450
Cumwhinton *T* 151 NY 4552
Cumwhitton *T* 151 NY 5052
Cundall *T* 147 SE 4272
Cunndal *W* 195 NB 5165
Cunnigill Hill *H* 203 HU 4367
Cunninghame 161 NS 4046
Cunninghamhead *T* 161 NS 3741
Cunningsburgh 203 HU 4130
Cunnister *T* 205 HU 5296
Cupar *T* 171 NO 3714
Cupar Muir *T* 171 NO 3613
Curbar *T* 139 SK 2574
Curbridge, Hants *T* 95 SU 5211
Curbridge, Oxon *T* 115 SP 3308
Curdridge *T* 95 SU 5213
Curdworth *T* 128 SP 1893
Curland *T* 92 ST 2717
Curragh's, The 144 SC 3695
Currarie 154 NX 1690
Currarie Port *W* 154 NX 0578
Currie *T* 163 NT 1867
Curr, The *H* 165 NT 8523
Curry Mallet *T* 92 ST 3221
Curry Rivel *T* 92 ST 3925
Curtisden Green *T* 97 TQ 7440
Curtisknowle *T* 89 SX 7353
Cury *T* 86 SW 6721
Cushat Law *H* 158 NT 9213
Cushnie *T* 185 NJ 7962
Cushuish *T* 92 ST 1930
Cusop *T* 113 SO 2341
Cut Hill *H* 89 SX 5982
Cutiau *T* 125 SH 6317
Cutnall Green *T* 117 SO 8868
Cutsdean *T* 114 SP 0830
Cutthorpe *T* 139 SK 3473
Cutts 203 HU 4038
Cuxham *T* 104 SU 6695
Cuxton *T* 98 TQ 7066
Cuxwold *T* 143 TA 1701
Cwm, Clwyd *T* 135 SJ 0677
Cwm, Gwent *T* 109 SO 1805
Cwmafan *T* 109 SS 7892
Cwmaman *T* 109 ST 0099
Cwmann *T* 111 SN 5847
Cwmavon *T* 113 SO 2706
Cwmbach, Dyfed *T* 111 SN 2526
Cwmbach, M. Glam *T* 109 SO 0202
Cwmbelan *T* 125 SN 9481
Cwmbran *P* 113 ST 2995
Cwm Bychan 135 SH 6431
Cwmcarn *T* 109 ST 2194
Cwmcarvan *T* 113 SO 4707
Cwm-Cewydd *T* 125 SH 8713
Cwm-Cou *T* 111 SN 2941
Cwm Croes 125 SH 8825
Cwm Cynllwyd 125 SH 8927
Cwmdare *T* 109 SN 9803
Cwmdu, Dyfed *T* 111 SN 6330
Cwmdu, Powys *T* 109 SO 1823
Cwmduad *T* 111 SN 3731
Cwm Einion 125 SN 7094
Cwmfelin Boeth *T* 111 SN 1919
Cwmfelinfach *T* 109 ST 1891
Cwmfelin Mynach *T* 111 SN 2324
Cwmffrwd *T* 111 SN 4217
Cwmgwrach *T* 109 SN 8605
Cwm Irfon *T* 112 SN 8549
Cwmisfael *T* 111 SN 4916
Cwm-Llinau *T* 125 SH 8407
Cwmllynfell *T* 109 SN 7412
Cwm Nantcol 125 SH 6425
Cwmparc *T* 109 SS 9596
Cwmpengraig *T* 111 SN 3536
Cwm Prysor 135 SH 7536
Cwmsychbant *T* 111 SN 4746
Cwmtillery *T* 109 SO 2105
Cwm-twrch Isaf *T* 109 SN 7610
Cwm-twrch Uchaf *T* 109 SN 7611
Cwmtydu 111 SN 3557
Cwm-y-glo *T* 134 SH 5562
Cwmyoy *T* 113 SO 3023
Cwmystwyth *T* 125 SN 7874
Cwn Ceulan 125 SN 6990
Cwrtnewydd *T* 111 SN 4847
Cwrt-y-cadno *T* 112 SN 6944
Cwrt-y-gollen *T* 113 SO 2317
Cyffylliog *T* 135 SJ 0657
Cyfronydd *T* 126 SJ 1307
Cymmer, M. Glam *T* 109 ST 0290
Cymmer, W. Glam *T* 109 SS 8696
Cymmer Abbey *A* 125 SH 7219
Cymyran Bay *W* 134 SH 2974
Cynghordy *T* 112 SN 8039
Cynwyd *T* 135 SJ 0541
Cynwyl Elfed *T* 111 SN 3727
Cyrn-y-Brain *H* 126 SJ 2149

D

Daaey 205 HU 6094
Dacre, Cumbr *T* 151 NY 4526
Dacre, N. Yks *T* 146 SE 1960
Dacre Banks *T* 146 SE 1961
Daddry Shield *T* 152 NY 8937
Dadford *T* 119 SP 6638
Dadlington *T* 128 SP 4098
Daer Reservoir *W* 156 NS 9707
Dafen *T* 108 SN 5201
Dagenham *P* 105 TQ 5084
Daglingworth *T* 114 SO 9905
Dagnall *T* 104 SP 9916
Daill 166 NR 3662
Dailly *T* 161 NS 2701
Dairsie or Osnaburgh *T* 171 NO 4117
Dalavich *T* 168 NM 9612
Dalbeattie *T* 156 NX 8361
Dalbeattie Forest *F* 156 NX 8558
Dalbeg *T* 195 NB 2345
Dalbeg Bay *W* 195 NB 2246
Dalblair *T* 156 NS 6419
Dalbog 177 NO 5771
Dalby *T* 144 SC 2278
Dalby Point 144 SC 2178
Dalcapon 176 NN 9754
Dalchalloch *T* 175 NN 7264
Dalchenna *T* 168 NN 0705
Dalchork 197 NC 5710
Dalchreichart *T* 182 NH 2912
Dalchruin 169 NN 7116
Dalcross 183 NH 7748
Dalderby *T* 141 TF 2466
Dale, Derby *T* 128 SK 4338
Dale, Dyfed *T* 110 SM 8005
Dale, Shetld *T* 202 HU 1852
Dale Dike Reservoir *W* 139 SK 2491
Dale Head *T* 151 NY 4316
Dalelia 173 NM 7369
Dale Point 110 SM 8205
Dales Head Dike *W* 141 TF 1563
Dales Voe, Shetld *W* 205 HU 4370
Dales Voe, Shetld *W* 203 HU 4545
Dalgarven *T* 161 NS 2945
Dalgety Bay, Fife *W* 170 NT 1783
Dalgety Bay, Strath *T* 170 NT 1684
Dalgig 161 NS 5512
Dalginross *T* 169 NN 7721
Dalguise 176 NN 9947
Dalhalvaig *T* 198 NC 8954
Dalham *T* 122 TL 7261
Daliburgh *T* 178 NF 7521
Dalinlongart Hill *H* 168 NS 1481
Dalkeith *T* 164 NT 3367
Dallas *T* 183 NJ 1252
Dallas Forest *F* 183 NJ 1253
Dall Burn *W* 175 NN 5754
Dalleagles *T* 161 NS 5110
Dalle Crucis Abbey *A* 126 SJ 2044
Dallinghoo *T* 123 TM 2655
Dallington *T* 97 TQ 6519
Dallowgill Moor 146 SE 1671
Dalmacallan Forest *F* 156 NX 8087
Dalmally *T* 168 NN 1627
Dalmary *T* 169 NS 5195
Dalmellington *T* 161 NS 4806
Dalmeny *T* 170 NT 1477
Dalmeny House 170 NT 1677
Dalmigavie 183 NH 7419
Dalmigavie Lodge 183 NH 7523
Dalmore, Highld *T* 183 NH 6668
Dalmore, W. Isles *T* 195 NB 2144
Dalmunzie Hotel 176 NO 0971
Dalnabreck *T* 173 NM 7069
Dalnacardoch Forest 175 NN 6875
Dalnacardoch Lodge 175 NN 7270
Dalnacreich *T* 182 NH 3155
Dalnaglar Castle 176 NO 1464
Dalnamein Forest 175 NN 7777
Dalnaspidal Lodge 175 NN 6473
Dalnavie *T* 192 NH 6473
Dalnawillan Lodge 199 ND 0340
Dalness 174 NN 1651
Dalnessie 197 NC 6315
Da Logat 202 HT 9541
Dalqueich 170 NO 0804
Dalquhairn 154 NX 3296
Dalquharran Castle 161 NS 2702
Dalreavoch *T* 193 NC 7508
Dalry *T* 161 NS 2949
Dalrymple *T* 161 NS 3544
Dalserf *T* 162 NS 7950
Dalston *T* 150 NY 3650
Dalswinton *T* 156 NX 9385
Dalton, D. & G *T* 157 NY 1174
Dalton, Lancs *T* 137 SD 4908
Dalton, Northum *T* 158 NY 9158
Dalton, Northum *T* 159 NZ 1172
Dalton, N. Yks *T* 152 NZ 1108
Dalton, N. Yks *T* 147 SE 4376
Dalton, S. Yks *T* 139 SK 4694
Dalton-in-Furness *T* 144 SD 2373
Dalton-le-Dale *T* 153 NZ 4048
Dalton-on-Tees *T* 152 NZ 2907
Dalton Piercy *T* 153 NZ 4631
Dalveich 169 NN 6124
Dalvina Lodge 197 NC 6943
Dalwhat Water *W* 156 NX 7294
Dalwhinnie *T* 175 NN 6385
Dalwood *T* 92 ST 2500
Damerham *T* 94 SU 1015
Damflask Reservoir *W* 139 SK 2791
Damgate *T* 133 TG 4009
Damnaglaur *T* 154 NX 1235
Dam of Hoxa *W* 200 ND 4294
Damsay 200 HY 3913
Danbury *T* 106 TL 7805
Danby *T* 148 NZ 7008
Danby Low Moor 153 NZ 7110
Danby Wiske *T* 152 SE 3398
Dandalieth 184 NJ 2846
Danderhall *T* 171 NT 3069
Danebridge, Ches *T* 138 SJ 9665
Danebridge, Staffs *T* 138 SJ 9665
Danebury *A* 94 SU 3237
Dane End *T* 105 TL 3321
Danehill *T* 97 TQ 4027
Dane's Brook *W* 91 SS 8331
Danes' Dyke *A* 149 TA 2171
Danskine 164 NT 5667
Dan-yr-Ogof 109 SN 8315
Darden Lough *W* 159 NY 9795
Darenth *T* 105 TQ 5671
Daresbury *T* 137 SJ 5782
Darfield *T* 139 SE 4104
Dargate *T* 99 TR 0761
Darite *T* 87 SX 2569
Darlaston *T* 128 SO 9897
Darley Dale *T* 139 SK 2763
Darlingscote *T* 118 SP 2342
Darlington *P* 152 NZ 2914
Darliston *T* 127 SJ 5833
Darlochan 160 NR 6723
Darlton *T* 140 SK 7773
Darnaw *H* 155 NX 5176
Darnaway Forest, Grampn *F* 183 NH 9852
Darnaway Forest, Highld *F* 183 NH 9852
Darnbrook Fell 146 SD 8872
Darowen *T* 125 SH 8301
Darra *T* 185 NJ 7447
Darras Hall *T* 159 NZ 1571
Darrington *T* 139 SE 4820
Darsham *T* 123 TM 4169
Dartford *T* 105 TQ 5474
Dartington *T* 89 SX 7862
Dartington Hall *A* 89 SX 7962
Dartmeet *T* 89 SX 6773
Dartmoor 89 SX 6276
Dartmoor Forest 89 SX 6180
Dartmouth *T* 89 SX 8751
Darton *T* 139 SE 3110
Darvel *T* 162 NS 5637
Darwell Reservoir *W* 97 TQ 7121
Darwen *T* 145 SD 6922
Da Scrodhurdins 202 HT 9339
Datchet *T* 104 SU 9877
Datchworth *T* 105 TL 2719
Daugh of Cairnborrow 184 NJ 4541
Daugh of Carron 184 NJ 2239
Daugh of Invermarkie 184 NJ 4141
Daugh of Kinermony *T* 184 NJ 2441
Dauntsey *T* 102 ST 9982
Davenham *T* 137 SJ 6671
Daventry *T* 119 SP 5762
Daventry Reservoir *W* 119 SP 5863
Davidstow *T* 88 SX 1587
Davington *T* 157 NT 2302
Daviot, Grampn *T* 185 NJ 7528
Daviot, Highld *T* 183 NH 7239
Davoch of Grange *T* 184 NJ 4751
Dawley *T* 127 SJ 6807
Dawlish *T* 89 SX 9676
Dawlish Warren *T* 89 SX 9778
Dawn *T* 135 SH 8672
Dawpool Bank 136 SJ 2381
Daws Heath *T* 106 TQ 8189
Dawsmere *T* 131 TF 4430
Daylesford *T* 115 SP 2426
Ddôl Cownwy *T* 125 SJ 0117
Ddyle *H* 125 SO 0575
Deadh Choimhead *H* 168 NM 9428
Deadwater 158 NY 6096
Deal *T* 99 TR 3752
Deal Hall 107 TR 0197
Dean, Cumbr *T* 150 NY 0725
Dean, Devon *T* 89 SX 7364
Dean, Hants *T* 95 SU 5619
Dean, Somer *T* 101 ST 6744
Deanburnhaugh *T* 157 NT 3911
Deane *T* 103 SU 5450
Dean Hill *H* 94 SU 2526
Deanich Lodge 191 NH 3683
Deanland *T* 94 ST 9918
Dean Prior *T* 89 SX 7363
Dean Row *T* 137 SJ 8781
Deans *T* 163 NT 0268
Deanscales *T* 150 NY 0926
Deanshanger *T* 119 SP 7639
Deanston *T* 169 NN 7101
Dean Water *W* 176 NO 4049
Dearg Abhainn *W* 174 NM 9739
Dearham *T* 150 NY 0736
Dearne *T* 139 SE 4604
Deasker 188 NF 6466
Debach *T* 123 TM 2454
Debden *T* 121 TL 5533
Debden Green *T* 121 TL 5732
Debenham *T* 123 TM 1763
Dechmont *T* 170 NT 0470
Deddington *T* 115 SP 4631
Dedham *T* 122 TM 0632
Dedridge *T* 163 NT 0666
Deene *T* 120 SP 9492
Deenethorpe *T* 120 SP 9591
Deepcar *T* 139 SK 2897
Deepcut *T* 103 SU 9057
Deepdale, Cumbr *T* 145 SD 7284
Deep Dale, Durham 152 NY 9715
Deeping Fen 130 TF 1916
Deeping Gate *T* 130 TF 1509
Deeping St James *T* 130 TF 1509
Deeping St Nicholas *T* 130 TF 2115
Deeps, The *W* 203 HU 3241
Deerhill *T* 184 NJ 4556
Deerhurst *T* 114 SO 8729
Deer Law *H* 163 NT 2225
Deerlee Knowe *H* 158 NT 7108
Deerness *T* 200 HY 5606
Deerplay Moor 146 SD 8627
Deer's Hill *H* 185 NJ 8045
Deer Sound *W* 200 HY 5308
Defford *T* 117 SO 9243
Defynnog *T* 109 SN 9227
Deganwy *T* 135 SH 7879
Deighton, N. Yks *T* 153 NZ 3801
Deighton, N. Yks *T* 147 SE 6244
Deil's Caldron *W* 169 NN 7623
Deil's Heid, The 177 NO 6741
Deiniolen *T* 134 SH 5863
Delabole *T* 88 SX 0683
Delamere *T* 137 SJ 5669
Delamere Forest *F* 137 SJ 5571
Delamere Station 137 SJ 5570
De Lank River *W* 87 SX 1376
Delfrigs *T* 185 NJ 9721
Delgatie Castle 185 NJ 7550
Delgaty Forest 185 NJ 7748
Dell *T* 195 NB 4961
Delliefure *T* 183 NJ 0730
Dell Lodge 183 NJ 0119
Dell River *W* 195 NB 5059
Delnadamph Lodge 184 NJ 2208
Delph *T* 138 SD 9808
Delph Bank 131 TF 3821
Delph Reservoir *W* 137 SD 7015
Delph, The 122 TL 7080
Delvine 176 NO 1240
Dembleby *T* 130 TF 0437
Denbigh *T* 135 SJ 0566
Denbury *T* 89 SX 8269
Denby *T* 128 SK 3946
Denby Dale *T* 139 SE 2208
Denchworth *T* 102 SU 3891
Dene Mouth *W* 153 NZ 4540
Denend 184 NJ 6038
Denford *T* 120 SP 9976
Denge Beach 99 TR 0718
Denge Marsh 99 TR 0520
Dengie, Essex *T* 107 TL 9801
Dengie, Essex *T* 107 TL 9901
Dengie Flat 107 TM 0404
Denham, Bucks *T* 104 TQ 0486
Denham, Suff *T* 122 TL 7561
Denham, Suff *T* 123 TM 1974
Denham Castle 122 TL 7462
Denham Green *T* 104 TQ 0388
Denham Street *T* 123 TM 1872
Denhead, Fife *T* 171 NO 4613
Denhead, Grampn *T* 185 NK 0052
Denhead of Arbirlot 177 NO 5742
Denhead of Gray 171 NO 3431
Denholm *T* 158 NT 5618
Denholme *T* 146 SE 0734
Denmead *T* 95 SU 6511
Denmore *T* 185 NJ 9411
Denne Park *T* 96 TQ 1629
Dennington *T* 123 TM 2867
Dennis Head 201 HY 7955
Denny *T* 169 NS 8182
Denny Island, Avon 101 ST 4581
Denny Island, Gwent 101 ST 4581
Dennyloanhead *T* 169 NS 8180
Denny Lodge 94 SU 3305
Denshaw *T* 138 SD 9710
Denside *T* 177 NO 8095
Densole *T* 99 TR 2141
Denston *T* 122 TL 7652
Denstone *T* 128 SK 0940
Dent *T* 145 SD 7086
Dentdale 145 SD 7186
Den, The *T* 161 NS 3251
Denton, Cambs *T* 120 TL 1587
Denton, Durham *T* 152 NZ 2118
Denton, E. Susx *T* 97 TQ 4502
Denton, G. Man *T* 137 SJ 9295
Denton, Kent *T* 99 TR 2147
Denton, Lincs *T* 130 SK 8632
Denton, Norf *T* 123 TM 2788
Denton, Northnts *T* 120 SP 8358
Denton, N. Yks *T* 146 SE 1448
Denton, Oxon *T* 115 SP 5902
Denton Fell *H* 158 NY 6262
Denver *T* 132 TF 6101
Denwick, Northum *T* 159 NU 2014
Den Wick, Orkney *W* 201 HY 5809
Deopham *T* 132 TG 0500
Deopham Green *T* 132 TM 0499
Depden Green *T* 122 TL 7757
Deptford, G. Lon *T* 105 TQ 3676
Deptford, Wilts *T* 94 SU 0537
Derby *P* 128 SK 3536
Derbyhaven *T* 144 SC 2867
Dere Street, Border *R* 164 NT 6326
Dere Street, Durham *A* 152 NZ 2119
Dere Street, Northum *R* 158 NY 9278
Dere Street, Northum *A* 152 NZ 0757
Dere Street, N. Yks *A* 147 SE 4363
Dergoals 154 NX 2459
Deri *T* 109 SO 1202
Dernaglar Loch *W* 154 NX 2658
Derringstone 99 TR 2049
Derrington *T* 127 SJ 8922
Derry Burn *W* 176 NO 0397
Derry Cairngorm *H* 176 NO 0198
Derryguaig *T* 173 NM 4935
Derry Hill *T* 102 ST 9670
Derrythorpe *T* 142 SE 8208
Dersalloch Hill *H* 161 NS 4203
Dersingham *T* 132 TF 6830
Dervaig *T* 173 NM 4352
Derventio Roman Fort *R* 150 NY 1131
Derwen *T* 135 SJ 0750
Derwent Reservoir, Derby *W* 138 SK 1791
Derwent Reservoir, Durham *W* 152 NZ 0152
Derwent Reservoir, Northum *W* 152 NZ 0152
Derwent Water *W* 150 NY 2420
Desborough *T* 119 SP 8083
Desford *T* 129 SK 4703
Deskry Water *W* 184 NJ 3807
Detchant *T* 165 NU 0836
Dethenydd 125 SO 0283
Detling *T* 98 TQ 7958
Deuchar Hill *H* 177 NO 4662
Deuchar Law *H* 163 NT 2829
Deuchary Hill *H* 176 NO 0348
Deuddwr *T* 126 SJ 2417
Deva *R* 136 SJ 4066
Devauden *T* 113 ST 4899
Devilla Forest *F* 170 NS 9688
Devil's Beef Tub 157 NT 0612
Devil's Bridge *T* 125 SN 7477
Devil's Causeway *R* 159 NU 1202
Devil's Ditch *A* 122 TL 6062
Devil's Dyke, Norf *A* 132 TF 7408
Devil's Dyke, W. Susx *A* 96 TQ 2611
Devil's Elbow 176 NO 1476
Devil's Point, The *H* 176 NN 9795
Devil's Water *W* 152 NY 9356
Devizes *T* 102 SU 0061
Devoke Water *W* 150 SD 1596
Devonport *T* 88 SX 4554
Devonside *T* 170 NS 9296
Devoran *T* 87 SW 7939
Dewlish *T* 93 SY 7798
Dewsall Court 113 SO 4833
Dewsbury *P* 147 SE 2422
Dhoon *T* 144 SC 4586
Dhoor *T* 144 SC 4496
Dhowin *T* 144 NX 4101
Dial Post *T* 96 TQ 1519
Diaval *H* 195 NB 4552
Dibden *T* 94 SU 4007
Dibden Purlieu *T* 94 SU 4106
Dibyn Du *H* 125 SN 7965
Dickleburgh *T* 123 TM 1782
Didbrook *T* 114 SP 0531
Didcot *T* 103 SU 5189
Diddington *T* 120 TL 1965
Diddlebury *T* 116 SO 5085
Didley *T* 113 SO 4532
Didmarton *T* 101 ST 8287
Didsbury *T* 137 SJ 8591
Didworthy *T* 89 SX 6862
Diebidale Forest 192 NH 4584
Diebidale River *W* 192 NH 4583
Diffwys *H* 125 SH 6623
Digby *T* 130 TF 0854
Diggle *T* 138 SE 0001
Dighty Water *W* 171 NO 4632
Dihewyd *T* 111 SN 4856
Dilham *T* 133 TG 3325
Dilhorne *T* 128 SJ 9743
Dilston *T* 159 NY 9763
Dilton Marsh *T* 101 ST 8549
Dilwyn *T* 113 SO 4154
Dinam 135 SJ 0133
Dinas, Dyfed *T* 111 SN 2730
Dinas, Gwyn *T* 134 SH 2736
Dinas Cross *T* 110 SN 0138
Dinas Dinorwig *A* 134 SH 5565
Dinas Head 110 SN 0141
Dinas Mawddwy *T* 125 SH 8514
Dinas Powys *T* 109 ST 1571
Dinchope *T* 116 SO 4584
Dinder *T* 101 ST 5744
Dinedor *T* 113 SO 5336
Dines Green *T* 117 SO 8255
Din Fell *H* 157 NY 4696
Dingestow *T* 113 SO 4510
Dingley *T* 119 SP 7787
Dingwall *T* 182 NH 5559
Din Lligwy *A* 134 SH 4986
Dinnet *T* 177 NO 4698
Dinnings Hill *H* 157 NY 2297
Dinnington, Somer *T* 92 ST 4012
Dinnington, S. Yks *T* 139 SK 5386
Dinnington, T. & W *T* 159 NZ 2073
Dinorwig *T* 134 SH 5861
Dinsdale Station 153 NZ 3413
Dinton, Bucks *T* 104 SP 7610
Dinton, Wilts *T* 94 SU 0131
Dinwoodie Mains *T* 157 NY 1090
Dinworthy *T* 90 SS 3115
Diollaid Mhòr *H* 160 NR 7739
Dippen *T* 160 NR 7937
Dippenhall *T* 103 SU 8146
Dippin *T* 160 NS 0422
Dippin Head 160 NS 0522
Dipple, Grampn *T* 184 NJ 3258
Dipple, Strath *T* 161 NS 2002
Diptford *T* 89 SX 7256
Dipton *T* 152 NZ 1553
Dirleton *T* 171 NT 5184
Dirrie More 191 NH 2375
Dirrington Great Law *H* 164 NT 6954
Dirrington Little Law *H* 164 NT 6853
Discoed *T* 116 SO 2764
Diseworth *T* 129 SK 4524
Dishes *T* 201 HY 6523
Dishforth *T* 147 SE 3873
Disley *T* 138 SJ 9784

E

F

Fife Ness Gallanach

Fife Ness 171 NO 6309
Fifield, Berks T 104 SU 9076
Fifield, Oxon T 115 SP 2418
Figheldean T 102 SU 1547
Figsbury Ring A 94 SU 1833
Filby T 133 TG 4613
Filey T 149 TA 1180
Filey Bay W 149 TA 1379
Filgrave T 120 SP 8748
Filkins T 115 SP 2404
Filla 205 HU 6668
Filleigh, Devon T 91 SS 6627
Filleigh, Devon T 91 SS 7410
Fill Geo 205 HP 5708
Fillingham T 140 SK 9485
Fillongley T 118 SP 2887
Filton T 101 ST 6079
Fimber T 149 SE 8960
Finalty Hill H 176 NO 2175
Finavon 177 NO 4956
Finavon Castle 177 NO 4956
Finbracks H 176 NO 4070
Finchale Priory A 152 NZ 2947
Fincham T 132 TF 6806
Fincharn 168 NM 9003
Finchdean T 95 SU 7312
Finchhampstead T 104 SU 7963
Finchingfield T 122 TL 6832
Finchley T 105 TQ 2590
Findern T 128 SK 3030
Findhorn T 183 NJ 0464
Findhorn Bay W 183 NJ 0462
Findhorn Bridge 183 NH 8027
Findhu Glen 169 NN 7214
Findochty T 184 NJ 4668
Findo Gask 170 NO 0020
Findon, Grampn T 177 NO 9397
Findon, W. Susx T 96 TQ 1208
Findon Mains 182 NH 6060
Findon Ness 177 NO 9497
Findrack House 184 NJ 6004
Finedon T 120 SP 9272
Fingal's Cave 172 NM 3235
Fingal Street T 123 TM 2369
Fingask T 185 NJ 7827
Fingask Castle 171 NO 2227
Fingest T 104 SU 7791
Finghall T 152 SE 1889
Fingland T 156 NS 7517
Fingland Fell H 157 NY 1494
Finglen Burn W 169 NN 6833
Finglen Rig H 163 NT 1332
Fingringhoe T 107 TM 0320
Finlarig 169 NN 5733
Finlas Water W 168 NS 3388
Finlaystone 169 NS 3673
Finmere T 119 SP 6332
Finnart 175 NN 5156
Finnarts Bay W 154 NX 0572
Finningham T 122 TM 0669
Finningley T 139 SK 6799
Finnygaud T 184 NJ 6054
Finsbay T 189 NG 0786
Finsbury T 105 TQ 3182
Finsthwaite T 145 SD 3687
Finstock T 115 SP 3616
Finstown T 200 HY 3513
Fintry, Grampn T 185 NJ 7554
Fintry, Strath T 169 NS 6186
Finzean T 177 NO 6092
Fiodday 178 NF 7502
Fionn Bheinn H 191 NH 1462
Fionn Bheinn Mhór H 191 NC 3704
Fionn Lighe W 174 NM 9682
Fionn Loch, Highld W 196 NC 1317
Fionn Loch, Highld W 190 NG 9478
Fionn Loch Mór W 196 NC 3323
Fionnphort, Strath T 172 NM 3023
Fionn Phort, Strath W 160 NR 9064
Firbank T 151 SD 6294
Firbeck T 139 SK 5688
Fire Beacon Point 88 SX 1092
Firgrove T 137 SD 9213
Firle Beacon H 97 TQ 4805
Firsby T 141 TF 4563
Firth T 205 HU 4473
Firth of Clyde W 161 NS 1456
Firth of Forth W 171 NT 3887
Firth of Lorn W 173 NM 7121
Firth of Tay W 171 NO 4028
Firths Voe W 205 HU 4473
Firth, The W 203 HU 3450
Fir Tree T 152 NZ 1434
Fishbourne, I. of W T 95 SZ 5592
Fishbourne, W. Susx T 95 SU 8304
Fishburn T 153 NZ 3631
Fishcross T 170 NS 9095
Fisherfield Forest 190 NH 0180
Fisherford T 184 NJ 6735
Fisher's Pond T 95 SU 4820
Fisherstreet T 96 SU 9531
Fisher Tarn Reservoir W 151 SD 5592
Fisherton, Highld T 183 NH 7451
Fisherton, Strath T 161 NS 2717
Fishguard P 110 SM 9537
Fishguard Bay W 110 SM 9739
Fish Holm 205 HU 4774
Fishlake T 139 SE 6513
Fishnish Bay W 173 NM 6442
Fishpool T 137 SD 8009
Fishtoft T 131 TF 3642
Fishtoft Drove T 131 TF 3149
Fishtown of Usan T 177 NO 7254
Fishwick T 165 NT 9151
Fiskavaig T 186 NG 3233
Fiskerton, Lincs T 140 TF 0572
Fiskerton, Notts T 129 SK 7351
Fistral Bay W 87 SW 7862
Fitful Head 203 HU 3413
Fittleton T 102 SU 1449
Fittleworth T 96 TQ 0119
Fitton End T 131 TF 4212
Fitty Hill H 200 HY 4244
Fitz T 126 SJ 4417
Fitzhead T 92 ST 1228
Fitzwilliam T 139 SE 4115
Fiunary T 173 NM 6246
Five Ashes T 97 TQ 5525
Fivehead T 92 ST 3522
Five Oak Green T 97 TQ 6445
Five Oaks T 96 TQ 0928
Five Penny Borve T 195 NB 4056
Five Penny Ness T 195 NB 5264
Five Roads T 111 SN 4905
Five Sisters H 180 NG 9716
Flackwell Heath T 104 SU 8989
Fladbury T 118 SO 9946
Fladda, Strath 172 NM 2943
Fladda, Strath 173 NM 7212
Fladdabister T 203 HU 4332
Fladda-chùain 189 NG 3681
Flag Fen 131 TL 2894
Flagg T 138 SK 1368
Flamborough T 149 TA 2270
Flamborough Head 149 TA 2570
Flamstead T 104 TL 0714
Flanders Moss, Central F 169 NS 5595
Flanders Moss, Central F 169 NS 6398
Flannan Isles 194 NA 7246
Flansham T 96 SU 9601
Flasby T 146 SD 9456
Flash T 138 SK 0267
Flashader T 186 NG 3553
Flashes, The 153 NZ 6125
Flat Holm 100 ST 2264
Flatt, The 158 NY 5678
Flaunden T 104 TL 0100
Flawborough T 129 SK 7842
Flawith T 147 SE 4865
Flax Bourton T 101 ST 5069
Flaxby T 147 SE 3958
Flaxfleet T 142 SE 8624
Flaxley T 114 SO 6915
Flaxpool T 92 ST 1435
Flaxton T 148 SE 6862
Fleam Dyke A 121 TL 5553
Fleckney T 129 SP 6493
Flecknoe T 119 SP 5163
Fleet, Hants T 103 SU 8154
Fleet, Lincs T 131 TF 3823
Fleet Bay W 155 NX 5652
Fleet Hargate T 131 TF 3924
Fleetwood P 145 SD 3247
Fleggburgh or Burgh St Margaret T 133 TG 4414
Flemingston T 109 ST 0170
Flemington T 162 NS 6559
Flempton T 122 TL 8170
Fleshwick Bay W 144 SC 2071
Fletching T 97 TQ 4323
Flexbury T 90 SS 2107
Flexford T 96 SU 9350
Flicham T 132 TF 7226
Flimby T 150 NY 0233
Flimwell T 97 TQ 7131
Flint T 136 SJ 2473
Flintham T 129 SK 7446
Flint Mountain T 136 SJ 2470
Flinton T 143 TA 2236
Flitcham T 132 TF 7226
Flitton T 120 TL 0535
Flitwick T 120 TL 0334
Flixborough T 142 SE 8715
Flixton, G. Man T 137 SJ 7494
Flixton, N. Yks T 149 TA 0479
Flixton, Suff T 123 TM 3186
Float Bay W 154 NX 0647
Flockton T 139 SE 2415
Flodabay T 189 NG 0988
Floday, W. Isles 195 NB 1033
Floday, W. Isles 195 NB 1241
Flodda 188 NF 8455
Flodday 178 NL 6192
Floddaybeg 188 NF 9257
Floddaymore 188 NF 9157
Flodden T 165 NT 9235
Flodigarry 187 NG 4671
Flookburgh T 145 SD 3675
Floors Castle 164 NT 7134
Flordon T 133 TM 1897
Flore T 119 SP 6460
Flossnan 186 NG 2337
Flotta, Orkney 200 ND 3593
Flotta, Shetld 203 HU 3746
Flotterton T 159 NT 9902
Flounden T 104 TL 0100
Flowerdale Forest 190 NG 8967
Flowton T 123 TM 0846
Flushing, Corn T 87 SW 8033
Flushing, Grampn T 185 NK 0546
Flyford Flavell T 118 SO 9855
Flyingdales Moor 149 SE 9199
Fobbing T 106 TQ 7184
Fochabers T 184 NJ 3458
Fochriw T 109 SO 1005
Fockerby T 142 SE 8419
Fodder Fen 121 TL 5387
Fodderletter 183 NJ 1421
Fodderty T 182 NH 5159
Foel T 125 SH 9911
Foel Cwmcerwyn H 110 SN 0931
Foel-drych H 110 SN 1630
Foel Eryr H 110 SN 0632
Foel Fenlli A 136 SJ 1660
Foel Figenau H 125 SH 9128
Foel Fraith H 109 SN 7518
Foel-fras H 135 SH 6968
Foel Fynyddau H 109 SS 7893
Foel Goch, Clwyd H 135 SH 9542
Foel Goch, Gwyn H 135 SH 9542
Foel Gurig H 125 SH 9078
Foell Rhudd H 125 SH 8923
Foel Rhiwlas H 126 SJ 2032
Foel Wen H 135 SJ 1033
Foel-y-ffridd H 125 SH 8311
Foel y Geifr H 125 SH 9327
Foffarty 176 NO 4145
Foggathorpe T 142 SE 7537
Fogla Skerry 202 HU 1461
Fogo T 164 NT 7749
Foinaven H 196 NC 3149
Foindle T 196 NC 1948
Folda T 176 NO 1864
Fole T 128 SK 0437
Foleshill T 118 SP 3582
Folke T 93 ST 6513
Folkestone P 99 TR 2235
Folkingham T 130 TF 0733
Folkington T 97 TQ 5503
Folksworth T 120 TL 1489
Folkton T 149 TA 0579
Folla Rule T 185 NJ 7333
Follifoot T 147 SE 3452
Folly Gate T 89 SX 5797
Fontburn Reservoir W 159 NZ 0493
Fonthill Bishop T 94 ST 9332
Fonthill Gifford T 93 ST 9231
Fontmell Magna T 93 ST 8616
Fontwell T 96 SU 9507
Foolow T 138 SK 1976
Foots Cray T 105 TQ 4770
Foot, The 200 HY 5315
Fora Ness, Shetld 203 HU 3517
Fora Ness, Shetld 205 HU 4571
Forcett T 152 NZ 1712
Ford, Bucks T 104 SP 7709
Ford, Devon T 89 SX 7840
Ford, Glos T 114 SP 0829
Ford, Mers T 136 SJ 3398
Ford, Northum T 165 NT 9437
Ford, Shrops T 126 SJ 4113
Ford, Staffs T 128 SK 0654
Ford, Strath T 168 NM 8603
Ford, Wilts T 101 ST 8474
Ford, W. Susx T 96 TQ 0003
Fordcombe T 97 TQ 5240
Forde Abbey A 92 ST 3505
Fordell T 170 NT 1588
Fordell Castle A 170 NT 1485
Forden T 126 SJ 2201
Ford End T 106 TL 6716
Forder Green T 89 SX 7867
Fordham, Cambs T 122 TL 6370
Fordham, Essex T 122 TL 9228
Fordham, Norf T 132 TL 6199
Fordham Abbey 122 TL 6369
Fordingbridge T 94 SU 1414
Fordon T 149 TA 0475
Fordoun T 177 NO 7575
Fordstreet, Essex T 122 TL 9226
Ford Street, Somer T 92 ST 1518
Fordwells T 115 SP 3013
Fordwich T 99 TR 1859
Fordyce T 184 NJ 5563
Fore Holm 203 HU 3544
Foreland 95 SZ 6687
Foreland House 166 NR 2764
Foreland Point 91 SS 7551
Foreland, The, or Handfast Point 94 SZ 0582
Foremark T 128 SK 3326
Foremark Resr W 128 SK 3324
Foreness Point 99 TR 3871
Forestburn Gate T 159 NZ 0696
Forest Coal Pit 113 SO 2820
Forestfield T 163 NS 8566
Forest Gate T 105 TQ 4085
Forest Green T 96 TQ 1241
Forest Hall 151 NY 5401
Forest Head T 151 NY 5857
Forest Hill T 115 SP 5907
Forest-in-Teesdale T 152 NY 8629
Forest Lodge, Highld 183 NJ 0216
Forest Lodge, Strath 174 NN 2742
Forest Lodge, Tays 175 NN 9374
Forest Mill T 170 NS 9593
Forest Moor 147 SE 2256
Forest of Ae F 156 NX 9991
Forest of Alyth 176 NO 1855
Forest of Atholl 175 NN 7973
Forest of Bere F 95 SU 6711
Forest of Birse 177 NO 5291
Forest of Bowland F 145 SD 6652
Forest of Clunie 176 NO 0750
Forest of Dean 113 SO 6311
Forest of Deer 185 NJ 9650
Forest of Glenartney 169 NN 6918
Forest of Glenavon 183 NJ 1105
Forest of Glen Tanar 177 NO 4794
Forest of Harris 194 NB 0609
Forest of Mamlorn 169 NN 4135
Forest of Mar 176 NO 0491
Forest of Pendle, The F 146 SD 8338
Forest of Rossendale F 146 SD 8525
Forest of Trawden, The F 146 SD 9338
Forest Row T 97 TQ 4234
Forestside T 95 SU 7512
Forest Town T 139 SK 5662
Forfar P 176 NO 4550
Forgandenny T 170 NO 0818
Forge Side T 113 SO 2408
Forgie T 184 NJ 3854
Forglen House 185 NJ 6952
Formartine 185 NJ 8730
Formby T 136 SD 2907
Formby Hills H 136 SD 2708
Forncett End T 133 TM 1493
Forncett St Mary T 133 TM 1693
Forncett St Peter T 123 TM 1692
Forneth T 176 NO 0945
Fornham All Saints T 122 TL 8367
Fornham St Martin T 122 TL 8567
Forres T 183 NJ 0358
Forrestburn Reservoir W 163 NS 8664
Forrestfield 163 NS 8567
Forrest Lodge 155 NX 5586
Forret Hill H 171 NO 3920
Forsbrook T 128 SJ 9641
Forse T 199 ND 2234
Forse House 199 ND 2135
Forsie 199 ND 0562
Forsinain Burn W 198 NC 9247
Forsinain Farm 198 NC 9149
Forsinard T 198 NC 8943
Forsnaval H 194 NB 0635
Forss House 199 ND 0368
Forss Water W 199 ND 0365
Forston T 93 SY 6695
Fort Augustus T 182 NH 3709
Forter 176 NO 1864
Forteviot T 170 NO 0517
Fort George T 183 NH 7656
Forth T 163 NS 9453
Forthampton T 114 SO 8532
Forth and Clyde Canal W 169 NS 6674
Forth Bridge, Fife 170 NT 1379
Forth Bridge, Lothn 170 NT 1379
Forth Road Bridge, Fife Q 170 NT 1279
Forth Road Bridge, Lothn Q 170 NT 1279
Fortingall T 175 NN 7447
Forton, Lancs T 145 SD 4851
Forton, Shrops T 126 SJ 4316
Forton, Somer T 92 ST 3307
Forton, Staffs T 127 SJ 7521
Fortree T 185 NJ 9640
Fortrie T 184 NJ 6645
Fortrose T 183 NH 7256
Fortuneswell T 93 SY 6873
Fort William P 174 NN 1073
Forty Foot or Vermuden's Drain W 121 TL 3588
Forty Hill T 105 TQ 3397
Forvie Ness or Hackley Head 185 NK 0226
Forward Green T 123 TM 0959
Fosbury T 102 SU 3158
Fosdyke T 131 TF 3133
Foss T 175 NN 7958
Fossdyke Navigation W 140 SK 9274
Fossebridge T 114 SP 0811
Foss Way, Devon R 92 ST 3102
Foss Way, Glos R 114 SP 0811
Foss Way, Lincs R 140 SK 8462
Foss Way, Notts R 129 SK 7347
Foss Way, Somer R 93 ST 5021
Foss Way, Warw R 118 SP 3358
Foss Way, Wilts R 101 ST 8378
Foss-y-ffin T 111 SN 4460
Foster Street T 105 TL 4808
Foston, Derby T 128 SK 1831
Foston, Lincs T 130 SK 8542
Foston, N. Yks T 148 SE 6965
Foston Beck W 130 SK 8740
Foston on the Wolds T 149 TA 1055
Fotherby T 141 TF 3191
Fotheringhay T 130 TL 0693
Fothringham Hill H 177 NO 4645
Foubister T 200 HY 5103
Foula 202 HT 9539
Foulden, Border T 165 NT 9255
Foulden, Norf T 132 TL 7699
Foulholme Sands 143 TA 1921
Foulis Castle 182 NH 5864
Foul Mile T 97 TQ 6215
Foulmire Heights H 158 NY 5895
Foulness W 133 TG 2341
Foulness Island 107 TR 0092
Foulness Point 107 TR 0495
Foulness Sands 107 TR 0796
Foulney Island 144 SD 2464
Foulridge T 146 SD 8942
Foulsham T 132 TG 0324
Fountainhall T 164 NT 4249
Fountains Abbey A 147 SE 2768
Fountains Fell 146 SD 8670
Four Ashes T 122 TM 0070
Four Crosses, Powys T 125 SJ 0508
Four Crosses, Powys T 126 SJ 2718
Four Crosses, Staffs T 128 SJ 9509
Four Elms T 97 TQ 4648
Four Forks T 92 ST 2336
Four Gotes T 131 TF 4416
Four Lanes T 86 SW 6838
Fourlanes End T 137 SJ 8059
Fourman Hill H 184 NJ 5745
Four Marks T 95 SU 6734
Four Mile Bridge T 134 SH 2878
Four Oaks, E. Susx T 98 TQ 8624
Four Oaks, W. Mids T 128 SP 1099
Four Oaks, W. Mids T 118 SP 2480
Fourpenny T 193 NH 8094
Fourstones T 158 NY 8867
Four Throws T 98 TQ 7729
Fovant T 94 SU 0029
Foveran T 185 NJ 9824
Foveran Burn W 185 NJ 9723
Fowberry Tower 165 NU 0329
Fowey T 87 SX 1251
Fowlis T 171 NO 3233
Fowlis Wester T 170 NN 9224
Fowlmere T 121 TL 4245
Fownhope T 113 SO 5834
Foxcote Reservoir W 119 SP 7136
Foxdale T 144 SC 2778
Foxearth T 122 TL 8344
Foxfield T 144 SD 2085
Foxham T 102 ST 9777
Foxhole T 87 SW 9654
Foxholes T 149 TA 0173
Fox Lane T 103 SU 8557
Foxley, Norf T 132 TG 0321
Foxley, Wilts T 101 ST 8986
Foxt T 128 SK 0348
Foxton, Cambs T 121 TL 4148
Foxton, Leic T 119 SP 7089
Foxup T 146 SD 8676
Foxwist Green T 137 SJ 6268
Foy T 113 SO 5928
Foyers T 182 NH 4920
Fraddon T 87 SW 9158
Fradley T 128 SK 1613
Fradswell T 128 SJ 9931
Fraisthorpe T 149 TA 1561
Framfield T 97 TQ 4920
Framingham Earl T 133 TG 2702
Framingham Pigot T 133 TG 2703
Framlingham T 123 TM 2863
Frampton, Dorset T 93 SY 6295
Frampton, Lincs T 131 TF 3239
Frampton Cotterell T 101 ST 6682
Frampton Mansell T 114 SO 9202
Frampton on Severn T 114 SO 7407
Frampton West End T 131 TF 3041
Framsden T 123 TM 1959
Framwellgate Moor T 152 NZ 2644
Franche T 117 SO 8278
Frankby T 136 SJ 2486
Frankley T 118 SO 9980
Frank Lockwood's Island 173 NM 6219
Frankton T 118 SP 4270
Frant T 97 TQ 5935
Fraochaidh, Highld H 174 NN 0251
Fraochaidh, Strath H 174 NN 0251
Fraserburgh P 185 NJ 9967
Fraserburgh Bay W 185 NK 0166
Frating Green T 107 TM 0923
Fratton T 95 SU 6500
Freathy T 88 SX 3952
Freckenham T 122 TL 6672
Freckleton T 145 SD 4329
Fredden Hill H 165 NT 9526
Freeby T 129 SK 8020
Freeland T 115 SP 4113
Freester T 203 HU 4553
Freethorpe T 133 TG 4005
Freevater Forest 191 NH 3488
Freiston T 131 TF 3743
Fremington, Devon T 90 SS 5132
Fremington, N. Yks T 152 SE 0499
Fremington, Strath T 162 NS 6559
Frenchbeer T 89 SX 6785
Freni-fawr H 111 SN 2035
Frensham T 103 SU 8441
Fresgoe T 198 NC 9566
Freshfield T 136 SD 2908
Freshford T 101 ST 7860
Freshwater T 94 SZ 3487
Freshwater Bay W 94 SZ 3485
Freshwater East T 110 SS 0198
Freshwater West W 110 SR 8899
Fressingfield T 123 TM 2677
Freston T 123 TM 1639
Freswick T 199 ND 3767
Freswick Bay W 199 ND 3867
Fretherne T 114 SO 7309
Frettenham T 133 TG 2417
Freuchie T 171 NO 2806
Friar's Gate T 97 TQ 4933
Friday Bridge T 131 TF 4604
Fridaythorpe T 149 SE 8759
Friern Barnet T 105 TQ 2892
Friesland 172 NM 1953
Friesthorpe T 140 TF 0783
Frieth T 104 SU 7990
Frilford T 115 SU 4497
Frilsham T 103 SU 5473
Frimley T 104 SU 8858
Frindsbury T 98 TQ 7469
Fring T 132 TF 7334
Fringford T 115 SP 6029
Frinsted T 98 TQ 8957
Frinton-on-Sea T 107 TM 2420
Friockheim T 177 NO 5949
Frisby on the Wreake T 129 SK 6917
Friskney T 131 TF 4655
Friskney Flats 131 TF 5051
Friston, E. Susx T 97 TV 5597
Friston, Suff T 123 TM 4160
Fritchley T 128 SK 3553
Fritham T 94 SU 2314
Frith Bank T 131 TF 3147
Frith Common T 117 SO 6969
Frithelstock T 90 SS 4619
Frithville T 131 TF 3150
Frittenden T 98 TQ 8141
Fritton, Norf T 133 TG 4600
Fritton, Norf T 123 TM 2292
Fritwell T 115 SP 5229
Frizington T 150 NY 0317
Frocester T 114 SO 7803
Frodesley T 127 SJ 5101
Frodsham T 137 SJ 5278
Froggatt T 139 SK 2476
Froghall T 128 SK 0247
Frogmore T 104 SU 8460
Frogmore House 104 SU 9776
Frolesworth T 119 SP 5090
Frome P 101 ST 7747
Fromes Hill T 117 SO 6846
Frome St Quintin T 93 ST 5902
Fron, Gwyn T 134 SH 3539
Fron, Powys T 126 SJ 2203
Fron, Powys T 125 SO 0965
Froncysyllte T 126 SJ 2741
Frongoch T 135 SH 9039
Frostenden T 123 TM 4881
Frosterley T 152 NZ 0337
Frosty Hill H 184 NJ 4610
Froxfield T 102 SU 2967
Froxfield Green T 95 SU 7025
Fruid Reservoir W 157 NT 0919
Fryerning T 106 TL 6400
Fryton T 148 SE 6875
Fuar Bheinn H 173 NM 8556
Fuar Larach H 160 NR 8154
Fuday 178 NF 7308
Fugla Ness, Shetld 204 HU 3191
Fugla Ness, Shetld 203 HU 3635
Fugla Ness, Shetld 205 HU 3774
Fugla Stack 203 HU 3530
Fugla Water W 205 HU 5172
Fuiay 178 NF 7402
Fulbeck T 130 SK 9450
Fulbourn T 121 TL 5156
Fulbrook T 115 SP 2613
Fulford, N. Yks T 147 SE 6149
Fulford, Somer T 92 ST 2029
Fulford, Staffs T 128 SJ 9538
Fulham T 105 TQ 2576
Fulking T 96 TQ 2410
Fuller's Moor T 127 SJ 4954
Fuller Street T 106 TL 7415
Fullerton T 102 SU 3739
Fulletby T 141 TF 2973
Full Sutton T 148 SE 7455
Fullwood T 161 NS 4450
Fulmer T 104 SU 9985
Fulmodeston T 132 TF 9931
Fulnetby T 141 TF 0979
Fulstow T 141 TF 3297
Fulwell T 159 NZ 3959
Fulwood, Lancs T 145 SD 5331
Fulwood, S. Yks T 139 SK 3085
Funtack Burn W 183 NH 7832
Funtington T 95 SU 8008
Funtley T 95 SU 5608
Funzie T 205 HU 6690
Funzie Bay W 205 HU 6689
Furnace T 168 NN 0200
Furness Fells 150 NY 3000
Furneux Pelham T 121 TL 4327
Furzehill 91 SS 7244
Fyfett T 92 ST 2314
Fyfield, Essex T 105 TL 5606
Fyfield, Glos T 115 SP 2004
Fyfield, Hants T 102 SU 2946
Fyfield, Oxon T 115 SU 4298
Fyfield, Wilts T 102 SU 1468
Fylingdales Moor 149 SE 9199
Fylingthorpe T 149 NZ 9404
Fyvie T 185 NJ 7638

G

Gablon 193 NH 7191
Gabroc Hill T 161 NS 4551
Gaddesby T 129 SK 6813
Gadfa T 134 SH 4689
Gadie Burn W 184 NJ 6324
Gaer T 109 SO 1721
Gaer-fawr T 113 ST 4498
Gaerllwyd T 113 ST 4496
Gaerwen T 134 SH 4871
Gagingwell T 115 SP 4025
Gaick Forest 175 NN 7584
Gaick Lodge 175 NN 7584
Gailey T 127 SJ 9110
Gainford T 152 NZ 1716
Gainsborough P 140 SK 8189
Gainsford End T 122 TL 7235
Gairbeinn H 175 NN 4698
Gairich H 174 NN 0299
Gairletter Point 168 NS 1984
Gairloch T 190 NG 8076
Gairlochy T 174 NN 1784
Gairney Bank 170 NT 1299
Gairnshiel Lodge 176 NJ 2900
Gairsay 200 HY 4422
Gairsay Sound W 200 HY 4424
Gairy Craig H 155 NX 5590
Gairy Hill H 199 ND 4685
Gaisgill T 151 NY 6305
Gaitnip Hill H 200 HY 4405
Gaitsgill T 151 NY 3846
Gala Lane, D. & G W 155 NX 4791
Gala Lane, Strath W 155 NX 4791
Galashiels P 164 NT 4936
Gala Water W 164 NT 4251
Galby T 129 SK 6901
Galgate T 145 SD 4855
Galhampton T 93 ST 6329
Gallanach, Strath 172 NM 2161

Gallanach Glen Iorsa

Gallanach, Strath 173 NM 8226
Gallan Head 194 NB 0539
Gallatown T 171 NT 2994
Galley Common T 118 SP 3192
Galleywood T 106 TL 7002
Galloway 155 NX 4766
Gallowfauld T 176 NO 4342
Gallow Hill, D. & G H 157 NT 0806
Gallow Hill, Tays H 176 NO 3941
Gallows Hill H 185 NJ 7118
Gallrope Bank 193 NH 7985
Galltair T 180 NG 8120
Galmisdale T 179 NM 4884
Galmpton, Devon T 89 SX 6840
Galmpton, Devon T 89 SX 8956
Galphay T 147 SE 2572
Galson T 195 NB 4458
Galston T 161 NS 5036
Galtachean 189 NG 3998
Galtrigill T 186 NG 1854
Galt, The 200 HY 4821
Gamallt, Dyfed H 112 SN 7856
Gamallt, Powys H 125 SN 9570
Gamblesby T 151 NY 6139
Gamhna Gigha 160 NR 6854
Gamlingay T 121 TL 2352
Gamrie T 185 NJ 7962
Gamrie Bay W 185 NJ 7965
Gamston, Notts T 129 SK 6037
Gamston, Notts T 140 SK 7176
Gana Hill H 156 NS 9501
Ganarew T 113 SO 5316
Ganavan 168 NM 8532
Ganllwyd T 125 SH 7224
Gannochy 177 NO 5970
Ganstead T 143 TA 1434
Ganthorpe T 148 SE 6870
Ganton T 149 SE 9877
Ganu Mór H 196 NC 3150
Gaodhail 173 NM 6138
Gaor Bheinn or Gulvain 174 NM 9987
Garadhban Forest F 169 NS 4790
Garbat T 182 NH 4167
Garbat Forest 182 NH 4368
Garbh-allt, Highld W 198 NC 7839
Garbhallt, Strath T 168 NS 0295
Garbh-bheinn, Highld H 187 NG 5323
Garbh Bheinn, Highld H 173 NM 9062
Garbh Bheinn, Highld H 174 NN 1660
Garbh Eileach 173 NM 6712
Garbh Eilean, Highld 190 NG 6153
Garbh Eilean, W. Isles 189 NG 4198
Garbh Ghaoir W 174 NN 4256
Garbh-mheall Mór H 175 NN 7292
Garbh Phort W 172 NM 3325
Garbh Reisa 167 NR 7598
Garbh Shlios 173 NM 7642
Garbh Thorr H 160 NR 9335
Garboldisham T 122 TM 0081
Gardenstown T 185 NJ 8064
Garderhouse T 203 HU 3347
Gardie House 203 HU 4842
Garelg Lâs H 109 SN 7720
Gare Hill T 101 ST 7840
Gare Loch W 168 NS 2486
Garelochhead T 168 NS 2491
Garenin T 195 NB 1944
Garford T 115 SU 4296
Garforth T 147 SE 4033
Garf Water W 163 NS 9232
Gargrave T 146 SD 9354
Gargunnock T 169 NS 7094
Gargunnock Hills H 169 NS 6891
Garioch 185 NJ 6924
Garleffin Fell H 154 NX 3599
Garleton Hills H 171 NT 5176
Garlick Hill H 155 NX 4372
Garlies Castle A 155 NX 4269
Garlieston T 155 NX 4746
Garlogie T 185 NJ 7805
Garmond T 185 NJ 8052
Garmony 173 NM 6740
Garmouth T 184 NJ 3464
Garmsley Camp A 117 SO 6261
Garmus Taing 204 HU 3694
Garn T 134 SH 2734
Garnant T 108 SN 6813
Garn Boduan A 134 SH 3139
Garn Caws H 109 SO 1216
Garn Ddu H 109 SO 0212
Garn Dolbenmaen T 134 SH 4944
Garnedd-goch H 134 SH 5149
Garnett Bridge T 151 SD 5299
Garnkirk T 162 NS 6768
Garn Prys H 135 SH 8848
Garn-yr-erw T 113 SO 2310
Garpol Water W 157 NT 0304
Garrabost T 195 NB 5133
Garragie Lodge 182 NH 5211
Garraron 173 NM 8008
Garras T 86 SW 7023
Garreg T 134 SH 6141
Garreg Bank T 126 SJ 2811
Garreg-ddu Reservoir W 125 SN 9165
Garrick 169 NN 8412
Garrigill T 151 NY 7441
Garrisdale Point 179 NG 2005
Garrison, The 86 SV 8910
Garroch 156 NX 5981
Garroch Head 161 NS 0951
Garron Point 177 NO 8987
Garros T 187 NG 4963
Garrow 175 NN 8240
Garrow Tor H 87 SX 1478
Garrygualach T 174 NH 1700
Garryhorn 155 NX 5493
Garrynamonie T 178 NF 7416
Garsdale, Cumbr 151 SD 7390
Garsdale, Cumbr T 151 SD 7489
Garsdale Head T 151 SD 7892
Garsdon T 102 ST 9687
Garshall Green T 128 SJ 9634
Garsington T 115 SP 5802
Garso Wick W 201 HY 7755
Garstang T 145 SD 4945
Garston T 136 SJ 4084
Garswood T 137 SJ 5599
Gartbreck 166 NR 2858
Gartcosh T 162 NS 6967
Garth, Clwyd T 126 SJ 2543
Garth, I. of M T 144 SC 3177
Garth, M. Glam T 109 SS 8690
Garth, Powys T 112 SN 9549
Garth, Shetld 202 HU 2157
Garthbrengy T 109 SO 0433
Gartheli T 111 SN 5856
Garth Head 199 ND 3188
Garthmyl T 126 SO 1999
Garthorpe, Humbs T 142 SE 8419
Garthorpe, Leic T 130 SK 8320
Garths Ness 203 HU 3611
Garths, The 205 HP 6615
Garths Voe W 205 HU 4073
Gartly T 184 NJ 5232
Gartmore T 169 NS 5297
Gartmore House 169 NS 5297
Gartnagrenach 160 NR 7959
Gartness, Central 169 NS 5086
Gartness, Strath 162 NS 7864
Gartocharn T 169 NS 4286
Garton T 143 TA 2635
Garton-on-the-Wolds T 149 SE 9859
Gartymore T 193 ND 0114
Garvald T 171 NT 5870
Garvard T 166 NR 3691
Garvary Burn W 193 NC 7321
Garve T 182 NH 3961
Garvellachs 173 NM 6511
Garvestone T 132 TG 0107
Garvock, Grampn T 177 NO 7470
Garvock, Strath 168 NS 2571
Garwall Hill H 154 NX 3483
Garway T 113 SO 4522
Garynahine T 195 NB 2331
Gasay 188 NF 8443
Gaskan 173 NM 8072
Gasker 194 NA 8711
Gastard T 101 ST 8868
Gasthorpe T 122 TL 9780
Gatcombe T 95 SZ 4984
Gatebeck T 145 SD 5586
Gate Burton T 140 SK 8383
Gateforth T 147 SE 5628
Gatehead T 161 NS 3936
Gate Helmsley T 148 SE 6955
Gateholm Island 110 SM 7707
Gatehouse 158 NY 7889
Gatehouse of Fleet T 155 NX 6056
Gatelawbridge T 156 NX 9096
Gateley T 132 TF 9624
Gatenby T 147 SE 3287
Gatescarth Pass 151 NY 4709
Gateshead P 159 NZ 2560
Gatesheath T 137 SJ 4760
Gateside, Fife T 170 NO 1809
Gateside, Strath T 161 NS 3653
Gateside, Tays T 176 NO 4344
Gathurst T 137 SD 5407
Gatley T 137 SJ 8488
Gat Sand 131 TF 4738
Gattonside T 164 NT 5435
Gauldry T 171 NO 3723
Gauls 170 NO 0734
Gaunt's Common T 94 SU 0205
Gautby T 141 TF 1772
Gavinton T 164 NT 7652
Gawber T 139 SE 3207
Gawcott T 119 SP 6831
Gawsworth T 137 SJ 8969
Gawthorpe Hall A 146 SD 8034
Gawthrop T 145 SD 6978
Gawthwaite T 145 SD 2784
Gaydon T 118 SP 3653
Gayhurst T 120 SP 8446
Gayle T 152 SD 8689
Gayle Moor 146 SD 7982
Gayles T 152 NZ 1207
Gay Street T 96 TQ 0820
Gayton, Mers T 136 SJ 2780
Gayton, Norf T 132 TF 7219
Gayton, Northnts T 119 SP 7054
Gayton, Staffs T 128 SJ 9828
Gayton le Marsh T 141 TF 4284
Gayton Sands 136 SJ 2578
Gayton Thorpe T 132 TF 7418
Gaywood T 132 TF 6320
Gazeley T 122 TL 7264
Geal Charn, Grampn H 184 NJ 2810
Geal Charn, Highld H 183 NJ 0912
Geal Charn, Highld H 174 NN 1594
Geal Charn, Highld H 175 NN 5081
Geal Charn, Highld H 175 NN 5698
Geal-Charn, Highld H 175 NN 5978
Geal-charn Mór H 183 NH 8312
Geallaig Hill H 176 NO 2998
Gealldruig Mhór 194 HW 8131
Geanies House 193 NH 8979
Gearr Garry W 174 NH 0801
Geary T 186 NG 2661
Geddes House 183 NH 8852
Gedding T 122 TL 9458
Geddington T 120 SP 8983
Gedintailor T 187 NG 5235
Gedney T 131 TF 4024
Gedney Broadgate T 131 TF 4022
Gedney Drove End T 131 TF 4629
Gedney Dyke T 131 TF 4126
Gedney Hill T 131 TF 3311
Gedney Marsh T 129 SK 4429
Gee Cross T 138 SJ 9593
Geifas H 125 SN 8272
Geilston 168 NS 3477
Geise T 199 ND 1064
Geldeston T 123 TM 3991
Geldie Burn W 176 NN 9687
Gell 135 SH 8569
Gelli T 110 SN 0819
Gellifor T 136 SJ 1262
Gelligaer T 109 ST 1397
Gelli-gaer Common 109 ST 1398
Gellilydan T 135 SH 6839
Gellioedd T 135 SH 9344
Gellyburn 176 NO 0939
Gellywen T 111 SN 2723
Gelston T 156 NX 7758
Geltsdale Middle 151 NY 6051
Genie Fea H 200 ND 2494
Genoch Mains 154 NX 1356
Gentlemen's Cave 200 HY 3948
Gentleshaw T 128 SK 0511
Geocrab T 189 NG 1191
Geoda nan Each 186 NG 1554
Geodh' a' Bhrideoin 197 NC 4967
Geodha Daraich 186 NG 3719
Geodha Mór, Highld 191 NC 0802
Geodha Mór, Highld 186 NG 2039
Geodha nan Calman 195 NB 1339
Geodha Nasavig 194 NB 0336
Geodha Ruadh 196 NC 2367
Geodha Ruadh na Fola 196 NC 2570
Geo Dubh 189 NB 2200
Geo Luon 200 HY 5429
Geo of Hellia 200 HY 1804
Geo of Markamouth 205 HP 4701
Geo of Odderaber 200 HY 4954
Geo of the Uin 203 HU 4118
Geo of Vigon 205 HP 4804
Geordie's Hill, Border H 157 NY 4396
Geordie's Hill, D. & G H 157 NY 4396
Georgeham T 90 SS 4639
Georgemas Junction Station 199 ND 1559
George Nympton T 91 SS 7022
Georgetown T 161 NS 4567
Georgia T 86 SW 4836
Germansweek T 88 SX 4394
Germoe T 86 SW 5829
Gerrans T 87 SW 8735
Gerrans Bay W 87 SW 9037
Gerrards Cross T 104 TQ 0088
Geshader T 195 NB 1131
Gestingthorpe T 122 TL 8138
Geuffordd T 126 SJ 2114
Geufron T 125 SN 8885
Geur Rubha 180 NG 5501
Ghlas-bheinn H 196 NC 3361
Giant's Leg 203 HU 5135
Giant, The A 93 ST 6601
Gibbet Hill H 95 SU 9035
Gibbieston 176 NO 0136
Gibbon Hill H 152 SE 0196
Gibraltar T 141 TF 5558
Gidea Park T 105 TQ 5390
Gidleigh T 89 SX 6788
Gifford T 164 NT 5368
Gigalum Island 160 NR 6446
Giggleswick T 146 SD 8063
Gigha Island 160 NR 6449
Gighay 178 NF 7604
Gilberdyke T 142 SE 8329
Gilchriston T 164 NT 4865
Gilcrux T 150 NY 1138
Gilderdale Forest 151 NY 6844
Gildersome T 147 SE 2429
Gildingwells T 139 SK 5585
Gileston T 109 ST 0267
Gilfach Goch T 109 SS 9889
Gilfachreda T 111 SN 4058
Gilgarran T 150 NY 0323
Gilkicker Point 95 SZ 6097
Gillamoor T 148 SE 6890
Gillaval Glas H 189 NB 1402
Gill Burn W 199 ND 3468
Gille-mhicheil 188 NF 9363
Gillen 186 NG 2659
Gillies Hill H 169 NS 7791
Gilling East T 147 SE 6177
Gillingham, Dorset T 93 ST 8026
Gillingham, Kent T 98 TQ 7767
Gillingham, Norf T 123 TM 4191
Gilling West T 152 NZ 1805
Gill of Garth 200 HY 4707
Gillow Heath T 137 SJ 8858
Gills T 199 ND 3272
Gills Bay W 199 ND 3373
Gilmanscleuch T 164 NT 3321
Gilmerton, Lothn T 164 NT 2968
Gilmerton, Tays T 170 NN 8823
Gilmorton T 119 SP 5787
Gilsay 188 NG 0280
Gilsland T 158 NY 6366
Gilsland Spa T 158 NY 6367
Gilston T 164 NT 4456
Giltar Point 110 SS 1298
Giltarump 202 HU 2742
Gilwern T 113 SO 2415
Gilwern Hill H 112 SO 0958
Gimingham T 133 TG 2836
Ginst Point 111 SN 3308
Gipping T 122 TM 0763
Gipsey Bridge T 131 TF 2850
Girdle Fell H 158 NT 7001
Girdle Ness 185 NJ 9705
Girlsta T 203 HU 4250
Girnock Burn W 176 NO 3293
Girsby T 153 NZ 3508
Girthon T 155 NX 6053
Girtley Hill H 161 NS 2361
Girton, Cambs T 121 TL 4262
Girton, Notts T 140 SK 8266
Girvan T 154 NX 1897
Gisborough Moor 153 NZ 6213
Gisburn T 146 SD 8348
Gisburn Forest F 145 SD 7457
Gisla T 195 NB 1225
Gisla River W 195 NB 1126
Gisleham T 123 TM 5188
Gislingham T 122 TM 0771
Gissing T 123 TM 1485
Gittisham T 92 SY 1398
Giùr-bheinn H 166 NR 3772
Gladestry T 113 SO 2355
Gladhouse Reservoir W 164 NT 2953
Gladsmuir T 171 NT 4573
Glais T 108 SN 7000
Glais Bheinn H 173 NM 7243
Glaisdale, N. Yks T 148 NZ 7603
Glaisdale, N. Yks T 148 NZ 7705
Glaisdale Moor 148 NZ 7201
Glaisdale Rigg H 148 NZ 7404
Glamaig H 187 NG 5130
Glam Burn W 190 NG 5542
Glame T 190 NG 5642
Glamis T 176 NO 3846
Glamis Castle A 176 NO 3848
Glanaber Terrace T 135 SH 7547
Glanaman T 108 SN 6813
Glan-Conwy 135 SH 8352
Glandford T 132 TG 0441
Glandwr, Dyfed T 111 SN 1928
Glandwr, Gwent T 109 SO 2001
Glangrwyney T 113 SO 2416
Glanmule T 116 SO 1690
Glanrhyd T 110 SN 1442
Glanton T 159 NU 0714
Glanton Pike T 159 NU 0514
Glanvilles Wootton T 93 ST 6708
Glan-y-don T 136 SJ 1679
Glan-yr-afon, Gwyn 135 SH 9141
Glan-yr-afon, Gwyn T 135 SJ 0242
Glapthorn T 120 TL 0290
Glapwell T 139 SK 4765
Glaramara H 150 NY 2410
Glas-allt-Shiel 176 NO 2782
Glas Bheinn, Highld H 196 NC 2526
Glas Bheinn, Highld H 190 NG 9043
Glas Bheinn, Highld H 174 NN 1397
Glas Bheinn, Highld H 174 NN 2564
Glas Bheinn, Strath H 166 NR 4359
Glas Bheinn, Strath H 166 NR 5070
Glas Bheinn Mhór H 180 NG 5525
Glasbury T 113 SO 1739
Glas-charn H 180 NM 8483
Glascoed, Clwyd T 135 SH 9974
Glascoed, Gwent T 113 SO 3301
Glascoed, Powys T 126 SJ 1108
Glascorrie 176 NO 4097
Glascote T 128 SK 2303
Glascwm T 112 SO 1553
Glascwm Hill H 113 SO 1652
Glasdrum T 174 NN 0046
Glas Eilean, Highld 180 NG 7000
Glas Eilean, Highld 180 NG 8425
Glas Eilean, Strath 166 NR 4465
Glas-eileanan 188 NF 8641
Glasfryn T 135 SH 9150
Glasfynydd Forest F 109 SN 8524
Glasgow P 162 NS 5865
Glasgow Airport 161 NS 4766
Glasha Burn W 191 NH 3691
Glasinfryn T 134 SH 5869
Glas-leac Beag 190 NB 9205
Glas-leac Mór 196 NB 9509
Glas-loch Mór W 197 NC 6719
Glaslyn W 125 SN 8294
Glas Maol H 176 NO 1676
Glas Mheall Mór H 175 NN 6877
Glasnakille T 187 NG 5313
Glaspwll T 125 SN 7397
Glassburn T 182 NH 3634
Glasserton T 155 NX 4238
Glassford T 162 NS 7247
Glasshouse Hill T 114 SO 7020
Glasshouses T 146 SE 1764
Glasslaw T 185 NJ 8659
Glasslie 171 NO 2305
Glasson, Cumbr T 157 NY 2560
Glasson, Lancs T 145 SD 4456
Glassonby T 151 NY 5738
Glass Water W 204 HU 2581
Glasterlaw 177 NO 5951
Glaston T 130 SK 8900
Glastonbury P 101 ST 4938
Glas Tulaichean H 176 NO 0576
Glatton T 120 TL 1586
Glazebury T 137 SJ 6797
Glazeley T 117 SO 7088
Gleadless Valley T 139 SK 3783
Gleadsmoss T 137 SJ 8268
Gleann a' Chilleine 175 NN 7336
Gleann a' Choilich 181 NH 1026
Gleann Airigh 168 NR 9195
Gleann an Dubh-Lochain 180 NG 8200
Gleann an Fhiodh 174 NN 0856
Gleann Aoistail 166 NR 6085
Gleann Astaile 166 NR 4871
Gleann Beag 191 NH 3283
Gleann Bhruthadail 195 NB 3343
Gleann Camgharaidh 174 NM 9888
Gleann Casaig 169 NN 5410
Gleann Cia-aig 174 NN 1891
Gleann Còsaidh 174 NG 9302
Gleann Dà-Eig 175 NN 6045
Gleann Da-Ghob 175 NN 6945
Gleann Diridh 175 NN 8775
Gleann Dubh, Highld 196 NC 2720
Gleann Dubh, Highld 196 NC 3033
Gleann Dubh, Highld 173 NM 7253
Gleann Dubh Lighe 174 NM 9482
Gleann Duibhe 175 NN 4554
Gleann Fearnach 176 NO 0368
Gleann Fhiodhaig 191 NH 1548
Gleann Fionnlighe 174 NM 9682
Gleann Geal 173 NM 7350
Gleann Gniomhaidh 181 NH 0519
Gleann Goibhre 182 NH 4248
Gleann Leireag 196 NC 1630
Gleann Leòra 166 NR 4354
Gleann Màma 180 NM 7485
Gleann Meadail 180 NM 8298
Gleann Meadhonach 180 NG 6005
Gleann Meinich W 182 NH 2553
Gleann Mór, Highld 191 NH 3885
Gleann Mór, Tays 176 NO 0276
Gleann Mór, W. Isles 178 NF 8125
Gleann Mór Barvas 195 NB 3746
Gleann na Guiserein 180 NG 7703
Gleann nam Fiadh 181 NH 1625
Gleann Oraid 186 NG 3330
Gleann Salach 174 NM 9739
Gleann Seilisdeir 173 NM 4731
Gleann Sithidh W 181 NH 0727
Gleann Sùileag 174 NN 0282
Gleann Tanagaidh 191 NH 0866
Gleann Udalain 180 NG 8730
Gleann Ullibh 166 NR 4666
Gleaston T 144 SD 2570
Glemanuilt Hill H 160 NR 6408
Glemsford T 122 TL 8348
Glen 155 NX 5457
Glenacardoch Point 160 NR 6538
Glen Achall 191 NH 2393
Glen Affric 182 NH 2022
Glenaffric Forest 181 NH 1220
Glen Albyn or Glen Mór 182 NH 4211
Glen Aldie 193 NH 7779
Glenalla Field H 154 NS 3500
Glen Almond, Tays 170 NN 9128
Glenalmond, Tays 170 NN 9627
Glen Ample 169 NN 5919
Glenan Bay W 168 NR 9170
Glenancross T 180 NM 6691
Glen App 154 NX 0774
Glenapp Castle 154 NX 0980
Glen Aray 168 NN 0814
Glen Arnisdale 180 NG 8609
Glenaros House 173 NM 5544
Glen Arroch 180 NG 7321
Glen Artney 169 NN 7318
Glenastle T 166 NR 3044
Glen Auldyn T 144 SC 4393
Glen Avon 183 NJ 1106
Glen Banchor 175 NN 6798
Glenbarr T 160 NR 6636
Glen Barrisdale 180 NG 8903
Glen Barry 184 NJ 5554
Glen Batrick 166 NR 5178
Glen Beasdale 180 NM 7385
Glenbeg, Highld 183 NJ 0028
Glenbeg, Highld T 173 NM 5862
Glen Bernisdale T 187 NG 4048
Glenbervie T 177 NO 7680
Glenboig T 162 NS 7268
Glenborrodale T 173 NM 6161
Glen Bragar 195 NB 3042
Glenbranter 168 NS 1097
Glenbranter Forest 168 NS 1097
Glen Breackerie 160 NR 6511
Glenbreck T 163 NT 0621
Glen Brein 182 NH 4707
Glenbrein Lodge 182 NH 4711
Glen Brerachan 176 NO 0263
Glen Brittle 187 NG 4123
Glen Brittle Forest 187 NG 4026
Glenbrittle House 187 NG 4121
Glen Bruar 175 NN 8273
Glenbuchat Lodge 184 NJ 3318
Glenbuck T 162 NS 7429
Glenburn T 161 NS 4761
Glencaird Hill H 154 NX 3580
Glen Callater 176 NO 1785
Glencalvie Forest 192 NH 4387
Glencalvie Lodge 192 NH 4689
Glencanisp Forest 196 NC 1619
Glencanisp Lodge 196 NC 1122
Glen Cannel 173 NM 5935
Glen Cannich 182 NH 2130
Glencannich Forest 182 NH 2333
Glencaple T 156 NX 9968
Glen Carron W 191 NH 0852
Glencarron and Glenuig Forest 191 NH 1249
Glencarron Lodge 191 NH 0651
Glencarse T 171 NO 1921
Glen Cassley 196 NC 4012
Glencassley Castle 192 NC 4407
Glenceitlein 174 NN 1447
Glen Clachaig 173 NM 5736
Glen Clova 176 NO 3570
Glencloy T 160 NS 0035
Glen Cochill 175 NN 9042
Glencoe, Highld T 174 NN 1058
Glen Coe, Highld 174 NN 1556
Glen Convinth 182 NH 5036
Glen Corodale 178 NF 8331
Glencorse Reservoir W 163 NT 2163
Glen Coul 196 NC 2829
Glencraig T 170 NT 1895
Glen Creran 174 NN 0449
Glencripesdale Burn W 173 NM 6859
Glen Croe 168 NN 2504
Glen Cross 195 NB 5060
Glen Dale 186 NG 1848
Glen Damff 176 NO 2567
Glendaruel 168 NR 9986
Glendaruel Forest F 168 NS 0288
Glendavan House 176 NJ 4301
Glendebadel Bay W 167 NR 6295
Glen Dee 176 NN 9893
Glen Dessarry 174 NM 9592
Glen Devon, Tays 170 NN 9504
Glendevon, Tays T 170 NN 9904
Glendevon Reservoirs, Central W 170 NN 9104
Glendevon Reservoirs, Tays W 170 NN 9104
Glendhu Forest 196 NC 2834
Glendhu Hill, Cumbr H 158 NY 5686
Glendhu Hill, Northum H 158 NY 5686
Glen Diebidale 192 NH 4583
Glen Dochart 169 NN 4727
Glen Docherty 191 NH 0560
Glendoebeg T 182 NH 4108
Glendoe Forest 182 NH 4304
Glendoe Lodge 182 NH 4009
Glendoick 171 NO 2022
Glen Doll 176 NO 2576
Glendoll Forest F 176 NO 2675
Glendoll Lodge 176 NO 2776
Glendon Hall T 120 SP 8481
Glen Douchary 191 NH 2591
Glen Douglas 168 NS 3098
Glen Drolla 188 NF 7672
Glenduckie 171 NO 2818
Glendue Fell H 153 NZ 6455
Glen Duror 174 NN 0154
Glen Dye 177 NO 6383
Glendye Lodge 177 NO 6486
Glen Eagles 170 NN 9307
Gleneagles Hotel 170 NN 9407
Gleneagles Station 170 NN 9210
Glen Effock 176 NO 4477
Glenegedale T 166 NR 3351
Glenegedale River W 166 NR 3452
Glen Einig 191 NH 3598
Glen Elchaig 180 NG 9627
Glenelg T 180 NG 8119
Glenelg Bay W 180 NG 8019
Glen Ernan 184 NJ 3112
Glen Errochty 175 NN 7663
Glen Esk 177 NO 5178
Glen Etive 174 NN 1751
Glen Euchar 173 NM 8419
Glen Ey 176 NO 0986
Glen Falloch 169 NN 3622
Glenfarg, Tays T 170 NO 1310
Glen Farg, Tays 170 NO 1513
Glenfarg Reservoir W 170 NO 1010
Glenfarquhar Lodge 177 NO 7281
Glen Fenzie 176 NJ 3201
Glen Feochan 168 NM 8924
Glenferness House 183 NH 9342
Glen Feshie 175 NN 8596
Glenfeshie Forest 175 NN 8890
Glenfeshie Lodge 175 NN 8493
Glen Fiag 197 NC 4524
Glen Fiddich 184 NJ 3234
Glenfiddich Forest 184 NJ 3130
Glenfiddich Lodge 184 NJ 3132
Glenfield T 129 SK 5306
Glen Finart 168 NS 1691
Glen Finglas 169 NN 5011
Glen Finglas Reservoir W 169 NN 5209
Glen Finlet 176 NO 2368
Glenfinnan, Highld T 180 NM 9080
Glen Finnan, Highld 180 NM 9183
Glenfoot T 170 NO 1715
Glen Fruin 168 NS 2888
Glen Fyne, Strath 168 NN 2316
Glen Fyne, Strath 168 NS 1172
Glenfyne Lodge 168 NN 2215
Glen Gairn 176 NO 3399
Glengap Forest F 156 NX 6460
Glengarnock T 161 NS 3252
Glengarrisdale Bay W 167 NR 6497
Glen Garry, Highld 174 NH 1400
Glen Garry, Tays 175 NN 7269
Glengarry Forest 174 NN 2296
Glen Garvan 174 NM 9675
Glengavel Reservoir W 162 NS 6634
Glengavel Water W 162 NS 6535
Glen Gelder 176 NO 2591
Glen Girnaig 175 NN 9366
Glen Glass 182 NH 5568
Glen Gloy 174 NN 2689
Glen Golly 197 NC 4243
Glen Golly River W 197 NC 4243
Glengorm Castle 173 NM 4357
Glen Gour 174 NM 9464
Glengrasco T 187 NG 4444
Glen Grudie 190 NG 9566
Glen Harris 179 NM 3696
Glenhead Farm 176 NO 2562
Glenhoul 156 NX 6087
Glen House 164 NT 2933
Glen Hurich 173 NM 8570
Glen Iorsa 160 NR 9239

Harmer Green High Grange

Harmer Green T 105 TL 2516
Harmer Hill T 127 SJ 4922
Harmston T 140 SK 9762
Harnham T 94 SU 1328
Harnhill T 114 SP 0700
Harold Hill T 105 TQ 5391
Haroldston West T 110 SM 8615
Haroldswick, Shetld T 205 HP 6312
Harold's Wick, Shetld W 205 HP 6411
Harold Wood T 105 TQ 5590
Harome T 147 SE 6482
Harpenden T 105 TL 1314
Harperleas Reservoir W 171 NO 2105
Harperrig Reservoir W 163 NT 0961
Harper's Brook W 120 SP 9286
Harpford T 92 SY 0990
Harpham T 149 TA 0961
Harpley, H. & W T 117 SO 6861
Harpley, Norf T 132 TF 7826
Harpole T 119 SP 6960
Harpsdale T 199 ND 1356
Harpsden T 104 SU 7680
Harpswell T 140 SK 9389
Harpurhey T 137 SD 8601
Harpur Hill T 138 SK 0671
Harrabrough Head 200 ND 4190
Harrapool T 180 NG 6523
Harray 200 HY 3319
Harrier 202 HT 9540
Harrietfield T 170 NN 9829
Harrietsham T 98 TQ 8652
Harrington, Cumbr T 150 NX 9925
Harrington, Lincs T 141 TF 3671
Harrington, Northnts T 119 SP 7780
Harringworth T 130 SP 9197
Harris, Highld 179 NM 3395
Harris, W. Isles 189 NG 1198
Harriseahead T 127 SJ 8656
Harrogate P 147 SE 3055
Harrold T 120 SP 9557
Harrow T 105 TQ 1588
Harrowbarrow T 88 SX 4070
Harrowden T 120 TL 0747
Harrow Hill H 96 TQ 0809
Harrow on the Hill T 105 TQ 1586
Harsgeir 195 NB 1140
Harston, Cambs T 121 TL 4250
Harston, Leic T 130 SK 8431
Hart T 153 NZ 4634
Harta Corrie 187 NG 4723
Hartamul 178 NF 8311
Hartburn T 159 NZ 0986
Harter Fell, Cumbr 151 NY 4609
Harter Fell, Cumbr 150 SD 2199
Hartest T 122 TL 8352
Hart Fell, D. & G H 157 NT 1113
Hart Fell, D. & G H 157 NY 2389
Hartfield T 97 TQ 4735
Hartford, Cambs T 121 TL 2572
Hartford, Ches T 137 SJ 6472
Hartfordbridge T 103 SU 7757
Hartford End T 106 TL 6817
Hartforth T 152 NZ 1706
Harthill, Ches T 127 SJ 5055
Harthill, Strath T 163 NS 9064
Harthill, S. Yks T 139 SK 4980
Harthope Burn W 165 NT 9623
Hartington T 138 SK 1260
Hartland T 90 SS 2624
Hartland Point 90 SS 2227
Hartland Quay T 90 SS 2224
Hartlebury T 117 SO 8470
Hartlepool P 153 NZ 5132
Hartlepool Bay W 153 NZ 5231
Hartley, Cumbr T 151 NY 7808
Hartley, Kent T 98 TQ 6166
Hartley, Kent T 97 TQ 7634
Hartley, Northum T 159 NZ 3375
Hartley Wespall T 104 SU 6958
Hartley Wintney T 103 SU 7656
Hartlip T 98 TQ 8364
Harton, N. Yks T 148 SE 7061
Harton, Shrops T 116 SO 4888
Harton, T. & W T 159 NZ 3764
Hartpury T 114 SO 8025
Hartshill T 128 SP 3294
Hartshorne T 128 SK 3221
Hartshorn Pike H 158 NT 6201
Hartsop T 151 NY 4013
Hartwell T 119 SP 7850
Hartwood T 163 NS 8459
Harvel T 98 TQ 6563
Harvington T 118 SP 0549
Harwell T 103 SU 4989
Harwich P 123 TM 2632
Harwich Harbour W 123 TM 2633
Harwood, Durham T 151 NY 8233
Harwood, G. Man T 137 SD 7411
Harwood Beck W 151 NY 8321
Harwood Dale T 149 SE 9695
Harwood Forest F 159 NY 9894
Harworth T 139 SK 6191
Hascombe T 96 SU 9940
Hascosay 205 HU 5592
Hascosay Sound W 205 HU 5492
Haselbech T 119 SP 7177
Haselbury Plucknett T 93 ST 4710
Haseley T 118 SP 2367
Haselor T 118 SP 1257
Hasfield T 114 SO 8227
Hasguard T 110 SM 8509
Haskayne T 136 SD 3508
Haskeir Eagach 188 NF 5980
Haskeir Island 188 NF 6182
Hasketon T 123 TM 2550
Hasland T 139 SK 3969
Haslemere T 95 SU 9032
Haslingden T 146 SD 7823
Haslingden Grane T 146 SD 7522
Haslingfield T 121 TL 4052
Haslington T 127 SJ 7356
Hassall T 137 SJ 7657
Hassall Green T 137 SJ 7858
Hassell Street T 99 TR 0946
Hassendean T 158 NT 5420
Hassingham T 133 TG 3705
Hassocks T 97 TQ 3015
Hassop T 139 SK 2272
Hastigrow T 199 ND 2661
Hastingleigh T 99 TR 0944
Hastings P 98 TQ 8109
Hastingwood T 105 TL 4807
Hastoe T 104 SP 9109
Haswell T 153 NZ 3743
Hatch, Beds T 120 TL 1547
Hatch, Hants T 103 SU 6752
Hatch, Wilts T 93 ST 9228
Hatch Beauchamp T 92 ST 3020
Hatch End T 105 TQ 1391
Hatching Green T 105 TL 1312
Hatchmere T 137 SJ 5571
Hatcliffe T 143 TA 2100
Hatfield, Herts P 105 TL 2208
Hatfield, H. & W T 113 SO 5959
Hatfield, S. Yks T 139 SE 6509
Hatfield Broad Oak T 105 TL 5416
Hatfield Chase 142 SE 7110
Hatfield Heath T 105 TL 5215
Hatfield House A 105 TL 2308
Hatfield Moors 142 SE 7006
Hatfield Peverel T 106 TL 7911
Hatfield Woodhouse T 142 SE 6808
Hatford T 115 SU 3394
Hatherden T 102 SU 3450
Hatherleigh T 91 SS 5404
Hathern T 129 SK 5022
Hatherop T 115 SP 1505
Hathersage T 139 SK 2381
Hatherton, Ches T 127 SJ 6847
Hatherton, Staffs T 128 SJ 9510
Hatley St George T 121 TL 2851
Hatt T 88 SX 3961
Hatterrall Hill H 113 SO 3025
Hattingley T 95 SU 6437
Hatton, Ches T 137 SJ 5982
Hatton, Derby T 128 SK 2130
Hatton, G. Lon T 104 TQ 0975
Hatton, Grampn T 185 NK 0537
Hatton, Lincs T 141 TF 1776
Hatton, Shrops T 116 SO 4690
Hatton, Warw T 118 SP 2467
Hatton Castle 185 NJ 7546
Hattoncrook T 185 NJ 8424
Hatton Heath T 136 SJ 4561
Hatton of Fintray T 185 NJ 8416
Hattons Lodge 102 SU 0688
Haugham T 141 TF 3381
Haugh Head T 165 NU 0026
Haughley T 122 TM 0262
Haughley Green T 122 TM 0364
Haugh of Glass T 184 NJ 4239
Haugh of Urr T 156 NX 8066
Haughs of Cromdale 183 NJ 0927
Haughton, Notts T 139 SK 6772
Haughton, Shrops T 126 SJ 3727
Haughton, Shrops T 127 SJ 5516
Haughton, Shrops T 127 SO 6896
Haughton, Staffs T 127 SJ 8620
Haughton Common 158 NY 8072
Haughton Green T 137 SJ 9393
Haughton Moss T 127 SJ 5756
Haunn 172 NM 3447
Haunton T 128 SK 2310
Hauxley T 159 NU 2703
Hauxley Haven W 159 NU 2802
Hauxton T 121 TL 4352
Havant T 95 SU 7106
Haven T 113 SO 4054
Havengore Island 107 TQ 9789
Havenstreet T 95 SZ 5690
Haven, The W 131 TF 3541
Haverfordwest P 110 SM 9515
Haverhill T 122 TL 6745
Haverigg T 144 SD 1578
Havering-atte-Bower T 105 TQ 5193
Haversham T 120 SP 8242
Haverthwaite T 145 SD 3483
Hawarden T 136 SJ 3165
Hawarden Airport 136 SJ 3565
Hawes T 152 SD 8789
Haweswater Reservoir W 151 NY 4814
Hawford T 117 SO 8460
Hawick, Border T 157 NT 5014
Ha Wick, Orkney W 200 ND 2489
Hawkchurch T 92 ST 3400
Hawkedon T 122 TL 7952
Hawkeridge T 101 ST 8653
Hawkerland T 92 SY 0588
Hawkesbury T 101 ST 7687
Hawkesbury Upton T 101 ST 7887
Hawkes End T 118 SP 2982
Hawkhill T 159 NU 2212
Hawkhope 158 NY 7189
Hawkhurst T 97 TQ 7630
Hawkinge T 99 TR 2140
Hawkley T 95 SU 7429
Hawkridge T 91 SS 8630
Hawkridge Reservoir W 92 ST 2036
Hawkshead T 150 SD 3598
Hawksland T 163 NS 8439
Hawks Ness 203 HU 4648
Hawkswick T 146 SD 9570
Hawksworth, Notts T 129 SK 7543
Hawksworth, W. Yks T 146 SE 1641
Hawkwell T 106 TQ 8491
Hawkwood Hill H 162 NS 6837
Hawley, Hants T 104 SU 8558
Hawley, Kent T 105 TQ 5571
Hawling T 114 SP 0623
Hawnby T 153 SE 5489
Haworth T 146 SE 0337
Haworth Moor 146 SE 0035
Hawsker T 149 NZ 9207
Hawstead T 122 TL 8659
Hawthorn T 153 NZ 4145
Hawthorn Hill T 104 SU 8774
Hawthornthwaite Fell H 145 SD 5751
Hawton T 129 SK 7851
Haxby T 147 SE 6057
Haxey T 142 SK 7699
Haxton Down H 102 SU 2050
Hay Bluff H 113 SO 2436
Haycock H 150 NY 1410
Haydock T 137 SJ 5696
Haydon T 93 ST 6715
Haydon Bridge T 158 NY 8464
Haydon Dean 165 NT 9844
Haydon Wick T 102 SU 1387
Haydown Hill H 102 SU 3156
Haye T 88 SX 3469
Hayes, G. Lon T 104 TQ 0980
Hayes, G. Lon T 105 TQ 4066
Hayfield T 138 SK 0387
Hayhillock 177 NO 5242
Hayle T 86 SW 5637
Hayling Bay W 95 SZ 7198
Hayling Island 95 SU 7201
Haylot Fell 145 SD 5961
Haynes T 120 TL 0942
Haynes Church End T 120 TL 0841
Hay-on-Wye T 113 SO 2342
Hayscastle T 110 SM 8925
Hayscastle Cross T 110 SM 9125
Hay Stacks 150 NY 1913
Hayton, Cumbr T 150 NY 1041
Hayton, Cumbr T 151 NY 5057
Hayton, Humbs T 142 SE 8245
Hayton, Notts T 140 SK 7284
Hayton's Bent T 116 SO 5280
Haytor Vale T 89 SX 7777
Haywards Heath T 97 TQ 3324
Haywood Oaks T 129 SK 6055
Hazelbank T 163 NS 8344
Hazelbury Bryan T 93 ST 7408
Hazeley T 104 SU 7459
Hazel Grove T 137 SJ 9286
Hazelrigg T 165 NU 0533
Hazelslade T 128 SK 0212
Hazelton Walls 171 NO 3322
Hazelwood T 128 SK 3246
Hazlemere T 104 SU 8995
Hazlerigg T 159 NZ 2372
Hazleton T 114 SP 0818
Heacham T 132 TF 6737
Headbourne Worhty T 95 SU 4932
Headcorn T 98 TQ 8344
Headingley T 147 SE 2836
Headington T 115 SP 5407
Headlam T 152 NZ 1818
Headless Cross T 118 SP 0365
Headley, Hants T 103 SU 5162
Headley, Hants T 95 SU 8236
Headley, Surrey T 96 TQ 2054
Head o' da Taing 202 HT 9739
Head of Bratta 205 HU 4799
Head of Brough 205 HU 4484
Head of Garness 185 NJ 7465
Head of Holland 200 HY 4912
Head of Hosta 205 HU 6791
Head of Lambhoga 205 HU 6287
Head of Moclett 200 HY 4949
Head of Muir T 169 NS 8181
Head of Stanshi 204 HU 2180
Head of Work 200 HY 4814
Headon T 140 SK 7477
Heads Nook T 151 NY 4955
Heads of Ayre 161 NS 2818
Heage T 128 SK 3750
Healabhal Bheag H 186 NG 2242
Healabhal Mhòr H 186 NG 2244
Healaugh, N. Yks T 152 SE 0199
Healaugh, N. Yks T 147 SE 5047
Healaval H 186 NG 2464
Heald Green T 137 SJ 8585
Heald Moor 146 SD 8826
Heale 91 SS 6446
Healey, Lancs T 137 SD 8815
Healey, Northum T 159 NZ 0158
Healey, N. Yks T 146 SE 1880
Healeyfield T 152 NZ 0648
Healing T 143 TA 2110
Heamoor T 86 SW 4631
Heanish T 172 NM 0343
Heanor T 128 SK 4346
Heanton Punchardon T 90 SS 5035
Heapham T 140 SK 8788
Hearnish 188 NF 6263
Hearthstane T 163 NT 1126
Heart Law H 164 NT 7166
Heasley Mill T 91 SS 7332
Heast T 180 NG 6417
Heath, Derby T 139 SK 4466
Heath, S. Glam T 109 ST 1779
Heath and Reach T 120 SP 9228
Heathcote T 138 SK 1460
Heath End, Hants T 103 SU 5962
Heath End, Hants T 103 SU 8449
Heather T 128 SK 3810
Heathfield, Devon T 89 SX 8376
Heathfield, E. Susx T 97 TQ 5821
Heathfield, Somer T 92 ST 1626
Heathfield, Strath T 161 NS 3262
Heathfield Moor 146 SE 1167
Heath Hayes T 128 SK 0110
Heath Hill T 127 SJ 7614
Heath House T 100 ST 4146
Heath, The T 133 TG 1821
Heathton T 117 SO 8192
Heatley T 137 SJ 7088
Heaton, Lancs T 145 SD 4460
Heaton, Staffs T 138 SJ 9562
Heaton, T. & W T 159 NZ 2766
Heaton Moor T 137 SJ 8791
Heaval H 178 NL 6799
Heaverham T 105 TQ 5758
Heaviley T 137 SJ 9088
Hebburn T 159 NZ 3164
Hebden T 146 SE 0263
Hebden Bridge T 146 SD 9927
Hebden Green T 137 SJ 6365
Hebden Moor 146 SE 0466
Hebden Water W 146 SD 9631
Hebrides or Western Isles, Highld 178 NG 0239
Hebrides or Western Isles, Strath 178 NG 0239
Hebrides or Western Isles, W. Isles 178 NG 0239
Hebron T 159 NZ 1989
Heckfield T 104 SU 7260
Heckington T 130 TF 1444
Heckmondwike T 146 SE 2123
Hecla H 178 NF 8234
Heddington T 102 ST 9966
Heddle T 200 HY 3512
Heddon-on-the-Wall T 159 NZ 1366
Heddon's Mouth 91 SS 6549
Hedenham T 133 TM 3193
Hedge End T 95 SU 4912
Hedgehope Hill H 158 NT 9419
Hedgerley T 104 SU 9787
Hedging T 92 ST 3029
Hedley on the Hill T 159 NZ 0759
Hednesford T 128 SK 0012
Hedon T 143 TA 1828
Hedsor T 104 SU 9086
Hegdon Hill T 113 SO 5854
Heggerscales T 151 NY 8210
Heglibister T 203 HU 3851
Heighington, Durham T 152 NZ 2422
Heighington, Lincs T 140 TF 0369
Heights of Brae T 182 NH 5161
Heights of Kinlochewe T 191 NH 0764
Heilam 197 NC 4560
Heillia 204 HU 2684
Heishival Mór H 178 NL 6296
Heisker or Monach Islands 188 NF 6262
Heiskers 178 NL 5886
Heiton T 164 NT 7130
Helbeck T 151 NY 7915
Heldale Water W 200 ND 2592
Heldon Hill 183 NJ 1358
Hele, Devon T 91 SS 5347
Hele, Devon T 91 SS 9902
Helensburgh T 168 NS 2982
Helford T 86 SW 7526
Helford River W 86 SW 7626
Helhoughton T 132 TF 8626
Helions Bumpstead T 122 TL 6541
Hellabrick's Wick W 202 HT 9636
Helland T 87 SX 0770
Hellesdon T 133 TG 2012
Helliar Holm 200 HY 4815
Hellidon T 119 SP 5158
Hellifield T 146 SD 8556
Helli Ness 203 HU 4628
Hellingly T 97 TQ 5912
Hellington T 133 TG 3103
Hellir 205 HU 3892
Hellisay 178 NF 7504
Hellister T 203 HU 3949
Hellmoor Loch W 157 NT 3816
Hell's Glen 168 NN 1706
Hell's Mouth or Porth Neigwl W 124 SH 2626
Helman Head 199 ND 3646
Helmdon T 119 SP 5843
Helmingham T 123 TM 1957
Helmsdale T 193 ND 0215
Helmshore T 146 SD 7821
Helmsley T 147 SE 6183
Helmsley Moor 153 SE 5991
Helperby T 147 SE 4369
Helperthorpe T 149 SE 9570
Helpringham T 130 TF 1340
Helpston T 130 TF 1205
Helsby T 137 SJ 4875
Helston P 86 SW 6527
Helstone T 87 SX 0881
Helton T 151 NY 5122
Helvellyn H 150 NY 3415
Helwick (lightship) 108 SS 3280
Helwith Bridge T 146 SD 8169
Hemblington T 133 TG 3411
Hembury A 92 ST 1103
Hemel Hempstead T 104 TL 0507
Hemingbrough T 147 SE 6730
Hemingby T 141 TF 2374
Hemingford Abbots T 121 TL 2970
Hemingford Grey T 121 TL 2970
Hemingstone T 123 TM 1553
Hemington, Northnts T 120 TL 0985
Hemington, Somer T 101 ST 7253
Hemley T 123 TM 2842
Hempholme T 149 TA 0850
Hempnall T 133 TM 2494
Hempnall Green T 133 TM 2493
Hempriggs T 183 NJ 1064
Hempriggs House 199 ND 3547
Hempstead, Essex T 122 TL 6338
Hempstead, Norf T 133 TG 1037
Hempstead, Norf T 133 TG 4028
Hempsted T 114 SO 8117
Hempton, Norf T 132 TF 9129
Hempton, Oxon T 115 SP 4431
Hemsby T 133 TG 4917
Hemsby Hole W 133 TG 5117
Hemswell T 140 SK 9390
Hemsworth T 139 SE 4213
Hemyock T 92 ST 1313
Henbury, Avon T 101 ST 5678
Henbury, Ches T 137 SJ 8873
Hendersyde Park 164 NT 7435
Hendon, G. Lon T 105 TQ 2389
Hendon, T. & W T 153 NZ 4055
Hendre T 136 SJ 1967
Hendreys Course H 163 NS 9758
Hendy T 111 SN 5803
Heneglwys T 134 SH 4276
Henfield T 96 TQ 2115
Hen Gerrig H 125 SH 9518
Hengistbury Head 94 SZ 1790
Hengoed, M. Glam T 109 ST 1595
Hengoed, Powys T 113 SO 2253
Hengoed, Shrops T 126 SJ 2933
Hengrave T 122 TL 8268
Henham T 121 TL 5428
Henley, Shrops T 116 SO 5476
Henley, Somer T 93 ST 4332
Henley, Suff T 123 TM 1551
Henley, W. Susx T 95 SU 8925
Henley-in-Arden T 118 SP 1566
Henley-on-Thames T 104 SU 7682
Henley Park T 96 SU 9352
Henllan, Clwyd T 135 SJ 0268
Henllan, Dyfed T 111 SN 3540
Henllan Amgoed T 111 SN 1820
Henllys T 113 ST 2694
Henlow T 120 TL 1738
Hennock T 89 SX 8380
Henryd T 135 SH 7774
Henry's Moat T 110 SN 0427
Hensall T 147 SE 5923
Hensbarrow Downs H 87 SW 9957
Henshaw T 158 NY 7664
Henstead T 123 TM 4986
Henstridge T 93 ST 7219
Henstridge Marsh T 93 ST 7420
Henton, Oxon T 104 SP 7602
Henton, Somer T 100 ST 4050
Henwood T 88 SX 2673
Heogan T 203 HU 4743
Heoga Ness 205 HU 5379
Heol Senni T 109 SN 9223
Heol-y-Cyw T 109 SS 9484
Hepburn T 165 NU 0624
Hepple T 159 NT 9800
Hepscott T 159 NZ 2284
Heptonstall T 146 SD 9828
Heptonstall Moor 146 SD 9430
Hepworth, Suff T 122 TL 9874
Hepworth, W. Yks T 138 SE 1606
Herbrandston T 110 SM 8707
Hereford P 113 SO 5140
Hergest T 113 SO 2755
Hergest Ridge, H. & W H 113 SO 2556
Hergest Ridge, Powys H 113 SO 2556
Heriot T 164 NT 3952
Herma Ness 205 HP 6018
Hermaness Hill H 205 HP 6017
Herman Law, Border H 157 NT 2115
Herman Law, D. & G H 157 NT 2115
Hermetray 188 NF 9874
Hermitage, Berks T 103 SU 5173
Hermitage, Border T 157 NY 5095
Hermitage, Dorset T 93 ST 6407
Hermitage, W. Susx T 95 SU 7505
Hermitage, The T 96 TQ 2253
Hermon, Dyfed T 111 SN 2131
Hermon, Dyfed T 111 SN 3630
Hermon, Gwyn T 134 SH 3969
Herne T 99 TR 1865
Herne Bay T 99 TR 1768
Herner T 91 SS 5826
Herne, The 121 TL 2490
Hernhill T 99 TR 0660
Herodsfoot T 87 SX 2160
Herongate T 106 TQ 6391
Heronsgate T 104 TQ 0294
Herra, The 205 HU 4693
Herriard T 103 SU 6645
Herringfleet T 133 TM 4797
Herringswell T 122 TL 7169
Herrington T 153 NZ 3653
Herscha Hill H 177 NO 7380
Hersden T 99 TR 2062
Hersham T 105 TQ 1164
Herstmonceux T 97 TQ 6312
Herston T 200 ND 4191
Herston Head 200 ND 4191
Hertford P 105 TL 3212
Hertford Heath T 105 TL 3511
Hertingfordbury T 105 TL 3012
Hesketh Bank T 145 SD 4423
Hesketh Lane T 145 SD 6141
Hesket Newmarket T 150 NY 3438
Heskin Green T 137 SD 5315
Hesleden T 153 NZ 4438
Hesleyside 158 NY 8183
Heslington T 147 SE 6250
Hessay T 147 SE 5253
Hessenford T 88 SX 3057
Hessett T 122 TL 9361
Hessle T 142 TA 0326
Hestan Island 155 NX 8350
Hest Bank T 145 SD 4766
Hesti Geo 202 HT 9736
Heston T 105 TQ 1277
Heswall T 136 SJ 2782
Hethe T 115 SP 5929
Hethersett T 133 TG 1505
Hethersgill T 157 NY 4767
Hethpool T 165 NT 8928
Hett T 152 NZ 2836
Hetton T 146 SD 9658
Hetton-le-Hole T 153 NZ 3547
Hetty Pegler's Tump A 114 SO 7900
Heugh T 159 NZ 0873
Heugh-head T 184 NJ 3811
Hevdadale Head 204 HU 3089
Heveningham T 123 TM 3372
Hever T 97 TQ 4744
Heversham T 145 SD 4983
Hevingham T 133 TG 1921
Hewelsfield T 113 SO 5602
Hewish, Avon T 100 ST 4064
Hewish, Somer T 93 ST 4208
Hexham P 158 NY 9364
Hexhamshire Common 152 NY 8853
Hextable T 105 TQ 5170
Hexton T 120 TL 1030
Hexworthy T 89 SX 6572
Heybridge, Essex T 106 TL 8508
Heybridge, Essex T 106 TQ 6498
Heybridge Basin T 106 TL 8707
Heybrook Bay T 88 SX 4949
Heydon, Cambs T 121 TL 4340
Heydon, Norf T 133 TG 1127
Heydon Hill H 92 ST 0327
Heydour T 130 TF 0039
Heylipol T 172 NL 9743
Heylor T 204 HU 2881
Heysham T 145 SD 4161
Heysham Lake W 145 SD 3758
Heyshott T 95 SU 8918
Heytesbury T 101 ST 9242
Heythrop T 115 SP 3527
Heywood, G. Man T 137 SD 8510
Heywood, Wilts T 101 ST 8753
Hibaldstow T 142 SE 9702
Hickleton T 139 SE 4805
Hickling, Norf T 133 TG 4124
Hickling, Notts T 129 SK 6928
Hickling Green T 133 TG 4023
Hickling Heath T 133 TG 4022
Hidcote Boyce T 118 SP 1742
High Ackworth T 139 SE 4417
Higham, Derby T 139 SK 3959
Higham, Kent T 98 TQ 7171
Higham, Lancs T 146 SD 8036
Higham, Suff T 122 TL 7465
Higham, Suff T 122 TM 0335
Higham Dykes T 159 NZ 1375
Higham Ferrers T 120 SP 9668
Higham Gobion T 120 TL 1032
Higham on the Hill T 128 SP 3895
Highampton T 90 SS 4804
Higham Wood T 97 TQ 6048
High Banton 169 NS 7480
High Beach T 105 TQ 4097
High Bentham T 145 SD 6669
High Bickington T 91 SS 6020
High Birkwith T 146 SD 8077
High Blantyre T 162 NS 6856
High Bonnybridge T 169 NS 8379
High Borve T 195 NB 4156
High Bradfield T 139 SK 2692
Highbridge, Highld T 174 NN 1981
Highbridge, Somer T 100 ST 3147
Highbrook T 97 TQ 3430
Highburton T 138 SE 1913
Highbury T 101 ST 6949
High Buston T 159 NU 2308
High Callerton T 159 NZ 1670
High Catton T 148 SE 7153
Highclere T 102 SU 4360
Highclere Castle 103 SU 4458
Highcliffe T 94 SZ 2093
High Cogges T 115 SP 3709
High Coniscliffe T 152 NZ 2215
High Cross, Hants T 95 SU 7126
High Cross, Herts T 105 TL 3618
High Cross Bank T 128 SK 2817
High Easter T 106 TL 6214
High Ellington T 146 SE 1983
Higher Ashton T 89 SX 8584
Higher Ballam T 145 SD 3630
Higher Ercall T 127 SJ 5917
Higher End T 137 SD 5303
Higher Penwortham T 145 SD 5128
Higher Poynton T 137 SJ 9483
Higher Sharpnose Point 90 SS 1914
Higher Tale T 92 ST 0601
Higher Town T 86 SV 9315
Higher Walreddon T 88 SX 4871
Higher Walton, Ches T 137 SJ 5985
Higher Walton, Lancs T 145 SD 5727
Higher Wych T 127 SJ 4943
Highfield, Northum 158 NY 7391
Highfield, Strath T 161 NS 3050
Highfield, T. & W T 159 NZ 1458
Highfields T 121 TL 3558
High Force W 152 NY 8727
High Garrett T 122 TL 7726
High Grange T 152 NZ 1731

High Green
Hubbert's Bridge

High Green, H. & W *T* 117 SO 8745
High Green, Norf *T* 133 TG 1305
High Green, S. Yks *T* 139 SK 3397
Highgreen Manor 158 NY 8091
High Halden *T* 98 TQ 8937
High Halstow *T* 98 TQ 7875
High Ham *T* 93 ST 4231
High Hatton *T* 127 SJ 6124
High Hesket *T* 151 NY 4744
High Hoyland *T* 139 SE 2710
High Hunsley *T* 142 SE 9535
High Hurstwood *T* 97 TQ 4926
High Knowes *H* 158 NT 9612
High Lane, G. Man *T* 138 SJ 9585
High Lane, H. & W *T* 117 SO 6760
High Laver *T* 105 TL 5208
Highleadon *T* 114 SO 7723
High Legh *T* 137 SJ 7084
Highleigh *T* 95 SZ 8498
Highley *T* 117 SO 7483
High Littleton *T* 101 ST 6458
High Melton *T* 139 SE 5001
Highmoor Cross *T* 104 SU 7084
Highmoor Hill *T* 101 ST 4689
High Moor of Killiemore 154 NX 3660
High Murdonochee *H* 154 NX 1775
Highnam *T* 114 SO 7919
High Neb *H* 139 SK 2285
High Newton *T* 145 SD 4082
High Newton-by-the-Sea *T* 165 NU 2325
High Offley *T* 127 SJ 7826
High Ongar *T* 105 TL 5603
High Onn *T* 127 SJ 8216
High Peak *H* 138 SK 1188
High Pike *H* 150 NY 3135
High Roding *T* 106 TL 6017
High Salvington *T* 96 TQ 1206
High Shaw *T* 152 SD 8792
High Spen *T* 159 NZ 1359
Highsted *T* 98 TQ 9061
High Stile *H* 150 NY 1614
High Street, Corn *T* 87 SW 9653
High Street, Cumbr *H* 151 NY 4411
High Street, Cumbr *R* 151 NY 4515
High Street, Suff *T* 123 TM 4355
High Street Green *T* 122 TM 0055
Hightae *T* 157 NY 0978
Hightown, Ches *T* 137 SJ 8761
Hightown, Mers *T* 136 SD 3003
High Toynton *T* 141 TF 2869
High Trewhill *T* 159 NU 0105
Highway, Corn *T* 87 SX 1453
Highway, Wilts *T* 102 SU 0474
High White Stones *H* 150 NY 2809
High Willhays *H* 89 SX 5789
Highworth *T* 102 SU 2092
High Wray *T* 151 SD 3799
High Wych *T* 105 TL 4614
High Wycombe *P* 104 SU 8593
Hilborough *T* 132 TF 8200
Hildasay 203 HU 3540
Hildenborough *T* 97 TQ 5648
Hildersham *T* 121 TL 5448
Hilderstone *T* 127 SJ 9434
Hilderthorpe *T* 149 TA 1765
Hilgay *T* 132 TL 6298
Hilgay Fen 131 TL 5895
Hill *T* 114 ST 6495
Hillam *T* 147 SE 5028
Hillberry *T* 144 SC 3879
Hillbrae, Grampn *T* 184 NJ 6047
Hillbrae, Grampn *T* 185 NJ 7923
Hill Brow *T* 95 SU 7926
Hilldyke *T* 131 TF 3447
Hill End, Durham *T* 152 NZ 0135
Hill End, Fife *T* 170 NT 0395
Hillend, Fife *T* 170 NT 1484
Hillend Reservoir *W* 163 NS 8367
Hillerton *T* 89 SX 7298
Hillesden *T* 119 SP 6828
Hillesley *T* 101 ST 7689
Hillfarrance *T* 92 ST 1624
Hillhead, Devon *T* 89 SX 9053
Hill Head, Hants *T* 95 SU 5402
Hillhead, Strath *T* 161 NS 4219
Hillhead of Auchentumb *T* 185 NJ 9258
Hillhead of Cocklaw *T* 185 NK 0844
Hilliard's Cross *T* 128 SK 1511
Hilliclay *T* 199 ND 1764
Hillingdon *T* 104 TQ 0783
Hillington *T* 132 TF 7125
Hillmorton *T* 119 SP 5373
Hill Mountain *T* 110 SM 9708
Hill Ness 205 HP 6517
Hillockhead *T* 184 NJ 3809
Hill of Aitnoch *H* 183 NH 9739
Hill of Alyth *H* 176 NO 2450
Hill of Arisdale *H* 205 HU 4984
Hill of Bakkanalee *H* 205 HP 4903
Hill of Barra *H* 185 NJ 8025
Hill of Beath *T* 170 NT 1490
Hill of Berran *H* 176 NO 4571
Hill of Camb *H* 205 HU 5092
Hill of Cammie, Grampn *H* 177 NO 5285
Hill of Cammie, Tays *H* 177 NO 5285
Hill of Cat, Grampn *H* 177 NO 4887
Hill of Cat, Tays *H* 177 NO 4887
Hill of Colvadale *H* 205 HP 6105
Hill of Corsegight *H* 185 NJ 8550
Hill of Couternach *H* 176 NO 3565
Hill of Crooksetter *H* 205 HU 4175
Hill of Dalsetter *H* 205 HU 5098
Hill of Dudwick *H* 185 NJ 9737
Hill of Edendocher *H* 177 NO 6085
Hill of Fare *H* 185 NJ 6803
Hill of Fearn *T* 193 NH 8377
Hill of Finavon *H* 177 NO 4955
Hill of Fingray, Grampn *H* 177 NO 5781
Hill of Fingray, Tays *H* 177 NO 5781
Hill of Fishrie *H* 185 NJ 8258
Hill of Foudland *H* 184 NJ 6033
Hill of Garbet *H* 177 NO 4668
Hill of Glansie *H* 176 NO 4369
Hill of Maud Crofts *T* 184 NJ 4662
Hill of Menmuir *H* 177 NO 5265
Hill of Miffia *H* 200 HY 2313
Hill of Mulderie *H* 184 NJ 3851
Hill of Nigg *H* 193 NH 8271
Hill of Oliclett *H* 199 ND 2946
Hill of Rangag *H* 199 ND 1844
Hill of Reafirth *H* 205 HU 5088
Hill of Saughs *H* 176 NO 4485
Hill of Shurton *H* 203 HU 4440
Hill of Skilmafilly *H* 185 NJ 9040
Hill of Stake *H* 161 NS 2763
Hill of the Wangie *H* 183 NJ 1453
Hill of Three Stones *H* 184 NJ 3422
Hill of Tillymorgan *H* 184 NJ 6534
Hill of Tomechole *H* 183 NJ 0649
Hill of Towie *H* 184 NJ 3847
Hill of Trusta *H* 177 NO 7886
Hill of Wirren *H* 177 NO 5273
Hill Ridware *T* 128 SK 0818
Hill Row Doles 121 TL 4176
Hillside, Grampn *T* 177 NO 9297
Hillside, Shetld *T* 203 HU 4063
Hillside, Tays *T* 177 NO 7061
Hills of Cromdale, Grampn *H* 183 NJ 1126
Hills of Cromdale, Highld *H* 183 NJ 1126
Hillswick *T* 204 HU 2877
Hill, The *T* 144 SD 1783
Hilltop 94 SU 4003
Hilmarton *T* 102 SU 0275
Hilperton *T* 101 ST 8759
Hilsea *T* 95 SU 6603
Hilton, Cambs *T* 121 TL 2966
Hilton, Cleve *T* 153 NZ 4611
Hilton, Cumbr *T* 151 NY 7320
Hilton, Derby *T* 128 SK 2430
Hilton, Dorset *T* 93 ST 7803
Hilton, Durham *T* 152 NZ 1621
Hilton, Grampn *T* 185 NJ 9434
Hilton, Shrops *T* 127 SO 7795
Hilton of Cadboll *T* 193 NH 8776
Himbleton *T* 117 SO 9458
Himley *T* 117 SO 8791
Hincaster *T* 145 SD 5184
Hinchingbrooke House *A* 121 TL 2271
Hinckley *P* 128 SP 4293
Hinderclay *T* 122 TM 0276
Hinderwell *T* 153 NZ 7916
Hindford *T* 126 SJ 3333
Hindhead *T* 95 SU 8835
Hindhope Law *H* 158 NY 7697
Hindlethwaite Moor 146 SE 0580
Hindley *T* 137 SD 6204
Hindley Green *T* 137 SD 6303
Hindlip *T* 117 SO 8758
Hindolveston *T* 132 TG 0329
Hindon *T* 93 ST 9132
Hindringham *T* 132 TF 9836
Hingham *T* 132 TG 0202
Hinkley Point Power Station *T* 100 ST 2146
Hinstock *T* 127 SJ 6926
Hintlesham *T* 123 TM 0843
Hinton, Avon *T* 101 ST 7376
Hinton, Hants *T* 94 SZ 2195
Hinton, Northnts *T* 119 SP 5352
Hinton, Shrops *T* 126 SJ 4108
Hinton Ampner *T* 95 SU 5927
Hinton Blewett *T* 101 ST 5956
Hinton Charterhouse *T* 101 ST 7758
Hinton-in-the-Hedges *T* 119 SP 5536
Hinton Martell *T* 94 SU 0106
Hinton on the Green *T* 118 SP 0240
Hinton Parva *T* 102 SU 2383
Hinton St George *T* 93 ST 4212
Hinton St Mary *T* 93 ST 7816
Hinton Waldrist *T* 115 SU 3899
Hints, Shrops *T* 117 SO 6175
Hints, Staffs *T* 128 SK 1503
Hinwick *T* 120 SP 9361
Hinxhill *T* 99 TR 0442
Hinxton *T* 121 TL 4945
Hinxworth *T* 121 TL 2340
Hipperholme *T* 146 SE 1225
Hipswell Moor 152 SE 1497
Hirddywell *H* 125 SO 0280
Hirfynydd *H* 109 SN 8206
Hirn *T* 177 NJ 7300
Hirnant *T* 125 SJ 0523
Hirst *T* 159 NZ 2887
Hirst Courtney *T* 147 SE 6124
Hirta or St Kilda 188 NF 0999
Hirwaun *T* 109 SN 9505
Hirwaun Common 109 SN 9404
Hiscott *T* 91 SS 5426
Hisehope Resr *W* 152 NZ 0246
Histon *T* 121 TL 4363
Hitcham *T* 122 TL 9851
Hitchin *T* 120 TL 1829
Hither Green *T* 105 TQ 3874
Hittisleigh *T* 89 SX 7395
Hixon *T* 128 SK 0026
Hoaden *T* 99 TR 2659
Hoaldalbert *T* 113 SO 3923
Hoar Cross *T* 128 SK 1223
Hoarwithy *T* 113 SO 5429
Hoath *T* 99 TR 2064
Hobarris *T* 116 SO 3178
Hobbister *T* 200 HY 3806
Hobhole Drain *W* 131 TF 3748
Hobkirk *T* 158 NT 5810
Hobland Hall 133 TG 5001
Hobson *T* 152 NZ 1755
Hoby *T* 129 SK 6617
Hockering *T* 132 TG 0713
Hockerton *T* 129 SK 7156
Hockley *T* 106 TQ 8492
Hockley Heath *T* 118 SP 1573
Hockliffe *T* 120 SP 9726
Hockwold cum Wilton *T* 122 TL 7288
Hockwold Fens 122 TL 7087
Hockworthy *T* 92 ST 0319
Hoddesdon *T* 105 TL 3708
Hoddlesden *T* 145 SD 7122
Hoddom Castle *A* 157 NY 1572
Hodge Beck *W* 153 SE 6294
Hodgeston *T* 110 SS 0399
Hod Hill *A* 93 ST 8510
Hodnet *T* 127 SJ 6128
Hodthorpe *T* 139 SK 5476
Hoe *T* 132 TF 9916
Hoe Gate *T* 95 SU 6213
Hoe Point 186 NG 1641
Hoe Rape 186 NG 1543
Hoff *T* 151 NY 6717
Hog Fell *H* 157 NY 3989
Hoggeston *T* 119 SP 8025
Hogh Bay *W* 172 NM 1657
Hog Hill *H* 157 NY 2895
Hoghton *T* 145 SD 6126
Hognaston *T* 128 SK 2350
Hog's Back *H* 96 SU 9248
Hogs Law *H* 164 NT 5555
Hogsthorpe *T* 141 TF 5372
Holbeach *T* 131 TF 3624
Holbeach Bank *T* 131 TF 3527
Holbeach Drove *T* 131 TF 3212
Holbeach Hurn *T* 131 TF 3927
Holbeach Marsh 131 TF 3829
Holbeach St Johns *T* 131 TF 3418
Holbeach St Marks *T* 131 TF 3731
Holbeach St Matthew *T* 131 TF 4132
Holbeck *T* 139 SK 5473
Holberrow Green *T* 118 SP 0259
Holbeton *T* 89 SX 6150
Holborn *T* 105 TQ 3181
Holborn Head 199 ND 1071
Holbrook, Derby *T* 128 SK 3644
Holbrook, Suff *T* 123 TM 1636
Holbrook Bay *W* 123 TM 1733
Holburn *T* 165 NU 0436
Holbury *T* 94 SU 4303
Holcombe, Devon *T* 89 SX 9574
Holcombe, Somer *T* 101 ST 6749
Holcombe Rogus *T* 92 ST 0518
Holcot *T* 119 SP 7969
Holden *T* 146 SD 7749
Holdenby *T* 119 SP 6967
Holderness Drain *W* 143 TA 1135
Holdgate *T* 116 SO 5689
Holdingham *T* 130 TF 0547
Holehouse Hill *H* 156 NY 0194
Hole in the Wall *T* 113 SO 6128
Holemoor *T* 90 SS 4205
Hole o' Row 200 HY 2219
Hole Park 98 TQ 8332
Holestane 156 NX 8799
Hole Stone Bay *W* 154 NX 0646
Holford *T* 100 ST 1541
Holker *T* 145 SD 3677
Holkham *T* 132 TF 8943
Holkham Bay *W* 132 TF 8846
Hollacombe, Devon *T* 90 SS 3703
Hollacombe, Devon *T* 91 SS 6311
Holland, Orkney 200 HY 4851
Holland, Orkney 201 HY 6622
Holland Fen 131 TF 2346
Holland-on-Sea *T* 107 TM 2016
Hollandstoun *T* 201 HY 7553
Hollesley *T* 123 TM 3544
Hollesley Bay *W* 123 TM 3944
Hollinfare *T* 137 SJ 6991
Hollingbourne *T* 98 TQ 8455
Hollington, Derby *T* 128 SK 2339
Hollington, E. Susx *T* 98 TQ 7911
Hollington, Staffs *T* 128 SK 0639
Hollingworth *T* 138 SK 0196
Hollingworth Lake *W* 137 SD 9314
Hollins *T* 137 SD 8108
Hollinsclough *T* 138 SK 0666
Hollinwood *T* 127 SJ 5236
Holliwell Point 107 TR 0296
Holloway *T* 128 SK 3256
Hollowell *T* 119 SP 6972
Hollowell Reservoir *W* 119 SP 6873
Holl Reservoir *W* 171 NO 2203
Holl's Green *T* 121 TL 2728
Hollybush, Gwent *T* 109 SO 1603
Hollybush, H. & W *T* 117 SO 7637
Hollybush, Strath *T* 161 NS 3914
Holly End *T* 131 TF 4906
Hollym *T* 143 TA 3425
Hollywood *T* 118 SP 0877
Holm, Orkney 200 HY 4703
Holm, W. Isles *T* 195 NB 4531
Holmbury St Mary *T* 96 TQ 1144
Holme, Cambs *T* 120 TL 1987
Holme, Cumbr *T* 145 SD 5279
Holme, Notts *T* 140 SK 8059
Holme, W. Yks *T* 138 SE 1006
Holme Chapel *T* 146 SD 8728
Holme Hale *T* 132 TF 8807
Holme Island 145 SD 4278
Holme Lacy *T* 113 SO 5535
Holme Marsh *T* 113 SO 3454
Holme next the Sea *T* 132 TF 7043
Holme-on-Spalding-Moor *T* 142 SE 8038
Holme on the Wolds *T* 142 SE 9646
Holmer *T* 113 SO 5042
Holmer Green *T* 104 SU 9096
Holmes Chapel *T* 137 SJ 7667
Holmesfield *T* 139 SK 3277
Holmeswood *T* 136 SD 4317
Holmewood *T* 139 SK 4265
Holmfirth *T* 138 SE 1508
Holmhead *T* 156 NS 5620
Holm Island 187 NG 5251
Holm of Helliness 203 HU 4628
Holm of Huip 201 HY 6231
Holm of Melby 202 HU 1958
Holm of Noss 203 HU 5539
Holm of Papa 200 HY 5052
Holm of Skaw 205 HP 6617
Holm of West Sandwick 205 HU 4389
Holmpton *T* 143 TA 3623
Holmrook *T* 150 SD 0799
Holmsgarth *T* 203 HU 4642
Holms of Ire 201 HY 6446
Holm Sound *W* 200 ND 5099
Holms Water *W* 163 NT 1033
Holmwood Station 96 TQ 1743
Holne *T* 89 SX 7069
Holnest *T* 93 ST 6509
Holoman Bay *W* 187 NG 5439
Holsworthy *T* 90 SS 3403
Holsworthy Beacon *T* 90 SS 3508
Holt, Clwyd *T* 126 SJ 4154
Holt, Dorset *T* 94 SU 0203
Holt, H. & W *T* 117 SO 8362
Holt, Norf *T* 132 TG 0738
Holt, Wilts *T* 101 ST 8661
Holtby *T* 147 SE 6754
Holt End *T* 118 SP 0769
Holt Heath *T* 117 SO 8163
Holton, Oxon *T* 115 SP 6006
Holton, Somer *T* 93 ST 6826
Holton, Suff *T* 123 TM 4077
Holton cum Beckering *T* 141 TF 1181
Holton Heath 94 SY 9591
Holton le Clay *T* 143 TA 2802
Holton le Moor *T* 142 TF 0898
Holton St Mary *T* 122 TM 0636
Holwell, Dorset *T* 93 ST 7010
Holwell, Herts *T* 120 TL 1633
Holwell, Leic *T* 129 SK 7323
Holwell, Oxon *T* 115 SP 2309
Holwick *T* 152 NY 9027
Holworth *T* 93 SY 7683
Holybourne *T* 103 SU 7340
Holy Cross *T* 117 SO 9279
Holyhead *P* 134 SH 2482
Holyhead Bay *W* 134 SH 2587
Holyhead Mountain *H* 134 SH 2283
Holy Island, Gwyn 134 SH 2579
Holy Island, Northum *T* 165 NU 1241
Holy Island, Northum 165 NU 1243
Holy Island, Strath 160 NS 0630
Holy Island Sands 165 NU 1042
Holy Loch *W* 168 NS 1781
Holymoorside *T* 139 SK 3369
Holyport *T* 104 SU 8977
Holystone *T* 158 NT 9502
Holytown *T* 162 NS 7660
Holywell, Cambs *T* 121 TL 3370
Holywell, Clwyd *T* 136 SJ 1876
Holywell, Corn *T* 86 SW 7658
Holywell, Dorset *T* 93 ST 5904
Holywell Bank 136 SJ 2179
Holywell Bay *W* 86 SW 7559
Holywell Green *T* 138 SE 0819
Holywell Lake *T* 92 ST 1020
Holywell Row *T* 122 TL 7077
Holywood *T* 156 NX 9480
Homer *T* 127 SJ 6101
Homersfield *T* 123 TM 2885
Hom Green *T* 113 SO 5822
Homington *T* 94 SU 1226
Honddu *W* 112 SO 0236
Honeybourne *T* 118 SP 1144
Honeychurch *T* 91 SS 6202
Honey Hill *T* 99 TR 1161
Honiley *T* 118 SP 2472
Honing *T* 133 TG 3227
Honingham *T* 133 TG 1011
Honington, Lincs *T* 130 SK 9443
Honington, Suff *T* 122 TL 9174
Honington, Warw *T* 118 SP 2642
Honister Pass 150 NY 2213
Honiton *P* 92 ST 1600
Honley *T* 138 SE 1311
Hoo *T* 123 TM 2558
Hooe, Devon *T* 88 SX 5052
Hooe, E. Susx *T* 97 TQ 6809
Hook, Dyfed *T* 110 SM 9811
Hook, G. Lon *T* 105 TQ 1764
Hook, Hants *T* 103 SU 7254
Hook, Humbs *T* 142 SE 7625
Hook, Wilts *T* 102 SU 0784
Hooke *T* 93 ST 5300
Hookgate *T* 127 SJ 7435
Hook Norton *T* 115 SP 3533
Hookway *T* 89 SX 8598
Hookwood *T* 96 TQ 2642
Hoole *T* 136 SJ 4267
Hoo Stack 203 HU 5052
Hoo St Werburgh *T* 98 TQ 7872
Hooton Levitt *T* 139 SK 5291
Hooton Pagnell *T* 139 SE 4808
Hooton Roberts *T* 139 SK 4897
Hope, Clwyd *T* 136 SJ 3158
Hope, Derby *T* 138 SK 1783
Hope, Devon *T* 89 SX 6740
Hope, Highld *T* 197 NC 4760
Hope, Powys *T* 126 SJ 2507
Hope, Shrops *T* 126 SJ 3401
Hope Bagot *T* 117 SO 5974
Hope Bowdler *T* 116 SO 4792
Hopehouse 158 NY 6780
Hopeman *T* 183 NJ 1469
Hope Mansell *T* 113 SO 6219
Hopesay *T* 116 SO 3983
Hope's Nose 89 SX 9563
Hopes Reservoir *W* 164 NT 5462
Hopes Water *W* 164 NT 5563
Hopetoun House 170 NT 0979
Hope under Dinmore *T* 113 SO 5052
Hopton, Staffs *T* 127 SJ 9426
Hopton, Suff *T* 122 TL 9979
Hopton Cangeford *T* 116 SO 5480
Hopton Castle *T* 116 SO 3678
Hopton on Sea *T* 133 TG 5300
Hopton Titterhill *H* 116 SO 3577
Hopton Wafers *T* 117 SO 6376
Hopwas *T* 128 SK 1805
Hopwood *T* 118 SP 0375
Horam *T* 97 TQ 5717
Horbling *T* 130 TF 1135
Horbury *T* 139 SE 2918
Horden *T* 153 NZ 4441
Horderley *T* 116 SO 4187
Hordle *T* 94 SZ 2795
Hordley *T* 126 SJ 3830
Horeb, Dyfed *T* 111 SN 3942
Horeb, Dyfed *T* 111 SN 5128
Horham *T* 123 TM 2172
Horkstowe *T* 142 SE 9818
Horley, Oxon *T* 118 SP 4143
Horley, Surrey *T* 97 TQ 2842
Hornblotton Green *T* 93 ST 5933
Hornby, Lancs *T* 145 SD 5868
Hornby, N. Yks *T* 153 NZ 3605
Horncastle *T* 141 TF 2669
Hornchurch *T* 105 TQ 5487
Horncliffe *T* 165 NT 9249
Horndean *T* 95 SU 7013
Horndon on the Hill *T* 106 TQ 6683
Horne *T* 97 TQ 3444
Horn Hill *T* 104 TQ 0192
Horniehaugh 176 NO 4161
Horning *T* 133 TG 3417
Horninghold *T* 129 SP 8097
Horninglow *T* 128 SK 2425
Horningsea *T* 121 TL 4962
Horningsham *T* 101 ST 8141
Horningtoft *T* 132 TF 9323
Hornish 178 NF 7309
Hornish Point *T* 188 NF 7547
Hornsby *T* 151 NY 5150
Hornsea *T* 143 TA 2047
Hornsea Mere *W* 143 TA 1947
Hornsey *T* 105 TQ 3089
Hornton *T* 118 SP 3945
Horrabridge *T* 88 SX 5169
Horringer *T* 122 TL 8261
Horsanish 188 NA 9908
Horsea Island 95 SU 6304
Horsebridge, E. Susx *T* 97 TQ 5811
Horsebridge, Hants *T* 94 SU 3430
Horse Bridge, Staffs *T* 128 SJ 9653
Horsebrook *T* 127 SJ 8810
Horsehay *T* 127 SJ 6707
Horseheath *T* 122 TL 6147
Horse Hope Hill *H* 163 NT 2130
Horsehouse *T* 146 SE 0481
Horse Island, Highld 190 NC 0204
Horse Island, Shetld 203 HU 3807
Horse Isle 161 NS 2142
Horseley Fen 121 TL 4083
Horseley Hill *H* 165 NT 8362
Horsell *T* 104 SU 9959
Horseman's Green *T* 126 SJ 4441
Horse of Burravoe 205 HU 5381
Horse of Copinsay 201 HY 6202
Horse Sound *W* 190 NC 0304
Horseway *T* 121 TL 4286
Horsey *T* 133 TG 4522
Horsey Island 107 TM 2324
Horsford *T* 133 TG 1916
Horsforth *T* 147 SE 2438
Horsham, H. & W *T* 117 SO 7358
Horsham, W. Susx *F* 96 TQ 1730
Horsham St Faith *T* 133 TG 2115
Horsington, Lincs *T* 141 TF 1968
Horsington, Somer *T* 93 ST 7023
Horsley, Derby *T* 128 SK 3744
Horsley, Glos *T* 114 ST 8398
Horsley, Northum *T* 158 NY 8496
Horsley, Northum *T* 159 NZ 0966
Horsley Cross *T* 123 TM 1227
Horsleycross Street *T* 123 TM 1228
Horsleyhill *T* 158 NT 5319
Horsley Woodhouse *T* 128 SK 3945
Horsmonden *T* 97 TQ 7040
Horspath *T* 115 SP 5704
Horstead *T* 133 TG 2619
Horsted Keynes *T* 97 TQ 3828
Horton, Avon *T* 101 ST 7584
Horton, Berks *T* 104 TQ 0175
Horton, Bucks *T* 104 SP 9219
Horton, Dorset *T* 94 SU 0307
Horton, Lancs *T* 146 SD 8550
Horton, Northnts *T* 120 SP 8254
Horton, Northum *T* 165 NU 0230
Horton, Somer *T* 92 ST 3214
Horton, Staffs *T* 137 SJ 9457
Horton, W. Glam *T* 108 SS 4785
Horton, Wilts *T* 102 SU 0463
Horton Court *A* 101 ST 7685
Horton-cum-Studley *T* 115 SP 5912
Horton Green *T* 126 SJ 4549
Horton Heath *T* 95 SU 4917
Horton in Ribblesdale *T* 146 SD 8072
Horton Kirby *T* 105 TQ 5668
Horton Moor 146 SD 8274
Horwich *T* 137 SD 6411
Horwood *T* 90 SS 5027
Hose *T* 129 SK 7329
Hoselaw Loch *W* 165 NT 8031
Hosh *T* 170 NN 8523
Hostingfield *T* 121 TL 4052
Hoswick *T* 203 HU 4123
Hotham *T* 142 SE 8934
Hothfield *T* 99 TQ 9644
Hoton *T* 129 SK 5722
Hot Point 86 SW 7112
Hott Hill *H* 157 NT 4210
Houbie 205 HU 6290
Hough *T* 127 SJ 7151
Hougham *T* 130 SK 8844
Hougharry *T* 188 NF 7071
Hough Bay *W* 172 NL 9346
Hough Green *T* 137 SJ 4887
Hough-on-the-Hill *T* 130 SK 9246
Hough Skerries 172 NL 9147
Houghton, Cambs *T* 121 TL 2872
Houghton, Cumbr *T* 157 NY 4059
Houghton, Dyfed *T* 110 SM 9807
Houghton, Hants *T* 94 SU 3432
Houghton, W. Susx *T* 96 TQ 0111
Houghton Conquest *T* 120 TL 0441
Houghton House *A* 120 TL 0339
Houghton-le-Spring *T* 153 NZ 3449
Houghton on the Hill *T* 129 SK 6703
Houghton Regis *T* 104 TL 0224
Houghton St Giles *T* 132 TF 9235
Houlsyke *T* 148 NZ 7308
Hound Green *T* 104 SU 7359
Houndslow *T* 164 NT 6347
Houndwood *T* 165 NT 8463
Hounslow *T* 105 TQ 1375
Housa Water *W* 202 HU 2844
Housay 205 HU 6871
Housedon Hill *H* 165 NT 9032
House of Auquhorthies *T* 185 NJ 7220
House of Daviot 183 NH 7240
House of Glenmuick 176 NO 3794
Housetter *T* 204 HU 3684
Houss Ness 203 HU 3729
Houston *T* 161 NS 4066
Houstry *T* 199 ND 1535
Houton Head 200 HY 3003
Hove *T* 97 TQ 2805
Hoveringham *T* 129 SK 6946
Hoveton *T* 133 TG 3018
Hovingham *T* 147 SE 6675
How *T* 151 NY 5056
Howardian Hills *H* 147 SE 6472
Howat's Hill *H* 157 NY 2279
How Caple *T* 113 SO 6130
Howden *T* 142 SE 7528
Howden-le-Wear *T* 152 NZ 1533
Howden Moors 138 SK 1697
Howden Reservoir, Derby *W* 138 SK 1793
Howden Reservoir, S. Yks *W* 138 SK 1793
Howe, Highld *T* 199 ND 3062
Howe, Norf *T* 133 TM 2799
Howe Green *T* 106 TL 7403
Howell *T* 130 TF 1346
Howe of Alford 184 NJ 5716
Howe of Fife 171 NO 2910
Howe of Teuchar *T* 185 NJ 7947
Howe of the Mearns 177 NO 7074
Howequoy Head 200 HY 4600
Howe Street, Essex *T* 106 TL 6914
Howe Street, Essex *T* 122 TL 6934
Howe, The, Cumbr *T* 145 SD 4588
Howe, The, I. of M *T* 144 SC 1967
Howey *T* 112 SO 0558
Howgate, Border *T* 158 NT 7820
Howgate, Lothn *T* 163 NT 2458
Howgate Hill *H* 163 NS 9134
Howgill Fells 151 SD 6799
Howick *T* 159 NU 2517
Howick Haven *W* 159 NU 2616
Howle *T* 127 SJ 6923
Howlett End *T* 122 TL 5934
Howmore *T* 178 NF 7536
Hownam *T* 158 NT 7719
Hownam Law *H* 165 NT 7921
Howsgarth *T* 201 HY 6539
Howsham, Humbs *T* 142 TA 0404
Howsham, N. Yks *T* 148 SE 7362
How Stean Beck *W* 146 SE 0572
Howton *T* 113 SO 4129
Howtown *T* 151 NY 4419
Howwood *T* 161 NS 3960
Hoxa *T* 200 ND 4193
Hoxne *T* 123 TM 1877
Hoy, Orkney 200 ND 2596
Hoy, Shetld 203 HU 3744
Hoylake *T* 136 SJ 2187
Hoyland Nether *T* 139 SE 3600
Hoyland Swaine *T* 139 SE 2604
Hoy Sound *W* 200 HY 2407
Hubberholme *T* 146 SD 9277
Hubbert's Bridge *T* 131 TF 2643

Huby Kelly Bray

Huby, N. Yks *T* 147 SE 2747
Huby, N. Yks *T* 147 SE 5665
Hucclecote *T* 114 SO 8717
Hucking *T* 98 TQ 8458
Hucknall *T* 129 SK 5349
Huddersfield *P* 138 SE 1416
Huddington *T* 117 SO 9457
Hudswell *T* 152 NZ 1400
Huggate *T* 149 SE 8855
Hughenden Valley *T* 104 SU 8696
Hughley *T* 127 SO 5698
Hugh Town *T* 86 SV 9010
Huip Ness 201 HY 6430
Huip Sound *W* 201 HY 6330
Huish, Devon *T* 91 SS 5311
Huish, Wilts *T* 102 SU 1463
Huish Champflower *T* 92 ST 0429
Huish Episcopi *T* 93 ST 4326
Hulcott *T* 104 SP 8516
Hule Moss *W* 164 NT 7149
Hulland *T* 128 SK 2446
Hulland Ward *T* 128 SK 2547
Hullavington *T* 101 ST 8982
Hullbridge *T* 106 TQ 8194
Hulme End *T* 138 SK 1059
Hulme Walfield *T* 137 SJ 8465
Hulne Park 159 NU 1615
Hulne Priory *A* 159 NU 1615
Hulver Street *T* 123 TM 4786
Humber (lightship) 143 TA 5813
Humber Bridge *O* 142 TA 0224
Humber Court *T* 113 SO 5356
Humberside Airport 143 TA 0910
Humberston *T* 143 TA 3005
Humbie *T* 164 NT 4562
Humbleton, Humbs *T* 143 TA 2234
Humbleton, Northum *T* 165 NT 9728
Hume *T* 164 NT 7041
Humla 179 NG 2000
Humphrey Head Point 145 SD 3973
Humshaugh *T* 158 NY 9271
Huna *T* 199 ND 3673
Huncoat *T* 146 SD 7730
Huncote *T* 129 SP 5197
Hunda 200 ND 4396
Hundalee *T* 158 NT 6418
Hunderthwaite *T* 152 NY 9821
Hunderthwaite Moor 152 NY 9319
Hundleby *T* 141 TF 3866
Hundleshope Heights *H* 163 NT 2534
Hundleton *T* 110 SM 9600
Hundon *T* 122 TL 7348
Hundred Acres *T* 95 SU 5911
Hundred End *T* 145 SD 4122
Hundred Foot Drain or New Bedford River *W* 121 TL 4987
Hundred Foot Washes, The 121 TL 4988
Hundred House *T* 112 SO 1154
Hundred Stream *W* 133 TG 4521
Hundred, The *T* 116 SO 5264
Huney 205 HP 6506
Hungarton *T* 129 SK 6907
Hungerford *P* 102 SU 3368
Hungerford Newtown *T* 102 SU 3571
Hungry Law, Border *H* 158 NT 7406
Hungry Law, Northum *H* 158 NT 7406
Hunmanby *T* 149 TA 0977
Hunningham *T* 118 SP 3768
Hunsdon *T* 105 TL 4114
Hunsingore *T* 147 SE 4253
Hunsonby *T* 151 NY 5835
Hunspow *T* 199 ND 2172
Hunstanton *T* 132 TF 6741
Hunstanworth *T* 152 NY 9449
Hunston, Suff *T* 122 TL 9768
Hunston, W. Susx *T* 95 SU 8601
Hunstrete *T* 101 ST 6462
Hunt End *T* 118 SP 0364
Hunter's Quay *T* 168 NS 1879
Hunterston House 161 NS 1851
Hunthill Lodge 177 NO 4771
Hunt House 148 SE 8198
Hunthwaite *T* 139 SK 4659
Huntingdon *P* 121 TL 2371
Huntingfield *T* 123 TM 3473
Huntington, H. & W *T* 113 SO 2553
Huntington, Lothn *T* 171 NT 4874
Huntington, N. Yks *T* 147 SE 6256
Huntington, Staffs *T* 128 SJ 9713
Huntingtower *T* 170 NO 0625
Hunt Law *H* 164 NT 5758
Huntley *T* 114 SO 7219
Huntly *T* 184 NJ 5340
Hunton, Kent *T* 97 TQ 7149
Hunton, N. Yks *T* 152 SE 1892
Hunt's Cross *T* 136 SJ 4385
Huntsham *T* 91 ST 0020
Huntspill *T* 100 ST 3045
Huntspill Level 100 ST 3245
Huntworth *T* 92 ST 3134
Hunwick *T* 152 NZ 1832
Hunworth *T* 132 TG 0735
Hurdsfield *T* 137 SJ 9274
Hurgin *H* 116 SO 2379
Hurlers, The *A* 87 SX 2571
Hurley, Berks *T* 104 SU 8283
Hurley, Warw *T* 128 SP 2496
Hurlford *T* 161 NS 4536
Hurliness *T* 200 ND 2789
Hurn *T* 94 SZ 1297
Hursley *T* 94 SU 4225
Hurst, Berks *T* 104 SU 7973
Hurst, G. Man *T* 137 SD 9400
Hurst, N. Yks *T* 152 NZ 0402
Hurstbourne Priors *T* 102 SU 4346
Hurstbourne Tarrant *T* 102 SU 3853
Hurst Castle *A* 94 SZ 3189
Hurst Green, E. Susx *T* 97 TQ 7327
Hurst Green, Lancs *T* 145 SD 6838
Hurst Green, Surrey *T* 97 TQ 3951
Hurst Moor 152 NZ 0403
Hurstpierpoint *T* 97 TQ 2816
Hurstwood Resr *W* 146 SD 8931
Hurt Wood *F* 96 TQ 0843
Hurworth Burn Reservoir *W* 153 NZ 4033
Hurworth-on-Tees *T* 152 NZ 3010
Hury *T* 152 NY 9519
Hury Resr *W* 152 NY 9618
Husbands Bosworth *T* 119 SP 6484
Husborne Crawley *T* 120 SP 9535
Hushinish *T* 194 NA 9812
Hushinish Bay *W* 196 NB 9911
Hushinish Point 194 NA 9811
Husival Mór *H* 194 NB 0211
Huskeiran 188 NF 5764
Husthwaite *T* 147 SE 5174
Hutcherleigh *T* 89 SX 7850
Huttoft *T* 141 TF 5176
Hutton, Avon *T* 100 ST 3558
Hutton, Border *T* 165 NT 9053
Hutton, Cumbr *T* 151 NY 4326
Hutton, Essex *T* 106 TQ 6394
Hutton, Lancs *T* 145 SD 4926
Hutton, N. Yks *T* 148 SE 7568
Hutton Bonville *T* 152 NZ 3300
Hutton Buscel *T* 149 SE 9784
Hutton Conyers *T* 147 SE 3273
Hutton Cranswick *T* 149 TA 0252
Hutton End *T* 151 NY 4538
Hutton Henry *T* 153 NZ 4236
Hutton-le-Hole *T* 148 SE 7090
Hutton Magna *T* 152 NZ 1212
Hutton Roof, Cumbr *T* 151 NY 3734
Hutton Roof, Cumbr *T* 145 SD 5678
Hutton Rudby *T* 153 NZ 4606
Hutton Sessay *T* 147 SE 4776
Hutton Wandesley *T* 147 SE 5050
Huxley *T* 137 SJ 5161
Huxter, Shetld 202 HU 1757
Huxter, Shetld 203 HU 3950
Huxter, Shetld 203 HU 5662
Huyton-with-Roby *T* 136 SJ 4391
Hycemoor *T* 150 SD 0989
Hyde, Glos *T* 114 SO 8801
Hyde, G. Man *T* 137 SJ 9494
Hyde, Hants *T* 94 SU 1612
Hyde Heath *T* 104 SP 9300
Hyde Park 105 TQ 2780
Hydestile *T* 96 SU 9740
Hynish *T* 172 NL 9839
Hynish Bay *W* 172 NM 0042
Hyssington *T* 126 SO 3194
Hythe, Hants *T* 94 SU 4208
Hythe, Kent *T* 99 TR 1634
Hythe End *T* 104 TQ 0172
Hythie *T* 185 NK 0051

I

Iarlshot *A* 203 HU 3909
Ibberton *T* 93 ST 7807
Ible *T* 139 SK 2557
Ibsley *T* 94 SU 1509
Ibstock *T* 128 SK 4010
Ibstone *T* 104 SU 7593
Ibthorpe *T* 102 SU 3753
Ibworth *T* 103 SU 5654
Icklburgh *T* 132 TL 8194
Ickenham *T* 104 TQ 0786
Ickford *T* 104 SP 6407
Ickham *T* 99 TR 2258
Ickleford *T* 120 TL 1831
Icklesham *T* 98 TQ 8716
Ickleton *T* 121 TL 4943
Icklingham *T* 122 TL 7772
Icknield Way *A* 121 TL 2836
Ickwell Green *T* 120 TL 1545
Ickworth House 122 TL 8161
Icomb *T* 115 SP 2122
Idbury *T* 115 SP 2320
Iddesleigh *T* 91 SS 5608
Ide *T* 89 SX 8990
Ideford *T* 89 SX 8977
Ide Hill *T* 97 TQ 4851
Iden *T* 98 TQ 9123
Iden Green *T* 98 TQ 8031
Idlicote *T* 118 SP 2844
Idmiston *T* 94 SU 2037
Idridgehay *T* 128 SK 2849
Idrigill *T* 186 NG 3863
Idrigill Point 186 NG 2536
Idstone *T* 102 SU 2584
Idvie 177 NO 5347
Ifield *T* 96 TQ 2537
Ifold *T* 96 TQ 0231
Iford *T* 97 TQ 4007
Ifton Heath *T* 126 SJ 3236
Ightfield *T* 127 SJ 5938
Ightham *T* 97 TQ 5956
Iken *T* 123 TM 4155
Ilam *T* 128 SK 1350
Ilchester *T* 93 ST 5222
Ilderton *T* 165 NU 0121
Ilford *T* 105 TQ 4586
Ilfracombe *T* 90 SS 5147
Ilkeston *T* 129 SK 4642
Ilketshall St Andrew *T* 123 TM 3787
Ilketshall St Lawrence *T* 123 TM 3883
Ilketshall St Margaret *T* 123 TM 3585
Ilkley *T* 146 SE 1147
Ilkley Moor 146 SE 1146
Illey *T* 118 SO 9881
Illingworth *T* 146 SE 0728
Illogan *T* 86 SW 6643
Illston on the Hill *T* 129 SP 7099
Ilmer *T* 104 SP 7605
Ilmington *T* 118 SP 2143
Ilminster *T* 92 ST 3514
Ilsington *T* 89 SX 7876
Ilston *T* 108 SS 5590
Ilton, N. Yks *T* 146 SE 1978
Ilton, Somer *T* 92 ST 3517
Imachar 160 NR 8640
Imber 102 ST 9648
Immingham *T* 143 TA 1814
Impington *T* 121 TL 4463
Inbirchworth Reservoir *W* 138 SE 2105
Ince *T* 136 SJ 4576
Ince Banks 136 SJ 4578
Ince Blundell *T* 136 SD 3203
Ince-in-Makerfield *T* 137 SD 5904
Inchbae Forest 191 NH 3776
Inchbae Lodge 182 NH 4069
Inchbare *T* 177 NO 6065
Inchberry *T* 184 NJ 3155
Inchcailloch 169 NS 4190
Inchcolm 170 NT 1882
Incheril *T* 190 NH 0362
Inchfad 169 NS 4091
Inch Garvie 170 NT 1379
Inchgrundle 176 NO 4179
Inchina *T* 190 NG 9690
Inchinnan *T* 169 NS 4769
Inchkeith 171 NT 2982
Inch Kenneth 173 NM 4335
Inchlaggan *T* 174 NH 1701
Inchlonaig 169 NS 3893
Inchmarnock 160 NS 0259
Inchmickery 171 NT 2080
Inchmore *T* 182 NH 3940
Inchmurrin 169 NS 3887
Inchnacardoch Forest 182 NH 3309
Inchnadamph *T* 196 NC 2521
Inchnadamph Forest 196 NC 2821
Inchnadamph National Nature Reserve 196 NC 2619
Inchture *T* 171 NO 2828
Inchyra 170 NO 1820
Indian Queens *T* 87 SW 9159
Inerval 166 NR 3242
Ingale Skerry 201 HY 6719
Inga Ness 200 HY 4143
Inganess Bay *W* 200 HY 4810
Ingatestone *T* 106 TQ 6499
Ingbirchworth *T* 139 SE 2206
Ingestre *T* 128 SJ 9724
Ingham, Lincs *T* 140 SK 9483
Ingham, Norf *T* 133 TG 3925
Ingham, Suff *T* 122 TL 8570
Ingleborough *H* 145 SD 7474
Ingleby Arncliffe *T* 153 NZ 4400
Ingleby Greenhow *T* 153 NZ 5806
Inglesbatch *T* 101 ST 7061
Inglesham *T* 115 SU 2098
Ingleton, Durham *T* 152 NZ 1720
Ingleton, N. Yks *T* 145 SD 6973
Inglewhite *T* 145 SD 5440
Inglewood Forest 151 NY 4639
Ingliston *T* 170 NT 1472
Ingmire Hall 151 SD 6391
Ingoe *T* 159 NZ 0374
Ingoldisthorpe *T* 132 TF 6832
Ingoldmells *T* 141 TF 5668
Ingoldmells Point 141 TF 5768
Ingoldsby *T* 130 TF 0130
Ingram *T* 159 NU 0116
Ingrave *T* 106 TQ 6292
Ings *T* 151 SD 4498
Ingst *T* 101 ST 5887
Ingtham Mote *A* 97 TQ 5853
Ingworth *T* 133 TG 1929
Inishail 168 NN 1024
Inkberrow *T* 118 SP 0157
Inkhorn *T* 185 NJ 9239
Inkpen *T* 102 SU 3764
Inkstack *T* 199 ND 2570
Innellan *T* 168 NS 1470
Innerdouny Hill *H* 170 NO 0307
Innerhadden 175 NN 6757
Innerhadden Burn *W* 175 NN 6756
Inner Hebrides, Highld 179 NM 1288
Inner Hebrides, Strath 179 NM 1288
Innerleithen *T* 164 NT 3336
Innerleven *T* 171 NO 3700
Innermessan *T* 154 NX 0863
Inner Sound *W* 190 NG 6443
Inner Sound *W* 165 NU 2035
Innerwell Port *W* 155 NX 4849
Innerwick, Lothn *T* 164 NT 7274
Innerwick, Tays *T* 175 NN 5847
Inninmore Bay *W* 173 NM 7241
Innis Chonain 168 NN 1025
Inns Holm 203 HU 3620
Innsworth *T* 114 SO 8621
Insch *T* 184 NJ 6328
Insh *T* 175 NH 8101
Insh Island 173 NM 7319
Inshore 196 NC 3262
Inshriach Forest *F* 175 NH 8302
Inskip *T* 145 SD 4638
Instow *T* 90 SS 4730
Inver, Grampn *T* 176 NO 2393
Inver, Highld *T* 193 NH 8682
Inver, Tays 176 NO 0142
Inverailort *T* 180 NM 7681
Inveralligin *T* 190 NG 8457
Inverallochy *T* 185 NK 0465
Inveramsay *T* 185 NJ 7424
Inveran *T* 192 NH 5797
Inveraray *T* 168 NN 0908
Inverarish *T* 180 NG 5535
Inverarity *T* 176 NO 4544
Inverarnan *T* 168 NN 3118
Inverasdale *T* 190 NG 8286
Inverbervie *T* 177 NO 8272
Inverbroom Lodge 191 NH 1883
Inverbrough *T* 183 NH 8130
Invercauld House 176 NO 1792
Inverchaolain Glen 168 NS 1076
Invercharnan 174 NN 1448
Invercharron House 192 NH 5991
Inverchoran *T* 182 NH 2650
Inver Cottage 166 NR 4471
Invercreran *T* 174 NN 0147
Inver Dalavil *W* 180 NG 5705
Inverdruie *T* 183 NH 9011
Inverebrie *T* 185 NJ 9233
Inverernan House 184 NJ 3211
Invereshie House 183 NH 8405
Inveresk *T* 171 NT 3472
Inverey *T* 176 NO 0889
Inverfarigaig *T* 182 NH 5224
Invergarry *T* 174 NH 3001
Invergeldie 169 NN 7427
Invergeldie Burn *W* 169 NN 7529
Inverghiusachan Point 174 NN 0940
Invergloy House 174 NN 2288
Invergordon *T* 183 NH 7068
Invergowrie *T* 171 NO 3430
Inverguhomery *T* 185 NK 0246
Inverguseran *T* 180 NG 7407
Inverharroch *T* 184 NJ 3831
Inverie *T* 180 NM 7699
Inverie Bay *W* 180 NM 7699
Inverinan 168 NM 9917
Inverinate *T* 180 NG 9122
Inverinate Forest 180 NG 9825
Inverkeilor *T* 177 NO 6649
Inverkeithing *T* 170 NT 1383
Inverkeithing Bay *W* 170 NT 1481
Inverkeithny *T* 184 NJ 6247
Inverkip *T* 168 NS 2072
Inverkirkaig *T* 196 NC 0819
Inverlael 191 NH 1885
Inverlael Forest 191 NH 2286
Inverliever Forest *F* 168 NM 9404
Inverliever Lodge 168 NM 8905
Inverlochlarig 169 NN 4318
Inverlochy Castle 174 NN 1476
Inver Mallie 174 NN 1388
Invermark Lodge 176 NO 4380
Invermoidart *T* 173 NM 6673
Invermoriston *T* 182 NH 4216
Invernaver *T* 197 NC 7060
Inverneill 167 NR 8481
Inverness (Dalcross) Airport 183 NH 7752
Inverness *P* 183 NH 6645
Invernoaden 168 NS 1297
Inveroran Hotel 174 NN 2741
Inverpattack Lodge 175 NN 5590
Inverpolly Forest 196 NC 1111
Inverpolly Lodge 196 NC 0714
Inverpolly National Nature Reserve 196 NC 1412
Inverquharity 176 NO 4057
Inverroy *T* 174 NN 2581
Inversanda Bay *W* 174 NM 9459
Inverscaddle Bay *W* 174 NN 0268
Invershin *T* 192 NH 5796
Inversnaid Hotel 168 NN 3308
Inverugie *T* 185 NK 1048
Inveruglas *T* 168 NN 3109
Inveruglas Water *W* 168 NN 2910
Inverurie *T* 185 NJ 7721
Invervar *T* 175 NN 6648
Inverwick Forest 182 NH 3413
Inwardleigh *T* 89 SX 5699
Inworth *T* 106 TL 8817
Inzie Head 185 NK 0662
Iona 172 NM 2724
Iorcail 179 NG 2606
Iping *T* 95 SU 8522
Ipplepen *T* 89 SX 8366
Ipsden *T* 104 SU 6385
Ipstones *T* 128 SK 0250
Ipswich *P* 123 TM 1644
Irby *T* 136 SJ 2584
Irby in the Marsh *T* 141 TF 4763
Irby upon Humber *T* 143 TA 1904
Irchester *T* 120 SP 9265
Ireby, Cumbr *T* 150 NY 2339
Ireby, Lancs *T* 145 SD 6575
Ireland, Orkney *T* 200 HY 3009
Ireland, Shetld *T* 203 HU 3722
Ireleth *T* 144 SD 2277
Ireshopeburn *T* 152 NY 8638
Ireshope Moor 151 NY 8436
Irfon *W* 112 SN 9649
Irish Law *H* 161 NS 2659
Irlam *T* 137 SJ 7294
Irnham *T* 130 TF 0226
Iron Acton *T* 101 ST 6883
Iron-Bridge *T* 127 SJ 6703
Iron Cross *T* 118 SP 0652
Ironmacannie *T* 156 NX 6675
Ironside *T* 185 NJ 8852
Ironville *T* 128 SK 4351
Irstead *T* 133 TG 3620
Irthington *T* 157 NY 4961
Irthlingborough *T* 120 SP 9470
Irton *T* 149 TA 0084
Irvine *P* 161 NS 3238
Irvine Bay *W* 161 NS 3038
Isauld *T* 198 NC 9765
Isay, Highld 186 NG 2157
Isay, W. Isles 189 NB 1002
Isbister, Orkney *T* 200 HY 2623
Isbister, Orkney *T* 200 HY 3918
Isbister, Shetld 205 HU 3791
Isbister, Shetld *T* 203 HU 5764
Isca *R* 89 SX 9292
Isca Roman Fort *R* 100 ST 3391
Isfield *T* 97 TQ 4517
Isham *T* 120 SP 8874
Islan Davaar 160 NR 7620
Island Macaskin 167 NR 7899
Island of Arran 160 NR 9536
Island of Bute 160 NS 0664
Island of Danna 167 NR 6978
Island of Mull 173 NM 6235
Island of Raasay *W* 190 NG 6257
Island of Rona *W* 190 NG 6257
Island of Skye 187 NG 4333
Island of Stroma 199 ND 3577
Islands of Fleet 155 NX 5749
Islawr-dref 125 SH 6815
Islay (Port Ellen) Airport 166 NR 3251
Islay 166 NR 3964
Islay House 166 NR 3362
Isle Abbotts *T* 92 ST 3520
Isle Brewers *T* 92 ST 3621
Isleham *T* 122 TL 6474
Isleham Fen 122 TL 6276
Isle Martin 191 NH 0999
Isle of Axholme 142 SE 7806
Isle of Dogs 105 TQ 3778
Isle of Ewe 190 NG 8588
Isle of Fethaland 205 HU 3794
Isle of Grain 98 TQ 8776
Isle of Harty 99 TR 0267
Isle of Lewis 195 NB 3138
Isle of Man (Ronaldsway) Airport 144 SC 2868
Isle of Man 144 SC 3281
Isle of May 171 NT 6599
Isle of Nibon 204 HU 3073
Isle of Noss 203 HU 5440
Isle of Oxney 98 TQ 9127
Isle of Portland 93 SY 6971
Isle of Purbeck 94 SY 9581
Isle of Sheppey 99 TQ 9769
Isle of Stenness 204 HU 2076
Isle of Thanet 99 TR 3267
Isle of Walney 144 SD 1768
Isle of West Burrafirth 202 HU 2558
Isle of Whithorn *T* 155 NX 4736
Isle of Wight 95 SZ 4985
Isleornsay or Eilean Iarmain *T* 180 NG 6912
Isle Ristol 196 NB 9711
Islesburgh *T* 204 HU 3369
Isles of Scilly 86 SV 8912
Isleworth *T* 105 TQ 1675
Isley Walton *T* 128 SK 4225
Islington *T* 105 TQ 3085
Islip, Northnts *T* 120 SP 9878
Islip, Oxon *T* 115 SP 5214
Islivig *T* 194 NA 9927
Istead Rise *T* 98 TQ 6369
Isurium *A* 147 SE 4066
Isycoed *T* 126 SJ 4050
Itchen Abbas *T* 95 SU 5333
Itchen Stoke *T* 95 SU 5632
Itchingfield *T* 96 TQ 1328
Itchington *T* 101 ST 6587
Itteringham *T* 133 TG 1430
Itton *T* 89 SX 6899
Itton Common *T* 113 ST 4896
Ivegill *T* 151 NY 4143
Ivelet *T* 152 SD 9398
Iver *T* 104 TQ 0381
Iver Heath *T* 104 TQ 0282
Iveston *T* 152 NZ 1350
Ivinghoe *T* 104 SP 9416
Ivinghoe Aston *T* 104 SP 9518
Ivington *T* 113 SO 4756
Ivington Green *T* 113 SO 4656
Ivybridge *T* 89 SX 6356
Ivychurch *T* 99 TR 0227
Ivy Hatch *T* 97 TQ 5854
Iwade *T* 98 TQ 8967
Iwerne Courtney or Shroton *T* 93 ST 8512
Iwerne Minster *T* 93 ST 8614
Ixworth *T* 122 TL 9370
Ixworth Thorpe *T* 122 TL 9172

J

Jack Hill *T* 146 SE 2051
Jackstown *T* 185 NJ 7531
Jackton *T* 162 NS 5953
Jacobstow *T* 88 SX 1995
Jacobstowe *T* 91 SS 5801
Jameston *T* 110 SS 0599
Jamestown, D. & G *T* 157 NY 2996
Jamestown, Highld *T* 182 NH 4756
Jamestown, Strath *T* 169 NS 3981
Jamieson's Point 154 NX 0371
Jarlshof *A* 203 HU 4039
Jarrow *T* 159 NZ 3265
Jawcraig *T* 170 NS 8575
Jaw Reservoir *W* 169 NS 4975
Jayes Park *T* 96 TQ 1440
Jaywick *T* 107 TM 1513
Jedburgh *P* 158 NT 6520
Jed Water *W* 158 NT 6710
Jeffreyston *T* 110 SN 0806
Jemimaville *T* 183 NH 7265
Jervaulx Abbey *A* 146 SE 1785
Jevington *T* 97 TQ 5601
Johnby *T* 151 NY 4333
John o' Groats *T* 199 ND 3872
Johnshaven *T* 177 NO 7967
Johnston *T* 110 SM 9310
Johnstone *T* 161 NS 4363
Johnstonebridge *T* 157 NY 1092
Johnston's Point 160 NR 7613
Jordans *T* 104 SU 9791
Jordanston *T* 110 SM 9132
Jumbles Reservoir *W* 136 SD 2314
Jump *T* 139 SE 3801
Juniper Green *T* 163 NT 1968
Jura 166 NR 5683
Jura Forest 166 NR 5072
Jura House 166 NR 4863
Jurby East *T* 144 SC 3899
Jurby Head 144 SC 3498
Jurby West *T* 144 SC 3598

K

Kaber *T* 151 NY 7911
Kaim Dam *W* 161 NS 3462
Kaimes *T* 163 NT 2768
Kaim Hill *H* 161 NS 2253
Kale Water *W* 164 NT 7326
Kalnakill *T* 190 NG 6954
Kame of Corrigall *H* 200 HY 3320
Kame of Flouravoug 205 HP 5916
Kame of Hoy 200 HY 1904
Kame of Sandwick *H* 205 HU 4787
Kames, Strath *T* 168 NR 9771
Kames, Strath *T* 162 NS 6926
Kames Bay *W* 160 NS 0767
Kame, The 202 HT 9340
Kea *T* 87 SW 8142
Keadby *T* 142 SE 8311
Keal *T* 141 TF 3763
Keal Cotes *T* 141 TF 3661
Kearsley *T* 137 SD 7505
Kearstay 194 NA 9617
Kearstwick *T* 145 SD 6080
Kearton *T* 152 SD 9999
Kearvaig 196 NC 2972
Kearvaig River *W* 196 NC 2970
Keasden *T* 145 SD 7266
Keava 195 NB 1935
Kebister Ness 203 HU 4746
Kebock Head 195 NB 4214
Keddington *T* 141 TF 3488
Kedington *T* 122 TL 7046
Kedleston *T* 128 SK 3041
Keelby *T* 143 TA 1609
Keele *T* 127 SJ 8045
Keeley Green *T* 120 TL 0046
Keelylang Hill *H* 200 HY 3710
Keen, The 203 HU 5057
Keeston *T* 110 SM 9019
Keevil *T* 101 ST 9258
Kegworth *T* 129 SK 4826
Kehelland *T* 86 SW 6241
Keig *T* 184 NJ 6119
Keighley *T* 146 SE 0540
Keighley Moor 146 SE 0039
Keilarsbrae *T* 170 NS 8993
Keilhill *T* 185 NJ 7159
Keillmore *T* 167 NR 6880
Keillor 176 NO 2640
Keillour 170 NN 9725
Keillour Forest 170 NN 9623
Keills *T* 166 NR 4168
Keills Cross *A* 167 NR 6980
Keil Point 160 NR 6707
Keils *T* 166 NR 5268
Keinton Mandeville *T* 93 ST 5430
Keir Hills *H* 156 NX 8491
Keir Mill *T* 156 NX 8593
Keisby *T* 130 TF 0328
Keiss *T* 199 ND 3461
Keith *T* 184 NJ 4350
Keith Hall *A* 185 NJ 7821
Keithock *T* 177 NO 6063
Kelbrook *T* 146 SD 9044
Kelburn *A* 161 NS 2156
Kelby *T* 130 TF 0041
Keld, Cumbr *T* 151 NY 5514
Keld, N. Yks *T* 152 NY 8901
Keldholme *T* 148 SE 7086
Keld, The *W* 201 HY 6033
Keldy Castle 148 SE 7791
Kelfield *T* 147 SE 5938
Kelham *T* 129 SK 7755
Kelk Beck *W* 149 TA 0957
Kellan *T* 173 NM 5240
Kellas, Grampn *T* 184 NJ 1754
Kellas, Tays *T* 171 NO 4535
Kellaton *T* 89 SX 8039
Kelleth *T* 151 NY 6605
Kellie Castle *A* 177 NO 6040
Kellie Law *H* 171 NO 5106
Kelling *T* 133 TG 0942
Kellington *T* 147 SE 5524
Kelloe *T* 153 NZ 3436
Kello Water *W* 156 NS 6708
Kelly *T* 88 SX 3981
Kelly Bray *T* 88 SX 3571

Kelmarsh Kirkmichael

Kelmarsh T 119 SP 7379
Kelmscot T 115 SU 2599
Kelsale T 123 TM 3865
Kelsall T 137 SJ 5268
Kelsey Head 86 SW 7660
Kelshall T 121 TL 3435
Kelso T 164 NT 7234
Kelston T 101 ST 7067
Keltie Water W 169 NN 6310
Keltney Burn, Tays W 175 NN 7650
Keltneyburn, Tays T 175 NN 7749
Kelton T 152 NY 9220
Kelton Hill or Rhonehouse T 156 NX 7459
Kelty T 170 NT 1394
Kelty Water W 169 NS 5095
Kelvedon T 106 TL 8618
Kelvedon Hatch T 105 TQ 5798
Kelynack T 86 SW 3729
Kemacott T 91 SS 6647
Kemback T 171 NO 4115
Kemberton T 127 SJ 7304
Kemble T 114 ST 9897
Kemerton T 117 SO 9437
Kemeys Commander T 113 SO 3504
Kemnay T 185 NJ 7316
Kempley T 114 SO 6729
Kempock Point 168 NS 2477
Kempsey T 117 SO 8549
Kempsford T 115 SU 1597
Kempston T 120 TL 0347
Kempston Hardwick T 120 TL 0344
Kempton T 116 SO 3683
Kemp Town T 97 TQ 3203
Kemsing T 105 TQ 5458
Kenardington T 99 TQ 9732
Kenchester T 113 SO 4442
Kencot T 115 SP 2504
Kendal P 151 SD 5192
Kendoon Loch W 156 NX 6190
Kenfig T 109 SS 8081
Kenfig Burrows 109 SS 7982
Kenfig Hill T 109 SS 8483
Kengharair Farm 173 NM 4348
Kenilworth T 118 SP 2972
Kenknock 175 NN 4636
Kenley, G. Lon T 105 TQ 3259
Kenley, Shrops T 127 SJ 5600
Kenmore, Highld T 190 NG 7557
Kenmore, Tays T 175 NN 7745
Kenmure Castle A 156 NX 6376
Kenn, Avon T 100 ST 4169
Kenn, Devon T 89 SX 9285
Kennacraig 160 NR 8262
Kennedy's Pass 154 NX 1593
Kennerleigh T 91 SS 8107
Kennet T 170 NS 9291
Kennet and Avon Canal, Wilts W 101 ST 8761
Kennet and Avon Canal, Wilts W 102 SU 2363
Kennethmont T 184 NJ 5429
Kennett T 122 TL 7068
Kennford T 89 SX 9186
Kennick Reservoir W 89 SX 8084
Kenninghall T 122 TM 0386
Kennington, Kent T 99 TR 0242
Kennington, Oxon T 115 SP 5202
Kennoway T 171 NO 3502
Kenny Hill T 122 TL 6679
Kennythorpe T 148 SE 7865
Kenovdy T 172 NL 9946
Kensaleyre T 187 NG 4251
Kensington T 105 TQ 2579
Kensworth T 104 TL 0218
Kentallen 174 NN 0057
Kentchurch T 113 SO 4125
Kentchurch Court A 113 SO 4225
Kentford T 122 TL 7166
Kentisbeare T 92 ST 0608
Kentisbury T 91 SS 6243
Kentmere T 151 NY 4504
Kentmere Reservoir W 151 NY 4408
Kenton, Devon T 89 SX 9583
Kenton, G. Lon T 105 TQ 1788
Kenton, Suff T 123 TM 1966
Kentra T 173 NM 6569
Kentra Bay W 173 NM 6469
Kents Bank T 145 SD 3976
Kent's Green T 114 SO 7423
Kent's Oak T 94 SU 3224
Kentwell Hall A 122 TL 8647
Kenwick T 126 SJ 4230
Kenwyn T 87 SW 8245
Kenyon T 137 SJ 6295
Keoldale T 196 NC 3866
Keose T 195 NB 3521
Keppanach 174 NN 0262
Keppoch T 180 NG 8924
Kepwick T 153 SE 4690
Keresley T 118 SP 3284
Kerloch H 177 NO 6987
Kerne Bridge T 113 SO 5819
Kerran Hill H 160 NR 7313
Kerrera 173 NM 8128
Kerridge T 137 SJ 9377
Kerris T 86 SW 4427
Kerry T 116 SO 1490
Kerrycroy T 161 NS 1061
Kerry Hill H 116 SO 1385
Kerrysdale T 190 NG 8273
Kerry's Gate T 113 SO 3933
Kersall T 140 SK 7162
Kersey T 122 TM 0044
Kershader T 195 NB 3420
Kershope Burn, Border W 158 NY 5285
Kershope Burn, Cumbr W 158 NY 5285
Kershopefoot T 157 NY 4782
Kershope Forest F 158 NY 5181
Kersoe T 118 SO 9940
Kerswell T 92 ST 0706
Kerswell Green T 117 SO 8646
Kesgrave T 123 TM 2145
Kessingland T 123 TM 5386
Kestle Mill T 87 SW 8459
Keston T 105 TQ 4164
Keswick, Cumbr T 150 NY 2623
Keswick, Norf T 133 TG 2004
Keswick, Norf T 133 TG 3533
Ketligill Head 204 HU 2784
Kettering P 120 SP 8678
Ketteringham T 133 TG 1602
Kettins T 176 NO 2339
Kettla Ness 203 HU 3428
Kettlebaston T 122 TL 9650
Kettlebridge 171 NO 3007
Kettlebrook T 128 SK 2103
Kettleburgh T 123 TM 2660
Kettleness T 153 NZ 8315
Kettleshulme T 138 SJ 9879
Kettlesing Bottom T 147 SE 2257
Kettlestone T 132 TF 9631
Kettlethorpe T 140 SK 8475
Kettletoft T 201 HY 6538
Kettletoft Bay W 201 HY 6638
Kettlewell T 146 SD 9772
Ketton T 130 SK 9804
Kew T 105 TQ 1877
Kewstoke T 100 ST 3363
Kex Beck W 146 SE 0953
Kexbrough T 139 SE 3009
Kexby, Lincs T 140 SK 8785
Kexby, N. Yks T 148 SE 7051
Kexwith Moor 152 NZ 0305
Key Green T 137 SJ 8963
Keyham T 129 SK 6706
Keyhaven T 94 SZ 3090
Keyingham T 143 TA 2425
Keymer T 97 TQ 3115
Keynsham T 101 ST 6568
Keysley Down H 93 ST 8634
Keysoe T 120 TL 0762
Keysoe Row T 120 TL 0861
Keyston T 120 TL 0475
Keyworth T 129 SK 6130
Kibblesworth T 152 NZ 2456
Kibworth Beauchamp T 129 SP 6893
Kibworth Harcourt T 129 SP 6894
Kidbrooke T 105 TQ 4076
Kiddemore Green T 127 SJ 8508
Kidderminster P 117 SO 8376
Kiddington T 115 SP 4122
Kidlington T 115 SP 4913
Kidmore End T 104 SU 6979
Kidsgrove T 127 SJ 8354
Kidstones T 146 SD 9581
Kidwelly T 111 SN 4106
Kielder T 158 NY 6293
Kielder Burn W 158 NY 6596
Kielder Castle 158 NY 6393
Kielder Forest F 158 NY 6691
Kielderhead Moor 158 NT 6800
Kielder Water W 158 NY 6788
Kiells T 166 NR 4168
Kierfea Hill H 200 HY 4232
Kierfiold House 200 HY 2418
Kiessimul Castle A 178 NL 6697
Kilbarchan T 161 NS 4063
Kilbeg T 180 NG 6406
Kilberry T 160 NR 7164
Kilberry Head 160 NR 7064
Kilbirnie T 161 NS 3154
Kilbirnie Loch W 161 NS 3354
Kilblaan Burn W 168 NN 1513
Kilbrannan Sound W 160 NR 8340
Kilbraur Hill H 193 NC 8208
Kilbride, Highld T 180 NG 5820
Kilbride, Strath T 168 NM 8525
Kilbride, W. Isles T 178 NF 7614
Kilbride Bay W 160 NR 9666
Kilbride Point 186 NG 3766
Kilbryde Castle 169 NN 7503
Kilburn, Derby T 128 SK 3845
Kilburn, N. Yks T 147 SE 5179
Kilby T 129 SP 6295
Kilchamaig 160 NR 8061
Kilchattan, Strath T 166 NR 3695
Kilchattan, Strath T 161 NS 1054
Kilchattan Bay W 161 NS 1055
Kilchenzie T 160 NR 6725
Kilcheran 173 NM 8238
Kilchiaran T 166 NR 2060
Kilchiaran Bay W 166 NR 1960
Kilchoan T 173 NM 4863
Kilchoan Bay W 173 NM 4863
Kilchoman T 166 NR 2163
Kilchrenan T 168 NN 0322
Kilchurn Castle A 168 NN 1327
Kilconquhar Loch W 171 NO 4801
Kilconquhar T 171 NO 4802
Kilcot T 114 SO 6925
Kilcoy T 182 NH 5751
Kilcreggon T 168 NS 2380
Kildale T 153 NZ 6009
Kildalloig T 160 NR 7518
Kildalton Cross A 166 NR 4550
Kildalton House 166 NR 4347
Kildary T 193 NH 7675
Kildavanan 160 NS 0266
Kildermorie Forest 192 NH 4678
Kildermorie Lodge 192 NH 5078
Kildonan T 160 NS 0321
Kildonan Burn W 198 NC 9224
Kildonan Lodge 193 NC 9022
Kildonnan T 179 NM 4885
Kildrummy T 184 NJ 4717
Kildwick T 146 SE 0146
Kilennan River W 166 NR 3858
Kilfinan T 168 NR 9378
Kilfinan Bay W 168 NR 9178
Kilfinichen Bay W 173 NM 4928
Kilfinnan T 174 NN 2795
Kilgetty T 110 SN 1207
Kilgwrrwg Common T 113 ST 4798
Kilham, Humbs T 149 TA 0664
Kilham, Northum T 165 NT 8832
Kili Holm 200 HY 4732
Kilkenneth T 172 NL 9444
Kilkerran 161 NS 3002
Kilkhampton T 90 SS 2511
Killamarsh T 139 SK 4580
Killay T 108 SS 6093
Killchianaig T 167 NR 6486
Killean T 160 NR 6944
Killearn T 169 NS 5286
Killegray 188 NF 9783
Killen T 183 NH 6758
Killerby T 152 NZ 1919
Killichonan T 175 NN 5458
Killichonan Burn W 175 NN 5660
Killiechonate T 174 NN 2481
Killiechonate Forest 174 NN 2173
Killiechronan T 173 NM 5441
Killiecrankie T 175 NN 9162
Killiemor T 173 NM 4839
Killilan T 180 NG 9430
Killilan Forest 180 NH 0231
Killimster T 199 ND 3156
Killin T 169 NN 5732
Killinallan 166 NR 3171
Killinghall T 147 SE 2858
Killingholme T 143 TA 1416
Killington T 145 SD 6188
Killington Reservoir W 151 SD 5991
Killin Lodge 182 NH 5209
Killochan Castle A 154 NS 2200
Killochyett T 164 NT 4545
Killocraw 160 NR 6628
Killundine T 173 NM 5849
Kilmacolm T 161 NS 3865
Kilmahumaig T 167 NR 7893
Kilmalieu 173 NM 8955
Kilmaluag T 187 NG 4274
Kilmaluag Bay W 187 NG 4475
Kilmannan Reservoir, Central W 169 NS 4978
Kilmannan Reservoir, Strath W 169 NS 4978
Kilmany T 171 NO 3821
Kilmarie T 187 NG 5417
Kilmarnock P 161 NS 4238
Kilmaron Castle 171 NO 3516
Kilmartin T 167 NR 8398
Kilmar Tor 87 SX 2574
Kilmaurs T 161 NS 4141
Kilmein Hill H 161 NS 4511
Kilmelford T 173 NM 8413
Kilmeny T 166 NR 3965
Kilmersdon T 101 ST 6952
Kilmeston T 95 SU 5926
Kilmichael Glassary T 168 NR 8593
Kilmichael of Inverlussa T 167 NR 7785
Kilmington, Devon T 92 SY 2798
Kilmington, Wilts T 93 ST 7736
Kilmonivaig T 174 NN 1783
Kilmorack T 182 NH 4944
Kilmore, Highld T 180 NG 6507
Kilmore, Strath 168 NM 8824
Kilmory, Highld 179 NG 3503
Kilmory, Highld T 173 NM 5270
Kilmory, Strath T 167 NR 7075
Kilmory, Strath T 160 NR 9621
Kilmory Bay W 167 NR 6974
Kilmory Castle 168 NR 8786
Kilmory Glen 179 NG 3602
Kilmory Lodge 167 NM 7105
Kilmory Water W 160 NR 9723
Kilmuir, Highld T 186 NG 2547
Kilmuir, Highld T 186 NG 3870
Kilmuir, Highld T 183 NH 6749
Kilmuir, Highld T 193 NH 7573
Kilnave T 166 NR 2871
Kilncadzow T 163 NS 8848
Kilndown T 97 TQ 7035
Kilnhurst T 139 SK 4597
Kilninian T 172 NM 4046
Kilninver T 173 NM 8221
Kiln Pit Hill T 152 NZ 0355
Kilnsea T 143 TA 4015
Kilnsey T 146 SD 9767
Kilnwick T 149 SE 9949
Kiloran T 166 NR 3996
Kiloran Bay W 166 NR 4098
Kilpatrick T 160 NR 9027
Kilpatrick Hills H 169 NS 4776
Kilpeck T 113 SO 4430
Kilpheder T 178 NF 7419
Kilphedir T 193 NC 9818
Kilpin T 142 SE 7727
Kilravock Castle 183 NH 8149
Kilrenny T 171 NO 5704
Kilsby T 119 SP 5671
Kilspindie T 171 NO 2225
Kilstay Bay W 154 NX 1338
Kilsyth T 169 NS 7177
Kilsyth Hills H 169 NS 6980
Kiltarlity T 182 NH 5041
Kilton T 100 ST 1643
Kilt Rock 187 NG 5066
Kilvaxter T 186 NG 3869
Kilve T 100 ST 1442
Kilvington T 129 SK 8043
Kilwinning T 161 NS 3043
Kimberley, Norf T 132 TG 0704
Kimberley, Notts T 129 SK 5044
Kimberley House 133 TG 0904
Kimble T 104 SP 8206
Kimblesworth T 152 NZ 2547
Kimble Wick T 104 SP 8007
Kimbolton, Cambs T 120 TL 0967
Kimbolton, H. & W T 116 SO 5261
Kimcote T 119 SP 5586
Kimmeridge T 93 SY 9179
Kimmerston T 165 NT 9535
Kimpton, Herts T 105 TL 1718
Kimpton, Wilts T 102 SU 2846
Kinbrace T 198 NC 8631
Kinbrace Burn W 198 NC 9029
Kinbuck T 169 NN 7905
Kincaple T 171 NO 4618
Kincardine, Fife T 170 NS 9387
Kincardine, Highld T 192 NH 6089
Kincardine Castle 170 NN 9411
Kincardine O'Neil T 177 NO 5999
Kinclaven 176 NO 1538
Kincorth T 185 NJ 9303
Kincorth House 183 NJ 0161
Kincraig T 183 NH 8305
Kincraigie 176 NN 9849
Kindallachan 176 NN 9949
Kinder Reservoir W 138 SK 0588
Kinder Scout H 138 SK 0988
Kineton, Glos T 114 SP 0926
Kineton, Warw T 118 SP 3351
Kinfauns T 170 NO 1622
Kingairloch 173 NM 8352
Kingairloch House 173 NM 8353
Kingarth T 161 NS 0956
Kingcoed T 113 SO 4305
Kingforth T 142 TA 0319
Kingham T 115 SP 2624
Kingholm Quay T 156 NX 9773
Kinghorn T 171 NT 2787
Kinglassie T 171 NT 2398
Kingoodie T 171 NO 3329
King Orry's Grave A 144 SC 4484
King's Acre T 113 SO 4741
Kingsand T 88 SX 4350
Kingsbarns T 171 NO 5912
Kingsbridge, Devon T 89 SX 7344
Kingsbridge, Somer T 91 SS 9837
King's Bromley T 128 SK 1216
Kingsburgh T 187 NG 3955
Kingsbury, G. Lon T 105 TQ 1989
Kingsbury, Warw T 128 SP 2196
Kingsbury Episcopi T 93 ST 4321
King's Caple T 113 SO 5629
King's Cave 193 NH 8371
Kingsclere T 103 SU 5258
King's Cliffe T 130 TL 0097
Kingscote T 101 ST 8190
Kingscott T 91 SS 5318
King's Coughton T 118 SP 0859
Kingscross T 160 NS 0428
Kingscross Point 160 NS 0528
King's Cross Station 105 TQ 3083
King's Delph 131 TL 2495
Kingsdon T 93 ST 5126
Kingsdown T 99 TR 3748
Kingseat T 170 NT 1290
Kingsey T 104 SP 7406
Kingsfold T 96 TQ 1636
Kingsford T 117 SO 8281
King's Forest of Geltsdale 151 NY 6053
Kingshall Street T 122 TL 9161
King's Heath T 118 SP 0781
Kingshouse 169 NN 5620
Kingskerswell T 89 SX 8868
Kingskettle T 171 NO 3008
Kingsland T 116 SO 4461
Kings Langley T 104 TL 0702
Kingsley, Ches T 137 SJ 5574
Kingsley, Hants T 103 SU 7838
Kingsley, Staffs T 128 SK 0147
Kingsley Green T 95 SU 8930
King's Lynn P 132 TF 6119
King's Meaburn T 151 NY 6221
Kings Muir, Border T 163 NT 2539
Kingsmuir, Tays T 177 NO 4749
Kingsnorth, Kent T 98 TQ 8072
Kingsnorth, Kent T 99 TR 0039
King's Norton, Leic T 129 SK 6800
King's Norton, W. Mids T 118 SP 0579
King's Nympton T 91 SS 6819
King's Nympton Station 91 SS 6616
King's Pyon T 113 SO 4450
Kings Ripton T 121 TL 2676
King's Seat H 171 NO 2333
King's Seat Hill H 170 NS 9399
King's Sedge Moor 92 ST 4133
King's Somborne T 94 SU 3631
King's Stag T 93 ST 7210
King's Stanley T 114 SO 8103
Kings Sutton T 119 SP 4936
Kingstanding T 128 SP 0794
Kingsteignton T 89 SX 8773
King Sterndale T 138 SK 0972
Kingsthorne T 113 SO 4932
Kingsthorpe T 119 SP 7563
Kingston, Cambs T 121 TL 3455
Kingston, Devon T 89 SX 6347
Kingston, Dorset T 93 ST 7509
Kingston, Grampn T 184 NJ 3365
Kingston, Hants T 94 SU 1402
Kingston, I. of W T 95 SZ 4781
Kingston, Kent T 99 TR 1951
Kingston, Lothn T 171 NT 5482
Kingston Bagpuize T 115 SU 4098
Kingston Blount T 104 SU 7399
Kingston by Sea T 96 TQ 2305
Kingston Deverill T 93 ST 8437
Kingstone, H. & W T 113 SO 4235
Kingstone, Somer T 92 ST 3713
Kingstone, Staffs T 128 SK 0629
Kingston Lisle T 102 SU 3287
Kingston near Lewes T 97 TQ 3908
Kingston on Soar T 129 SK 5027
Kingston Seymour T 100 ST 4067
Kingston St Mary T 92 ST 2229
Kingston upon Hull P 143 TA 0928
Kingston upon Thames P 105 TQ 1869
Kingstown T 157 NY 3959
King Street, Cambs R 130 TF 1108
King Street, Ches R 137 SJ 6969
King Street, Lincs R 130 TF 1108
King's Walden T 105 TL 1623
Kingswear T 89 SX 8851
Kingswells T 185 NJ 8606
Kingswinford T 117 SO 8888
Kingswood, Avon T 101 ST 6573
Kingswood, Bucks T 104 SP 6819
Kingswood, Glos T 101 ST 7492
Kingswood, H. & W T 113 SO 2954
Kingswood, Kent T 98 TQ 8450
Kingswood, Powys T 126 SJ 2402
Kingswood, Surrey T 96 TQ 2456
Kingswood, Warw T 118 SP 1871
Kings Worthy T 95 SU 4933
Kington, Dorset T 94 SY 9579
Kington, H. & W T 118 SO 9955
Kington, Powys T 113 SO 3056
Kington Langley T 101 ST 9277
Kington Magna T 93 ST 7623
Kington St Michael T 101 ST 9077
Kingussie T 175 NH 7500
King Water W 158 NY 5466
Kingweston T 93 ST 5231
Kinharrachie T 185 NJ 9231
Kininvie House 184 NJ 3144
Kinkell Bridge 170 NN 9316
Kinkell Church A 185 NJ 7819
Kinkell Ness 171 NO 5315
Kinknockie T 185 NK 0041
Kinlet T 117 SO 7280
Kinloch, Fife 171 NO 2812
Kinloch, Highld T 196 NC 3434
Kinloch, Highld T 180 NG 6917
Kinloch, Highld T 179 NM 4099
Kinloch, Tays T 176 NO 1444
Kinloch, Tays 176 NO 2644
Kinlochard T 169 NN 4502
Kinlochbervie T 196 NC 2256
Kinlocheil T 174 NM 9779
Kinlochewe T 190 NH 0261
Kinlochewe Forest 191 NH 0666
Kinloch Glen 179 NG 3800
Kinloch Hourn T 180 NG 9507
Kinloch Laggan T 175 NN 5489
Kinlochleven T 174 NN 1861
Kinloch Lodge 197 NC 5552
Kinlochluichart Forest 182 NH 2769
Kinlochmore T 174 NN 1962
Kinlochourn Forest 180 NG 9409
Kinloch Rannoch T 175 NN 6658
Kinloch River W 197 NC 5451
Kinlochspelve T 173 NM 6526
Kinloss T 183 NJ 0661
Kinmel Bay T 135 SH 9880
Kinmount House 157 NY 1468
Kinmuck T 185 NJ 8119
Kinmundy T 185 NJ 8918
Kinnadie T 185 NJ 9743
Kinnaird T 171 NO 2428
Kinnaird Castle 177 NO 6357
Kinnaird Head 185 NJ 9967
Kinneff 177 NO 8574
Kinneil House A 170 NS 9880
Kinnelhead 157 NT 0301
Kinnell T 177 NO 6050
Kinnel Water W 157 NY 0692
Kinnerley T 126 SJ 3321
Kinnersley, H. & W T 113 SO 3449
Kinnersley, H. & W T 117 SO 8743
Kinnerton, Clwyd T 136 SJ 3361
Kinnerton, Powys T 116 SO 2463
Kinnesswood T 170 NO 1703
Kinninvie T 152 NZ 0521
Kinnordy 176 NO 3655
Kinnoull Hill H 170 NO 1322
Kinoulton T 129 SK 6730
Kinpurney Hill H 176 NO 3241
Kinrive Hill H 192 NH 6875
Kinross T 170 NO 1102
Kinrossie T 170 NO 1832
Kinsham T 116 SO 3664
Kinsley T 139 SE 4114
Kintail Forest 180 NG 9917
Kintarvie T 195 NB 2317
Kintbury T 102 SU 3866
Kintessack T 183 NJ 0060
Kintillo T 170 NO 1317
Kintocher T 184 NJ 5709
Kintore T 185 NJ 7916
Kintour T 166 NR 4551
Kintra 166 NR 3248
Kintra River W 166 NR 3349
Kintyre 160 NR 7439
Kinuachdrachd T 167 NR 7098
Kinuachdrachd Harbour W 167 NR 7098
Kinveachy T 183 NH 9118
Kinver T 117 SO 8484
Kippax T 147 SE 4130
Kippen T 169 NS 6594
Kippenross House 169 NS 7899
Kippford or Scaur T 155 NX 8354
Kirbister, Orkney T 200 HY 3507
Kirbister, Orkney 201 HY 6823
Kirbuster T 200 HY 2825
Kirby Bedon T 133 TG 2805
Kirby Bellars T 129 SK 7117
Kirby Cane T 133 TM 3794
Kirby Cross T 107 TM 2220
Kirby Grindalythe T 149 SE 9067
Kirby Hall A 120 SP 9292
Kirby Hill, N. Yks T 152 NZ 1306
Kirby Hill, N. Yks T 147 SE 3968
Kirby Knowle T 147 SE 4787
Kirby-le-Soken T 107 TM 2221
Kirby Mills T 148 SE 7085
Kirby Misperton T 148 SE 7779
Kirby Muxloe T 129 SK 5204
Kirby Row T 123 TM 3792
Kirby Sigston T 153 SE 4194
Kirby Underdale T 148 SE 8058
Kirby Wiske T 147 SE 3784
Kirdford T 96 TQ 0126
Kiribost Island 188 NF 7564
Kirivick T 195 NB 1941
Kirk T 199 ND 2858
Kirkabister 203 HU 4938
Kirkaig Point 196 NC 0621
Kirkandrews-on-Eden T 157 NY 3558
Kirkbampton T 150 NY 3056
Kirkbean T 156 NX 9759
Kirk Bramwith T 139 SE 6211
Kirkbride T 150 NY 2356
Kirkbuddo T 177 NO 5043
Kirk Burn, Highld W 199 ND 3164
Kirkburn, Humbs T 149 SE 9855
Kirkburton T 138 SE 1912
Kirkby, Lincs T 140 TF 0692
Kirkby, Mers T 136 SJ 4198
Kirkby, N. Yks T 153 NZ 5305
Kirkby Fell 146 SD 8763
Kirkby Fleetham T 152 SE 2894
Kirkby Green T 140 TF 0857
Kirkby in Ashfield T 129 SK 5056
Kirkby Industrial Estate 136 SJ 4398
Kirkby-in-Furness T 144 SD 2282
Kirkby la Thorpe T 130 TF 0945
Kirkby Lonsdale P 145 SD 6178
Kirkby Malham T 146 SD 8961
Kirkby Mallory T 129 SK 4500
Kirkby Malzeard T 147 SE 2374
Kirkby Mills T 148 SE 7085
Kirkbymoorside T 148 SE 6986
Kirkby on Bain T 141 TF 2462
Kirkby Overblow T 147 SE 3249
Kirkby Stephen T 151 NY 7708
Kirkby Thore T 151 NY 6325
Kirkby Underwood T 130 TF 0727
Kirkcaldy P 171 NT 2791
Kirkcambeck T 158 NY 5368
Kirkcarswell T 155 NX 7549
Kirkcolm T 154 NX 0368
Kirkconnel, D. & G T 156 NS 7312
Kirkconnel, D. & G A 157 NY 2575
Kirkconnell 156 NX 9868
Kirkcowan T 154 NX 3260
Kirkcudbright T 155 NX 6851
Kirkcudbright Bay W 155 NX 6645
Kirk Deighton T 147 SE 3950
Kirk Ella T 142 TA 0229
Kirk Fell H 150 NY 1910
Kirkfieldbank T 163 NS 8643
Kirkgunzeon T 156 NX 8666
Kirkham, Lancs T 145 SD 4232
Kirkham, N. Yks T 148 SE 7365
Kirkhamgate T 147 SE 2922
Kirk Hammerton T 147 SE 4655
Kirkharle T 159 NZ 0182
Kirkheaton, Northum T 159 NZ 0177
Kirkheaton, W. Yks T 138 SE 1818
Kirkhill, Highld T 182 NH 5545
Kirkhill, Tays T 177 NO 6860
Kirkhope, Border T 164 NT 3823
Kirk Hope, Orkney W 200 ND 3389
Kirkhouse T 164 NT 3233
Kirkhouse Point 200 ND 4790
Kirkibost, Highld T 180 NG 5517
Kirkibost, W. Isles T 195 NB 1834
Kirkibost Island 188 NF 7564
Kirkinch 176 NO 3144
Kirkinner T 155 NX 4251
Kirkintilloch T 169 NS 6573
Kirk Ireton T 128 SK 2650
Kirkland, Cumbr T 150 NY 0717
Kirkland, Cumbr T 151 NY 6432
Kirkland, D. & G T 156 NS 7214
Kirkland, D. & G T 156 NX 8190
Kirkland Hill H 156 NS 7216
Kirk Langley T 128 SK 2838
Kirkleatham T 153 NZ 5921
Kirklevington T 153 NZ 4209
Kirkley T 123 TM 5391
Kirklington, Notts T 139 SK 6757
Kirklington, N. Yks T 147 SE 3181
Kirklinton T 157 NY 4367
Kirkliston T 171 NT 1274
Kirkmaiden T 154 NX 1236
Kirk Merrington T 152 NZ 2631
Kirk Michael, I. of M T 144 SC 3190
Kirkmichael, Strath T 161 NS 3408

Kirkmichael Ledbeg River

Kirkmichael, Tays T 176 NO 0860
Kirkmond le Mire T 141 TF 1892
Kirkmuirhill T 162 NS 7942
Kirknewton, Lothn T 163 NT 1167
Kirknewton, Northum T 165 NT 9130
Kirkney Water W 184 NJ 4831
Kirk of Shotts T 163 NS 8462
Kirkoswald, Cumbr T 151 NY 5541
Kirkoswald, Strath T 161 NS 2407
Kirkpatrick Durham T 156 NX 7870
Kirkpatrick-Fleming T 157 NY 2670
Kirk Sandall T 139 SE 6108
Kirksanton T 144 SD 1380
Kirk Smeaton T 139 SE 5116
Kirkstile T 184 NJ 5235
Kirkstone Pass 151 NY 4009
Kirk Taing 200 HY 5632
Kirkton, Border T 158 NT 5413
Kirkton, D. & G T 156 NX 9781
Kirkton, Fife T 171 NO 3625
Kirkton, Grampn T 184 NJ 6113
Kirkton, Grampn T 184 NJ 6425
Kirkton, Grampn T 185 NJ 6950
Kirkton, Grampn T 185 NJ 8243
Kirkton, Grampn T 185 NK 1050
Kirkton, Highld T 190 NG 9141
Kirkton, Highld T 193 NH 7998
Kirkton, Strath T 163 NS 9321
Kirkton, Tays 170 NN 9618
Kirkton, Tays T 176 NO 4246
Kirkton Head 185 NK 1250
Kirkton Manor T 163 NT 2238
Kirkton of Airlie 176 NO 3151
Kirkton of Auchterhouse T 176 NO 3438
Kirkton of Barevan T 183 NH 8347
Kirkton of Bourtie T 185 NJ 8024
Kirkton of Collace T 171 NO 1931
Kirkton of Craig T 177 NO 7055
Kirkton of Culsalmond T 184 NJ 6532
Kirkton of Durris T 177 NO 7796
Kirkton of Glenbuchat T 184 NJ 3715
Kirkton of Glenisla T 176 NO 2160
Kirkton of Kingoldrum T 176 NO 3355
Kirkton of Largo T 171 NO 4203
Kirkton of Lethendy T 176 NO 1241
Kirkton of Logie Buchan T 185 NJ 9829
Kirkton of Maryculter T 177 NO 8599
Kirkton of Menmuir T 177 NO 5364
Kirkton of Monikie T 177 NO 5138
Kirkton of Rayne T 185 NJ 6930
Kirkton of Skene T 185 NJ 8007
Kirkton of Strathmartine T 171 NO 3735
Kirkton of Tealing 176 NO 4038
Kirktown T 185 NK 0952
Kirktown of Alvah T 184 NJ 6760
Kirktown of Auchterless T 185 NJ 7141
Kirktown of Bourtie T 185 NJ 8125
Kirktown of Deskford T 184 NJ 5061
Kirktown of Fetteresso T 177 NO 8585
Kirkwall T 200 HY 4410
Kirkwall Airport 200 HY 4808
Kirkwhelpington T 159 NY 9984
Kirk Yetholm T 165 NT 8228
Kirmington T 143 TA 1011
Kirmond le Mire T 141 TF 1892
Kirn T 168 NS 1877
Kirriemuir T 176 NO 3853
Kirriereoch Hill H 155 NX 4286
Kirroughtree Forest F 155 NX 4372
Kirstead Green T 133 TM 2997
Kirtlebridge T 157 NY 2372
Kirtle Water W 157 NY 2577
Kirtling T 122 TL 6856
Kirtling Green T 122 TL 6855
Kirtlington T 115 SP 5019
Kirtomy T 198 NC 7463
Kirtomy Point 198 NC 7465
Kirton, Highld T 180 NG 8227
Kirton, Lincs T 131 TF 3038
Kirton, Notts T 140 SK 6969
Kirton, Suff T 123 TM 2739
Kirton End T 131 TF 2840
Kirton Holme T 131 TF 2642
Kirton in Lindsey T 142 SK 9398
Kishorn Island 180 NG 8037
Kislingbury T 119 SP 6959
Kites Hardwick T 119 SP 4768
Kit Hill H 88 SX 3771
Kithurst Hill H 96 TQ 0712
Kit's Coty House A 98 TQ 7460
Kittybrewster T 185 NJ 9308
Kitwood T 95 SU 6633
Kiveton Park T 139 SK 4983
Klibreck 197 NC 5834
Klibreck Burn W 197 NC 5832
Knaith T 140 SK 8384
Knapdale 167 NR 8176
Knaphill T 104 SU 9658
Knap of Howar A 200 HY 4851
Knap of Trowieglen H 200 ND 2398
Knapp, Somer T 92 ST 3025
Knapp, Tays 171 NO 2831
Knaps Longpeak 90 SS 2018
Knapton, Norf T 133 TG 3034
Knapton, N. Yks T 147 SE 5652
Knapton, N. Yks T 149 SE 8875
Knapwell T 121 TL 3362
Knaresborough T 147 SE 3557
Knarsdale T 151 NY 6753
Knaven T 185 NJ 8943
Knayton T 147 SE 4387
Knebworth T 105 TL 2420
Kneep T 195 NB 0936
Kneesall T 139 SK 6364
Kneesworth T 121 TL 3444
Kneeton T 129 SK 7146
Knelston T 108 SS 4689
Knightacott T 91 SS 6439
Knightcote T 118 SP 3954
Knighton, Devon T 89 SX 5249
Knighton, Leic T 129 SK 6001
Knighton, Powys T 116 SO 2872
Knighton, Staffs T 137 SJ 7360
Knighton, Staffs T 127 SJ 7427
Knighton Down H 102 SU 1144
Knightwick T 117 SO 7355
Knill T 113 SO 2960
Knipe, The H 156 NS 6511
Knipton T 130 SK 8231
Knipton Reservoir W 130 SK 8130
Knitsley T 152 NZ 1148
Kniveton T 128 SK 2150
Knochenkelly T 160 NS 0427
Knock, Cumbr T 151 NY 6627
Knock, Grampn T 184 NJ 5452
Knock, Strath T 173 NM 5438
Knock, W. Isles T 195 NB 4931
Knockally T 199 ND 1429
Knockan T 196 NC 2110
Knockandhu T 184 NJ 2123
Knockando T 184 NJ 1941
Knockando House 184 NJ 2042
Knockandy Hill H 184 NJ 5531
Knockangle Point 166 NR 3151
Knockbain T 182 NH 6255
Knock Bay W 180 NG 6608
Knockbrex T 155 NX 5849
Knock Castle T 161 NS 1962
Knockcoid 154 NX 0169
Knockdaw Hill H 154 NX 1688
Knockdee T 199 ND 1761
Knockdhu W 154 NX 1483
Knockdolian W 154 NX 1184
Knockdolian Castle 154 NX 1285
Knockdow 168 NS 1070
Knockendon Reservoir W 161 NS 2452
Knockenkelly T 160 NS 0426
Knockentiber T 161 NS 3939
Knockespock House 184 NJ 5424
Knock Fell 151 NY 7230
Knockfin Heights H 198 NC 9234
Knock Head 184 NJ 6566
Knock Hill, Fife H 170 NT 0593
Knock Hill, Grampn H 184 NJ 5355
Knockholt T 105 TQ 4759
Knockholt Pound T 105 TQ 4859
Knockie Lodge 182 NH 4413
Knockin T 126 SJ 3322
Knockinlochie W 154 NX 3188
Knock Moss 154 NX 2657
Knocknaha T 160 NR 6918
Knocknain 154 NW 9764
Knocknevis H 155 NX 5573
Knock of Balmyle H 176 NO 1156
Knock of Braemoray H 183 NJ 0141
Knockrome T 166 NR 5571
Knocksharry T 144 SC 2785
Knock, The H 157 NY 2291
Knodishall T 123 TM 4261
Knole A 97 TQ 5354
Knolls Green T 137 SJ 8079
Knolton T 126 SJ 3738
Knook T 102 ST 9341
Knossington T 129 SK 8008
Knott H 150 NY 2933
Knott End-on-Sea T 145 SD 3548
Knotting T 120 TL 0063
Knottingley T 147 SE 4923
Knotty Green T 104 SU 9391
Knowbury T 116 SO 5775
Knowe 154 NX 3171
Knowehead T 156 NX 6190
Knowesgate T 159 NY 9885
Knowes Hill H 164 NT 4338
Knoweside T 161 NS 2512
Knowetownhead T 158 NT 5418
Knowle, Avon T 101 ST 6070
Knowle, Devon T 90 SS 4938
Knowle, Devon T 91 SS 7801
Knowle, Shrops T 117 SO 5973
Knowle, W. Mids T 118 SP 1877
Knowle Green T 145 SD 6338
Knowl Hill T 104 SU 8279
Knowlton T 99 TR 2853
Knowsley T 136 SJ 4395
Knowsley Hall T 136 SJ 4493
Knowstone T 91 SS 8223
Knox Hill H 177 NO 8171
Knox Knowe, Border H 158 NT 6502
Knox Knowe, Northum H 158 NT 6502
Knoydart 180 NG 7802
Knucklas T 116 SO 2574
Knutsford T 137 SJ 7578
Knypersley T 127 SJ 8756
Kokoarrah 116 SO 0497
Kuggar T 86 SW 7216
Kyle 161 NS 5022
Kyleakin, Highld T 180 NG 7526
Kyle Akin, Highld W 180 NG 7526
Kyle of Durness W 196 NC 3865
Kyle of Lochalsh P 180 NG 7627
Kyle of Sutherland W 192 NH 5894
Kyle of Tongue W 197 NC 5858
Kylerhea, Highld T 180 NG 7820
Kyle Rhea, Highld W 180 NG 7922
Kyles Lodge 188 NF 9987
Kylesmorar T 180 NM 8093
Kyles of Bute, Strath W 160 NR 9968
Kyles of Bute, Strath W 168 NS 0472
Kyles Scalpay T 189 NG 2198
Kyles Stockinish T 189 NG 1391
Kylestrome T 196 NC 2234
Kyllachy House 183 NH 7825
Kyloe T 165 NU 0540
Kyloe Hills H 165 NU 0439
Kynance Cove W 86 SW 6813
Kynnersley T 127 SJ 6716
Kype Muir 162 NS 7139
Kype Water W 162 NS 7439
Kyre Park T 117 SO 6263

L

Labost T 195 NB 2749
Lacastal W 195 NB 4240
Laceby T 143 TA 2106
Lacey Green T 104 SP 8200
Lach Dennis T 137 SJ 7072
Lache T 136 SJ 3964
Lachlan Bay W 168 NS 0095
Lackalee T 189 NG 1392
Lackford T 122 TL 7970
Lacock T 101 ST 9168
Ladbroke T 118 SP 4158
Ladder Burn W 176 NO 4184
Ladder Hills H 184 NJ 2819
Laddingford T 97 TQ 6948
Laddus Fens 131 TF 4801
Lade Bank T 131 TF 3954
Ladhar Bheinn H 180 NG 8204
Ladock T 87 SW 8950
Ladybank, Fife T 171 NO 3009
Ladybank, Strath 161 NS 2102
Ladybower Reservoir W 138 SK 1986
Lady Isle 161 NS 2729
Ladykirk T 165 NT 8847
Ladyland Moor 161 NS 3059
Ladylea Hill H 184 NJ 3416
Lady Port W 144 SC 2887
Ladysford T 185 NJ 9060
Lady's Holm 203 HU 3709
Ladyside Height H 164 NT 3647
Lael Forest 191 NH 1982
Lagars Geo 203 HU 4422
Lagavulin T 166 NR 4045
Lagg, Strath T 166 NR 5978
Lagg, Strath T 160 NR 9521
Laggan, Highld T 174 NN 2997
Laggan, Highld T 175 NN 6194
Laggan, Strath 166 NR 2855
Laggan, Strath 154 NX 2582
Laggan Bay, Strath W 173 NM 4541
Laggan Bay, Strath W 166 NR 3052
Laggan Deer Forest 173 NM 6321
Laggan Lodge 173 NM 6224
Laggan Point 166 NR 2755
Laggantalluch Head 154 NX 0836
Lagganulva T 173 NM 4541
Laid 196 NC 4159
Laide T 190 NG 9092
Laiken Forest F 183 NH 9052
Laindon T 106 TQ 6889
Lair T 190 NH 0148
Lairg T 192 NC 5806
Lairg Lodge 192 NC 5707
Lairgmore T 182 NH 5937
Lairg Station 192 NC 5803
Lairig a' Mhuic 175 NN 5749
Lairig Breisleich, Central 175 NN 5541
Lairig Breisleich, Tays 175 NN 5541
Lairig Ghru 183 NH 9603
Lairig Leacach 174 NN 2872
Lair of Aldararie, Grampn H 176 NO 3178
Lair of Aldararie, Tays H 176 NO 3178
Laival a Tuath H 194 NB 0224
Lake T 102 SU 1339
Lake Cottage 154 NX 0948
Lakenham T 133 TG 2307
Lakenheath T 122 TL 7182
Lakenheath Station 122 TL 7186
Lakenheath Warren 122 TL 7680
Lake of Menteith W 169 NN 5700
Lakesend T 131 TL 5196
Lakeside T 145 SD 3787
Laleham T 104 TQ 0568
Laleston T 109 SS 8779
Lamachan Hill H 155 NX 4377
Lamahip H 177 NO 5592
Lamaload Reservoir W 138 SJ 9775
Lamarsh T 122 TL 8935
Lamas T 133 TG 2422
Lamba 205 HU 3981
Lamba Ness 205 HP 6715
Lamba Taing 203 HU 4326
Lamba Water W 203 HU 3856
Lambden T 164 NT 7443
Lamberhurst T 97 TQ 6736
Lamberton T 165 NT 9657
Lamberton Beach 165 NT 9758
Lambeth T 105 TQ 3078
Lambfell Moar T 144 SC 2984
Lambgarth Head 203 HU 4550
Lamb Head 201 HY 6921
Lamb Hill H 154 NX 1068
Lamb Hoga 205 HU 6088
Lambhoga Head 203 HU 4014
Lamb Holm 200 HY 4800
Lamblair Hill H 158 NT 5701
Lambley, Northum T 158 NY 6858
Lambley, Notts T 129 SK 6245
Lambourn T 102 SU 3379
Lambourn Downs H 102 SU 3382
Lambourne End T 105 TQ 4894
Lambrigg Fell 151 SD 5894
Lambs Green T 96 TQ 2136
Lambston T 110 SM 9017
Lamerton T 88 SX 4576
Lamesley T 159 NZ 2558
Lamford Hill H 155 NX 5398
Lamh Dearg H 176 NO 1263
Lamington, Highld T 193 NH 7577
Lamington, Strath T 163 NS 9831
Lamlash T 160 NS 0231
Lamlash Bay W 160 NS 0330
Lammer Law H 164 NT 5261
Lammermuir 164 NT 7358
Lammermuir Hills, Border H 164 NT 5762
Lammermuir Hills, Lothn H 164 NT 5762
Lamonby T 151 NY 4135
Lamorna T 86 SW 4424
Lamorran T 87 SW 8741
Lampeter T 111 SN 5748
Lampeter Velfry T 110 SN 1514
Lamphey T 110 SN 0100
Lamplugh T 150 NY 0820
Lamport T 119 SP 7574
Lamyatt T 93 ST 6535
Lana T 88 SX 3396
Lanark T 163 NS 8843
Lancaster P 145 SD 4761
Lancaster Canal W 145 SD 5041
Lancaster Sound W 145 SD 3366
Lanchester T 152 NZ 1647
Landbeach T 121 TL 4764
Landcross T 90 SS 4523
Landerberry T 185 NJ 7504
Landford T 94 SU 2518
Landford Manor 94 SU 2620
Landimore T 108 SS 4693
Landkey T 91 SS 5931
Landore T 108 SS 6695
Landrake T 88 SX 3760
Landscove T 89 SX 7766
Land's End 86 SW 3425
Landshipping T 110 SN 0211
Landulph T 88 SX 4361
Landwade T 122 TL 6267
Landywood T 128 SJ 9906
Laneast T 88 SX 2283
Lane End T 104 SU 8091
Lane Green T 128 SJ 9607
Laneham T 140 SK 8076
Lanercost Priory A 158 NY 5563
Laneshaw Bridge T 146 SD 9240
Laneshaw Reservoir, Lancs W 146 SD 9441
Laneshaw Reservoir, N. Yks W 146 SD 9441
Langa 203 HU 3739
Langar T 129 SK 7234
Langaton Point 199 ND 3579
Langay 188 NG 0181
Langbank T 169 NS 3873
Langbar T 146 SE 0951
Langcliffe T 146 SD 8265
Lang Clodie Wick W 204 HU 3088
Lang Craig 177 NO 7048
Langdale End T 149 SE 9391
Langdale Fell 151 NY 6500
Langdale Pikes H 150 NY 2707
Langdon Beck T 151 NY 8531
Langdon Common 151 NY 8533
Langdon Hills T 106 TQ 6786
Langdyke 171 NO 3304
Langenhoe T 107 TM 0018
Langford, Beds T 120 TL 1840
Langford, Devon T 92 ST 0203
Langford, Essex T 106 TL 8309
Langford, Notts T 140 SK 8258
Langford, Oxon T 115 SP 2402
Langford Budville T 92 ST 1122
Langford Grounds 100 ST 3567
Langham, Essex T 122 TM 0231
Langham, Leic T 130 SK 8411
Langham, Norf T 132 TG 0041
Langham, Suff T 122 TL 9769
Langham Hall 122 TM 0333
Lang Head 204 HU 3070
Langho T 145 SD 7034
Langholm T 157 NY 3684
Langlee Crags H 165 NT 9622
Langleeford T 165 NT 9421
Langley, Berks T 104 TQ 0079
Langley, Ches T 137 SJ 9471
Langley, Essex T 121 TL 4334
Langley, Hants T 95 SU 4401
Langley, Herts T 105 TL 2122
Langley, Kent T 98 TQ 8051
Langley, Warw T 118 SP 1963
Langley, W. Susx T 95 SU 8029
Langley Burrell T 102 ST 9375
Langley Hill H 114 SP 0029
Langley Marsh T 92 ST 0729
Langley Park T 152 NZ 2144
Langley Street T 133 TG 3701
Langness 144 SC 2966
Langney T 97 TQ 6202
Langney Point 97 TQ 6401
Langold T 139 SK 5887
Langore T 88 SX 3086
Langport T 93 ST 4226
Langrick T 131 TF 2648
Langridge T 101 ST 7469
Langrigg T 150 NY 1645
Langrish T 95 SU 7023
Langsett T 138 SE 2100
Langsett Reservoir W 138 SE 2000
Langshaw T 164 NT 5139
Langskaill 200 HY 4842
Langstone T 95 SU 7105
Langstone Harbour W 95 SU 6802
Langstrothdale Chase 146 SD 8979
Langthorne T 152 SE 2491
Langthorpe T 147 SE 3867
Langthwaite T 152 NZ 0022
Langtoft, Humbs T 149 TA 0167
Langtoft, Lincs T 130 TF 1212
Langton, Durham T 152 NZ 1619
Langton, Lincs T 141 TF 2368
Langton, Lincs T 141 TF 3970
Langton, N. Yks T 148 SE 7967
Langton by Wragby T 141 TF 1476
Langton Green T 97 TQ 5439
Langton Herring T 93 SY 6182
Langton Matravers T 94 SZ 0078
Langtree T 90 SS 4515
Langwathby T 151 NY 5633
Langwell Forest 196 NC 0425
Langwell House 193 ND 1122
Langwell Lodge 191 NC 1702
Langwell Water W 193 ND 0423
Langwith T 139 SK 5269
Langwith Junction T 139 SK 5168
Langwood Fen 121 TL 4385
Langworth T 140 TF 0676
Lanherne or Vale of Mawgan 87 SW 8964
Lanhydrock House A 87 SX 0863
Lanivet T 87 SX 0364
Lank Rigg H 150 NY 0912
Lanlivery T 87 SX 0758
Lanlluest H 116 SO 1974
Lanner T 86 SW 7139
Lanreath T 87 SX 1856
Lanrick 169 NN 6803
Lansallos T 87 SX 1750
Lanton, Border T 164 NT 6221
Lanton, Northum T 165 NT 9231
Lanyar Taing 205 HU 3893
Lapford T 91 SS 7308
Laphroaig T 166 NR 3845
Lapley T 127 SJ 8712
Lapworth T 118 SP 1671
Larachbeg 173 NM 6948
Larbert T 170 NS 8682
Larg Hill H 155 NX 4275
Largie T 184 NJ 6131
Largie Castle 160 NR 7046
Largiemore 168 NR 9486
Largo Bay W 171 NO 4201
Largo Law H 157 NT 4205
Largoward T 171 NO 4607
Largs T 161 NS 2059
Largs Bay W 161 NS 2059
Largybeg T 160 NS 0423
Largybeg Point 160 NS 0523
Largymore T 160 NS 0424
Larig Hill H 183 NJ 0840
Larkfield T 168 NS 2375
Larkhall T 162 NS 7651
Larkhill T 102 SU 1244
Larling T 122 TL 9889
Larriston T 158 NY 5494
Larriston Fells H 158 NY 5792
Lartington T 152 NZ 0117
Lary T 176 NJ 3300
Lasham T 103 SU 6742
Lashy Sound W 201 HY 5937
Laskentyre T 189 NG 0799
Lassodie T 170 NT 1292
Lastingham T 148 SE 7290
Latchingdon T 106 TL 8800
Latchley T 88 SX 4073
Lately Common T 137 SJ 6698
Lathbury T 120 SP 8745
Latheron T 199 ND 2033
Latheronwheel T 199 ND 1932
Latheronwheel House 199 ND 1832
Lathones T 171 NO 4708
Latimer T 104 TQ 0099
Latrigg H 150 NY 2724
Latteridge T 101 ST 6684
Lattiford T 93 ST 6926
Latton T 114 SU 0995
Lauchintilly T 185 NJ 7412
Laudale House 173 NM 7459
Lauder T 164 NT 5347
Lauder Common 164 NT 5046
Lauderdale 164 NT 5645
Laugharne T 111 SN 3010
Laugharne Sands 111 SN 3207
Laughterton T 140 SK 8375
Laughton, E. Susx T 97 TQ 5013
Laughton, Leic T 119 SP 6689
Laughton, Lincs T 140 SK 8497
Laughton-en-le-Morthen T 139 SK 5287
Launcells T 90 SS 2405
Launceston P 88 SX 3384
Launde Abbey T 129 SK 7904
Launton T 115 SP 6022
Laurencekirk T 177 NO 7171
Laurieston T 156 NX 6864
Laurieston Forest F 156 NX 6464
Lauriston Castle 177 NO 7666
Lavan Sands or Traeth Lafan 135 SH 6375
Lavant T 95 SU 8508
Lavendon T 120 SP 9153
Lavenham T 122 TL 9149
Laverhay T 157 NY 1498
Lavernock Point 109 ST 1968
Laverstock T 94 SU 1530
Laverstoke T 103 SU 4948
Laverton, Glos T 114 SP 0735
Laverton, N. Yks T 147 SE 2273
Laverton, Somer T 101 ST 7753
Law T 163 NS 8252
Lawers, Tays T 175 NN 6739
Lawers, Tays 169 NN 7923
Lawers Burn W 175 NN 6741
Lawford T 123 TM 0830
Lawhitton T 88 SX 3582
Lawkland T 146 SD 7766
Law Kneis H 157 NT 2913
Lawley T 127 SJ 6708
Lawnhead T 127 SJ 8324
Lawrenny T 110 SN 0107
Lawshall T 122 TL 8654
Lawton T 113 SO 4459
Laxa Burn W 205 HU 4988
Laxay T 195 NB 3321
Laxdale T 195 NB 4234
Laxdale Lochs W 189 NB 1801
Laxey T 144 SC 4384
Laxey Bay W 144 SC 4382
Laxey Head 144 SC 4483
Laxfield T 123 TM 2972
Laxfirth, Shetld T 203 HU 4346
Lax Firth, Shetld W 203 HU 4447
Laxford Bridge 196 NC 2346
Laxo T 203 HU 4463
Laxobigging T 205 HU 4173
Laxton, Humbs T 142 SE 7925
Laxton, Northnts T 130 SP 9596
Laxton, Notts T 140 SK 7266
Layaval H 178 NF 7723
Laycock T 146 SE 0341
Layer Breton T 106 TL 9418
Layer de la Haye T 107 TL 9720
Layham T 122 TM 0340
Laytham T 142 SE 7439
Lazenby T 153 NZ 5719
Lazonby T 151 NY 5439
Lea, Derby T 139 SK 3257
Lea, H. & W T 114 SO 6621
Lea, Lincs T 140 SK 8286
Lea, Shrops T 126 SJ 4108
Lea, Shrops T 116 SO 3589
Lea, Wilts T 102 ST 9586
Leacann Doire Bainneir H 174 NN 2994
Leac Dhonn 190 NH 0199
Leac Eskadale T 189 NG 2399
Leachie Hill H 177 NO 7385
Leachkin T 182 NH 6444
Leac nam Faoileann 187 NG 4214
Leac Shoilleir H 173 NM 6065
Leac Tressirnish 187 NG 5257
Leadburn T 163 NT 2355
Leadenham T 130 SK 9552
Leaden Roding T 106 TL 5913
Leader Water W 164 NT 5251
Leadgate, Cumbr T 151 NY 7043
Leadgate, Durham T 152 NZ 1251
Leadhills T 156 NS 8814
Leafield T 115 SP 3215
Leagrave T 104 TL 0523
Leake Commonside T 131 TF 3952
Leake Hurn's End T 131 TF 4249
Lealholm T 148 NZ 7607
Lealholm Moor 148 NZ 7509
Lealt, Highld T 187 NG 5060
Lealt, Strath T 167 NR 6690
Lealt Burn W 167 NR 6693
Lealt River W 187 NG 4960
Lea Marston T 128 SP 2093
Leamington Hastings T 119 SP 4467
Leamington Spa, Royal P 118 SP 3265
Leanachan Forest F 174 NN 2078
Leanoch Burn W 184 NJ 1951
Leap Hill, Border H 158 NT 5101
Leap Hill, Border H 158 NT 7207
Leap Hill, Northum H 158 NT 7207
Leap Moor 168 NS 2370
Leargybreck T 166 NR 5371
Learmouth T 165 NT 8637
Leasgill T 145 SD 4984
Leasingham T 130 TF 0548
Leask T 185 NK 0232
Lea Taing 200 HY 5410
Leatherhead T 96 TQ 1656
Leathley T 147 SE 2347
Leaton T 126 SJ 4618
Lea Town T 145 SD 4731
Leaveland T 99 TR 0054
Leavening T 148 SE 7862
Leaves Green T 105 TQ 4162
Lebberston T 149 TA 0782
Lechlade T 115 SU 2199
Lecht Road 184 NJ 2413
Leck Beck W 145 SD 6376
Leck Fell 145 SD 6678
Leckford T 94 SU 3737
Leckfurin T 197 NC 7059
Leckhampstead, Berks T 102 SU 4375
Leckhampstead, Bucks T 119 SP 7237
Leckhampton T 114 SO 9419
Leckie 169 NS 6894
Leckmelm T 191 NH 1690
Leckwith T 109 ST 1574
Leconfield T 142 TA 0143
Ledaig T 173 NM 9037
Ledaig Point 168 NM 8935
Ledbeg River W 196 NC 2413

Llandinabo Loch Etive

Llandinabo *T* 113 SO 5128
Llandinam *T* 125 SO 0288
Llandissilio *T* 110 SN 1221
Llandogo *T* 113 SO 5204
Llandough, S. Glam *T* 109 SS 9973
Llandough, S. Glam *T* 109 ST 1773
Llandovery *P* 110 SN 7634
Llandow *T* 109 SS 9473
Llandre, Dyfed *T* 125 SN 6287
Llandre, Dyfed *T* 112 SN 6742
Llandrillo *T* 135 SJ 0337
Llandrillo-yn-Rhôs *T* 135 SH 8480
Llandrindod Wells *P* 125 SO 0661
Llandrinio *T* 126 SJ 2917
Llandudno *P* 135 SH 7882
Llandudno Junction *T* 135 SH 8078
Llandudwen *T* 134 SH 2736
Llandwrog *T* 134 SH 4556
Llandybie *T* 111 SN 6115
Llandyfalle Hill *H* 112 SO 0737
Llandyfan *T* 111 SN 6417
Llandyfriog *T* 111 SN 3341
Llandyfrydog *T* 134 SH 4485
Llandygwydd *T* 111 SN 2443
Llandyrnog *T* 135 SJ 1065
Llandyssil *T* 126 SO 1995
Llandysul *T* 111 SN 4141
Llanegryn *T* 124 SH 6005
Llanegwad *T* 111 SN 5221
Llanelian-yn-Rhôs *T* 135 SH 8676
Llanelidan *T* 135 SJ 1050
Llanelieu *T* 109 SO 1834
Llanellen *T* 113 SO 3010
Llanelli *P* 108 SN 5100
Llanelltyd *T* 125 SH 7119
Llanelly *T* 113 SO 2314
Llanelly Hill *T* 109 SO 2212
Llanelwedd *T* 112 SO 0552
Llanelwy or St Asaph *T* 135 SJ 0374
Llanenddwyn *T* 124 SH 5823
Llanengan *T* 124 SH 2927
Llanerchymedd *T* 134 SH 4184
Llanerfyl *T* 125 SJ 0309
Llanfachraeth *T* 134 SH 3182
Llanfachreth *T* 125 SH 7522
Llanfaelog *T* 134 SH 3373
Llanfaes *T* 134 SH 6077
Llanfaethlu *T* 134 SH 3187
Llanfaglan *T* 134 SH 4760
Llanfair *T* 134 SH 5729
Llanfair Caereinion *T* 125 SJ 1006
Llanfair Clydogau *T* 111 SN 6251
Llanfair Dyffryn Clwyd *T* 126 SJ 1355
Llanfairfechan *T* 135 SH 6874
Llanfair Kilgeddin *T* 113 SO 3407
Llanfair-Nant-Gwyn *T* 110 SN 1637
Llanfairpwllgwyngyll *T* 134 SH 5372
Llanfair Talhaiarn *T* 135 SH 9270
Llanfair Waterdine *T* 116 SO 2476
Llanfairyneubwll *T* 134 SH 3076
Llanfairynghornwy *T* 134 SH 3291
Llanfallteg *T* 110 SN 1519
Llanfaredd *T* 112 SO 0750
Llanfarian *T* 124 SN 5977
Llanfechain *T* 126 SJ 1820
Llanfechan *T* 112 SN 9750
Llanfechell *T* 134 SH 3691
Llanfendigaid *T* 124 SH 5605
Llanferres *T* 136 SJ 1860
Llanfflewyn *T* 134 SH 3589
Llanfihangel-ar-arth *T* 111 SN 4539
Llanfihangel Crucorney *T* 113 SO 3220
Llanfihangel Glyn Myfyr *T* 135 SH 9949
Llanfihangel Nant Bran *T* 109 SN 9434
Llanfihangel-nant-Melan *T* 113 SO 1858
Llanfihangel Rhydithon *T* 116 SO 1566
Llanfihangel Rogiet *T* 101 ST 4587
Llanfihangel Tal-y-llyn *T* 109 SO 1128
Llanfihangel-uwch-Gwili *T* 111 SN 4922
Llanfihangel-y-Creuddyn *T* 125 SN 6676
Llanfihangel-yng-Ngwynfa *T* 125 SJ 0816
Llanfihangel yn Nhowyn *T* 134 SH 3277
Llanfihangel-y-pennant, Gwyn *T* 134 SH 5244
Llanfihangel-y-pennant, Gwyn *T* 125 SH 6708
Llanfihangel Ystum Llwern *T* 113 SO 4313
Llanfihangel-y-traethau *T* 134 SH 5935
Llanfilo *T* 109 SO 1233
Llanfoist *T* 113 SO 2913
Llanfor *T* 135 SH 9336
Llanfrechfa *T* 113 ST 3193
Llanfrothen *T* 135 SH 6241
Llanfrynach *T* 109 SO 0725
Llanfwrog, Clwyd *T* 136 SJ 1157
Llanfwrog, Gwyn *T* 134 SH 3084
Llanfyllin *T* 126 SJ 1419
Llanfynydd, Clwyd *T* 126 SJ 2856
Llanfynydd, Dyfed *T* 111 SN 5527
Llanfyrnach *T* 111 SN 2231
Llangadfan *T* 125 SJ 0110
Llangadog *T* 108 SN 7028
Llangadwaladr, Clwyd *T* 126 SJ 1830
Llangadwaladr, Gwyn *T* 134 SH 3869
Llangaffo *T* 134 SH 4468
Llangain *T* 111 SN 3816
Llangammarch Wells *T* 112 SN 9347
Llangan *T* 109 SS 9577
Llangarron *T* 113 SO 5321
Llangasty-Talyllin *T* 109 SO 1326
Llangathen *T* 111 SN 5822
Llangattock *T* 109 SO 2117
Llangattock Lingoed *T* 113 SO 3620
Llangattock-Vibon-Avel *T* 113 SO 4515
Llangedwyn *T* 126 SJ 1824
Llangefni *T* 134 SH 4675
Llangeinor *T* 109 SS 9187
Llangeitho *T* 111 SN 6259
Llangeler *T* 111 SN 3739
Llangelynnin *T* 124 SH 5707
Llangendeirne *T* 111 SN 4514
Llangennech *T* 108 SN 5601
Llangennith *T* 108 SS 4291
Llangenny *T* 113 SO 2418
Llangernyw *T* 135 SH 8767
Llangian *T* 134 SH 2929
Llangiwg *T* 108 SN 7205
Llanglydwen *T* 111 SN 1826
Llangoed *T* 134 SH 6179
Llangoedmor *T* 111 SN 2046
Llangollen *P* 126 SJ 2142
Llangollen Canal, Ches *W* 127 SJ 5747
Llangollen Canal, Clwyd *W* 126 SJ 2342
Llangolman *T* 110 SN 1127
Llangorse *T* 109 SO 1327
Llangorse Lake *W* 109 SO 1326
Llangorwen *T* 124 SN 6083
Llangovan *T* 113 SO 4505
Llangower *T* 135 SH 9032
Llangranog *T* 111 SN 3154
Llangristiolus *T* 134 SH 4373
Llangrove *T* 113 SO 5219
Llangua *T* 113 SO 3925
Llangunllo *T* 116 SO 2171
Llangunnor *T* 111 SN 4320
Llangurig *P* 125 SN 9180
Llangwm, Clwyd *T* 135 SH 9644
Llangwm, Dyfed *T* 110 SM 9909
Llangwm, Gwent *T* 113 SO 4200
Llangwnnadl *T* 134 SH 2033
Llangwyfan *T* 136 SJ 1266
Llangwyllog *T* 134 SH 4379
Llangwyryfon *T* 124 SN 6070
Llangybi, Dyfed *T* 111 SN 6153
Llangybi, Gwent *T* 113 ST 3796
Llangybi, Gwyn *T* 134 SH 4241
Llangyfelach *T* 108 SS 6499
Llangynhafal *T* 136 SJ 1263
Llangynidr *T* 109 SO 1519
Llangynin *T* 111 SN 2519
Llangynog, Dyfed *T* 111 SN 3416
Llangynog, Powys *T* 125 SJ 0526
Llangynwyd *T* 109 SS 8588
Llanhamlach *T* 109 SO 0926
Llanharan *T* 109 ST 0083
Llanharry *T* 109 ST 0180
Llanhennock *T* 100 ST 3592
Llanhilleth *T* 109 SO 2200
Llanidloes *T* 125 SN 9584
Llaniestyn *T* 134 SH 2733
Llanigon *T* 113 SO 2140
Llanilar *T* 125 SN 6275
Llanild *T* 109 SS 9881
Llanishen, Gwent *T* 113 SO 4703
Llanishen, S. Glam *T* 109 ST 1782
Llaniwared *H* 125 SN 8977
Llanllechid *T* 135 SH 6268
Llanlleonfel *T* 112 SN 9449
Llanllowell *T* 113 ST 3998
Llanllugan *T* 125 SJ 0502
Llanllwch *T* 111 SN 3818
Llanllwchaiarn *T* 116 SO 1292
Llanllwni *T* 111 SN 4940
Llanllyfni *T* 134 SH 4752
Llanmadoc *T* 108 SS 4493
Llanmaes *T* 109 SS 9869
Llanmartin *T* 100 ST 3989
Llanmerewig *T* 126 SO 1693
Llanmihangel *T* 109 SS 9872
Llanmiloe *T* 111 SN 2508
Llanmorlais *T* 108 SS 5394
Llannefydd *T* 135 SH 9870
Llannerch Hall 135 SJ 0572
Llannon *T* 111 SN 5408
Llannor *T* 134 SH 3537
Llanon *T* 124 SN 5166
Llanover *T* 113 SO 3108
Llanpumsaint *T* 111 SN 4129
Llanrhaeadr *T* 135 SJ 0863
Llanrhaeadr-ym-Mochnant *T* 126 SJ 1226
Llanrhian *T* 110 SM 8231
Llanrhidian *T* 108 SS 4992
Llanrhidian Sands 108 SS 4995
Llanrhos *T* 135 SH 7980
Llanrhyddlad *T* 134 SH 3389
Llanrhystud *T* 124 SN 5469
Llanrothal *T* 113 SO 4718
Llanrug *T* 134 SH 5363
Llanrwst *T* 135 SH 8062
Llansadurnen *T* 111 SN 2810
Llansadwrn, Dyfed *T* 108 SN 6931
Llansadwrn, Gwyn *T* 134 SH 5676
Llansaint *T* 111 SN 3808
Llansamlet *T* 108 SS 6897
Llansannan *T* 135 SH 9365
Llansannor *T* 109 SS 9977
Llansantffraed, Dyfed *T* 124 SN 5167
Llansantffraed, Powys *T* 109 SO 1223
Llansantffraed-Cwmdeuddwr *T* 125 SN 9667
Llansantffraed-in-Elwel *T* 112 SO 0954
Llansantffraid Glan Conwy *T* 135 SH 8076
Llansantffraid-ym-Mechain *T* 126 SJ 2220
Llansawel *T* 111 SN 6236
Llansilin *T* 126 SJ 2128
Llansoy *T* 113 SO 4402
Llanspyddid *T* 109 SO 0128
Llanstadwell *T* 110 SM 9505
Llanstephan, Dyfed *T* 111 SN 3510
Llanstephan, Powys *T* 112 SO 1142
Llanthony *T* 113 SO 2827
Llantilio Crossenny *T* 113 SO 3914
Llantilio Pertholey *T* 113 SO 3116
Llantrisant, Gwent *T* 113 ST 3997
Llantrisant, Gwyn *T* 134 SH 3683
Llantrisant, M. Glam *T* 109 ST 0483
Llantrithyd *T* 109 ST 0473
Llantwit Fardre *T* 109 ST 0785
Llantwit Major *T* 109 SS 9768
Llantysilio Hall 126 SJ 1943
Llantysilio Mountain *H* 126 SJ 1545
Llanuwchllyn *T* 135 SH 8730
Llanvaches *T* 101 ST 4391
Llanvair Discoed *T* 101 ST 4492
Llanvapley *T* 113 SO 3614
Llanvetherine *T* 113 SO 3617
Llanveynoe *T* 113 SO 3031
Llanvihangel Crucorney *T* 113 SO 3220
Llanvihangel Gobion *T* 113 SO 3409
Llanvihangel-Ystern-Llewern *T* 113 SO 4313
Llanwarne *T* 113 SO 5028
Llanwddyn *T* 125 SJ 0219
Llan-wen Hill *H* 116 SO 2969
Llanwenog *T* 111 SN 4945
Llanwern *T* 100 ST 3688
Llanwinio *T* 111 SN 2626
Llanwnda, Dyfed *T* 110 SM 9339
Llanwnda, Gwyn *T* 134 SH 4758
Llanwnnen *T* 111 SN 5347
Llanwnog *T* 125 SO 0293
Llanwrda *T* 108 SN 7131
Llanwrin *T* 125 SH 7803
Llanwrthwl *T* 125 SN 9763
Llanwrtyd *T* 112 SN 8647
Llanwrtyd-Wells *T* 112 SN 8846
Llanwyddelan *T* 125 SJ 0801
Llanybldwel *T* 126 SJ 2423
Llanybri *T* 111 SN 3312
Llanybydder *T* 111 SN 5244
Llanycefn *T* 110 SN 0923
Llanychaer *T* 110 SM 9835
Llanycil *T* 135 SH 9134
Llanycrwys *T* 111 SN 6445
Llanymawddwy *T* 125 SH 9019
Llanymynech, Powys *T* 126 SJ 2620
Llanymynech, Shrops *T* 126 SJ 2620
Llanynghenedl *T* 134 SH 3181
Llanynys *T* 135 SJ 1062
Llan-y-pwll *T* 126 SJ 3651
Llanyre *T* 125 SO 0462
Llanystumdwy *T* 134 SH 4738
Llanywern *T* 109 SO 1028
Llawhaden *T* 110 SN 0717
Llawlech *H* 125 SH 6321
Llawnt *T* 126 SJ 2531
Llawr Dref *T* 124 SH 2828
Llawryglyn *T* 125 SN 9391
Llay *T* 126 SJ 3355
Llechcynfarwy *T* 134 SH 3881
Llechfaen *T* 109 SO 0828
Llechryd, Dyfed *T* 111 SN 2143
Llechryd, M. Glam *T* 109 SO 1009
Llechrydau 126 SJ 2234
Lledrod *T* 125 SN 6470
Lleyn Peninsula 134 SH 3035
Llidiad-Nenog *T* 111 SN 5437
Llithfaen *T* 134 SH 3543
Lliw Resrs *W* 111 SN 6505
Llong *T* 136 SJ 2662
Llowes *T* 113 SO 1941
Llwchmynydd *T* 124 SH 1526
Llwn-y-groes *T* 111 SN 5956
Llwydcoed *T* 109 SN 9904
Llwyn *T* 116 SO 2880
Llwyncelyn *T* 111 SN 4459
Llwyndafydd *T* 111 SN 3755
Llwynderw *T* 126 SJ 2003
Llwyndyrys *T* 134 SH 3741
Llwyngwril *T* 124 SH 5909
Llwynhendy *T* 108 SS 5499
Llwynmawr *T* 126 SJ 2237
Llŵyn-on Reservoir *W* 109 SO 0012
Llwynypia *T* 109 SS 9993
Llyn Alaw *W* 134 SH 3986
Llyn Aled *W* 135 SH 9157
Llyn Alwen *W* 135 SH 9056
Llyn Arenig-Fawr *W* 135 SH 8438
Llyn Berwyn *W* 112 SN 7457
Llyn Bodlyn *W* 125 SH 6424
Llyn Brân *W* 135 SH 9659
Llyn Brenig *W* 135 SH 9755
Llyn Brianne Reservoir, Dyfed *W* 112 SN 8050
Llyn Brianne Reservoir, Powys *W* 112 SN 8050
Llyn Celyn *W* 135 SH 8640
Llynclys *T* 126 SJ 2824
Llyn Clywedog *W* 125 SN 9088
Llyn Coch-hwyad *W* 125 SH 9211
Llyn Conwy *W* 135 SH 7846
Llyn Coron *W* 134 SH 3870
Llyn Cowlyd Reservoir *W* 135 SH 7262
Llyn Crafnant Reservoir *W* 135 SH 7561
Llyn Cwellyn *W* 134 SH 5655
Llyn Cwm Dulyn *W* 134 SH 4949
Llyn Cwmystradllyn *W* 134 SH 5644
Llyn Dinas *W* 134 SH 6149
Llyn Efyrnwy *W* 125 SH 9921
Llyn Eigiau Reservoir *W* 135 SH 7265
Llyn Elsi Reservoir *W* 135 SH 7855
Llynfaes *T* 134 SH 4178
Llyn Gwyddior *W* 125 SH 9307
Llyn Gwynant *W* 135 SH 6452
Llyn Gynon *W* 125 SN 8064
Llyn Helyg *W* 136 SJ 1177
Llyn Hywel *W* 125 SH 6626
Llyn Llydaw *W* 135 SH 6254
Llyn Llywenan *W* 134 SH 3481
Llyn Mawr *W* 125 SO 0097
Llyn Nantlle Uchaf *W* 134 SH 5153
Llyn Ogwen *W* 135 SH 6660
Llyn Padarn *W* 134 SH 5761
Llyn Peris *W* 134 SH 5959
Llyn Syfydrin *W* 125 SN 7284
Llyn Tegid or Bala Lake *W* 135 SH 9133
Llyn Teifi *W* 125 SN 7867
Llyn Trawsfynydd *W* 135 SH 6936
Llyn y Fan Fach *W* 109 SN 8021
Llyn y Fan Fawr *W* 109 SN 8321
Llyn y Tarw *W* 125 SO 0297
Llysfaen *T* 135 SH 8977
Llyswen *T* 112 SO 1338
Llysworney *T* 109 SS 9674
Llys-y-frân *T* 110 SN 0424
Llys-y-frân Reservoir *W* 110 SN 0325
Llywel *T* 109 SN 8730
Loadpot Hill *H* 151 NY 4518
Loan 170 NS 9575
Loanend *T* 165 NT 9450
Loanhead *T* 163 NT 2765
Loans *T* 161 NS 3431
Lòba Sgeir 194 HW 8031
Lochaber *T* 174 NN 1492
Lochaber Loch *W* 156 NX 9270
Loch a' Bhaid-luachraich *W* 190 NG 8986
Loch a' Bhealaich, Highld *W* 197 NC 6027
Loch a' Bhealaich, Highld *W* 190 NG 8664
Loch a' Bhealaich, Highld *W* 180 NH 0221
Loch a' Bhealaich Bheithe *W* 175 NN 5172
Loch a' Bhràige *W* 190 NG 6260
Loch a' Bhraoin *W* 191 NH 1374
Loch a Bhùrra *W* 167 NR 6696
Loch a' Chàirn Bhàin *W* 196 NC 2034
Loch Achall *W* 191 NH 1795
Loch Achanalt *W* 182 NH 2761
Loch a' Chaorainn *W* 192 NH 4678
Loch a' Chaoruinn *W* 160 NR 7866
Loch Achilty *W* 182 NH 4356
Loch Achnamoine *W* 198 NC 8132
Loch a' Chnuic Bhric *W* 166 NR 4473
Loch a' Choire *W* 173 NM 8552
Loch a' Choire Mhóir *W* 191 NH 3088
Loch Achonachie *W* 182 NH 4354
Loch a' Chracaich *W* 190 NG 7657
Loch a' Chrathaich *W* 182 NH 3621
Loch Achray *W* 169 NN 5106
Loch a' Chroisg *W* 191 NH 1258
Loch Affric *W* 181 NH 1622
Loch a' Garbh-bhaid Mór *W* 196 NC 2748
Loch a' Gheoidh *W* 167 NR 6695
Loch a' Ghlinne *W* 194 NB 0212
Loch a' Ghorm-choire *W* 197 NC 4432
Loch a' Ghriama *W* 196 NC 3926
Loch Ailort, Highld *W* 180 NM 7379
Lochailort, Highld *T* 180 NM 7682
Loch Ailsh *W* 196 NC 3111
Loch Ainort *W* 180 NG 5528
Loch Airdeglais *W* 173 NM 6228
Loch Airigh na Beinne *W* 196 NC 3266
Loch Airigh na h-Airde *W* 195 NB 2123
Loch Akran *W* 198 NC 9260
Loch a' Laip *W* 188 NF 8647
Lochaline, Strath *T* 173 NM 6744
Loch Aline, Strath *W* 173 NM 6946
Loch Alsh *W* 180 NG 8025
Loch Alvie *W* 183 NH 8609
Loch a' Mhuilinn *W* 199 ND 0142
Loch a' Mhuillidh *W* 182 NH 2738
Lochan a' Chairn *W* 192 NH 5184
Loch an Aircill *W* 166 NR 5077
Loch an Alltan Fheàrna *W* 198 NC 7533
Lochan Breaclaich *W* 169 NN 6231
Lochan Burn *W* 157 NT 0300
Loch an Daimh, Highld *W* 191 NH 2794
Loch an Daimh, Tays *W* 175 NN 4846
Loch an Dherue *W* 197 NC 5448
Loch an Doire Dhuibh *W* 196 NC 1310
Loch an Draing *W* 190 NG 7790
Lochan Dubh nan Geodh *W* 199 ND 0647
Loch an Dùin, Highld *W* 175 NN 7280
Loch an Dùin, Tays *W* 175 NN 7280
Loch an Easain Uaine *W* 196 NC 3246
Loch an Eion *W* 190 NG 9251
Loch an Eircill *W* 196 NC 3027
Lochan Fada *W* 190 NH 0271
Lochan Gaineamhach *W* 174 NN 3053
Loch an Iasaich *W* 180 NG 9535
Loch an Laoigh *W* 190 NH 0241
Loch an Leathaid Bhuain *W* 196 NC 2736
Loch an Leothaid *W* 196 NC 1729
Lochan na Bi *W* 168 NN 3031
Lochan na h-Achlaise *W* 174 NN 3148
Lochan na h-Earba *W* 175 NN 4883
Lochan na Lairige *W* 175 NN 5940
Loch an Ruathair *W* 198 NC 8637
Lochans *T* 154 NX 0656
Lochan Shira *W* 168 NN 1720
Lochan Sron Mór *W* 168 NN 1519
Loch an Tachdaidh *W* 181 NH 0938
Lochan Thulachan *W* 199 ND 1041
Loch an t-Seilich *W* 175 NN 7586
Loch Arail *W* 167 NR 8079
Locharbriggs *T* 156 NX 9980
Loch Ard *W* 168 NN 4601
Loch Ard Forest *F* 169 NS 4898
Loch Arichlinie *W* 198 NC 8435
Loch Arienas *W* 173 NM 6851
Loch Arkaig *W* 174 NN 0791
Loch Arklet *W* 168 NN 3709
Lochar Moss 157 NY 0371
Loch Arnish *W* 190 NG 5848
Loch Arthur *W* 156 NX 9068
Lochar Water *W* 156 NY 0272
Loch Ascaig *W* 198 NC 8525
Loch a' Sguirr *W* 190 NG 6052
Loch Ashie *W* 182 NH 6335
Loch Assapol *W* 172 NM 4020
Loch Assynt *W* 196 NC 2124
Lochassynt Lodge 196 NC 1726
Loch a Tuath or Broad Bay *W* 195 NB 5036
Loch Aulasary *W* 188 NF 9473
Loch Avich *W* 168 NM 9314
Loch Avon *W* 176 NJ 0102
Loch Awe, Highld *W* 196 NC 2415
Loch Awe, Strath *W* 168 NM 9914
Lochawe, Strath *T* 168 NN 1227
Loch Bà, Highld *W* 174 NN 3149
Loch Bà, Strath *W* 173 NM 5737
Loch Bad a' Chreamh *W* 190 NG 8180
Loch Bad a' Ghaill *W* 196 NC 0710
Loch Badanloch *W* 198 NC 7734
Loch Bad an Sgalaig *W* 190 NG 8571
Loch Baligill *W* 198 NC 8562
Loch Ballygrant *W* 166 NR 4066
Loch Bay *W* 186 NG 2655
Loch Beanacharan *W* 182 NH 3039
Loch Beanie *W* 176 NO 1668
Loch Beannach, Highld *W* 196 NC 1326
Loch Beannach, Highld *W* 197 NC 6814
Loch Beannacharain *W* 182 NH 2351
Loch Bee *W* 188 NF 7743
Loch Beinn a' Mheadhoin *W* 182 NH 2324
Loch Beinn Uraraidh *W* 166 NR 4053
Loch Benachally *W* 176 NO 0750
Loch Beoraid *W* 180 NM 8285
Loch Bhac *W* 175 NN 8262
Loch Bharcasaig *W* 186 NG 2542
Loch Bhrodainn *W* 175 NN 7483
Loch Bhrollum *W* 189 NB 3103
Loch Blàir *W* 174 NN 0594
Loch Bodavat *W* 194 NB 0619
Lochboisdale, W. Isles *T* 178 NF 7919
Loch Boisdale, W. Isles *W* 178 NF 8018
Loch Boltachan *W* 169 NN 6926
Loch Borralan *W* 196 NC 2610
Loch Borralie *W* 196 NC 3867
Loch Bracadale *W* 186 NG 2838
Loch Bradan Reservoir *W* 155 NX 4297
Loch Bràigh an Achaidh *W* 180 NG 7440
Loch Brandy *W* 176 NO 3475
Loch Breac *W* 199 ND 0637
Loch Breachacha *W* 172 NM 1653
Loch Breivat *W* 195 NB 3345
Loch Brittle *W* 187 NG 4019
Loch Broom, Highld *W* 191 NH 1392
Loch Broom, Tays *W* 176 NO 0158
Loch Brora *W* 193 NC 8508
Loch Bruicheach *W* 182 NH 4536
Loch Buidhe *W* 192 NH 6698
Loch Buidhe Mór *W* 198 NC 7758
Loch Buie, Strath *W* 173 NM 6023
Lochbuie, Strath *T* 173 NM 6125
Loch Builg *W* 184 NJ 1803
Loch Calavie *W* 181 NH 0538
Loch Calder *W* 199 ND 0760
Loch Callater *W* 176 NO 1884
Loch Caluim *W* 199 ND 0252
Loch Càm *W* 166 NR 3466
Loch Caoldair *W* 175 NN 6189
Loch Caolisport *W* 167 NR 7374
Loch Caravat *W* 188 NF 8461
Loch Carloway *W* 195 NB 1842
Lochcarnan, W. Isles *T* 188 NF 8044
Loch Càrnan, W. Isles *W* 188 NF 8243
Loch Caroy *W* 186 NG 3042
Loch Carron, Highld *W* 180 NG 8735
Lochcarron, Highld *T* 180 NG 8939
Loch Ceann Dibig *W* 189 NG 1597
Loch Chaolartan *W* 194 NB 0624
Loch Chaorunn Reservoir *W* 167 NR 8371
Loch Choire *W* 197 NC 6328
Loch Choire Forest 197 NC 6329
Loch Choire Lodge 197 NC 6530
Loch Chon *W* 169 NN 4205
Loch Ciaran *W* 160 NR 7754
Loch Claidh *W* 189 NB 2603
Loch Clàir, Highld *W* 190 NG 7771
Loch Clair, Highld *W* 190 NG 9957
Loch Clash *W* 196 NC 2156
Loch Cliad *W* 172 NM 2058
Loch Cluanie *W* 181 NH 1309
Loch Coire na Saidhe Duibhe *W* 197 NC 4536
Loch Coirigerod *W* 195 NB 1721
Loch Con *W* 175 NN 6867
Loch Connan *W* 186 NG 3843
Loch Connell *W* 154 NX 0168
Loch Coruisk *W* 187 NG 4820
Lochcote Reservoir *W* 170 NS 9773
Loch Coulin *W* 190 NH 0155
Loch Coulside *W* 197 NC 5843
Loch Coulter Reservoir *W* 169 NS 7686
Loch Coultrie *W* 190 NG 8545
Loch Cracail Mór *W* 192 NC 6202
Loch Craggie, Highld *W* 191 NC 3205
Loch Craggie, Highld *W* 197 NC 6152
Loch Craggie, Highld *W* 192 NC 6207
Lochcraig Head *H* 157 NT 1617
Loch Craignish *W* 167 NM 7901
Lochcraig Reservoir *W* 161 NS 5351
Loch Cravadale *W* 194 NB 0212
Loch Creran *W* 174 NM 9442
Loch Crinan *W* 167 NR 7995
Loch Cròcach, Highld *W* 196 NC 1027
Loch Cròcach, Highld *W* 196 NC 1939
Loch Cròcach, Highld *W* 197 NC 4249
Loch Cròcach, Highld *W* 198 NC 8043
Loch Crò Criosdaig *W* 195 NB 0820
Loch Crunachdan *W* 175 NN 5493
Loch Cruoshie *W* 181 NH 0536
Loch Cuaich *W* 175 NN 6987
Loch Culag *W* 196 NC 0921
Loch Dallas *W* 183 NJ 0947
Loch Damh *W* 190 NG 8650
Loch Davan *W* 176 NJ 4400
Loch Dee *W* 155 NX 4779
Loch Derculich *W* 175 NN 8654
Loch Derry *W* 154 NX 2573
Lochdhu Hotel 199 ND 0144
Loch Diabaigas Airde *W* 190 NG 8159
Loch Dionard *W* 196 NC 3549
Loch Dochard *W* 174 NN 2142
Loch Dochart *W* 169 NN 4025
Lochdochart House 169 NN 4327
Loch Doilet *W* 173 NM 8067
Loch Doine *W* 169 NN 4719
Lochdon, Strath *T* 173 NM 7333
Loch Don, Strath *W* 173 NM 7431
Loch Doon, D. & G *W* 155 NX 4998
Loch Doon, Strath *W* 155 NX 4998
Loch Dornal, D. & G *W* 154 NX 2976
Loch Dornal, Strath *W* 154 NX 2976
Loch Droma *W* 191 NH 2675
Loch Druidibeg *W* 178 NF 7937
Loch Druim a' Chliabhain *W* 198 NC 8141
Loch Drunkie *W* 169 NN 5404
Loch Duagrich *W* 187 NG 4040
Loch Dubh *W* 199 ND 0537
Loch Dubh a' Chuail *W* 196 NC 3428
Loch Dùghaill, Highld *W* 196 NC 1952
Loch Dughaill, Highld *W* 190 NG 9947
Loch Duich *W* 180 NG 9021
Loch Dungeon *W* 155 NX 5284
Loch Duntelchaig *W* 182 NH 6231
Loch Dunvegan *W* 186 NG 2153
Lochead 167 NR 7778
Loch Earn, Central *W* 169 NN 6423
Loch Earn, Tays *W* 169 NN 6423
Lochearnhead *T* 169 NN 5823
Loch Eatharna *W* 172 NM 2256
Loch Eck *W* 168 NS 1392
Loch Eck Forest 168 NS 1493
Lochee *T* 171 NO 3631
Loch Eigheach *W* 175 NN 4557
Loch Eil *W* 174 NN 0277
Loch Eilde Beag *W* 174 NN 2565
Loch Eilde Mór *W* 174 NN 2464
Loch Eileanach, Highld *W* 197 NC 5940
Loch Eileanach, Highld *W* 199 ND 0747
Locheil Forest 174 NN 0888
Locheilside Station 174 NM 9978
Loch Eilt *W* 180 NM 8182
Loch Einich *W* 175 NN 9199
Loch Eishort *W* 180 NG 6114
Lochenbreck Loch *W* 156 NX 6465
Lochend, Highld *T* 199 ND 2668
Lochend, Highld *T* 182 NH 5937
Loch Enoch *W* 155 NX 4485
Locheport, W. Isles *T* 188 NF 8563
Loch Eport, W. Isles *W* 188 NF 8863
Locherben *T* 156 NX 9597
Loch Eriboll *W* 197 NC 4460
Loch Ericht, Highld *W* 175 NN 5676
Loch Ericht, Tays *W* 175 NN 5676
Loch Ericht Forest *F* 175 NN 5981
Loch Erisort *W* 195 NB 3420
Loch Errochty *W* 175 NN 6865
Locher Water *W* 161 NS 3763
Loch Esk *W* 176 NO 2379
Loch Etchachan *W* 176 NJ 0000
Loch Etive *W* 168 NN 0535

Loch Ewe
Lower Beeding

Loch Ewe W 190 NG 8486
Loch Eye W 193 NH 8379
Loch Eynort, Highld W 186 NG 3624
Loch Eynort, W. Isles W 178 NF 8026
Loch Fad W 160 NS 0761
Loch Fada, Highld W 187 NG 4949
Loch Fada, Highld W 190 NG 9186
Loch Fada, Strath W 166 NR 3895
Loch Fada, W. Isles W 188 NF 8770
Loch Fannich W 182 NH 2065
Loch Faskally W 175 NN 9258
Loch Fèith an Leòthaid W 196 NC 1822
Loch Fell H 157 NT 1704
Loch Feochan W 168 NM 8523
Loch Fiag W 197 NC 4529
Loch Fiart W 173 NM 8037
Loch Finlaggan W 166 NR 3867
Loch Finlas W 155 NX 4698
Loch Finsbay W 189 NG 0886
Loch Fitty W 170 NT 1291
Loch Fleet W 193 NH 7996
Loch Flodabay W 189 NG 1088
Lochfoot T 156 NX 8973
Loch Freuchie W 175 NN 8637
Loch Frisa W 173 NM 4849
Loch Fuaroil W 195 NB 1224
Loch Fuaron W 173 NM 5826
Loch Fyne W 168 NR 9286
Loch Gaineamhach, Highld W 197 NC 5824
Loch Gaineamhach, Highld W 190 NG 7553
Loch Gaineanhach W 168 NM 9100
Lochgair T 168 NR 9290
Loch Gairloch W 190 NG 7776
Lochganvich T 195 NB 2929
Loch Garasdale W 160 NR 7651
Loch Garbhaig W 190 NH 0070
Loch Garry, Highld W 174 NH 2302
Loch Garry, Tays W 175 NN 6270
Loch Garten W 183 NH 9718
Lochgarthside T 182 NH 5219
Loch Garve W 182 NH 4060
Lochgelly, Fife T 170 NT 1893
Loch Gelly, Fife W 171 NT 2092
Loch Ghuilbinn W 174 NN 4174
Loch Gilp W 168 NR 8684
Lochgilphead T 168 NR 8688
Loch Glascarnoch W 191 NH 3172
Loch Glashan W 168 NR 9193
Loch Glass W 192 NH 5172
Loch Glencoul W 196 NC 2531
Loch Glendhu W 196 NC 2633
Loch Glow W 170 NT 0895
Loch Goil W 168 NS 2096
Lochgoilhead T 168 NN 1901
Lochgoin Reservoir W 161 NS 5347
Loch Gorm W 166 NR 2365
Loch Gowan W 191 NH 1556
Loch Grannoch W 155 NX 5469
Loch Greshornish W 186 NG 3453
Loch Grosebay W 189 NG 1592
Loch Gruinart W 166 NR 2970
Loch Grunavat W 195 NB 0827
Loch Haluim W 197 NC 5645
Loch Harport W 186 NG 3433
Loch Harrow W 155 NX 5286
Loch Heilen W 199 ND 2568
Loch Hempriggs W 199 ND 3447
Loch Heouravay W 188 NF 8251
Loch Heron W 154 NX 2764
Loch-hill T 184 NJ 2964
Loch Hoil W 175 NN 8643
Loch Hope W 197 NC 4654
Loch Hourn W 180 NG 8309
Loch Humphrey W 169 NS 4575
Loch Huna W 188 NF 8166
Loch Hunish W 187 NG 4076
Loch Inchard W 196 NC 2355
Lochinch Castle 154 NX 1061
Loch Indaal W 166 NR 2758
Lochindorb W 183 NH 9736
Lochindorb Lodge 183 NH 9735
Loch Insh W 183 NH 8304
Loch Inshore W 196 NC 3369
Lochinvar W 156 NX 6585
Loch Inver, Highld W 196 NC 0722
Lochinver, Highld T 196 NC 0922
Loch Iubhair W 169 NN 4226
Loch Kanaird W 191 NH 1099
Loch Katrine W 169 NN 4509
Loch Keisgaig W 196 NC 2668
Loch Ken W 156 NX 6870
Loch Kennard W 175 NN 9046
Loch Kernsary W 190 NG 8880
Loch Kildonan W 178 NF 7327
Loch Killin W 182 NH 5310
Loch Kinardochy W 175 NN 7755
Loch Kindar W 156 NX 9664
Loch Kinnabus W 166 NR 3042
Loch Kinord W 176 NO 4499
Loch Kirkaig W 196 NC 0719
Loch Kishorn W 180 NG 8138
Loch Knockie W 182 NH 4513
Loch Laggan W 175 NN 4886
Loch Laidon, Highld W 174 NN 3955
Loch Laidon, Tays W 174 NN 3955
Lochlane T 169 NN 8321
Loch Langass W 188 NF 8464
Loch Langavat, W. Isles W 195 NB 1819
Loch Langavat, W. Isles W 195 NB 5254
Loch Langavat, W. Isles W 188 NG 0489
Loch Laro W 192 NH 6199
Loch Laxavat Ard W 195 NB 2438
Loch Laxford W 196 NC 2049
Loch Leacann W 168 NN 0003
Loch Leathan W 187 NG 5051
Loch Leathann an Sgorra W 166 NR 4052
Loch Lednoch Reservoir W 169 NN 7129
Loch Lee W 176 NO 4279
Loch Lesgamaill W 166 NR 5777
Loch Leven, Highld W 174 NN 1060
Loch Leven, Tays W 170 NO 1401
Loch Linnhe W 174 NM 9354
Loch Loch W 176 NN 9874
Loch Lochy W 174 NN 2390
Loch Lomond, Central W 168 NS 3599
Loch Lomond, Strath W 168 NS 3599
Loch Long, Highld W 180 NG 8928
Loch Long, Strath W 168 NS 2292
Loch Losait W 186 NG 2759
Loch Loyal W 197 NC 6247
Loch Loyal Lodge 197 NC 6146
Loch Loyne W 181 NH 1504
Loch Lubnaig W 169 NN 5813
Lochluichart, Highld T 182 NH 3262
Loch Luichart, Highld 182 NH 3661
Loch Lundie W 190 NG 8049
Loch Lurgainn W 196 NC 1109
Loch Lyon W 174 NN 4141
Lochmaben T 157 NY 0882
Lochmaben Stone A 157 NY 3165
Loch Maberry, D. & G W 154 NX 2875
Loch Maberry, Strath W 154 NX 2875
Loch Macaterick W 155 NX 4491
Lochmaddy, W. Isles T 188 NF 9168
Loch Maddy, W. Isles W 188 NF 9368
Loch Mahaick W 169 NN 7006
Loch Mannoch W 156 NX 6660
Loch Maree W 190 NG 9570
Loch ma Stac W 182 NH 3421
Loch Meadaidh W 196 NC 4064
Loch Meadie, Highld W 197 NC 5041
Loch Meadie, Highld W 198 NC 7560
Loch Meadie, Highld W 199 ND 0948
Loch Meala W 198 NC 7857
Loch Meallbrodden W 170 NN 9125
Loch Mealt W 187 NG 5065
Loch Meig W 182 NH 3655
Loch Meiklie W 182 NH 4330
Loch Melfort W 173 NM 8012
Loch Merkland W 196 NC 3931
Loch Mhairc W 175 NN 8879
Loch Mhòr W 182 NH 5419
Loch Migdale W 192 NH 6391
Loch Moan W 154 NX 3485
Loch Moidart W 173 NM 6873
Loch Monar 181 NH 1440
Loch Moraig W 175 NN 9066
Loch Mòr an Stàirr W 195 NB 3938
Loch Morar W 180 NM 7790
Loch More, Highld W 196 NC 3237
Loch More, Highld W 199 ND 0845
Lochmore Cottage 199 ND 0846
Lochmore Lodge 196 NC 2938
Loch Morie W 192 NH 5375
Loch Morlich W 183 NH 9609
Loch Mòr na Caorach W 198 NC 7654
Loch Mòr Sandavat W 195 NB 4952
Loch Morsgail W 195 NB 1322
Loch Moy W 183 NH 7734
Loch Muck W 155 NS 5100
Loch Mudle W 173 NM 5466
Loch Muick W 176 NO 2983
Loch Mullardoch 181 NH 1530
Loch na Beinne Baine W 182 NH 2819
Loch na Caoidhe W 182 NH 2246
Loch na Cille W 167 NR 6879
Loch na Claise Càrnaich W 196 NC 2852
Loch na Claise Mòire W 191 NC 3805
Loch na Conaire W 167 NR 6796
Loch na Craige W 175 NN 8845
Loch na Creige Duibhe W 196 NC 2936
Loch na Creitheach W 187 NG 5120
Loch na Dal W 180 NG 7014
Loch na Fuaralaich W 192 NC 4806
Loch na Gainimh, Highld W 196 NC 1718
Loch na Gainimh, Highld W 196 NC 2061
Lochnagar H 176 NO 2585
Loch na h-Oidhche W 190 NG 8965
Loch na Keal W 173 NM 5038
Loch na Làthaich W 172 NM 3723
Loch na Leitreach W 180 NH 0227
Loch nam Bonnach W 182 NH 4848
Loch nam Brac W 196 NC 1848
Loch nam Breac W 198 NC 8248
Loch nam Breac Dearga W 182 NH 4522
Loch na Mile W 166 NR 5470
Loch nan Ceall W 180 NM 6486
Loch nan Clach, Highld W 198 NC 7753
Loch nan Clach, Strath W 173 NM 7846
Loch nan Clàr W 198 NC 7635
Loch nan Eilean W 195 NB 3617
Loch nan Eun, Highld W 190 NG 7048
Loch nan Eun, Highld W 180 NG 9526
Loch nan Eun, Highld W 182 NH 3120
Loch nan Eun, Highld W 182 NH 4648
Loch nan Eun, Tays W 176 NO 0678
Loch nan Falcag W 195 NB 2926
Loch nan Geireann W 188 NF 8472
Loch nan Stearnag W 195 NB 3237
Loch Nant W 168 NN 0024
Loch nan Torran W 160 NR 7568
Loch Nan Uamh W 180 NM 7083
Loch na Saobhaidhe W 198 NC 8047
Loch na Scaravat W 195 NB 3540
Loch na Sealga W 190 NH 0383
Loch na Seilg W 197 NC 4951
Loch na Seilge W 198 NC 9258
Loch Naver W 197 NC 6136
Lochnaw Castle 154 NW 9962
Loch Nedd W 196 NC 1332
Loch Neldricken W 155 NX 4483
Loch Nell W 168 NM 8927
Lochnell House 173 NM 8839
Loch Ness W 182 NH 5023
Loch Nevis W 180 NM 7695
Loch Niarsco W 187 NG 3947
Loch Obisary W 188 NF 8961
Loch Ochiltree W 154 NX 3174
Loch Odhairn W 195 NB 4114
Loch of Boardhouse W 200 HY 2625
Loch of Cliff W 205 HP 6011
Loch of Girlsta W 203 HU 4352
Loch of Harray W 200 HY 2915
Loch of Hundland W 200 HY 2926
Loch of Kirbister W 200 HY 3608
Loch of Lintrathen W 176 NO 2754
Loch of Lowes W 176 NO 0544
Loch of Mey W 199 ND 2773
Loch of Skaill W 200 HY 2418
Loch of Skellister W 203 HU 4656
Loch of Skene W 185 NJ 7807
Loch of Spiggie W 203 HU 3716
Loch of Stenness W 200 HY 2812
Loch of Strathbeg W 185 NK 0759
Loch of Strom W 203 HU 4048
Loch of St Tredwell W 200 HY 4950
Loch of Swannay W 200 HY 2926
Loch of the Lowes W 157 NT 2319
Loch of Tingwall W 203 HU 4142
Loch of Toftingall W 199 ND 1952
Loch of Vaara W 203 HU 3256
Loch of Vatsetter W 205 HU 5389
Loch of Voxterby W 202 HU 2653
Loch of Watlee W 205 HP 5905
Loch of Wester W 199 ND 3259
Loch of Yarrows W 199 ND 3144
Loch Oich W 174 NH 3201
Loch Olginey W 199 ND 0957
Loch Ollay W 178 NF 7531
Loch Orasay W 195 NB 3827
Loch Ordie W 176 NO 0350
Loch Ore, Fife W 170 NT 1695
Lochore, Fife T 170 NT 1796
Loch Osgaig W 196 NC 0412
Loch Ossian W 174 NN 3968
Loch Pattack W 175 NN 5479
Loch Poit na h-I W 172 NM 3122
Loch Poll W 196 NC 1030
Loch Pooltiel W 186 NG 1650
Loch Quien W 160 NS 0659
Loch Quoich W 174 NH 0102
Loch Rangag W 199 ND 1741
Loch Rannoch W 175 NN 5957
Lochranza, Strath T 160 NR 9250
Loch Ranza, Strath W 160 NR 9351
Loch Resort W 194 NB 0617
Loch Riddon W 168 NS 0077
Loch Riecawr W 155 NX 4393
Loch Righ Mòr W 166 NR 5485
Loch Rimsdale W 198 NC 7336
Loch Roag W 195 NB 1234
Loch Ronald W 154 NX 2664
Lochrosque Forest 182 NH 2162
Loch Ruard W 199 ND 1443
Loch Rumsdale W 198 NC 9641
Loch Rusky W 169 NN 6103
Loch Ruthven W 182 NH 6127
Lochrutton Loch W 156 NX 8972
Loch Ryan W 154 NX 0565
Loch Sand W 199 ND 0941
Loch Scadavay W 188 NF 8568
Loch Scammadale W 168 NM 8920
Loch Scarmclate W 199 ND 1959
Loch Scaslavat W 194 NB 0231
Loch Scavaig W 187 NG 5015
Loch Scoly W 175 NN 9147
Loch Scresort W 179 NM 4199
Loch Scridain W 173 NM 4726
Loch Scye W 199 ND 0055
Loch Seaforth W 188 NB 2106
Loch Sealg or Loch Shell W 195 NB 3510
Loch Sgamhain W 191 NH 0952
Loch Sgeireach Mòr W 195 NB 4945
Loch Sgibacleit W 195 NB 3116
Loch Sguabain W 173 NM 6330
Loch Sguod W 190 NG 8187
Loch Shanndabhat W 195 NB 3413
Loch Shell or Loch Sealg W 195 NB 3510
Loch Shiel W 173 NM 8072
Loch Shieldaig W 190 NG 8055
Loch Shin W 197 NC 4916
Loch Shira W 168 NN 1009
Loch Shurrery W 199 ND 0455
Lochside, Grampn T 177 NO 7364
Lochside, Highld 197 NC 4759
Lochside, Highld 198 NC 8735
Loch Sionascaig W 196 NC 1214
Loch Skealtar W 188 NF 8968
Loch Skeen W 157 NT 1716
Loch Skerrow W 156 NX 6068
Loch Skiach W 176 NN 9547
Lochskipport, W. Isles T 178 NF 8238
Loch Skipport, W. Isles W 178 NF 8338
Loch Slapin W 180 NG 5717
Loch Sletill W 198 NC 9547
Loch Sligachan W 187 NG 5132
Lochslin T 193 NH 8480
Loch Sloy W 168 NN 2812
Loch Smigeadail W 166 NR 3875
Loch Smuaisaval W 195 NB 2030
Loch Snigisclett W 178 NF 8025
Loch Snizort W 186 NG 3261
Loch Snizort Beag W 186 NG 3954
Lochs of Beosetter W 203 HU 4943
Lochs of Lumbister W 205 HU 4896
Loch Spallander Reservoir W 161 NS 3908
Loch Spelve W 173 NM 6927
Loch Spey W 174 NN 4293
Loch Spynie W 184 NJ 2366
Loch Stack W 196 NC 2942
Lochstack Lodge 196 NC 2643
Loch Staosnaig W 166 NR 3993
Loch Steisevat W 188 NG 0187
Loch Stornoway W 160 NR 7361
Loch Strandavat W 195 NB 2519
Loch Strathy W 198 NC 7747
Loch Striven W 168 NS 0777
Loch Stulaval W 178 NF 8022
Loch Suainaval W 194 NB 0629
Loch Sunart W 173 NM 7361
Loch Sween W 167 NR 7382
Loch Syre W 197 NC 6644
Loch Tamanavay W 194 NB 0320
Loch Tanna W 160 NR 9243
Loch Tarbert W 166 NR 5581
Loch Tarff W 182 NH 4209
Loch Tay W 175 NN 6838
Loch Teacuis W 173 NM 6455
Loch Tealasavay W 194 NB 0218
Loch Teàrnait W 173 NM 7547
Loch Thom W 168 NS 2672
Loch Thota Bridein W 195 NB 3327
Loch Tollaidh W 190 NG 8478
Lochton T 177 NO 7592
Loch Torridon W 190 NG 7659
Loch Tralaig W 168 NM 8816
Loch Trealaval W 195 NB 2723
Loch Treig W 174 NN 3372
Loch Trollamarig W 189 NB 2201
Loch Tromlee W 168 NN 0425
Loch Trool W 154 NX 4179
Loch Truderscaig W 198 NC 7133
Loch Tuath W 172 NM 4043
Loch Tuim Ghlais W 198 NC 9852
Loch Tulla W 174 NN 2942
Loch Tummel W 175 NN 8159
Loch Tungavat W 195 NB 1628
Loch Turret Reservoir W 169 NN 8027
Loch Uisg W 173 NM 6425
Lochuisge, Highld 173 NM 7955
Loch Uisge, Highld W 173 NM 8055
Loch Uiskevagh W 188 NF 8551
Loch Uraval W 195 NB 3032
Loch Urigill W 196 NC 2410
Loch Urr W 156 NX 7684
Loch Urrahag W 195 NB 3247
Loch Ussie W 182 NH 5057
Loch Vaich W 191 NH 3477
Loch Valigan W 176 NN 9769
Loch Valley W 155 NX 4481
Loch Venachar W 169 NN 5705
Loch Veyatie W 196 NC 1813
Loch Voil W 169 NN 5020
Loch Vrotachan W 176 NO 1278
Loch Walton W 169 NS 6686
Loch Watten W 199 ND 2356
Loch Whinyeon W 156 NX 6260
Lochwinnoch T 161 NS 3558
Lochwood, D. & G 157 NY 0896
Lochwood, Strath T 162 NS 6966
Lockengate T 87 SX 0361
Lockerbie T 157 NY 1381
Lockeridge T 102 SU 1467
Lockerley T 94 SU 3026
Lockerley Hall 94 SU 2928
Locking T 100 ST 3659
Lockington, Humbs T 142 SE 9947
Lockington, Leic T 129 SK 4627
Lockleywood T 127 SJ 6928
Locks Heath T 95 SU 5107
Lockton T 148 SE 8489
Lockwood Beck Reservoir W 153 NZ 6713
Loddington, Leic T 129 SK 7802
Loddington, Northnts T 120 SP 8178
Loddiswell T 89 SX 7248
Loddon T 133 TM 3698
Lode T 121 TL 5362
Loder Head 203 HU 5243
Loders T 93 SY 4994
Lodsworth T 96 SU 9223
Loe, The W 86 SW 6425
Loft Hill H 158 NT 8513
Lofthouse T 146 SE 1073
Lofthouse Gate T 147 SE 3324
Loftus T 153 NZ 7118
Logan T 156 NS 5820
Loganlea Reservoir W 163 NT 1962
Logan Mains 154 NX 0943
Logan Rock 86 SW 3922
Logan Water W 162 NS 7537
Loggerheads T 127 SJ 7336
Loggie T 191 NH 1490
Logie, Fife T 171 NO 4020
Logie, Grampn T 185 NK 0357
Logie, Tays 176 NO 1245
Logie, Tays T 177 NO 6963
Logiealmond 170 NN 9731
Logiealmond Lodge 170 NN 9631
Logie Coldstone T 184 NJ 4304
Logie Head 184 NJ 5268
Logie Hill T 193 NH 7676
Logie Newton T 184 NJ 6638
Logie Pert T 177 NO 6664
Logierait T 176 NN 9751
Login T 110 SN 1623
Lolworth T 121 TL 3663
Lomond Hills H 171 NO 2206
Lonbain T 190 NG 6852
Londesborough T 142 SE 8645
Londinium R 105 TQ 3181
London (Gatwick) Airport O 96 TQ 2640
London (Heathrow) Airport O 104 TQ 0875
London (Stansted) Airport 105 TL 5322
London T 105 TQ 3079
London Bridge Station 105 TQ 3280
London Colney T 105 TL 1704
Londonderry T 147 SE 3087
Londonthorpe T 130 SK 9538
Lòndubh T 190 NG 8680
Lonemore, Highld T 190 NG 7877
Lonemore, Highld T 193 NH 7688
Longa Island 190 NG 7377
Longannet Point 170 NS 9485
Long Ashton T 101 ST 5470
Longay 180 NG 6531
Long Bennington T 130 SK 8344
Longbenton T 159 NZ 2668
Longborough T 115 SP 1829
Long Bredy T 93 SY 5690
Longbridge, Warw T 118 SP 2762
Longbridge, W. Mids T 118 SP 0177
Longbridge Deverill T 101 ST 8640
Long Buckby T 119 SP 6267
Longburton T 93 ST 6412
Long Clawson T 129 SK 7227
Longcliffe T 128 SK 2255
Long Common T 95 SU 5014
Long Compton, Staffs T 127 SJ 8522
Long Compton, Warw T 115 SP 2833
Longcot T 102 SU 2790
Long Crag H 159 NU 0606
Long Craig 177 NO 7254
Long Crendon T 104 SP 6908
Long Crichel T 94 ST 9710
Longcroft T 169 NS 7979
Longden T 126 SJ 4406
Longdendale 138 SK 0498
Long Ditton T 105 TQ 1665
Longdon, H. & W T 117 SO 8336
Longdon, Staffs T 128 SK 0814
Longdon on Tern T 127 SJ 6115
Longdown T 89 SX 8691
Longdowns T 86 SW 7434
Long Drax T 142 SE 6828
Long Duckmanton T 139 SK 4471
Long Eaton T 129 SK 4933
Long Fell H 156 NX 9064
Longfield T 98 TQ 6068
Longford, Derby T 128 SK 2137
Longford, G. Lon T 104 TQ 0476
Longford, Glos T 114 SO 8421
Longford, Shrops T 127 SJ 6434
Longford, Shrops T 127 SJ 7218
Longford, W. Mids T 118 SP 3583
Longforgan T 171 NO 3130
Longformacus T 164 NT 6957
Longframlington T 159 NU 1301
Long Geo 200 HY 4404
Long Gill T 146 SD 7858
Longham, Dorset T 94 SZ 0698
Longham, Norf T 132 TF 9415
Long Hanborough T 115 SP 4114
Long Haven W 185 NK 1240
Long Hermiston T 170 NT 1770
Longhirst T 159 NZ 2289
Long Holcombe 91 SS 7636
Longhope, Glos T 114 SO 6818
Longhope, Orkney T 200 ND 3090
Longhope, Orkney W 200 ND 3191
Longhorsley T 159 NZ 1494
Longhoughton T 159 NU 2415
Long Itchington T 118 SP 4165
Long Lawford T 119 SP 4775
Longleat House A 101 ST 8043
Longley Green T 117 SO 7350
Long Load T 93 ST 4623
Long Loch, Strath W 161 NS 4752
Long Loch, Tays W 176 NO 2838
Longmanhill T 185 NJ 7462
Longman Point 183 NH 6747
Long Man, The A 97 TQ 5403
Long Marston, Herts T 104 SP 8915
Long Marston, N. Yks T 147 SE 5051
Long Marston, Warw T 118 SP 1548
Long Marton T 151 NY 6624
Long Melford T 122 TL 8645
Longmoor Camp T 95 SU 7930
Longmorn T 184 NJ 2358
Long Mountain H 126 SJ 2707
Long Mynd, The H 126 SO 4193
Longness 144 SC 2866
Long Newnton T 101 ST 9192
Longnewton, Border T 164 NT 5827
Longnewton, Cleve T 153 NZ 3816
Longnewton Forest F 164 NT 6227
Longney T 114 SO 7612
Longniddry T 171 NT 4476
Longnor, Shrops T 127 SJ 4800
Longnor, Staffs T 138 SK 0965
Long Nose Spit 99 TR 3872
Longparish T 102 SU 4344
Long Preston T 146 SD 8358
Longridge, Lancs T 145 SD 6037
Longridge, Lothn T 163 NS 9562
Longridge Fell H 145 SD 6540
Longridge Towers 165 NT 9549
Longriggend T 169 NS 8270
Long Riston T 143 TA 1242
Long Sand 131 TF 5447
Longsdon T 128 SJ 9654
Longships 86 SW 3225
Longside T 185 NK 0347
Longsleddale 151 NY 5002
Longslow T 127 SJ 6535
Longstanton T 121 TL 3966
Longstock T 94 SU 3537
Longstowe T 121 TL 3055
Long Stratton T 123 TM 1992
Long Street T 119 SP 7947
Long Sutton, Hants T 103 SU 7347
Long Sutton, Lincs T 131 TF 4322
Long Sutton, Somer T 93 ST 4625
Long Tain 205 HU 3785
Longthorpe T 130 TL 1698
Longton, Lancs T 145 SD 4725
Longton, Staffs T 127 SJ 9143
Longtown, Cumbr T 157 NY 3868
Longtown, H. & W T 113 SO 3229
Long Valley 103 SU 8352
Longville in the Dale T 127 SO 5493
Long Whatton T 129 SK 4823
Longwick T 104 SP 7904
Long Wittenham T 115 SU 5493
Longwitton T 159 NZ 0788
Longwood House 95 SU 5424
Longwood Warren 95 SU 5326
Longworth T 115 SU 3999
Longyester T 164 NT 5465
Lòn Liath W 180 NM 6590
Lonmore T 186 NG 2646
Looe T 87 SX 2553
Looe Bay W 88 SX 2753
Looe or St George's Island 87 SX 2551
Loose T 97 TQ 7652
Loosley Row T 104 SP 8100
Lootcherbrae T 184 NJ 6054
Lopcombe Corner T 94 SU 2535
Lopen T 93 ST 4214
Lop Ness 201 HY 7643
Loppington T 127 SJ 4729
Lopwell T 88 SX 4764
Lorbottle T 159 NU 0306
Lorbottle Hall 159 NU 0408
Lord Arthur's Cairn H 184 NJ 5119
Lord's Seat H 150 NY 2026
Lorn 168 NN 0835
Lornty 176 NO 1746
Lornty Burn W 176 NO 1447
Lorton T 150 NY 1525
Lorton Vale 150 NY 1526
Loscoe T 128 SK 4247
Lossie Forest F 184 NJ 2767
Lossiemouth T 184 NJ 2370
Lossit 166 NR 1856
Lossit Bay W 166 NR 1756
Lossit Point 166 NR 1756
Lostock Gralam T 137 SJ 6975
Lostock Junction T 137 SD 6708
Lostwithiel T 87 SX 1059
Lothbeg T 193 NC 9410
Lothbeg Point 193 NC 9609
Lothersdale T 146 SD 9646
Lothmore T 193 NC 9711
Lotus Hill H 156 NX 9067
Loudoun Hill H 162 NS 6037
Loudwater T 104 SU 9090
Loughborough P 129 SK 5319
Loughor T 108 SS 5798
Loughton, Bucks T 120 SP 8337
Loughton, Essex T 105 TQ 4296
Loughton, Shrops T 117 SO 6183
Lound, Lincs T 130 TF 0618
Lound, Notts T 140 SK 6986
Lound, Suff T 133 TM 5099
Lount T 128 SK 3819
Louth T 141 TF 3387
Love Clough T 146 SD 8127
Lover T 94 SU 2120
Loversall T 139 SK 5798
Loves Green T 106 TL 6404
Loveston T 110 SN 0808
Lovington T 93 ST 5930
Low Bentham T 145 SD 6469
Low Bradfield T 139 SK 2692
Low Bradley T 146 SE 0048
Low Braithwaite T 151 NY 4242
Lowbridge House 151 NY 5401
Low Brunton T 158 NY 9270
Low Burnham T 142 SE 7802
Lowca T 150 NX 9821
Low Catton T 148 SE 7053
Low Coniscliffe T 152 NZ 2413
Low Crosby T 157 NY 4459
Lowdham T 129 SK 6646
Low Dinsdale T 153 NZ 3410
Low Dovengill T 151 SD 7299
Low Eggborough T 147 SE 5623
Low Ellington T 146 SE 2083
Lower Aisholt T 92 ST 2035
Lower Ashton T 89 SX 8484
Lower Assendon T 104 SU 7484
Lower Basildon T 104 SU 6178
Lower Bayble T 195 NB 5130
Lower Beeding T 96 TQ 2227

Lower Benefield Marybank

Lower Benefield T 120 SP 9988
Lower Boddington T 119 SP 4852
Lower Breinton T 113 SO 4739
Lower Bullingham T 113 SO 5238
Lower Cam T 114 SO 7400
Lower Chapel T 109 SO 0235
Lower Chute T 102 SU 3153
Lower Darwen T 145 SD 6825
Lower Diabaig T 190 NG 7960
Lower Down T 116 SO 3384
Lower Dunsforth T 147 SE 4464
Lower Farringdon T 95 SU 7035
Lower Frankton T 126 SJ 3732
Lower Froyle T 103 SU 7644
Lower Gledfield T 192 NH 5990
Lower Green T 132 TF 9837
Lower Halstow T 98 TQ 8567
Lower Hardres T 99 TR 1553
Lower Heyford T 115 SP 4824
Lower Higham T 98 TQ 7172
Lower Hope, The W 98 TQ 7077
Lower Hordley T 126 SJ 3929
Lower Icknield Way A 104 SP 9212
Lower Killeyan T 166 NR 2743
Lower Langford T 101 ST 4560
Lower Largo T 171 NO 4102
Lower Lemington T 115 SP 2234
Lower Lye T 116 SO 4066
Lower Machen T 109 ST 2288
Lower Maes-coed T 113 SO 3530
Lower Moor T 118 SO 9847
Lower Nazeing T 105 TL 3906
Lower Penarth T 109 ST 1870
Lower Penn T 127 SO 8696
Lower Pennington T 94 SZ 3193
Lower Peover T 137 SJ 7474
Lower Quinton T 118 SP 1847
Lower Sharpnose Point 90 SS 1912
Lower Shelton T 120 SP 9942
Lower Shiplake T 104 SU 7779
Lower Shuckburgh T 119 SP 4962
Lower Slaughter T 115 SP 1622
Lower Stanton St Quintin T 101 ST 9180
Lower Stoke T 98 TQ 8376
Lower Stondon T 120 TL 1535
Lower Sundon T 120 TL 0527
Lower Swanwick T 95 SU 5009
Lower Swell T 115 SP 1725
Lower Tamar Lake W 90 SS 2911
Lower Thurlton T 133 TM 4299
Lower Tysoe T 118 SP 3445
Lower Upham T 95 SU 5219
Lower Vexford T 92 ST 1135
Lower Weare T 100 ST 4053
Lower Welson T 113 SO 2949
Lower Wield T 103 SU 6340
Lower Winchendon or Nether Winchendon T 104 SP 7312
Lower Woodend T 104 SU 8187
Lower Woodford T 94 SU 1235
Lowesby T 129 SK 7207
Lowestoft P 133 TM 5493
Loweswater, Cumbr W 150 NY 1221
Loweswater, Cumbr T 150 NY 1420
Loweswater Fell 150 NY 1319
Lowford T 123 TM 0931
Low Gate T 158 NY 9063
Low Gill, Cumbr T 151 SD 6297
Lowgill, Lancs T 145 SD 6564
Low Ham T 93 ST 4329
Low Hesket T 151 NY 4646
Low Hesleyhurst T 159 NZ 0897
Lowick, Cumbr T 145 SD 2986
Lowick, Northnts T 120 SP 9780
Lowick, Northum T 165 NU 0139
Lowlandman's Bay W 166 NR 5672
Low Leighton T 138 SK 0085
Low Mill T 153 SE 6795
Low Moor T 145 SD 7341
Lownie Moor T 177 NO 4848
Lowood T 164 NT 5235
Low Row, Cumbr T 158 NY 5863
Low Row, N. Yks T 152 SD 9897
Lowsonford T 118 SP 1868
Lowther T 151 NY 5323
Lowther Castle 151 NY 5223
Lowther Hill H 156 NS 8910
Lowther Hills, Border H 156 NT 0006
Lowther Hills, D. & G H 156 NS 8911
Lowther Hills, Strath H 156 NS 8911
Lowther Hills, Strath H 156 NT 0006
Lowthorpe T 149 TA 0860
Lowton T 137 SJ 6297
Lowton Common T 137 SJ 6397
Low Torry T 170 NT 0186
Low Waters T 162 NS 7254
Low Worsall T 153 NZ 3909
Loxbeare T 91 SS 9116
Loxhill T 96 TQ 0038
Loxhore T 91 SS 6138
Loxley T 118 SP 2453
Loxton T 100 ST 3755
Loxwood T 96 TQ 0331
Lubcroy 191 NC 3501
Lubenham T 119 SP 7087
Lub Score W 187 NG 3973
Luccombe T 91 SS 9144
Luccombe Chine 95 SZ 5879
Luccombe Village T 95 SZ 5879
Luce Bay W 154 NX 2342
Luce Sands 154 NX 1554
Lucker T 165 NU 1530
Luckett T 88 SX 3873
Luckington T 101 ST 8384
Lucklawhill T 171 NO 4221
Luckwell Bridge T 91 SS 9038
Lucton T 116 SO 4364
Ludag T 178 NF 7713
Ludborough T 141 TF 2995
Ludchurch T 110 SN 1410
Luddenden T 146 SE 0426
Luddenham Court 99 TQ 9963
Luddesdown T 98 TQ 6766
Luddington T 142 SE 8216
Lude House 175 NN 8865
Ludford T 141 TF 1989
Ludgershall, Bucks T 104 SP 6617
Ludgershall, Wilts T 102 SU 2650
Ludgvan T 86 SW 5033
Ludham T 133 TG 3818
Ludlow T 116 SO 5175
Ludwell T 93 ST 9122
Ludworth T 153 NZ 3641
Luffincott T 88 SX 3394
Lugar T 162 NS 5921
Lugar Water W 161 NS 5023
Lugate Water W 164 NT 4345
Luggate Burn T 171 NT 6074
Luggiebank T 169 NS 7672
Lugton T 161 NS 4152
Lugton Water W 161 NS 3849
Luguvalium R 151 NY 4055
Lugwardine T 113 SO 5541
Luib T 180 NG 5627
Luing 173 NM 7410
Luinga Bheag 180 NM 6187
Luinga Mhòr 180 NM 6085
Luinne Bheinn H 180 NG 8600
Luirsay Dubh 178 NF 8640
Luithaid H 195 NB 1713
Lui Water W 176 NO 0592
Lulham T 113 SO 4041
Lullingstone Castle 105 TQ 5364
Lullington, Derby T 128 SK 2513
Lullington, Somer T 101 ST 7851
Lulsgate Bottom T 101 ST 5165
Lulsley T 117 SO 7455
Lulworth Camp T 93 SY 8381
Lulworth Cove W 93 SY 8279
Lumb T 146 SE 0321
Lumby T 147 SE 4830
Lumley Moor Reservoir W 147 SE 2270
Lumloch 169 NS 6369
Lumphanan T 184 NJ 5804
Lumphinnans T 170 NT 1792
Lumsdaine T 165 NT 8769
Lumsden T 184 NJ 4722
Lunan T 177 NO 6851
Lunan Bay W 177 NO 7051
Lunan Burn W 176 NO 1741
Lunanhead T 177 NO 4752
Lunan Water W 177 NO 6549
Luncarty T 170 NO 0929
Lund, Humbs T 149 SE 9748
Lund, N. Yks T 147 SE 6532
Lund, Shetld 205 HP 5703
Lunda Wick W 205 HP 5604
Lunderston Bay W 168 NS 2073
Lundie T 176 NO 2936
Lundin Links T 171 NO 4102
Lundy 90 SS 1345
Lune Forest F 151 NY 8323
Lune Moor 152 NY 8923
Lunga, Strath 172 NM 2741
Lunga, Strath 173 NM 7008
Lunga, Strath 167 NM 7906
Lunna T 205 HU 4869
Lunna Holm 205 HU 5274
Lunnasting 203 HU 4865
Lunning T 203 HU 5066
Lunning Sound W 203 HU 5165
Lunsford's Cross T 97 TQ 7110
Lunt T 136 SD 3401
Luntley T 113 SO 3955
Luppitt T 92 ST 1606
Lupton T 145 SD 5581
Lupton Beck W 145 SD 5580
Lurgashall T 96 SU 9327
Lurg Hill H 184 NJ 5057
Lurg Mhòr H 181 NH 0639
Lusby T 141 TF 3367
Luskentyre T 189 NG 0699
Lusragan Burn W 168 NM 9032
Luss T 168 NS 3592
Lussa Loch W 160 NR 7130
Lussa Point 167 NR 6486
Lussa River, Strath W 173 NM 6531
Lussa River, Strath W 167 NR 6391
Lusta T 186 NG 2656
Lustleigh T 89 SX 7881
Luston T 116 SO 4863
Luthermuir T 177 NO 6568
Luther Water W 177 NO 6869
Luthrie T 171 NO 3319
Luton, Beds P 104 TL 0921
Luton, Devon T 89 SX 9076
Luton, Kent T 98 TQ 7666
Luton International Airport 105 TL 1220
Lutterworth T 119 SP 5484
Lutton, Devon T 89 SX 5959
Lutton, Lincs T 131 TF 4325
Lutton, Northnts T 120 TL 1187
Lutworthy T 91 SS 7616
Luxborough T 91 SS 9737
Luxhay Reservoir W 92 ST 2017
Luxulyan T 87 SX 0558
Lybster T 199 ND 2435
Lychett Matravers T 94 SY 9495
Lydbury North T 116 SO 3586
Lydcott 91 SS 6936
Lydd T 99 TR 0421
Lydd Airport 99 TR 0621
Lydden T 99 TR 2645
Lyddington T 130 SP 8797
Lydd-on-Sea T 99 TR 0820
Lydeard St Lawrence T 92 ST 1232
Lydford, Devon T 88 SX 5185
Lydford, Somer T 93 ST 5631
Lydgate T 146 SD 9225
Lydham T 116 SO 3391
Lydiard Millicent T 102 SU 0986
Lydiate T 136 SD 3704
Lydlinch T 93 ST 7413
Lydney T 113 SO 6303
Lydney Sand 113 ST 6399
Lydstep T 110 SS 0898
Lye T 117 SO 9284
Lye Green T 104 SP 9703
Lyford T 115 SU 3994
Lymbridge Green T 99 TR 1243
Lyme Bay W 92 SY 3886
Lyme Park A 138 SJ 9682
Lyme Regis T 92 SY 3392
Lyminge T 99 TR 1641
Lyminge Forest F 99 TR 1545
Lymington T 94 SZ 3295
Lymington River W 94 SU 3102
Lyminster T 96 TQ 0204
Lymm T 137 SJ 6887
Lymore T 94 SZ 2993
Lympne T 99 TR 1235
Lympne Castle A 99 TR 1134
Lympsham T 100 ST 3354
Lympstone T 89 SX 9984
Lynaberack 175 NN 7694
Lynchat T 175 NH 7801
Lyndale House 186 NG 3654
Lyndale Point 186 NG 3657
Lyndhurst T 94 SU 3008
Lyndhurst Road Station 94 SU 3310
Lyndon T 130 SK 9004
Lyne T 104 TQ 0166
Lyneal T 126 SJ 4433
Lyneham, Oxon T 115 SP 2720
Lyneham, Wilts T 102 SU 0279
Lyne House 96 TQ 1938
Lynemouth T 159 NZ 2991
Lyne of Gorthleck T 182 NH 5420
Lyne of Skene T 185 NJ 7610
Lyness T 200 ND 3094
Lyne Water W 163 NT 1645
Lyng, Norf T 132 TG 0617
Lyng, Somer T 92 ST 3228
Lynmouth T 91 SS 7249
Lynn Deeps W 132 TF 5946
Lynn of Lorn W 173 NM 8640
Lynsted T 98 TQ 9460
Lynton T 91 SS 7149
Lyon's Gate T 93 ST 6505
Lyonshall T 113 SO 3355
Lype Hill H 91 SS 9537
Lyrawa Burn W 200 ND 2798
Lyrie Geo 200 ND 2096
Lytchett Minster T 94 SY 9693
Lyte's Cary A 93 ST 5326
Lyth T 199 ND 2863
Lytham T 145 SD 3627
Lytham St Anne's T 145 SD 3228
Lythe T 153 NZ 8413
Lythes T 200 ND 4589
Lyveden New Building A 120 SP 9885

M

Maaey Riabhach 188 NF 8850
Maaruig T 189 NB 2006
Maa Water W 203 HU 3755
Mabe Burnthouse T 86 SW 7634
Mabie T 156 NX 9570
Mablethorpe T 141 TF 5084
Macaterick H 155 NX 4390
Macclesfield P 137 SJ 9173
Macclesfield Canal W 137 SJ 9066
Macclesfield Forest T 138 SJ 9772
Macduff T 185 NJ 7064
Macduff's Castle A 171 NT 3497
Machany Water W 170 NN 8615
Macharioch T 160 NR 7309
Machars, The 154 NX 3854
Machen T 109 ST 2189
Machir Bay W 166 NR 1962
Machrie Bay W 160 NR 8834
Machrie Water W 160 NR 9335
Machrihanish T 160 NR 6320
Machrihanish Airport 160 NR 6622
Machrihanish Bay W 160 NR 6323
Machrihanish Water W 160 NR 6621
Machynlleth P 125 SH 7400
Mackworth T 128 SK 3137
Maclean's Nose 173 NM 5361
Macleod's Maidens H 186 NG 2436
Macleod's Tables H 186 NG 2243
Macmerry T 171 NT 4372
Madadh Gruamach 188 NF 9566
Madderty T 170 NN 9521
Maddiston T 170 NS 9476
Madehurst T 96 SU 9810
Madeley T 127 SJ 7744
Madeley Heath T 127 SJ 7845
Madingley T 121 TL 3960
Madley T 113 SO 4238
Madresfield T 117 SO 8047
Madron T 86 SW 4531
Mad Wharf 136 SD 2608
Maelienydd H 116 SO 1371
Maenaddwyn T 134 SH 4684
Maenclochog T 110 SN 0827
Maendy T 109 ST 0176
Mae Ness 200 HY 4831
Maentwrog T 135 SH 6640
Maer T 127 SJ 7938
Maerdy, Clwyd T 135 SJ 0144
Maerdy, M. Glam T 109 SS 9798
Maesbrook T 126 SJ 3021
Maesbury Marsh T 126 SJ 3125
Maes-glas T 100 ST 3086
Maeshafn T 136 SJ 2061
Maes Howe A 200 HY 3112
Maesllyn T 111 SN 3644
Maesmynis T 112 SO 0147
Maesteg T 109 SS 8691
Maesybont T 111 SN 5616
Maesycrugiau T 111 SN 4741
Maesycwmmer T 109 ST 1594
Maesyrychen Mountain H 126 SJ 1946
Magdalen Laver T 105 TL 5108
Maggieknockater T 184 NJ 3146
Magham Down T 97 TQ 6110
Maghannan 195 NB 0821
Maghull T 136 SD 3702
Magor T 101 ST 4287
Maiden Bradley T 101 ST 8038
Maiden Castle A 93 SY 6688
Maidencombe T 89 SX 9268
Maidenhead P 104 SU 8881
Maidenhead Bay W 161 NS 2108
Maiden Island 173 NM 8432
Maiden Law T 152 NZ 1749
Maiden Newton T 93 SY 5997
Maidenpap, D. & G H 156 NX 8961
Maiden Pap, Highld H 199 ND 0429
Maiden Paps H 157 NT 5002
Maidens T 161 NS 2107
Maiden Stone A 185 NJ 7024
Maiden Way, Cumbr R 151 NY 6537
Maiden Way, Northum R 151 NY 6756
Maidenwell T 87 SX 1470
Maidford T 119 SP 6052
Maids Moreton T 119 SP 7035
Maidstone P 97 TQ 7655
Maidwell T 119 SP 7476
Mail T 203 HU 4228
Main T 182 NH 4239
Mainland, Orkney 200 HY 3711
Mainland, Shetld 203 HU 4051
Mains of Ardestie 171 NO 5034
Mains of Balhall 177 NO 5163
Mains of Ballindarg 176 NO 4051
Mains of Clunas T 183 NH 8846
Mains of Dalvey 183 NJ 1132
Mains of Dellavaird 177 NO 7481
Mains of Drum T 177 NO 8099
Mains of Loch T 184 NJ 3062
Mains of Melgund 177 NO 5456
Mains of Thornton 177 NO 6871
Mainstone T 116 SO 2787
Main Water of Luce W 154 NX 1469
Maisemore T 114 SO 8121
Maisgeir 172 NM 3439
Makerstoun T 164 NT 6732
Malasgair H 195 NB 3017
Malash T 99 TR 0251
Malborough T 89 SX 7039
Malcolm's Head 201 HZ 1970
Malcom's Point 173 NM 4918
Maldon T 106 TL 8506
Malham T 146 SD 9063
Malham Tarn W 146 SD 8966
Mallaig P 180 NM 6796
Mallart River W 197 NC 6834
Mallerstang Common 151 SD 7798
Mallowdale Fell H 145 SD 6259
Malltraeth T 134 SH 4069
Malltraeth Bay W 134 SH 3864
Malltraeth Marsh W 134 SH 4571
Malltraeth Sands 134 SH 4067
Mallwyd T 125 SH 8612
Malmesbury T 102 ST 9387
Malpas, Ches T 127 SJ 4847
Malpas, Corn T 87 SW 8442
Malpas, Gwent T 100 ST 3091
Maltby, Cleve T 153 NZ 4613
Maltby, S. Yks T 139 SK 5392
Maltby le Marsh T 141 TF 4681
Maltman's Hill T 98 TQ 9043
Malton T 148 SE 7871
Malvern Hills H 117 SO 7742
Malvern Link T 117 SO 7847
Malvern Wells T 117 SO 7742
Màm an Staing 180 NG 7813
Mamble T 117 SO 6971
Mam na Gualainn H 174 NN 1162
Mamore Forest 174 NN 2265
Màm Sodhail H 181 NH 1225
Mam Tor A 138 SK 1283
Manaccan T 86 SW 7625
Manacle Point 87 SW 8121
Manacles, The 87 SW 8120
Manafon T 126 SJ 1102
Manar House 185 NJ 7319
Manaton T 89 SX 7581
Manby T 141 TF 3986
Mancetter T 128 SP 3296
Manchester P 137 SJ 8397
Manchester International Airport 137 SJ 8184
Manchester Ship Canal, Ches W 137 SJ 6990
Manchester Ship Canal, G. Man W 137 SJ 6990
Mancot T 136 SJ 3267
Mandally T 174 NH 2900
Manea T 121 TL 4889
Manfield T 152 NZ 2213
Mangaster 204 HU 3270
Mangersta T 194 NB 0031
Mangotsfield T 101 ST 6577
Manish, W. Isles 194 NA 9513
Manish, W. Isles T 189 NG 1089
Manish Point, Highld 190 NG 5648
Manish Point, W. Isles 188 NF 7173
Mankinholes T 146 SD 9623
Manley T 137 SJ 5071
Manmoel T 109 SO 1803
Mannal T 172 NL 9840
Manningford Bohune T 102 SU 1357
Manningford Bruce T 102 SU 1358
Mannings Heath T 96 TQ 2028
Mannington T 94 SU 0605
Manningtree T 123 TM 1031
Mannofield T 185 NJ 9104
Manorbier T 110 SS 0698
Manordeilo T 108 SN 6726
Manorowen T 110 SM 9336
Manor Water W 163 NT 2134
Man o' Scord H 204 HU 3283
Manquhill Hill H 156 NX 6694
Mansell Gamage T 113 SO 3944
Mansell Lacy T 113 SO 4245
Mansfield, Notts P 139 SK 5361
Mansfield, Strath T 156 NS 6214
Mansfield Woodhouse T 139 SK 5463
Mansie's Berg 203 HU 5341
Manston T 93 ST 8115
Manston Airport 99 TR 3366
Manswood T 94 ST 9707
Manthorpe T 130 TF 0715
Manton, Humbs T 142 SE 9302
Manton, Leic T 130 SK 8804
Manton, Wilts T 102 SU 1768
Manton Dyke A 116 SO 2090
Manuden T 121 TL 4926
Maoile Lunndaidh H 191 NH 1345
Maol Breac H 168 NN 2515
Maol Buidhe H 166 NR 2945
Maol Chean-dearg H 190 NG 9249
Maol Chinn-dearg H 181 NH 0408
Maol nan Damh H 167 NR 6288
Maovally H 196 NC 3721
Maplebeck T 140 SK 7160
Maple Cross T 104 TQ 0292
Mapledurham T 104 SU 6776
Mapledurwell T 103 SU 6851
Maplehurst T 96 TQ 1824
Mapleton T 128 SK 1648
Maplin Sands 107 TR 0188
Mapperley T 128 SK 4343
Mapperton T 93 SY 5099
Mappleborough Green T 118 SP 0866
Mappleton T 143 TA 2243
Mappowder T 93 ST 7306
Maragay Mór 188 NF 8952
Marazion T 86 SW 5130
Marbury T 127 SJ 5645
March P 131 TL 4196
Marcham T 115 SU 4596
Marchamley T 127 SJ 5929
Marchbankwood 157 NT 0800
March Ghyll Reservoir W 146 SE 1251
Marchington T 128 SK 1330
Marchington Woodlands T 128 SK 1128
Marchnant W 125 SN 7470
Marchwiel T 126 SJ 3547
Marchwood T 94 SU 3810
Marcross T 109 SS 9269
Mardale Common 151 NY 4811
Marden, H. & W T 113 SO 5147
Marden, Kent T 97 TQ 7444
Marden, Wilts T 102 SU 0857
Mardy T 113 SO 3015
Mare Fen 121 TL 5588
Marefield T 129 SK 7407
Mareham le Fen T 141 TF 2761
Mareham on the Hill T 141 TF 2868
Maresfield T 97 TQ 4624
Mare Tail 131 TF 4437
Marfleet T 143 TA 1429
Margam T 109 SS 7887
Margam Burrows 109 SS 7785
Margaret Marsh T 93 ST 8218
Margaret Roding T 106 TL 5912
Margaretting T 106 TL 6701
Margate P 99 TR 3571
Marg na Craige H 175 NN 6297
Margnaheglish T 160 NS 0331
Marham T 132 TF 7009
Marhamchurch T 90 SS 2203
Marholm T 130 TF 1402
Marian-glas T 134 SH 5084
Mariansleigh T 91 SS 7422
Marishader T 187 NG 4964
Mark T 100 ST 3847
Marka Ber 201 HY 5907
Markbeech T 97 TQ 4742
Markby T 141 TF 4878
Mark Causeway T 100 ST 3647
Mark Cross T 97 TQ 5831
Market Bosworth T 128 SK 4003
Market Deeping T 130 TF 1310
Market Drayton T 127 SJ 6734
Market Harborough P 119 SP 7387
Markethill T 176 NO 2239
Market Lavington T 102 SU 0154
Market Overton T 130 SK 8816
Market Rasen T 141 TF 1089
Market Stainton T 141 TF 2279
Market Weighton T 142 SE 8841
Market Weston T 122 TL 9877
Markfield T 129 SK 4810
Markham T 109 SO 1701
Markinch T 171 NO 2901
Markington T 147 SE 2965
Marksbury T 101 ST 6662
Marks Tey T 106 TL 9023
Markwell 88 SX 3658
Markyate T 104 TL 0616
Marlborough P 102 SU 1969
Marlborough Downs H 102 SU 1575
Marlcliff T 118 SP 0950
Marldon T 89 SX 8663
Marlesford T 123 TM 3258
Marley Green T 127 SJ 5845
Marlingford T 133 TG 1309
Marloes T 110 SM 7908
Marlow T 104 SU 8586
Marlpit Hill T 97 TQ 4447
Marnhull T 93 ST 7818
Marnoch T 184 NJ 5950
Marnock T 162 NS 7168
Marple T 138 SJ 9588
Marr T 139 SE 5105
Marrick T 152 SE 0798
Marrister 203 HU 5464
Marrival H 188 NF 8070
Marros T 111 SN 2009
Marscalloch Hill H 156 NX 6192
Marsco H 187 NG 5025
Marsden T 138 SE 0411
Marsden Bay W 159 NZ 3965
Marsett T 146 SD 9086
Marsh T 92 ST 2510
Marshalls Heath T 105 TL 1615
Marsham T 133 TG 1923
Marshaw T 145 SD 5953
Marsh Baldon T 115 SU 5699
Marshborough T 99 TR 3057
Marshbrook T 116 SO 4489
Marshchapel T 143 TF 3599
Marshfield, Avon T 101 ST 7873
Marshfield, Gwent T 100 ST 2682
Marshgate T 88 SX 1591
Marsh Gibbon T 104 SP 6423
Marsh Green, Devon T 92 SY 0493
Marsh Green, Kent T 97 TQ 4444
Marsh Green, Shrops T 127 SJ 6014
Marshland, Humbs 142 SE 7920
Marshland, Norf 131 TF 5312
Marshland Fen 131 TF 5508
Marshland St James T 131 TF 5209
Marshside, Kent T 99 TR 2265
Marshside, Mers T 136 SD 3619
Marshside Sands 145 SD 3421
Marsh, The T 126 SO 3197
Marshwood T 92 SY 3899
Marshwood Vale 92 SY 4097
Marske T 152 NZ 1000
Marske-by-the-Sea T 153 NZ 6322
Marston, Ches T 137 SJ 6775
Marston, H. & W T 113 SO 3657
Marston, Lincs T 130 SK 8943
Marston, Oxon T 115 SP 5208
Marston, Staffs T 127 SJ 8314
Marston, Staffs T 127 SJ 9227
Marston, Warw T 128 SP 2095
Marston, Wilts T 102 ST 9656
Marston Green T 118 SP 1785
Marston Magna T 93 ST 5922
Marston Meysey T 115 SU 1297
Marston Montgomery T 128 SK 1338
Marston Moor 147 SE 4953
Marston Moretaine T 120 SP 9941
Marston on Dove T 128 SK 2329
Marston Stannett T 113 SO 5755
Marston St Lawrence T 119 SP 5342
Marston Trussell T 119 SP 6985
Marstow T 113 SO 5519
Marsworth T 104 SP 9214
Marten T 102 SU 2860
Marthall T 137 SJ 8075
Martham T 133 TG 4518
Martin, Hants T 94 SU 0619
Martin, Lincs T 141 TF 1259
Martindale T 151 NY 4319
Martindale Common 151 NY 4317
Martin Dales T 141 TF 1761
Martin Drove End T 94 SU 0520
Martinhoe T 91 SS 6648
Martin Hussingtree T 117 SO 8860
Martinscroft T 137 SJ 6589
Martinstown T 93 SY 6488
Martlesham T 123 TM 2446
Martlesham Heath T 123 TM 2445
Martletwy T 110 SN 0310
Martley T 117 SO 7560
Martnaham Loch W 161 NS 3917
Martock T 93 ST 4619
Marton, Ches T 137 SJ 8568
Marton, Cleve T 153 NZ 5216
Marton, Lincs T 140 SK 8481
Marton, N. Yks T 147 SE 4162
Marton, N. Yks T 148 SE 7383
Marton, Shrops T 126 SJ 2802
Marton, Warw T 118 SP 4068
Marton Abbey 147 SE 5869
Marvig T 195 NB 4119
Mar Wick, Orkney W 200 HY 2224
Marwick, Orkney T 200 HY 2324
Marwick Head 200 HY 2225
Marwood T 91 SS 5437
Marybank T 182 NH 4853

Maryburgh Milton Ernest

Maryburgh T 182 NH 5456
Marygold T 165 NT 8160
Maryhill T 185 NJ 8245
Marykirk T 177 NO 6865
Marylebone, G. Lon T 105 TQ 2881
Marylebone, G. Man T 137 SD 5807
Marypark T 184 NJ 1938
Maryport, Cumbr T 150 NY 0336
Maryport, D. & G T 154 NX 1434
Maryport Bay W 154 NX 1434
Marystow T 88 SX 4382
Mary Tavy T 88 SX 5079
Maryton T 177 NO 6856
Marywell, Grampn T 177 NO 5895
Marywell, Tays T 177 NO 6544
Masham T 147 SE 2280
Masham Moor 146 SE 1079
Mashbury T 106 TL 6511
Masongill T 145 SD 6675
Massacamber 188 NF 9382
Massingham Heath 132 TF 7721
Mastrick T 185 NJ 9007
Matching T 105 TL 5211
Matching Green T 105 TL 5311
Matching Tye T 105 TL 5111
Matfen T 159 NZ 0371
Matfield T 97 TQ 6541
Mathern T 101 ST 5291
Mathon T 117 SO 7345
Mathry T 110 SM 8832
Matlaske T 133 TG 1534
Matlock P 139 SK 3060
Matlock Bath T 139 SK 2958
Matson T 114 SO 8515
Matterdale End T 151 NY 3923
Mattersey T 140 SK 6989
Matthew's Port W 161 NS 1903
Mattingley T 103 SU 7357
Mattishall T 132 TG 0511
Mattishall Burgh T 132 TG 0511
Mauchline T 161 NS 4927
Maud T 185 NJ 9248
Maugersbury T 115 SP 2025
Maughold T 144 SC 4991
Maughold Head 144 SC 4891
Maulden T 120 TL 0538
Maulds Meaburn T 151 NY 6216
Maunby T 147 SE 3586
Maund Bryan T 113 SO 5650
Mautby T 133 TG 4812
Mavesyn Ridware T 128 SK 0717
Mavis Enderby T 141 TF 3666
Mavis Grind 204 HU 3468
Mawbray T 150 NY 0846
Mawdesley T 137 SD 4914
Mawgan T 86 SW 7025
Mawla T 86 SW 7045
Mawnan T 87 SW 7827
Mawnan Smith T 86 SW 7728
Maxey T 130 TF 1208
Maxstoke T 118 SP 2386
Maxton T 164 NT 6130
Maxwellheugh T 164 NT 7233
Maxwellston 154 NS 2600
Mayar H 176 NO 2473
Maybole T 161 NS 2909
Mayfield, E. Susx T 97 TQ 5826
Mayfield, Lothn T 164 NT 3564
Mayfield, Staffs T 128 SK 1545
Mayfield, Surrey T 96 TQ 0056
Mayford T 96 SU 9956
May Hill H 114 SO 6921
Mayland T 106 TL 9101
Maypole T 113 SO 4716
Maypole Green T 133 TM 4195
Maywick T 203 HU 3724
McArthur's Head 166 NR 4659
McFarlane's Rock 186 NG 3031
McFarquhar's Cave 183 NH 7965
Meadie Burn W 197 NC 5137
Meadle T 104 SP 8005
Meadowtown T 126 SJ 3101
Meal a' Chaorainn H 191 NH 1360
Mealasta 194 NB 0022
Mealasta Island 194 NA 9721
Meal Bank T 151 SD 5495
Mealdarroch Point 160 NR 8868
Mealista T 194 NA 9924
Mealisval H 194 NB 0226
Meall a' Bhata H 197 NC 6326
Meall a' Bhreacraibh H 183 NH 7935
Meall a' Bhuachaille H 183 NH 9911
Meall a' Chàise H 173 NM 7517
Meall a' Chaorainn H 191 NH 1360
Meallach Mhòr H 175 NN 7790
Meall a' Choire Bhuidhe H 176 NO 0671
Meall a' Chrasgaidh H 191 NH 1873
Meall a' Chràthaich H 182 NH 3622
Meall a' Churain H 169 NN 4632
Meall a' Ghrianain H 191 NH 3677
Meall a' Mhadaidh H 169 NN 5925
Meall a' Mhuic W 175 NN 5750
Meall an Aonaich H 196 NC 3316
Meall an Arbhair 166 NR 3890
Meallan Buidhe, Highld H 181 NH 1337
Meallan Buidhe, Highld H 182 NH 3344
Meall an Damhain H 173 NM 7259
Meall an Doirein H 190 NG 8575
Meall an Fhuarain, Highld H 191 NC 2802
Meall an Fhuarain, Highld H 197 NC 5130
Meall an Fhuarain, Highld H 187 NG 4535
Meall an Inbhire H 173 NM 4656
Meallan Liath H 197 NC 5150
Meallan Liath Beag H 193 NC 8815
Meallan Liath Coire Mhic Dhughaill H 196 NC 3539
Meallan Liath Mòr H 197 NC 6517
Meall an t-Seallaidh H 169 NN 5423
Meall an t-Sithe H 191 NH 1476
Meall an Tuirc H 192 NH 5372
Meall a' Phiobaire H 197 NC 6915
Meall a'Phubuill H 174 NN 0285
Meall Bhenneit H 192 NH 5483
Meall Blair H 174 NN 0795
Meall Buidhe, Highld H 180 NM 8498
Meall Buidhe, Highld H 175 NN 8095
Meall Buidhe, Strath H 174 NN 4244
Meall Buidhe, Strath H 160 NR 7332
Meall Buidhe, Tays H 174 NN 4244
Meall Buidhe, Tays H 175 NN 4949
Meall Cala H 169 NN 5012
Meall Cruaidh H 175 NN 5780
Meall Cruinn H 175 NN 4547
Meall Dearg H 175 NN 8841
Meall Dheirgidh H 192 NH 4794
Meall Dubh, Highld H 191 NH 2089
Meall Dubh, Highld H 182 NH 2407
Meall Dubh, Strath H 168 NS 0789
Meall Fuar-mhonaidh H 182 NH 4522
Meall Gainmheich H 169 NN 5009
Meall Garbh, Strath H 174 NN 1636
Meall Garbh, Tays H 175 NN 6443
Meall Geal 195 NB 5660
Meall Ghaordaidh H 175 NN 5139
Meall Ghaordaigh H 175 NN 5139
Meall Ghiubhais H 190 NG 9763
Meall Gorm, Grampn H 176 NO 1894
Meall Gorm, Highld H 180 NG 7740
Meall Gorm, Highld H 182 NH 2269
Meall Leacachain H 191 NH 2477
Meall Liath Choire H 191 NH 2296
Meall Loch Airigh Alasdair H 180 NG 7436
Meall Luaidhe H 175 NN 5843
Meall Luidh Mòr H 174 NN 4179
Meall Meadhonach H 196 NC 4162
Meall Mhic Lomhair H 182 NH 3167
Meall Mòr, Highld 196 NC 1237
Meall Mòr, Highld H 192 NH 5174
Meall Mòr, Highld H 183 NH 7335
Meall Mòr, Highld H 174 NN 1055
Meall Moraig H 192 NH 6694
Meall na Caorach H 199 ND 1027
Meall na Drochaide H 182 NH 5069
Meall na h-Aisre H 175 NH 5100
Meall na h-Eilrig H 182 NH 5332
Meall na h-Uamha H 190 NG 7765
Meall na Leitreach H 175 NN 6370
Meall nam Bràdhan H 191 NH 2690
Meall na Mèine H 190 NG 9081
Meall nam Fuaran H 175 NN 8236
Meall nan Caorach, Highld H 182 NH 4735
Meall nan Caorach, Tays H 170 NN 9233
Meall nan Con, Highld H 197 NC 5829
Meall nan Con, Highld H 173 NM 5068
Meall nan Creag Leac H 173 NM 8674
Meall nan Damh H 160 NR 9146
Meall nan Each H 173 NM 6364
Meall nan Ruadhag H 174 NN 2957
Meall nan Tarmachan H 175 NN 5839
Meall nan Tighearn, Central H 168 NN 2323
Meall nan Tighearn, Strath H 168 NN 2323
Meall na Speireig H 182 NH 4966
Meall na Suiramach H 187 NG 4469
Meall Odhar, Central H 169 NN 6414
Meall Odhar, Strath H 168 NM 9416
Meall Odhar, Tays H 169 NN 6414
Meall Odhar, Tays H 175 NN 6639
Meall Reamhar, Strath H 167 NR 8369
Meall Reamhar, Tays H 169 NN 6621
Meall Reamhar, Tays H 175 NN 8670
Meall Reamhar, Tays H 170 NN 8732
Meall Reamhar, Tays H 176 NO 0356
Meall Tairneachan H 175 NN 8054
Meall Tarsuinn H 170 NN 8729
Meall Taurnie, Central H 175 NN 4838
Meall Taurnie, Tays H 175 NN 4838
Meall Uaine H 176 NO 1167
Mealna Letter or Duchray Hill H 176 NO 1667
Meal nan Damh H 160 NR 9146
Mealsgate T 150 NY 2042
Mearbeck T 146 SD 8260
Mearbrook T 146 SD 8160
Meare T 101 ST 4541
Meare Green T 92 ST 3326
Mears Ashby T 120 SP 8366
Measham T 128 SK 3312
Meathop T 145 SD 4380
Meaul H 155 NX 5091
Meaux T 143 TA 0939
Meavag T 189 NG 1596
Meavaig T 189 NB 0905
Meavaig River W 189 NB 1007
Meavy T 89 SX 5467
Medbourne T 129 SP 8093
Medburn T 159 NZ 1370
Meddon T 90 SS 2717
Meden Vale T 139 SK 5769
Medmenham T 104 SU 8084
Medstead T 95 SU 6537
Meerbrook T 138 SJ 9960
Meer End T 118 SP 2474
Meesden T 121 TL 4232
Meeth T 91 SS 5408
Meggat Water W 157 NY 2996
Meggernie Castle 175 NN 5546
Meggethead T 163 NT 1621
Megget Reservoir W 163 NT 1922
Meg's Craig 177 NO 6844
Meidrim T 111 SN 2921
Meifod T 126 SJ 1513
Meigle 176 NO 2844
Meigle Hill H 164 NT 4636
Meikle Black Law H 165 NT 8268
Meikle Carewe Hill H 177 NO 8292
Meikle Conval H 184 NJ 2937
Meikle Craigs 161 NS 3228
Meikle Earnock T 162 NS 7153
Meikle Float 154 NX 0648
Meikle Hard Hill H 156 NX 9362
Meikle Hill H 183 NJ 1450
Meikleour T 176 NO 1539
Meikle Says Law H 164 NT 5861
Meikle Strath 177 NO 6471
Meikle Tarty T 185 NJ 9928
Meikle Wartle T 185 NJ 7230
Meinciau T 111 SN 4610
Meir T 127 SJ 9342
Meir Heath T 127 SJ 9340
Meith Bheinn H 180 NM 8287
Melbecks Moor 152 NY 9400
Melbost T 195 NB 4632
Melbost Borve T 195 NB 4157
Melbost Sands 195 NB 4535
Melbourn T 121 TL 3844
Melbourne, Derby T 128 SK 3825
Melbourne, Humbs T 142 SE 7544
Melbury 90 SS 3719
Melbury Abbas T 93 ST 8820
Melbury Bubb T 93 ST 5906
Melbury Osmond T 93 ST 5707
Melbury Sampford 93 ST 5706
Melby T 202 HU 1857
Melchbourne T 120 TL 0265
Melchet Court 94 SU 2722
Melcombe Bingham T 93 ST 7602
Meldon, Devon T 89 SX 5592
Meldon, Northum T 159 NZ 1183
Meldon Reservoir W 89 SX 5691
Meldreth T 121 TL 3746
Meldrum House 185 NJ 8129
Melfort T 173 NM 8314
Melgarve T 175 NN 4695
Meliden T 135 SJ 0681
Melincourt T 109 SN 8201
Melin-y-coed T 135 SH 8160
Melin-y-ddôl T 125 SJ 0907
Melin-y-grug T 125 SJ 0507
Melin-y-Wig T 135 SJ 0448
Melkinthorpe T 151 NY 5525
Melkridge T 158 NY 7363
Melksham T 101 ST 9063
Melldalloch T 168 NR 9374
Mellerstain House 164 NT 6439
Mell Head 199 ND 3476
Melling, Lancs T 145 SD 6071
Melling, Mers T 136 SD 3900
Mellis T 123 TM 1074
Mellon Charles T 190 NG 8491
Mellon Udrigle T 190 NG 8895
Mellor, G. Man T 138 SJ 9888
Mellor, Lancs T 145 SD 6530
Mellor Brook T 145 SD 6430
Mells, Somer T 101 ST 7249
Mells, Suff T 123 TM 4076
Melmerby, Cumbr T 151 NY 6137
Melmerby, N. Yks T 146 SE 0785
Melmerby, N. Yks T 147 SE 3376
Melmerby Fell 151 NY 6538
Melowther Hill H 162 NS 5648
Melplash T 93 SY 4898
Melrose T 164 NT 5434
Melsetter 200 ND 2689
Melsonby T 152 NZ 1908
Meltham T 138 SE 0910
Melton T 123 TM 2850
Meltonby T 148 SE 7952
Melton Constable T 132 TG 0433
Melton Mowbray P 129 SK 7519
Melton Ross T 142 TA 0710
Meluncart H 177 NO 6382
Melvaig T 190 NG 7486
Melverley T 126 SJ 3316
Melvich T 198 NC 8864
Melvich Bay W 198 NC 8865
Membury T 92 ST 2703
Memsie T 185 NJ 9762
Memus 176 NO 4258
Menabilly 87 SX 0951
Menai Bridge T 134 SH 5572
Menai Strait W 134 SH 5270
Mendham T 123 TM 2782
Mendick Hill H 163 NT 1250
Mendip Forest 101 ST 5054
Mendip Hills H 101 ST 5255
Mendlesham T 123 TM 1065
Mendlesham Green T 123 TM 0963
Menheniot T 88 SX 2862
Mennock T 156 NS 8008
Men of Mey 199 ND 3175
Menston T 146 SE 1744
Menstrie T 169 NS 8496
Menteith Hills H 169 NN 5502
Mentmore T 104 SP 9019
Meòir Langwell W 192 NH 4298
Meole Brace T 127 SJ 4810
Meon Hill H 118 SP 1745
Meonstoke T 95 SU 6119
Meon Valley 95 SU 6016
Meopham T 98 TQ 6466
Meopham Station T 98 TQ 6467
Mepal T 121 TL 4480
Meppershall T 120 TL 1436
Merbach T 113 SO 3045
Mere, Ches T 137 SJ 7281
Mere, Wilts T 93 ST 8132
Mere Brow T 136 SD 4118
Mereclough T 146 SD 8730
Mere Green T 128 SP 1299
Mere, The W 126 SJ 4035
Mereworth T 97 TQ 6553
Mereworth Castle 97 TQ 6653
Mergie T 177 NO 7988
Meriden T 118 SP 2482
Merkadale T 186 NG 3831
Merkland 154 NX 2491
Merkland Lodge 196 NC 4029
Merkland Point 160 NS 0238
Merlin's Bridge T 110 SM 9414
Merrick 154 NX 4185
Merrington T 127 SJ 4720
Merriott T 93 ST 4412
Merrivale T 89 SX 5475
Merrymeet T 88 SX 2766
Merse 165 NT 8146
Mersea Flats 107 TM 0513
Mersea Island 107 TM 0314
Mersehead Sands 150 NX 9254
Mersham T 99 TR 0539
Merstham T 97 TQ 2953
Merston T 95 SU 8903
Merstone T 95 SZ 5284
Merther T 87 SW 8644
Merthyr T 111 SN 3521
Merthyr Cynog T 112 SN 9837
Merthyr Dyfan T 109 ST 1170
Merthyr Mawr T 109 SS 8877
Merthyr Tydfil P 109 SO 0506
Merthyr Vale T 109 ST 0799
Merton, Devon T 91 SS 5212
Merton, G. Lon T 105 TQ 2569
Merton, Norf T 132 TL 9098
Merton, Oxon T 115 SP 5717
Mervinslaw T 158 NT 6713
Meshaw T 91 SS 7519
Messing T 106 TL 8918
Messingham T 142 SE 8904
Metfield T 123 TM 2980
Metheringham T 140 TF 0761
Methil T 171 NT 3699
Methley T 147 SE 3926
Methlick T 185 NJ 8537
Methven T 170 NO 0226
Methwold T 132 TL 7394
Methwold Fens 132 TL 6593
Methwold Hythe T 132 TL 7194
Mettingham T 123 TM 3689
Mevagissey T 87 SX 0144
Mevagissey Bay W 87 SX 0246
Mew Stone 89 SX 9149
Mexborough T 139 SE 4700
Mey T 199 ND 2872
Meysey Hampton T 115 SP 1200
Miavaig T 195 NB 0834
Michael T 144 SC 3290
Michaelchurch T 113 SO 5225
Michaelchurch Escley T 113 SO 3134
Michaelchurch-on-Arrow T 113 SO 2450
Michaelstone-y-Fedw T 100 ST 2484
Michaelston-le-Pit T 109 ST 1573
Michaelstow T 87 SX 0878
Micheldever T 103 SU 5139
Micheldever Station 103 SU 5142
Micheldever Wood F 95 SU 5337
Michelmersh T 94 SU 3426
Mickfield T 123 TM 1361
Mickleby T 153 NZ 8013
Mickle Fell 151 NY 8124
Micklefield T 147 SE 4433
Mickleham T 96 TQ 1753
Mickleover T 128 SK 3135
Mickleton, Durham T 152 NY 9623
Mickleton, Glos T 118 SP 1643
Mickle Trafford T 136 SJ 4469
Mickley T 147 SE 2577
Mickley Square T 159 NZ 0762
Mid Ardlaw T 185 NJ 9463
Midbarrow (lightship) 107 TR 1992
Midbea T 200 HY 4444
Mid Beltie T 177 NJ 6200
Midberg 205 HU 5988
Middle Assendon T 104 SU 7485
Middle Aston T 115 SP 4726
Middle Barton T 115 SP 4325
Middlebie T 157 NY 2176
Middle Claydon T 119 SP 7125
Middle Drums 177 NO 5957
Middle Fell H 151 NY 7444
Middle Fen 121 TL 5779
Middlefield Law H 162 NS 6830
Middle Grounds 100 ST 3576
Middleham T 146 SE 1287
Middlehope T 116 SO 4988
Middlehope Moor 152 NY 8841
Middle Level Main Drain W 131 TF 5405
Middle Littleton T 118 SP 0747
Middle Maes-coed T 113 SO 3333
Middlemarsh T 93 ST 6707
Middle Mill T 110 SM 8026
Middle Moor, Cambs 121 TL 2789
Middle Moor, Northum 165 NU 1423
Middle Mouse 134 SH 3895
Middle Muir 163 NS 8525
Middlemuir Farm 185 NJ 9420
Middle Rasen T 140 TF 0889
Middle Rigg 170 NO 0608
Middlesbrough P 153 NZ 4920
Middle Shield Park 158 NY 6070
Middlesmoor T 146 SE 0974
Middleston Moor T 152 NZ 2533
Middlestown T 139 SE 2617
Middleton, Cumbr T 145 SD 6286
Middleton, Derby T 138 SK 1963
Middleton, Derby T 128 SK 2756
Middleton, Essex T 122 TL 8739
Middleton, G. Man T 137 SD 8606
Middleton, Grampn T 185 NJ 8419
Middleton, Hants T 102 SU 4244
Middleton, H. & W T 116 SO 5469
Middleton, Lancs T 145 SD 4258
Middleton, Lothn T 164 NT 3658
Middleton, Norf T 132 TF 6615
Middleton, Northnts T 120 SP 8490
Middleton, Northum T 165 NU 0023
Middleton, Northum T 165 NU 1035
Middleton, Northum T 159 NZ 0685
Middleton, N. Yks T 146 SE 1249
Middleton, N. Yks T 148 SE 7885
Middleton, Shrops T 126 SJ 3129
Middleton, Shrops T 126 SO 2999
Middleton, Shrops T 116 SO 5477
Middleton, Strath T 172 NL 9443
Middleton, Suff T 123 TM 4367
Middleton, Tays 170 NO 1206
Middleton, Tays 176 NO 1447
Middleton, Warw T 128 SP 1798
Middleton, W. Yks T 147 SE 3028
Middleton Cheney T 119 SP 4942
Middleton Common 152 NY 9531
Middleton Green T 128 SJ 9935
Middle Tongue 146 SD 9181
Middleton Hall T 165 NT 9825
Middleton-in-Teesdale T 152 NY 9425
Middleton-on-Sea T 96 SZ 9799
Middleton on the Hill T 116 SO 5464
Middleton-on-the-Wolds T 149 SE 9449
Middleton Priors T 117 SO 6290
Middleton Scriven T 117 SO 6887
Middleton St George T 153 NZ 3413
Middleton Stoney T 115 SP 5323
Middleton Tyas T 152 NZ 2205
Middletown T 126 SJ 3012
Middle Tysoe T 118 SP 3444
Middle Wallop T 94 SU 2937
Middlewich T 137 SJ 7066
Middle Winterslow T 94 SU 2432
Middle Witchyburn T 184 NJ 6356
Middle Woodford T 94 SU 1136
Middlewood Green T 123 TM 0961
Middlewood Station 137 SJ 9484
Middlezoy T 92 ST 3732
Middridge T 152 NZ 2526
Midfield T 197 NC 5865
Midge Hall T 145 SD 5123
Midgeholme T 158 NY 6358
Midgham T 103 SU 5567
Midgley T 146 SE 0326
Mid Hill, D. & G H 156 NS 6907
Mid Hill, Orkney H 200 HY 3324
Mid Hill, Strath H 154 NX 2889
Midhope Moors 138 SK 1998
Midhopestones T 139 SK 2399
Midhurst P 95 SU 8821
Mid Kame H 203 HU 4158
Midland Ness 200 HY 3203
Midlem T 164 NT 5227
Midmar Forest F 185 NJ 7004
Mid Moile H 154 NX 0971
Mid Sannox T 160 NS 0145
Midsomer Norton T 101 ST 6654
Mid Thundergay 160 NR 8846
Midtown T 190 NG 8285
Midtown of Buchromb T 184 NJ 3143
Mid Urchany 183 NH 8849
Midville T 141 TF 3857
Mid Walls T 202 HU 2050
Mid Yell T 205 HU 5090
Mid Yell Voe W 205 HU 5191
Migneint 135 SH 7842
Migvie T 184 NJ 4306
Milborne Port T 93 ST 6718
Milborne St Andrew T 93 SY 8097
Milborne Wick T 93 ST 6620
Milbourne T 159 NZ 1175
Milburn T 151 NY 6529
Milburn Forest F 151 NY 7232
Milburn Geo 203 HU 4012
Milbury Heath T 101 ST 6690
Milcombe T 115 SP 4134
Milden T 122 TL 9546
Mildenhall, Suff T 122 TL 7174
Mildenhall, Wilts T 102 SU 2169
Mildenhall Fen 122 TL 6678
Milebrooke T 116 SO 3172
Milebush T 97 TQ 7545
Mile Elm T 102 ST 9969
Mile End, Essex T 122 TL 9927
Mile End, Glos T 113 SO 5911
Mileham T 132 TF 9119
Mile Hill H 176 NO 3157
Milesmark T 170 NT 0788
Milfield T 165 NT 9333
Milford, Derby T 128 SK 3545
Milford, Devon T 90 SS 2322
Milford, Staffs T 128 SJ 9721
Milford, Surrey T 96 SU 9442
Milford Haven, Dyfed W 110 SM 8504
Milford Haven, Dyfed P 110 SM 9006
Milford on Sea T 94 SZ 2892
Milk Hill H 102 SU 1064
Milkieston Rings 163 NT 2445
Milkwall T 113 SO 5809
Milland T 95 SU 8327
Mill Bank T 146 SE 0321
Mill Bay, Orkney W 200 HY 5736
Mill Bay, Orkney W 201 HY 6626
Mill Bay, Orkney W 200 ND 3095
Millbounds T 200 HY 5635
Millbreck T 185 NK 0045
Millbridge T 103 SU 8442
Millbrook, Beds T 120 TL 0138
Millbrook, Corn T 88 SX 4252
Millbrook, Hants T 94 SU 3813
Millbrook Station 120 TL 0040
Mill Buie, Grampn H 183 NJ 0950
Millbuie, Highld 182 NH 6459
Millburn T 161 NS 4429
Millburn Geo, Shetld 203 HU 4012
Millburn Geo, Shetld 203 HU 5239
Mill Corner T 98 TQ 8223
Millden Lodge 177 NO 5479
Milldens 177 NO 5450
Milldoe H 200 HY 3520
Mill End, Bucks T 104 SU 7885
Mill End, Herts T 121 TL 3032
Millerhill T 171 NT 3269
Miller's Bay W 160 NR 7067
Miller's Dale T 138 SK 1473
Milleur Point 154 NX 0273
Millfire H 155 NX 5084
Mill Green, Essex T 106 TL 6401
Mill Green, Shrops T 127 SJ 6828
Millheugh T 162 NS 7551
Mill Hill T 105 TQ 2292
Millholme T 151 SD 5690
Millhouse, Cumbr T 150 NY 3637
Millhouse, Strath T 168 NR 9570
Millikenpark T 161 NS 4162
Millington T 148 SE 8351
Milljoan Hill H 154 NX 1177
Mill Lane T 103 SU 7850
Millmeece T 127 SJ 8333
Mill of Kingoodie 185 NJ 8325
Millom T 144 SD 1780
Millport T 161 NS 1655
Mill Rig H 162 NS 6334
Mill Side T 145 SD 4484
Millstone Edge H 157 NT 4300
Millstone Hill, Grampn H 184 NJ 4257
Millstone Hill, Grampn H 184 NJ 6720
Millstone Point 160 NR 9950
Mill Street T 132 TG 0118
Millthrop T 151 SD 6691
Milltimber T 177 NJ 8501
Milton of Corsindale T 185 NJ 6809
Milton of Murtle T 177 NJ 8702
Milltown, Derby T 139 SK 3561
Milltown, Devon T 91 SS 5538
Milltown, D. & G T 157 NY 3375
Milltown, Grampn T 184 NJ 4716
Milltown, Grampn T 184 NJ 5448
Milltown of Aberdalgie T 170 NO 0720
Milltown of Auchindoun T 184 NJ 3540
Milltown of Campfield T 177 NJ 6400
Milltown of Craigston T 185 NJ 7655
Milltown of Edinvillie T 184 NJ 2640
Milltown of Towie T 184 NJ 4612
Milnathort T 170 NO 1204
Milne Height H 157 NY 1597
Milngavie T 169 NS 5574
Milnrow T 137 SD 9212
Milnthorpe T 145 SD 4981
Milovaig T 186 NG 1450
Milray Hill H 156 NS 5905
Milson T 117 SO 6473
Milstead T 98 TQ 9058
Milston T 102 SU 1645
Milton, Cambs T 121 TL 4762
Milton, Central T 169 NN 5001
Milton, Cumbr T 158 NY 5560
Milton, D. & G T 154 NX 2154
Milton, D. & G T 156 NX 8470
Milton, Dyfed T 110 SN 0403
Milton, Grampn 184 NJ 1719
Milton, Grampn T 184 NJ 5163
Milton, Highld T 199 ND 3451
Milton, Highld T 182 NH 3055
Milton, Highld T 182 NH 4930
Milton, Highld T 182 NH 5749
Milton, Highld T 193 NH 7674
Milton, Highld T 183 NH 9553
Milton, Oxon T 115 SP 4535
Milton, Oxon T 103 SU 4891
Milton, Staffs T 127 SJ 9050
Milton, Strath T 169 NS 4274
Milton, Tays 175 NN 9138
Milton, Tays 176 NO 3843
Milton Abbas T 93 ST 8001
Milton Abbot T 88 SX 4079
Milton Bridge T 163 NT 2462
Milton Bryan T 120 SP 9730
Milton Burn W 170 NN 9532
Milton Clevedon T 93 ST 6637
Milton Coldwells T 185 NJ 9538
Milton Combe T 88 SX 4865
Milton Damerel T 90 SS 3810
Miltonduff T 184 NJ 1860
Milton Ernest T 120 TL 0156

Mynydd Sylen Norbury

Mynydd Sylen H 111 SN 5108
Mynydd Tan-y-coed H 125 SH 6604
Mynydd Tarw H 126 SJ 1132
Mynydd Trawsnant H 112 SN 8248
Mynydd Troed H 109 SO 1728
Mynydd Waun Fawr H 125 SJ 0105
Mynydd y Betws H 108 SN 6710
Mynydd y Cemais H 125 SH 8708
Mynydd y Drum, Powys H 109 SN 8110
Mynydd y Drum, W. Glam H 109 SN 8110
Mynydd y Gadfa H 125 SH 9914
Mynydd y Gaer H 109 SS 9585
Mynydd y Garreg H 111 SN 4409
Mynydd-y-glog H 109 SN 9808
Mynydd y Gwair H 111 SN 6507
Mynytho T 134 SH 3031
Myrebird T 177 NO 7498
Mytchett T 103 SU 8855
Mytholm T 146 SD 9827
Mytholmroyd T 146 SE 0126
Myton-on-Swale T 147 SE 4366

N

Naast T 190 NG 8283
Naburn T 147 SE 6045
Nackington T 99 TR 1554
Nacton T 123 TM 2240
Na Cùiltean 166 NR 5464
Naden Reservoir W 137 SD 8516
Na Dromannan H 191 NC 2101
Nafferton T 149 TA 0559
Na Gamhnaichean 187 NG 4312
Nailsea T 101 ST 4770
Nailstone T 128 SK 4107
Nailsworth T 114 ST 8499
Nairn T 183 NH 8856
Nancegollan T 86 SW 6332
Nancledra T 86 SW 4936
Nanhoron T 134 SH 2831
Nannau 125 SH 7420
Nannerch T 136 SJ 1669
Nanpantan T 129 SK 5017
Nanpean T 87 SW 9656
Nanstallon T 87 SX 0366
Nant Brân W 109 SN 9632
Nantclwyd Hall 126 SJ 1151
Nant Cynnen W 111 SN 3522
Nant-ddû T 109 SO 0015
Nanternis T 111 SN 3756
Nant Ffrancon 135 SH 6462
Nantgaredig T 111 SN 4921
Nantgarw T 109 ST 1285
Nant Glâs T 125 SN 9965
Nantglyn T 135 SJ 0062
Nantgwynant 134 SH 6149
Nantlle T 134 SH 5153
Nantmawr T 126 SJ 2524
Nantmel T 125 SO 0366
Nantmor T 134 SH 6046
Nant Peris T 134 SH 6058
Nantwich P 127 SJ 6552
Nant-y-derry T 113 SO 3306
Nantyffyllon T 109 SS 8592
Nantyglo T 109 SO 1910
Nant-y-moch Reservoir W 125 SN 7587
Nant-y-moel T 109 SS 9393
Nant yr Eira 125 SH 9606
Naphill T 104 SU 8596
Nappa T 146 SD 8553
Napton on the Hill T 119 SP 4661
Narachan Burn W 160 NR 7648
Narberth T 110 SN 1114
Narborough, Leic T 129 SP 5497
Narborough, Norf T 132 TF 7412
Nare Head 87 SW 9136
Nare Point 87 SW 7925
Narrows of Raasay W 187 NG 5435
Nasareth T 134 SH 4750
Naseby T 119 SP 6877
Naseby Field 119 SP 6879
Naseby Reservoir W 119 SP 6677
Nash, Bucks T 119 SP 7834
Nash, Gwent T 100 ST 3483
Nash, H. & W T 116 SO 3062
Nash, Shrops T 117 SO 6071
Nash Lee T 104 SP 8408
Nash Point 109 SS 9168
Nassington T 130 TL 0696
Nass, The 107 TL 9911
Nasty T 105 TL 3524
Nateby, Cumbr T 151 NY 7706
Nateby, Lancs T 145 SD 4644
National Exhibition Centre 118 SP 1983
Natland T 151 SD 5289
Naughton T 122 TM 0249
Naunton, Glos T 114 SP 1123
Naunton, H. & W T 117 SO 8739
Naunton Beauchamp T 118 SO 9652
Navax Point 86 SW 5944
Nave Island 166 NR 2976
Navenby T 140 SK 9857
Naver Forest F 197 NC 6840
Navestock Heath T 105 TQ 5397
Navestock Side T 105 TQ 5697
Naworth Castle A 158 NY 5662
Nawton T 147 SE 6584
Nayland T 122 TL 9734
Nazeing T 105 TL 4106
Naze, The 107 TM 2624
Neacroft T 94 SZ 1896
Neal's Green T 118 SP 3384
Neap 203 HU 5058
Neap of Skea 205 HU 3783
Neasham T 152 NZ 3310
Neath P 109 SS 7497
Neatishead T 133 TG 3421
Neaty Burn W 182 NH 3541
Neave or Coomb Island 197 NC 6664
Neban Point 200 HY 2113
Neblonga 200 HY 2111
Nebo, Dyfed T 124 SN 5465
Nebo, Gwyn T 134 SH 4750
Nebo, Gwyn T 135 SH 8356
Necton T 132 TF 8709
Nedd T 196 NC 1332
Nedd Fechan W 109 SN 9113
Nedging Tye T 122 TM 0149
Needham T 123 TM 2281
Needham Market T 123 TM 0954
Needingworth T 121 TL 3472
Needles, The 94 SZ 2984
Needs Law H 158 NT 6002
Needs Ore Point 94 SZ 4397
Needwood Forest F 128 SK 1624
Neegirth 205 HU 5171
Neen Savage T 117 SO 6777
Neen Sollars T 117 SO 6672
Neenton T 117 SO 6388
Nefyn T 134 SH 3040
Neidpath Castle A 163 NT 2340
Neil's Helly 200 HY 5054
Neilston T 161 NS 4756
Neilston Pad H 161 NS 4755
Neist 186 NG 1247
Nelson, Lancs T 146 SD 8637
Nelson, M. Glam T 109 ST 1195
Nelson Village T 159 NZ 2577
Nemphlar T 163 NS 8544
Nempnett Thrubwell T 101 ST 5360
Nenthead T 151 NY 7843
Nenthorn T 164 NT 6837
Nercwys T 136 SJ 2361
Nereabolls T 166 NR 2255
Nerston T 162 NS 6456
Nesbit T 165 NT 9833
Ness, Ches T 136 SJ 3076
Ness, N. Yks T 148 SE 6978
Ness, W. Isles 195 NB 5261
Nesscliffe T 126 SJ 3819
Ness Glen 161 NS 4702
Ness Head 199 ND 3866
Ness of Boray 200 HY 4421
Ness of Brough 201 HY 6542
Ness of Burravoe 205 HU 3890
Ness of Gossabrough 205 HU 5383
Ness of Hillswick 204 HU 2775
Ness of Houlland, Shetld 205 HP 5205
Ness of Houlland, Shetld 205 HU 3788
Ness of Ireland 203 HU 3723
Ness of Olnesfirth 204 HU 3076
Ness of Ork 200 HY 5422
Ness of Ramnageo 205 HU 6299
Ness of Sound, Shetld 205 HU 4482
Ness of Sound, Shetld 203 HU 4638
Ness of Trebister 203 HU 4538
Ness Point or North Cheek 149 NZ 9606
Ness, The, Orkney 200 HY 5408
Ness, The, Orkney 201 HY 6630
Ness, The, Shetld 203 HU 3626
Neston, Ches T 136 SJ 2977
Neston, Wilts T 101 ST 8668
Nether Alderley T 137 SJ 8476
Netheravon T 102 SU 1449
Nether Blainslie T 164 NT 5443
Netherbrae T 185 NJ 7959
Nether Broughton T 129 SK 6925
Netherburn T 163 NS 8047
Nether Burrow T 145 SD 6175
Netherbury T 93 SY 4799
Netherby 157 NY 3971
Nether Cerne T 93 SY 6698
Nether Compton T 93 ST 5917
Nether Crimond 185 NJ 8222
Nether Dallachy T 184 NJ 3664
Netherend T 113 SO 5900
Nether Exe T 89 SS 9300
Netherfield T 97 TQ 7118
Netherhampton T 94 SU 1129
Nether Handwick 176 NO 3741
Nether Haugh T 139 SK 4196
Nether Heyford T 119 SP 6558
Nether Howecleuch T 157 NT 0312
Nether Kellet T 145 SD 5068
Nether Kinmundy T 185 NK 0544
Nether Kirkton T 161 NS 4857
Netherlaw T 155 NX 7445
Netherley T 177 NO 8593
Nethermill T 157 NY 0487
Nethermuir 185 NJ 9144
Nether Padley T 139 SK 2578
Netherplace T 161 NS 5255
Nether Poppleton T 147 SE 5655
Nether Row T 150 NY 3237
Netherseal T 128 SK 2813
Nether Silton T 153 SE 4592
Nether Stowey T 100 ST 1939
Netherthird T 156 NS 5718
Netherthong T 138 SE 1309
Netherton, Central T 169 NS 5579
Netherton, Devon T 89 SX 8971
Netherton, H. & W T 118 SO 9941
Netherton, Mers T 136 SD 3500
Netherton, Northum T 159 NT 9807
Netherton, Tays 176 NO 1452
Netherton, Tays T 177 NO 5457
Netherton, W. Yks T 139 SE 2716
Nethertown, Cumbr T 150 NX 9907
Nethertown, Highld T 199 ND 3578
Nether Urquhart 170 NO 1808
Nether Wallop T 94 SU 3036
Nether Wasdale T 150 NY 1204
Nether Whitacre T 128 SP 2393
Nether Winchendon or Lower Winchendon T 104 SP 7312
Netherwitton T 159 NZ 0990
Netherwood 162 NS 6628
Nether Worton T 115 SP 4230
Nethy Bridge T 183 NJ 0020
Netley T 95 SU 4508
Netley Marsh T 94 SU 3313
Nettlebed T 104 SU 7086
Nettlebridge T 101 ST 6448
Nettlecombe T 93 SY 5195
Nettleden T 104 TL 0210
Nettleham T 140 TF 0075
Nettle Hill H 151 NY 7107
Nettlestead T 97 TQ 6852
Nettlestead Green T 97 TQ 6850
Nettlestone T 95 SZ 6290
Nettlestone Point 95 SZ 6291
Nettleton, Lincs T 143 TA 1000
Nettleton, Wilts T 101 ST 8278
Neuadd Reservoirs W 109 SO 0318
Neuk, The T 177 NO 7397
Nevendon T 106 TQ 7590
Nevern T 110 SN 0840
Nevis Forest F 174 NN 1270
Nev of Stuis 205 HU 4697
Nev, The, Orkney 200 HY 4452
Nev, The, Shetld 205 HP 6611
Nev, The, Shetld 202 HU 2544
Nev, The, Shetld 203 HU 3414
New Abbey T 156 NX 9666
New Aberdour T 185 NJ 8863
New Addington T 105 TQ 3863
New Alresford T 95 SU 5832
New Alyth T 176 NO 2447
Newark, Cambs T 130 TF 2100
Newark, Orkney T 201 HY 7242
Newark Bay, Orkney W 201 HY 5704
Newark Bay, Orkney W 200 ND 4689
Newark Castle, Border A 164 NT 4229
Newark Castle, Strath A 161 NS 3217
Newark Castle, Strath A 168 NS 3374
Newark-on-Trent P 129 SK 7953
Newarthill T 162 NS 7859
New Ash Green T 98 TQ 6065
New Bedford River or Hundred Foot Drain W 121 TL 4987
New Bewick T 159 NU 0620
Newbiggin, Cumbr T 151 NY 4729
Newbiggin, Cumbr T 151 NY 5549
Newbiggin, Cumbr T 151 NY 6228
Newbiggin, Cumbr T 144 SD 2669
Newbiggin, Durham T 152 NY 9127
Newbiggin, N. Yks T 152 SD 9591
Newbiggin, N. Yks T 146 SD 9985
Newbiggin-by-the-Sea T 159 NZ 3087
Newbiggin Common 152 NY 9131
Newbigging, Strath T 163 NT 0145
Newbigging, Tays T 176 NO 2842
Newbigging, Tays T 177 NO 4237
Newbigging, Tays T 177 NO 4936
Newbiggin-on-Lune T 151 NY 7005
Newbold, Derby T 139 SK 3773
Newbold, Leic T 128 SK 4019
Newbold on Avon T 119 SP 4976
Newbold-on-Stour T 118 SP 2446
Newbold Pacey T 118 SP 2957
Newbold Verdon T 129 SK 4403
New Bolingbroke T 141 TF 3057
Newborough, Cambs T 130 TF 2006
Newborough, Gwyn T 134 SH 4265
Newborough, Staffs T 128 SK 1325
Newborough Warren 134 SH 4263
Newbottle T 119 SP 5237
Newbourne T 123 TM 2742
New Brancepeth T 152 NZ 2241
Newbridge, Clwyd T 126 SJ 2841
Newbridge, Corn T 86 SW 4231
Newbridge, Gwent T 109 ST 2197
Newbridge, Hants T 94 SU 2915
Newbridge, I. of W T 94 SZ 4187
Newbridge, Lothn T 170 NT 1272
Newbridge-on-Usk T 113 ST 3894
Newbridge-on-Wye T 112 SO 0158
New Brighton T 136 SJ 3093
New Brinsley T 129 SK 4650
Newbrough T 158 NY 8767
New Buckenham T 123 TM 0890
Newbuildings T 91 SS 7903
Newburgh, Fife T 171 NO 2318
Newburgh, Grampn T 185 NJ 9925
Newburgh, Lancs T 137 SD 4810
Newburgh Bar 185 NK 0123
Newburgh Priory A 147 SE 5476
Newburn T 159 NZ 1965
Newbury P 103 SU 4767
Newby, Cumbr T 151 NY 5921
Newby, N. Yks T 153 NZ 5012
Newby, N. Yks T 145 SD 7270
Newby Bridge T 145 SD 3786
Newby East T 157 NY 4758
Newby Hall A 147 SE 3467
Newby Moss 145 SD 7472
New Byth T 185 NJ 8254
Newby West T 150 NY 3653
Newby Wiske T 147 SE 3687
Newcastle, Gwent T 113 SO 4417
Newcastle, Shrops T 116 SO 2482
Newcastle Airport 159 NZ 1971
Newcastle Emlyn T 111 SN 3040
Newcastleton T 157 NY 4887
Newcastleton Forest F 158 NY 5287
Newcastle-under-Lyme P 127 SJ 8546
Newcastle upon Tyne P 159 NZ 2464
Newchapel, Dyfed T 111 SN 2339
Newchapel, Staffs T 127 SJ 8654
Newchapel, Surrey T 97 TQ 3642
New Cheriton T 95 SU 5827
Newchurch, Dyfed T 111 SN 3824
Newchurch, Gwent T 113 ST 4597
Newchurch, I. of W T 95 SZ 5685
Newchurch, Kent T 99 TR 0531
Newchurch, Powys T 113 SO 2150
Newchurch in Pendle T 146 SD 8239
New Clipstone T 139 SK 5863
New Costessey T 133 TG 1809
Newcott T 92 ST 2308
New Cross T 125 SN 6377
New Cumnock T 156 NS 6113
New Deer T 185 NJ 8847
Newdigate T 96 TQ 1942
New Duston T 119 SP 7162
New Earswick T 147 SE 6155
New Edlington T 139 SK 5498
New Ellerby T 143 TA 1639
Newell Green T 104 SU 8871
New Eltham T 105 TQ 4573
New End T 118 SP 1060
Newenden T 98 TQ 8327
Newent T 114 SO 7226
New Farnley T 147 SE 2431
New Ferry T 136 SJ 3485
Newfield, Durham T 152 NZ 2033
Newfield, Highld T 193 NH 7877
New Forest F 94 SU 2806
New Fryston T 147 SE 4527
Newgale T 110 SM 8422
New Galloway T 156 NX 6377
Newgate T 132 TG 0543
Newgate Street T 105 TL 3005
Newgord 205 HP 5706
New Grimsby T 86 SV 8815
New Grounds 114 SO 7205
Newhall, Ches T 127 SJ 6145
Newhall, Derby T 128 SK 2921
Newhall, Lothn 163 NT 1756
Newhall House 183 NH 6965
Newham T 165 NU 1728
Newham Hall T 165 NU 1729
New Hartley T 159 NZ 3076
Newhaven P 97 TQ 4401
New Hedges T 110 SN 1302
Newhey T 137 SD 9311
New Holland T 142 TA 0823
Newholm T 153 NZ 8610
New Horndean T 165 NT 8949
New Horton Grange 159 NZ 1975
New Houghton, Derby T 139 SK 4965
New Houghton, Norf T 132 TF 7927
Newhouse T 162 NS 7961
New Houses T 146 SD 8073
New Hutton T 151 SD 5691
New Hythe T 98 TQ 7159
Newick T 97 TQ 4121
Newington, Kent T 98 TQ 8564
Newington, Kent T 99 TR 1837
Newington, Oxon T 115 SU 6096
New Inn, Dyfed T 111 SN 4736
New Inn, Gwent T 113 SO 4800
New Inn, Gwent T 113 ST 3099
New Invention T 116 SO 2976
New Kelso T 190 NG 9342
New Lanark T 163 NS 8842
Newland, Glos T 113 SO 5509
Newland, H. & W T 117 SO 7948
Newland, N. Yks T 142 SE 6924
Newlandrig T 164 NT 3362
Newlands, Border T 157 NY 5094
Newlands, Grampn T 184 NJ 3051
Newlands, Highld T 183 NH 7645
Newlands, Northum T 152 NZ 0955
Newlands Hause 150 NY 1917
Newlands of Fleenas Wood F 183 NH 9146
Newlands of Geise T 199 ND 0865
New Lane T 136 SD 4213
New Leake T 141 TF 4057
New Leeds T 185 NJ 9954
New Longton T 145 SD 5025
Newlot 200 HY 5215
New Luce T 154 NX 1764
Newlyn T 86 SW 4628
Newlyn Downs H 87 SW 8354
Newmachar T 185 NJ 8819
Newmains T 163 NS 8256
New Malden T 105 TQ 2168
Newmarket, Suff P 122 TL 6463
Newmarket, W. Isles T 195 NB 4235
Newmarket Heath 122 TL 6163
New Marske T 153 NZ 6220
New Marton T 126 SJ 3434
Newmill, Border T 157 NT 5010
New Mill, Corn T 86 SW 4534
Newmill, Grampn T 184 NJ 4352
New Mill, Herts T 104 SP 9212
New Mill, W. Yks T 138 SE 1609
Newmill of Inshewan T 176 NO 4260
New Mills, Ches T 137 SJ 7782
New Mills, Corn T 87 SW 9052
New Mills, Derby T 138 SJ 9985
New Mills, Gwent T 113 SO 5107
New Mills, Powys T 125 SJ 0901
Newmiln T 170 NO 1230
Newmilns T 161 NS 5237
New Milton T 94 SZ 2495
New Moat T 110 SN 0625
Newnham, Glos T 114 SO 6911
Newnham, Hants T 103 SU 7153
Newnham, Herts T 121 TL 2437
Newnham, H. & W T 117 SO 6469
Newnham, Kent T 98 TQ 9557
Newnham, Northnts T 119 SP 5759
New Ollerton T 139 SK 6668
New Park F 94 SU 2905
New Pitsligo T 185 NJ 8856
New Polzeath T 87 SW 9379
New Pool W 125 SN 7492
Newport, Devon T 91 SS 5632
Newport, Dyfed T 110 SN 0539
Newport, Essex T 121 TL 5233
Newport, Glos T 114 ST 7097
Newport, Gwent P 100 ST 3188
Newport, Highld T 199 ND 1324
Newport, Humbs T 142 SE 8530
Newport, I. of W T 95 SZ 5089
Newport, Norf T 133 TG 5016
Newport, Shrops T 127 SJ 7419
Newport Bay W 110 SN 0340
Newport-on-Tay T 171 NO 4227
Newport Pagnell T 120 SP 8743
Newpound Common T 96 TQ 0627
New Prestwick T 161 NS 3424
Newquay, Corn T 87 SW 8161
New Quay, Dyfed T 111 SN 3959
Newquay Bay W 87 SW 8162
New Rackheath T 133 TG 2812
New Radnor T 116 SO 2161
New River, Cambs W 121 TL 5869
New River, Lincs W 131 TF 2518
New River Ancholme W 142 SE 9718
New Romney T 99 TR 0624
New Rossington T 139 SK 6197
New Row T 145 SD 6438
New Sauchie T 170 NS 8994
New Scone T 170 NO 1326
Newseat, Grampn T 185 NJ 7032
Newseat, Grampn 185 NK 0748
Newsham, Northum T 159 NZ 3079
Newsham, N. Yks T 152 NZ 1010
Newsholme, Humbs T 142 SE 7229
Newsholme, Lancs T 146 SD 8451
New Silksworth T 153 NZ 3753
Newstead, Border T 164 NT 5634
Newstead, Northum T 165 NU 1527
Newstead, Notts T 129 SK 5252
New Stevenston T 162 NS 7659
Newthorpe T 147 SE 4632
Newtimber Place 96 TQ 2613
New Tolsta T 195 NB 5348
Newton, Border T 158 NT 5920
Newton, Cambs T 131 TF 4314
Newton, Cambs T 121 TL 4349
Newton, Ches T 137 SJ 5059
Newton, Ches T 137 SJ 5375
Newton, Cumbr T 144 SD 2371
Newton, D. & G T 157 NY 1194
Newton, Grampn T 184 NJ 1663
Newton, Highld 196 NC 2331
Newton, Highld T 199 ND 3449
Newton, Highld T 183 NH 7448
Newton, Highld T 183 NH 7766
Newton, H. & W T 113 SO 3433
Newton, H. & W T 113 SO 5054
Newton, Lancs T 145 SD 4431
Newton, Lancs T 145 SD 5974
Newton, Lancs T 145 SD 6950
Newton, Lincs T 130 TF 0436
Newton, Lothn T 170 NT 0977
Newton, M. Glam T 109 SS 8477
Newton, Norf T 132 TF 8315
Newton, Northnts T 120 SP 8883
Newton, Northum T 159 NZ 0364
Newton, S. Glam T 100 ST 2478
Newton, Staffs T 128 SK 0325
Newton, Strath T 168 NS 0498
Newton, Strath T 163 NS 6660
Newton, Strath T 163 NS 9331
Newton, Suff T 122 TL 9140
Newton, Warw T 119 SP 5378
Newton, W. Glam T 108 SS 6088
Newton, Wilts T 94 SU 2322
Newton, W. Isles T 188 NF 8977
Newton Abbot T 89 SX 8671
Newton Arlosh T 150 NY 1955
Newton Aycliffe T 152 NZ 2724
Newton Bewley T 153 NZ 4626
Newton Blossomville T 120 SP 9251
Newton Bromswold T 120 SP 9965
Newton Burgoland T 128 SK 3709
Newton by Toft T 140 TF 0587
Newton Dale 148 SE 8290
Newton Ferrers T 89 SX 5448
Newtonferry T 188 NF 8978
Newton Flotman T 133 TM 2098
Newtongarry Croft T 184 NJ 5735
Newtongrange T 164 NT 3364
Newton Harcourt T 129 SP 6397
Newton Heath 94 SZ 0084
Newtonhill T 177 NO 9193
Newton House 184 NJ 6629
Newton Kyme T 147 SE 4645
Newton-le-Willows, Mers T 137 SJ 5894
Newton-le-Willows, N. Yks T 152 SE 2189
Newton Longville T 120 SP 8431
Newton Mearns T 161 NS 5455
Newtonmill 177 NO 6064
Newtonmore P 175 NN 7199
Newton of Ardtoe T 173 NM 6470
Newton of Balcanquhal T 170 NO 1510
Newton-on-Ouse T 147 SE 5159
Newton-on-Rawcliffe T 148 SE 8190
Newton on the Moor T 159 NU 1705
Newton on Trent T 140 SK 8374
Newton or St Mary's Haven W 165 NU 2424
Newton Poppleford T 92 SY 0889
Newton Purcell T 119 SP 6230
Newton Regis T 128 SK 2707
Newton Reigny T 151 NY 4731
Newton Solney T 128 SK 2825
Newton Stacey T 102 SU 4140
Newton St Cyres T 89 SX 8797
Newton Stewart T 154 NX 4065
Newton St Faith T 133 TG 2217
Newton St Loe T 101 ST 7064
Newton St Petrock T 90 SS 4112
Newton Tony T 102 SU 2140
Newton Tors H 165 NT 9127
Newton Tracey T 91 SS 5226
Newton under Roseberry T 153 NZ 5613
Newton upon Derwent T 148 SE 7249
Newton Valence T 95 SU 7232
Newtown, Ches T 127 SJ 6248
Newtown, Ches T 138 SJ 9784
Newtown, Cumbr T 157 NY 5062
Newtown, Derby T 138 SJ 9984
Newtown, Dorset T 94 SZ 0493
Newtown, Grampn T 183 NJ 1469
Newtown, Hants T 94 SU 2710
Newtown, Hants T 94 SU 3023
Newtown, Hants T 103 SU 4763
Newtown, Hants T 95 SU 6113
Newtown, Highld T 182 NH 3504
Newtown, H. & W T 113 SO 6145
Newtown, I. of M T 144 SC 3273
Newtown, I. of W T 94 SZ 4290
New Town, Lothn T 171 NT 4470
Newtown, Northum T 165 NT 9731
Newtown, Northum T 159 NU 0300
Newtown, Northum T 165 NU 0425
Newtown, Powys P 116 SO 1191
Newtown, Shrops T 127 SJ 4731
Newtown, Staffs T 137 SJ 9060
Newtown, Wilts T 93 ST 9128
Newtown Bay W 94 SZ 4192
Newtown-in-St-Martin T 86 SW 7423
Newtown Linford T 129 SK 5110
Newtown St Boswells T 164 NT 5731
New Tredegar T 109 SO 1403
Newtyle T 176 NO 2941
Newtyle Forest F 183 NJ 0552
Newtyle Hill H 176 NO 0542
New Ulva 167 NR 7080
New Waltham T 143 TA 2804
New Wimpole T 121 TL 3449
New Winton T 171 NT 4271
New Yatt T 115 SP 3713
New York, Lincs T 131 TF 2455
New York, T. & W T 159 NZ 3270
Neyland T 110 SM 9605
Niarbyl Bay W 144 SC 2176
Nibley T 101 ST 6982
Nibon 204 HU 3073
Nicholashayne T 92 ST 1016
Nicholaston T 108 SS 5288
Nidd T 147 SE 3060
Nidderdale 146 SE 0976
Nigg, Grampn T 185 NJ 9403
Nigg, Highld T 193 NH 8071
Nigg Bay, Grampn W 185 NJ 9704
Nigg Bay, Highld W 193 NH 7771
Nikka Vord H 205 HP 6210
Nilig 135 SJ 0255
Nine Ashes T 106 TL 5902
Ninebanks T 151 NY 7853
Nine Barrow Down H 94 SZ 0081
Ninemile Bar or Crocketford T 156 NX 8372
Nine Standards Rigg H 151 NY 8206
Ninfield T 97 TQ 7012
Ningwood T 94 SZ 4088
Nisbet T 164 NT 6725
Nithsdale 156 NX 8990
Niton T 95 SZ 5076
Nitshill T 161 NS 5160
Noak Hill T 105 TQ 5493
Nobottle T 119 SP 6763
Nocton T 140 TF 0664
Noddsdale Water W 161 NS 2263
Noke T 115 SP 5413
Noltland Castle A 200 HY 4248
Nolton T 110 SM 8618
Nolton Haven T 110 SM 8518
No Man's Heath, Ches T 127 SJ 5148
No Man's Heath, Warw T 128 SK 2909
Nomansland, Devon T 91 SS 8313
Nomansland, Wilts T 94 SU 2517
Noneley T 127 SJ 4828
No Ness 203 HU 4421
Nonington T 99 TR 2552
Nook 157 NY 4679
Nookton Fell H 152 NY 9148
Noonsbrough T 202 HU 2957
Noose, The 114 SO 7207
Nor T 165 NT 9047
Noranside T 177 NO 4760
Noran Water W 177 NO 4760
Norbury, Ches T 127 SJ 5647
Norbury, Derby T 128 SK 1242
Norbury, Glos A 114 SO 9915

Norbury Osgathorpe

Norbury, Shrops *T* 126 SO 3693
Norbury, Staffs *T* 127 SJ 7823
Nordelph *T* 131 TF 5500
Norden, Dorset *T* 94 SY 9483
Norden, G. Man *T* 137 SD 8514
Nordley *T* 127 SO 6996
Norham *T* 165 NT 9047
Norley *T* 137 SJ 5772
Norleywood *T* 94 SZ 3597
Normanby, Humbs *T* 142 SE 8816
Normanby, N. Yks *T* 148 SE 7381
Normanby-by-Spital *T* 140 TF 0088
Normanby le Wold *T* 141 TF 1295
Norman Cross *T* 120 TL 1690
Normandy *T* 96 SU 9351
Norman's Green *T* 92 ST 0503
Norman's Law *H* 171 NO 3020
Normanton, Derby *T* 128 SK 3433
Normanton, Lincs *T* 130 SK 9446
Normanton, Notts *T* 129 SK 7054
Normanton, W. Yks *T* 147 SE 3822
Normanton le Heath *T* 128 SK 3712
Normanton on Soar *T* 129 SK 5123
Normanton-on-the-Wolds *T* 129 SK 6233
Normanton on Trent *T* 140 SK 7968
Normoss *T* 145 SD 3337
Norrington Common *T* 101 ST 8864
Norris Hill *T* 128 SK 3216
Northallerton *T* 153 SE 3794
Northam, Devon *T* 90 SS 4429
Northam, Hants *T* 94 SU 4312
Northampton *P* 119 SP 7560
North Ascot *T* 104 SU 9069
North Aston *T* 115 SP 4728
Northaw *T* 105 TL 2802
North Baddesley *T* 94 SU 3919
North Ballachulish *T* 174 NN 0560
North Barrow *T* 93 ST 6029
North Barrule *H* 144 SC 4490
North Barsham *T* 132 TF 9134
North Bay, Orkney *W* 201 HY 6542
North Bay, Orkney *W* 200 ND 2990
North Bay, W. Isles *W* 178 NF 7302
North Benfleet *T* 106 TQ 7589
North Berwick *T* 171 NT 5585
North Berwick Law *H* 171 NT 5584
North Birny Fell *H* 157 NY 4791
North Boarhunt *T* 95 SU 6010
Northborough *T* 130 TF 1508
Northbourne *T* 99 TR 3352
North Bovey *T* 89 SX 7483
North Bradley *T* 101 ST 8555
North Brentor *T* 88 SX 4881
North Buckland *T* 90 SS 4740
North Burlingham *T* 133 TG 3610
North Burnt Hill *H* 161 NS 2566
North Cadbury *T* 93 ST 6327
North Cairn *T* 154 NW 9770
North Carlton *T* 140 SK 9477
North Carr (lightship) 171 NO 6714
North Cave *T* 142 SE 8932
North Cerney *T* 114 SP 0208
Northchapel *T* 96 SU 9529
North Charford *T* 94 SU 1919
North Charlton *T* 165 NU 1622
North Cheek or Ness Point 149 NZ 9606
North Cheriton *T* 93 ST 6925
North Chideock *T* 93 SY 4294
Northchurch *T* 104 SP 9709
North Cliffe *T* 142 SE 8737
North Clifton *T* 140 SK 8272
Northcote Manor 91 SS 6218
North Cotes *T* 143 TA 3500
Northcott *T* 88 SX 3392
North Cove *T* 123 TM 4689
North Cowton *T* 152 NZ 2803
North Crawley *T* 120 SP 9244
North Cray *T* 105 TQ 4972
North Creake *T* 132 TF 8538
North Curry *T* 92 ST 3125
North Dalton *T* 149 SE 9352
North Dawn 200 HY 4703
North Deep *W* 171 NO 2219
North Deighton *T* 147 SE 3951
North Downs, Kent *H* 98 TQ 6762
North Downs, Surrey *H* 103 SU 8147
North Drove Drain *W* 130 TF 1817
North Duffield *T* 142 SE 6837
Northdyke *T* 200 HY 2320
North Elkington *T* 141 TF 2890
North Elmham *T* 132 TF 9820
North End, Avon *T* 100 ST 4167
Northend, Avon *T* 101 ST 7768
Northend, Bucks *T* 104 SU 7392
North End, Hants *T* 102 SU 4163
North End, Hants *T* 95 SU 6502
Northend, Warw *T* 118 SP 3952
North End, W. Susx *T* 96 TQ 1209
North Erradale *T* 190 NG 7481
North Esk Reservoir, Border *W* 163 NT 1558
North Esk Reservoir, Lothn *W* 163 NT 1558
Northey Island 104 TL 0806
North Fearns *T* 180 NG 5935
North Fen, Cambs 131 TF 3009
North Fen, Cambs 121 TL 5169
North Ferriby *T* 142 SE 9825
Northfield, Border *T* 165 NT 9167
Northfield, Grampn *T* 185 NJ 9008
Northfield, W. Mids *T* 118 SP 0279
Northfleet *T* 98 TQ 6274
North Foreland 99 TR 4069
North Frodingham *T* 149 TA 0953
North Glen Sannox 160 NR 9947
North Gorley *T* 94 SU 1611
North Green *T* 123 TM 2288
North Greetwell *T* 140 TF 0173
North Grimston *T* 148 SE 8467
North Harris 189 NB 1307
North Haven, Grampn *W* 185 NK 1138
North Haven, Shetld *W* 201 HZ 2272
North Havra 203 HU 3642
North Hayling *T* 95 SU 7303
North Head, Highld 199 ND 3850
North Head, Orkney 199 ND 3985
North Heasley *T* 91 SS 7333
North Heath *T* 96 TQ 0621
North Hill, Cambs *T* 121 TL 4476
North Hill, Corn *T* 88 SX 2776
North Hill, Orkney *H* 200 HY 4048
North Hill, Orkney *H* 200 HY 4954
North Hill, Somer *H* 91 SS 9447
North Hinksey Village *T* 115 SP 4905
North Holms 205 HP 5611
North Holmwood *T* 96 TQ 1647
North Huish *T* 89 SX 7156
North Hykeham *T* 140 SK 9466
Northiam *T* 98 TQ 8225
Northill *T* 120 TL 1546
Northington *T* 95 SU 5737
North Kelsey *T* 142 TA 0401
North Kelsey Beck, Humbs *W* 142 TA 0302
North Kelsey Beck, Lincs *W* 142 TA 0302
North Kessock *T* 182 NH 6548
North Kilvington *T* 147 SE 4285
North Kilworth *T* 119 SP 6183
North Kyme *T* 130 TF 1552
North Lancing *T* 96 TQ 1804
Northlands *T* 131 TF 3453
Northleach *T* 114 SP 1114
North Lee, Bucks *T* 104 SP 8309
North Lee, W. Isles *H* 188 NF 9366
Northleigh, Devon *T* 92 SY 1995
North Leigh, Oxon *T* 115 SP 3812
North Leverton with Habblesthorpe *T* 140 SK 7882
Northlew *T* 88 SX 5099
North Littleton *T* 118 SP 0847
North Loch *W* 201 HY 7545
North Lopham *T* 122 TM 0383
North Luffenham *T* 130 SK 9303
North Marden *T* 95 SU 8016
North Marston *T* 104 SP 7722
North Medwin *W* 163 NT 0150
North Middleton *T* 164 NT 3559
North Molton *T* 91 SS 7329
Northmoor *T* 115 SP 4203
Northmoor Green or Moorland *T* 92 ST 3332
North Morar 180 NM 7892
North Moreton *T* 103 SU 5689
Northmuir *T* 176 NO 3855
North Muskham *T* 140 SK 7959
North Neaps 205 HP 4905
North Ness 202 HU 1861
North Nesting 203 HU 4558
North Nevi 201 HY 6101
North Newbold *T* 142 SE 9136
North Newington *T* 118 SP 4239
North Newnton *T* 102 SU 1257
North Newton *T* 92 ST 2930
North Nibley *T* 114 ST 7495
North Oakley *T* 103 SU 5354
North Ockendon *T* 106 TQ 5984
Northolt *T* 105 TQ 1285
Northop *T* 136 SJ 2468
Northop Hall *T* 136 SJ 2767
North Ormsby *T* 141 TF 2993
Northorpe, Lincs *T* 140 SK 8997
Northorpe, Lincs *T* 130 TF 0917
North Otterington *T* 153 SE 3689
North Owersby *T* 140 TF 0694
Northowram *T* 146 SE 1126
North Perrott *T* 93 ST 4709
North Petherton *T* 92 ST 2933
North Petherwin *T* 88 SX 2889
North Pickenham *T* 132 TF 8606
North Piddle *T* 118 SO 9654
Northpunds *T* 203 HU 4022
North Queensferry *T* 170 NT 1380
North Radworthy 91 SS 7534
Northrepps *T* 133 TG 2439
North Rigton *T* 147 SE 2849
North Rode *T* 137 SJ 8966
North Roe, Shetld 204 HU 3487
North Roe, Shetld *T* 204 HU 3689
North Ronaldsay 201 HY 7654
North Ronaldsay Firth *W* 201 HY 7549
North Runcton *T* 132 TF 6415
North Sandwick *T* 205 HU 5497
North Scale *T* 144 SD 1870
North Scarle *T* 140 SK 8466
North Seaton *T* 159 NZ 2986
North Shian 173 NM 9143
North Shields *T* 159 NZ 3568
North Shoebury *T* 106 TQ 9386
North Shore *T* 145 SD 3038
North Side *T* 131 TL 2799
North Somercotes *T* 141 TF 4296
North Sound, The *W* 200 HY 5745
North Stack 134 SH 2184
North Stainley *T* 147 SE 2877
North Stainmore *T* 151 NY 8315
North Stane 205 HP 6613
North Stifford *T* 106 TQ 6080
North Stoke, Avon *T* 101 ST 7069
North Stoke, Oxon *T* 104 SU 6186
North Stoke, W. Susx *T* 96 TQ 0210
North Street *T* 95 SU 6433
North Sunderland *T* 165 NU 2131
North Sutor 183 NH 8168
North Taing, Orkney 201 HY 6225
North Taing, Orkney 201 HY 6716
North Tamerton *T* 88 SX 3197
North Tawton *T* 91 SS 6601
North Third Reservoir *W* 169 NS 7588
North Thoresby *T* 143 TF 2998
North Tidworth *T* 102 SU 2349
North Tolsta *T* 195 NB 5347
Northton *T* 188 NF 9989
Northtown *T* 200 ND 4797
North Tuddenham *T* 132 TG 0414
North Ugie Water *W* 185 NJ 9753
North Uist 188 NF 8370
Northwall *T* 201 HY 7544
North Walsham *T* 133 TG 2830
North Waltham *T* 103 SU 5646
North Warnborough *T* 103 SU 7351
North Water Bridge *T* 177 NO 6566
North Watten *T* 199 ND 2458
Northway *T* 114 SO 9233
North Weald Bassett *T* 105 TL 4904
North West Passage *W* 86 SV 8411
North West Point 90 SS 1348
North Wharf 145 SD 3249
North Wheatley *T* 140 SK 7585
North Whilborough *T* 89 SX 8766
Northwich *P* 137 SJ 6573
Northwick, Avon *T* 101 ST 5686
North Wick, Avon *T* 101 ST 5865
North Widcombe *T* 101 ST 5758
North Willingham *T* 141 TF 1688
North Wingfield *T* 139 SK 4165
North Witham *T* 130 SK 9221
Northwold *T* 132 TL 7597
Northwood, Derby *T* 139 SK 2664
Northwood, G. Lon *T* 104 TQ 0991
Northwood, I. of W *T* 95 SZ 4894
Northwood, Shrops *T* 126 SJ 4633
Northwood Green *T* 114 SO 7216
North Wootton, Dorset *T* 93 ST 6514
North Wootton, Norf *T* 132 TF 6424
North Wootton, Somer *T* 101 ST 5641
North Wraxall *T* 101 ST 8175
North Yardhope 158 NT 9201
North York Moors 148 SE 7398
North Yorkshire Moors Railway 148 SE 8497
Norton, Ches *T* 137 SJ 5582
Norton, Cleve *T* 153 NZ 4421
Norton, Glos *T* 114 SO 8524
Norton, Herts *T* 121 TL 2334
Norton, H. & W *T* 117 SO 8851
Norton, H. & W *T* 118 SP 0447
Norton, I. of W *T* 94 SZ 3489
Norton, Northnts *T* 119 SP 6063
Norton, Notts *T* 139 SK 5772
Norton, N. Yks *T* 148 SE 7971
Norton, Powys *T* 116 SO 3067
Norton, Shrops *T* 127 SJ 5609
Norton, Shrops *T* 127 SJ 7200
Norton, Shrops *T* 116 SO 4681
Norton, Suff *T* 122 TL 9565
Norton, S. Yks *T* 139 SE 5415
Norton, S. Yks *T* 139 SK 3682
Norton, Wilts *T* 101 ST 8884
Norton, W. Susx *T* 96 SU 9206
Norton Bavant *T* 101 ST 9043
Norton Bridge *T* 127 SJ 8730
Norton Canes *T* 128 SK 0108
Norton Canon *T* 113 SO 3847
Norton Disney *T* 140 SK 8959
Norton East *T* 128 SK 0208
Norton Ferris *T* 93 ST 7936
Norton Fitzwarren *T* 92 ST 1925
Norton Green *T* 94 SZ 3488
Norton Hawkfield *T* 101 ST 5964
Norton Heath *T* 106 TL 6004
Norton in Hales *T* 127 SJ 7038
Norton-in-the-Moors *T* 127 SJ 8951
Norton-Juxta-Twycross *T* 128 SK 3207
Norton-le-Clay *T* 147 SE 4071
Norton Lindsey *T* 118 SP 2263
Norton Malreward *T* 101 ST 6065
Norton Mandeville *T* 105 TL 5804
Norton Marshes 133 TG 4100
Norton St Philip *T* 101 ST 7755
Norton Subcourse *T* 133 TM 4198
Norton sub Hamdon *T* 93 ST 4615
Norwell *T* 140 SK 7761
Norwell Woodhouse *T* 140 SK 7462
Norwich *P* 133 TG 2308
Norwich Airport 133 TG 2113
Norwick, Shetld *T* 205 HP 6514
Nor Wick, Shetld *W* 205 HP 6514
Norwood Green *T* 105 TQ 1378
Norwood Hill *T* 96 TQ 2443
Noseley *T* 129 SP 7398
Noss Head 199 ND 3855
Noss Mayo *T* 89 SX 5447
Nosterfield *T* 147 SE 2780
Nostie *T* 180 NG 8527
Notgrove *T* 114 SP 1120
Nottage *T* 109 SS 8278
Nottingham *P* 129 SK 5741
Nottington *T* 93 SY 6682
Notton, Wilts *T* 101 ST 9169
Notton, W. Yks *T* 139 SE 3413
Nounsley *T* 106 TL 7910
Noup Head 200 HY 3950
Noup of Noss 203 HU 5539
Noup, The 205 HP 6318
Noutard's Green *T* 117 SO 7966
Novar House 182 NH 6168
Nox *T* 126 SJ 4110
Nuffield *T* 104 SU 6787
Nunburnholme *T* 148 SE 8548
Nuneaton *P* 118 SP 3691
Nuneham Courtenay *T* 115 SU 5599
Nun Monkton *T* 147 SE 5057
Nunney *T* 101 ST 7345
Nunnington *T* 147 SE 6679
Nunnykirk *T* 159 NZ 0892
Nunthorpe *T* 153 NZ 5314
Nunton, Wilts *T* 94 SU 1526
Nunton, W. Isles *T* 188 NF 7653
Nunwick 158 NY 8774
Nursling *T* 94 SU 3716
Nursted *T* 95 SU 7621
Nutberry Hill *H* 162 NS 7433
Nutbourne *T* 96 TQ 0718
Nutfield *T* 97 TQ 3049
Nuthall *T* 129 SK 5144
Nuthampstead *T* 121 TL 4034
Nuthurst *T* 96 TQ 1926
Nutley *T* 97 TQ 4427
Nutwell *T* 139 SE 6304
Nybster *T* 199 ND 3663
Nyetimber *T* 95 SZ 8998
Nyewood *T* 95 SU 8021
Nyland Hill *H* 101 ST 4550
Nymet Rowland *T* 91 SS 7108
Nymet Tracey *T* 89 SS 7200
Nympsfield *T* 114 SO 8000
Nynehead *T* 92 ST 1422
Nyton *T* 96 SU 9305

O

Oadby *T* 129 SK 6200
Oad Street *T* 98 TQ 8662
Oakamoor *T* 128 SK 0544
Oakbank *T* 163 NT 0766
Oakdale *T* 109 ST 1898
Oake *T* 92 ST 1525
Oaken *T* 127 SJ 8502
Oakenclough *T* 145 SD 5447
Oakengates *T* 127 SJ 7010
Oakenshaw, Durham *T* 152 NZ 2037
Oakenshaw, W. Yks *T* 146 SE 1727
Oakford, Devon *T* 91 SS 9021
Oakford, Dyfed *T* 111 SN 4558
Oakgrove *T* 137 SJ 9169
Oakham *T* 130 SK 8508
Oakhanger *T* 95 SU 7735
Oakhill *T* 101 ST 6347
Oakington *T* 121 TL 4164
Oaklands, Gwyn 135 SH 8158
Oaklands, Herts *T* 105 TL 2417
Oakle Street *T* 114 SO 7517
Oakley, Beds *T* 120 TL 0153
Oakley, Bucks *T* 104 SP 6312
Oakley, Fife *T* 170 NT 0289
Oakley, Hants *T* 103 SU 5650
Oakley, Suff *T* 123 TM 1677
Oakley Green *T* 104 SU 9276
Oakley Park *T* 125 SN 9887
Oakridge *T* 114 SO 9103
Oaks *T* 126 SJ 4204
Oaksey *T* 114 ST 9993
Oakthorpe *T* 128 SK 3213
Oakwoodhill *T* 96 TQ 1337
Oakworth *T* 146 SE 0338
Oare, Kent *T* 99 TR 0062
Oare, Wilts *T* 102 SU 1563
Oasby *T* 130 TF 0039
Oa, The 166 NR 3144
Oathlaw *T* 177 NO 4756
Oban *P* 168 NM 8530
Oban Bay *W* 168 NM 8530
Obney 176 NO 0336
Obney Hills *H* 176 NO 0238
Oborne *T* 93 ST 6518
Occlestone Green *T* 137 SJ 6962
Occold *T* 123 TM 1570
Ochil Hills *H* 170 NO 0610
Ochiltree *T* 161 NS 5021
Ochtermuthill 169 NN 8316
Ochtertyre 169 NN 8323
Ockbrook *T* 128 SK 4236
Ockham *T* 96 TQ 0756
Ockle *T* 173 NM 5570
Ockle Point 173 NM 5471
Ockley *T* 96 TQ 1440
Ockran Head 204 HU 2484
Ocle Pychard *T* 113 SO 5946
Odcombe *T* 93 ST 5015
Odda's Chapel *A* 114 SO 8729
Odd Down *T* 101 ST 7362
Oddendale *T* 151 NY 5913
Oddingley *T* 117 SO 9159
Oddington, Glos *T* 115 SP 2225
Oddington, Oxon *T* 115 SP 5515
Odell *T* 120 SP 9657
Odie 201 HY 6229
Odiham *T* 103 SU 7451
Odin Bay *W* 201 HY 6924
Odness 201 HY 6926
Odstock *T* 94 SU 1426
Odstock Down *H* 94 SU 1324
Odstone *T* 128 SK 3907
Offa's Dyke, Clwyd *A* 135 SJ 1079
Offa's Dyke, Clwyd *A* 126 SJ 2948
Offa's Dyke, Glos *A* 113 SO 5407
Offa's Dyke, H. & W *A* 113 SO 2959
Offa's Dyke, Powys *A* 126 SJ 2507
Offa's Dyke, Shrops *A* 116 SO 2678
Offchurch *T* 118 SP 3565
Offenham *T* 118 SP 0546
Offham, E. Susx *T* 97 TQ 4012
Offham, Kent *T* 97 TQ 6557
Offord Cluny *T* 121 TL 2267
Offord D'Arcy *T* 121 TL 2266
Offton *T* 122 TM 0649
Offwell *T* 92 SY 1999
Ogbourne Maizey *T* 102 SU 1871
Ogbourne St Andrew *T* 102 SU 1972
Ogbourne St George *T* 102 SU 2074
Ogden Reservoir *W* 146 SD 8039
Ogil 176 NO 4561
Ogle *T* 159 NZ 1378
Ogmore *T* 109 SS 8876
Ogmore-by-Sea *T* 109 SS 8675
Ogmore Forest *F* 109 SS 9489
Ogmore Vale *T* 109 SS 9390
Ogston Reservoir *W* 139 SK 3760
Oh Me Edge *H* 158 NY 7099
Oigh-sgeir 179 NM 1596
Oisgill Bay *W* 186 NG 1349
Oitir Fhiadhaich 188 NF 7465
Oitir Mhór, W. Isles *W* 178 NF 7306
Oitir Mhór, W. Isles 188 NF 8157
Okeford Fitzpaine *T* 93 ST 8010
Okehampton *P* 89 SX 5895
Okehampton Camp *T* 89 SX 5893
Okehampton Common 89 SX 5790
Okraquoy 203 HU 4331
Olantigh 99 TR 0548
Old *T* 119 SP 7873
Old Aberdeen *T* 185 NJ 9408
Old Alresford *T* 95 SU 5834
Oldany Island 196 NC 0934
Old Basing *T* 103 SU 6752
Old Bedford River *W* 131 TL 5496
Oldberrow *T* 118 SP 1266
Old Bewick *T* 165 NU 0621
Old Bolingbroke *T* 141 TF 3565
Oldborough *T* 91 SS 7706
Old Brampton *T* 139 SK 3371
Old Bridge of Urr *T* 156 NX 7767
Old Buckenham *T* 122 TM 0691
Old Burghclere *T* 103 SU 4657
Oldbury, Shrops *T* 117 SO 7192
Oldbury, Warw *T* 128 SP 3194
Oldbury, Wilts *A* 102 SU 0569
Oldbury, W. Mids *T* 118 SO 9889
Oldbury Castle *A* 102 SU 0469
Oldbury-on-Severn *T* 101 ST 6192
Oldbury on the Hill *T* 101 ST 8188
Oldbury Sands 113 ST 5893
Old Byland *T* 147 SE 5585
Oldcastle *T* 113 SO 3224
Old Castle Head 110 SS 0796
Old Castleton 158 NY 5190
Oldchapel Hill *H* 125 SN 9780
Old Cleeve *T* 100 ST 0341
Old Clipstone *T* 139 SK 6064
Old Colwyn *T* 135 SH 8678
Oldcotes *T* 139 SK 5988
Old Croft River, Cambs *W* 131 TL 5098
Old Croft River, Norf *W* 131 TL 5098
Old Dailly *T* 154 NX 2299
Old Dalby *T* 129 SK 6723
Old Deer *T* 185 NJ 9747
Old Denaby *T* 139 SK 4899
Old Ellerby *T* 143 TA 1636
Old Felixstowe *T* 123 TM 3135
Oldfield *T* 117 SO 8465
Oldford *T* 101 ST 7850
Old Hall *A* 136 SD 4616
Old Hall, The *T* 143 TA 2717
Oldham *P* 137 SD 9204
Oldhamstocks *T* 164 NT 7470
Old Head 199 ND 4783
Old Heath *T* 107 TM 0123
Old Howe *W* 149 TA 1156
Oldhurst *T* 121 TL 3077
Old Hutton *T* 145 SD 5688
Old Kea *T* 87 SW 8441
Old Kilpatrick *T* 169 NS 4673
Old Kinnernie *T* 185 NJ 7209
Old Knebworth *T* 105 TL 2320
Oldland *T* 101 ST 6771
Old Leake *T* 131 TF 4050
Old Lynn Channel *W* 131 TF 5233
Old Malton *T* 148 SE 7972
Old Man of Coniston, The *H* 150 SD 2797
Old Man of Hoy 200 HY 1700
Old Man of Storr *H* 187 NG 5053
Oldmeldrum *T* 185 NJ 8127
Old Milverton *T* 118 SP 3067
Old Monkland *T* 162 NS 7163
Old Newton *T* 122 TM 0562
Old Oswestry *A* 126 SJ 2931
Oldpark *T* 127 SJ 6909
Old Peak or South Cheek 149 NZ 9802
Old Philpstoun *T* 170 NT 0577
Old Radnor *T* 113 SO 2559
Old Rayne *T* 184 NJ 6728
Old River Ancholme *W* 142 SE 9715
Old Romney *T* 99 TR 0325
Old Sarum *A* 94 SU 1332
Old Scone 170 NO 1126
Oldshore Beg *T* 196 NC 1959
Oldshoremore *T* 196 NC 2058
Old Soar Manor *A* 97 TQ 6154
Old Sodbury *T* 101 ST 7581
Old Somerby *T* 130 SK 9633
Old South 131 TF 4735
Oldstead *T* 147 SE 5380
Old Swarland *T* 159 NU 1601
Old Town, Cumbr *T* 145 SD 5983
Old Town, Northum *T* 158 NY 8891
Oldtown of Ord *T* 184 NJ 6259
Old Warden *T* 120 TL 1343
Oldways End *T* 91 SS 8624
Old Weston *T* 120 TL 1077
Oldwhat *T* 185 NJ 8651
Old Winchester Hill *A* 95 SU 6420
Old Windsor *T* 104 SU 9874
Old Wives Lees *T* 99 TR 0754
Olenacum Roman Fort *R* 150 NY 2646
Olgrinmore *T* 199 ND 0955
Oliver's Battery *T* 95 SU 4527
Ollaberry *T* 204 HU 3680
Ollach *T* 187 NG 5136
Ollerton, Ches *T* 137 SJ 7776
Ollerton, Notts *T* 139 SK 6567
Ollerton, Shrops *T* 127 SJ 6525
Ollinsgarth 203 HU 4430
Ollisdal Geo 186 NG 2138
Olna Firth *W* 203 HU 3864
Olney *T* 120 SP 8851
Olrig House 199 ND 1866
Olton *T* 118 SP 1382
Olveston *T* 101 ST 6087
Ombersley *T* 117 SO 8464
Ompton *T* 140 SK 6865
Onchan *T* 144 SC 4078
Onchan Head 144 SC 4077
Onecote *T* 128 SK 0555
Ongar Hill *T* 131 TF 5824
Ongar Street *T* 116 SO 3967
Onibury *T* 116 SO 4579
Onich *T* 174 NN 0261
Onllwyn *T* 109 SN 8410
Onneley *T* 127 SJ 7543
Onslow Village *T* 96 SU 9949
Opinan, Highld *T* 190 NG 7472
Opinan, Highld *T* 190 NG 8796
Opsay 188 NF 9876
Orbost 186 NG 2543
Orby *T* 141 TF 4967
Orby Marsh 141 TF 5167
Orchard *T* 93 ST 8215
Orchard Portman *T* 92 ST 2421
Orcheston *T* 102 SU 0545
Orcheston Down *H* 102 SU 0748
Orcop *T* 113 SO 4726
Orcop Hill *T* 113 SO 4828
Ord *T* 180 NG 6113
Ordhead *T* 184 NJ 6610
Ordie *T* 176 NJ 4501
Ordie Burn *W* 170 NO 0733
Ordiequish *T* 184 NJ 3357
Ord Point 193 ND 0617
Ord River *W* 180 NG 6212
Ords, The 203 HU 3413
Ord, The 203 HU 4936
Ore *T* 98 TQ 8311
Ore Bay *W* 200 ND 3094
Oreton *T* 117 SO 6580
Oreval *H* 195 NB 0810
Orfasay 205 HU 4977
Orford, Ches *T* 137 SJ 6190
Orford, Suff *T* 123 TM 4250
Orford Ness 123 TM 4549
Orgreave *T* 128 SK 1516
Orinsay *T* 195 NB 3612
Orka Voe *W* 205 HU 4077
Orknagable 205 HP 5713
Orkney Islands 200 HY 4821
Orleton, H. & W *T* 116 SO 4967
Orleton, H. & W *T* 117 SO 6967
Orlingbury *T* 120 SP 8672
Ormesby *T* 153 NZ 5317
Ormesby St Margaret *T* 133 TG 4915
Ormesby St Michael *T* 133 TG 4814
Ormiclate Castle 178 NF 7331
Ormiscaig *T* 190 NG 8590
Ormiston *T* 171 NT 4169
Ormsaigmore *T* 173 NM 4763
Ormsary House 167 NR 7472
Ormskirk *T* 136 SD 4108
Ornish Island 178 NF 8538
Ornsay 180 NG 7012
Oronsay, Highld 186 NG 3136
Oronsay, Highld 173 NM 5859
Oronsay, Strath 166 NR 3588
Orosay, W. Isles 188 NF 8476
Orosay, W. Isles 178 NF 7106
Orosay, W. Isles 178 NF 7217
Orphir 200 HY 3406
Orpington *P* 105 TQ 4665
Orrell *T* 137 SD 5305
Orrin Falls *W* 182 NH 4751
Orrin Reservoir *W* 182 NH 3749
Orrisdale Head 144 SC 3192
Orroland *T* 155 NX 7746
Orsay 166 NR 1651
Orsett *T* 106 TQ 6481
Orslow *T* 127 SJ 8015
Orston *T* 129 SK 7741
Orton, Cumbr *T* 151 NY 6208
Orton, Northnts *T* 119 SP 8079
Orton Longueville *T* 130 TL 1796
Orton-on-the-Hill *T* 128 SK 3003
Orval *H* 179 NM 3399
Orwell *T* 121 TL 3650
Osbaldeston *T* 145 SD 6431
Osbaston *T* 128 SK 4204
Osborne Bay *W* 95 SZ 5395
Osborne House 95 SZ 5194
Osbournby *T* 130 TF 0638
Oscroft *T* 137 SJ 5067
Ose *T* 186 NG 3141
Osea Island 105 TL 1106
Osgathorpe *T* 128 SK 4319

Osgodby Picton

Osgodby, Lincs T 140 TF 0792
Osgodby, N. Yks T 147 SE 6433
Osgodby, N. Yks T 149 TA 0584
Oskaig T 187 NG 5438
Oskamull T 173 NM 4540
Osmaston T 128 SK 2043
Osmington T 93 SY 7283
Osmington Mills T 93 SY 7381
Osmotherley T 153 SE 4597
Osnaburgh or Dairsie T 171 NO 4117
Ospisdale T 193 NH 7189
Ospringe T 99 TR 0060
Ossett T 139 SE 2820
Ossington T 140 SK 7564
Ostend T 106 TQ 9397
Osterley Park 105 TQ 1577
Oswaldkirk T 147 SE 6279
Oswaldtwistle T 145 SD 7327
Oswestry P 126 SJ 2929
Otford T 105 TQ 5259
Otham T 98 TQ 7953
Othery T 92 ST 3831
Otley, Suff T 123 TM 2055
Otley, W. Yks T 146 SE 2045
Ot Moor 115 SP 5614
Otterbourne T 95 SU 4623
Otterburn, Northum T 158 NY 8893
Otterburn, N. Yks T 146 SD 8857
Otterburn Camp T 158 NY 8995
Otterden Place T 98 TQ 9454
Otter Ferry T 168 NR 9384
Otterham T 88 SX 1690
Ottershaw T 104 TQ 0264
Otters Wick, Orkney W 201 HY 7044
Otterswick, Shetld T 205 HU 5185
Otters Wick, Shetld W 205 HU 5285
Otterton T 92 SY 0885
Ottery St Mary T 92 SY 1095
Ottringham T 143 TA 2624
Oughtershaw T 146 SD 8681
Oughtibridge T 139 SK 3093
Oulston T 147 SE 5474
Oulton, Cumbr T 150 NY 2450
Oulton, Norf T 133 TG 1328
Oulton, Staffs T 127 SJ 9135
Oulton, Suff T 133 TM 5294
Oulton, W. Yks T 147 SE 3628
Oulton Broad T 123 TM 5292
Oulton Street T 133 TG 1527
Oundle T 120 TL 0488
Ousby T 151 NY 6135
Ousdale 193 ND 0720
Ousden T 122 TL 7459
Ouseburn T 147 SE 4461
Ousefleet T 142 SE 8223
Ouse Ness 200 HY 4549
Ouston T 152 NZ 2554
Outer Hebrides 188 NF 9080
Outertown T 200 HY 2310
Outgate T 150 SD 3599
Outhgill T 151 NY 7801
Outlane T 138 SE 0818
Out Newton T 143 TA 3821
Out Rawcliffe T 145 SD 4042
Outshore Point 200 HY 2222
Out Skerries 205 HU 6871
Out Stack 205 HP 6120
Outwell, Cambs T 131 TF 5103
Outwell, Norf T 131 TF 5103
Outwood, Surrey T 97 TQ 3245
Outwood, W. Yks T 147 SE 3323
Ovenden T 146 SE 0827
Over, Avon T 101 ST 5882
Over, Cambs T 121 TL 3770
Overbister T 201 HY 6940
Overbury T 118 SO 9537
Overcombe T 93 SY 6982
Over Haddon T 138 SK 2066
Over Kellet T 145 SD 5269
Over Kiddington T 115 SP 4122
Over Norton T 115 SP 3128
Overseal T 128 SK 2915
Over Silton T 153 SE 4593
Overstone T 119 SP 8066
Overstrand T 133 TG 2440
Overton, Clwyd T 126 SJ 3741
Overton, D. & G T 156 NX 9864
Overton, Grampn T 185 NJ 8714
Overton, Hants T 103 SU 5149
Overton, Lancs T 145 SD 4358
Overton, Shrops T 116 SO 5072
Overtown T 163 NS 8052
Over Wallop T 102 SU 2838
Over Water W 150 NY 2535
Over Whitacre T 118 SP 2591
Oving, Bucks T 104 SP 7821
Oving, W. Susx T 95 SU 9005
Ovingdean T 97 TQ 3503
Ovingham T 159 NZ 0863
Ovington, Durham T 152 NZ 1314
Ovington, Essex T 122 TL 7642
Ovington, Hants T 95 SU 5631
Ovington, Norf T 132 TF 9202
Ovington, Northum T 159 NZ 0663
Ower T 94 SU 3216
Owermoigne T 93 SY 7685
Owlswick T 104 SP 7906
Owmby-by-Spital T 140 TF 0087
Owslebury T 95 SU 5123
Owston T 129 SK 7707
Owston Ferry T 142 SE 8000
Owstwick T 143 TA 2732
Owthorpe T 129 SK 6733
Oxborough T 132 TF 7401
Oxcars 171 NT 2081
Oxenfoord Castle 164 NT 3865
Oxenholme T 151 SD 5289
Oxenhope T 146 SE 0335
Oxen Park T 145 SD 3187
Oxenton T 114 SO 9531
Oxenwood T 102 SU 3059
Oxford P 115 SP 5106
Oxford Canal W 119 SP 4837
Ox Hill, D. & G H 156 NS 7200
Oxhill, Warw T 118 SP 3145
Oxley T 127 SJ 9102
Oxley's Green T 97 TQ 6921
Oxna 203 HU 3537
Oxnam T 158 NT 6918
Oxnam Water W 158 NT 7216
Oxshott T 105 TQ 1460
Oxspring T 139 SE 2602
Oxted T 97 TQ 3952
Oxton, Border T 164 NT 4953
Oxton, Notts T 129 SK 6351
Oxwich T 108 SS 4986
Oxwich Bay W 108 SS 5286
Oxwick T 132 TF 9124
Oykel Bridge T 191 NC 3800
Oyne T 184 NJ 6725

P

Pabay 180 NG 6727
Pabay Mòr 195 NB 1038
Pabbay, W. Isles 188 NF 8988
Pabbay, W. Isles 178 NL 6087
Packington T 128 SK 3614
Padanaram T 176 NO 4251
Padbury T 119 SP 7230
Paddaburn Moor 158 NY 6578
Paddington T 105 TQ 2482
Paddington Station 105 TQ 2681
Paddlesworth T 99 TR 1939
Paddockhaugh T 184 NJ 2058
Paddock Wood T 97 TQ 6745
Paddolgreen T 127 SJ 5032
Padeswood T 136 SJ 2762
Padiham T 146 SD 8033
Padon Hill H 158 NY 8192
Padstow T 87 SW 9175
Padstow Bay W 87 SW 9179
Pagham T 95 SZ 8897
Pagie Hill H 163 NS 8428
Paglesham Churchend T 106 TQ 9293
Paglesham Eastend T 106 TQ 9492
Paible, W. Isles T 188 NF 7367
Paible, W. Isles T 188 NG 0399
Paignton T 89 SX 8960
Pailton T 119 SP 4781
Painscastle T 113 SO 1646
Painshawfield T 159 NZ 0660
Painswick T 114 SO 8609
Pairc or Park 195 NB 3212
Paisley P 161 NS 4864
Pakefield T 123 TM 5390
Pakenham T 122 TL 9267
Pale T 135 SH 9836
Palestine T 102 SU 2640
Paley Street T 104 SU 8676
Palgowan 154 NX 3783
Palgrave T 123 TM 1178
Pallinsburn House 165 NT 8939
Palmaddie Hill H 154 NX 3291
Palmerstown T 109 ST 1369
Palnackie T 155 NX 8256
Palnure T 155 NX 4563
Palnure Burn W 155 NX 4768
Palterton T 139 SK 4768
Pamber End T 104 SU 6158
Pamber Green T 103 SU 6059
Pamber Heath T 104 SU 6162
Pamphill T 94 ST 9900
Pampisford T 121 TL 4948
Pan 200 ND 3794
Panbride T 171 NO 5635
Pancrasweek T 90 SS 2905
Pandy, Clwyd T 126 SJ 1935
Pandy, Gwent T 113 SO 3322
Pandy, Powys T 125 SH 9004
Pandy Tudur T 135 SH 8564
Panfield T 122 TL 7325
Pangbourne T 104 SU 6376
Pan Hope W 200 ND 3794
Pannal T 147 SE 3051
Pannanich Hill H 176 NO 3994
Panorama Walk 125 SH 6216
Pant T 126 SJ 2722
Panteg T 110 SM 9234
Pant-glas, Gwyn T 134 SH 4747
Pant-glâs, Powys 125 SN 7798
Pantglas Hall 111 SN 5525
Pantgwyn T 111 SN 2446
Pant Mawr T 125 SN 8582
Panton T 141 TF 1778
Pant-pastynog T 135 SJ 0461
Pantperthog T 125 SH 7404
Pant Sychbant 109 SN 9909
Pant-y-dwr T 125 SN 9875
Pant-y-ffridd T 126 SJ 1502
Pantyffynnon T 111 SN 6210
Panxworth T 133 TG 3112
Papa 203 HU 3637
Papa Little 203 HU 3360
Papa Sound W 200 HY 4752
Papa Stour 202 HU 1760
Papa Stronsay 201 HY 6629
Papa Westray 200 HY 4952
Papa Westray Airport 200 HY 4852
Papcastle T 150 NY 1131
Papil Ness 205 HP 5404
Papley T 200 ND 4691
Pap of Glencoe H 174 NN 1259
Papple T 171 NT 5972
Papplewick T 129 SK 5451
Paps of Jura H 166 NR 4974
Papworth Everard T 121 TL 2863
Papworth St Agnes T 121 TL 2664
Par T 87 SX 0753
Parbold T 137 SD 4911
Parbrook T 93 ST 5636
Parcllyn T 111 SN 2451
Parc Seymour T 100 ST 4091
Pardshaw T 150 NY 0924
Parham T 123 TM 3060
Parham House A 96 TQ 0614
Park 174 NM 9340
Park Corner T 104 SU 6988
Parkend, Glos T 113 SO 6108
Park End, Northum T 158 NY 8775
Parkeston T 123 TM 2332
Parkgate, Ches T 136 SJ 2878
Parkgate, Ches T 137 SJ 7874
Parkgate, D. & G T 156 NY 0288
Park Gate, Hants T 95 SU 5208
Parkgate, Surrey T 96 TQ 2044
Parkham T 90 SS 3821
Parkham Ash T 90 SS 3620
Park Head 87 SW 8470
Parkhill House 185 NJ 8914
Parkhouse T 113 SO 5003
Parkhurst T 95 SZ 4991
Parkhurst Forest F 95 SZ 4790
Parkmill T 108 SS 5589
Park or Pairc 195 NB 3212
Parkstone T 94 SZ 0391
Parley Common 94 SZ 0999
Parley Cross T 94 SZ 0897
Parracombe T 91 SS 6644
Parrog T 110 SN 0439
Parson Cross T 139 SK 3592
Parson Drove T 131 TF 3708
Partick T 161 NS 5467
Partington T 137 SJ 7191
Partney T 141 TF 4168
Parton, Cumbr T 150 NX 9720
Parton, D. & G T 156 NX 6970
Partridge Green T 96 TQ 1919
Parwich T 128 SK 1854
Parys Mountain H 134 SH 4490
Passenham T 119 SP 7939
Pass of Brander 168 NN 0527
Pass of Drumochter, Highld 175 NN 6376
Pass of Drumochter, Tays 175 NN 6376
Pass of Killiecrankie 175 NN 9162
Pass of Leny 169 NN 5908
Pass of Llanberis 135 SH 6356
Pass of Melfort 173 NM 8415
Paston T 133 TG 3234
Patcham T 97 TQ 3008
Patching T 96 TQ 0806
Patchole T 91 SS 6142
Patchway T 101 ST 6081
Pateley Bridge T 146 SE 1565
Pateley Moor 146 SE 1967
Pathfinder Village T 89 SX 8493
Pathhead, Fife T 171 NT 2892
Pathhead, Lothn T 164 NT 3964
Pathhead, Strath T 156 NS 6114
Path of Condie 170 NO 0711
Patmore Heath T 121 TL 4425
Patna T 161 NS 4110
Patney T 102 SU 0758
Patrick T 144 SC 2482
Patrick Brompton T 152 SE 2290
Patrington T 143 TA 3122
Patrixbourne T 99 TR 1855
Patshull Hall 127 SJ 8001
Patterdale T 151 NY 3915
Patterton Station 161 NS 5357
Pattingham T 127 SO 8299
Pattishall T 119 SP 6754
Patton Bridge T 151 SD 5597
Paul T 86 SW 4627
Paulerspury T 119 SP 7245
Paull T 143 TA 1626
Paull Holme Sands 143 TA 1823
Paulton T 101 ST 6556
Pauperhaugh 159 NZ 1099
Pavenham T 120 SP 8955
Pawlaw Pike H 152 NZ 0032
Pawston T 165 NT 8532
Paxford T 118 SP 1837
Paxhill Park 97 TQ 3526
Paxton T 165 NT 9352
Payhembury T 92 ST 0801
Paythorne T 146 SD 8352
Pcaston T 164 NT 4265
Peacehaven T 97 TQ 4101
Peak Dale T 138 SK 0976
Peak Forest T 138 SK 1179
Peakirk T 130 TF 1606
Peanmeanach T 180 NM 7180
Pearsie 176 NO 3659
Peasedown St John T 101 ST 7057
Peasemore T 103 SU 4577
Peasenhall T 123 TM 3569
Peaslake T 96 TQ 0844
Peasmarsh T 98 TQ 8823
Peaston Bank T 164 NT 4466
Peathill, Grampn T 185 NJ 9366
Peat Hill, Tays H 177 NO 5067
Peat Inn 171 NO 4509
Peatling Magna T 119 SP 5992
Peatling Parva T 119 SP 5989
Peaton T 116 SO 5385
Pebmarsh T 122 TL 8533
Pebworth T 118 SP 1346
Pecket Well T 146 SD 9929
Peckforton T 127 SJ 5356
Peckleton T 129 SK 4701
Peddars Way R 132 TF 7724
Pedmore T 117 SO 9182
Pedwell T 93 ST 4236
Peebles P 163 NT 2540
Peel T 144 SC 2484
Peel Fell, Border H 158 NY 6299
Peel Fell, Northum H 158 NY 6299
Peffer Burn W 171 NT 5980
Pegal Burn W 200 ND 2797
Pegswood T 159 NZ 2287
Pegwell Bay W 99 TR 3563
Peil Bar 144 SD 2361
Peinchorran T 187 NG 5233
Peinlich T 187 NG 4158
Pelaw T 159 NZ 2962
Pelcomb Cross T 110 SM 9218
Peldon T 107 TL 9816
Pelsall T 128 SK 0203
Pelton T 152 NZ 2553
Peluth T 150 NY 1249
Pelynt T 87 SX 2055
Pembrey T 108 SN 4201
Pembrey Forest F 108 SN 3802
Pembridge T 113 SO 3958
Pembroke T 110 SM 9801
Pembroke Dock T 110 SM 9603
Pembury T 97 TQ 6241
Penallt T 113 SO 5209
Pen Allt-mawr H 109 SO 2024
Penally T 110 SS 1199
Penare T 87 SW 9940
Penarth T 109 ST 1871
Pen-bont Rhydybeddau T 125 SN 6883
Pen Brush 110 SM 8839
Penbryn T 111 SN 2952
Penbwchdy 110 SM 8737
Pencader T 111 SN 4436
Pen Caer 110 SM 9140
Pencaitland T 164 NT 4468
Pencarreg T 111 SN 5345
Pencarreg-gopa H 125 SN 7294
Pencarrow Head 87 SX 1550
Pencelli T 109 SO 0925
Pen Cerrig-calch H 109 SO 2122
Pen-Clawdd T 108 SS 5495
Penclegyr, Dyfed 110 SM 7629
Pencleygr, Dyfed 110 SM 8032
Pencoed, M. Glam T 109 SS 9581
Pen Coed, Powys H 125 SH 9809
Pencombe T 113 SO 6052
Pencoyd T 113 SO 5126
Pencraig, H. & W T 113 SO 5621
Pencraig, Powys T 125 SJ 0427
Pendeen T 86 SW 3734
Pendeen Watch 86 SW 3735
Pendennis Point 87 SW 8231
Penderry Hill H 154 NX 0675
Penderyn T 109 SN 9408
Penderyn Reservoir W 109 SN 9407
Pen Dinas A 124 SN 5880
Pendine T 111 SN 2308
Pendine Sands 110 SN 0727
Pendlebury T 137 SD 7801
Pendle Hill H 146 SD 7941
Pendleton T 146 SD 7639
Pendock T 114 SO 7832
Pendoggett T 87 SX 0279
Pendoylan T 109 ST 0676
Penegoes T 125 SH 7701
Penffordd T 110 SN 0722
Penffridd T 134 SH 5057
Penge T 105 TQ 3570
Pengorffwysfa T 134 SH 4692
Pengwern 135 SJ 0276
Pen Gwyllt Meirch H 113 SO 2525
Penhale Point 86 SW 7559
Penhale Sands 86 SW 7656
Penhalurick T 86 SW 7037
Penhill H 146 SE 0486
Penhow T 101 ST 4290
Penhurst T 97 TQ 6916
Peniarth 124 SH 6105
Penicuik T 163 NT 2360
Peniel T 135 SJ 0363
Peniel Heugh H 164 NT 6526
Penifiler T 187 NG 4841
Peninver T 160 NR 7524
Penisa'r Waun T 134 SH 5564
Penistone T 139 SE 2403
Penketh T 137 SJ 5687
Penkill 154 NX 2398
Penkiln Burn W 155 NX 4368
Penkridge T 127 SJ 9213
Penlee Point 88 SX 4449
Penley T 126 SJ 4140
Penllechwen 110 SM 7429
Penllergaer T 108 SS 6198
Pen Llithrig-y-wrâch H 135 SH 7162
Pen-llyn, Gwyn T 134 SH 3582
Penllyn, S. Glam T 109 SS 9776
Penmachno T 135 SH 7950
Penmaen, Gwent T 109 ST 1897
Penmaen, W. Glam T 108 SS 5388
Penmaenmawr T 135 SH 7176
Penmaenpool T 125 SH 6918
Penmaen Swatch W 135 SH 6577
Penmark T 109 ST 0568
Pen Milan H 109 SN 9923
Penmon T 135 SH 6380
Penmorfa T 134 SH 5440
Penmynydd T 134 SH 5174
Penn T 104 SU 9193
Pennal T 125 SH 7000
Pennan T 185 NJ 8465
Pennan Head 185 NJ 8565
Pennant, Dyfed T 124 SN 5163
Pennant, Powys T 125 SN 8797
Pennant-Melangell T 125 SJ 0226
Pennard T 108 SS 5688
Pennerley T 126 SO 3599
Pennines, The H 146 SE 0077
Pennington T 144 SD 2677
Pennjerick T 86 SW 7730
Penn Street T 104 SU 9295
Penny Bridge T 145 SD 3083
Pennycross T 173 NM 5026
Pennygown 173 NM 5942
Pennymoor T 91 SS 8611
Penparc T 111 SN 2148
Penparcau T 124 SN 5980
Penperlleni T 113 SO 3204
Penpillick T 87 SX 0756
Penpol T 87 SW 8139
Penpoll T 87 SX 1454
Penpont T 156 NX 8494
Pen Pumlumon-Arwystli H 125 SN 8187
Penrherber T 111 SN 2939
Penrhiwceiber T 109 ST 0598
Pen Rhiwclochdy H 112 SN 7552
Penrhiw-llan T 111 SN 3742
Penrhiwpal T 111 SN 3445
Penrhos, Gwent T 113 SO 4111
Penrhos, Gwyn T 134 SH 2781
Penrhos, Gwyn T 134 SH 3433
Penrhos, Powys T 109 SN 8011
Penrhyn Bay T 135 SH 8281
Penrhyn Castle A 134 SH 6072
Penrhyn-coch T 125 SN 6484
Penrhyn Colmon 134 SH 1934
Penrhyndeudraeth T 134 SH 6139
Penrhyn-gwyr or Worms Head 108 SS 3887
Penrhyn Mawr, Gwyn 134 SH 1632
Penrhyn Mawr, Gwyn 134 SH 2179
Penrhyn-side T 135 SH 8181
Penrice T 108 SS 4988
Penrith T 151 NY 5130
Penrose T 87 SW 8770
Penruddock T 151 NY 4227
Penryn T 87 SW 7834
Pensarn, Clwyd T 135 SH 9578
Pen-sarn, Gwyn T 134 SH 4344
Pen-sarn, Gwyn T 124 SH 5828
Pensax T 117 SO 7269
Pensby T 136 SJ 2683
Penselwood T 93 ST 7531
Pensford T 101 ST 6263
Penshaw T 152 NZ 3253
Penshurst T 97 TQ 5243
Penshurst Place A 97 TQ 5244
Penshurst Station 97 TQ 5146
Pensilva T 88 SX 2969
Pentewan T 87 SX 0147
Pentir T 134 SH 5767
Pentire T 87 SW 7961
Pentire Point 87 SW 9280
Pentland Firth W 199 ND 3082
Pentland Hills, Border H 163 NT 1358
Pentland Hills, Lothn H 163 NT 1358
Pentland Hills, Strath H 163 NT 1358
Pentland Skerries 199 ND 4777
Pentney T 132 TF 7213
Penton Mewsey T 102 SU 3347
Pentraeth T 134 SH 5278
Pentre, Clwyd T 135 SJ 0862
Pentre, Clwyd T 126 SJ 1334
Pentre, Clwyd T 126 SJ 2940
Pentre, Powys T 125 SO 0686
Pentre, Shrops T 126 SJ 3617
Pentre-bâch, Dyfed T 111 SN 5547
Pentrebach, M. Glam T 109 SO 0604
Pentre-bach, Powys T 109 SN 9133
Pentre Berw T 134 SH 4772
Pentre-bont T 135 SH 7352
Pentre-celyn, Clwyd T 126 SJ 1553
Pentre-celyn, Powys 125 SH 8905
Pentre-cwrt T 111 SN 3838
Pentre Dolau Honddu T 112 SN 9943
Pentredwr, Clwyd T 126 SJ 1946
Pentre-dwr, W. Glam T 108 SS 6996
Pentrefelin, Gwyn T 134 SH 5239
Pentrefelin, Gwyn T 135 SH 8074
Pentrefoelas T 135 SH 8751
Pentregat T 111 SN 3552
Pentre-Gwenlais T 111 SN 6116
Pentre Halkyn T 136 SJ 2072
Pentre-llyn-cymmer T 135 SJ 9752
Pentre'r beirdd T 126 SJ 1914
Pentre'r-felin T 109 SN 9230
Pentre-tafarn-y-fedw T 135 SH 8162
Pentre-ty-gwyn T 109 SN 8135
Pentrich T 128 SK 3852
Pentridge T 94 SU 0317
Pentridge Hill H 94 SU 0417
Pen Trum-gwr H 125 SH 6503
Pentwyn T 109 ST 2081
Pentwyn Reservoir W 109 SO 0515
Pentyrch T 109 ST 1082
Penuwch T 124 SN 5962
Penwhapple Reservoir W 154 NX 2697
Penwhirn Reservoir W 154 NX 1269
Penwithick T 87 SX 0256
Penybanc T 111 SN 6124
Pen y Bedw H 135 SH 7847
Pen-y-bont, Clwyd T 126 SJ 2123
Pen-y-bont, Dyfed T 111 SN 3027
Penybont, Powys T 116 SO 1164
Penybontfawr T 125 SJ 0824
Pen-y-bryn, Gwyn T 125 SH 6919
Penybryn, M. Glam T 109 ST 1396
Pen-y-bwlch H 125 SN 7863
Penycae, Clwyd T 126 SJ 2845
Pen-y-cae, Powys T 109 SN 8413
Pen-y-cae-mawr T 113 ST 4196
Pen-y-cefn T 136 SJ 1175
Pen-ychain 134 SH 4335
Pen y Cil 124 SH 1524
Pen-y-clawdd T 113 SO 4507
Penycloddiau A 136 SJ 1267
Pen-y-coedcae T 109 ST 0687
Pen-y-crug A 109 SO 0330
Penycwm T 110 SM 8523
Penyffordd T 136 SJ 3061
Pen y Ffrid Gownwy H 125 SH 9717
Pen-y-garn T 111 SN 5731
Pen-y-garnedd, Gwyn T 134 SH 5376
Penygarnedd, Powys T 125 SJ 1023
Penygarreg Reservoir W 125 SN 9067
Pen-y-ghent H 146 SD 8473
Pen y Gogarth or Great Ormes Head 135 SH 7584
Penygraig T 109 SS 9991
Pen-y-groes, Dyfed T 111 SN 5813
Penygroes, Gwyn T 134 SH 4753
Pen y Gurnos H 112 SN 7751
Pen y Manllwyn H 109 SO 2031
Penysarn T 134 SH 4690
Pen-y-stryt T 126 SJ 1951
Penywaun T 109 SN 9704
Penzance P 86 SW 4730
Peopleton T 117 SO 9350
Peover Heath T 137 SJ 7973
Peper Harow T 96 SU 9344
Peplow T 127 SJ 6324
Percie T 177 NO 5992
Percyhorner T 185 NJ 9665
Perivale T 105 TQ 1682
Perlethorpe T 139 SK 6571
Perranarworthal T 86 SW 7738
Perran or Ligger Bay W 86 SW 7256
Perranporth T 86 SW 7554
Perranuthnoe T 86 SW 5329
Perranzabuloe T 86 SW 7752
Perry Barr T 118 SP 0692
Perry Green T 105 TL 4317
Pershore T 117 SO 9446
Pert T 177 NO 6565
Pertenhall T 120 TL 0865
Perth P 170 NO 1123
Perthy T 126 SJ 3633
Perton T 127 SO 8598
Peter Black Sand 132 TF 6231
Peterborough P 130 TL 1998
Peterburn T 190 NG 7483
Peterchurch T 113 SO 3438
Peterculter T 177 NJ 8401
Peterhead P 185 NK 1346
Peterhead Bay W 185 NK 1345
Peter Hill H 177 NO 5788
Peterlee T 153 NZ 4240
Petersfield P 95 SU 7423
Peter's Green T 105 TL 1419
Peter's Hill H 176 NJ 3600
Peters Marland T 90 SS 4713
Peterstone Wentlooge T 100 ST 2680
Peterston-super-Ely T 109 ST 0876
Peterstow T 113 SO 5624
Peter Tavy T 88 SX 5177
Petertown T 200 HY 3004
Petham T 99 TR 1251
Petrockstowe T 90 SS 5109
Pett T 98 TQ 8714
Pettaugh T 123 TM 1659
Pettinain T 163 NS 9542
Pettistree T 123 TM 2954
Petton, Devon T 91 ST 0024
Petton, Shrops T 126 SJ 4326
Petty T 185 NJ 7636
Pettycur T 171 NT 2686
Pettymuick T 185 NJ 9024
Petworth T 96 SU 9721
Petworth House A 96 SU 9721
Pevensey Bay, E. Susx T 97 TQ 6504
Pevensey Bay, E. Susx W 97 TQ 6603
Pevensey Levels 97 TQ 6307
Peveril Castle A 138 SK 1482
Peveril Point 94 SZ 0478
Pewsey T 102 SU 1660
Pewsey Down H 102 SU 1757
Philham T 90 SS 2522
Philiphaugh T 164 NT 4427
Philip Law H 158 NT 7210
Phillack T 86 SW 5638
Philleigh T 87 SW 8739
Philpstoun T 170 NT 0476
Phoenix Green T 103 SU 7555
Pibble Hill H 155 NX 5360
Pica T 150 NY 0222
Picardy Stone A 184 NJ 6130
Piccotts End T 104 TL 0509
Pickering T 148 SE 7984
Picket Piece T 102 SU 3947
Picket Post 94 SU 1906
Pickhill T 147 SE 3483
Picklescott T 126 SO 4399
Pocklington Canal W 142 SE 7445
Pickmere T 137 SJ 6977
Pickwell, Devon T 90 SS 4540
Pickwell, Leic T 129 SK 7811
Pickworth, Leic T 130 SK 9913
Pickworth, Lincs T 130 TF 0433
Picton, Ches T 136 SJ 4371
Picton, N. Yks T 153 NZ 4107

Purton River Arun

Purton, Wilts *T* 102 SU 0987
Purton Stoke *T* 102 SU 0990
Pury End *T* 119 SP 7045
Pusey *T* 115 SU 3596
Putley *T* 117 SO 6437
Putney *T* 105 TQ 2274
Puttenham, Herts *T* 104 SP 8814
Puttenham, Surrey *T* 96 SU 9348
Puxton *T* 100 ST 4063
Pwll *T* 108 SN 4700
Pwllcrochan *T* 110 SM 9202
Pwlldu Head 108 SS 5786
Pwllheli *T* 134 SH 3735
Pwllmeyric *T* 101 ST 5292
Pwll-y-glaw *T* 109 SS 7993
Pwllygranant 110 SN 1247
Pyecombe *T* 97 TQ 2813
Pye Corner *T* 100 ST 3485
Pykestone Hill *H* 163 NT 1731
Pyle, I. of W *T* 95 SZ 4778
Pyle, M. Glam *T* 109 SS 8282
Pylle *T* 101 ST 6038
Pymore *T* 121 TL 4986
Pyrford *T* 104 TQ 0359
Pyrton *T* 104 SU 6895
Pytchley *T* 120 SP 8574
Pyworthy *T* 90 SS 3103

Q

Quabbs *T* 116 SO 2180
Quadring *T* 131 TF 2233
Quainton *T* 104 SP 7420
Quandale 200 HY 3732
Quanter Ness 200 HY 4114
Quantock Hills *H* 92 ST 1537
Quarley *T* 102 SU 2743
Quarndon *T* 128 SK 3341
Quarrier's Homes *T* 161 NS 3666
Quarrington *T* 130 TF 0544
Quarrington Hill *T* 152 NZ 3337
Quarrybank, Ches *T* 137 SJ 5465
Quarry Bank, W. Mids *T* 117 SO 9386
Quarry Head 185 NJ 9066
Quarryhill 193 NH 7481
Quarry, The *T* 114 ST 7399
Quarrywood *T* 184 NJ 1864
Quarter *T* 162 NS 7251
Quarter Fell *H* 154 NX 2070
Quatford *T* 117 SO 7490
Quatt *T* 117 SO 7588
Quebec *T* 152 NZ 1743
Quedgeley *T* 114 SO 8013
Queen Adelaide *T* 121 TL 5681
Queenborough *T* 98 TQ 9172
Queen Camel *T* 93 ST 5924
Queen Charlton *T* 101 ST 6367
Queensberry *H* 156 NX 9899
Queensbury *T* 146 SE 1030
Queen's Carn *H* 192 NH 4672
Queensferry, Clwyd *P* 136 SJ 3168
Queensferry, Lothn *T* 170 NT 1378
Queen's Forest, The *F* 183 NH 9710
Queen's Ground 132 TL 6893
Queenside Muir 161 NS 2864
Queen's View 175 NN 8659
Queenzieburn *T* 169 NS 6977
Quenby Hall *A* 129 SK 7006
Quendale *T* 203 HU 3713
Quendon *T* 121 TL 5130
Queniborough *T* 129 SK 6412
Quenington *T* 115 SP 1404
Quernmore *T* 145 SD 5160
Quethiock *T* 88 SX 3164
Quey Firth *W* 204 HU 3682
Quholm *T* 200 HY 2412
Quidenham *T* 122 TM 0287
Quidhampton, Hants *T* 103 SU 5150
Quidhampton, Wilts *T* 94 SU 1130
Quidnish *T* 189 NG 0987
Quien Hill *H* 160 NS 0559
Quies 87 SW 8376
Quilquox *T* 185 NJ 9038
Quilva Taing 202 HU 1757
Quinag *H* 196 NC 2028
Quindry *T* 200 ND 4392
Quine's Hill *T* 144 SC 3473
Quinish, Strath 173 NM 4254
Quinish, W. Isles 188 NF 8886
Quinish Point 172 NM 4057
Quintin Knowe *H* 156 NS 6507
Quinton *T* 119 SP 7754
Quoditch *T* 88 SX 4097
Quoig 169 NN 8222
Quorndon or Quorn *T* 129 SK 5616
Quorn or Quorndon *T* 129 SK 5616
Quothquan *T* 163 NS 9939
Quoyloo *T* 200 HY 2420
Quoy Ness 201 HY 6236
Quoys *T* 205 HP 6112

R

Raasay House 187 NG 5436
Rabbit Islands 197 NC 6063
Raby *T* 136 SJ 3180
Raby Castle *A* 152 NZ 1221
Rachub *T* 135 SH 6268
Rackenford *T* 91 SS 8518
Rackham *T* 96 TQ 0513
Rackheath *T* 133 TG 2715
Racks *T* 157 NY 0374
Rackwick, Orkney *T* 200 HY 4449
Rack Wick, Orkney *W* 200 HY 4450
Rack Wick, Orkney *W* 200 HY 5042
Rack Wick, Orkney *W* 200 ND 2098
Rackwick, Orkney *T* 200 ND 2099
Radcliffe, G. Man *T* 137 SD 7807
Radcliffe, Northum *T* 159 NU 2602
Radcliffe on Trent *T* 129 SK 6439
Radclive *T* 119 SP 6733
Radcot *T* 115 SU 2899
Raddery *T* 183 NH 7159
Radernie *T* 171 NO 4609
Radford Semele *T* 118 SP 3464
Radlett *T* 105 TQ 1699
Radley *T* 115 SU 5299
Radnage *T* 104 SU 7897
Radnor Forest *F* 116 SO 2064
Radstock *T* 101 ST 6854
Radstone *T* 119 SP 5840
Radway *T* 118 SP 3748
Radway Green *T* 127 SJ 7754
Radwell *T* 121 TL 2335
Radwinter *T* 122 TL 6037
Radyr *T* 109 ST 1080
Raera 173 NM 8320
Raerinish Point 195 NB 4324
Raes Knowes *H* 157 NY 2983
Rafford *T* 183 NJ 0656
Ragdale *T* 129 SK 6619
Raglan *T* 113 SO 4107
Ragnall *T* 140 SK 8073
Rainberg Mór *H* 166 NR 5687
Rainford *T* 137 SD 4801
Rainham, G. Lon *T* 105 TQ 5282
Rainham, Kent *T* 98 TQ 8165
Rainhill *T* 137 SJ 4991
Rainow *T* 138 SJ 9576
Rainton *T* 147 SE 3775
Rainworth *T* 139 SK 5958
Raisbeck *T* 151 NY 6407
Rait *T* 171 NO 2226
Raithby, Lincs *T* 141 TF 3184
Raithby, Lincs *T* 141 TF 3767
Raitts Burn *W* 183 NH 7704
Rake *T* 95 SU 8027
Rake Law *H* 156 NS 8717
Ralfland Forest *F* 151 NY 5413
Ramasaig 186 NG 1644
Rame, Corn *T* 86 SW 7233
Rame, Corn *T* 88 SX 4249
Rame Head 88 SX 4148
Ram Lane *T* 99 TQ 9646
Ramna Stacks 205 HU 3797
Rampisham *T* 93 ST 5602
Rampside *T* 144 SD 2466
Rampton, Cambs *T* 121 TL 4268
Rampton, Notts *T* 140 SK 7978
Ramsbottom *T* 137 SD 7816
Ramsbury *T* 102 SU 2771
Ramscraigs *T* 199 ND 1427
Ramsdean *T* 95 SU 7022
Ramsdell *T* 103 SU 5857
Ramsden *T* 115 SP 3515
Ramsden Bellhouse *T* 106 TQ 7194
Ramsden Heath *T* 106 TQ 7195
Ramsey, Cambs *T* 121 TL 2885
Ramsey, Essex *T* 123 TM 2130
Ramsey, I. of M *T* 144 SC 4594
Ramsey Bay *W* 144 SC 4695
Ramseycleuch *T* 157 NT 2714
Ramsey Forty Foot *T* 121 TL 3087
Ramsey Hollow 121 TL 3286
Ramsey Island, Dyfed 110 SM 7023
Ramsey Island, Essex *T* 106 TL 9505
Ramsey Knowe *H* 157 NT 2516
Ramsey Mereside *T* 121 TL 2889
Ramsey Sound *W* 110 SM 7124
Ramsey St Mary's *T* 121 TL 2588
Ramsgate *P* 99 TR 3765
Ramsgill *T* 146 SE 1171
Ramshorn *T* 128 SK 0845
Rams Ne 205 HU 6087
Ranachan Hill *H* 160 NR 6825
Ranby *T* 139 SK 6581
Rand *T* 141 TF 1078
Randwick *T* 114 SO 8306
Ranfurly *T* 168 NS 3569
Rangemore *T* 128 SK 1823
Rangeworthy *T* 101 ST 6986
Ranish *T* 195 NB 4024
Rankinston *T* 161 NS 4514
Rannoch Forest 175 NN 4565
Rannoch Moor, Highld 174 NN 3852
Rannoch Moor, Tays 174 NN 3852
Rannoch River *W* 173 NM 7147
Rannoch Station 174 NN 4257
Ranskill *T* 139 SK 6587
Ranson Moor 131 TG 3993
Ranton *T* 127 SJ 8524
Ranworth *T* 133 TG 3514
Rapness *T* 200 HY 5141
Rapness Sound *W* 200 HY 5138
Rappach 191 NC 2401
Rappach Water *W* 191 NH 2998
Rascarrel *T* 155 NX 7948
Rascarrel Bay *W* 155 NX 8148
Raskelf *T* 147 SE 4971
Rassau *T* 109 SO 1512
Rastrick *T* 146 SE 1321
Ratae *R* 129 SK 5804
Ratagan *T* 180 NG 9119
Ratagan Forest *F* 180 NG 9020
Ratby *T* 129 SK 5105
Ratcliffe Culey *T* 128 SP 3299
Ratcliffe on the Wreake *T* 129 SK 6314
Rathen *T* 185 NK 0060
Rathillet *T* 171 NO 3620
Rathmell *T* 146 SD 8059
Ratho *T* 170 NT 1370
Ratho Station *T* 170 NT 1372
Rathven *T* 184 NJ 4465
Rat Island 90 SS 1443
Ratley *T* 118 SP 3847
Ratlinghope *T* 126 SO 4097
Rattar *T* 199 ND 2673
Ratten Row *T* 145 SD 4241
Rattery *T* 89 SX 7461
Rattlesden *T* 122 TL 9759
Rattray *T* 176 NO 1845
Rattray Head 185 NK 1058
Rauceby *T* 130 TF 0245
Rauceby Station *T* 130 TF 0344
Raughton Head *T* 151 NY 3845
Raunds *T* 120 SP 9972
Ravenfield *T* 139 SK 4895
Ravenglass *T* 150 SD 0896
Raveningham *T* 133 TM 3996
Ravenscar *T* 149 NZ 9801
Ravensdale *T* 144 SC 3591
Ravensden *T* 120 TL 0754
Ravenseat *T* 152 NY 8603
Ravenshall Point 155 NX 5252
Ravenshead *T* 129 SK 5654
Ravens Knowe *H* 158 NT 7806
Ravensmoor *T* 127 SJ 6250
Ravensthorpe, Northnts *T* 119 SP 6670
Ravensthorpe, W. Yks *T* 139 SE 2220
Ravensthorpe Reservoir *W* 119 SP 6770
Ravenstone *T* 120 SP 8550
Ravenstonedale *T* 151 NY 7204
Ravenstonedale Common 151 NY 6900
Ravenstown *T* 145 SD 3675
Ravenstruther *T* 163 NS 9245
Ravensworth *T* 152 NZ 1407
Raw *T* 149 NZ 9405
Rawcliffe, Humbs *T* 142 SE 6822
Rawcliffe, N. Yks *T* 147 SE 5855
Rawcliffe Bridge *T* 142 SE 7021
Rawdon *T* 146 SE 2139
Rawmarsh *T* 139 SK 4496
Rawreth *T* 106 TQ 7893
Rawridge *T* 92 ST 2006
Rawtenstall *T* 146 SD 8123
Rayburn Lake *W* 159 NZ 1192
Raydon *T* 122 TM 0538
Raylees *T* 158 NY 9291
Rayleigh *T* 106 TQ 8090
Rayne *T* 106 TL 7222
Ray Sand 107 TM 0400
Rea Brook *W* 117 SO 6586
Reach *T* 121 TL 5666
Read *T* 146 SD 7634
Reading *P* 104 SU 7173
Reading Street *T* 98 TQ 9230
Read's Island 142 SE 9622
Reagill *T* 151 NY 6017
Rearquhar *T* 193 NH 7492
Rearsby *T* 129 SK 6514
Rease Heath *T* 127 SJ 6454
Reaster *T* 199 ND 2565
Reawick *T* 203 HU 3244
Reay *T* 198 NC 9664
Reay Forest 196 NC 2939
Rechullin *T* 190 NG 8557
Reculver *T* 99 TR 2269
Redberth *T* 110 SN 0804
Redbourn *T* 105 TL 1012
Redbourne *T* 142 SE 9700
Redbrook *T* 113 SO 5310
Redburn, Highld 182 NH 5767
Redburn, Highld *T* 183 NH 9447
Redcar *T* 153 NZ 6024
Redcastle, Highld *T* 182 NH 5849
Redcastle, Tays 177 NO 6850
Redcleuch Edge *H* 157 NT 3410
Redcliff Bay *T* 101 ST 4475
Red Dial *T* 150 NY 2546
Redding *T* 170 NS 9278
Reddingmuirhead *T* 170 NS 9177
Reddish *T* 137 SJ 8998
Redditch *P* 118 SP 0467
Red Down 88 SX 2685
Rede *T* 122 TL 8055
Redenhall *T* 123 TM 2684
Redesdale *F* 158 NY 8396
Redesdale Camp *T* 158 NY 8298
Redesdale Forest *F* 158 NT 7501
Redesmouth *T* 158 NY 8682
Redford, Durham *T* 152 NZ 0730
Redford, Tays *T* 177 NO 5644
Redfordgreen *T* 157 NT 3616
Redgrave *T* 122 TM 0477
Red Head, Highld 199 ND 3477
Red Head, Orkney 200 HY 5640
Red Head, Tays 177 NO 7047
Redheugh 176 NO 4463
Redhill, Avon *T* 101 ST 4963
Redhill, Grampn *T* 185 NJ 6836
Redhill, Grampn *T* 185 NJ 7704
Red Hill, Powys *H* 112 SO 1550
Redhill, Surrey *P* 97 TQ 2850
Redhythe Point 184 NJ 5767
Redisham *T* 123 TM 4084
Redland, Avon *T* 101 ST 5875
Redland, Orkney *T* 200 HY 3724
Redlingfield *T* 123 TM 1870
Red Lion Hill *H* 125 SO 0577
Redlynch, Somer *T* 93 ST 7033
Redlynch, Wilts *T* 94 SU 2021
Redmarley D'Abitot *T* 114 SO 7531
Redmarshall *T* 153 NZ 3821
Redmile *T* 129 SK 7935
Redmire *T* 152 SE 0491
Redmire Moor 152 SE 0493
Redmires Reservoirs *W* 139 SK 2685
Redmoor *T* 87 SX 0861
Redmyre Loch *W* 171 NO 2833
Rednal *T* 126 SJ 3628
Red Nev 200 HY 4145
Redpath *T* 164 NT 5835
Red Pike *H* 150 NY 1615
Red Point, Highld 198 NC 9365
Redpoint, Highld *T* 190 NG 7369
Red Rock *T* 137 SD 5809
Red Roses *T* 111 SN 2011
Red Row *T* 159 NZ 2599
Redruth *P* 86 SW 7042
Redshin Cove *W* 165 NU 0150
Red Street *T* 127 SJ 8351
Red Wharf Bay, Gwyn *T* 134 SH 5381
Red Wharf Bay, Gwyn *W* 134 SH 5481
Redwick, Avon *T* 101 ST 5486
Redwick, Gwent *T* 100 ST 4184
Redworth *T* 152 NZ 2423
Reed *T* 121 TL 3636
Reedham *T* 133 TG 4101
Reedness *T* 142 SE 7923
Reed Point 165 NT 7872
Reef *T* 195 NB 1134
Reeker Pike *H* 158 NY 6682
Reepham, Lincs *T* 140 TF 0373
Reepham, Norf *T* 133 TG 1023
Reeth *T* 152 SE 0399
Regaby *T* 144 SC 4397
Regent's Park 105 TQ 2882
Regoul *T* 183 NH 8851
Regulbium *R* 99 TR 2169
Rèidh Eilean 172 NM 2426
Reiff *T* 196 NB 9614
Reigate *P* 96 TQ 2750
Reighton *T* 149 TA 1375
Reighton Sands 149 TA 1476
Rèisa an t-Sruith 167 NR 7399
Rèisa Mhic Phaidean 167 NM 7501
Reisgill Burn *W* 199 ND 2337
Reiss *T* 199 ND 3354
Rejerrah *T* 86 SW 8056
Relubbus *T* 86 SW 5631
Relugas *T* 183 NH 9948
Remenham *T* 104 SU 7784
Remenham Hill *T* 104 SU 7882
Remony 175 NN 7644
Rempstone *T* 129 SK 5724
Remuil Hill *H* 160 NR 6212
Rendall 200 HY 3819
Rendcomb *T* 114 SP 0209
Rendham *T* 123 TM 3564
Rendlesham *T* 123 TM 3253
Rendlesham Forest *F* 123 TM 3449
Renfrew *T* 161 NS 5067
Renhold *T* 120 TL 0852
Renishaw *T* 139 SK 4477
Renish Point 188 NG 0481
Rennington *T* 159 NU 2118
Renton *T* 169 NS 3878
Renwick *T* 151 NY 5943
Repps *T* 133 TG 4117
Repton *T* 128 SK 3027
Rerwick Head 200 HY 5411
Rescobie 177 NO 5052
Resipole 173 NM 7264
Resolis *T* 183 NH 6765
Resolven *T* 109 SN 8302
Rest and be thankful 168 NN 2307
Reston *T* 165 NT 8862
Reswallie 177 NO 5051
Retew *T* 87 SW 9257
Rettendon *T* 106 TQ 7796
Rettendon Place *T* 106 TQ 7796
Revesby *T* 141 TF 2961
Rewe *T* 89 SX 9499
Reydon *T* 123 TM 4977
Reymerston *T* 132 TG 0206
Reynalton *T* 110 SN 0908
Reynoldston *T* 108 SS 4890
Rhadmad *T* 124 SN 5974
Rhaeadr Cynfal *W* 135 SH 7041
Rhandirmwyn *T* 112 SN 7843
Rhayader *P* 125 SN 9768
Rhedyn *T* 134 SH 2932
Rheindown *T* 182 NH 5247
Rhemore 173 NM 5750
Rhenigidale 189 NB 2201
Rhes-y-cae *T* 136 SJ 1971
Rhewl, Clwyd *T* 135 SJ 1060
Rhewl, Clwyd *T* 126 SJ 1844
Rhian 197 NC 5616
Rhicarn 196 NC 0825
Rhiconich *T* 196 NC 2552
Rhicullen *T* 192 NH 6971
Rhidorroch Forest 191 NH 2398
Rhidorroch House 191 NH 1795
Rhidorroch River *W* 191 NH 2194
Rhifail 198 NC 7349
Rhigos *T* 109 SN 9205
Rhilean Burn *W* 183 NH 8937
Rhilochan *T* 193 NC 7407
Rhinns of Islay 166 NR 2157
Rhinns of Kells 155 NX 5083
Rhinns Point 166 NR 1851
Rhinog Fawr *H* 135 SH 6579
Rhins, The 154 NX 0653
Rhiroy *T* 191 NH 1589
Rhiw *T* 124 SH 2228
Rhiwbryfdir *T* 135 SH 6946
Rhiwderin *T* 100 ST 2687
Rhiwlas, Clwyd *T* 126 SJ 1932
Rhiwlas, Gwyn *T* 134 SH 5766
Rhiwlas, Gwyn *T* 135 SH 9237
Rhobell Fawr *H* 125 SH 7825
Rhodesia *T* 139 SK 5680
Rhodes Minnis *T* 99 TR 1542
Rhondda *T* 109 SS 9896
Rhondda Fach 109 ST 0096
Rhondda Fawr 109 SS 9994
Rhonehouse or Kelton Hill *T* 156 NX 7459
Rhoose *T* 109 ST 0666
Rhos, Dyfed *T* 111 SN 3835
Rhos, W. Glam *T* 108 SN 7303
Rhoscefnhir *T* 134 SH 5276
Rhoscolyn *T* 134 SH 2775
Rhoscrowther *T* 110 SM 9002
Rhos Dirion *H* 109 SO 2133
Rhosesmor *T* 136 SJ 2168
Rhos-fawr *T* 134 SH 3839
Rhosgadfan *T* 134 SH 5057
Rhosgoch, Gwyn *T* 134 SH 4189
Rhos-goch, Powys *T* 113 SO 1847
Rhoshirwaun *T* 134 SH 1929
Rhoslan *T* 134 SH 4841
Rhoslefain *T* 124 SH 5705
Rhosllanerchrugog *T* 126 SJ 2946
Rhosmeirch *T* 134 SH 4677
Rhosneigr *T* 134 SH 3273
Rhosnesni *T* 126 SJ 3551
Rhôs-on-Sea *T* 135 SH 8481
Rhossili *T* 108 SS 4188
Rhossili Bay *W* 108 SS 4089
Rhosson *T* 110 SM 7325
Rhostrehwfa *T* 134 SH 4474
Rhostryfan *T* 134 SH 4957
Rhostyllen *T* 126 SJ 3148
Rhosybol *T* 134 SH 4288
Rhos-y-brithdir *T* 126 SJ 1323
Rhos-y-gwaliau *T* 135 SH 9434
Rhos-y-llan *T* 134 SH 2337
Rhos-y-mawn 135 SH 8566
Rhu, Strath 160 NR 8364
Rhu, Strath *T* 168 NS 2684
Rhuallt *T* 135 SJ 0775
Rhuddlan *T* 135 SJ 0278
Rhue *T* 191 NH 0997
Rhulen *T* 112 SO 1349
Rhum 179 NM 3697
Rhunahaorine *T* 160 NR 7048
Rhu Nòa 190 NH 0064
Rhyd, Gwyn *T* 135 SH 6341
Rhyd, Powys *T* 125 SH 9700
Rhydargaeau *T* 111 SN 4326
Rhydcymerau *T* 111 SN 5839
Rhydd *T* 117 SO 8345
Rhyd-Ddu *T* 134 SH 5753
Rhydding *T* 109 SS 7598
Rhŷd-foel *T* 135 SH 9176
Rhydlewis *T* 111 SN 3447
Rhydlios *T* 134 SH 1830
Rhydlydan *T* 135 SH 8950
Rhydowen *T* 111 SN 4445
Rhyd-Rosser *T* 124 SN 5667
Rhydtalog *T* 126 SJ 2355
Rhydwyn *T* 134 SH 3189
Rhyd-y-clafdy *T* 134 SH 3235
Rhydycroesau *T* 126 SJ 2430
Rhydyfelin, Dyfed *T* 124 SN 5979
Rhydyfelin, M. Glam *T* 109 ST 0988
Rhyd-y-fro *T* 108 SN 7105
Rhydymain *T* 125 SH 8022
Rhydymwyn *T* 136 SJ 2066
Rhyd-yr-onen *T* 124 SH 6102
Rhyl *T* 135 SJ 0181
Rhymney *T* 109 SO 1107
Rhymney River, M. Glam *W* 109 ST 1888
Rhymney River, S. Glam *W* 109 ST 2180
Rhymney Valley 109 ST 1592
Rhynd *T* 170 NO 1520
Rhynie, Grampn *T* 184 NJ 4927
Rhynie, Highld 193 NH 8479
Ribbesford *T* 117 SO 7874
Ribble Head *T* 146 SD 7779
Ribblesdale *H* 146 SD 8158
Ribbleton *T* 145 SD 5630
Ribchester *T* 145 SD 6535
Ribigill 197 NC 5854
Riby *T* 143 TA 1807
Riccall *T* 147 SE 6237
Riccarton *T* 161 NS 4235
Richards Castle *T* 116 SO 4969
Richmond, G. Lon *P* 105 TQ 1874
Richmond, N. Yks *T* 152 NZ 1701
Richmond Park 105 TQ 1972
Rickarton *T* 177 NO 8189
Rickets Head 110 SM 8519
Rickinghall *T* 122 TM 0475
Rickling *T* 121 TL 4931
Rickmansworth *T* 104 TQ 0494
Riddell *T* 164 NT 5124
Riddlecombe *T* 91 SS 6113
Riddlesden *T* 146 SE 0842
Ridge, Dorset *T* 94 SY 9386
Ridge, Herts *T* 105 TL 2100
Ridge, Wilts *T* 94 ST 9532
Ridgehill, Avon *T* 101 ST 5362
Ridge Hill, H. & W *H* 113 SO 5035
Ridge Lane *T* 128 SP 2995
Ridge Way, Berks *A* 103 SU 5481
Ridge Way, Oxon *A* 102 SU 3683
Ridge Way, Wilts *A* 102 SU 0151
Ridge Way, Wilts *A* 102 SU 1168
Ridge Way, Wilts *A* 102 SU 1677
Ridgeway Cross *T* 117 SO 7147
Ridgewell *T* 122 TL 7340
Ridgewood *T* 97 TQ 4719
Ridgmont *T* 120 SP 9736
Riding Mill *T* 159 NZ 0161
Ridlees Cairn *H* 158 NT 8404
Ridlington, Leic *T* 130 SK 8402
Ridlington, Norf *T* 133 TG 3430
Ridsdale *T* 158 NY 9084
Riechip 176 NO 0647
Riemore Lodge 176 NO 0449
Rienachait *T* 196 NC 0430
Riereach Burn *W* 183 NH 8445
Rievaulx *T* 147 SE 5785
Rigg *T* 157 NY 2966
Riggend *T* 169 NS 7670
Riggs Moor 146 SE 0373
Rigg, The *H* 158 NY 6483
Rigmaden Park 145 SD 6184
Rig of the Shalloch *H* 154 NX 3891
Rigside *T* 163 NS 8735
Rileyhill *T* 128 SK 1115
Rilla Mill *T* 88 SX 2973
Rillington *T* 148 SE 8574
Rimington *T* 146 SD 8045
Rimpton *T* 93 ST 6021
Rimsdale Burn *W* 198 NC 7440
Rimswell *T* 143 TA 3128
Rinaston *T* 110 SM 9825
Ringasta *T* 203 HU 3714
Ringford *T* 155 NX 6857
Ringland *T* 133 TG 1313
Ringmer *T* 97 TQ 4412
Ringmore *T* 89 SX 6545
Ringorm *T* 184 NJ 2644
Ring's End *T* 131 TF 3902
Ringsfield *T* 123 TM 4088
Ringshall, Herts *T* 104 SP 9814
Ringshall, Suff *T* 122 TM 0452
Ringshall Stocks *T* 122 TM 0551
Ringstead, Norf *T* 132 TF 7040
Ringstead, Northnts *T* 120 SP 9875
Ringstead Bay *W* 93 SY 7581
Ringwood *P* 94 SU 1405
Ringwood Forest *F* 94 SU 1108
Ringwould *T* 99 TR 3648
Rinmore *T* 184 NJ 4117
Rinn Druim Tallig 195 NB 3150
Rinnigill *T* 200 ND 3193
Rinn Thorbhais 172 NL 9340
Rinsey *T* 86 SW 5927
Ripe *T* 97 TQ 5110
Ripley, Derby *T* 128 SK 4050
Ripley, Hants *T* 94 SZ 1698
Ripley, N. Yks *T* 147 SE 2860
Ripley, Surrey *T* 96 TQ 0456
Riplingham *T* 142 SE 9631
Ripon *P* 147 SE 3171
Rippingale *T* 130 TF 0928
Ripple, H. & W *T* 117 SO 8737
Ripple, Kent *T* 99 TR 3450
Ripponden *T* 138 SE 0319
Rippon Tor *H* 89 SX 7475
Rireavach *T* 190 NH 0295
Risabus *T* 166 NR 3143
Risbury *T* 113 SO 5556
Risby, Humbs *T* 142 SE 9214
Risby, Suff *T* 122 TL 8066
Risca *T* 100 ST 2491
Rise *T* 143 TA 1542
Risegate *T* 130 TF 2129
Rise Hill *H* 145 SD 7388
Riseley, Beds *T* 120 TL 0462
Riseley, Berks *T* 104 SU 7263
Risga 173 NM 6160
Rishangles *T* 123 TM 1668
Rishton *T* 145 SD 7230
Rishworth *T* 138 SE 0318
Rishworth Moor 138 SE 0017
Rising Bridge *T* 146 SD 7825
Risley, Ches *T* 137 SJ 6592
Risley, Derby *T* 129 SK 4635
Risplith *T* 147 SE 2468
Rispond 197 NC 4565
Rivar *T* 102 SU 3161
Rivenhall End *T* 106 TL 8316
River Add *W* 167 NR 8293
River Adur *W* 96 TQ 2118
River Affric *W* 181 NH 0920
River Aire, Humbs *W* 147 SE 6723
River Aire, N. Yks *W* 147 SE 6723
River Aire, W. Yks *W* 147 SE 3630
River Alde *W* 123 TM 2967
River Allen, Corn *W* 87 SX 0678
River Allen, Dorset *W* 94 ST 9906
River Allen, Northum *W* 158 NY 7961
River Almond, Lothn *W* 163 NT 0266
River Almond, Tays *W* 169 NN 7733
River Almond, Tays *W* 170 NO 0228
River Aln *W* 159 NU 1314
River Alne *W* 118 SP 1562
River Alport *W* 138 SK 1292
River Alt, Lancs *W* 136 SD 3403
River Alt, Mers *W* 136 SD 3403
River Alun *W* 110 SM 7627
River Alwin *W* 158 NT 9208
River Alyn or Afon Alun *W* 126 SJ 3756
River Amber *W* 139 SK 4363
River Anker *W* 128 SK 2305
River Annan *W* 157 NY 1373
River Ant *W* 133 TG 3618
River Applecross *W* 190 NG 7347
River Ardle *W* 176 NO 0761
River Arnol *W* 195 NB 3045
River Arrow, H. & W *W* 113 SO 4058
River Arrow, Warw *W* 118 SP 0861
River Arun *W* 96 TQ 0422

Skelfhill Pen Staffin Island

Skelfhill Pen H 157 NT 4403
Skellingthorpe T 140 SK 9271
Skellister T 203 HU 4654
Skellow T 139 SE 5210
Skelmanthorpe T 139 SE 2310
Skelmersdale P 136 SD 4605
Skelmonae 185 NJ 8839
Skelmorlie T 161 NS 1967
Skelmuir 185 NJ 9842
Skelpick T 198 NC 7256
Skelpick Burn W 198 NC 7355
Skelton, Cleve T 153 NZ 6518
Skelton, Cumbr T 151 NY 4335
Skelton, N. Yks T 152 NZ 0900
Skelton, N. Yks T 147 SE 3668
Skelton, N. Yks T 147 SE 5756
Skelwick, Orkney T 200 HY 4844
Skel Wick, Orkney W 200 HY 4945
Skelwith Bridge T 150 NY 3403
Skendleby T 141 TF 4369
Skene House 185 NJ 7709
Skenfrith T 113 SO 4520
Skerne T 149 TA 0455
Skeroblingarry 160 NR 7026
Skerray T 197 NC 6563
Skerries 134 SH 2794
Skerry of Eshaness 204 HU 2076
Skervuile Lighthouse 166 NR 6071
Sketty T 108 SS 6293
Skewen T 108 SS 7297
Skewsby T 147 SE 6271
Skeyton T 133 TG 2425
Skiag Bridge 196 NC 2324
Skibo Castle 193 NH 7389
Skidbrooke T 141 TF 4492
Skidby T 142 TA 0133
Skiddaw H 150 NY 2529
Skiddaw Forest F 150 NY 2729
Skigersta T 195 NB 5461
Skilgate T 91 SS 9827
Skillington T 130 SK 8925
Skinburness T 150 NY 1255
Skinflats T 170 NS 9083
Skinidin T 186 NG 2247
Skinningrove T 153 NZ 7119
Skipness T 160 NR 9057
Skipness Bay W 160 NR 9057
Skipness Point 160 NR 9157
Skipsea T 149 TA 1655
Skipton T 146 SD 9951
Skipton-on-Swale T 147 SE 3679
Skipwith T 147 SE 6638
Skirling T 163 NT 0739
Skirmett T 104 SU 7790
Skirpenbeck T 148 SE 7457
Skirwith T 151 NY 6132
Skirza T 199 ND 3868
Skirza Head 199 ND 3968
Skokholm Island 110 SM 7305
Skomer Island 110 SM 7209
Skroo 201 HZ 2274
Skuda Sound W 205 HU 6099
Skulamus T 180 NG 6622
Skullomie T 197 NC 6161
Skye (Broadford) Airport 180 NG 6924
Skye of Curr T 183 NH 9924
Slack T 146 SD 9728
Slackhall T 138 SK 0781
Slackhead T 184 NJ 4063
Slacks of Cairnbanno T 185 NJ 8446
Slad T 114 SO 8707
Slade T 90 SS 5146
Slade Green T 105 TQ 5276
Slaggan Bay W 190 NG 8394
Slaggyford T 151 NY 6752
Slaidburn T 145 SD 7152
Slaithwaite T 138 SE 0814
Slaley T 151 NY 9757
Slaley Forest F 152 NY 9555
Slamannan T 170 NS 8573
Slapton, Bucks T 104 SP 9320
Slapton, Devon T 89 SX 8245
Slapton, Northnts T 119 SP 6446
Slate, The H 160 NR 6316
Slaugham T 96 TQ 2527
Slawston T 129 SP 7794
Sleach Water W 199 ND 0344
Sleaford, Hants T 103 SU 8038
Sleaford, Lincs P 130 TF 0645
Sleagill T 151 NY 5919
Sleapford T 127 SJ 6315
Sledge Green T 114 SO 8134
Sledmere T 149 SE 9364
Sleightholme T 152 NY 9510
Sleightholme Moor 152 NY 9207
Sleights T 148 NZ 8607
Slepe T 93 SY 9293
Sletill Hill H 198 NC 9346
Sliabh Gaoil H 167 NR 8174
Slickly T 199 ND 3066
Sliddery T 160 NR 9322
Sliddery Water W 160 NR 9527
Slidderywater Foot 160 NR 9321
Slieau Dhoo H 144 SC 3589
Slieau Ruy H 144 SC 3282
Sliemore 183 NJ 0320
Sligachan Hotel 187 NG 4829
Slimbridge T 114 SO 7403
Slindon, Staffs T 127 SJ 8232
Slindon, W. Susx T 96 SU 9608
Slinfold T 96 TQ 1131
Slingsby T 148 SE 6974
Slioch, Grampn 184 NJ 5638
Slioch, Highld H 190 NH 0069
Slios Garbh H 180 NM 8384
Slip End T 104 TL 0818
Slipton T 120 SP 9579
Slitrig Water W 158 NT 5107
Slochd T 183 NH 8424
Slockavullin T 167 NR 8297
Sloc nam Feàrna 168 NR 8673
Sloley T 133 TG 2924
Sloothby T 141 TF 4970
Slouchnawen Bay W 154 NW 9563
Slough, Berks P 104 SU 9780
Slough, Powys T 116 SO 3063
Slugaide Glas W 166 NR 2846
Slymaback, Central H 169 NN 7510
Slymaback, Tays H 169 NN 7510
Slyne T 145 SD 4765
Sma' Glen 170 NN 9030
Smailholm T 164 NT 6436
Smallbridge T 137 SD 9115
Smallburgh T 133 TG 3324
Smallburn, Grampn T 185 NK 0141
Smallburn, Strath T 162 NS 6826
Small Dole T 96 TQ 2112
Small Downs W 99 TR 3955
Smalley T 128 SK 4044
Smallfield T 97 TQ 3143
Small Hythe T 98 TQ 8930
Small Isles 166 NR 5468
Smallridge T 92 ST 3000
Smardale T 151 NY 7308
Smarden T 98 TQ 8842
Smasha Hill H 157 NT 4416
Smeatharpe T 92 ST 1910
Smeeth T 99 TR 0739
Smeeton Westerby T 119 SP 6792
Smerclate T 178 NF 7515
Smerral T 199 ND 1733
Smethwick T 118 SP 0288
Smiddy Shaw Reservoir W 152 NZ 0446
Smigel Burn W 198 NC 9257
Smirisary T 180 NM 6477
Smisby T 128 SK 3419
Smithey Fen 121 TL 4570
Smithfield T 157 NY 4465
Smithincott T 92 ST 0611
Smith Sound W 86 SV 8706
Smithton T 183 NH 7146
Snaefell H 144 SC 3988
Snaigow House 176 NO 0843
Snailbeach T 126 SJ 3702
Snailwell T 122 TL 6467
Snainton T 149 SE 9282
Snaip Hill H 163 NT 0232
Snaith T 147 SE 6422
Snape, N. Yks T 147 SE 2684
Snape, Suff T 123 TM 3958
Snap, The 205 HU 6587
Snarestone T 128 SK 3409
Snarford T 140 TF 0582
Snargate T 99 TQ 9828
Snarravoe 205 HP 5601
Snave T 99 TR 0129
Snead T 116 SO 3192
Sneaton T 149 NZ 8907
Sneatonthorpe T 149 NZ 9006
Snelland T 140 TF 0780
Snelston T 128 SK 1543
Snettisham T 132 TF 6834
Sneug, The H 202 HT 9439
Sneuk Head 200 ND 2095
Snilesworth Moor 153 SE 5296
Snishival T 178 NF 7634
Snitter T 159 NU 0203
Snitterby T 140 SK 9894
Snitterfield T 118 SP 2160
Snitton T 116 SO 5575
Snodhill T 113 SO 3240
Snodland T 98 TQ 7061
Snook Point 165 NU 2426
Snowdon H 134 SH 6154
Snowhope Hill H 152 NY 9434
Snowshill T 114 SP 0933
Soa, Strath 172 NM 0746
Soa, Strath 172 NM 1551
Soa Island 172 NM 2419
Soa Mòr 189 NB 0605
Soay, Highld 180 NG 4413
Soay, W. Isles 188 NA 0601
Soay Sound W 180 NG 4416
Soberton T 95 SU 6116
Soberton Heath T 95 SU 6014
Socach Burn W 168 NR 8999
Socach, The H 184 NJ 2714
Soham T 122 TL 5973
Soham Mere 121 TL 5773
Soldon Cross T 90 SS 3210
Soldridge T 95 SU 6535
Solent W 95 SZ 4797
Sole Street, Kent T 98 TQ 6567
Sole Street, Kent T 99 TR 0949
Solihull P 118 SP 1579
Sollas T 188 NF 8174
Sollers Dilwyn T 113 SO 4255
Sollers Hope T 113 SO 6033
Sollom T 136 SD 4518
Solva T 110 SM 8024
Solway Firth W 150 NX 9845
Solway Moss 157 NY 3469
Somerby T 129 SK 7710
Somercotes T 128 SK 4253
Somerford Keynes T 114 SU 0295
Somerley T 95 SZ 8198
Somerleyton T 133 TM 4796
Somersal Herbert T 128 SK 1335
Somersby T 141 TF 3472
Somersham, Cambs T 121 TL 3678
Somersham, Suff T 123 TM 0848
Somersham High North Fen 121 TL 3681
Somerton, Norf T 133 TG 4719
Somerton, Oxon T 115 SP 4928
Somerton, Somer T 93 ST 4828
Sompting T 96 TQ 1704
Sonachan Hotel 173 NM 4566
Sonning T 104 SU 7575
Sonning Common T 104 SU 7080
Soonhope Burn W 164 NT 5356
Sopley T 94 SZ 1697
Sopworth T 101 ST 8286
Sorbie T 155 NX 4346
Sor Brook W 119 SP 4437
Sordale T 199 ND 1561
Sorisdale T 172 NM 2763
Sorn T 161 NS 5526
Sornhill 161 NS 5134
Soroba Hill H 167 NM 7905
Sortat T 199 ND 2863
Sotby T 141 TF 2078
Sots Hole T 141 TF 1164
Sotterley T 123 TM 4584
Soudley T 127 SJ 7229
Soughton or Sychdyn T 136 SJ 2466
Soulbury T 120 SP 8827
Soulby T 151 NY 7410
Souldern T 115 SP 5231
Souldrop T 120 SP 9861
Soulseat Loch W 154 NX 1058
Sound, Shetld T 203 HU 3850
Sound, Shetld T 203 HU 4640
Sound Gruney 205 HU 5896
Sound of Arisaig W 180 NM 6580
Sound of Barra W 178 NF 7509
Sound of Berneray, W. Isles W 188 NF 9079
Sound of Berneray, W. Isles W 178 NL 5581
Sound of Bute W 160 NS 0155
Sound of Canna W 179 NG 3002
Sound of Eigg W 179 NM 4382
Sound of Eriskay W 178 NF 7913
Sound of Faray W 200 HY 5437
Sound of Fiaray W 178 NF 7009
Sound of Fuday W 178 NF 7208
Sound of Gigha W 160 NR 6749
Sound of Handa W 196 NC 1547
Sound of Harris W 188 NF 9681
Sound of Hellisay W 178 NF 7503
Sound of Hoxa W 200 ND 3993
Sound of Insh W 173 NM 7419
Sound of Iona W 172 NM 2923
Sound of Islay W 166 NR 4369
Sound of Jura W 167 NR 6580
Sound of Kerrera W 173 NM 8228
Sound of Luing W 173 NM 7209
Sound of Mingulay W 178 NL 5885
Sound of Monach W 188 NF 7063
Sound of Mull W 173 NM 6145
Sound of Pabbay, W. Isles W 188 NF 9085
Sound of Pabbay, W. Isles W 178 NL 6288
Sound of Papa W 202 HU 1758
Sound of Pladda W 160 NS 0320
Sound of Raasay W 190 NG 5654
Sound of Rhum W 179 NM 4390
Sound of Sandray W 178 NL 6493
Sound of Shiant W 189 NB 3701
Sound of Shillay W 188 NF 8890
Sound of Shuna W 173 NM 9249
Sound of Sleat W 180 NG 6806
Sound of Spuir W 188 NF 8685
Sound of Taransay W 188 NG 0599
Sound of Ulva W 173 NM 4439
Sound of Vatersay W 178 NL 6297
Sound, The W 88 SX 4752
Soundwell T 101 ST 6575
Sourhope T 158 NT 8420
Sourin T 200 HY 4331
Sourton T 89 SX 5390
Soutergate T 144 SD 2281
Souter Head 177 NJ 9601
South Acre T 132 TF 8114
Southall T 105 TQ 1280
South Allington T 89 SX 7938
South Alloa T 170 NS 8791
Southam, Glos T 114 SO 9725
Southam, Warw T 118 SP 4161
South Ambersham T 96 SU 9120
Southampton (Eastleigh) Airport 95 SU 4517
Southampton P 94 SU 4112
Southampton Water W 95 SU 4506
South Bank T 153 NZ 5320
South Barrow T 93 ST 6027
South Barrule H 144 SC 2575
South Bay W 201 HY 7551
South Benfleet T 106 TQ 7785
Southborough T 97 TQ 5842
Southbourne, Dorset T 94 SZ 1491
Southbourne, W. Susx T 95 SU 7705
South Brent T 89 SX 6960
Southburgh T 132 TF 9904
South Burlingham T 133 TG 3707
South Burn W 200 ND 2299
South Cadbury T 93 ST 6325
South Cairn 154 NW 9769
South Carlton T 140 SK 9576
South Cave T 142 SE 9231
South Cerney T 114 SU 0597
South Channel W 99 TR 3272
South Channel W 142 SE 9621
South Chard T 92 ST 3205
South Charlton T 159 NU 1620
South Cheek or Old Peak 149 NZ 9802
South Cheriton T 93 ST 6925
Southchurch T 106 TQ 9085
South Cliffe T 142 SE 8736
South Clifton T 140 SK 8270
South Cove T 123 TM 4980
South Creake T 132 TF 8536
South Croxton T 129 SK 6810
South Dalton T 142 SE 9645
South Darenth T 105 TQ 5669
South Deep W 171 NO 2218
South District 131 TL 5298
South Downs, E. Susx H 97 TQ 3707
South Downs, W. Susx H 96 SU 9214
South Drove Drain W 130 TF 2114
South Duffield T 142 SE 6833
Southease T 97 TQ 4205
South Elkington T 141 TF 2988
South Elmsall T 139 SE 4711
Southend, Berks T 103 SU 5970
South End, Cumbr T 144 SD 2063
Southend, Strath T 160 NR 6908
Southend Airport 106 TQ 8789
Southend-on-Sea P 106 TQ 8785
Southerndown T 109 SS 8874
Southerness T 150 NX 9754
Southerness Point 150 NX 9754
South Erradale T 190 NG 7471
Southery T 132 TL 6294
Southery Fens 132 TL 6193
South Fambridge T 106 TQ 8595
South Fawley T 102 SU 3980
South Ferriby T 142 SE 9820
Southfield Reservoir W 139 SE 6519
Southfleet T 98 TQ 6171
South Foreland 99 TR 3643
South Forty Foot Drain W 130 TF 1633
South Galson River W 195 NB 4557
South Garth 205 HU 5499
South Garvan T 174 NM 9977
Southgate, G. Lon T 105 TQ 3094
Southgate, Norf T 132 TF 6833
Southgate, Norf T 133 TG 1424
Southgate, W. Glam T 108 SS 5588
South Godstone T 97 TQ 3648
South Goodwin (lightship) 99 TR 4342
South Gorley T 94 SU 1610
South Green T 106 TQ 6893
South Hanningfield T 106 TQ 7497
South Harbour W 201 HZ 2069
South Harris 189 NG 0993
South Harris Forest 189 NG 1098
South Harting T 95 SU 7819
South Havra 203 HU 3627
South Hayling T 95 SZ 7299
South Head, Highld 199 ND 3749
South Head, Shetld 204 HU 2382
South Heath T 104 SP 9102
South Heighton T 97 TQ 4503
South Hetton T 153 NZ 3745
South Hiendley T 139 SE 3912
South Hill T 88 SX 3372
South Hole T 90 SS 2219
South Holland Main Drain W 131 TF 3718
South Holms 205 HP 5710
South Holmwood T 96 TQ 1745
South Hornchurch T 105 TQ 5283
South Hylton T 153 NZ 3556
Southill T 120 TL 1542
South Isle of Gletness 203 HU 4750
South Kelsey T 142 TF 0498
South Kilvington T 147 SE 4284
South Kilworth T 119 SP 6081
South Kirkby T 139 SE 4510
South Kirkton T 185 NJ 7405
South Kyme T 130 TF 1749
South Kyme Fen 130 TF 1848
South Laggan Forest F 174 NN 2794
South Lancing T 96 TQ 1803
South Lee H 188 NF 9165
Southleigh, Devon T 92 SY 2093
South Leigh, Oxon T 115 SP 3908
South Level 122 TL 5985
South Leverton T 140 SK 7881
South Littleton T 118 SP 0746
South Lochboisdale T 178 NF 7717
South Lopham T 122 TM 0481
South Luffenham T 130 SK 9401
South Malling T 97 TQ 4111
South Marston T 102 SU 1988
South Medwin W 163 NT 0244
South Milford T 147 SE 4931
South Milton T 89 SX 6942
South Mimms T 105 TL 2201
Southminster T 106 TQ 9599
South Molton T 91 SS 7125
South Moor, Durham T 152 NZ 1851
Southmoor, Oxon T 115 SU 4098
South Morar 180 NM 7588
South Moreton T 103 SU 5688
South Mundam T 95 SU 8700
South Muskham T 140 SK 7957
South Ness 202 HT 9636
South Nesting 203 HU 4554
South Nesting Bay W 203 HU 4856
South Nevi 201 HY 6000
South Newington T 115 SP 4033
South Newton T 94 SU 0834
South Normanton T 129 SK 4456
South Norwood T 105 TQ 3468
South Nuffield T 97 TQ 3049
South Ockendon T 106 TQ 5982
Southoe T 120 TL 1860
Southolt T 123 TM 1968
South Ormsby T 141 TF 3775
Southorpe T 130 TF 0803
South Otterington T 147 SE 3787
Southowram T 146 SE 1123
South Oxhey T 105 TQ 1193
South Perrott T 93 ST 4706
South Petherton T 93 ST 4316
South Petherwin T 88 SX 3182
South Pickenham T 132 TF 8504
South Pool T 89 SX 7740
Southport P 136 SD 3316
South Queich W 170 NO 0303
South Radworthy 91 SS 7432
South Raynham T 132 TF 8724
Southrepps T 133 TG 2536
South Reston T 141 TF 4083
Southrey T 141 TF 1366
South Ronaldsay 200 ND 4490
Southrop T 115 SP 2003
Southrope T 103 SU 6744
South Runcton T 132 TF 6308
South Scarle T 140 SK 8463
Southsea T 95 SZ 6498
South Shian 173 NM 9042
South Shields P 159 NZ 3666
South Shore T 145 SD 3033
South Skirlaugh T 143 TA 1439
South Somercotes T 141 TF 4193
South Sound W 205 HU 5390
South Stack 134 SH 2082
South Stainley T 147 SE 3063
South Stainmore T 151 NY 8413
Southstoke, Avon T 101 ST 7461
South Stoke, Oxon T 103 SU 5983
South Stoke, W. Susx T 96 TQ 0210
South Street T 97 TQ 3917
South Tawton T 89 SX 6594
South Thoresby T 141 TF 4076
South Tidworth T 102 SU 2448
South Town, Hants T 95 SU 6536
Southtown, Orkney T 200 ND 4895
South Ugie Water W 185 NK 0046
South Uist 178 NF 7829
South View 203 HU 3842
Southwaite T 151 NY 4545
South Walls 200 ND 3189
South Walsham T 133 TG 3613
South Ward H 203 HU 3264
South Warnborough T 103 SU 7247
Southwater T 96 TQ 1525
Southway T 101 ST 5142
South Weald T 105 TQ 5793
Southwell, Dorset T 93 SY 6870
Southwell, Notts T 129 SK 7054
South Weston T 104 SU 7098
South West Point 90 SS 1343
South Wheatley T 88 SX 2492
Southwick, Hants T 95 SU 6208
Southwick, Northnts T 120 TL 0292
South Wick, Shetld W 204 HU 3191
Southwick, T. & W T 159 NZ 3758
Southwick, Wilts T 101 ST 8355
Southwick, W. Susx T 96 TQ 2405
South Widcombe T 101 ST 5856
South Wigston T 129 SP 5898
South Willingham T 141 TF 1983
South Wingfield T 128 SK 3755
South Witham T 130 SK 9219
Southwold T 123 TM 5076
South Wonston T 95 SU 4635
Southwood, Norf T 133 TG 3905
Southwood, Somer 93 ST 5533
South Woodham Ferrers T 106 TQ 8097
South Wootton T 132 TF 6422
South Zeal T 89 SX 6593
Soutra Mains T 164 NT 4559
Soval Lodge 195 NB 3424
Sowerby, N. Yks T 147 SE 4381
Sowerby, W. Yks T 146 SE 0423
Sowerby Bridge T 146 SE 0623
Sowerby Row T 151 NY 3940
Sow of Atholl, The H 175 NN 6274
Sow, The 200 HY 1802
Sowton T 89 SX 9791
Soyea Island 196 NC 0422
Soyland Moor 138 SD 9819
Spa Common T 133 TG 2930
Spadeadam Fm 158 NY 5870
Spadeadam Forest F 158 NY 6373
Spade Mill Reservoirs W 145 SD 6237
Spalding P 131 TF 2422
Spaldington T 142 SE 7633
Spaldwick T 120 TL 1272
Spalford T 140 SK 8369
Spango Hill H 156 NS 8118
Spanish Head 144 SC 1865
Sparham T 132 TG 0719
Spark Bridge T 145 SD 3084
Sparkford T 93 ST 6026
Sparkwell T 89 SX 5857
Sparrowpit T 138 SK 0980
Sparsholt, Hants T 94 SU 4331
Sparsholt, Oxon T 102 SU 3487
Spartleton Edge H 164 NT 6565
Spaunton T 148 SE 7289
Spaunton Moor 148 SE 7293
Spaxton T 92 ST 2237
Spean Bridge T 174 NN 2281
Spear Head 199 ND 0971
Speen, Berks T 103 SU 4668
Speen, Bucks T 104 SU 8499
Speeton T 149 TA 1574
Speinne Mòr H 173 NM 4949
Speke T 136 SJ 4483
Speldhurst T 97 TQ 5541
Spellbrook T 105 TL 4817
Spelsbury T 115 SP 3521
Spencers Wood T 104 SU 7166
Spennithorne T 146 SE 1388
Spennymoor T 152 NZ 2534
Spetchley T 117 SO 8954
Spetisbury T 93 ST 9102
Spexhall T 123 TM 3780
Spey Bay, Grampn T 184 NJ 3565
Spey Bay, Grampn W 184 NJ 3767
Speybridge T 183 NJ 0326
Speymouth Forest 184 NJ 3557
Spilsby T 141 TF 4066
Spindlestone T 165 NU 1533
Spinningdale T 192 NH 6789
Spirthill T 102 ST 9975
Spital Burn W 177 NO 6583
Spithead W 95 SZ 6396
Spithurst T 97 TQ 4217
Spittal, Dyfed T 110 SM 9723
Spittal, Highld T 199 ND 1654
Spittal, Lothn T 171 NT 4677
Spittal, Northum T 165 NU 0051
Spittalfield T 176 NO 1040
Spittal of Glenmuick T 176 NO 3085
Spittal of Glenshee T 176 NO 1070
Spixworth T 133 TG 2415
Spofforth T 147 SE 3651
Spondon T 128 SK 4035
Spo Ness 200 HY 4846
Spooner Row T 133 TM 0997
Spoo Ness 205 HP 5607
Sporle T 132 TF 8411
Spott T 171 NT 6775
Spratton T 119 SP 7170
Spreakley T 103 SU 8341
Spreyton T 89 SX 6996
Spridlington T 140 TF 0084
Springburn T 162 NS 6068
Springcorrie T 195 NB 2332
Springfield, Fife T 171 NO 3411
Springfield, Grampn T 183 NJ 0560
Springfield, W. Mids T 118 SP 0981
Springfield Reservoir W 163 NS 9052
Springholm T 156 NX 8069
Springkell 157 NY 2575
Spring Mill Reservoir W 137 SD 8717
Springside T 161 NS 3738
Springthorpe T 140 SK 8789
Sproatley T 143 TA 3419
Sproston Green T 137 SJ 7366
Sprotbrough T 139 SE 5402
Sproughton T 120 TL 1244
Sprouston T 164 NT 7535
Sprowston T 133 TG 2411
Sproxton, Leic T 130 SK 8524
Sproxton, N. Yks T 147 SE 6181
Spuir 188 NF 8584
Spurn (lightship) 143 TA 4809
Spur Ness 201 HY 6033
Spurness Sound W 201 HY 6232
Spurn Head 143 TA 3910
Spurstow T 137 SJ 5557
Spur, The 199 ND 1769
Spùt Rollà W 169 NN 7228
Square and Compass T 110 SM 8531
Srath a' Chràisg 197 NC 5324
Srath Beag 196 NC 3853
Srath Dionard 196 NC 3453
Srath Lungard 190 NG 9164
Srath nan Lòn 191 NC 2401
Srath na Seilge 197 NC 7019
Srianach 195 NB 4010
Sròn Ach' a' Bhacaidh H 192 NH 6198
Sròn a' Chleirich H 175 NN 7876
Sròn a' Choire Ghairbh H 174 NN 2294
Sron a' Gheodha Dhuibh 190 NG 7792
Sròn Bheag, Highld 173 NM 4662
Sròn Bheag, Tays H 175 NN 5262
Sròn Mhòr H 169 NN 6526
Sròn na Carra 190 NG 7473
Sròn na Clèite 190 NG 7389
Sròn na h-Iolaire 179 NM 3891
Sronphadruig Lodge 175 NN 7178
Sròn Romul H 194 NA 9615
Sròn Ruadh 195 NB 4636
Sron Rubha na Gaoithe 193 NC 9911
Stab Hill H 154 NX 1471
Staca Leathann 194 NA 9828
Stac a' Mheadais 186 NG 3325
Stac an Aoineidh 172 NM 2522
Stac an Tuill 186 NG 3521
Stack Clò Kearvaig 196 NC 2973
Stackhouse T 146 SD 8165
Stack Islands 178 NF 7807
Stack o' da Noup 203 HU 3516
Stack of Billyageo 203 HU 4421
Stack of Birrier 205 HU 6494
Stack of the Brough 203 HU 4015
Stackpole T 110 SR 9896
Stackpole Head 110 SR 9994
Stack Rocks 110 SM 8113
Stacks of Duncansby 199 ND 4071
Stacksteads T 146 SD 8421
Stac na Cathaig H 182 NH 6430
Stac na h-Iolaire H 183 NJ 0109
Stac Pollaidh H 196 NC 1010
Stac Shuardail 195 NB 4830
Staddiscombe T 88 SX 5151
Staddlethorpe T 142 SE 8428
Stadhampton T 115 SU 6098
Staffa 172 NM 3235
Staffield T 151 NY 5442
Staffin T 187 NG 4867
Staffin Bay W 187 NG 4869
Staffin Island 187 NG 4969

Stafford Strensham

Stafford *P*	127	SJ 9223
Staffs & Worcs Canal *W*	117	SO 8788
Stagsden *T*	120	SP 9849
Stainacre *T*	149	NZ 9108
Stainburn *T*	147	SE 2448
Stainby *T*	130	SK 9022
Staincross *T*	139	SE 3310
Stain Dale	148	SE 8690
Staindrop *T*	152	NZ 1220
Staines *P*	104	TQ 0471
Stainfield, Lincs *T*	130	TF 0725
Stainfield, Lincs *T*	141	TF 1073
Stainforth, N. Yks *T*	146	SD 8267
Stainforth, S. Yks *T*	139	SE 6411
Stainforth and Keadby Canal *W*	142	SE 7311
Staining *T*	145	SD 3536
Stainland *T*	138	SE 0719
Stainmore Common	151	NY 8517
Stainmore Forest	152	NY 9410
Stainsacre *T*	149	NZ 9108
Stainton, Cleve *T*	153	NZ 4814
Stainton, Cumbr *T*	151	NY 4828
Stainton, Cumbr *T*	145	SD 5285
Stainton, Durham *T*	152	NZ 0718
Stainton, N. Yks *T*	152	SE 1096
Stainton, S. Yks *T*	139	SK 5593
Stainton by Langworth *T*	140	TF 0677
Staintondale *T*	149	SE 9998
Stainton le Vale *T*	141	TF 1794
Stainton with Adgarley *T*	144	SD 2572
Stair, Cumbr *T*	150	NY 2321
Stair, Strath *T*	161	NS 4323
Staithes *T*	153	NZ 7818
Stakeford *T*	159	NZ 2785
Stake Pass	150	NY 2608
Stake Pool *T*	145	SD 4148
Stalbans *P*	105	TL 1407
Stalbridge *T*	93	ST 7317
Stalbridge Weston *T*	93	ST 7216
Stalham *T*	133	TG 3725
Stalham Green *T*	133	TG 3824
Stalisfield Green *T*	98	TQ 9552
Stallingborough *T*	143	TA 2011
Stalling Busk *T*	146	SD 9185
Stalmine *T*	145	SD 3745
Stalybridge *T*	138	SJ 9698
Stambourne *T*	122	TL 7238
Stambourne Green *T*	122	TL 7038
Stamford *P*	130	TF 0307
Stamford Bridge *T*	148	SE 7155
Stamfordham *T*	159	NZ 0872
Stanborough *T*	105	TL 2211
Stanbridge, Beds *T*	104	SP 9624
Stanbridge, Dorset *T*	94	SU 0004
Stand *T*	162	NS 7668
Standard *W*	154	NX 3085
Standburn *T*	170	NS 9274
Standeford *T*	127	SJ 9108
Standen *T*	98	TQ 8540
Standford *T*	95	SU 8134
Standish *T*	137	SD 5610
Standlake *T*	115	SP 3903
Standon, Hants *T*	94	SU 4226
Standon, Herts *T*	105	TL 3922
Standon, Staffs *T*	127	SJ 8235
Stane *T*	163	NS 8859
Stanegate, Cumbr *R*	157	NY 4760
Stanegate, Northum *R*	158	NY 7866
Stane Street, Essex *R*	105	TL 5421
Stane Street, Surrey *R*	96	TQ 1440
Stanfield *T*	132	TF 9320
Stanford, Beds *T*	120	TL 1641
Stanford, Kent *T*	99	TR 1238
Stanford Bishop *T*	117	SO 6851
Stanford Bridge *T*	117	SO 7165
Stanford Dingley *T*	103	SU 5771
Stanford in the Vale *T*	115	SU 3493
Stanford-le-Hope *T*	106	TQ 6882
Stanford on Avon *T*	119	SP 5878
Stanford on Soar *T*	129	SK 5422
Stanford on Teme *T*	117	SO 7066
Stanford Reservoir, Leic *W*	119	SP 6080
Stanford Reservoir, Northnts *W*	119	SP 6080
Stanford Rivers *T*	105	TL 5300
Stanger Head	200	HY 5142
Stanghow *T*	153	NZ 6715
Stang, The	152	NZ 0208
Stanhoe *T*	132	TF 8036
Stanhope, Border *T*	163	NT 1229
Stanhope, Durham *T*	152	NY 9939
Stanhope Common	152	NY 9642
Stanion *T*	120	SP 9187
Stanley, Derby *T*	128	SK 4140
Stanley, Durham *T*	152	NZ 1952
Stanley, Staffs *T*	127	SJ 9352
Stanley, Tays *T*	170	NO 1033
Stanley, W. Yks *T*	147	SE 3424
Stanley Crook *T*	152	NZ 1638
Stanley Force *W*	150	SD 1799
Stanmer *T*	97	TQ 3309
Stanmore, Berks *T*	103	SU 4778
Stanmore, G. Lon *T*	105	TQ 1692
Stannery Knowe *H*	161	NS 4912
Stannington, Northum *T*	159	NZ 2179
Stannington, S. Yks *T*	139	SK 3088
Stansbatch *T*	116	SO 3561
Stansfield *T*	122	TL 7852
Stansore Point	95	SZ 4698
Stanstead *T*	122	TL 8449
Stanstead Abbotts *T*	105	TL 3911
Stansted *T*	98	TQ 6062
Stansted House	95	SU 7610
Stansted Mountfitchet *T*	105	TL 5124
Stanton, Derby *T*	128	SK 2719
Stanton, Glos *T*	114	SP 0734
Stanton, Gwent *T*	113	SO 3121
Stanton, Northum	159	NZ 1390
Stanton, Staffs *T*	128	SK 1246
Stanton, Suff *T*	122	TL 9673
Stanton by Bridge *T*	128	SK 3727
Stanton-by-Dale *T*	129	SK 4638
Stanton Drew *T*	101	ST 5963
Stanton Fitzwarren *T*	102	SU 1790
Stanton Harcourt *T*	115	SP 4105
Stanton Hill *T*	139	SK 4860
Stanton in Peak *T*	139	SK 2464
Stanton Lacy *T*	116	SO 4978
Stanton Long *T*	116	SO 5790
Stanton-on-the-Wolds *T*	129	SK 6330
Stanton Prior *T*	101	ST 6762
Stanton St Bernard *T*	102	SU 0962
Stanton St John *T*	115	SP 5709
Stanton St Quintin *T*	101	ST 9080
Stanton Street *T*	122	TL 9566
Stanton under Bardon *T*	129	SK 4610
Stanton upon Hine Heath *T*	127	SJ 5724
Stanton Wick *T*	101	ST 6162
Stanwardine in the Fields *T*	126	SJ 4124
Stanway, Essex *T*	106	TL 9424
Stanway, Glos *T*	114	SP 0632
Stanwell *T*	104	TQ 0574
Stanwell Moor *T*	104	TQ 0474
Stanwick *T*	120	SP 9771
Stanwick-St-John *T*	152	NZ 1811
Stanydale *T*	202	HU 2850
Stape *T*	148	SE 7993
Stapehill *T*	94	SU 0501
Stapeley *T*	127	SJ 6749
Staple *T*	99	TR 2756
Staplecross *T*	98	TQ 7822
Staplefield *T*	96	TQ 2728
Staple Fitzpaine *T*	92	ST 2618
Stapleford, Cambs *T*	121	TL 4751
Stapleford, Herts *T*	105	TL 3116
Stapleford, Leic *T*	130	SK 8118
Stapleford, Lincs *T*	140	SK 8757
Stapleford, Notts *T*	129	SK 4837
Stapleford, Wilts *T*	94	SU 0737
Stapleford Abbotts *T*	105	TQ 5095
Stapleford Tawney *T*	105	TQ 5099
Staplegrove *T*	92	ST 2126
Staplehay *T*	92	ST 2121
Staple Hill *H*	92	ST 2416
Staplehurst *T*	98	TQ 7843
Staplers *T*	95	SZ 5189
Staple Sound *W*	165	NU 2337
Stapleton, Avon *T*	101	ST 6176
Stapleton, Cumbr *T*	157	NY 5071
Stapleton, H. & W *T*	116	SO 3265
Stapleton, Leic *T*	128	SP 4398
Stapleton, N. Yks *T*	152	NZ 2612
Stapleton, Shrops *T*	127	SJ 4704
Stapleton, Somer *T*	93	ST 4621
Stapley *T*	92	ST 1813
Staploe *T*	120	TL 1460
Star, Dyfed *T*	111	SN 2435
Star, Fife *T*	171	NO 3103
Star, Somer *T*	101	ST 4358
Starbotton *T*	146	SD 9574
Starcross *T*	89	SX 9781
Stare Dam *W*	176	NO 0438
Starkigarth *T*	203	HU 4329
Starston *T*	123	TM 2384
Start Bay *W*	89	SX 8444
Startforth *T*	152	NZ 0316
Startley *T*	102	ST 9482
Start Point, Corn	88	SX 0486
Start Point, Devon	89	SX 8237
Start Point, Orkney	201	HY 7843
Startup Hill *H*	163	NS 9729
Stathe *T*	92	ST 3728
Stathern *T*	129	SK 7731
Station Town *T*	153	NZ 4036
Stattic Point	190	NG 9796
Staughton Highway *T*	120	TL 1364
Staunton, Glos *T*	113	SO 5512
Staunton, Glos *T*	114	SO 7929
Staunton Harold Hall	128	SK 3721
Staunton Harold Reservoir *W*	128	SK 3723
Staunton in the Vale *T*	129	SK 8043
Staunton on Arrow *T*	113	SO 3760
Staunton on Wye *T*	113	SO 3645
Stava Ness	203	HU 5060
Staveley, Cumbr *T*	151	SD 4698
Staveley, Derby *T*	139	SK 4374
Staveley, N. Yks *T*	147	SE 3662
Staveley-in-Cartmel *T*	145	SD 3886
Staverton, Devon *T*	89	SX 7964
Staverton, Glos *T*	114	SO 8923
Staverton, Northnts *T*	119	SP 5361
Staverton, Wilts *T*	101	ST 8560
Stawell *T*	100	ST 3638
Staxigoe *T*	199	ND 3852
Staxton *T*	149	TA 0179
Staylittle *T*	125	SN 8892
Staythorpe *T*	129	SK 7553
Steam Dyke *A*	121	TL 5553
Stean *T*	146	SE 0873
Stean Moor	146	SE 0671
Stearsby *T*	147	SE 6171
Steart *T*	100	ST 2745
Stebbing *T*	106	TL 6624
Stedham *T*	95	SU 8622
Steele Road *T*	158	NY 5293
Steele's Knowe *H*	170	NN 9607
Steen's Bridge *T*	113	SO 5457
Steep *T*	95	SU 7425
Steep Holm	100	ST 2260
Steeping River *W*	141	TF 4661
Steeple, Dorset *T*	93	SY 9181
Steeple, Essex *T*	106	TL 9303
Steeple Ashton, Oxon *T*	115	SP 4725
Steeple Ashton, Wilts *T*	101	ST 9056
Steeple Barton *T*	115	SP 4425
Steeple Bumpstead *T*	122	TL 6841
Steeple Claydon *T*	119	SP 6926
Steeple Gidding *T*	120	TL 1381
Steeple Langford *T*	94	SU 0437
Steeple Morden *T*	121	TL 2842
Steer Rig, Border *H*	165	NT 8524
Steer Rig, Northum *H*	165	NT 8524
Steeton *T*	146	SE 0344
Steinacleit *A*	195	NB 3954
Steinmanhill *T*	185	NJ 7642
Steisay *T*	188	NF 8544
Stelling Minnis *T*	99	TR 1446
Stemster *T*	199	ND 1861
Stemster Hill *H*	199	ND 2041
Stemster House	199	ND 1860
Stenalees *T*	87	SX 0157
Stenbury Down *H*	95	SZ 5379
Stenhousemuir *T*	170	NS 8783
Stenhouse Reservoir *W*	171	NT 2187
Stenness, Orkney	200	HY 3211
Stenness, Shetld	204	HU 2177
Stenton *T*	171	NT 6274
Stepney *T*	105	TQ 3581
Steppingley *T*	120	TL 0135
Stepps *T*	162	NS 6568
Sternfield *T*	123	TM 3961
Stert *T*	102	SU 0359
Stert Flats	100	ST 2647
Stetchworth *T*	122	TL 6458
Stevenage *P*	105	TL 2324
Stevenston *T*	161	NS 2642
Steventon, Hants *T*	103	SU 5447
Steventon, Oxon *T*	103	SU 4791
Stevington *T*	120	SP 9853
Stewartby *T*	120	TL 0242
Stewarton *T*	161	NS 4246
Stewkley *T*	120	SP 8526
Stewton *T*	141	TF 3686
Stey Fell *H*	155	NX 5560
Steyning *T*	96	TQ 1811
Steynton *T*	110	SM 9107
Stibb *T*	90	SS 2210
Stibbard *T*	132	TF 9828
Stibb Cross *T*	90	SS 4214
Stibb Green *T*	102	SU 2262
Stibbington *T*	130	TL 0898
Stichill *T*	164	NT 7138
Sticker *T*	87	SW 9750
Stickford *T*	141	TF 3559
Sticklepath *T*	89	SX 6494
Stickle Pike *H*	150	SD 2193
Stickle Tarn *W*	150	NY 2807
Stickney *T*	131	TF 3456
Stiffkey *T*	132	TF 9742
Stifford's Bridge *T*	117	SO 7348
Stilligarry *T*	178	NF 7638
Stillingfleet *T*	147	SE 5941
Stillington, Cleve *T*	153	NZ 3723
Stillington, N. Yks *T*	147	SE 5867
Stilton *T*	120	TL 1689
Stinchcombe *T*	114	ST 7398
Stinsford *T*	93	SY 7191
Stiperstones *H*	126	SO 3698
Stirchley *T*	127	SJ 7006
Stirkoke House	199	ND 3150
Stirling *P*	169	NS 7993
Stisted *T*	106	TL 8024
Stithians *T*	86	SW 7336
Stithians Reservoir *W*	86	SW 7136
Stittenham *T*	192	NH 6574
Stivichall *T*	118	SP 3376
Stixwould *T*	141	TF 1766
Stoak *T*	136	SJ 4273
Stob a' Choin *H*	169	NN 4116
Stob a' Ghrianain *H*	174	NN 0882
Stob an Aonaich Mhòir *H*	175	NN 5369
Stob an Eas *H*	168	NN 1807
Stob an t-Sluichd *H*	176	NJ 1102
Stob Binnein *H*	169	NN 4322
Stob Choire Claurigh *H*	174	NN 2673
Stob Coir' an Albannaich, Highld *H*	174	NN 1644
Stob Coir' an Albannaich, Strath *H*	174	NN 1644
Stob Coire a' Chearcaill *H*	174	NN 0172
Stob Coire Easain, Highld *H*	174	NN 2372
Stob Coire Easain, Highld *H*	174	NN 3073
Stob Dubh *H*	174	NN 1648
Stob Ghabhar, Highld *H*	174	NN 2345
Stob Ghabhar, Strath *H*	174	NN 2345
Stobieside	162	NS 6239
Stob Law *H*	163	NT 2333
Stob na Cruaiche, Highld *H*	174	NN 3657
Stob na Cruaiche, Tays *H*	174	NN 3657
Stobo *T*	163	NT 1837
Stoborough *T*	93	SY 9286
Stoborough Green *T*	93	SY 9285
Stock *T*	106	TQ 6998
Stockay	188	NF 6663
Stockbridge *T*	94	SU 3635
Stockbriggs *T*	162	NS 7936
Stockbury *T*	98	TQ 8461
Stockcross *T*	102	SU 4368
Stockdalewath *T*	151	NY 3845
Stockeinteignhead *T*	89	SX 9170
Stockerston *T*	130	SP 8397
Stock Gaylard House	93	ST 7213
Stock Green *T*	118	SO 9959
Stockingford *T*	118	SP 3491
Stocking Pelham *T*	121	TL 4529
Stockinish Island *T*	189	NG 1390
Stockland *T*	92	ST 2404
Stockland Bristol *T*	100	ST 2443
Stockleigh English *T*	91	SS 8506
Stockleigh Pomeroy *T*	91	SS 8703
Stockley *T*	102	SU 0067
Stockport *T*	137	SJ 8990
Stocksbridge *T*	139	SK 2698
Stocksfield *T*	159	NZ 0561
Stocks Reservoir *W*	145	SD 7356
Stockton, H. & W *T*	116	SO 5161
Stockton, Norf *T*	133	TM 3894
Stockton, Shrops *T*	127	SO 7299
Stockton, Warw *T*	118	SP 4363
Stockton, Wilts *T*	102	ST 9838
Stockton Heath *T*	137	SJ 6186
Stockton-on-Tees *P*	153	NZ 4419
Stockton on Teme *T*	117	SO 7167
Stockton on the Forest *T*	147	SE 6555
Stock Wood *T*	118	SP 0058
Stodmarsh *T*	99	TR 2160
Stoer *T*	196	NC 0428
Stoford, Somer *T*	93	ST 5613
Stoford, Wilts *T*	94	SU 0835
Stogumber *T*	92	ST 0937
Stogursey *T*	100	ST 2042
Stoke, Devon *T*	90	SS 2324
Stoke, Hants *T*	103	SU 4051
Stoke, Hants *T*	95	SU 7202
Stoke, Kent *T*	98	TQ 8275
Stoke Abbott *T*	93	ST 4500
Stoke Albany *T*	119	SP 8088
Stoke Ash *T*	123	TM 1170
Stoke Bardolph *T*	129	SK 6441
Stoke Bliss *T*	117	SO 6562
Stoke Bruerne *T*	119	SP 7449
Stoke by Clare *T*	122	TL 7443
Stoke-by-Nayland *T*	122	TL 9836
Stoke Canon *T*	89	SX 9397
Stoke Charity *T*	103	SU 4839
Stoke Climsland *T*	88	SX 3674
Stoke D'Abernon *T*	105	TQ 1259
Stoke Doyle *T*	120	TL 0286
Stoke Dry *T*	130	SP 8596
Stoke Ferry *T*	132	TF 7000
Stoke Fleming *T*	89	SX 8648
Stokeford *T*	93	SY 8687
Stoke Gabriel *T*	89	SX 8457
Stoke Gifford *T*	101	ST 6280
Stoke Golding *T*	128	SP 3997
Stoke Goldington *T*	120	SP 8748
Stokeham *T*	140	SK 7876
Stoke Hammond *T*	120	SP 8829
Stoke Heath *T*	127	SJ 6529
Stoke Holy Cross *T*	133	TG 2301
Stoke Lacy *T*	113	SO 6249
Stoke Lyne *T*	115	SP 5628
Stoke Mandeville *T*	104	SP 8310
Stokenchurch *T*	104	SU 7696
Stoke Newington *T*	105	TQ 3286
Stokenham *T*	89	SX 8042
Stoke on Tern *T*	127	SJ 6428
Stoke-on-Trent *P*	127	SJ 8745
Stoke Orchard *T*	114	SO 9228
Stoke Poges *T*	104	SU 9884
Stoke Point	89	SX 5645
Stoke Prior, H. & W *T*	113	SO 5256
Stoke Prior, H. & W *T*	117	SO 9467
Stoke Rivers *T*	91	SS 6335
Stoke Rochford *T*	130	SK 9127
Stoke Row *T*	104	SU 6884
Stokesay *T*	116	SO 4381
Stokes Bay *W*	95	SZ 5898
Stokesby *T*	133	TG 4310
Stokesley *T*	153	NZ 5208
Stoke St Gregory *T*	92	ST 3427
Stoke St Mary *T*	92	ST 2622
Stoke St Michael *T*	101	ST 6646
Stoke St Milborough *T*	116	SO 5782
Stoke sub Hamdon *T*	93	ST 4717
Stoke Talmage *T*	104	SU 6799
Stoke Trister *T*	93	ST 7428
Stolford *T*	100	ST 2245
Stondon Massey *T*	105	TL 5800
Stone, Bucks *T*	104	SP 7812
Stone, Glos *T*	114	ST 6895
Stone, H. & W *T*	117	SO 8675
Stone, Kent *T*	105	TQ 5774
Stone, Staffs *P*	127	SJ 9033
Stone Allerton *T*	100	ST 4051
Ston Easton *T*	101	ST 6253
Stonebroom *T*	139	SK 4159
Stone Cross *T*	97	TQ 6204
Stonefield *T*	162	NS 6857
Stonefield Castle Hotel	168	NR 8671
Stonegate *T*	97	TQ 6628
Stonegate Crofts *T*	185	NK 0339
Stonegrave *T*	147	SE 6577
Stonehaugh *T*	158	NY 7976
Stonehaven *T*	177	NO 8786
Stonehenge *A*	102	SU 1242
Stone House, Cumbr *T*	146	SD 7686
Stonehouse, Glos *T*	114	SO 8005
Stonehouse, Northum *T*	158	NY 6958
Stonehouse, Strath *T*	162	NS 7546
Stone in Oxney *T*	98	TQ 9427
Stoneleigh *T*	118	SP 3372
Stonely *T*	120	TL 1067
Stonesby *T*	130	SK 8224
Stonesdale Moor	152	NY 8904
Stonesfield *T*	115	SP 3917
Stones Green *T*	123	TM 1626
Stoneside Hill *H*	150	SD 1489
Stone Street, Kent *R*	99	TR 1348
Stone Street, Suff *R*	123	TM 3686
Stone, The	86	SW 5526
Stoneybridge *T*	178	NF 7433
Stoneyburn *T*	163	NS 9762
Stoney Cross *T*	94	SU 2611
Stoneygate *T*	129	SK 6002
Stoneyhills *T*	106	TQ 9597
Stoneykirk *T*	154	NX 0953
Stoney Middleton *T*	139	SK 2375
Stoney Stanton *T*	129	SP 4994
Stoney Stratton *T*	101	ST 6539
Stoney Stretton *T*	126	SJ 3809
Stoneywood *T*	185	NJ 8911
Stonga Banks	204	HU 2985
Stonganess	205	HP 5402
Stonham Aspal *T*	123	TM 1359
Stonnall *T*	128	SK 0704
Stonor *T*	104	SU 7388
Stonton Wyville *T*	129	SP 7395
Stonybreck *T*	201	HZ 2071
Stonyfield	192	NH 6973
Stonyhurst College	145	SD 6939
Stony Stratford *T*	119	SP 7940
Stood Hill *H*	156	NS 8512
Stoodleigh *T*	91	SS 9218
Stoodleigh Beacon *H*	91	SS 8818
Stopham *T*	96	TQ 0219
Stopsley *T*	105	TL 1023
Storeton *T*	136	SJ 3084
Stornoway *T*	195	NB 4233
Stornoway Airport	195	NB 4633
Storridge *T*	117	SO 7548
Storrington *T*	96	TQ 0814
Storrs *T*	151	SD 4094
Storr, The *H*	187	NG 4065
Storth *T*	145	SD 4779
Stotfold *T*	120	TL 2136
Stottesdon *T*	117	SO 6782
Stoughton, Leic *T*	129	SK 6402
Stoughton, Surrey *T*	96	SU 9851
Stoughton, W. Susx *T*	95	SU 8011
Stoul *T*	180	NM 7594
Stoulton *T*	117	SO 9049
Stourbridge *T*	117	SO 9084
Stourbrough Hill *H*	202	HU 2152
Stourhead *A*	93	ST 7734
Stourpaine *T*	93	ST 8609
Stourport-on-Severn *T*	117	SO 8171
Stour Provost *T*	93	ST 7921
Stour Row *T*	93	ST 8221
Stourton, Staffs *T*	117	SO 8685
Stourton, Warw *T*	118	SP 2936
Stourton, Wilts *T*	93	ST 7734
Stourton Caundle *T*	93	ST 7115
Stove	201	HY 6035
Stoven *T*	123	TM 4481
Stow *T*	140	SK 8882
Stow Bardolph *T*	132	TF 6205
Stow Bardolph Fen	131	TF 5604
Stow Bedon *T*	132	TL 9596
Stowbridge *T*	132	TF 6007
Stow cum Quy *T*	121	TL 5160
Stowe *T*	116	SO 3073
Stowe-by-Chartley *T*	128	SK 0027
Stowell *T*	93	ST 6822
Stowe School	119	SP 6737
Stowford *T*	88	SX 4386
Stowlangtoft *T*	122	TL 9668
Stow Longa *T*	120	TL 1070
Stow Maries *T*	106	TQ 8399
Stowmarket *T*	122	TM 0458
Stow-on-the-Wold *P*	115	SP 1925
Stowting *T*	99	TR 1242
Stowupland *T*	120	TL 0660
Straad *T*	160	NS 0462
Strachan *T*	177	NO 6792
Strachur *T*	168	NN 0901
Strachur Bay *W*	168	NN 0801
Stradbroke *T*	123	TM 2374
Stradishall *T*	122	TL 7452
Stradsett *T*	132	TF 6605
Stragglethorpe *T*	130	SK 9152
Strait of Dover *W*	99	TR 3828
Straiton, Lothn *T*	163	NT 2766
Straiton, Strath *T*	161	NS 3804
Straloch, Grampn	185	NJ 8621
Straloch, Tays *T*	176	NO 0463
Stramshall *T*	128	SK 0835
Strandburgh Ness	205	HU 6792
Stranraer *P*	154	NX 0660
Strata Florida *T*	125	SN 7465
Stratfield Mortimer *T*	104	SU 6664
Stratfield Saye *T*	104	SU 6861
Stratfield Turgis *T*	104	SU 6960
Stratford *T*	105	TQ 3884
Stratford St Andrew *T*	123	TM 3560
Stratford St Mary *T*	122	TM 0434
Stratford Tony *T*	94	SU 0926
Stratford-upon-Avon *P*	118	SP 2055
Stratford-upon-Avon Canal *W*	118	SP 1765
Strath *T*	190	NG 7977
Strathaird	187	NG 5418
Strathallan, Central	169	NN 8408
Strathallan, Tays	169	NN 8408
Strathallan Castle	170	NN 9115
Strathan, Highld *T*	196	NC 0821
Strathan, Highld *T*	174	NM 9791
Strath an Lòin	197	NC 4417
Strathardle	176	NO 1055
Strathaven *T*	162	NS 7044
Strath Avon	183	NJ 1526
Strath Beag	191	NH 1087
Strath Beg	198	NC 8531
Strath Blane, Central	169	NS 5380
Strathblane, Central *T*	169	NS 5679
Strathblane Hills *H*	169	NS 5681
Strathbogie, Grampn	184	NJ 4937
Strath Bogie, Grampn	184	NJ 5238
Strathbraan	176	NN 9739
Strath Bran	182	NH 2461
Strath Brora	193	NC 7408
Strath Burn *W*	199	ND 2551
Strathcarron	192	NH 5391
Strathcoil	173	NM 6830
Strathconon	182	NH 4056
Strathconon Forest	182	NH 2447
Strath Cuileannach	192	NH 4393
Strathdearn	183	NH 7624
Strathdon *T*	184	NJ 3512
Strath Dores	182	NH 6138
Strath Eachaig	168	NS 1385
Strathearn	170	NN 9118
Stratherrick, Highld	182	NH 5016
Stratherrick, Highld	182	NH 5118
Strath Fillan	169	NN 3627
Strath Finella	177	NO 6979
Strathfinella Hill *H*	177	NO 6878
Strath Fleet	193	NC 7003
Strath Gartney	169	NN 4511
Strathgarve Forest	182	NH 4164
Strathglass	182	NH 3734
Strathgryfe	168	NS 3370
Strath Halladale	198	NC 8953
Strath Isla	184	NJ 4251
Strath Kanaird, Highld *T*	191	NC 1501
Strath Kanaird, Highld	191	NC 1602
Strathkinness *T*	171	NO 4616
Strathlachlan Forest	168	NS 0093
Strath Mashie	175	NN 5992
Strathmashie House	175	NN 5891
Strath Melness Burn *W*	197	NC 5663
Strathmiglo *T*	171	NO 2110
Strath More, Highld	197	NC 4544
Strath More, Highld	191	NH 1882
Strathmore, Tays	176	NO 4354
Strathmore Lodge	199	ND 1048
Strathmore River *W*	197	NC 4647
Strath Mulzie	191	NH 3193
Strathnairn	183	NH 6731
Strath nan Lùb	168	NS 0791
Strath na Sealga	191	NH 0780
Strathnashealiag Forest	191	NH 0583
Strathnaver	198	NC 7147
Strath of Appin	174	NM 9545
Strath of Kildonan or Strath Ullie	193	NC 9219
Strath of Orchy	168	NN 1827
Strath Oykel	192	NC 4201
Strathpeffer *T*	182	NH 4858
Strath Rannoch, Highld	191	NH 3872
Strathrannoch, Highld *T*	191	NH 3874
Strath Rory	192	NH 6877
Strath Rusdale	192	NH 5777
Strath Sgitheach	182	NH 5263
Strath Shinary	196	NC 2461
Strath Skinsdale	193	NC 7620
Strathspey, Grampn	184	NJ 1840
Strathspey, Highld	184	NJ 1840
Strath Stack	196	NC 2740
Strath Suardal	180	NG 6221
Strathtay, Tays *T*	175	NN 9153
Strath Tay, Tays	176	NO 0242
Strath Tirry	197	NC 5319
Strath Ullie or Strath of Kildonan	193	NC 9219
Strath Vagastie	197	NC 5430
Strath Vaich	191	NH 3572
Strathvaich Forest	191	NH 3176
Strathvaich Lodge	191	NH 3474
Strathwhillan *T*	160	NS 0235
Strathy *T*	198	NC 8365
Strathy Bay *W*	198	NC 8366
Strathy Forest, Highld *F*	198	NC 8255
Strathy Forest, Highld *F*	198	NC 8262
Strathy Point	198	NC 8269
Strathyre, Central *T*	169	NN 5617
Strathyre, Central	169	NN 5618
Strathyre Forest	169	NN 5718
Stratton, Corn *T*	90	SS 2206
Stratton, Dorset *T*	93	SY 6593
Stratton, Glos *T*	114	SP 0103
Stratton Audley *T*	115	SP 6026
Stratton-on-the-Fosse *T*	101	ST 6550
Stratton St Margaret *T*	102	SU 1787
Stratton St Michael *T*	133	TM 2093
Stratton Strawless *T*	133	TG 2220
Stravanan Bay *W*	160	NS 0756
Stravithie	171	NO 5311
Strawarren Fell *W*	154	NX 1679
Streap *H*	174	NM 9486
Streat *T*	97	TQ 3515
Streatham *T*	105	TQ 2972
Streatley, Beds *T*	120	TL 0728
Streatley, Berks *T*	103	SU 5980
Streens	183	NH 8639
Street, Lancs *T*	145	SD 5252
Street, N. Yks *T*	148	NZ 7304
Street, Somer *T*	93	ST 4836
Street End *T*	95	SZ 8599
Streethay *T*	128	SK 1410
Streetly *T*	128	SP 0898
Strefford *T*	116	SO 4485
Strem Ness	202	HT 9741
Strensall *T*	147	SE 6360
Strensham *T*	117	SO 9140

Thelwall Treforest Industrial Estate

Thelwall T 137 SJ 6487
Themelthorpe T 132 TG 0523
Thenford T 119 SP 5241
Therfield T 121 TL 3377
Thetford P 122 TL 8783
Thetford Warren 122 TL 8383
Theydon Bois T 105 TQ 4598
Thickwood T 101 ST 8272
Thieves Holm 200 HY 4614
Thimbleby, Lincs T 141 TF 2369
Thimbleby, N. Yks T 153 SE 4595
Thirkleby T 147 SE 4778
Thirlby T 147 SE 4884
Thirlestane T 164 NT 5647
Thirlestane Castle A 164 NT 5347
Thirlmere W 150 NY 3116
Thirl, The 199 ND 1872
Thirlwall Castle A 158 NY 6666
Thirlwall Common 158 NY 6769
Thirn T 146 SE 2186
Thirsk P 147 SE 4382
Thirstane Hill H 156 NS 8709
Thistleton T 130 SK 9117
Thistley Green T 122 TL 6676
Thixendale T 148 SE 8461
Thockrington 158 NY 9579
Tholomas Drove T 131 TF 4006
Tholthorpe T 147 SE 4766
Thomas Chapel T 110 SN 1008
Thomastown T 184 NJ 5736
Thompson T 132 TL 9296
Thomshill T 184 NJ 2157
Thong T 98 TQ 6770
Thoralby T 146 SE 0086
Thoresby Hall A 139 SK 6371
Thoresway T 141 TF 1696
Thorganby, Lincs T 141 TF 2197
Thorganby, N. Yks T 142 SE 6942
Thorgill 148 SE 7096
Thorington T 123 TM 4274
Thorington Street T 122 TM 0135
Thorlby T 146 SD 9652
Thorley T 105 TL 4718
Thormanby T 147 SE 4974
Thornaby-on-Tees T 153 NZ 4516
Thornage T 132 TG 0536
Thornborough, Bucks T 119 SP 7433
Thornborough, N. Yks T 147 SE 2979
Thornbury, Avon T 101 ST 6390
Thornbury, Devon T 90 SS 4008
Thornbury, H. & W T 113 SO 6259
Thornby T 119 SP 6775
Thorncliffe T 138 SK 0158
Thorncombe T 92 ST 3703
Thorncombe Street T 96 TQ 0042
Thorndon T 123 TM 1369
Thorndon Cross T 89 SX 5393
Thorne T 142 SE 6913
Thorne Moors or Waste 142 SE 7315
Thorner T 147 SE 3840
Thorness Bay W 95 SZ 4594
Thorne St Margaret T 92 ST 0921
Thorne Waste or Moors 142 SE 7315
Thorney, Cambs T 131 TF 2804
Thorney, Notts T 140 SK 8573
Thorney Hill T 94 SZ 2099
Thorney Island 95 SU 7503
Thornfalcon T 92 ST 2823
Thornford T 93 ST 6013
Thorngumbald T 143 TA 2026
Thornham T 132 TF 7343
Thornham Magna T 123 TM 1071
Thornham Parva T 123 TM 1172
Thornhaugh T 130 TF 0600
Thornhill, Central T 169 NS 6699
Thornhill, Derby T 138 SK 1983
Thornhill, D. & G T 156 NX 8795
Thornhill, Hants T 95 SU 4712
Thornhill, M. Glam T 109 ST 1584
Thornhill Edge T 139 SE 2518
Thornicombe T 93 ST 8703
Thornley, Durham T 152 NZ 1137
Thornley, Durham T 153 NZ 3639
Thornliebank T 161 NS 5559
Thorns T 122 TL 7455
Thornthwaite, Cumbr T 150 NY 2225
Thornthwaite, N. Yks T 146 SE 1758
Thornton, Bucks T 119 SP 7535
Thornton, Fife T 171 NT 2897
Thornton, Humbs T 142 SE 7645
Thornton, Humbs T 142 TA 0817
Thornton, Lancs T 145 SD 3442
Thornton, Lincs T 141 TF 2467
Thornton, Mers T 136 SD 3300
Thornton, Northum T 165 NT 9547
Thornton, Tays 176 NO 3946
Thornton Beck W 148 SE 8381
Thornton Castle 177 NO 6871
Thornton Dale T 148 SE 8382
Thorntonhall T 162 NS 5955
Thornton Hough T 136 SJ 3081
Thornton-in-Craven T 146 SD 9048
Thornton-le-Beans T 153 SE 3990
Thornton-le-Clay T 148 SE 6865
Thornton le Moor, Lincs T 140 TF 0596
Thornton-le-Moor, N. Yks T 147 SE 3988
Thornton-le-Moors T 136 SJ 4474
Thorntonloch T 164 NT 7574
Thornton Moor Reservoir W 146 SE 0533
Thornton Reservoir, Leic W 129 SK 4707
Thornton Reservoir, N. Yks W 146 SE 1888
Thornton Rust T 146 SD 9788
Thornton Steward T 146 SE 1787
Thornton Watlass T 147 SE 2385
Thornwood Common T 105 TL 4704
Thorny Hill H 155 NX 5388
Thornyhive Bay W 177 NO 8882
Thoroton T 129 SK 7642
Thorp Arch T 147 SE 4345
Thorpe, Cumbr T 151 NY 4926
Thorpe, Derby T 128 SK 1550
Thorpe, Lincs T 141 TF 4982
Thorpe, Norf T 133 TM 4398
Thorpe, Notts T 129 SK 7649
Thorpe, N. Yks T 146 SE 0161
Thorpe, Surrey T 104 TQ 0268
Thorpe Abbotts T 123 TM 1979
Thorpe Acre T 129 SK 5120
Thorpe Arnold T 129 SK 7720
Thorpe Audlin T 139 SE 4716
Thorpe Bassett T 148 SE 8673
Thorpe Bay T 106 TQ 9185
Thorpe by Water T 130 SP 8996
Thorpe Constantine T 128 SK 2609
Thorpe End T 133 TG 2811
Thorpe Fendykes T 141 TF 4560
Thorpe Green T 122 TL 9354
Thorpe Hall 147 SE 5776
Thorpe Hesley T 139 SK 3796
Thorpe in Balne T 139 SE 5910
Thorpe Langton T 119 SP 7492
Thorpe Larches T 153 NZ 3826
Thorpe le Fallows T 140 SK 9180
Thorpe-le-Soken T 107 TM 1822
Thorpe Malsor T 120 SP 8379
Thorpe Mandeville T 119 SP 5344
Thorpe Market T 133 TG 2435
Thorpe Morieux T 122 TL 9453
Thorpeness T 123 TM 4759
Thorpe on the Hill T 140 SK 9065
Thorpe Salvin T 139 SK 5281
Thorpe Satchville T 129 SK 7311
Thorpe St Andrew T 133 TG 2609
Thorpe Thewles T 153 NZ 4023
Thorpe Underwood T 147 SE 4659
Thorpe Waterville T 120 TL 0281
Thorpe Willoughby T 147 SE 5730
Thorp St Peter T 141 TF 4860
Thorrington T 107 TM 0920
Thorverton T 91 SS 9202
Thrandeston T 123 TM 1176
Thrapston T 120 SP 9978
Threapwood T 126 SJ 4445
Threave Castle A 156 NX 7362
Three Bridges T 97 TQ 2837
Three Cocks T 113 SO 1737
Three Crosses T 108 SS 5794
Three Holes T 131 TF 5000
Three Hundreds of Aylesbury, The 104 SP 8607
Threekingham T 130 TF 0836
Three Leg Cross T 97 TQ 6831
Three Legged Cross T 94 SU 0506
Three Mile Cross T 104 SU 7167
Threemilestone T 87 SW 7844
Three Pikes H 151 NY 8334
Three Sisters, The H 174 NN 1656
Threipmuir Reservoir W 163 NT 1763
Threlkeld T 150 NY 3125
Threshfield T 146 SD 9863
Thrigby T 133 TG 4612
Thringarth T 152 NY 9322
Thringstone T 128 SK 4217
Thrintoft T 152 SE 3293
Thriplow T 121 TL 4346
Throcking T 121 TL 3330
Throckley T 159 NZ 1566
Throckmorton T 118 SO 9849
Throphill T 159 NZ 1385
Thropton T 159 NU 0202
Throsk 170 NS 8591
Throwleigh T 89 SX 6690
Throwley T 99 TQ 9955
Throwley Forestal T 99 TQ 9854
Thrumpton T 129 SK 5031
Thrumster T 199 ND 3345
Thrunton T 159 NU 0810
Thrunton Wood F 159 NU 0709
Thrupp, Glos T 114 SO 8603
Thrupp, Oxon T 115 SP 4815
Thruscross Reservoir W 146 SE 1558
Thrushelton T 88 SX 4487
Thrushgill T 145 SD 6562
Thruxton, Hants T 102 SU 2945
Thruxton, H. & W T 113 SO 4334
Thrybergh T 139 SK 4695
Thundersley T 106 TQ 7988
Thurcaston T 129 SK 5610
Thurcroft T 139 SK 4988
Thurgarton, Norf T 133 TG 1834
Thurgarton, Notts T 129 SK 6949
Thurgoland T 139 SE 2901
Thurlaston, Leic T 129 SP 5099
Thurlaston, Warw T 119 SP 4670
Thurlby, Lincs T 140 SK 9061
Thurlby, Lincs T 130 TF 0916
Thurleigh T 120 TL 0558
Thurlestone T 89 SX 6742
Thurloxton T 92 ST 2730
Thurlstone T 139 SE 2303
Thurlton T 133 TM 4198
Thurmaston T 129 SK 6109
Thurnham, Kent T 98 TQ 8057
Thurnham, Lancs T 145 SD 4554
Thurning, Norf T 132 TG 0829
Thurning, Northnts T 120 TL 0883
Thurnscoe T 139 SE 4505
Thursby T 150 NY 3250
Thursford T 132 TF 9833
Thursley T 103 SU 9039
Thurso P 199 ND 1168
Thurso Bay W 199 ND 1170
Thurstaston T 136 SJ 2484
Thurston T 122 TL 9265
Thurstonfield T 150 NY 3156
Thurstonland T 138 SE 1610
Thurton T 133 TG 3200
Thurvaston T 128 SK 2437
Thuxton T 132 TG 0307
Thwaite, N. Yks T 152 SD 8998
Thwaite, Suff T 123 TM 1168
Thwaite St Mary T 133 TM 3395
Thwing T 149 TA 0570
Tianavaig Bay W 187 NG 5138
Tibbermore T 170 NO 0523
Tibber's Castle A 156 NX 8698
Tibberton, Glos T 114 SO 7622
Tibberton, H. & W T 117 SO 9057
Tibberton, Shrops T 127 SJ 6820
Tibbie Sheils Inn 157 NT 2420
Tibshelf T 139 SK 4360
Tibthorpe T 149 SE 9655
Ticehurst T 97 TQ 6930
Tichborne T 95 SU 5730
Tickencote T 130 SK 9809
Tickenham T 101 ST 4471
Tick Fen 121 TL 3484
Tickhill T 139 SK 5893
Ticklerton T 116 SO 4890
Ticknall T 128 SK 3523
Tickton T 142 TA 0641
Tidcombe T 102 SU 2958
Tiddington, Oxon T 104 SP 6504
Tiddington, Warw T 118 SP 2255
Tidebrook T 97 TQ 6129
Tideford T 88 SX 3459
Tidenham T 113 ST 5596
Tidenham Chase 113 ST 5598
Tideswell T 138 SK 1575
Tidmarsh T 104 SU 6374
Tidmington T 118 SP 2638
Tidpit T 94 SU 0719
Tiers Cross T 110 SM 9010
Tiffield T 119 SP 6951
Tifty T 185 NJ 7740
Tigerton T 177 NO 5464
Tigharry T 188 NF 7172
Tigh-na-Blair 169 NN 7716
Tighnabruaich T 168 NR 9772
Tighnafiline T 190 NG 8789
Tighvein H 160 NR 9927
Tigley T 89 SX 7560
Tilbrook T 120 TL 0869
Tilbury P 98 TQ 6376
Tile Cross T 118 SP 1686
Tile Hill T 118 SP 2878
Tilehurst T 104 SU 6673
Tilford T 103 SU 8743
Tillathrowie T 184 NJ 4735
Tillicoultry T 170 NS 9196
Tillingham T 107 TL 9903
Tillington, H. & W T 113 SO 4645
Tillington, W. Susx T 96 SU 9621
Tillington Common T 113 SO 4546
Tillyarblet 177 NO 5267
Tillycorthie T 185 NJ 9023
Tillydrine T 177 NO 6098
Tillyfourie T 184 NJ 6412
Tillygarmond 177 NO 6393
Tillygreig T 185 NJ 8823
Tillykerrie 185 NJ 8321
Tilly Whim Caves 94 SZ 0376
Tilmanstone T 99 TR 3051
Tilney All Saints T 131 TF 5617
Tilney High End T 131 TF 5617
Tilney St Lawrence T 131 TF 5413
Tilshead T 102 SU 0347
Tilstock T 127 SJ 5437
Tilston T 126 SJ 4651
Tilstone Fearnall T 137 SJ 5660
Tilsworth T 104 SP 9724
Tilton on the Hill T 129 SK 7405
Timberland T 141 TF 1258
Timberland Delph W 141 TF 1560
Timbersbrook T 137 SJ 8962
Timberscombe T 91 SS 9542
Timble T 146 SE 1853
Timperley T 137 SJ 7888
Timsbury, Avon T 101 ST 6658
Timsbury, Hants T 94 SU 3424
Timsgarry T 194 NB 0534
Timworth Green T 122 TL 8669
Tincleton T 93 SY 7791
Tindale T 158 NY 6159
Tindale Tarn, Cumbr W 158 NY 6058
Tindale Tarn, Northum W 158 NY 6058
Tind, The 205 HU 6790
Tingewick T 119 SP 6532
Tingley T 147 SE 2826
Tingrith T 120 TL 0032
Tingwall 200 HY 4023
Tinhay T 88 SX 3985
Tinnis Castle A 163 NT 1434
Tinnis Hill H 157 NY 4385
Tinshill T 147 SE 2539
Tinsley T 139 SK 4090
Tintagel T 88 SX 0588
Tintagel Head 88 SX 0489
Tintern Abbey A 113 SO 5300
Tintern Parva T 113 SO 5301
Tintinhull T 93 ST 4919
Tinto H 163 NS 9534
Tinto Hills H 163 NS 9434
Tintwistle T 138 SK 0297
Tinwald T 156 NY 0081
Tinwell T 130 TF 0006
Tipperty T 185 NJ 9627
Tipperweir H 177 NO 6885
Tipton T 118 SO 9592
Tipton St John T 92 SY 0991
Tiptree T 106 TL 8916
Tirabad T 112 SN 8841
Tiree 172 NM 0045
Tiree Airport 172 NM 0045
Tirfergus Hill H 160 NR 6617
Tirga Mòr H 194 NB 0511
Tirley T 114 SO 8328
Tirphil T 109 SO 1303
Tir Rhiwiog H 125 SH 9316
Tirymynach 125 SH 9201
Tisbury T 94 ST 9429
Tissington T 128 SK 1752
Titchberry T 90 SS 2427
Titchfied T 95 SU 5305
Titchmarsh T 120 TL 0279
Titchwell T 132 TF 7643
Titley T 113 SO 3360
Titlington T 159 NU 0915
Tittensor T 127 SJ 8738
Titterstone Clee Hill H 117 SO 5978
Tittesworth Reservoir W 138 SJ 9959
Tittleshall T 132 TF 8921
Tiumpan Head 195 NB 5737
Tiverton, Ches T 137 SJ 5560
Tiverton, Devon T 91 SS 9512
Tiverton Junction Station 92 ST 0311
Tivetshall St Margaret T 123 TM 1686
Tivetshall St Mary T 123 TM 1686
Tixall T 128 SJ 9722
Tixover T 130 SK 9700
Toab, Orkney T 200 HY 5106
Toab, Shetld T 203 HU 3811
Toa Galson 195 NB 4560
Tobermory T 173 NM 5055
Toberonochy T 173 NM 7408
Tobson T 195 NB 1338
Tocher T 185 NJ 6932
Tockenham T 102 SU 0479
Tockenham Wick T 102 SU 0381
Tockholes T 145 SD 6623
Tockington T 101 ST 6086
Tockwith T 147 SE 4752
Todber T 93 ST 7920
Toddington, Beds T 120 TL 0028
Toddington, Glos T 114 SP 0332
Toddun H 189 NB 2102
Todenham T 118 SP 2436
Todhead Point 177 NO 8777
Tod Hill H 160 NR 7211
Todhills T 157 NY 3663
Tod Law H 162 NS 7735
Todmorden T 146 SD 9324
Todwick T 139 SK 4984
Toes 110 SR 8994
Toft, Cambs T 121 TL 3656
Toft, Lincs T 130 TF 0617
Toft Hill T 152 NZ 1528
Toft Monks T 133 TM 4294
Toft next Newton T 140 TF 0488
Toftrees T 132 TF 8927
Toft Sand 131 TF 4440
Tofts Voe W 205 HU 4375
Toftwood T 132 TF 9911
Togston T 159 NU 2401
Tokavaig T 180 NG 6011
Tokers Green T 104 SU 6977
Tolland T 92 ST 1032
Tollard Royal T 94 ST 9417
Toll Bar T 139 SE 5508
Toll Creagach H 181 NH 1928
Toller Fratrum T 93 SY 5797
Toller Porcorum T 93 SY 5697
Tollerton, Notts T 129 SK 6034
Tollerton, N. Yks T 147 SE 5164
Tollesbury T 106 TL 9510
Tolleshunt D'Arcy T 106 TL 9211
Tolleshunt Major T 106 TL 9011
Toll of Birness 185 NK 0034
Tollomuick Forest 191 NH 3380
Tolmount, Grampn H 176 NO 2180
Tolmount, Tays H 176 NO 2180
Tolpuddle T 93 SY 7994
Tolquhon Castle A 185 NJ 8728
Tolsta Chaolais T 195 NB 1937
Tolsta Head 195 NB 5647
Tolworth T 105 TQ 1965
Tom a' Chòinich H 181 NH 1627
Tom an t-Saighdeir H 168 NM 9715
Tom an t-Suidhe Mhòir H 183 NJ 1118
Tomatin T 183 NH 8029
Tom Bailgeann H 182 NH 5829
Tombane Burn W 175 NN 9341
Tombreck T 183 NH 6934
Tomchrasky T 182 NH 2512
Tomdoun T 174 NH 1501
Tomich, Highld T 182 NH 3027
Tomich, Highld T 193 NH 7071
Tomich House 182 NH 5347
Tomintoul, Grampn T 184 NJ 1618
Tomintoul, Grampn T 176 NO 1490
Tomlachlan Burn W 183 NH 9337
Tom na h-Iolaire H 168 NR 9484
Tomnaven 184 NJ 4033
Tomnavoulin T 184 NJ 2126
Tomont End 161 NS 1859
Tom's Cairn H 177 NO 6194
Tomsléibhe 173 NM 6137
Tom Soilleir H 173 NM 8409
Tomtain H 169 NS 7281
Tonbridge T 97 TQ 5947
Tondu T 109 SS 8984
Tong, Shrops T 127 SJ 7907
Tong, W. Isles T 195 NB 4436
Tonga 205 HP 5815
Tonge T 128 SK 4123
Tongham T 103 SU 8849
Tongland T 155 NX 6953
Tongue (lightship) 107 TR 3485
Tongue T 197 NC 5956
Tongue Bay W 197 NC 6061
Tongue House 197 NC 5958
Tongwynlais T 109 ST 1382
Tòn Mhòr H 166 NR 2371
Tonna T 109 SS 7799
Ton-teg T 109 ST 0986
Tòn Tire 173 NM 6020
Tonwell T 105 TL 3317
Tonypandy T 109 SS 9992
Tonyrefail T 109 ST 0188
Toot Baldon T 115 SP 5600
Toot Hill, Essex T 105 TL 5102
Toothill, Hants T 94 SU 3818
Topcliffe T 147 SE 4026
Topcroft T 123 TM 2692
Topcroft Street T 123 TM 2691
Toppesfield T 122 TL 7337
Toppings T 137 SD 7213
Topsham T 89 SX 9688
Torbay, Devon P 89 SX 8962
Tor Bay, Devon W 89 SX 9259
Torbeg T 160 NR 9029
Torboll Farm 193 NH 7599
Torbreck Burn W 193 NC 7006
Torbryan T 89 SX 8166
Torcastle 174 NN 1378
Torcross T 89 SX 8242
Tore T 182 NH 6052
Tore Hill H 183 NH 9917
Torfichen Hill, Border H 164 NT 3353
Torfichen Hill, Lothn H 164 NT 3353
Torhousemuir 154 NX 3957
Torksey T 140 SK 8378
Torlum, Tays H 169 NN 8119
Torlum, W. Isles T 188 NF 7851
Torlum Wood F 169 NN 8218
Torlundy T 174 NN 1477
Tormarton T 101 ST 7778
Tormisdale 166 NR 1958
Tormitchell T 154 NX 2394
Tormore T 160 NR 8932
Tornsdale 199 ND 1450
Tornagrain T 183 NH 7649
Tornahaish T 184 NJ 2908
Tornashean Forest F 184 NJ 3710
Tornaveen T 184 NJ 6106
Torness, Highld T 182 NH 5827
Tor Ness, Orkney 200 HY 4219
Tor Ness, Orkney 201 HY 6520
Tor Ness, Orkney 201 HY 7555
Tor Ness, Orkney 199 ND 2588
Torogay 188 NF 9178
Torosay Castle 173 NM 7235
Torpantau H 109 SO 0418
Torpenhow T 150 NY 2039
Torphichen T 170 NS 9672
Torphins T 177 NJ 6202
Torpoint T 88 SX 4355
Torquay T 89 SX 9164
Torquhan T 164 NT 4447
Torrachilty Wood F 182 NH 4355
Torran, Highld T 190 NG 5948
Torran, Strath 168 NM 8704
Torrance T 169 NS 6274
Torran Rocks 172 NM 2814
Torrans 173 NM 4825
Torran Tùrach H 168 NS 0070
Torran Water W 199 ND 0553
Torrent Walk 125 SH 7518
Torridon T 190 NG 8956
Torridon Forest 190 NG 9058
Torridon House 190 NG 8657
Torrin T 180 NG 5720
Torrisdale, Highld T 197 NC 6761
Torris Dale, Strath 160 NR 7837
Torrisdale Bay W 197 NC 6962
Torrisdale Castle 160 NR 7936
Torrish 193 NC 9718
Torrisholme T 145 SD 4564
Torr Meadhonach H 160 NR 9551
Tòrr Mòr H 161 NS 1052
Torr Nead an Eoin H 160 NR 9549
Torroble T 192 NC 5904
Torrs Warren 154 NX 1454
Torr, The H 160 NR 9125
Torry, Grampn T 184 NJ 4340
Torry, Grampn T 185 NJ 9505
Torry Bay W 170 NT 0185
Torryburn 170 NT 0286
Torrylin T 160 NR 9521
Torrylinwater Foot 160 NR 9520
Torsa 173 NM 7613
Torside Reservoir W 138 SK 0698
Torterston T 185 NK 0747
Torthorwald T 157 NY 0378
Tortington T 96 TQ 0005
Tortworth T 114 ST 7093
Torvaig T 187 NG 4944
Torver T 150 SD 2894
Torwood T 169 NS 8485
Torworth T 139 SK 6586
Toscaig T 180 NG 7138
Toseland T 121 TL 2362
Tosside T 146 SD 7756
Tosside Beck, Lancs W 146 SD 7853
Tosside Beck, N. Yks W 146 SD 7853
Tosson Hill H 159 NZ 0098
Tostock T 122 TL 9563
Totaig T 186 NG 2050
Totarol T 195 NB 1834
Tote, Highld T 187 NG 4149
Tote, Highld T 187 NG 5159
Totegan T 198 NC 8268
Totland T 94 SZ 3287
Totland Bay W 94 SZ 3186
Totley T 139 SK 3079
Totnes T 89 SX 8060
Totronald 172 NM 1656
Totscore T 186 NG 3866
Tottenham T 105 TQ 3390
Tottenhill T 132 TF 6410
Totteridge, Bucks T 104 SU 8793
Totteridge, G. Lon T 105 TQ 2494
Totternhoe T 104 SP 9821
Tottiford Reservoir W 89 SX 8183
Tottington T 137 SD 7712
Totton T 94 SU 3613
Touch Hills H 169 NS 7291
Tournaig T 190 NG 8783
Toux, Grampn T 184 NJ 5459
Toux, Grampn T 185 NJ 9850
Tovil T 97 TQ 7554
Towan Head 87 SW 7962
Toward T 156 NS 6812
Toward Point 161 NS 1367
Towcester T 119 SP 6948
Towednack T 86 SW 4838
Tower Point 110 SM 7910
Towersey T 104 SP 7305
Towie T 184 NJ 4412
Towiemore T 184 NJ 3945
Tow Law T 152 NZ 1139
Towneley Hall A 146 SD 8530
Town End T 131 TL 4195
Townhead, Cumbr T 151 NY 6334
Townhead, D. & G T 155 NX 6946
Townhead of Greenlaw T 156 NX 7464
Townhill T 170 NT 1089
Townshend T 86 SW 5932
Town Yetholm T 165 NT 8228
Towthorpe T 147 SE 6258
Towton T 147 SE 4839
Towyn T 135 SH 9779
Toynton All Saints T 141 TF 3964
Toynton Fen Side T 141 TF 3962
Toynton St Peter T 141 TF 4063
Toy's Hill T 97 TQ 4651
Trabboch T 161 NS 4321
Trabbochburn T 161 NS 4621
Traboe T 86 SW 7421
Tradespark, Highld T 183 NH 8656
Tradespark, Orkney T 200 HY 4508
Traeth Bach 134 SH 5836
Traeth Lafan or Lavan Sands 135 SH 6375
Trafford Park T 137 SJ 7896
Trahenna Hill H 163 NT 1337
Traigh House 180 NM 6590
Tràigh Mhòr 178 NF 7005
Trallong T 109 SN 9629
Trallwng or Welshpool P 126 SJ 2207
Tranent T 171 NT 4072
Trannon H 125 SN 9196
Trantlemore T 198 NC 8953
Tranwell T 159 NZ 1883
Trapp T 111 SN 6519
Traprain T 171 NT 5975
Traprain Law A 171 NT 5874
Traquair T 164 NT 3334
Traquair House A 164 NT 3335
Trawden T 146 SD 9138
Trawsallt H 125 SN 7870
Trawsfynydd T 135 SH 7035
Trealaval H 195 NB 2623
Trealaw T 109 ST 0092
Treales T 145 SD 4433
Trearddur T 134 SH 2579
Treaslane T 187 NG 3953
Trebartha T 88 SX 2677
Trebetherick T 87 SW 9377
Treborough T 92 ST 0136
Trebudannon T 87 SW 8961
Treburley T 88 SX 3477
Trecastle T 109 SN 8829
Trecwn T 110 SM 9632
Trecynon T 109 SN 9903
Tredavoe T 86 SW 4528
Tredegar T 109 SO 1409
Tredegar Park A 100 ST 2885
Tredington T 118 SP 2543
Tredinnick T 87 SW 9270
Tredomen T 109 SO 1231
Tredrizzick T 87 SW 9576
Tredunnock T 113 ST 3894
Treen T 86 SW 3923
Treeton T 139 SK 4387
Trefdraeth T 134 SH 4070
Trefeca T 109 SO 1432
Trefeglwys T 125 SN 9790
Trefenter T 124 SN 6068
Treffgarne T 110 SM 9523
Treffynnon T 110 SM 8428
Trefil T 109 SO 1212
Trefilan T 111 SN 5557
Trefnanney T 126 SJ 2015
Trefnant T 135 SJ 0570
Trefonen T 126 SJ 2527
Trefor T 134 SH 3780
Treforest T 109 ST 0889
Treforest Industrial Estate 109 ST 1186

Trefriw Vale of Evesham

Trefriw T 135 SH 7863
Tregadillett T 88 SX 2983
Tregaian T 134 SH 4579
Tregare T 113 SO 4110
Tregaron T 112 SN 6860
Tregarth T 134 SH 6068
Tregeare T 88 SX 2486
Tregeare Rounds A 87 SX 0380
Tregeiriog T 126 SJ 1733
Tregele T 134 SH 3592
Tregidden T 86 SW 7522
Treglemais T 110 SM 8229
Tregole T 88 SX 1998
Tregonetha T 87 SW 9563
Tregonning Hill H 86 SW 6029
Tregony T 87 SW 9244
Tregoyd T 113 SO 1937
Tre-groes T 111 SN 4044
Tregurrian T 87 SW 8565
Tregynon T 125 SO 0998
Trehafod T 109 ST 0491
Treharris T 109 ST 0997
Treherbert T 109 SS 9498
Treknow T 88 SX 0586
Trelan T 86 SW 7418
Trelawnyd T 135 SJ 0979
Trelech T 111 SN 2830
Treleddyd-fawr T 110 SM 7527
Trelewis T 109 ST 1097
Treligga T 88 SX 0584
Trelights T 87 SW 9979
Trelill T 87 SX 0478
Trelissik T 87 SW 8339
Trelleck T 113 SO 5005
Trelleck Grange T 113 SO 4901
Trelogan T 136 SJ 1180
Trelowarren A 86 SW 7124
Trelystan 126 SJ 2603
Tremadog T 134 SH 5640
Tremadog Bay W 134 SH 5334
Tremail T 88 SX 1686
Tremain T 111 SN 2348
Tremaine T 88 SX 2388
Tremar T 87 SX 2568
Trematon T 88 SX 3959
Tremeirchion T 135 SJ 0873
Trenance T 87 SW 8567
Trenarren T 87 SX 0348
Trench T 127 SJ 6913
Trenchford Reservoir W 89 SX 8082
Trendrine Hill H 86 SW 4738
Treneglos T 88 SX 2088
Trenewan T 87 SX 1753
Trent T 93 ST 5918
Trent and Mersey Canal, Ches W 137 SJ 7164
Trent and Mersey Canal, Derby W 128 SK 3529
Trent and Mersey Canal, Staffs W 128 SK 2018
Trentham T 127 SJ 8741
Trentishoe T 91 SS 6448
Trent Valley 128 SJ 9922
Treoes T 109 SS 9478
Treorchy T 109 SS 9596
Tre'r Ceiri A 134 SH 3744
Tre'r-ddôl T 125 SN 6692
Trerice A 87 SW 8458
Tresaith T 111 SN 2851
Tresco 86 SV 8914
Trescott T 127 SO 8497
Trescowe T 86 SW 5730
Tresham T 101 ST 7991
Treshnish Isles 172 NM 2741
Treshnish Point 172 NM 3348
Tresillian T 87 SW 8646
Tresinwen T 110 SM 9040
Tresmeer T 88 SX 2387
Tres Ness 201 HY 7137
Tressait T 175 NN 8160
Tresta, Shetld T 203 HU 3651
Tresta, Shetld 205 HU 6190
Treswell T 140 SK 7879
Tre Taliesin T 125 SN 6591
Trethevy Quoit A 87 SX 2568
Trethewey T 86 SW 3823
Trethomas T 109 ST 1889
Trethurgy T 87 SX 0355
Tretio T 110 SM 7829
Tretire T 113 SO 5224
Tretower T 109 SO 1821
Tretower Court & Castle A 109 SO 1821
Treuddyn T 136 SJ 2558
Trevalga T 88 SX 0890
Trevanson T 87 SW 9772
Trevarren T 87 SW 9160
Trevarrick T 87 SW 9843
Trevellas T 86 SW 7452
Treverva T 86 SW 7531
Trevethin T 113 SO 2802
Trevigro T 88 SX 3369
Trevine T 110 SM 8432
Treviscoe T 87 SW 9456
Trevone T 87 SW 8975
Trevor T 134 SH 3746
Trevose Head W 87 SW 8576
Trewarmett T 88 SX 0686
Trewarthenick T 87 SW 9044
Trewassa T 88 SX 1486
Trewavas Head 86 SW 5926
Trewellard T 86 SW 3733
Trewen T 88 SX 2583
Trewent Point 110 SS 0297
Trewidland T 87 SX 2559
Trewint T 88 SX 1897
Trewithian T 87 SW 8737
Trewoon T 87 SW 9952
Treyarnon T 87 SW 8673
Treyford T 95 SU 8218
Triangular Lodge A 120 SP 8382
Trichrug H 108 SN 7023
Trickett's Cross T 94 SU 0901
Trigon Hill H 93 SY 8989
Trimdon T 153 NZ 3633
Trimdon Colliery 153 NZ 3835
Trimdon Grange T 153 NZ 3635
Trimingham T 133 TG 2738
Trimley St Martin T 123 TM 2738
Trimley St Mary T 123 TM 2836
Trimpley T 117 SO 7978
Trimpley Reservoir W 117 SO 7778
Trimsaran T 111 SN 4504
Trimstone T 90 SS 5043
Trinant T 109 SO 2000
Tring T 104 SP 9211
Trinity T 177 NO 6062
Trislaig T 174 NN 0874
Trispen T 87 SW 8450
Tritlington T 159 NZ 2092
Triuirebheinn H 178 NF 8121
Trochry T 176 NN 9740
Troedyraur T 111 SN 3245
Troedyrhiw T 109 SO 0702
Trofarth T 135 SH 8571
Troisgeach H 168 NN 2919
Trondavoe T 205 HU 3770
Troon, Corn T 86 SW 6638
Troon, Strath T 161 NS 3230
Trossachs, The 169 NN 5007
Troston T 122 TL 8972
Troswick Ness 203 HU 4117
Trotternish 187 NG 4653
Trottiscliffe T 98 TQ 6460
Trotton T 95 SU 8322
Troughend Common 158 NY 8591
Troup Head 185 NJ 8267
Troutbeck T 151 NY 4003
Troutbeck Bridge T 151 NY 4000
Trowbridge P 101 ST 8557
Trow Green T 113 SO 5706
Trowie Glen 200 HY 2300
Trowle Common T 101 ST 8458
Trows T 164 NT 6932
Trowse Newton T 133 TG 2406
Trudoxhill T 101 ST 7443
Trull T 92 ST 2122
Truman H 109 SN 7420
Trumau H 125 SN 8667
Trum Gelli H 125 SH 6501
Trumisgarry T 188 NF 8675
Trumland House 200 HY 4227
Trumpan T 186 NG 2261
Trumpet T 117 SO 6539
Trumpington T 121 TL 4454
Trunch T 133 TG 2834
Trundle, The A 95 SU 8711
Truro P 87 SW 8244
Trusham T 89 SX 8582
Trusley T 128 SK 2535
Trusthorpe T 141 TF 5183
Trwyn Cilan 124 SH 2923
Trwyn Llanbedrog 134 SH 3330
Trwyn Maen Dylan 134 SH 4252
Trwyn y Bwa 110 SN 0543
Trwyn y Gorlech 134 SH 3445
Trwyn yr Wylfa 124 SH 3224
Trysull T 127 SO 8594
Tuarie Burn W 193 NC 8220
Tubney T 115 SU 4398
Tuckenhay T 89 SX 8156
Tuckhill T 117 SO 7888
Tuddenham, Suff T 122 TL 7371
Tuddenham, Suff T 123 TM 1948
Tudeley T 97 TQ 6245
Tudhoe T 152 NZ 2635
Tudhope Hill, Border H 157 NY 4399
Tudhope Hill, D. & G H 157 NY 4399
Tudweiliog T 134 SH 2336
Tuffley T 114 SO 8315
Tufton T 110 SN 0428
Tugby T 129 SK 7600
Tugford T 116 SO 5587
Tulach Hill H 175 NN 8564
Tulliallan Castle 170 NS 9388
Tullibody T 170 NS 8695
Tullibole Castle A 170 NO 0500
Tullich, Highld 193 NH 8576
Tullich, Strath T 168 NN 0815
Tullich Hill H 175 NN 7036
Tullich Muir T 193 NH 7373
Tulliemet 176 NN 9952
Tulliemet House 176 NN 9954
Tulloch, Grampn T 177 NO 7771
Tulloch, Highld 192 NH 6192
Tulloch, Highld 183 NH 9816
Tulloch Castle 182 NH 5460
Tullochgorm 168 NR 9695
Tulloch Station 174 NN 3580
Tulloes 177 NO 5146
Tullo Hill H 177 NO 4964
Tullybannocher 169 NN 7521
Tullybothy Craigs 171 NO 6410
Tullyfergus 176 NO 2149
Tullymurdoch 176 NO 1952
Tullynessle T 184 NJ 5519
Tulm Bay W 187 NG 4175
Tumble T 111 SN 5411
Tumby Woodside T 141 TF 2657
Tummel Bridge T 175 NN 7659
Tummer Hill Scar 144 SD 1867
Tunbridge Wells, Royal T 97 TQ 5839
Tungadal River W 187 NG 4239
Tunstall, Humbs T 143 TA 3031
Tunstall, Kent T 98 TQ 8961
Tunstall, Lancs T 145 SD 6073
Tunstall, Norf T 133 TG 4108
Tunstall, N. Yks T 152 SE 2196
Tunstall, Staffs T 127 SJ 8651
Tunstall, Suff T 123 TM 3655
Tunstall Forest F 123 TM 3854
Tunstall Reservoir W 152 NZ 0641
Tunstead T 133 TG 2921
Tunworth T 103 SU 6748
Tupsley T 113 SO 5340
Tupton T 139 SK 3966
Turgis Green T 104 SU 6959
Turin 177 NO 5353
Turin Hill H 177 NO 5153
Turkdean T 114 SP 1017
Tur Langton T 129 SP 7194
Turls Head 204 HU 2886
Turnastone T 113 SO 3536
Turnberry T 161 NS 2005
Turnberry Bay W 161 NS 1906
Turnditch T 128 SK 2946
Turners Hill T 97 TQ 3135
Turners Puddle T 93 SY 8393
Turnworth T 93 ST 8207
Turriff T 185 NJ 7250
Turton Bottoms T 137 SD 7415
Turton Moor 137 SD 6918
Turvalds Head 204 HU 3268
Turves T 131 TL 3396
Turvey T 120 SP 9452
Turville T 104 SU 7691
Turville Heath T 104 SU 7491
Turweston T 119 SP 6037
Tushielaw 157 NT 3018
Tusker Rock 109 SS 8474
Tutbury T 128 SK 2128
Tutnall T 118 SO 9970
Tutshill T 113 ST 5494
Tuttington T 133 TG 2227
Tuxford T 140 SK 7370
Twa Havens W 185 NK 1036
Twatt, Orkney T 200 HY 2724
Twatt, Shetld T 203 HU 3253
Twechar T 169 NS 7075
Tweedmouth T 165 NT 9952
Tweedsmuir T 163 NT 1024
Tweed's Well W 157 NT 0514
Twelveheads T 86 SW 7642
Twemlow Green T 137 SJ 7868
Twenty T 130 TF 1520
Twenty Foot River W 131 TF 3600
Twerton T 101 ST 7264
Twickenham T 105 TQ 1473
Twigworth T 114 SO 8522
Twineham T 96 TQ 2519
Twiness 200 HY 4941
Twinhoe T 101 ST 7459
Twinlaw Cairns A 164 NT 6254
Twinstead T 122 TL 8636
Twinyess 201 HY 7452
Twitchen, Devon T 91 SS 7830
Twitchen, Shrops T 116 SO 3779
Twmpa H 109 SO 2235
Two Bridges T 89 SX 6074
Two Dales T 139 SK 2863
Two Gates T 128 SK 2101
Twopenny Knowe H 162 NS 6232
Twycross T 128 SK 3305
Twyford, Berks T 104 SU 7975
Twyford, Bucks T 119 SP 6626
Twyford, Hants T 95 SU 4825
Twyford, Leic T 129 SK 7210
Twyford, Norf T 132 TG 0124
Twyford Common T 113 SO 5135
Twyn-du H 109 SO 0820
Twynholm T 155 NX 6654
Twyning T 117 SO 9037
Twyning Green T 117 SO 9036
Twynllanan T 109 SN 7524
Twyn Rhyd-car H 112 SN 9642
Twyn-y-Sheriff T 113 SO 4005
Twywell T 120 SP 9578
Tyberton T 113 SO 3839
Tyburn T 118 SP 1391
Tycroes T 111 SN 6010
Ty Croes Station 134 SH 3472
Tycrwyn T 125 SJ 1018
Tydd Gote T 131 TF 4517
Tydd St Giles T 131 TF 4216
Tydd St Giles Fen 131 TF 3914
Tydd St Mary T 131 TF 4418
Tŷ-hen T 134 SH 1731
Tyldesley T 137 SD 7001
Tyler Hill T 99 TR 1460
Tylers Green T 104 SU 9094
Tylorstown T 109 ST 0195
Tylwch T 125 SN 9780
Ty Mawr Cwm 135 SH 9047
Ty-nant, Clwyd T 135 SH 9944
Ty-nant, Gwyn T 125 SH 9026
Tyndrum T 168 NN 3330
Tyneham T 93 SY 8880
Tynehead T 164 NT 3959
Tyne Mouth, Lothn W 171 NT 6480
Tynemouth, T. & W P 159 NZ 3669
Tyne Water W 164 NT 3863
Tynewydd T 109 SS 9399
Tyninghame T 171 NT 6079
Tynron T 156 NX 8092
Tyn-y-ffridd T 126 SJ 1130
Tynygraig, Dyfed T 125 SN 6969
Tyn-y-graig, Powys T 112 SO 0250
Ty'n-y-groes T 135 SH 7771
Tyrebagger Hill H 185 NJ 8412
Ty Rhiw T 109 ST 1284
Tyringham T 120 SP 8547
Tythby T 129 SK 6936
Tythegston T 109 SS 8578
Tytherington, Avon T 101 ST 6688
Tytherington, Ches T 137 SJ 9175
Tytherington, Somer T 101 ST 7645
Tytherington, Wilts T 101 ST 9141
Tytherleigh T 92 ST 3103
Tŷ-uchaf 125 SH 9921
Tywardreath T 87 SX 0854
Tywi Forest, Dyfed F 112 SN 8151
Tywi Forest, Powys F 112 SN 8151
Tywyn, Gwyn T 124 SH 5800
Tywyn, Gwyn T 135 SH 7978
Tywyn Trewan 134 SH 3175

U

Uachdar T 188 NF 8055
Uags T 180 NG 7234
Uair, The W 198 NC 8254
Uamh Bheag, Central H 169 NN 6911
Uamh Bheag, Tays H 169 NN 6911
Ubbeston Green T 123 TM 3272
Ubley T 101 ST 5258
Uchd a' Chlàrsair H 175 NN 8181
Uckerby T 152 NZ 2402
Uckfield T 97 TQ 4721
Uckington T 114 SO 9124
Udairn 187 NG 5142
Udale Bay W 183 NH 7166
Uddingston T 162 NS 6960
Uddington T 163 NS 8633
Udimore T 98 TQ 8619
Udny Green T 185 NJ 8826
Udny Station T 185 NJ 9124
Udstonhead 162 NS 7046
Uffcott T 102 SU 1277
Uffculme T 92 ST 0612
Uffington, Lincs T 130 TF 0607
Uffington, Oxon T 102 SU 3089
Uffington, Shrops T 127 SJ 5213
Uffington Castle A 102 SU 3086
Ufford, Cambs T 130 TF 0904
Ufford, Suff T 123 TM 2952
Ufton T 118 SP 3762
Ufton Nervet T 104 SU 6367
Ugadale T 160 NR 7828
Ugadale Point 160 NR 7828
Ugborough T 89 SX 6755
Ugborough Beacon H 89 SX 6659
Ugborough Moor 89 SX 6462
Uggeshall T 123 TM 4480
Ugglebarnby T 149 NZ 8807
Ugley T 121 TL 5228
Ugley Green T 121 TL 5227
Ugthorpe T 153 NZ 7911
Uig, Highld T 186 NG 1952
Uig, Highld T 187 NG 3963
Uig Bay W 186 NG 3862
Uigshader T 187 NG 4246
Uisenis H 189 NB 3306
Uisge Labhair W 175 NN 4471
Uisge Misgeach W 181 NH 1938
Uisge Toll a' Mhadaidh W 190 NG 9784
Uisgnaval Mòr H 189 NB 1208
Uisken T 172 NM 3919
Ukna Skerry 203 HU 3531
Ulbster T 199 ND 3241
Ulceby, Humbs T 143 TA 1215
Ulceby, Lincs T 141 TF 4272
Ulcombe T 98 TQ 8449
Uldale T 150 NY 2537
Uldale Head H 151 NY 6400
Uldale House 151 SD 7396
Uley T 114 ST 7998
Ulfhart Point 187 NG 4716
Ulgham T 159 NZ 2392
Ulladale River W 194 NB 0713
Ullapool P 191 NH 1294
Ullapool River W 191 NH 1495
Ullaval H 195 NB 0811
Ullenhall T 118 SP 1267
Ullenwood T 114 SO 9416
Ulleskelf T 147 SE 5240
Ullesthorpe T 119 SP 5087
Ulley T 139 SK 4687
Ullingswick T 113 SO 5950
Ullinish T 186 NG 3238
Ullock T 150 NY 0724
Ulscarf H 150 NY 2912
Ullswater W 151 NY 4220
Ulpha T 150 SD 1993
Ulsta T 205 HU 4680
Ultrome T 149 TA 1656
Ulva 172 NM 4140
Ulva House 173 NM 4439
Ulverston T 145 SD 2877
Ulzieside T 156 NS 7708
Umberleigh T 91 SS 6023
Unapool T 196 NC 2333
Underbarrow T 151 SD 4691
Undercliff, The, I. of W 94 SZ 3882
Undercliff, The, I. of W 95 SZ 5376
Underhoull 205 HP 5704
Underriver T 97 TQ 5552
Underwood, Gwent T 100 ST 3889
Underwood, Notts T 129 SK 4750
Undy T 101 ST 4387
Unifirth T 202 HU 2856
Union Canal W 170 NS 9976
Union Cottage 177 NO 8290
Union Mills T 144 SC 3577
Unst 205 HP 6009
Unst Airport 205 HP 6207
Unstone T 139 SK 3777
Unthank T 151 NY 4536
Upavon T 102 SU 1355
Up Cerne T 93 ST 6502
Upchurch T 98 TQ 8467
Upcott T 113 SO 3251
Upend T 122 TL 7058
Up Exe T 91 SS 9402
Uphall T 170 NT 0672
Uphall Station T 170 NT 0670
Upham, Devon T 91 SS 8808
Upham, Hants T 95 SU 5320
Up Hatherley T 114 SO 9120
Uphill T 100 ST 3158
Up Holland T 137 SD 5105
Uplawmoor T 161 NS 4355
Upleadon T 114 SO 7527
Upleatham T 153 NZ 6319
Uplees 99 TQ 9964
Uploders T 93 SY 5093
Uplowman T 92 ST 0115
Uplyme T 92 SY 3293
Upminster T 105 TQ 5686
Up Nately T 103 SU 6951
Upnor T 98 TQ 7570
Upottery T 92 ST 2007
Uppark A 95 SU 7717
Upper Affcot T 116 SO 4486
Upper Ardchronie T 192 NH 6188
Upper Arley T 117 SO 7680
Upper Astrop T 119 SP 5137
Upper Basildon T 103 SU 5976
Upper Bayble T 195 NB 5331
Upper Beeding T 96 TQ 2010
Upper Benefield T 120 SP 9889
Upper Boddington T 119 SP 4853
Upper Borth T 124 SN 6088
Upper Breinton T 113 SO 4640
Upper Broughton T 129 SK 6826
Upper Bucklebury T 103 SU 5468
Upper Burnhaugh 177 NO 8394
Upper Caldecote T 120 TL 1645
Upper Chapel T 112 SO 0040
Upper Chute T 102 SU 2953
Upper Clatford T 102 SU 3543
Upper Clynnog T 134 SH 4646
Upper Coll T 195 NB 4539
Upper Dallachy T 184 NJ 3662
Upper Dean T 120 TL 0467
Upper Denby T 139 SE 2207
Upper Derraid T 183 NJ 0233
Upper Dicker T 97 TQ 5510
Upper Dunsforth T 147 SE 4463
Upper Elkstone T 138 SK 0559
Upper End T 138 SK 0976
Upper Ethie T 183 NH 7663
Upper Farringdon T 95 SU 7135
Upper Framilode T 114 SO 7510
Upper Froyle T 103 SU 7543
Upper Glenfintaig 174 NN 2588
Upper Gravenhurst T 120 TL 1136
Upper Green T 102 SU 3763
Upper Hackney T 139 SK 2961
Upper Hale T 103 SU 8449
Upper Hambleton T 130 SK 9007
Upper Hardres Court T 99 TR 1550
Upper Hartfield T 97 TQ 4734
Upper Heath T 116 SO 5685
Upper Helmsley T 148 SE 6956
Upper Heyford, Northnts T 119 SP 6659
Upper Heyford, Oxon T 115 SP 4926
Upper Heyford Airfield 115 SP 5126
Upper Hill T 113 SO 4753
Upper Hopton T 138 SE 1918
Upper Hulme T 138 SK 0161
Upper Icknield Way A 104 SP 8912
Upper Inglesham T 115 SU 2096
Upper Killay T 108 SS 5892
Upper Knockando T 184 NJ 1843
Upper Lambourne T 102 SU 3180
Upper Lochton T 177 NO 6997
Upper Loch Torridon W 190 NG 8556
Upper Longdon T 128 SK 0614
Upper Longwood T 127 SJ 6007
Upper Lydbrook T 113 SO 6015
Upper Maes-coed T 113 SO 3334
Uppermill T 138 SD 9905
Upper Minety T 102 SU 0090
Upper North Dean T 104 SU 8498
Upper Poppleton T 147 SE 5554
Upper Quinton T 118 SP 1746
Upper Sanday T 200 HY 5403
Upper Sapey T 117 SO 6863
Upper Seagry T 102 ST 9480
Upper Shelton T 120 SP 9943
Upper Sheringham T 133 TG 1441
Upper Skelmorlie T 161 NS 1967
Upper Slaughter T 115 SP 1523
Upper Soudley T 114 SO 6610
Upper Stondon T 120 TL 1435
Upper Stowe T 119 SP 6456
Upper Street, Hants T 94 SU 1518
Upper Street, Norf T 133 TG 3517
Upper Sundon T 120 TL 0427
Upper Swainswick T 101 ST 7568
Upper Swell T 115 SP 1726
Upper Tamar Lake W 90 SS 2812
Upper Tean T 128 SK 0139
Upperthong T 138 SE 1308
Upper Tillyrie T 170 NO 1006
Upperton T 96 SU 9522
Upper Tooting T 105 TQ 2772
Uppertown T 199 ND 3576
Upper Tysoe T 118 SP 3343
Upper Upham T 102 SU 2277
Upper Wardington T 119 SP 4945
Upper Weald T 119 SP 8037
Upper Weedon T 119 SP 6258
Upper Wield T 103 SU 6238
Upper Winchendon T 104 SP 7414
Upper Woodford T 94 SU 1237
Uppingham T 130 SP 8699
Uppington T 127 SJ 5909
Upsall T 147 SE 4587
Upshire T 105 TL 4101
Up Somborne T 94 SU 3932
Upstreet T 99 TR 2263
Up Sydling T 93 ST 6201
Upton, Berks T 104 SU 9879
Upton, Bucks T 104 SP 7711
Upton, Cambs T 130 TF 1000
Upton, Cambs T 120 TL 1778
Upton, Ches T 136 SJ 4169
Upton, Dorset T 94 SY 9693
Upton, Hants T 102 SU 3655
Upton, Hants T 94 SU 3717
Upton, Leic T 128 SP 3699
Upton, Lincs T 140 SK 8686
Upton, Mers T 136 SJ 2788
Upton, Norf T 133 TG 3912
Upton, Northnts T 119 SP 7160
Upton, Notts T 129 SK 7354
Upton, Notts T 140 SK 7476
Upton, Oxon T 103 SU 5186
Upton, Somer T 91 SS 9929
Upton, W. Yks T 139 SE 4713
Upton Bishop T 114 SO 6527
Upton Cheyney T 101 ST 6969
Upton Cressett T 117 SO 6592
Upton Cross T 88 SX 2872
Upton Grey T 103 SU 6948
Upton Hellions T 91 SS 8403
Upton Lovell T 102 ST 9440
Upton Magna T 127 SJ 5512
Upton Noble T 101 ST 7139
Upton Pyne T 89 SX 9197
Upton Scudamore T 101 ST 8647
Upton Snodsbury T 117 SO 9454
Upton St Leonards T 114 SO 8615
Upton upon Severn T 117 SO 8540
Upton Warren T 117 SO 9367
Upwaltham T 96 SU 9413
Upware T 121 TL 5370
Upwell, Cambs T 131 TF 5002
Upwell, Norf T 131 TF 5002
Upwell Fen, Cambs 131 TL 4995
Upwell Fen, Norf 131 TL 5599
Upwey T 93 SY 6684
Upwood T 121 TL 2682
Uradale 203 HU 4037
Ura Firth, Shetld W 204 HU 2977
Urafirth, Shetld T 204 HU 3078
Urchfont T 102 SU 0457
Urdimarsh T 113 SO 5249
Ure 204 HU 2280
Urgha T 189 NG 1799
Urie Lingey 205 HU 5995
Urie Ness 205 HU 5994
Urishay Common T 113 SO 3137
Urit Hill H 162 NS 7626
Urlar Burn W 175 NN 8345
Urlay Nook T 153 NZ 4014
Urmston T 137 SJ 7594
Urquhart T 184 NJ 2862
Urquhart Bay W 182 NH 5229
Urquhart Castle A 182 NH 5328
Urra T 153 NZ 5701
Urrall Fell H 154 NX 2870
Urray T 182 NH 5052
Urr Water W 156 NX 7674
Urswick T 144 SD 2673
Urvaig 172 NM 0850
Ushaw Moor T 152 NZ 2242
Usinish 178 NF 8635
Usk T 113 SO 3701
Uskie Geo 202 HU 2047
Usk Reservoir, Dyfed W 109 SN 8228
Usk Reservoir, Powys W 109 SN 8228
Usselby T 141 TF 0993
Usta Ness 203 HU 3841
Usway Burn W 158 NT 8713
Utley T 146 SE 0542
Uton T 89 SX 8298
Utterby T 141 TF 3093
Uttoxeter P 128 SK 0933
Uwchmynydd, Gwyn T 124 SH 1525
Uwch-mynydd, Gwyn 125 SH 6519
Uxbridge T 104 TQ 0583
Uyea, Shetld 204 HU 3193
Uyea, Shetld 205 HU 6099
Uyea Sound, Shetld W 205 HP 5900
Uyeasound, Shetld T 205 HP 5901
Uynarey 205 HU 4480
Uzmaston T 110 SM 9714

V

Vacsay 195 NB 1136
Vaila 202 HU 2346
Vaila Hall 202 HU 2246
Vaila Sound W 202 HU 2347
Vaitam 188 NF 9380
Vale Catmose 130 SK 8709
Vale of Belvoir, Leic 129 SK 7838
Vale of Belvoir, Notts 129 SK 7838
Vale of Berkeley 114 SO 6900
Vale of Clwyd 135 SJ 0768
Vale of Conwy 135 SH 7866
Vale of Evesham 118 SP 0942

Vale of Gloucester West Bradley

Vale of Gloucester 114 SO 8320
Vale of Mawgan or Lanherne 87 SW 8964
Vale of Neath 109 SN 8303
Vale of Pewsey 102 SU 1158
Vale of Taunton Deane 92 ST 1727
Vale of White Horse, Oxon 102 SU 2689
Vale of White Horse, Wilts 102 SU 2689
Valla Field 205 HP 5807
Vallay, W. Isles 188 NF 7776
Vallay, W. Isles 188 NG 0582
Vallay Strand 188 NF 7875
Valle Crucis Abbey A 126 SJ 2044
Valley Airport 134 SH 3075
Valleyfield T 170 NT 0086
Valsgarth T 205 HP 6413
Valtos, Highld T 187 NG 5163
Valtos, W. Isles T 195 NB 0937
Vange T 106 TQ 7287
Varne (lightship) 99 TR 3830
Varragill River W 187 NG 4738
Varteg T 113 SO 2606
Vatersay, W. Isles 178 NL 6296
Vatersay, W. Isles T 178 NL 6394
Vatersay Bay W 178 NL 6495
Vatisker Point 195 NB 4939
Vatten T 186 NG 2843
Vaul 172 NM 0448
Vaul Bay W 172 NM 0548
Vauld, The T 113 SO 5349
Vaynol Hall 134 SH 5369
Vaynor T 109 SO 0510
Vaynor Park T 126 SJ 1700
Veantrow Bay W 200 HY 5020
Veensgarth T 203 HU 4244
Veilish Point 188 NF 8178
Velindre T 113 SO 1836
Vell 205 HU 4890
Vellan Head 86 SW 6614
Vementry 202 HU 2860
Ve Ness, Orkney 200 HY 3705
Veness, Orkney T 200 HY 5729
Venford Reservoir W 89 SX 6870
Vennington T 126 SJ 3409
Venn Ottery T 92 SY 0791
Venta, Gwent R 101 ST 4790
Venta, Hants R 95 SU 4729
Ventnor T 95 SZ 5677
Vercovicium R 158 NY 7968
Vere, The 205 HP 6403
Vernham Dean T 102 SU 3456
Vernham Street T 102 SU 3557
Vernolds Common T 116 SO 4780
Verran Island T 178 NF 7234
Verulamium R 105 TL 1307
Verwig T 111 SN 1849
Verwood T 94 SU 0908
Veryan T 87 SW 9139
Veryan Bay W 87 SW 9640
Ve Skerries 202 HU 1065
Vestra Fiold H 200 HY 2322
Vicarage T 92 SY 2088
Vickerstown T 144 SD 1868
Victoria T 87 SW 9861
Victoria Station 105 TQ 2979
Vidlin T 203 HU 4765
Vidlin Voe W 203 HU 4866
Viewing Hill H 151 NY 7833
Viewpark T 162 NS 7161
Village Abberley, The T 117 SO 7567
Village, The T 117 SO 8989
Vinehall Street T 97 TQ 7520
Vines Cross T 97 TQ 5917
Vinessan 178 NL 6695
Virda Field H 202 HU 1561
Virginia Water T 104 SU 9967
Virginstow T 88 SX 3792
Virley Channel W 107 TM 0011
Viroconium R 127 SJ 5608
Vobster T 101 ST 7049
Voe, Shetld 204 HU 3381
Voe, Shetld W 203 HU 4015
Voe, Shetld T 203 HU 4062
Voe of Cullingsburgh W 203 HU 5142
Voe of Dale W 202 HU 1751
Voe of Snarraness W 202 HU 2356
Vord Hill H 205 HU 6293
Voreda R 151 NY 4938
Vorogay 188 NF 7864
Vowchurch T 113 SO 3636
Voxter 205 HU 3770
Voy 200 HY 2514
Vuia Beag 195 NB 1233
Vuia Mòr 195 NB 1234
Vyne, The A 103 SU 6357

W

Waberthwaite T 150 SD 1093
Wackerfield T 152 NZ 1522
Wacton T 123 TM 1791
Wadbister Voe W 203 HU 4450
Wadborough T 117 SO 9047
Waddesdon T 104 SP 7416
Waddingham T 140 SK 9896
Waddington, Lancs T 145 SD 7243
Waddington, Lincs T 140 SK 9764
Wadebridge P 87 SW 9872
Wadeford T 92 ST 3110
Wadenhoe T 120 TL 0183
Wadesmill T 105 TL 3517
Wadhurst T 97 TQ 6332
Wadshelf T 139 SK 3171
Wadsworth Moor 146 SD 9833
Wadworth T 139 SK 5797
Waen-fâch T 126 SJ 2017
Wag 199 ND 0126
Wainfleet All Saints T 141 TF 4958
Wainfleet Bank T 141 TF 4759
Wainfleet Sand 131 TF 5455
Wainhope 158 NY 6790
Wainhouse Corner T 88 SX 1895
Wainscott T 98 TQ 7471
Wainstalls T 146 SE 0428
Waitby T 151 NY 7508
Wakefield P 139 SE 3320
Wakerley T 130 SP 9599
Wakes Colne T 122 TL 8928
Walberswick T 123 TM 4974
Walberton T 96 SU 9705
Walbury Hill H 102 SU 3761
Walcot, Lincs T 130 TF 0635
Walcot, Shrops T 127 SJ 5912
Walcot, Shrops T 116 SO 3485
Walcot, Warw T 118 SP 1258
Walcote T 119 SP 5683
Walcott, Lincs T 130 TF 1356
Walcott, Norf T 133 TG 3632
Walden T 146 SE 0083
Walden Head T 146 SD 9880
Walden Stubbs T 139 SE 5516
Waldersey 131 TF 4204
Waldershare House 99 TR 2848
Walderslade T 98 TQ 7663
Walderton T 95 SU 7810
Walditch T 93 SY 4892
Waldridge T 152 NZ 2550
Waldringfield T 123 TM 2844
Waldron T 97 TQ 5419
Wales T 139 SK 4882
Walesby, Lincs T 141 TF 1392
Walesby, Notts T 140 SK 6870
Walford, H. & W T 116 SO 3972
Walford, H. & W T 113 SO 5820
Walford, Shrops T 126 SJ 4320
Walgherton T 127 SJ 6949
Walgrave T 119 SP 8072
Walkden T 137 SD 7403
Walker T 159 NZ 2964
Walkerburn T 164 NT 3637
Walker Fold T 145 SD 6741
Walkeringham T 140 SK 7692
Walkerith T 140 SK 7893
Walkern T 121 TL 2826
Walker's Green T 113 SO 5247
Walkerwood Reservoir W 138 SJ 9898
Walkhampton T 89 SX 5369
Walkington T 142 SE 9937
Walk Mill T 146 SD 8630
Wall, Northum T 158 NY 9169
Wall, Staffs T 128 SK 1006
Wallace's Hill H 164 NT 3036
Wallacetown T 161 NS 3522
Walland Marsh 99 TQ 9923
Wallasey P 136 SJ 2992
Wallbury A 105 TL 4917
Waller's Haven W 97 TQ 6607
Wall Hill H 155 NX 7344
Wall Hills A 113 SO 6359
Walling Fen 142 SE 8829
Wallingford T 103 SU 6089
Wallington, G. Lon T 105 TQ 2863
Wallington, Hants T 95 SU 5806
Wallington, Herts T 121 TL 2933
Wallington Hall A 132 TF 6211
Wallis T 110 SN 0125
Walliswood T 96 TQ 1238
Walls T 202 HU 2449
Wallsend T 159 NZ 2966
Walls, The A 127 SO 7896
Wall under Heywood T 116 SO 5092
Wallyford T 171 NT 3672
Walmer T 99 TR 3750
Walmer Bridge T 145 SD 4824
Walmersley T 137 SD 8013
Walmley T 128 SP 1393
Walpole T 123 TM 3674
Walpole Highway T 131 TF 5113
Walpole St Andrew T 131 TF 5017
Walpole St Peter T 131 TF 5016
Walsall P 128 SP 0198
Walsall Wood T 128 SK 0503
Walsden T 146 SD 9322
Walsgrave on Sowe T 118 SP 3881
Walsham le Willows T 122 TM 0071
Walshaw Dean Reservoir W 146 SD 9633
Walsoken T 131 TF 4710
Walston T 163 NT 0545
Walter's Ash T 104 SU 8398
Walterstone T 113 SO 3425
Waltham, Humbs T 143 TA 2603
Waltham, Kent T 99 TR 1048
Waltham Abbey T 105 TL 3800
Waltham Chase T 95 SU 5615
Waltham Cross T 105 TL 3601
Waltham on the Wolds T 129 SK 8025
Waltham St Lawrence T 104 SU 8276
Walthamstow T 105 TQ 3788
Walton, Bucks T 120 SP 8836
Walton, Cumbr T 158 NY 5264
Walton, Derby T 139 SK 3569
Walton, Leic T 119 SP 5986
Walton, Powys T 113 SO 2559
Walton, Shrops T 127 SJ 5918
Walton, Somer T 93 ST 4636
Walton, Suff T 123 TM 2935
Walton, Warw T 118 SP 2853
Walton, W. Yks T 139 SE 3517
Walton, W. Yks T 147 SE 4447
Walton Cardiff T 114 SO 9032
Walton East T 110 SN 0223
Walton Highway T 131 TF 4912
Walton-in-Gordano T 101 ST 4273
Walton-le-Dale T 145 SD 5527
Walton-on-Thames T 105 TQ 1066
Walton-on-the-Hill, Staffs T 128 SJ 9521
Walton on the Hill, Surrey T 96 TQ 2254
Walton-on-the-Naze T 107 TM 2521
Walton on the Wolds T 129 SK 5919
Walton-on-Trent T 128 SK 2118
Walton West T 110 SM 8612
Walworth T 152 NZ 2318
Walwyn's Castle T 110 SM 8711
Wambrook T 92 ST 2908
Wamphray Water W 157 NT 1400
Wanborough T 102 SU 2183
Wandlebury A 121 TL 4953
Wandsworth T 105 TQ 2673
Wangford T 123 TM 4679
Wangford Fen 122 TL 7484
Wangford Warren 122 TL 7782
Wanlip T 129 SK 5910
Wanlockhead T 156 NS 8712
Wansdyke, Avon A 101 ST 6763
Wansdyke, Wilts A 102 SU 1264
Wansford, Cambs T 130 TL 0799
Wansford, Humbs T 149 TA 0656
Wanstead T 105 TQ 4087
Wanstrow T 101 ST 7141
Wanswell T 114 SO 6801
Wantage T 102 SU 4088
Wantyn's Dyke A 116 SO 1990
Wapley T 101 ST 7179
Wappenbury T 118 SP 3769
Wappenham T 119 SP 6245
Warbleton T 97 TQ 6118
Warborough T 103 SU 5993
Warboys T 121 TL 3080
Warbstow T 88 SX 2090
Warburton T 137 SJ 7089
Warcop T 151 NY 7415
Warcop Fell 151 NY 7820
Warden T 99 TR 0271
Warden Point 99 TR 0272
Ward Green T 122 TM 0463
Ward Hill, Orkney H 200 HY 2202
Ward Hill, Orkney H 200 HY 3307
Ward Hill, Orkney H 200 HY 5530
Ward Hill, Orkney H 199 ND 4588
Wardington T 119 SP 4946
Wardlaw Hill H 162 NS 6822
Wardle, Ches T 137 SJ 6157
Wardle, G. Man T 137 SD 9116
Wardley T 130 SK 8300
Wardlow T 138 SK 1874
Ward of Bressay H 203 HU 5038
Ward of Culswick H 202 HU 2645
Ward of Redland H 200 HY 3617
Ward of Scousburgh H 203 HU 3818
Ward of Veester H 203 HU 4126
War Down H 95 SU 7219
Ward's Stone 145 SD 5858
Wardy Hill T 121 TL 4782
Ware T 105 TL 3514
Wareham T 93 SY 9287
Wareham Forest F 93 SY 8792
Warehorne T 99 TQ 9832
Warenford T 165 NU 1328
Waren Mill T 165 NU 1434
Warenton T 165 NU 1030
Wareside T 105 TL 3915
Waresley T 121 TL 2554
Warfield T 104 SU 8872
Wargrave T 104 SU 7878
Warham T 132 TF 9441
Wark, Northum T 165 NT 8238
Wark, Northum T 158 NY 8677
Wark Forest F 158 NY 7377
Warkleigh T 91 SS 6422
Warks Burn W 158 NY 8176
Warkton T 120 SP 8979
Warkworth T 159 NU 2406
Warlaby T 153 SE 3591
Warland T 137 SD 9420
Warland Reservoir W 138 SD 9620
Warleggan T 87 SX 1569
Warley Moor Reservoir W 146 SE 0331
Warlingham T 105 TQ 3458
Warmfield T 139 SE 3720
Warmingham T 137 SJ 7161
Warmington, Northnts T 120 TL 0791
Warmington, Warw T 118 SP 4147
Warminster P 101 ST 8644
Warmsworth T 139 SE 5400
Warmwell T 93 SY 7585
Warndon T 117 SO 8857
War Ness 200 HY 5528
Warnford T 95 SU 6223
Warnham T 96 TQ 1533
Warninglid T 96 TQ 2526
Warren, Ches T 137 SJ 8970
Warren, Dyfed T 110 SR 9397
Warren Row T 104 SU 8180
Warren Street T 98 TQ 9253
Warrington, Bucks T 120 SP 8953
Warrington, Ches P 137 SJ 6088
Warsash T 95 SU 4906
Warslow T 138 SK 0858
Warsop T 139 SK 5667
Warter T 149 SE 8750
Warth Hill, Cumbr H 145 SD 5684
Warth Hill, Highld H 199 ND 3769
Warthill T 147 SE 6755
Wart Holm 200 HY 4838
Wartling T 97 TQ 6509
Wartnaby T 129 SK 7123
Warton, Lancs T 145 SD 4028
Warton, Lancs T 145 SD 5072
Warton, Northum T 159 NU 0002
Warton, Warw T 128 SK 2803
Warton Sands 145 SD 4472
Wart, The, Orkney H 201 HY 6337
Wart, The, Orkney H 200 ND 4393
Warwick, Cumbr T 151 NY 4656
Warwick, Warw P 118 SP 2865
Warwick Bridge T 151 NY 4756
Wasbister T 200 HY 3932
Wasdale Head T 150 NY 1808
Washaway T 87 SX 0369
Washbourne T 89 SX 7954
Washfield T 91 SS 9315
Washford T 100 ST 0441
Washford Pyne T 91 SS 8111
Washingborough T 140 TF 0270
Washington, T. & W T 152 NZ 3056
Washington, W. Susx T 96 TQ 1212
Wash W 131 TF 5342
Wash, The W 110 SR 9294
Wasing T 103 SU 5764
Waskerley, Durham W 152 NZ 0244
Waskerley, Durham T 152 NZ 0545
Wasperton T 118 SP 2658
Wass T 147 SE 5579
Wass Wick W 200 HY 4122
Wast Water W 150 NY 1606
Watchet T 100 ST 0743
Watchfield, Oxon T 102 SU 2590
Watchfield, Somer T 100 ST 3446
Watchgate T 151 SD 5299
Watch Hill, Border H 157 NY 4390
Watch Hill, Cumbr H 151 NY 6246
Watch Hill, D. & G H 157 NY 4390
Watch Water Reservoir W 164 NT 6656
Watendlath T 150 NY 2716
Water T 146 SD 8425
Waterbeach T 121 TL 4965
Waterbeck T 157 NY 2477
Waterden T 132 TF 8836
Water End, Herts T 104 TL 0310
Water End, Herts T 105 TL 2204
Waterfall T 128 SK 0851
Waterfoot, Lancs T 146 SD 8321
Waterfoot, Strath T 162 NS 5655
Waterford T 105 TL 3114
Watergate Bay W 87 SW 8264
Watergrove Resr W 137 SD 9017
Waterhead, Cumbr T 151 NY 3703
Waterhead, Strath T 161 NS 5411
Waterhead Hill H 156 NS 5700
Waterhead Moor 161 NS 2662
Waterheads 163 NT 2450
Waterhouses, Durham T 152 NZ 1841
Waterhouses, Staffs T 128 SK 0850
Wateringbury T 97 TQ 6853
Waterlip T 101 ST 6544
Waterloo, Dorset T 94 SZ 0094
Waterloo, Mers T 136 SJ 3198
Waterloo, Norf T 133 TG 2219
Waterloo, Strath T 163 NS 8054
Waterloo, Tays T 176 NO 0536
Waterloo Station 105 TQ 3179
Waterlooville T 95 SU 6809
Watermeetings T 156 NS 9512
Watermillock T 151 NY 4422
Water Newton T 130 TL 1097
Waternish 186 NG 2757
Waternish Point 186 NG 2367
Water of Ae W 157 NY 0485
Water of Ailnack, Grampn W 183 NJ 1313
Water of Ailnack, Highld W 183 NJ 1313
Water of App W 154 NX 0774
Water of Aven W 177 NO 6088
Water of Buchat W 184 NJ 3716
Water of Caiplich, Grampn W 183 NJ 0910
Water of Caiplich, Highld W 183 NJ 0910
Water of Charr W 177 NO 6180
Water of Coyle W 161 NS 4713
Water of Dye W 177 NO 6587
Water of Feugh W 177 NO 6792
Water of Girvan W 161 NS 3004
Water of Ken W 156 NX 6394
Water of Leith W 163 NT 1364
Water of Luce W 154 NX 1761
Water of Mark W 176 NO 3883
Water of May W 170 NO 0611
Water of Milk W 157 NY 1781
Water of Minnoch W 154 NX 3782
Water of Nevis W 174 NN 1868
Water of Nochty W 184 NJ 3215
Water of Ruchill W 169 NN 7418
Water of Saughs W 176 NO 4373
Water of Tanar W 176 NO 4594
Water of Tarf W 177 NO 4883
Water of Tig W 154 NX 1482
Water of Tulla W 174 NN 3647
Water of Unich W 176 NO 3679
Water Orton T 118 SP 1891
Waterperry T 104 SP 6206
Waterrow T 92 ST 0525
Watersfield T 96 TQ 0115
Waterside, Strath T 161 NS 4308
Waterside, Strath T 161 NS 4843
Waterside, Strath T 161 NS 5160
Waterside, Strath T 169 NS 6773
Water Sound W 200 ND 4695
Waterstein Head 186 NG 1547
Waterstock T 104 SP 6305
Waterston T 110 SM 9306
Water Stratford T 119 SP 6534
Waters Upton T 127 SJ 6319
Watertborpe T 139 SK 4382
Water Yeat T 150 SD 2889
Watford, Herts P 105 TQ 1097
Watford, Northnts T 119 SP 6068
Wath, N. Yks T 146 SE 1467
Wath, N. Yks T 147 SE 3276
Wath upon Dearne T 139 SE 4300
Watling Street, G. Lon R 105 TQ 1792
Watling Street, Herts R 105 TL 1110
Watling Street, Leic R 119 SP 4490
Watling Street, Staffs R 127 SJ 8310
Watling Street, Warw R 128 SK 2500
Watlington, Norf T 132 TF 6110
Watlington, Oxon T 104 SU 6894
Watnall T 129 SK 5045
Wat's Dyke A 136 SJ 2762
Wats Ness 202 HU 1650
Watten T 199 ND 2454
Watterow T 92 ST 0525
Wattisfield T 122 TM 0174
Wattisham T 122 TM 0151
Watton, Humbs T 149 TA 0150
Watton, Norf T 132 TF 9100
Watton at Stone T 105 TL 3019
Watton Beck W 149 TA 0448
Wattston T 169 NS 7769
Wattstown T 109 ST 0294
Wattsville T 109 ST 2091
Watty Bell's Cairn H 158 NT 8901
Wauchope Forest F 158 NT 6104
Waulkmill Bay W 200 HY 3806
Waunarlwydd T 108 SS 6095
Waun Fâch H 109 SO 2130
Waunfawr T 134 SH 5259
Waun Lysiog 109 SO 0216
Waun-oer H 125 SH 7814
Wavendon T 120 SP 9037
Waverley Abbey A 103 SU 8645
Waverton, Ches T 136 SJ 4564
Waverton, Cumbr T 150 NY 2247
Wawne T 143 TA 0937
Waxham T 133 TG 4326
Waxholme T 143 TA 3229
Wayford T 92 ST 4006
Wayland's Smithy A 102 SU 2885
Way Village T 91 SS 8810
Wealdstone T 105 TQ 1689
Weald, The 97 TQ 6035
Weare T 100 ST 4152
Weare Giffard T 90 SS 4721
Wearhead T 151 NY 8539
Weasdale T 151 NY 6903
Weasenham All Saints T 132 TF 8421
Weasenham St Peter T 132 TF 8522
Weather Ness 200 HY 5240
Weaverham T 137 SJ 6174
Weaver Hills H 128 SK 0946
Weaver's Point 188 NF 9568
Weaverthorpe T 149 SE 9670
Webheath T 118 SP 0266
Weddel Sound W 200 ND 3394
Wedder Dod H 156 NS 8215
Wedder Holm 205 HU 6197
Wedderlairs T 185 NJ 8532
Wedder Law H 156 NS 9302
Weddington T 128 SP 3693
Wedhampton T 102 SU 0657
Wedholme Flow 150 NY 2253
Wedmore T 101 ST 4347
Wednesbury T 128 SO 9995
Wednesfield T 128 SJ 9500
Weedon T 104 SP 8118
Weedon Bec T 119 SP 6359
Weedon Lois T 119 SP 6047
Weeford T 128 SK 1404
Week T 91 SS 7316
Weekley T 120 SP 8880
Week St Mary T 88 SX 2397
Weeley T 107 TM 1422
Weeley Heath T 107 TM 1520
Weem T 175 NN 8449
Weem Hill H 175 NN 8351
Weeping Cross T 127 SJ 9421
Wee Queensberry H 156 NX 9897
Weeting T 122 TL 7788
Weeton, Lancs T 145 SD 3834
Weeton, N. Yks T 147 SE 2847
Weeton Station 147 SE 2747
Weets Hill H 146 SD 8544
Weetwood Hall 165 NU 0129
Weir T 146 SD 8725
Weir Dike W 142 SE 9714
Weir Wood Reservoir W 97 TQ 3934
Weisdale 203 HU 3953
Weisdale Voe W 203 HU 3747
Welbeck Abbey T 139 SK 5574
Welborne T 132 TG 0609
Welbourn T 130 SK 9654
Welburn T 148 SE 7268
Welbury T 153 NZ 3902
Welby T 130 SK 9738
Welches Dam T 121 TL 4686
Welcombe T 90 SS 2218
Weldon T 120 SP 9289
Weldrake T 142 SE 6845
Welford, Berks T 102 SU 4173
Welford, Northnts T 119 SP 6480
Welford-on-Avon T 118 SP 1552
Welham T 119 SP 7692
Welham Green T 105 TL 2305
Well, Hants T 103 SU 7646
Well, Lincs T 141 TF 4473
Well, N. Yks T 147 SE 2681
Welland T 117 SO 7940
Wellbank T 177 NO 4736
Wellesbourne T 118 SP 2855
Wellgrain Dod H 156 NS 9017
Well Hill, D. & G H 156 NS 9106
Well Hill, Kent T 105 TQ 4963
Welling T 105 TQ 4775
Wellingborough T 120 SP 8967
Wellingham T 132 TF 8722
Wellingore T 130 SK 9856
Wellington, H. & W T 113 SO 4948
Wellington, Shrops T 127 SJ 6511
Wellington, Somer T 92 ST 1320
Wellington Heath T 117 SO 7140
Welloe 86 SW 5825
Well of Kildinguie 201 HY 6527
Wellow, Avon T 101 ST 7358
Wellow, I. of W T 94 SZ 3888
Wellow, Notts T 139 SK 6766
Wells P 101 ST 5445
Wellsborough T 128 SK 3602
Wells-next-the-Sea T 132 TF 9143
Wellwood T 170 NT 0989
Welney T 131 TL 5293
Welshampton T 126 SJ 4335
Welsh Bicknor T 113 SO 5917
Welsh Channel W 135 SJ 1086
Welsh End T 127 SJ 5136
Welsh Frankton T 126 SJ 3633
Welsh Grounds 101 ST 4381
Welsh Hook T 110 SM 9327
Welsh Newton T 113 SO 5018
Welshpool or Trallwng P 126 SJ 2207
Welsh St Donats T 109 ST 0276
Welton, Cumbr T 150 NY 3544
Welton, Humbs T 142 SE 9527
Welton, Lincs T 140 TF 0179
Welton, Northnts T 119 SP 5866
Welton le Marsh T 141 TF 4768
Welton le Wold T 141 TF 2787
Welwick T 143 TA 3421
Welwyn T 105 TL 2316
Welwyn Garden City T 105 TL 2313
Wem T 127 SJ 5129
Wembdon T 92 ST 2837
Wembley T 105 TQ 1985
Wembury T 88 SX 5148
Wembury Bay W 88 SX 5147
Wembworthy T 91 SS 6609
Wemyss Bay T 168 NS 1969
Wenallt 135 SH 9842
Wendens Ambo T 121 TL 5135
Wendlebury T 115 SP 5619
Wendling T 132 TF 9312
Wendover T 104 SP 8607
Wendron T 86 SW 6731
Wendy T 121 TL 3247
Wenhaston T 123 TM 4275
Wenlock Edge H 116 SO 5190
Wennington, Cambs T 121 TL 2379
Wennington, G. Lon T 105 TQ 5381
Wennington, Lancs T 145 SD 6170
Wensley, Derby T 139 SK 2661
Wensley, N. Yks T 152 SE 0989
Wensleydale 146 SD 9888
Wentbridge T 139 SE 4817
Wentnor T 116 SO 3892
Wentwood F 113 ST 4294
Wentworth, Cambs T 121 TL 4878
Wentworth, S. Yks T 139 SK 3898
Wentworth Castle 139 SE 3203
Wenvoe T 109 ST 1273
Weobley T 113 SO 4051
Weobley Marsh T 113 SO 4151
Wereham T 132 TF 6801
Wergs T 127 SJ 8701
Wernrheolydd T 113 SO 3912
Werrington, Cambs T 130 TF 1603
Werrington, Corn T 88 SX 3287
Werrington, Staffs T 127 SJ 9447
Wervin T 136 SJ 4272
Wesham T 145 SD 4232
Wessington T 139 SK 3757
West Acre T 132 TF 7815
West Allerdean T 165 NT 9646
West Alvington T 89 SX 7243
West Anstey T 91 SS 8527
West Ashby T 141 TF 2672
West Ashling T 95 SU 8107
West Ashton T 101 ST 8755
West Auckland T 152 NZ 1726
West Bagborough T 92 ST 1633
West Barns T 171 NT 6578
West Barsham T 132 TF 9033
West Baugh Fell 151 SD 7394
West Bay, Dorset T 93 SY 4690
West Bay, Dorset W 93 SY 6773
West Beckham T 133 TG 1339
West Benula Forest 181 NH 0827
Westbere T 99 TR 1961
West Bergholt T 122 TL 9627
West Bexington T 93 SY 5386
West Bilney T 132 TF 7115
West Blatchington T 97 TQ 2806
Westborough T 130 SK 8544
Westbourne, Dorset T 94 SZ 0791
Westbourne, W. Susx T 95 SU 7507
West Bradford T 145 SD 7444
West Bradley T 93 ST 5536

West Bretton
Whyle

West Bretton T 139 SE 2813
West Bridgford T 129 SK 5837
West Bromwich P 118 SP 0092
West Buckland, Devon T 91 SS 6531
West Buckland, Somer T 92 ST 1720
West Burra 203 HU 3632
West Burrafirth T 202 HU 2657
West Burton, Lancs T 146 SD 9961
West Burton, N. Yks T 146 SE 0186
West Burton, W. Susx T 96 SU 9913
Westbury, Bucks T 119 SP 6235
Westbury, Shrops T 126 SJ 3509
Westbury, Wilts T 101 ST 8751
Westbury Leigh T 101 ST 8650
Westbury-on-Severn T 114 SO 7214
Westbury-sub-Mendip T 101 ST 5048
Westby T 145 SD 3831
West Caister T 133 TG 5111
West Calder T 163 NT 0163
West Camel T 93 ST 5724
West Challow T 102 SU 3688
West Charleton T 89 SX 7542
West Chelborough T 93 ST 5405
West Chevington T 159 NZ 2297
West Chiltington T 96 TQ 0918
West Chinnock T 93 ST 4613
West Clandon T 96 TQ 0452
West Cliffe T 99 TR 3544
Westcliff-on-Sea T 106 TQ 8685
West Clyne T 193 NC 8805
West Coker T 93 ST 5113
Westcombe T 101 ST 6739
West Compton, Dorset T 93 SY 5694
West Compton, Somer T 101 ST 5942
Westcote T 115 SP 2220
Westcott, Bucks T 104 SP 7117
Westcott, Devon T 92 ST 0204
Westcott, Surrey T 96 TQ 1448
Westcott Barton T 115 SP 4225
West Cross T 108 SS 6189
West Cullerley T 185 NJ 7603
West Curry 88 SX 2893
West Curthwaite T 150 NY 3248
West Dart River W 89 SX 6373
Westdean, E. Susx T 97 TV 5299
West Dean, Hants T 94 SU 2527
West Dean, W. Susx T 95 SU 8612
West Deeping T 130 TF 1008
West Derby T 136 SJ 3993
West Dereham T 132 TF 6500
West Ditchburn T 159 NU 1320
West Down, Devon T 90 SS 5142
West Down, Wilts H 102 SU 0548
West Drayton, G. Lon T 104 TQ 0679
West Drayton, Notts T 140 SK 7074
West End, Avon T 101 ST 4469
West End, Beds T 120 SP 9853
West End, Hants T 95 SU 4614
West End, Humbs T 142 SE 9130
West End, Norf T 133 TG 4911
West End, N. Yks T 146 SE 1457
West End, Oxon T 115 SP 4204
West End, Surrey T 104 SU 9460
West End Green T 104 SU 6661
Wester Culbeuchly Crofts T 184 NJ 6562
Westerdale, Highld T 199 ND 1251
Westerdale, N. Yks T 153 NZ 6605
Westerdale Moor 153 NZ 6602
Wester Denoon 176 NO 3443
Wester Fearn Burn W 192 NH 6086
Westerfield, Shetld T 203 HU 3551
Westerfield, Suff T 123 TM 1747
Wester Fintray T 185 NJ 8116
Westergate T 96 SU 9305
Wester Gruinards T 192 NH 5192
Westerham T 97 TQ 4454
Wester Hoevdi 202 HT 9338
Wester Lealty 192 NH 6073
Westerleigh T 101 ST 7079
Western Cleddau W 110 SM 9521
Wester Newburn 171 NO 4405
Westernhope Moor 152 NY 9133
Western Isles or Hebrides, Highld 178 NG 0239
Western Isles or Hebrides, Strath 178 NG 0239
Western Isles or Hebrides, W. Isles 178 NG 0239
Western Rocks 86 SV 8306
Wester Quarff T 203 HU 4135
Wester Ross 191 NH 0562
Wester Skeld T 202 HU 2943
Westerton T 177 NO 6654
Westerwick, Shetld T 202 HU 2842
Wester Wick, Shetld W 202 HU 2842
West Farleigh T 97 TQ 7152
West Fell H 151 NY 6601
West Felton T 126 SJ 3425
West Fen, Cambs 131 TL 3799
West Fen, Cambs 121 TL 5182
West Fen, Lincs 131 TF 3154
Westfield, E. Susx T 98 TQ 8115
Westfield, Highld T 199 ND 0664
Westfield, Lothn T 170 NS 9472
Westfield, Norf T 132 TF 9909
West Firle T 97 TQ 4707
West Fleetham T 165 NU 1928
Westgate, Durham T 152 NY 9038
Westgate, Humbs T 142 SE 7707
Westgate, Norf T 132 TF 9740
Westgate on Sea T 99 TR 3270
West Gerinish T 188 NF 7741
West Ginge T 103 SU 4486
West Glen River W 130 TF 0022
West Grafton T 102 SU 2460
West Green T 103 SU 7456
West Grimstead T 94 SU 2126
West Grinstead T 96 TQ 1720
West Haddlesey T 147 SE 5626
West Haddon T 119 SP 6371
West Hagbourne T 103 SU 5187
West Hall, Cumbr T 158 NY 5667
Westhall, Grampn 184 NJ 6726
Westhall, Suff T 123 TM 4181
West Hallam T 128 SK 4341
West Halton T 142 SE 9021
Westham, E. Susx T 97 TQ 6304
West Ham, G. Lon T 105 TQ 4083
Westham, Somer T 100 ST 4046
Westhampnett T 95 SU 8806
West Handley T 139 SK 3977
West Hanney T 102 SU 4092
West Hanningfield T 106 TQ 7399
West Hardwick T 139 SE 4118
West Harptree T 101 ST 5656
West Hatch T 92 ST 2820
Westhay T 101 ST 4342
Westhead T 136 SD 4307
West Heath T 103 SU 8556
West Helmsdale T 193 ND 0115
West Hendred T 103 SU 4488
West Heslerton T 149 SE 9175
Westhide T 113 SO 5844
West Hill, Devon T 92 SY 0693
Westhill, Grampn T 185 NJ 8307
West Hoathly T 97 TQ 3632
West Holme T 93 SY 8885
Westhope, H. & W T 113 SO 4651
Westhope, Shrops T 116 SO 4786
West Horndon T 106 TQ 6288
Westhorpe, Lincs T 130 TF 2131
Westhorpe, Suff T 122 TM 0569
West Horrington T 101 ST 5747
West Horsley T 96 TQ 0752
West Hougham T 99 TR 2640
Westhoughton T 137 SD 6505
Westhouse T 145 SD 6774
Westhouses T 139 SK 4258
West Hoyle Bank 135 SJ 1087
Westhumble T 96 TQ 1651
West Hyde T 104 TQ 0391
West Ilsley T 103 SU 4782
Westing T 205 HP 5705
West Itchenor T 95 SU 7901
West Kame H 203 HU 3959
West Kennett T 102 SU 1168
West Kilbride T 161 NS 2147
West Kingsdown T 105 TQ 5762
West Kington T 101 ST 8177
West Kirby T 136 SJ 2186
West Knighton T 93 SY 7387
West Knock H 177 NO 4775
West Knoyle T 93 ST 8532
Westlake T 89 SX 6253
West Langdon T 99 TR 3247
West Langwell T 197 NC 6909
West Lavington, Wilts T 102 SU 0053
West Lavington, W. Susx T 95 SU 8920
West Lavington Down H 102 ST 9949
West Layton T 152 NZ 1409
West Leake T 129 SK 5226
Westleigh, Devon T 90 SS 4728
Westleigh, Devon T 92 ST 0616
Westleton T 123 TM 4469
West Lexham T 132 TF 8417
Westley, Shrops T 126 SJ 3607
Westley, Suff T 122 TL 8264
Westley Waterless T 122 TL 6156
West Lilling T 147 SE 6465
West Linga 203 HU 5364
Westlington T 104 SP 7610
West Linton, Border T 163 NT 1551
Westlinton, Cumbr T 157 NY 3964
West Littleton T 101 ST 7675
West Loch Tarbert, Strath W 160 NR 8163
West Loch Tarbert, W. Isles W 189 NB 0903
West Lomond H 171 NO 1906
West Lulworth T 93 SY 8280
West Lutton T 149 SE 9369
West Mains 163 NS 8549
West Malling T 97 TQ 6757
West Malvern T 117 SO 7646
West Marden T 95 SU 7713
West Markham T 140 SK 7272
Westmarsh T 99 TR 2761
West Marton T 146 SD 8950
West Meon T 95 SU 6423
West Mersea T 107 TM 0112
Westmeston T 97 TQ 3313
Westmill T 121 TL 3627
West Milton T 93 SY 5096
Westminster P 105 TQ 2979
West Monar Forest 191 NH 0842
West Monkton T 92 ST 2628
West Moors T 94 SU 0802
West Moulie Geo 202 HU 2940
West Mouse 134 SH 3094
Westmuir, Tays T 176 NO 3652
West Muir, Tays T 177 NO 5661
West Ness, Fife 171 NO 6106
Westness, Orkney 200 HY 3829
Westnewton, Cumbr T 150 NY 1344
West Newton, Humbs T 143 TA 1937
West Newton, Norf T 132 TF 6927
West Norwood T 105 TQ 3171
West Ogwell T 89 SX 8270
Weston, Avon T 101 ST 7266
Weston, Berks T 102 SU 4073
Weston, Ches T 137 SJ 5080
Weston, Ches T 127 SJ 7352
Weston, Dorset T 93 SY 6871
Weston, Hants T 95 SU 7221
Weston, Herts T 121 TL 2630
Weston, Lincs T 131 TF 2925
Weston, Northnts T 119 SP 5847
Weston, Notts T 140 SK 7767
Weston, N. Yks T 146 SE 1747
Weston, N. Yks T 148 SE 7565
Weston, Shrops T 127 SJ 5629
Weston, Shrops T 127 SO 5993
Weston, Staffs T 128 SJ 9727
Weston Bampfylde T 93 ST 6124
Weston Bay W 100 ST 3060
Weston Beggard T 113 SO 5841
Westonbirt T 101 ST 8589
Weston by Welland T 119 SP 7791
Weston Colville T 122 TL 6153
Weston Green T 122 TL 6252
Weston Heath T 127 SJ 7713
Weston Hill H 116 SO 5582
Weston Hills T 131 TF 2720
Westoning T 120 TL 0332
Weston-in-Gordano T 101 ST 4474
Weston Jones T 127 SJ 7624
Weston Longville T 133 TG 1115
Weston Lullingfields T 126 SJ 4224
Weston-on-the-Green T 115 SP 5318
Weston-on-Trent T 128 SK 4028
Weston Patrick T 103 SU 6946
Weston Rhyn T 126 SJ 2835
Weston-sub-Edge T 118 SP 1241
Weston-super-Mare P 100 ST 3261
Weston Turville T 104 SP 8511
Weston-under-Lizard T 127 SJ 8010
Weston under Penyard T 113 SO 6323
Weston under Wetherley T 118 SP 3669
Weston Underwood, Bucks T 120 SP 8650
Weston Underwood, Derby T 128 SK 2942
Westonzoyland T 92 ST 3534
West Overton T 102 SU 1367
West Parley T 94 SZ 0898
West Peckham T 97 TQ 6452
West Pennard T 101 ST 5438
West Pentire T 86 SW 7760
West Perry T 120 TL 1466
Westport T 92 ST 3820
West Putford T 90 SS 3515
West Quantoxhead T 100 ST 1141
West Rainton T 152 NZ 3146
West Rasen T 140 TF 0689
Westray 200 HY 4446
Westray Airport 200 HY 4552
Westray Firth W 200 HY 4735
West Raynham T 132 TF 8725
West Reef 172 NM 2414
Westrigg T 163 NS 9067
West Road W 99 TR 0015
West Row T 122 TL 6775
West Rudham T 132 TF 8127
West Runton T 133 TG 1842
Westruther T 164 NT 6350
Westry T 131 TL 3998
West Saltoun T 164 NT 4667
West Sandwick T 205 HU 4588
West Scar 153 NZ 6026
West Scrafton T 146 SE 0783
West Sedge Moor 92 ST 3625
Westside 200 HY 3729
West Somerset Railway 92 ST 1334
West Stafford T 93 SY 7289
West Stockwith T 140 SK 7994
West Stoke T 95 SU 8308
West Stonesdale T 152 NY 8802
West Stoughton T 100 ST 4148
West Stour T 93 ST 7822
West Stourmouth T 99 TR 2562
West Stow T 122 TL 8170
West Stowell T 102 SU 1362
West Street T 98 TQ 9054
West Tanfield T 147 SE 2678
West Tarbert T 160 NR 8467
West Tarbert Bay W 160 NR 6553
West Thorney T 95 SU 7602
West Thurrock T 105 TQ 5877
West Tilbury T 98 TQ 6677
West Tisted T 95 SU 6529
West Tofts T 170 NO 1034
West Torrington T 141 TF 1382
West Town T 101 ST 4868
West Tytherley T 94 SU 2729
West Tytherton T 102 ST 9574
West Voe W 203 HU 3730
West Voe of Sumburgh W 203 HU 3909
West Walton T 131 TF 4713
Westward T 150 NY 2744
Westward Ho! T 90 SS 4329
West Water W 177 NO 5367
West Water Reservoir W 163 NT 1152
Westwell, Kent T 99 TQ 9947
Westwell, Oxon T 115 SP 2210
Westwell Leacon T 99 TQ 9647
West Wellow T 94 SU 2919
West Wemyss T 171 NT 3294
West Wick, Avon T 100 ST 3661
Westwick, Cambs T 121 TL 4265
Westwick, Norf T 133 TG 2726
West Wickham, Cambs T 122 TL 6149
West Wickham, G. Lon T 105 TQ 3866
West Winch T 132 TF 6315
West Winterslow T 94 SU 2332
West Wittering T 95 SZ 7898
West Witton T 146 SE 0688
Westwood, Devon T 92 SY 0198
Westwood, Wilts T 101 ST 8059
West Woodburn T 158 NY 8986
West Woodhay T 102 SU 3963
West Woodlands T 101 ST 7743
Westwoodside T 142 SK 7499
West Worldham T 95 SU 7436
West Wratting T 122 TL 6051
West Wycombe T 104 SU 8394
West Yell T 205 HU 4583
Wetheral T 151 NY 4654
Wetherby T 147 SE 4048
Wether Cairn H 158 NT 9411
Wetherden T 122 TM 0062
Wether Fell 146 SD 8787
Wether Hill, D. & G H 156 NX 7087
Wether Hill, D. & G H 156 NX 7094
Wether Hill, Tays H 170 NN 9205
Wetheringsett T 123 TM 1266
Wether Lair H 158 NY 7096
Wether Law H 163 NT 1948
Wethersfield T 122 TL 7131
Wethersta T 203 HU 3665
Wetherup Street T 123 TM 1464
Wetley Rocks T 128 SJ 9649
Wet Sleddale Reservoir W 151 NY 5411
Wettenhall T 137 SJ 6261
Wetton T 128 SK 1155
Wetwang T 149 SE 9359
Wetwood T 127 SJ 7733
Wexcombe T 102 SU 2759
Weybourne T 133 TG 1143
Weybread T 123 TM 2480
Weybridge T 104 TQ 0764
Weydale T 199 ND 1564
Weyhill T 102 SU 3146
Weymouth P 93 SY 6779
Weymouth Bay W 93 SY 6980
Whaddon, Bucks T 119 SP 8034
Whaddon, Cambs T 121 TL 3546
Whaddon, Glos T 114 SO 8313
Whaddon, Wilts T 94 SU 1926
Whaddon Chase 119 SP 8032
Whale T 151 NY 5221
Whale Chine 95 SZ 4678
Whale Firth W 205 HU 4694
Whale Geo 205 HU 4493
Whale Island 95 SU 6302
Whaley T 139 SK 5171
Whaley Bridge T 138 SK 0181
Whaley Thorns T 139 SK 5371
Whaligoe 199 ND 3240
Whalley T 145 SD 7336
Whalsay 203 HU 5563
Whalsay Airport 203 HU 5966
Whalton T 159 NZ 1381
Whalwick Taing 204 HU 2381
Wham T 146 SD 7762
Whaness T 200 HY 2502
Whaplode T 131 TF 3224
Whaplode Drove T 131 TF 3113
Whaplode Fen 131 TF 3320
Whaplode River W 131 TF 3429
Wharfe T 146 SD 7869
Wharfedale 147 SE 2646
Wharles T 145 SD 4435
Wharncliffe Side T 139 SK 2994
Wharram le Street T 148 SE 8666
Wharton, Ches T 137 SJ 6666
Wharton, H. & W T 113 SO 5055
Whashton T 152 NZ 1406
Whatcombe T 93 ST 8301
Whatcote T 118 SP 3044
Whatfield T 122 TM 0246
Whatley T 101 ST 7347
Whatlington T 97 TQ 7518
Whatstandwell T 128 SK 3354
Whatton T 129 SK 7439
Whauphill T 154 NX 4049
Whaw 152 NY 9804
Wheatacre T 133 TM 4693
Wheathampstead T 105 TL 1713
Wheathill T 117 SO 6282
Wheatley, Hants T 103 SU 7840
Wheatley, Oxon T 115 SP 5905
Wheatley Hill T 153 NZ 3738
Wheatley Lane T 146 SD 8338
Wheaton Aston T 127 SJ 8512
Wheat Stack 165 NT 8671
Wheddon Cross T 91 SS 9238
Wheedlemont T 184 NJ 4726
Wheeldale Moor 148 SE 7898
Wheelerstreet T 96 SU 9440
Wheelock T 137 SJ 7559
Wheelton T 145 SD 6021
Wheen 176 NO 3671
Whelford T 115 SU 1799
Whelpley Hill T 104 SP 9904
Whenby T 147 SE 6369
Whepstead T 122 TL 8358
Whernside 145 SD 7382
Wherstead T 123 TM 1540
Wherwell T 102 SU 3840
Wheston T 138 SK 1376
Whetsted T 97 TQ 6545
Whetstone T 129 SP 5597
Whicham T 144 SD 1382
Whichford T 115 SP 3134
Whickham T 159 NZ 2061
Whiddon Down T 89 SX 6992
Whigstreet T 177 NO 4844
Whillan Beck W 150 NY 1802
Whilton T 119 SP 6364
Whimple T 92 SY 0497
Whimpwell Green T 133 TG 3829
Whinburgh T 132 TG 0009
Whinfell Beacon H 151 NY 5700
Whinlatter Pass 150 NY 1924
Whinnyfold T 185 NK 0833
Whins Brow H 145 SD 6353
Whippingham T 95 SZ 5193
Whipsnade T 104 TL 0118
Whipsnade Park Zoo 104 TL 0017
Whipton T 89 SX 9493
Whissendine T 130 SK 8214
Whissonsett T 132 TF 9123
Whistley Green T 104 SU 7974
Whiston, Mers T 137 SJ 4791
Whiston, Northnts T 120 SP 8460
Whiston, Staffs T 127 SJ 8914
Whiston, Staffs T 128 SK 0347
Whiston, S. Yks T 139 SK 4590
Whitaloo Point 200 HY 2628
Whitbeck T 144 SD 1184
Whitbourne T 117 SO 7256
Whitburn, Lothn T 163 NS 9464
Whitburn, T. & W T 159 NZ 4062
Whitby, Ches T 136 SJ 3975
Whitby, N. Yks P 149 NZ 8910
Whitchurch, Avon T 101 ST 6167
Whitchurch, Bucks T 104 SP 8020
Whitchurch, Devon T 88 SX 4972
Whitchurch, Dyfed T 110 SM 8025
Whitchurch, Hants T 103 SU 4648
Whitchurch, H. & W T 113 SO 5517
Whitchurch, Oxon T 104 SU 6377
Whitchurch, S. Glam T 109 ST 1580
Whitchurch, Shrops P 127 SJ 5441
Whitchurch Canonicorum T 92 SY 3995
Whitchurch Hill T 104 SU 6478
Whitcott Keysett T 116 SO 2782
Whiteacen 184 NJ 2545
Whiteadder Reservoir W 164 NT 6563
Whiteadder Water, Border W 165 NT 9154
Whiteadder Water, Lothn W 164 NT 6366
Whiteash Hill Wood F 184 NJ 3758
Whitebridge T 182 NH 4815
Whitebrook T 113 SO 5306
Whitecairns T 185 NJ 9218
White Cart Water W 161 NS 5263
White Castle A 113 SO 3716
White Caterthun 177 NO 5466
Whitechapel T 145 SD 5541
Whitecliff Bay W 95 SZ 6486
White Coomb H 157 NT 1615
White Coppice T 137 SD 6119
Whitecraig, Lothn T 171 NT 3570
White Craig, Strath H 163 NT 0753
Whitecroft T 113 SO 6206
White Esk W 157 NY 2598
Whiteface T 193 NH 7089
Whitefarland Point 160 NR 8642
Whitefauld Hill H 156 NY 0293
White Fen 121 TL 3492
Whitefield, G. Man T 137 SD 8105
Whitefield, Tays 170 NO 1734
Whitefield Loch W 154 NX 2355
Whiteford T 185 NJ 7226
Whiteford Point 108 SS 4496
Whitegate T 137 SJ 6369
Whitehall T 201 HY 6528
Whitehaugh Forest F 184 NJ 5723
Whitehaven T 150 NX 9717
White Hill, Border H 158 NT 5212
White Hill, Grampn H 177 NO 5388
Whitehill, Hants T 95 SU 7934
White Hill, Lancs H 145 SD 6758
White Hill, Strath H 156 NS 8820
White Hill, Tays H 176 NO 4073
Whitehills T 184 NJ 6565
White Hope Edge H 157 NY 3397
Whitehope Law H 164 NT 3344
White Horse A 93 SY 7184
Whitehouse, Grampn T 184 NJ 6115
Whitehouse, Strath T 160 NR 8161
White Island 86 SV 9217
Whitekirk T 171 NT 5981
White Kirkley T 152 NZ 0235
White Knowes H 156 NS 6104
White Lackington T 93 SY 7198
White Ladies Aston T 117 SO 9252
Whitelake W 101 ST 5240
White Law, Border H 165 NT 8526
White Law, Northum H 165 NT 8526
Whitelaw Hill, Border H 163 NT 1935
Whitelaw Hill, Lothn H 171 NT 5771
Whitelee Forest F 161 NS 5443
Whiteley Village T 104 TQ 0962
White Loch W 154 NX 1060
White Lyne W 158 NY 5473
Whitemans Green T 97 TQ 3025
White Meldon H 163 NT 2142
Whitemill Bay W 201 HY 6946
Whitemill Point 201 HY 7046
Whitemire T 183 NH 9754
Whitemoor T 87 SW 9757
Whitemoor Reservoir W 146 SD 8743
White Mounth H 176 NO 2383
White Ness, Kent 99 TR 3971
White Ness, Shetld 203 HU 3844
Whiteness, Shetld 203 HU 4147
Whiteness Head 183 NH 8058
Whiteness Sands 193 NH 8386
Whiteness Voe W 203 HU 3943
Whiten Head or An Ceann Geal 197 NC 5068
White Notley T 106 TL 7818
Whiteparish T 94 SU 2423
White Preston H 158 NY 5977
Whiterashes T 185 NJ 8523
White Rocks T 113 SO 4424
White Roding or White Roothing T 105 TL 5613
White Roothing or White Roding T 105 TL 5613
Whiterow T 199 ND 3548
Whitesand Bay W 86 SW 3527
Whitesand Bay or Porth-mawr W 110 SM 7227
White Sands 136 SJ 2772
White Shank H 157 NT 2006
White Sheet Hill, Wilts H 93 ST 8034
Whitesheet Hill, Wilts H 94 ST 9524
Whiteshill T 114 SO 8407
Whiteshoot Hill H 94 SU 2833
Whiteside, Lothn T 163 NS 9668
Whiteside, Northum 158 NY 7069
Whitesmith T 97 TQ 5214
Whitestaunton T 92 ST 2810
Whitestone T 89 SX 8693
Whitestone Hill H 158 NT 7915
White Top of Culreoch H 156 NX 6063
White Waltham T 104 SU 8577
Whiteway T 114 SO 9210
Whiteway House 89 SX 8782
Whitewell T 145 SD 6547
Whiteworks 89 SX 6071
Whitewreath T 184 NJ 2357
Whitfell H 150 SD 1593
Whitfield, Avon T 101 ST 6791
Whitfield, Bucks T 119 SP 6039
Whitfield, Kent T 99 TR 3045
Whitfield, Northum T 158 NY 7858
Whitfield Moor 151 NY 7453
Whitford, Clwyd T 136 SJ 1478
Whitford, Devon T 92 SY 2595
Whitgift T 142 SE 8122
Whitgreave T 127 SJ 8928
Whithorn T 155 NX 4440
Whithorse Hill H 102 SU 3086
Whiting Bay, Strath T 160 NS 0425
Whiting Bay, Strath W 160 NS 0526
Whitland T 111 SN 2016
Whitletts T 161 NS 3622
Whitley, Berks T 104 SU 7170
Whitley, Ches T 137 SJ 6179
Whitley, N. Yks T 147 SE 5621
Whitley, Wilts T 101 ST 8866
Whitley Bay T 159 NZ 3572
Whitley Chapel T 152 NY 9257
Whitley Row T 97 TQ 4952
Whitlock's End T 118 SP 1077
Whitminster T 114 SO 7708
Whit Moor 145 SD 5964
Whitmore T 127 SJ 8141
Whitnage T 92 ST 0215
Whitnash T 118 SP 3263
Whitney-on-Wye, H. & W T 113 SO 2747
Whitney-on-Wye, H. & W T 113 SO 2747
Whitrigg, Cumbr T 150 NY 2038
Whitrigg, Cumbr 150 NY 2257
Whitsand Bay W 88 SX 3751
Whitsbury T 94 SU 1219
Whitsome T 165 NT 8650
Whitson T 100 ST 3883
Whitstable T 99 TR 1166
Whitstone T 88 SX 2698
Whittingham T 159 NU 0611
Whittingslow T 116 SO 4389
Whittington, Derby T 139 SK 3874
Whittington, Glos T 114 SP 0121
Whittington, H. & W T 117 SO 8752
Whittington, Lancs T 145 SD 6076
Whittington, Norf T 132 TL 7199
Whittington, Shrops T 126 SJ 3231
Whittington, Staffs T 128 SK 1608
Whittington, Staffs T 117 SO 8682
Whittlebury T 119 SP 6943
Whittle-le-Woods T 145 SD 5821
Whittlesey T 131 TL 2797
Whittlesey Mere 121 TL 2290
Whittlesford T 121 TL 4748
Whittlewood Forest F 119 SP 7242
Whitton, Border T 164 NT 7622
Whitton, Cleve T 153 NZ 3822
Whitton, Humbs T 142 SE 9024
Whitton, Northum T 159 NU 0501
Whitton, Powys T 116 SO 2767
Whitton, Shrops T 116 SO 5772
Whitton, Suff T 123 TM 1447
Whittonditch T 102 SU 2972
Whittonstall T 152 NZ 0757
Whitwell, Derby T 139 SK 5276
Whitwell, Herts T 105 TL 1820
Whitwell, I. of W T 95 SZ 5278
Whitwell, Leic T 130 SK 9208
Whitwell, N. Yks T 152 SE 2899
Whitwell-on-the-Hill T 148 SE 7265
Whitwick T 128 SK 4316
Whitwood T 147 SE 4024
Whitworth T 137 SD 8818
Whixall T 127 SJ 5134
Whixley T 147 SE 4458
Whorlton, Durham T 152 NZ 1014
Whorlton, N. Yks T 153 NZ 4802
Whorlton Moor 153 SE 5098
Whygate 158 NY 7776
Whyle T 116 SO 5661

ORDNANCE SURVEY PRODUCTS

Ordnance Survey produces and publishes maps in a variety of forms and scales described below, beginning with large-scale maps from which the wide range of small-scale maps are derived.

LARGE SCALE MAPS

Highly detailed maps of Great Britain for people that need accurate large-scale information.

1:1250 scale maps (1 cm to 12·5 metres or 50 inches to 1 mile)
These are the largest scale maps published by the Ordnance Survey and are available for cities and other significant urban areas throughout Britain. There are over 50,000 maps in this series. Each map represents an area of 500 m by 500 m and carries Natioanl Grid lines at 100 metre intervals. Every building, road and most other features are shown, even post boxes. Street names, house names or numbers are included as well as administrative amd parliamentary boundaries. Height information and some survey control points are also shown.

1:2500 scale maps (1 cm to 25 metres or 25 inches to 1 mile)
These maps cover all parts of the country other than significant urban areas (1:1250) and mountain and moorland areas (1:10 000 scale). Normally each plan covers an area of 2 km east to west by 1 km north to south. National Grid lines are shown at 100 metre intervals. Areas of land parcels are given in acres and hectares as well as features shown on 1:1250 scale maps.

1:10 000 scale maps (1 cm to 100 metres or about 6 inches to 1 mile)
These maps cover the whole country. They are also the largest scale of mapping to cover mountain and moorland and to show contours. Some maps are at 1:10 560 scale with contours at 25 feet intervals, but they are being replaced by 1:10 000 scale maps with contours at 10 metre intervals in mountainous areas and 5 metre intervals elsewhere.

Updated Survey Information
Two services are provided to make the latest 1:1250 and 1:2500 scales survey information available before a new edition map is printed.

SUSI (Supply of Updated Survey Information) provides the most up-to-date large-scale information available. Anyone can call at their local Ordnance Survey office (listed in the Telephone Directory) and order a copy of the surveyor's working document known as Master Survey Drawings (MSD's) on paper or film.

SIM (Survey Information on Microfilm) provides copies of MSD's after a fixed amount of survey change has been recorded. These copies at original map scale are available through Ordnance Survey Agents either on paper or film. Copies of current edition 1:1250 and 1:2500 maps are also provided through the SIM service.

DIGITAL MAPPING

A growing number of 1:1250 and 1:2500 scale maps are available on magnetic tape in the form of numerical co-ordinates suitable for computer manipulation. Data on the tape can be recalled to produce an exact scale map copy or a larger or smaller scale copy as required. Furthermore selected detail can be recalled rather than the whole map.

A digital topographic database from maps at 1:625 000 scale (10 miles to 1 inch) has also been developed by Ordnance Survey and is now available. The structure of the data allows feature selection by location, type or name, the extraction of information for a named area, and the analysis of road or river networks.

SMALL SCALE MAPS

Pathfinder Maps 1:25 000 scale (4 cm to 1 km or 2½ inches to 1 mile)
These coloured maps are ideal for the walker or rambler showing the countryside in great detail with footpaths, rights of way in England and Wales and field boundaries. The maps normally cover an area 20 km (12½ miles) east to west by 10 km (6¼ miles) north to south. Coverage of the country by Pathfinder mapping will be complete by 1990.

Outdoor Leisure Maps 1:25 000 scale (4 cm to 1 km or 2½ inches to 1 mile)
This series covers selected popular leisure and recreation areas of the country. Packed with detail they are invaluable to the serious walker or climber. A wealth of tourist information makes them equally popular with the less dedicated outdoor enthusiast. The area covered by the map varies but is much larger than the Pathfinder.

Landranger Maps 1:50 000 scale (2 cm to 1 km or about 1¼ inches to 1 mile)
Landranger maps are suitable for motoring, walking, educational and business purposes. The series covers the whole of the country in 204 sheets. Each map covers an area of 40 km by 40 km (25 miles by 25 miles). All show tourist information, and sheets covering England and Wales include public rights of way. Like other Ordnance Survey maps National Grid squares are provided so that any feature can be given a unique reference number.

Tourist Maps 1:63 360 scale (1 inch to 1 mile) and 1:50 000 scale
These maps cover popular touring and holiday areas and are designed to help visitors explore the countryside in detail. The mapping is enhanced with additional tourist information and some include a useful guide to the area. Public rights of way are also shown.

Routemaster Maps 1:250 000 scale (1 cm to 2·5 km or 1 inch to 4 miles)
Nine Routemaster maps cover Great Britain. They are designed for the motorist to help find the shortest or most scenic route. The maps are regularly revised and show motorways, trunk main and secondary routes prominently depicted to ease map reading. Colour shading and contours are used to depict relief. Road distances and tourist information are also included.

Great Britain Routeplanner 1:625 000 scale (1 cm to 6·25 km or approximately 1 inch to 10 miles)
This map covers the whole of Great Britain on one sheet. Southern England and Wales appear on one side with Northern England and Scotland on the other. Frequently updated, the map also features inset diagrams of major towns, and National Parks, Forest Parks and areas of outstanding natural beauty. A mileage chart and gazetteer of towns and cities is also included.

OTHER PRODUCTS AND FURTHER INFORMATION

Further information on Ordnance Survey products and services can be obtained from Information and Enquiries, Ordnance Survey, Romsey Road, Maybush, Southampton, SO9 4DH.

Key to 1:250 000 Maps, atlas pages 86-205

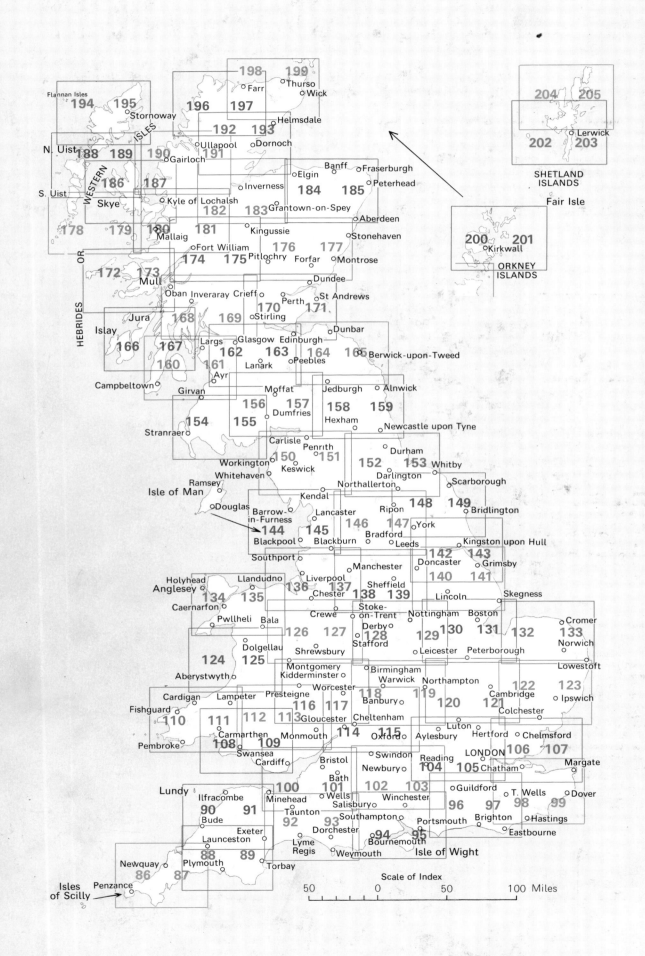

Flannan Isles
194 **195**
Stornoway

196 **197**
Farr Thurso Wick

192 **193**
Helmsdale
Ullapool Dornoch

N. Uist **188** **189** **190** **191**
Gairloch Inverness Banff Fraserburgh
Elgin Peterhead

S. Uist **186** **187**
Skye Kyle of Lochalsh
182 **183** Grantown-on-Spey
Aberdeen

178 **179** **180** **181** Kingussie
Mallaig Stonehaven
176 **177**
Fort William
174 **175** Pitlochry Forfar Montrose
172 **173**
Mull Dundee
Oban Inveraray Crieff
170 Perth St Andrews
Jura **168** **169** Stirling **171**
Islay Dunbar
166 **167** Largs Glasgow Edinburgh
160 **162** **163** **164** **165** Berwick-upon-Tweed
161 Lanark Peebles
Ayr
Campbeltown
Girvan Moffat Jedburgh Alnwick
156 **157** **158** **159**
154 **155** Dumfries Hexham
Stranraer Newcastle upon Tyne
Carlisle Penrith Durham
Workington **150** **151** **152** **153** Whitby
Whitehaven Keswick Darlington Scarborough
Ramsey Northallerton
Isle of Man Kendal
Douglas Lancaster Ripon **148** **149** Bridlington
Barrow- **144** **145** **146** **147** York
in-Furness Bradford
Blackpool Blackburn Leeds Kingston upon Hull
Southport **142** **143**
Manchester Doncaster Grimsby
140 **141**
Holyhead Llandudno Liverpool Sheffield
Anglesey **134** **135** **136** **137** Chester **138** **139** Lincoln Skegness
Caernarfon Crewe Stoke- Boston
Pwllheli Bala on-Trent Nottingham Cromer
126 **127** Derby **129** **130** **131** **132** **133**
Dolgellau **128** Norwich
124 **125** Shrewsbury Stafford Leicester Peterborough Lowestoft
Aberystwyth Montgomery Birmingham
Kidderminster Warwick Northampton **122** **123**
Cardigan Lampeter Presteigne **118** Banbury **119** Cambridge Ipswich
Fishguard **116** **117** **120** **121** Colchester
110 **111** **112** **113** Gloucester Cheltenham Luton
Pembroke Carmarthen Monmouth **114** **115** Aylesbury Hertford Chelmsford
108 **109** Oxford LONDON **106** **107**
Swansea Swindon Reading Margate
Cardiff **104** **105** Chatham
Bristol Newbury Dover
Bath
Lundy **100** **101** **102** **103** Guildford T. Wells
Ilfracombe Minehead Wells Winchester **96** **97** **98** **99**
90 **91** Salisbury Southampton Brighton Hastings
Bude Taunton **93** Portsmouth Eastbourne
92 Dorchester **94** **95**
Exeter Lyme Weymouth Isle of Wight
Launceston Regis Bournemouth
88 **89**
Newquay Plymouth Torbay
86 **87**
Isles Penzance
of Scilly

204 **205**

202 **203**
Lerwick

SHETLAND
ISLANDS

Fair Isle

200 **201**
Kirkwall

ORKNEY
ISLANDS

WESTERN ISLES
HEBRIDES
OR
HEBRIDES

Scale of Index

50 0 50 100 Miles